Anne Boleyn

JOSEPHINE WILKINSON received a First from the University of Newcastle where she also read for her PhD. Her other books include *The Early Loves of Anne Boleyn, Mary Boleyn: Henry VIII's Favourite Mistress, Divorcing Catherine: Henry VIII's Quest to Marry Anne Boleyn, Anne Boleyn: The Young Queen to Be* and *Richard III: The Young King to Be*. She lives in York.

Anne Boleyn

PAUL FRIEDMANN

Edited by Josephine Wilkinson

AMBERLEY

LIST OF ILLUSTRATIONS

This edition first published 2013

First published 1884

Amberley Publishing
The Hill, Stroud
Gloucestershire, GL5 4EP

www.amberley-books.com

Copyright © Josephine Wilkinson, 2010, 2013

The right of Josephine Wilkinson to be identified as the Author of this work has been asserted in accordance with the Copyrights, Designs and Patents Act 1988.

British Library Cataloguing in Publication Data.
A catalogue record for this book is available from the British Library.

ISBN 978 1 4456 1761 9

Typesetting and Origination by Amberley Publishing.
Printed in Great Britain.

CONTENTS

Part 1:

FROM COURTIER'S DAUGHTER TO QUEEN OF ENGLAND, 1502–MARCH 1534

INTRODUCTION

To understand the history of Anne Boleyn's rise and fall, it is absolutely necessary to have a clear and correct idea of the state of England during her lifetime, and of the character of the people she had to deal with. This knowledge, I am sorry to say, cannot be found in any of the numerous works relating to the period of Henry VIII. The writers of these works do not mark with sufficient distinctness the immense difference between England in 1530 and England at the present time; and many of their judgements on Henry VIII and on his contemporaries are superficial and fantastic. I may therefore be allowed as far as possible to attempt to remedy these defects.

Towards the end of the fifteenth century, England was neither like the kingdom of the early Plantagenets, which included nearly a third of France, and ranked among the foremost powers of Europe, nor like the country which under the able rule of Elizabeth developed its internal resources, and profited by the weakness and strife of its neighbours. The country had been ruined by civil wars: its foreign possessions were nearly all gone: the population had been much thinned, had grown unruly, and had lost its habits of industry: the revenue was small, the treasury empty, the administration bad. When Henry VII ascended the throne he set himself to improve the condition of his realm, and in many respects he succeeded. He reorganised the administration, and made it as good and strong as possible. He broke the turbulent spirit of barons and knights, and enforced strict obedience to the royal power. He paid his debts and filled the exchequer, so that at his death a very considerable sum was found in the royal coffers. But with all his talent and energy he could not in a few years change a weak and poor country into a strong and prosperous one. Trade and industry could not be called forth at a moment's notice; and without these England, with an indifferent soil and a bad climate, was unable to support a large population, or to amass any great wealth.

Consequently we find that during the first half of the sixteenth century the population of England was about three and a half millions, while that of France was estimated at fourteen millions, and Charles V could boast of sixteen millions of subjects in Europe alone. Even the states of such a prince as Ferdinand of Austria, or of the Republic of Venice, contained a larger population than England. Of Poland, Muscovy and Turkey, I do not speak, for they did not belong to Western Europe; but each of them was more populous than the realms of Henry.

The capital shared the comparative insignificance of the country; presenting an aspect very different from that of today. To the east it was bounded by the Tower and the Minories, to the north by Houndsditch and the London Wall, while to the west it went as far as the Old Bailey. But the population was by no means crowded. The houses were generally two storeys high, and many of them had gardens or even orchards, so that Thomas Cromwell, for example, was able to grow apples and pears close to Lothbury. Even a part of the ground where the Bank of England now stands was at that time covered with trees. Outside the city walls to the north and east the town was surrounded by orchards and open fields, cattle grazing where now Finsbury Circus and Liverpool Street are crowded with houses. To the west were little suburbs round Smithfield and Holborn, and along the south side of the Strand the houses of the nobility stood in their spacious gardens up to Charing Cross. Southwark consisted of a few hundred houses clustered round the southern end of London Bridge, while Westminster could not boast of a thousand. The most trustworthy estimate of the population makes it amount to 90,000 in the city, and 40,000 more in the suburbs. Paris at that time had more than 400,000 inhabitants, Milan and Ghent 250,000 each. Rome, Bruges, Venice, Genoa and Naples were all of them larger than London, which could rank only with third-rate towns, such as Lyons, Seville, Florence, Luebeck, and Antwerp.

England did not make up by wealth and energy or by other qualities for the smallness of its population. To compare it with the Low Countries or with Upper Italy in regard to trade, industry and wealth would of course be preposterous; it could not be compared even with France, Germany or Spain. At that time England was almost exclusively an agricultural or grazing country; besides the various trades ministering to the daily wants of the inhabitants there was little industry. The chief exports were tin, wool, hides, unfinished cloth, and a few other articles of an average annual value of £400,000. The imports were wine, steel, wax, the finer qualities of cloth and linen, and all kinds of manufactured wares.

Small as it was, this trade was, in great part, in the hands of foreigners. The Hanseatic merchants of the Steelyard, the Italian and Dalmatian traders of Lombard Street were the leading importers and exporters, and nearly monopolised the banking trade. A great part of English merchandise was carried under foreign flags. Notwithstanding the disfavour of the laws, large fleets of Hanseatic hulks, Venetian galleons and Spanish carracks went to nearly every port of the south of England; and Flemish and French ships passed constantly between their own countries and this island. The only trade which was exclusively in English hands was the very inconsiderable coasting trade, and the trade with Calais. The English sent every year from twenty to thirty well-sized ships to the Baltic; from 150 to 200 craft, mostly small, went to fish near Iceland or Newfoundland; the rest, scarcely more than 100, traded with the Low Countries, France, and the north of Spain. Few English ships went as far as Cadiz or Seville, while in the Mediterranean the flag was as yet nearly unknown.

The royal revenue was in proportion to the poverty of the country. It consisted of the rents of the royal domains, about £50,000; of the customs and other taxes on import and export, about £35,000; of the receipts of the courts of wards and liveries, about £15,000; of the receipts of the courts of law, of fines and forfeitures, of duties on the production of tin, and of other small sums, bringing up the total to about £125,000 a year. The revenue of Charles V was about £1.1 million, that of Francis I, £800,000. The Signory of Venice was richer than the King of England. The revenues of the Sultan were ten times as great as those of Henry. Even Ferdinand of Austria, the King of Poland or the Grand Duke of Muscovy, if all their revenues had been taken into account, would not have been found poorer.

Had the English at that time still possessed those military qualities which had decided the day at Crécy and at Agincourt, King Henry VIII might, notwithstanding the poverty of his realms, have had a very real and lasting political influence in Europe. But his father had been essentially a pacific king, and had discouraged among his subjects a martial spirit which might have led to rebellion. The English therefore had made no progress in the art of war; they had never learnt the exact drill and the iron discipline which had come in with the increased use of firearms. Bows and bills were no match for hackbut and pike, the loose fighting order of the English yeomen – so well adapted to their temper – could not resist the shock of the serried ranks of Swiss or Landsknechts. The day of the English archer was gone.

On sea the English might have proved more formidable, for they were as good and daring sailors as they are now. Only they lacked ships. The royal fleet consisted of some thirty ships of 150 tons on an average and one huge unwieldy vessel of 1,000 tons. Of the merchantmen 100 perhaps might have been pressed into service, but most of them were not fit to carry heavy cannon. France, Spain, the Low Countries or the Hanseatic towns were each able to equip fleets two or three times as numerous as any force Henry VIII could have fitted out.

Thus Henry VIII could never occupy that position among Christian princes which was held by Francis I, Charles V, or the Pope. But on his accession he found himself with two advantages by which he might have continually augmented his power. The first of these was the geographical position of England, separating France from the northern seas and Spain from the Low Countries. If he had chosen to do so, Henry VIII could have rendered all communication between the French and their friends the Scots most difficult, and could have made it nearly impossible for Spain to trade with the Low Countries or to send soldiers to them. Hence both the French and the Spanish faction desired his alliance, and were always ready to pay a good price even for his neutrality. Henry VII, profiting by this advantage, had exerted considerable influence on the politics of his neighbours, and had obtained all kinds of benefits with very little outlay. While other kings got heavily into debt, Henry VII accumulated large sums of money, which his son on his accession found in the exchequer. This was another great advantage: with ready money armies of foreign mercenaries could be levied, and fleets fitted out; and the bare ability to appear at any moment in the field gave an additional importance to the King of England.

Had Henry VIII been an able and really patriotic king he might with very little trouble to himself and to his subjects have made his country strong and prosperous; after a happy and quiet reign he might have left it one of the foremost powers of Europe. Unhappily for England he was not such a king; the advantages he inherited from his father he wasted; the position he occupied he spoilt as much as it could be spoilt by fickleness and incapacity.

Henry VIII had the ill luck to arrive at the crown at the age of nineteen. His education had been very bad, and quite unfitted for a future king. Henry VII had been no scholar, and having sometimes felt the lack of learning had come to set an unreasonable value on it. He had therefore taken care that his son should be taught many things which he himself knew not; so that the young prince got a smattering of several sciences law, theology, and medicine of the Latin and French languages and of the polite literature then in favour. Of that science by which his father had obtained and consolidated his power Henry VIII learned very little; it was not considered necessary to train him in the methods of administration, finance, politics and war.

Nevertheless he was praised as a most remarkable king. The methodical tyranny of Henry VII had in twenty-four years changed the most turbulent into the most subservient nation in Europe. Everybody in England bowed before the king, and the young man in his teens was surrounded by a host of most obedient servants and of most fulsome flatterers. He had moreover the mischance to marry a woman six years his senior, who was incapable of exercising a wholesome influence on her husband.

His good natural qualities were not, therefore, developed, while his faults and vices were fostered with tender care. He had a certain breadth of mind; and if he seemed to care for details, it was not, I think, because he had a predilection for them, but rather because his ministers left nothing else to his decision. He had natural shrewdness; except when his vanity was in play, it was not easy to dupe him; and in small intrigues he was able to overreach many a cleverer man. In a way he was good-natured; he was fond of children, he was liberal towards those of his courtiers whom he liked and as long as he liked them; for a little flattery he would often be very kind to a suitor. He spoke well, wrote, except upon business, very tolerably, and knew how to blend dignity with affability. But most of his good qualities were stifled in the bud.

The faults and vices of Henry were so great that, if the unhappy position in which he grew up were not taken into account, he would seem a contemptible monster. He was immensely vain, foolish, weak and thoroughly dishonest. In this age of rehabilitations an attempt has been made to represent Henry as upon the whole a good man and an able sovereign. Every favourable saying of his contemporaries has been adduced as if it were incontrovertible evidence, every damning statement has been dismissed as the outcome of spleen, malice or folly. Those who argue in this way overlook the fact that in the sixteenth century every prince found numerous panegyrists. Alexander VI and Caesar Borgia, Charles IX, and Henry III of France had their virtues extolled. Lucrezia Borgia and Marguerite de Valois were spoken of as most chaste and moral ladies. Francis I and Kaiser Max live to this day in popular fancy as patterns of excellent, high-minded and chivalrous sovereigns. Praise bestowed on a king means very little.

The state papers of Henry's reign show that he was exceedingly vain. He inquired eagerly whether Francis I was as tall and broad as himself; and he exhibited the royal legs to the Venetian ambassador Pasqualigo, complacently praising the size of his calves.[1] From Chapuis we learn that Henry thought the highest compliment he could pay the French was to say they were as handsome and tall as the English.[2] We may still see the numerous portraits of himself which he caused to be painted, and compare them with the very few pictures or other works of art he bought or ordered.

In the correspondence of nearly every ambassador at his court we read of some foolish boast about his riches, his power, and his wisdom. 'He never forgets his own greatness,' Castillon writes, 'and is silent as to that of others.'[3] 'The emperor is stupid,' Henry declared to Peter Schwaben, 'he knows no Latin, the princes ought to have asked me and the King of France to arbitrate, we would have settled the matter very quickly.'[4] 'Your master,' said Francis to the English ambassadors, 'thinks himself very wise, but is nothing more than a fool.'[5] Reading the despatches we find that Henry put himself on a par with such princes as Charles V or Francis I, princes whose realms were four times as populous as England, whose revenues were even greater in proportion, and who commanded the services of captains and armies such as Henry could never dream of bringing into the field. And as if the king had feared that these boasts might not be transmitted to the proper quarter, as if he had been anxious to show that they were not the result of a momentary feeling, as if he had wished to hand them down to posterity, we find them embodied in his letters and instructions to his ambassadors. To the imperial court he wrote that it was wholly due to his influence that Charles had been elected emperor, and that it was he, not Charles, who had gained the battle of Pavia.[6] The French court, on the other hand, was informed in 1536 that no King of England had ever held France so much in his power as Henry VIII did at that time.[7]

Henry's acts corresponded with his words. They aimed much more at show and momentary renown than at any real and lasting advantage. They were intended to make the king appear for the hour a noble, wise, rich and powerful monarch, not to make his people happy, or to strengthen his realms. The court of Henry was of the most magnificent description; the treasure accumulated by his father was squandered in jousts, balls, and mummeries. Foreign ambassadors, literary men, even simple visitors, received large presents or were regaled in right royal fashion, that they might praise the splendour of the court and the liberality of the king. Occasions of ostentatious display were eagerly sought; really useful undertakings – buildings, public works, the founding of schools or charities – on the contrary, were generally avoided. Other men during Henry's reign built and founded a good deal, the king has scarcely left any monument to perpetuate his name. What Henry wanted was immediate praise and glory, and this he was well aware he could more easily obtain by mere show than by lasting deeds.

And as at home so abroad. Henry's policy during peace and during war was always one of show. He paid dearly for mere names. Defender of the faith, protector of the Italian league, even Most Christian King or King of the Romans were empty titles with which he allowed himself to be beguiled. His campaigns were either fruitless or worse than fruitless; the successes he obtained were merely outward, and any fortress he conquered he was finally compelled either to raze or to restore for a tenth or twentieth part of the money it had cost him.

When he allied himself with Ferdinand, Maximilian, or Charles, there was always a kind of tacit understanding that Henry was to have the glory, and his ally the profit, of the war. Had this result been obtained but a few times, one might have thought that Henry had been baffled by the craftier statesmen of Spain or Germany. But as it was repeated over and over again, he must have been satisfied with the share allotted to him. Marilhac, the French ambassador, stated that such was the case. 'He cares more,' he said, 'for a fair show than for the greatest good you can do him.'[8]

His courage in the field was not tested, for Henry was never present at a battle. As to his courage in facing the danger of disease, Jean du Bellay records that, when in 1528 a servant of Anne Boleyn fell ill of the sweat, the lady, notwithstanding the king's passion for her, was forthwith sent from court, while Henry fled from place to place to escape the danger of infection.[9] In 1540 he was again in mortal terror, so much so that Marilhac called him 'the most timid person in such matters you could meet with.'[10] At a time when it was the custom to speak of kings in the most guarded terms and with the greatest respect, Eustache Chapuis, Charles's ambassador, excused Henry, saying that he was not so very wicked but entirely led by others, but that even these could not wholly trust him on account of his levity.[11] Castillon, the French ambassador, did not scruple to call him plainly a fool.[12] Badoer, Carroz, Giustinian, du Bellay, Mendoza, Dinteville, Chapuis, Marilhac all asserted that he was invariably under the influence of some other person, some *alter rex*. And this was not said in spleen or in anger, but generally by those diplomatists who were in favour with the king, and had the best opportunity of judging of his character and position.

Events fully justified the statements of the ambassadors. Scarcely anything could be more contemptible than the way in which Henry allowed himself to be led. He never dared openly to rebel against any one under whose sway he had come, he never dared to meet a man face to face. Though he might bitterly resent the treatment he received, he never mustered sufficient courage to put a stop to it himself. He conspired against his ministers or his wives, secretly he sought for allies to overthrow the hated tyrants, but until he found a strong and decided hand to carry him forward and to destroy his victim, he never ventured to assert his authority. Wolsey ousted Fox and Catherine, Anne Boleyn overthrew Wolsey. When Henry became thoroughly tired of Anne he dared not attack her until Cromwell took the lead and brought her to the scaffold. Norfolk and Gardiner avenged Anne's fate on the Earl of Essex, to be in their turn overthrown by Seymour and Dudley. From first to last, supreme power was vested in some other person than the king; there was an *alter rex*.

Henry's obstinacy has been advanced as a proof of a strong will. But obstinacy is by no means a sign of a strong mind, it is rather a sign of weakness. A man of strong will and quick decision will never fear to change his mind and follow a new course, for he feels sure that his energy and determination will not fail him. A weak man, on the contrary, is so very glad when for once he has come to a decision that he is loath to give it up. The consciousness of his vacillating temper impels him to cling to his resolution; he fears that if he abandons it he will float about like a ship without rudder. This was true of Henry, but it was not the whole truth; for often, when he insisted upon some important point, the explanation was that the person under whose guidance he had placed himself would have it so. The persistency with which he acted in the matter of the divorce, for instance, was due mainly to the influence of Anne Boleyn. In matters of detail he could be obstinate enough without receiving encouragement; and then he frequently held by his own opinion in order to irritate those whose yoke he had to bear. If he felt some humiliation in nearly always allowing his ministers to have their will, he felt a corresponding pride in the annoyance his sudden resistance gave them. The prayers of those who wished to dissuade him from his purpose flattered him; he gloried in the sham strength which enabled him to withstand their entreaties. He thus often rendered more difficult or even impossible the attainment of what he himself desired, and inflicted a great deal of vexation and misery on his servants.

But the most terrible fault of Henry, and that for which outward circumstances are no excuse, was his utter want of truth. His dishonesty cannot be denied; his own handwriting is still extant to show it. Nor can it be excused on the plea that in the sixteenth century falsehood was general. There was a wide difference between the falsehood Machiavelli advised and that which Henry practised. The Florentine secretary was decidedly the more honest of the two. He approved of falsehood and deceit towards an enemy, towards a doubtful friend, or towards the general public. According to him, official documents may contain false statements, lies may be boldly told to an adversary, and the assurances of diplomatists are to be held of small account, for their rule is generally not to speak the truth. But untruthfulness and double-dealing towards one's own servants and counsellors Machiavelli did not advise. Charles V and Francis I, who followed the worst maxims of the secretary, told no lies to their chief ministers. Duprat and Gattinara, Montmorency and Covos, Chabot and Granville were not deceived by their masters. The ministers of Henry VIII were deceived constantly. He intrigued with one to counteract the doings of another; none of them ever felt sure that he possessed the confidence of the king. When Henry hated any of his servants and lacked the energy to dismiss them, he showed them as good natured a face as Holbein ever painted on his most flattering portrait. All the time he was accumulating a store of hatred, was laying snares for his intended victims; and at last he handed them over to their enemies, as ruthlessly as if he had never smiled on them. In the skilful acting of his part the king often showed real talent; nobody could be certain that his amiability was not a mask. And this of course made most people afraid to commit themselves, and weakened the salutary action of the Government.

Even this was not the worst. Had Machiavelli heard of it, he would simply have said that Henry was a fool, who by deceiving too much, lost the fruit of his deceit. But if the secretary had seen how Henry was constantly intent on deceiving himself, even Machiavelli would have turned with disgust from so miserable a liar. Henry was a liar to his own conscience. He was a thoroughly immoral man, and he dared not own it to himself. He tried by all kinds of casuistic subterfuges to make his most dishonest acts appear pure virtue, to make himself believe in his own goodness. And this he did not only after the deed had been committed, so as to stifle the pangs of his conscience: before the act he contrived by sophisms to convince himself that what he desired was quite moral and right. It was his constant practice to use fine phrases about questionable acts, and to throw upon somebody else the blame for a misdeed which could not be denied. We find him urging others to do that which he has not the moral courage to do himself. We see him prompting deeds from which he afterwards shrinks back full of pious horror, never admitting for a moment that he has been the cause of them. The morality of Henry was the very type of what is commonly called 'cant'.

One more fault has been laid to Henry's charge, the coarseness which he always manifested in his relations with the other sex. Even his great panegyrist has been forced to admit the truth of this. Nor can it be excused by the general coarseness of the times. The French under Francis I were perhaps even more dissolute than the English, but Francis was a model of delicacy when compared with Henry. The Spaniards, Italians, and Germans, were all more refined in this respect than the King of England. But this is to be said in favour of Henry, that neither his parents nor those who surrounded him had given him an example of refinement. Henry VII was quite as coarse as his son; there is scarcely anything so disgusting to be found in the correspondence of the latter as his father's instructions to John Stile when he intended to marry the Queen Dowager of Naples. Henry grew up in the most brutal and dissolute atmosphere; there was nobody to teach him better; his courtiers were as bad as their king.

If such was the character of King Henry, Catherine of Aragon was altogether different. She was not vain at all, but on the contrary very simple and careless of show, praise, or glory. If she occasionally insisted on being treated with the ceremonies due to her rank, this was not for vanity's sake, but because she considered it one of the duties of her station. Nor was she weak; she came quickly to a decision, and was most firm in doing what she considered right. She was courageous and did not shrink from responsibility; threats or danger had no influence on her, and it was impossible to deter her from what she thought her duty by any fear of worldly consequences. She was more truthful than most people around her, infinitely more so than Henry. She was pious in the Spanish fashion, following the precepts of her Church, but taking no interest in their real sense. She was charitable and kind, true and devoted to her friends, and of a forgiving temper towards her enemies. One of the fairest praises bestowed on Catherine is a passage in a letter of Eustache Chapuis, where he deplores that she will lose the goodwill of the Duke of Norfolk by showing compassion for the pitiable state of Wolsey, the man whom she believed to be the author of all her trouble.[13]

But on the other hand Catherine was narrow-minded, violent, and wanting in delicacy and tact. She was unable to understand any but the very simplest issues; as soon as a question became complicated it passed the limits of her intelligence. Consequently she committed gross errors of judgement which entailed a great deal of trouble on her and on her friends. She could never look at any question from a high standpoint, or gain a general view of things. She had many individual aims, many single duties, but no comprehensive scheme. Thus she was wholly unfit to strike out a way for herself, especially in the difficult position in which she found herself. She had to rely on others, first on her father Ferdinand and on her confessor, afterwards on Charles V and on his ambassador. Even when she was striving with all her might to defend her own and her daughter's rights, she never formed any independent plan. She only resolved that she would not give way, that no threat or violence should induce her to lay aside her character as the wife of Henry, or to admit her marriage to have been questionable.

While the narrowness of her mind prevented Catherine from carrying out any great plan, her want of delicacy and tact made her commit many blunders, and put her from the outset into a false position. According to two successive Spanish ambassadors, Don Gutiere Gomez de Fuensalida and Don Luis Carroz, the intimacy in which she lived with her confessor was decidedly scandalous.[14] Her father Ferdinand most certainly thought so. For in the spring of 1509, Catherine sent one of her servants, Juan de Ascoytia, with a letter to her father exculpating herself, and asking him to do all in his power that Father Diego Fernandez, such was the confessor's name, might remain with her.[15] When Ferdinand learned the facts from Juan, who was a familiar servant of the princess and could tell all that went on in her household, he became so alarmed that at the next interview with the English ambassador he told a direct lie. He said that his daughter had written to him to send her another confessor, which he intended shortly to do.[16] It is evident that Ferdinand had heard enough to make him fear that on account of this scandal the marriage with Henry might fall through. By a falsehood he hoped somewhat to shield the reputation of his daughter, or at least to gain time. With all the papers before us it cannot be disputed that Catherine acted with extraordinary imprudence in persisting in having the friar with her as her confessor and most intimate servant. Though we may hold that there was no guilt of the kind suspected at the time, we cannot much admire a person who utterly disregarded her own reputation.

But it was not only in this way that her want of tact prevented Catherine from obtaining a good position. The same defect caused her to omit a good many little acts of amiability which, by a man of Henry's temper, are generally much more prized than serious devotion. That Catherine was quite incapable of flattering Henry may not be imputed to her as a fault, but it was a disadvantage to her. That she was equally incapable of humouring the whims and caprices of her husband, and of coaxing him into any course she wished him to follow, was a real defect. Instead of leading her husband with 'iron hand in glove of velvet', she allowed him to feel the whole harshness of her grasp. If she wanted anything, she asked for it directly, without charm of manner; when she was displeased, she too plainly showed her resentment. There was no pliancy in her disposition, and this must have been terribly wounding to the feelings of such a man as Henry. Still, such was his weakness that for nearly four years he accepted her guidance; rather than stand alone he submitted to her disagreeable rule. As to the broad features of foreign politics Catherine followed the advice of her father, but she was incompetent to deal with purely English questions. She disliked the English system of government as it had been carried on under Henry VII, and as, with little modification, it remained during the reign of his son. Since she was not strong enough to change it, she simply opposed now and then some of the measures proposed by the royal ministers. The part she played in home politics was unimportant, but such influence as she exerted was not exerted generally to the advantage of the Crown. The blunders she committed in this manner helped to prepare the way for her ruin.

The two great parties into which Englishmen who took any interest in politics were then divided were the party of the aristocracy and the party of the officials. The aristocratic party was composed of nearly all the peers with their relatives and dependants, and of the great majority of the independent gentry. The party of the officials consisted of all those royal servants who, by their talents and industry, had risen in the bureaucratic hierarchy, with their families and clients, and of those courtiers who depended entirely on the favour of the king. Both parties were very powerful, both had their distinct traditions and aims, the foremost of which was to ruin the rival faction.

Nearly all the lay peers at that time were great landowners, some of them to an extent altogether unknown now. At their country seats they kept large establishments, 100 servants not being considered extravagant for a simple baron, while dukes and marquises had two or three times as many. Some of these servants were of the better classes – the sons of knights, of gentlemen, and sometimes even of nobles. Young men attached themselves to the households of the great barons, partly to lead at the country seats or at the town houses of their patrons a pleasant and carefree life, partly to learn with them the ways of the world, partly to rise and to make their fortune by the influence of their masters. The lords found among them energetic and faithful agents both for political intrigue and for military service. And as every peer had at his house a well-stocked armoury, he had at his command the nucleus of a small administration and a miniature army, the ranks of which he could at any time swell by the aid of his tenants and clients.

The latter were generally very numerous. In those troubled times a man of the middle classes – unless he happened to possess extraordinary energy and capacity – could not stand by himself. In the greater towns men were formed into guilds and could defend themselves jointly, but in small towns, in villages and in the country, this was not the case. Here they were obliged to look out for patrons able and willing to defend them against oppression and violence. In the peers they generally found such protectors. Most peers had influence at court and at quarter sessions, and were held in respect by the sheriff and the other officials of the county. A peer therefore who was ready to assist the yeomen and small burghers around him readily found a great many clients, who in return for the protection he gave them stood by him in his quarrels. Even the severe laws of Henry VII against retainers had not been able to change this order of things. Many peers boasted that with their household servants, their clients, their tenants, and their sons and servants, they could bring 10,000 men into the field; and it was the bare truth. Each single lord was still a powerful baron, and when they all stood together they represented a force which it would not have been easy to subdue.

The peers were divided on many questions, there were frequent quarrels among them, and they regarded one another with a good deal of jealousy. But they had common interests which held them together. As great landlords they wished for the same financial and administrative measures. As men whose fortune was already made, they naturally combined against those who were striving to rise. Being nearly all men of the sword, they disliked the clerkly official. These were ties strong enough to bind the whole peerage into a party with very specific aims.

The independent gentry generally sided with the lords. They too were great landowners, and if they rose in rank, it was only to become peers. They led a life very similar to that of the barons, to whom most of them were related; so that all their interests and sympathies were akin to those of the class above them, and they followed their natural bent, and stood by their party.

Nor was this all that contributed to the power of the lords. Tradition was in their favour. The offices of high treasurer, high steward, lord chamberlain and chamberlain of the household were reserved for them. The command of the armies, the wardenship of the northern marches, the deputyship of Ireland and of Calais, were generally held by some of them. They were also employed on great embassies, and on all great occasions of state. Those peers who sat on the royal council had, therefore, considerable influence as heads of a party holding many high offices.

But what was all this power and influence when compared with the position their grandfathers had enjoyed? The lords thought of the time when a Warwick could make and unmake the king, when there was no power in England equal to that of their class. They regretted those halcyon days, which tradition rendered more bright; and they wished to see the king reduced once more to the position of *primus inter pares*, to diminish the authority of the administration and to augment that of parliament. In fact, they desired a total reversal of the policy of the Tudors. For a long time they had been in opposition, now openly, now secretly, withstanding the constant extension of the royal prerogative.

The fact that they had never within the remembrance of the people been placed at the head of the administration, that they had never held undisputed sway in the councils of the two Henrys, was in some respects of great advantage to the lords. For they had never had any occasion to show their incapacity, nor had they been obliged to impose taxes, to enforce odious laws, or to annoy people by fiscal regulations. They had, on the contrary, persistently clamoured against the harshness of the existing system. They were therefore looked upon as the faithful defenders of the liberty of the subject, and as the only safeguard against the tyranny of the king and the rapacity of the officials. And this made them not a little popular.

The officials formed a party less numerous, but much better organised, than the peers and their adherents. As a political power they were but of recent origin. Henry VII, on coming to the throne, had fully realised that it would be impossible to establish a strong and durable government without having at his command a body of men, thoroughly versed in all the arts of administration, owing obedience to no one but the king, and wholly devoted to him. Such a body of officials he had set himself to form, and before the end of his reign, he had brought together a large number of able and energetic civil servants. Henry VIII sacrificed a few of the most hated of his father's ministers, but he was clever enough to know the value of the bureaucracy Henry VII had left behind him. He was careful not to disorganise so admirable an instrument of arbitrary rule. Under Richard Fox, Bishop of Winchester, and subsequently under Cardinal Wolsey, the body of officials was strengthened and made even more effective than it had been under Henry VII.

Nearly all officials had risen from the lower ranks of life. Such men were preferred, for those who had no connection with any of the great houses were less likely to be led astray by family influence. As the salaries were very small, it was their interest to compete for extraordinary grants in return for good and zealous work. They were eager to please their superiors, that they might be recommended to the royal bounty; and when they rose high enough to attract the attention of the king, their chief object was to win his favour. The officials vied with each other in fulfilling his wishes, their promotion being wholly dependent on his goodwill.

The officials were most corrupt. To the grants they obtained from the king they added the bribes they extorted from the public. Bribery was practised in every form in a most shameful way. Many of those who had frequent occasion to transact business in the royal courts conferred some sinecure or pension on the most influential members of the bureaucracy, others made a present every time they appeared. With the exception of a few persons known to enjoy the special favour of the king, no man could obtain the speedy discharge of his business without offering a bribe. The clearest right could not obtain a hearing, the simplest formality could not be gone through, all manner of obstacles were raised, if no present was forthcoming. Nor was this all. Besides being rapacious the royal officials were generally ill-bred and overbearing. They were upstarts, who had to undergo many a humiliation, and who avenged themselves on the public for the slavish cringing demanded of them by the king. As a body, therefore, they were detested by the nation, while the most conspicuous among them were held in special execration.

Their unpopularity greatly enhanced their value in the eyes of Henry VIII. Had he withdrawn his protection from them, innumerable enemies would have risen against them and hunted them down. The officials were as much at the king's mercy in this respect as in any other; with them the loss of the royal favour meant ruin, if not death. And as they knew that the throne was their only safeguard, they stood most faithfully by it. In fact, during the reign of Henry VII and of his son, although we hear of many a conspiracy of the nobles, we never hear of a conspiracy of the officials against the king. Even if they had preferred some pretender they would not have dared to favour him; for in case of a revolution they would have fared very badly; the mob would have risen against them. So the officials were constantly on their guard against the dangers which beset the throne, and were always ready to put down with the greatest sternness any attempt at rebellion. It was this quality which made them most valuable to a king who by his arbitrary proceedings excited the ill will of his subjects. Henry VIII without his officials would have had but a brief career.

The peers and the officials were of course deadly enemies. The lords hated the officials for their rapacity and insolence, but even more on account of the power they gave to the Crown. The officials, on the other hand, hated the lords for the resistance they offered to their exactions and tyrannical bearing, and for the share they had in the royal favour. Every grant, every office which the peers were able to secure for one of their party, seemed to the members of the bureaucracy a clear loss to themselves. Every suitor introduced directly to the king detracted from their income, for he paid them no bribes. The lords spoiled their trade, making it far less lucrative than it would otherwise have been.

Their political creeds, too, were wholly opposed to one another. While the peers wished to limit the power of the Crown, the officials, as the chief agents of the royal authority, were eager to extend it. On this account a constant war raged between the two parties; under the smooth surface of the court a bitter enmity lay hidden. Any measures favoured by the one party were sure to arouse the suspicions of the other. To be friends with both was not possible; whoever wished to have some influence in politics was obliged to ally himself either with the officials or with the peers.

Catherine generally sided with the peers. Not only were all her instincts in favour of the aristocracy, she was disgusted at the way in which the officials used their power; and she incurred their very hearty aversion by occasionally trying to resist their tyranny. Henry was well aware that the tone which Catherine adopted towards the officials was not to his advantage, but he could not muster sufficient energy to prevent her from thwarting them. A party secretly hostile to Catherine continued to have a large share of his favour and confidence; and they missed no opportunity of undermining the queen's influence.

That Ferdinand of Aragon cheated his beloved son-in-law more than even Henry would submit to may have been one of the reasons why in 1513 Catherine suddenly lost the control she had exercised over her husband. Another reason is to be found in the considerable humiliation which the queen in that year inflicted on poor Henry. The king had in the spring of 1513 crossed the Channel for the purpose of leading the army with which he intended to conquer the whole of France. To begin this modest undertaking he had sat down before Therouenne, a place which could be of no earthly use to him, but which greatly annoyed the town of St Omer belonging to Archduke Charles. Near Therouenne he was joined by the Emperor Max, who brought him no soldiers, but gained his heart by compliments. Shortly afterwards Max won for Henry that famous cavalry engagement known as the Battle of the Spurs; Henry trumpeted this victory all over the world, but the world was just for once. Even in England Max, not Henry, was credited with the result, and the country rang with the praise of the 'second Mavors'. Therouenne, being taken, had to be razed to the ground; after which, by the advice of the emperor, Tournay was attacked, a place 80 miles from the nearest English fort, but wedged in between Charles's territories. After the capture of Tournay, in which an English garrison was placed, the campaign came to an end, and Henry could not but be a little ashamed when he compared the small result with his gigantic anticipations. During his absence the Scots, as hereditary allies of France, had invaded the northern borders; and Catherine, who had been left as regent in England, acted with energy and courage. An army was soon collected of which the Earl of Surrey assumed the command. But this was not sufficient for the queen; the martial ardour of her forefathers rekindled in her; she took to horse and rode towards the north to place herself at the head of the troops.[17] Surrey's speedy and complete success prevented her from going farther than Woburn, but her vigorous behaviour gained for her the esteem and admiration of the English people. The Battle of Flodden, fought by Englishmen in defence of English soil, interested them much more than a brilliant cavalry engagement fought for no national purpose, somewhere in Artois, by German and Burgundian mercenaries. Catherine and Surrey were the heroes of the day, not Henry and his favourites.

And Catherine, with her usual awkwardness, did her best to bring this truth home to Henry. He had sent the Duc de Longueville, made prisoner at Guinegatte, to England, to be kept there in confinement. Catherine in return sent three Scots over to Henry, with a letter saying that it was no great thing for a man to make another man prisoner, but that here were three men made prisoners by a woman.[18] She was made to pay very dearly for the coarse way in which she showed her exultation. Henry, jealous of her fame and glory, stung to the quick by her taunt, looked out for a new counsellor.

Among the brilliant courtiers of Henry there were none who could take the place; they were ornamental nullities. Supple enough to humour Henry's whims, just clever enough to flatter his vanity, they had no qualities which would have enabled them to guide him. There were, indeed, a few noblemen who might have filled the post of prime minister tolerably well; but Henry distrusted them, not without reason, for even the most loyal of them would never have defended his interests with that energy which was necessary for the safety of the throne.

But there was at court one Thomas Wolsey, a priest, who as a young man had entered the service of Sir John Nanfan, had afterwards passed to that of Fox, Bishop of Winchester, and towards the end of Henry VII's reign had obtained a place in the royal chapel. He was an able man, and when Henry VIII succeeded, he knew how to flatter the new king: clever, light-hearted, witty, and pliant, he amused and pleased his royal master. Not long afterwards he was made royal almoner, which was already an important position, for the almoner was employed in all kinds of secular business. Wolsey was grateful for the favour shown to him, and proved his gratitude by zealous and able service. At the same time he made his company agreeable to the king, who often went to sup with him, Wolsey being quite ready to forget the gravity of his cloth and to amuse his royal visitor by all kinds of jokes. He was chosen to accompany Henry to France as head of the commissariat of the army; and this was most advantageous to him. Henry, far from Catherine, was no longer under her sway; he allowed himself to be guided and advised by his almoner, whose knowledge of business contrasted agreeably with her incapacity. Wolsey, who was of unbounded ambition, seized the opportunity, and determined to become, if possible, the king's prime minister.

He had an immense advantage over all his lay competitors for the post. Henry could not be jealous of any fame or glory he might gain, for Wolsey was but a priest.

In modern England a clergyman is treated in much the same way as other men: if any difference is made it is rather in his favour. During the Middle Ages this was not the case. The Church was certainly held sacred, and its ministers shared in some measure the respect paid to the institution. But the respect shown to them was not the respect shown to an equal; there was always a mixture of contempt in it. In an age when every man had to defend his liberty, security, and honour by force of arms, military courage was the paramount virtue. The peaceful citizen, the inoffensive villein were despised; every one of their occupations was looked upon with scorn. A true knight spent his time in fighting, jousting, and love-making – three occupations specially forbidden to the clergy. No wonder, then, that the proud warrior looked down on the priest with that feeling which the strong and courageous have for the weak and craven. A priest for him was a special kind of being, something between a man and a woman, with most of the privileges of the latter, with none of the rights of the former. 'Friars and women cannot insult' was a typical mediaeval saying.

England, indeed, had during thirty years of peace and strong government gained more modern ideas about knights and priests, but Henry still cherished many of the notions of the Middle Ages. He aspired to the glory and fame of a valiant knight, a fame which Brandon or Carew, Compton or Pointz, might share with him, but which could never fall to the lot of Wolsey. There was no danger that by being raised to high position he would become a rival whose fame might eclipse that of the king. Let Mr Almoner be ever so clever, active, witty, and brilliant, neither in the field nor with fair ladies could he boast of any success. He would for ever remain but a priest.

Henry had not, therefore, the slightest hesitation in raising his new favourite to the highest dignities. The bishopric of Tournay, the archbishopric of York were bestowed upon him; the Pope was induced to make him a cardinal; and he became lord chancellor. Henry handed over the reins of government to him, trusting his ability and devotion, and relying on his quick and firm decision. And Wolsey, though he took good care of his own interests, in a way served his master faithfully enough. The policy he pursued was more brilliant than really wise, but it was just what Henry appreciated. His alliance was courted, he was flattered by pope, emperor, and Christian king; he thought himself one of the greatest sovereigns on earth.

But Wolsey committed a mistake which was committed by all Henry's ministers; he became rather too forgetful of the feelings of his master. By and by the king began to be annoyed at the way in which the cardinal carried on the whole government of the realm. He had not courage to rebel, for he could neither govern by himself nor had he anybody else to guide him; he submitted to the rule of Wolsey as something inevitable. But he brooded over many a grievance, and, if he had seen a chance, would have planned the destruction of his minister. His friendship became a mask to hide the humiliation he felt at being so utterly set aside by the cardinal.

During the reign of Wolsey, Catherine sank into utter insignificance. Henry's hatred for Ferdinand was, indeed, easily allayed by a splendid present sent to him by the Catholic king with flattering messages; and the anger excited by Catherine did not last long, for when she ceased to rule Henry he found her a very tolerable wife. But one thing told heavily against her: all the sons she bore to the king died shortly after birth; of her children, but one girl, Princess Mary, survived. To Henry, who ardently longed for a son and heir to succeed him in England and in those realms he always dreamt of conquering, this was a bitter disappointment. When Anne Boleyn began to be a prominent figure at court he had ceased to have any hope of an heir by Catherine, who was then more than forty years of age.

1

ANNE & WOLSEY

Nowhere has the making of false pedigrees been so extensively practised as it was in England during the sixteenth century. Every man or woman who rose in the royal favour had but to apply to the heralds, to have – for a consideration – some genealogical tree made out, the root of which was a fabulous Saxon chieftain or an equally imaginary Norman knight. In the case of Anne Boleyn we know the exact date when this service was rendered to her by Henry's kings-at-arms. In December 1530 it was found that the Boleyns had sprung from a Norman lord who had settled in England during the twelfth century, and somewhat later it was discovered that during the fourteenth century there had been in Picardy a man called Walter Boulen who had held a piece of land in fee of the Lord of Avesnes.[1] Although Lady Anne was already a very important person at court, whom it was rather dangerous to annoy, the new pedigree was received with derision by nobles of ancient descent.[2] The whole structure seems to have been most fantastic, and all that is really known of Anne's origin is that her great-grandfather, Geffrey Boleyn, was a wealthy London merchant. He was elected alderman, and in due time arrived at knighthood and the dignity of Lord Mayor.

Sir Geffrey married a daughter of Lord Hoo and Hastings, by whom he had several children. William, his eldest son, was in turn knighted by Richard III, retired from business, bought large estates in Norfolk, Essex and Kent, and married Margaret Butler, one of the daughters of the Earl of Ormond. Sir William was happy enough to escape the dangers of a war of succession and of several bloody insurrections; he held to the last the position of a wealthy country gentleman with some influence even at court. He had three sons and several daughters. James Boleyn, the eldest son, was to inherit the bulk of the family property. Edward Boleyn married Anne, daughter of Sir John Tempest, who was a favourite attendant of Queen Catherine and seems to have always remained attached to her party. Thomas Boleyn, the second son of Sir William, inherited some of his grandfather's ability, and went to court to make his fortune in the royal service. Being a young man of good address he succeeded in obtaining the hand of Lady Elizabeth Howard, one of the daughters of the Earl of Surrey.

This marriage, at the time it was concluded, was not so brilliant for Thomas Boleyn as it might now appear. After the Battle of Bosworth, where the Duke of Norfolk had fallen, his son, the Earl of Surrey, had been attainted and deprived of his estates. A few years later he was pardoned and restored to the earldom of Surrey, but most of his lands remained with the Crown. With a very numerous family he found himself in straitened circumstances, and as he was able to give his daughters but small marriage portions, they could not expect to become the wives of men of great wealth and rank. Of the sisters of Lady Elizabeth one married Thomas Bryan, another Sir Henry Wyatt, a third Sir Griffith ap Rice. Thomas Boleyn, therefore, could well aspire to the hand of Lady Elizabeth.

The young couple at first resided chiefly at Hever, in Kent, a place belonging to Sir William Boleyn. Besides the house and the yield of the home farm, they seem to have had in money only £50 a year. But that sum was not so small as it appears: it entitled to the honour of knighthood, and enabled its possessor to lead a simple but easy life in the country. In all probability it was at Hever that Anne was born either in 1502 or in the first half of 1503.[3] She had a good many brothers and sisters, but most of them died young. The only survivors were her brother George and her sister Mary, both younger than Anne.

While Anne was still a child the position of her father steadily improved. In 1505 Sir William Boleyn died, and his son Thomas inherited a considerable part of his wealth. At the same time the Earl of Surrey, by his prudence, energy and skill, gradually gained the favour of Henry VII. On the accession of Henry VIII the cloud which had hung over the house of Howard was entirely dispelled, and Surrey became one of the chief counsellors of the new king. He naturally advanced the interests of his sons-in-law. Thomas Boleyn, who had been knighted, was employed by the Government. In 1511 he and his brother-in-law, Sir Henry Wyatt, were made joint governors of Norwich Castle. In 1512 Sir Thomas was sent as ambassador to Margaret of Savoy, the ruler of the Low Countries; and henceforward we find him taking rank among the regular ministers of the Crown.

Sir Thomas had now a large income, of which he made a very creditable use by giving his children a good education. He kept several masters to teach them, and though, measured by our standard, their accomplishments were but small, they were well brought up according to the ideas of their time. But Sir Thomas did even more for Anne. The French court being considered in England the pattern of grace and refinement, he secured for Anne in 1514 the privilege of accompanying Mary Tudor, who went to marry Louis XII of France.[4] Mary promised to look after the child, who on her part seems to have been delighted at the prospect of escaping from the monotony of Hever, and of living at the liveliest of courts. It was on this occasion that she wrote to her father a most grateful letter, by the strange spelling of which some students have been sorely puzzled.[5]

Towards the end of 1514 Mary Tudor, accompanied by Surrey, now created Duke of Norfolk, by Sir Thomas Boleyn, and by her little attendant Anne, crossed the Channel. At Abbeville the marriage ceremony was performed, after which Louis, jealous of English influence, dismissed the servants his young wife had brought over. Exceptions were made, however, in favour of Anne and of her cousin the Lady Elizabeth Grey, as both were children and could have no influence on the queen. Shortly afterwards King Louis died, and his widow hastened to marry Charles Brandon, Duke of Suffolk, and returned to England. But Anne, who by this time had learned a good many French ways, remained behind. By the wish of her father she was entrusted to the care of the new queen, Claude of France, an excellent woman, who is said to have taken the greatest pleasure in the education of young girls.

Under this superintendence Anne remained six years in France, learning French and Italian, and acquiring all those arts and graces by which she was afterwards to shine. When towards the end of 1521 the political aspect became rather threatening, Sir Thomas recalled his daughter. She had now become a young woman, not very handsome, but of elegant and graceful figure, with very fine black eyes and hair and well-shaped hands. She was naturally quick and witty, gifts her French education had fully developed. Being extremely vain and fond of praise and admiration, Anne laid herself out to please, a task not very difficult for a young lady just returned from the centre of all elegance. Being so closely related to one of the greatest noblemen in the realm, she soon obtained a good position at court, and shared its gaieties and pastimes.

Already, before Anne's return, it had been proposed that she should marry Sir James Butler, son of Sir Piers Butler, an Irish chieftain, who had set up a claim to the earldom of Ormond, and had seized the Irish estates of the late lord. The Earl of Surrey, Anne's uncle, who was at the time lord deputy of Ireland, wished by this marriage to conciliate the conflicting claims of the late earl's English legitimate descendants and of his illegitimate son, Sir Piers, whom the Irish people preferred. Anne was to receive as her dowry the claims of the Boleyn and Saintleger families, and her father-in-law was to be created Earl of Ormond. Cardinal Wolsey was favourable to the plan, and Sir Thomas Boleyn and his English relations were ready to accept the compromise; but the pretensions of the Irish chieftain were exorbitant. A year passed during which Surrey and he haggled about the terms, and at the end of 1522 the matter was given up.

The events of Anne's life from 1523 to 1526 are not exactly known. Her fortunes were at that time thrown into the shade by those of her younger sister Mary. Early in 1521 the latter had married William Carey, one of the gentlemen of Henry's chamber. As she resided constantly at court and seems to have been rather handsome, she attracted the attention of the king, and soon became his mistress.[6] But Mary Carey did not contrive to make her position profitable either to herself or to her husband: it was her father, Sir Thomas Boleyn, who reaped the golden harvest. Mr Brewer in his Calendar has recorded a few of the grants he obtained from the king: on 24 April 1522, the patent of treasurer of the household; five days later the stewardship of Tunbridge, the receivership of Bransted, and the keepership of the manor of Penshurst; in 1523 the keepership of Thunderley and Westwood Park, and in 1524 the stewardship of Swaffham. Having by all these lucrative employments obtained sufficient means to sustain his dignity, Sir Thomas was in 1525 created Lord Rochford.

Her father holding an office which obliged him to be nearly always at court, Anne spent a good part of her time with him in the vicinity of the royal palace. Although there was much gaiety around her, she appears to have felt rather dissatisfied. Being long past twenty and still only plain Mistress Anne, what wonder if she thought that, as her elders were not eager to provide a husband for her, she might look out for herself? There was at that time in the household of Cardinal Wolsey a foolish, wayward, violent young man, Sir Henry Percy, eldest son and heir of the Earl of Northumberland. He had been sent to Wolsey to learn under his roof the manners and customs of the court, and to gain the patronage of the great cardinal. Not being able to do any more useful work, Sir Henry simply followed Wolsey when the latter went to court. On these occasions he frequently met Mistress Anne; a flirtation began between them; and Percy being a very fair prize, she tried her best arts on him. The young knight soon fell desperately in love, and did not hide his intention of making her his wife. Wolsey was greatly displeased when he heard of it, and immediately sent for Sir Henry. The latter made a frank avowal, and ingenuously begged that his betrothal with Lady Mary Talbot, which had taken place in 1523 or 1524, might be formally cancelled. But he met with no favour; Wolsey soundly rated him for his presumption, and, when Sir Henry proved obstinate, called in the old Earl of Northumberland to carry off his son. Both Anne and Percy were enraged at this interference with their affairs, and retained a grudge against the cardinal to the end of his life.

One of the reasons which have been assigned for Wolsey's opposition to Sir Henry Percy's wishes is that the cardinal was already aware that the king was in love with Anne. There is nothing improbable in this. The reign of Mary Carey was past, her fickle lover had turned to other beauties, and it is pretty certain that in 1526 there was already a flirtation between him and Anne. This may have been known to Wolsey, and may have influenced his conduct.

For some time Anne kept her royal adorer at an even greater distance than the rest of her admirers. She had good reason to do so, for the position which Henry offered her had nothing very tempting to an ambitious and clever girl. Unlike his contemporary Francis I, and some of his successors on the English throne, Henry VIII behaved rather shabbily towards those of his fair subjects whom he honoured with his caprice. The mother of his son, Henry Fitzroy, had been married to a simple knight, and had received little money and few jewels or estates. Mary Boleyn had not even fared so well; her husband remained plain Mr Carey, and the grants bestowed on her were small. Nor had these or the other ladies who had become royal mistresses ever held a brilliant position at court. Their names are scarcely mentioned in contemporary records, and they would all have been utterly forgotten had not a few of them been otherwise remarkable. Under these circumstances it cannot be considered an act of great virtue that Anne showed no eagerness to become the king's mistress. She certainly was at first rather reticent, for we know from one of Henry's letters that she kept him in suspense for more than a year.[7] She was pleased to have the king among her admirers, but she wished for something better than the position of Elizabeth Blount or of her sister Mary.

Still, if a more brilliant prospect had not opened before Anne, it is highly probable that after having secured what would have seemed to her a fair equivalent she would have put aside her scruples. For whatever her good qualities may have been, modesty did not hold a prominent place among them. Sir Henry Percy was not the only man with whom she had an intrigue. Thomas Wyatt, her cousin, though already married, was her ardent admirer. She gave him a golden locket, and, if we may believe their contemporaries, he received from her very different treatment from that which she now accorded to Henry.[8]

It is not, therefore, uncharitable to suppose that if Anne had had no chance of becoming Henry's wife she might have tried to obtain by her ability and charms that position in England which her famous namesake, Anne d'Etampes, held in France. She might have become the first duchess of the Portsmouth, Cleveland and Kendal class, and her offspring might to this day have been the mighty and highly respected Dukes of Pembroke.

But when Henry began to pay court to Anne there was already a rumour that he was tired of his queen, that he was greatly annoyed at having no legitimate son to succeed him, and that he might possibly discard Catherine and look out for a younger bride. There were rumours to this effect whenever Henry was on bad terms with the family of the queen. When, in 1514, he had quarrelled with King Ferdinand, his father-in-law, it had been said that he would divorce Catherine, who had then no child living.[9] The political troubles of 1526 were in some respects very similar to those of 1514, and they naturally gave rise to the same reports.

At this time both king and prime minister had been deeply offended by Charles V, the nephew of the queen. The emperor, after the battle of Pavia, had taken but little account of the wishes and pretensions of Henry. He knew that the king and Wolsey had been negotiating a private peace with France, that they had intentionally delayed the payment of subsidies, and that they had been quite ready to betray him. After his victory, therefore, with more justice than prudence, he treated his faithless ally with scarcely hidden contempt. Henry resented the slight, and was unwilling to give up the foolish hope that he might one day become King of France. The cardinal was equally displeased. In 1521 the emperor had promised him an indemnity for his pension from France, and had undertaken to support him at the next conclave; but the new pensions had been paid most irregularly, and at the two conclaves of 1521 and 1523 the imperialist cardinals had not voted in his favour. Tempting offers being made to him by Louise de Savoye, he advised Henry to go over to the French, and both king and minister now freely abused the emperor. Catherine, who liked her nephew, was far too honest to hide her feelings; she defended him, and thereby drew on herself a part of her husband's anger. In these circumstances the possibility of a divorce began once more to be talked about.

A divorce such as may be obtained now was not possible in the time of Henry VIII. Marriage being a sacrament was held to be indissoluble. Consequently, when a man wished to get rid of his wife without killing her, he had to prove that his marriage had never been good and valid. This was done with a facility of which nobody can form an idea without being acquainted with the composition and practice of the courts before which such cases were brought. They were most corrupt, and always ready to please the strongest. Mr Brewer, in his Calendar, cites but one example, that of the Duke of Suffolk, who twice committed bigamy and was three times divorced, who began by marrying his aunt and ended by marrying his daughter-in-law.[10] But his case was by no means extraordinary; during the reign of Henry VIII and Edward VI there were many similar instances. The repudiation of a wife was a matter of nearly daily occurrence.

Anne, who had seen people repudiate their old wives and take new and younger brides, who knew that Henry was on bad terms with the queen and that he ardently wished to have a legitimate son, began to consider what effect all this might have upon her own fortunes. Perceiving that she might be able to displace Catherine, she resolved to spurn every lower prize and to strive with all her might for the crown. From this time she ceased to be merely a clever coquette, and became an important political personage.

If Anne wished to keep her power over Henry unimpaired, to increase her influence and finally to reach the desired end, she had to play a difficult game. She had to refuse the king's dishonourable proposals, yet had to make her society agreeable to him. Had she yielded, he would very soon have grown tired of her, for he was the most fickle of lovers, having hitherto changed his loves with even greater facility than his good brother of France. But Anne was quite clever enough to succeed; Henry bitterly complained of her severity, but never found her company tiresome. The longer this lasted the more his love for her increased: what had at first been a simple caprice became a violent passion for which he was ready to make great sacrifices.

Although the idea of a divorce had presented itself to many minds at an earlier date, no allusion whatever is made to it in the state papers before 1527. A letter of John Clerk, Bishop of Bath, of 13 September 1526, in which occur the words that there will be great difficulty *circa istud benedictum divortium*, clearly refers to the divorce between Margaret of Scotland and the Earl of Angus.[11] Margaret had just obtained at Rome a sentence in her favour, the revocation of which was desired by Henry. It is only in the spring of 1527, long after the king had been sighing at Anne's feet, that the divorce is first seriously mentioned.

In the spring of 1527 Henry consulted some of his most trusted counsellors about the legality of his marriage with his late brother's widow. Fully understanding in what direction the royal wishes lay, they immediately showed great scruples. Wolsey himself seems to have been eager to please the king; he was perhaps not aware that Henry had some other motive than a simple dislike of Catherine and the desire for a son and heir. That Lord Rochford, Anne's father, was in favour of the divorce awakened no suspicion, for he was a French pensioner, decidedly hostile to the emperor. The notion that Anne might profit by the intrigue, or even that she had anything to do with it, would have seemed preposterous. Wolsey thought that Anne had become Henry's mistress; and as he knew from long experience that in such cases the king was tired of his conquest in a few months, he confidently expected that long before the divorce could be obtained Anne would be cast off. In that case he hoped to make a good bargain by selling the hand of his master to the highest bidder.

Consequently the cardinal had no reason to object to Henry's wish to get rid of Catherine. He lent himself to a most odious attempt to cheat Catherine out of her 'good right'. On 17 May 1527, Wolsey, with Warham, the Archbishop of Canterbury, held secretly a court at Westminster, before which Henry was cited. Proceedings were begun nominally against the king for having lived for eighteen years in incestuous intercourse with the widow of his late brother, and Henry pretended to defend himself against the accusation. A second sitting was held on the 20th, a third on the 31st. At the latter sitting, Dr John Bell appeared as proctor of the king, while Dr Richard Wolman, a trusted royal servant, was appointed to plead against him.[12]

But it was felt that the authority of the two archbishops alone might not be sufficient to overcome the public feeling against the divorce. Wolsey, therefore, proposed that the question whether a man might marry his late brother's wife should be submitted to a number of the most learned bishops in England. The question was put in such a way that it was thought all the bishops would answer as the king desired. It was intended that the court should meet once more in secret after receipt of the answer of the bishops, that it should declare the marriage of Henry and Catherine to have been null and void from the beginning, and that it should condemn them to separate and to undergo some penance for the sin they had lived in. After this, Henry would have been free to marry whom he chose.[13]

Unhappily the bishops did not prove quite so subservient as had been expected; perhaps, too, they had not perceived the drift of the question. Most of them answered that such a marriage with papal dispensation would be perfectly valid.[14] This of course made it difficult for the archbishops to decide in Henry's favour; and even if they did decide in his favour, Catherine would still have the right of appeal from their judgement to that of the Pope. At this time all the world was startled by the tidings that the Pope was shut up by the imperial troops in the castle of St Angelo, and it was pretty certain that Clement would not in these circumstances dare to give judgement against the emperor's aunt. The news of the Pope's imprisonment was therefore as disagreeable as the reply of the bishops. Henry was further disconcerted by learning that the secret had not been well kept, and that Catherine was perfectly aware of the steps taken against her.

Cardinal Wolsey was so much hated by most Englishmen, Catherine was so popular, and the course which Henry pursued was so repugnant to his people, that even his most trusted agents did not scruple to betray his confidence. On the day after the first sitting at Westminster Don Iñigo de Mendoza, the imperial ambassador, was informed of all that had been done. A friend of Catherine told him, and although the man denied that he acted by her order, Mendoza felt sure that he came with the consent of the queen, and that the help of the emperor was wanted.[15]

Under these conditions it was not easy to proceed, for Catherine might make great difficulties, and the matter, if rendered public by her, might lead to the serious embarrassment of the government. But Henry was so much bent on having his way at once that he made an attempt to wring from Catherine some acknowledgment of the justice of his pretended scruples. On 22 June he spoke to her, saying that since he had married her he had been living in a state of mortal sin, and that henceforward he would abstain from her company; and he asked her to retire to some place far from court. If Henry expected that Catherine would give way he was mistaken. She was very much moved and burst into tears, but she neither admitted the justice of Henry's scruples, nor made choice of a separate residence. The king, seeing his error, was afraid to press her further. He blandly told her that all would be done for the best, and asked her to keep the matter secret.[16]

All proceedings were for the moment abandoned; but Henry was very angry at his defeat, and would have liked to carry matters with a high hand, and to bully his bishops into a favourable opinion. He was especially indignant with Wolsey for not taking definite action, and startled him by the violence of his expostulations.[17]

The negotiations with France had now proceeded so far that it was necessary to send a special embassy to treat with Francis about the league against the emperor. Wolsey was undoubtedly the person most fitted for such a mission, and at any other time he would have acted wisely in undertaking it himself. At this juncture, however, he committed a great blunder in deciding to go to Amiens. Henry was urging him to reopen the legatine court, and to continue the proceedings in the divorce case; and Wolsey may have wished to leave the country for a time in order to escape from this difficulty. He certainly hoped that during his absence Henry's passion would become less violent, and that he would find means to satisfy the king without making himself even more odious to the people than he already was. With these thoughts and hopes Wolsey left at the beginning of July with a numerous retinue, and crossed over to France.

The cardinal had not been absent a month before it became plain to most courtiers that the divorce was sought in favour of Anne.[18] She now almost constantly resided at court, remained for hours with the king, and scarcely thought it worthwhile to hide her purpose. This made the divorce very unpopular, for Lord Rochford, mean and grasping, was not beloved, while Anne had but a sorry reputation, and, owing to the violence of her temper and the insolence of her language, was disliked by the court in general. Such decency as still survived among English courtiers was shocked by the remembrance of the king's relation to Anne's sister, and everybody saw through the lie of Henry's scruples. When Wolsey started for France he probably anticipated that the king, left to himself, would be cowed by the strength of the opposition, and would abandon his design.

If such were the thoughts of Wolsey, he underrated the ability of Anne. She could not reckon upon a single ally, but she had by this time come to understand the character of Henry, and had learned how he might be ruled. The secret of Wolsey's success was no longer hidden from her. She had the same kind of advantages as those to which the cardinal had owed his elevation: for Henry might raise her to the highest rank without fearing her rivalry; and as Wolsey had consolidated his power during Henry's absence from Catherine, so Anne was now intent on gaining a lasting influence during the absence of Wolsey. She played her game with such tact that week after week her empire became stronger. Henry allowed himself to be guided by her in matters of state, she succeeded in making him suspicious of the cardinal's judgement and intentions, and she encouraged him to act independently behind the back of his prime minister.

After the failure of the attempt to secure the divorce by surreptitious means, Wolsey, seeing the king so bent on it, had formed a plan by which he hoped the end might be attained in a more effective manner and with less responsibility to himself. From Abbeville he communicated it to Henry. Catherine, he said, might decline his jurisdiction or appeal to the Pope. Now if Clement were free he would certainly favour the king, but he was the prisoner of Charles, and likely to continue so for some time. The cardinals who remained at liberty might, however, meet at Avignon, where Wolsey would join them; and as Perpignan was not far off the emperor might be induced to go to that place to arrange with Louise of Savoy, mother of Francis I, and with Wolsey for the conclusion of peace, and for the liberation of the Pope. If Charles refused reasonable conditions Henry might declare against him, the cardinals at Avignon would easily be induced to take steps for the government of the Church during the captivity of the pontiff, and matters might be handled in such a way that Henry would in the meanwhile gain his end.[19]

But this method seemed too dilatory to the king, who was eager to be at liberty to marry, and to Anne, who wished soon to be queen;

and Wolsey was suspected of having proposed the plan in order to gain time. It was thought that a direct appeal to the Pope might be successful, and it was decided that the attempt should be made without the cardinal's knowledge. The instrument chosen by Henry and Anne was Dr William Knight, the king's first secretary, an old and apparently somewhat conceited man, while their chief adviser seems to have been John Barlow, the chaplain of Lord Rochford.[20] Knight was to proceed to Italy, where he was to try by all means to get access to the Pope. He was to ask Clement to grant a dispensation to Henry to marry at once, even if the woman he might select should be related to him within the prohibited degrees of affinity, provided only she was not the wife of somebody else. This power was to be conceded to Henry before the declaration of the invalidity of his marriage with Catherine. If the Pope would not grant so much, then Knight was to ask that the king might have a dispensation to marry immediately after the dissolution of the first marriage.[21] Moreover, he was to obtain a bull, delegating for the time of the Pope's captivity the whole of his spiritual power to Cardinal Wolsey.[22] To conceal this mission Knight received another set of instructions which he was to show to Wolsey, ordering him to act in accordance with the proceedings of the cardinal's agents.

Knight left England early in September, and first proceeded to Compiègne, where he met Wolsey.[23] The latter, though not yet informed of the secret intrigue, was very little pleased with the secretary whom Henry had chosen to negotiate with the Pope.[24] He feared that his own position would be rendered even more difficult by Knight, whom he knew to be totally unfit for such an errand. Still, he could not prevent the secretary from leaving, and he had to own that his own plan was impracticable. There was a difficulty at the very beginning; the cardinals did not feel inclined to do Wolsey's bidding, and would not go to Avignon.[25]

The cardinal was of course aware of Anne's intentions; they were no longer a secret to anybody. But he seems to have retained his feeling of security, the long empire which he had held over Henry's mind having made him overbearing and blind to danger. He believed himself to be indispensable to the king, and was sure that he would not be dismissed. His negotiations in France had now come to an end, the treaty of alliance which Francis desired having been signed at Amiens; and about the middle of September Wolsey started for home.

On his arrival in England he repaired on 30 September to Richmond, where the court was residing. He sent in a gentleman to inquire of the king where it would please his highness to receive him. On such occasions it had been Henry's custom for many years to retire to a private room, where the cardinal met him alone, that they might be able to speak freely. But now Anne Boleyn was nearly always with the king; she already ruled him in most matters of detail, and had changed many an old custom. When Wolsey's messenger met the king in the great hall she was present. The man having delivered his message, she broke in before the king could answer. 'And where else,' she exclaimed, 'is the cardinal to come but here where the king is?' Wolsey's servant, not yet accustomed to the new fashions at court, looked rather astonished, and waited for an answer from the king. But Henry had no wish to contradict the lady; he confirmed what she had said, and the cardinal was obliged to go to the hall. He found the king dallying with Anne and chatting with his favourites;[26] and in their presence he had his first audience, and could not of course transact any business, or exert any influence on Henry. He was taught that he was no longer the only person by whom the king allowed himself to be ruled; the days of his absolute empire were gone.

There is no doubt that Wolsey deeply resented the affront put upon him; but he was prudent enough to dissemble. He did not wish to irritate the king by showing his anger at the treatment he had received; for he knew that Henry required from his courtiers meek submission to any indignity he might inflict on them. Nor did the cardinal wish to gratify his enemies by an exhibition of his feelings. He kept very quiet, and was soon rewarded, for Anne's empire was not yet so complete that she could hope to deprive Wolsey of all influence at once. The cardinal was called to several private audiences with the king, and professed much eagerness to serve Henry in the matter of the divorce. He thereby regained in part the confidence of his master, who showed him a fair face and continued to leave to him the chief management of affairs. Still, Wolsey was not unmindful of the warning he had received; he indicated that he was ready to ally himself with Anne and to help her to attain her end. Such was the result which in a few months she had obtained.

2

THE LEGATINE COURT

In forming an alliance for the purpose of furthering the divorce of Henry, Anne and Wolsey did not act in good faith towards each other. The true reason why Anne sought his aid was that she found it impossible to win the battle with the support of such friends as the Duke of Norfolk and the Duke of Suffolk. She wanted the cardinal to obtain the divorce, and thereby to prepare the way for her own marriage with the king. The friendship would then have been at an end; Anne would have turned against the cardinal as soon as she had been proclaimed queen. Henry might still have been ready to submit to Wolsey's rule, but Anne was of far too imperious a temper to brook the authority of the prime minister. Wolsey, on the other hand, saw how much ground he had lost, and did not wish to excite the enmity of so important a person as Anne. As he was well aware that the divorce could not be obtained at once, and as he thought with the rest of the court that Anne was the king's mistress, he still expected the passion of Henry to cool down long before he could be set free. If this anticipation proved to be correct, he would be able to influence Henry either to give up the demand for a divorce or to persevere, as might seem to be most expedient. He continued to hope that, if Catherine were divorced and Anne abandoned, he might find an opportunity of selling his master's alliance, and perhaps even his hand, for a yet higher price than that which the French were actually paying him.

The alliance between Wolsey and Anne was concluded all the more quickly, because the former soon after his return from France had learned the secret of Knight's mission. He was informed of the contents of the secretary's instructions, and discovered the draft of a proposed bull of dispensation for bigamy. This gave him an immediate advantage. He went to Henry and explained how dangerous such an attempt might be to the royal cause, since it would afford the clearest proof that what the king really wanted was to marry Anne, and that his scruples had their origin in this wish. The Pope, knowing the whole truth, would scarcely dare to grant a dispensation, and even if he did so, it would not have much authority with the English people. Europe would cry shame on the Pope and on the king, and Henry would find himself in so difficult a position that he might be glad to escape from it by retracing every step he had taken.

Henry felt the force of Wolsey's arguments; he was cowed by his minister's firmness and decision. He agreed that new instructions should be sent to Knight, who had not yet reached Rome; that the dispensation for bigamy should be abandoned; and that the Pope should be asked only to commit the matter to a legatine court in England. But Henry, though he followed the advice of his minister, did not do it cheerfully or honestly. He never admitted to Wolsey that he had all the time intentionally kept him in the dark, and he now wrote to Knight asking him not to let the cardinal know what had been done. If Wolsey made any inquiries, Knight was to answer that he had received his instructions after he had left the cardinal at Amiens. Knight would receive a new draft of a bull of dispensation – to be made use of only after the dissolution of the marriage with Catherine – 'which no man does know but they which I am sure will never disclose it to no man living for any craft the Lord Cardinal or any other can find.' This bull the secretary was entreated to obtain as quickly as possible in due form, keeping it, however, secret. A draft of a bull very like it would be sent by the king and cardinal jointly, but this was only *pro forma.*[1]

This letter, which Henry took the trouble to write entirely with his own hand, is a very curious document. It reads more like the composition of a schoolboy found out by the master against whom he plots than like the letter of an absolute king, who might have dismissed and ruined Wolsey at a moment's notice. It shows the awe with which he regarded the cardinal, and the secret but strong dislike he had for him. It shows how eager and impatient he was to marry Anne, and how confidently he believed that the divorce would be shortly obtained. It shows how foolish, rash and weak Henry was, how entirely he depended on others more capable and energetic than himself.

From Amiens, Knight had first gone to Parma, in the hope that he might reach Rome without further difficulty. But the country was very unsafe, and as his mission was to remain secret he could not apply to the imperial generals for a safe conduct, without which it was difficult to proceed. Finally he went to Foligno, whence he reported to the king what obstacles he had found in his way.[2] A few days later he received Henry's letter, together with the new instructions brought by John Barlow, chaplain to Lord Rochford. Knight, who was ordered to proceed at all hazards to Rome, accordingly set out, and after some difficulty was able to reach the city. But he could not gain admittance to the castle of St Angelo, where the Pope was still a prisoner; and he was warned that he had been detected, and advised to be off at once. He therefore sent a memorial in writing to Clement and returned to Foligno.[3] A few days later the Pope was free, and the secretary hastened to meet him at Orvieto, where he repeated the demands he had already made in the memorial. On this occasion Knight seems to have committed the grossest blunders and indiscretions. He revealed what his instructions had originally been, and foolishly told the papal officials the name of the person whom Henry wished to marry and what was the exact nature of the impediments.[4] Details so disgusting and showing so clearly the thorough bad faith of Henry, and the utter hollowness of his pretences of conscientious motives, could not but influence the Pope and his advisers against granting the request. But Clement was not in a position to refuse point-blank a demand made in so urgent a manner by the King of England. He gave Knight fair words; but his chief minister Pucci, Cardinal of Santi Quattro, an able lawyer and canonist, introduced into the two documents the Pope was to sign some changes which made them of no force.[5] The English secretary was not able to detect the difference between the two sets of papers; he accepted the corrected version, and left Orvieto convinced that he had obtained everything that was wanted. On his way home he once more met John Barlow, who brought him fresh and more detailed instructions from Henry and Wolsey. The secretary was so confident he had succeeded that he did not return to Orvieto but stopped at Asti, expecting high praise for his cleverness.[6]

The poor secretary was grievously mistaken. He had sent forward by a special courier the two briefs which Clement had signed. They were handed to Wolsey, who at once perceived their real meaning and was but too glad to point out the flaws in them to the king. The commission was worth nothing; whatever Wolsey might decree, appeal would still be permitted to the Pope, and the cardinal's judgement would have no effect.[7] And as the commission had been so cleverly worded by Cardinal Pucci, it was clear that the Pope wished to retain the power of giving final judgement, and meant, if convenient, to make use of it. Wolsey was triumphant, for Knight, by allowing himself to be duped so easily, had given signal proof that nobody but the cardinal and his chosen agents were able to carry on so difficult a negotiation. Henry and Anne, thoroughly convinced of their incapacity to obtain their end without Wolsey's help, gave themselves up to his guidance and assented to all he proposed.

Wolsey, having now learned how strongly Henry was bent on the divorce, thought it prudent to display some energy in support of his demand. Two new agents chosen by the cardinal were sent off to Orvieto: Dr Stephen Gardiner, hitherto chief secretary to Wolsey, and Dr Edward Foxe, of the royal chapel. In order to gratify Anne, the two ambassadors were ordered to take Hever on their way and to communicate to her the tenor of their instructions.[8]

The instructions were twofold. The ambassadors were to press the Pope to give to Wolsey and to a special legate such powers as would enable them to pronounce final judgement of divorce; and as Clement might be prepossessed against Henry and attribute to him unworthy motives, they were to dispel his misapprehensions. The legate, so ran their instructions, had heard that the king was supposed by the Pope to have undertaken this cause not from fear of a disputed succession, but out of vain affection or undue love to a gentlewoman, not so excellent as she was in England esteemed. The ambassadors were to assure the Pope that this was not the case; that Wolsey would never have favoured such a scheme. On the one hand, the cardinal considered the marriage of Henry with Catherine to be invalid, and the king agreed with his opinion. On the other:

> The approved excellent virtuous qualities of the said gentlewoman, the purity of her life, her constant virginity, her maidenly and womanly pudicity, her soberness, chasteness, meekness, humility, wisdom, descent right noble and high through regal blood, education in all good and laudable qualities and manners, apparent aptness to procreation of children, with her other infinite good qualities, more to be regarded and esteemed than the only progeny.

This explained the king's desire to be quickly divorced, a desire which Wolsey regarded as honest and necessary.[9]

Could there be anything more flattering and agreeable to Anne? Not only had the proud cardinal been brought to praise her to the Pope in the most fulsome terms, he had declared that he approved of the king's wish to marry her. No wonder that Anne received the two ambassadors most graciously, and that she declared herself quite satisfied with the efforts made in her cause. Her former agents were now discarded. Knight was ordered to remain in France.[10] Barlow, who at least had committed no blunder, was to be rewarded for his several journeys by the gift of the parsonage of Sonridge, for which Lord Rochford and Anne interceded with Wolsey.[11] All secret negotiations were for the moment abandoned, and both Henry and Anne manifested perfect confidence in the legate. He was beginning to feel safe again, and thought that he had regained his former position.

He was confirmed in this opinion by the success which seemed to attend the mission of Foxe and Gardiner. The two ambassadors, after protracted struggles, wrung from Clement such concessions as made the case appear hopeful to those who were unacquainted with the character of the Pope and the ways of the Roman court. A joint commission was to be issued for Cardinal Campeggio and Wolsey to hear and decide the cause in England. Campeggio had been expressly chosen by Henry and Wolsey as most favourable to the king. He was Cardinal Protector of England, an office worth several thousand ducats a year, and held the bishopric of Hereford in commend. He was therefore greatly dependent on Henry's goodwill, and had hitherto shown himself a steadfast friend. It was hoped that in this case too he would prove to be an obedient servant of Henry, and give such sentence as the king desired.[12]

As the good news of the continuous success of Wolsey's agents was received in England, Anne loudly proclaimed her gratitude to the cardinal. There was among the gentlemen of Henry's court a certain Thomas Henneage, specially employed to wait on mistress Anne, to whom he carried chosen dishes from the royal table and little gifts from the king. Many of his letters to Wolsey, containing sayings of Anne and of Lady Rochford, her mother, have been preserved. We learn from them that the cardinal and Anne kept up a frequent correspondence, although only a few letters of the lady have escaped destruction. Anne's letters, and the messages delivered by Henneage, show that she was on most friendly terms with the cardinal. She was always asking little services or gifts from him. One day it is a morsel of tunny she wants, another day a dish of carps or shrimps. When she is for a time without some small remembrance of the kind, Anne complains in the most charming way, and expresses a fear that the cardinal has forgotten her. There is no longer any trace of opposition or of rivalry; Anne decidedly acknowledges the superiority of Wolsey, and is grateful for his friendship and for the services he renders her.[13]

On 2 May 1528, Dr Foxe returned to England to report on the mission entrusted to him and to Gardiner, and on the following day he arrived at Greenwich, where the court was staying. His presence having been announced to the king, he was ordered to repair to the apartment of Mistress Anne. He found her alone, and had time to explain to her what endeavours had been made to obtain the appointment of the legates, praising his colleague Gardiner, whose energy and zeal he extolled and whose most hearty and humble commendations he transmitted. Anne listened with pleasure, promised both Foxe and Gardiner large recompense for the good service done to her, and was evidently desirous of attaching two such able and zealous men to her cause. While they were talking Henry came in, and Anne left him alone with Foxe to receive the report the latter had to make. The king was delighted by what he heard; he called in Mistress Anne, and made Foxe repeat in her presence all he had said. In further conversation the doctor said the Pope had been assured, so the Pope himself had told him, that Henry wished for this divorce only in order to marry Mistress Anne, and that such haste was made because she was already with child, being a worthless person. At first Clement had believed this, but after reading Wolsey's letters he had entirely changed his mind, and he was now favourably inclined towards the king. An account which was gladly accepted by both the king and the lady.

Foxe was not allowed to leave the royal presence until late at night; nevertheless, he was ordered to go straight to Durham Place in the Strand, where Wolsey lodged, and to show him the commission granted by the Pope. The cardinal saw immediately that the document was not worth much more than the bull obtained by Knight, since the Pope retained the right of pronouncing final judgement. But next morning, having weighed all the circumstances, he thought it best to conceal his disappointment. Henry and Anne were so highly elated by what they had heard from Foxe that if the truth had been told they would have been greatly enraged. They might have suspected the sincerity of the legate; they might have thought that he was making these difficulties only in order to retard or prevent the divorce. All the ground he had gained during the last six months would thus have been lost, Anne would have been violently hostile and Henry alienated. To such a danger Wolsey dared not expose himself, and in the afternoon, when Lord Rochford and Dr Bell came from Greenwich to confer with him, he declared himself better satisfied with the commission.[14] But he wanted a papal decretal defining the question of law in a manner favourable to Henry's claim, so that the legates would have to decide on nothing but on the question of fact. Such a decretal Gardiner was now instructed to obtain, and he was to press for the speedy departure of Campeggio.[15]

The next six weeks Henry and Anne spent pleasantly enough at Greenwich. But in the middle of June they were rudely torn asunder by a danger they had not foreseen. The sweating sickness, a peculiar epidemic disease, very contagious and rather dangerous, had made its appearance, and on 16 June one of Anne's maids was taken ill with it.[16] The court broke up at once, and the king hastily went to Waltham. However much he might like the company of Anne, he feared infection even more, and she did not accompany him, but retired to Hever. Here she and her father, Lord Rochford, fell ill.[17] Henry by this time had gone to Hunsdon, six of his attendants having shown symptoms of the disease at Waltham; and from Hunsdon, he had written to Anne asking her to leave Surrey, and to come to the healthier northern side of the river. When he heard of her illness,[18] he was in great alarm, and at once despatched Doctor Butts, his physician, to look after father and daughter at Hever.[19] To Anne he wrote entreating her to follow the doctor's advice, hoping soon to have news of her amendment.[20] His hope was realised, for a few days later he received a message that both father and daughter were out of danger.[21] Henry now left Hunsdon, frequently changing his abode until he finally settled at Tittenhanger, which Wolsey had put at his disposal.[22] Several of his courtiers died, William Carey, the husband of Anne's sister Mary, being one of them.[23] But after a time the epidemic subsided, and the king began to breathe more freely, for the danger seemed past.[24]

The sweating sickness gave occasion to an incident which was very characteristic of the kind of influence exerted by Anne over the king. The abbess of the convent of Wilton had died, and the choice of her successor lay with Cardinal Wolsey. Among the candidates was a nun, Eleanor Carey, sister of William Carey, Anne's brother-in-law.[25] She was favoured by the Boleyn family and by their friends. But Wolsey's agents reported that Eleanor had led a dissolute life, that she had several illegitimate children, and that she was most unfit to be at the head of a convent. Wolsey wished to appoint Dame Isabel Jordan, the prioress of Wilton, an aged, sad and discreet woman, but the friends of Eleanor Carey raked up an old scandal, pretending that the prioress had also in youth committed some offence against chastity, and they brought the matter before Henry. As it was impossible to deny Eleanor's guilt, the king did not wish to interfere in her favour, but he decided that the office should not be granted to her rival. This resolution was communicated to Wolsey by Dr Bell, and to Anne by the king himself.[26]

Wolsey disregarded the indirect message of Henry. He had most probably already bound himself to nominate Isabel Jordan, and, notwithstanding Dr Bell's letter, he signed the document appointing her.[27]

A few years before, the cardinal might have done this with impunity, for Henry at that time did not feel ashamed of the almost unlimited power he conceded to his prime minister. The ladies whom he had formerly courted had been so insignificant that they had not attempted to awaken in him a spirit of independence; they had been dazzled by the splendour of his nominal authority. Anne could not be so easily imposed upon. Henry was well aware of her penetration, and knew that she did not mistake appearance for reality. She had often spoken to him of his greatness, cleverly mixing flattery with a veiled reproof that he did not exert his power as much as he ought. Henry had made some efforts to convince her that his will was supreme; and she had affected to believe him, inciting him at the same time to act with even greater vigour. Now this awkward move of Wolsey came to spoil everything; if it were not immediately condemned, it would seem that the cardinal was more the sovereign than Henry himself. Anne, even if she did not taunt her lover with the disregard shown to his orders, would silently rebuke him by showing that she was vexed by what had happened; and Henry would no longer dare to brag of what he could do, since he could not even prevent the nomination of an abbess.

So the king was greatly annoyed by Wolsey's conduct, and expressed himself in rather strong terms.[28] The cardinal, as soon as he heard of Henry's anger, felt that he had committed a blunder. He hastened to apologise in the most humble manner, saying that he had not known the king's will. [29] But this did not pacify Henry, because Anne might complain that he had deceived her and had taken no interest in the cause she supported. Accordingly he sent to Wolsey a lengthy and very strong reprimand, on the composition of which he apparently bestowed great pains. Before sending off the letter, he read it to Anne's friend, Thomas Henneage, and to Sir John Russell. Whether he sent a copy to Anne is uncertain; but, if not, Henneage was expected, no doubt, to give her a full account of it.[30] Quoting some words from Dr Bell's letter, the king declared that the cardinal had been perfectly apprised of his wish, and wound up by speaking of the bad behaviour of Wolsey's officials and of the frequent bribes he received from religious communities.[31] Wolsey thereupon unreservedly admitted the truth of all that Henry had said, and humbly begged the king's pardon. This was enough: Henry was cleared before Anne; and, having shown that he was quite able to humiliate his minister, he now graciously accorded entire forgiveness.[32] Isabel Jordan remained abbess, and the matter was allowed to drop.[33]

Anne herself had not actively interfered in this affair. She had continued to write amiably to the cardinal, declaring in a letter from Hever that the king and he were the two persons for whom she cared most. When, after her recovery, towards the end of July, she joined the court at Ampthill, she wrote to him again in most flattering terms, and, showing her letter to the king, insisted that he should add a postscript to it.[34] She wished it to be known that she was Wolsey's friend and using her influence in his favour. It was already probable that by the force of circumstances Wolsey's power would decline, and Anne may have been unwilling to risk a battle and the loss of a useful ally, when she was pretty sure that time would rid her of her rival. Wolsey, misled by her apparent friendliness, allowed himself to drift into danger and ruin.

During the autumn of 1528 Anne was sometimes at court, sometimes at one or other of her father's country houses. She did not wish to be constantly with the king, as her position was still rather difficult; and there seemed to be some danger that if he saw her constantly his passion for her might cool. By remaining away for a few weeks occasionally, she kept up his ardour and made her position more easy. Moreover, Campeggio was at last on his way to England to sit as judge in the divorce cause, and it was not considered advantageous to parade Anne before the Italian legate. Campeggio might retain some feeling of decency, and object to have the real cause of Henry's conscientious scruples flaunted before his eyes. A certain degree of decorum was to be practised a little longer.

Campeggio was bringing the decretal which Wolsey had asked for. With the law expounded in a manner favourable to the king, it seemed scarcely doubtful that the divorce would be granted. But Clement, though he had allowed himself to be bullied into this extreme concession, had maintained one point. The decretal was to remain with Campeggio; he might communicate its contents to Henry and Wolsey, but the document itself was not to pass into their possession. Campeggio had left Rome in June 1528 for Orvieto to receive the decretal and the last instructions of the Pope.[35] Some galleys having been obtained from the French commanders, the cardinal embarked at Corneto on 24 July, crossed over to Provence, and arrived towards the end of August at Lyons.[36] On 8 September he was at Orléans, and on the 14th made his entry into Paris.[37] On the 18th he left Paris, pressed by the English agents to make haste, but owing to unfavourable winds and to fits of gout he did not reach London before 8 October.[38]

So much obloquy has been thrown on Clement VII for his behaviour in the matter of the divorce that it is necessary to inquire whether he was guilty of all the offences laid to his charge. His policy has been compared with that of the great popes of the Middle Ages; but such a comparison cannot hold good, for the mediaeval popes found themselves in totally different circumstances. Gregory VII was the champion of great ideas, of reforms approved of by the vast majority of believers; and his chief adversary was a wayward emperor, opposed by strong vassals and rival sovereigns. Besides, Gregory was not entirely successful. He and his immediate successors, during their struggles with the empire, laid the foundations of those powers which were to ruin their work.

Gregory VII and his successors, in order to fight the emperor, were obliged to buy the alliance of the kings of France, England, and Spain by considerable concessions, and they thereby helped to strengthen the royal authority in those countries. In order to withstand the imperial cause in Italy, they befriended the petty princes, the lords and the towns. They aided every rebel, until the spirit of revolt spread to Rome itself; and then the Popes had to take shelter in France, where they became dependent on the goodwill of the French kings. Meanwhile, the Italian republics and small states consolidated their power; and with political freedom and growing wealth a spirit of research and inquiry arose which led to the foundation of numerous schools. Learning ceased to be a privilege of the clergy; it could be got elsewhere than in the cloister; it took a decidedly secular turn. Lay lawyers began to be appointed to many of those places in the political world which for centuries had been held almost exclusively by clergymen. From Italy the new movement passed to the rest of Western

Europe, and during the thirteenth and fourteenth centuries universities were founded in Germany, France, Spain and England, and soon trained a sufficient number of scholars to fill the public offices. Kings availed themselves of these facilities to form good administrations. With the help of the lawyers, they enlarged their own functions and curtailed those of the barons, and at the close of the fifteenth century three remarkable men, each in his own kingdom, put an end to the mediaeval system of government. Louis XI in France, Ferdinand the Catholic in Spain and Henry VII in England established the royal authority on so strong a basis that for a while no attempt to resist it could prove successful. The power of the barons was broken, and these three kings ruled almost directly and absolutely over all their subjects.

The increase of strength which the royal power received in France, England and Spain was all the greater because no effective safeguard had as yet been invented against the abuse of it, and because, the malpractices of the barons being so recent and so well remembered, people loyally adhered to the Crown as a means of escape from feudal tyranny. Kings who found themselves in so advantageous a position were not much inclined to allow any other power to have sway in their dominions. The independence of the Church was soon as little to their taste as the independence of the barons had been. Louis XI renewed the Pragmatic Sanction, which had fallen into a state of disuse, and Francis I concluded the Concordat, which made the clergy even more dependent on the royal will. Ferdinand firmly maintained his right to rule the Church in Sicily, to the Monarchia as it was called, and – notwithstanding papal protests – used the royal central inquisition in a way diametrically opposed to the wishes of the Roman court. When the Pope fulminated censures against him, Ferdinand threatened with death any person who should dare to publish the papal mandate; and the Pope, powerless to hurt the king, had to give way. So low had the papacy sunk, so little was its authority regarded.

The rise of these great national monarchies led to the manifestation of a new spirit of patriotism. People began to feel very strongly as Frenchmen and Germans, as Englishmen and Italians. This national spirit was of course opposed to any foreign authority; and when heresiarchs in Germany and Switzerland denounced the vices, the greed and the arrogance of Rome, they commanded immediate attention, and soon obtained the support of some of the most important German princes. The Roman Church had become so unpopular with all but Italians that the ground was ready to receive the seed.

The difficulties of the papacy were increased by the political changes which took place in Europe after the death of Ferdinand of Aragon. Up to the end of the fifteenth century several great European powers, France,

Spain, the Empire, Burgundy, balanced each other, while the second-rate states, England, Hungary, Venice, Naples, occupied an independent and influential position. This balance had now been destroyed; there were but two great powers striving for absolute ascendancy: the Empire and France. Of the second-rate powers, Naples had been annexed to Spain, Burgundy had been divided, the power of Venice had been broken, while Bohemia and Hungary were soon to fall to the house of Austria. In 1520 the struggle between Charles and Francis had broken out; the following year found it in full blaze; and nearly every state of western Europe took one side or the other.

Had the Pope held aloof from the conflict, he would have angered both parties. Leo X, obliged to act with one of the two sovereigns, decided to act with the emperor.

The old pretensions of the Pope to stand above the emperor had long been abandoned in all but outward form; there was no rivalry on this account. On the contrary, the emperor, who wanted to reconstitute the universal Christian republic, of which he was to be the secular chief, seemed the natural ally of the universal Christian Church against heretics and schismatics, against those who claimed national independence. The interests of the Pope and the emperor were in so many respects almost identical that Leo's choice was inevitable.

Adrian VI followed Leo's policy, and Clement, when he ascended the throne, was bound by treaties to assist the emperor. At first he kept his obligations tolerably well, but after a time, listening to the advice of visionary counsellors, in an evil hour for the Church, he allowed his Italian patriotism to overrule his better judgement. He began to oppose, first secretly, then openly, the policy of the emperor. Charles, at the height of his power, was not the man to forgive such resistance. The Colonna, his adherents, entered Rome and spent several days in plundering it. As this had not the desired effect of frightening the Pope into submission, Bourbon led his soldiers against the Eternal City, and the result was the sack of Rome. Clement found himself shut up a prisoner in St Angelo, and it was only after paying a heavy ransom that he was allowed to escape to Orvieto.

Here he had leisure to reflect on the difficulties of his situation. Even a stronger man than Clement might have been appalled by them. The allegiance of the emperor to the Church seemed well-nigh lost. His German and Spanish soldiers had acted outrageously in Rome; and neither the German nor the Spanish clergy had shown themselves greatly shocked by the insult offered to the Holy See, while the people of Charles's dominions received the news with pleasure rather than with pain.

Charles – it must be remembered – had been brought up by his grandfather Maximilian, and had been imbued by him with very fantastic and exaggerated notions about the imperial dignity and power. It was not impossible that he might do as some of his predecessors on the imperial throne had done: call a Council, and with its assistance depose the Pope. Clement knew that to withstand such an assertion of imperial authority he would have to rely on the help of Francis I, Henry VIII and the princes of the Italian League. But the devotion of the kings of France and England to the Holy See was less ardent than he could have wished. The French clergy adopted a very independent tone, Francis jealously guarded his new privileges, and politically he did very little for the Pope. Henry VIII, indeed, had for years shown himself a zealous champion of the Holy See; but he had done so only on the tacit understanding that the whole government of the Church in his states was to be left to him and his ministers, the Holy See simply enjoying a few revenues.

Clement could not but fear that if he threw himself entirely on the alliance with Francis and Henry, he would lose his independence. He foresaw that they would wring from him every possible concession, and that he would soon be regarded as their tool. Such a position he would not accept; he preferred to attempt to regain his power even at the cost of great inconvenience, labour and danger to himself.

The policy which Clement now adopted was entirely suited to his temper and abilities. He resolved to forgive past offences, and to come to terms with Charles, but at the same time secretly to throw as many difficulties as possible in his way. For Charles V in difficulties might prove a more obedient son of the Church than Charles V triumphant; if the emperor were hard pressed by his enemies, he would probably set a higher value on the friendship and favour of the Holy See. The Pope might then become the mediator and umpire between the contending parties, and re-establish much of his lost authority.

The steps taken by Henry in the matter of the divorce seemed most convenient for Clement's purpose, for Charles could not but be anxious to obtain the assistance of the Pope in favour of his aunt. Like other people, Clement thought that the passion of Henry for Anne Boleyn would not last, and that after a time he would either abandon his demand for a divorce or acquiesce in a sentence declaring the validity of his marriage. Clement supposed, therefore, that at first, without committing himself too far, he might safely show some favour to Henry's views.

In consequence of this policy the breach between the empire and the papacy was well-nigh healed; but unhappily the English business became more difficult than had been expected. Henry did not give up his purpose; Wolsey, instead of acting as the Pope expected his legate to act, entirely sided with the king; and both insisted on the mission of Campeggio with exorbitant powers to the legates. These powers Clement was very loath to grant, for he dreaded the revival of Charles's hostility. On the other hand, he was afraid to exasperate Henry, or to anger his mighty patron the King of France. Threats of open rebellion against his authority filled him with alarm; he dared not face such a danger. As long as he was not quite certain of the lasting allegiance of Charles, he saw that it would be folly to come to an open rupture with the party united against the emperor. He could not run the risk of losing the obedience of both.

Clement did all he could to gain time and to evade an absolutely binding act. He invented every kind of excuse for delay, hoping that in the interval he might make quite sure of Charles, draw Francis away from Henry, and persuade the latter to abandon his design. The first two of these objects he attained; in the third he failed, because he was hampered by perplexities which rendered success impossible.

In the treatment of Henry's claim Clement could never strike out the bold and honest line which Bishop Fisher, John Clerk, Bishop of Bath, and some of the Lutheran divines adopted. Clerk had the courage to declare that the passage in Leviticus does not refer to the widow of a late but to the wife of a living brother, that it does not relate to a marriage but only emphasises the prohibition against adultery in a case where it seems particularly shocking, that the prohibition of canon law is consequently not based upon the passage and can derive no authority from the Bible. Fisher agreed with Clerk;[39] but this the Pope could not do.

The revolt of the Lutherans had in part been caused by the system of clerical exactions, many innocent acts having been declared sinful in order that the clergy might obtain money and influence by granting dispensations or giving absolution. Lutherans assailed the canon law as a fabric which had been reared independently of the Bible, while Catholic divines tried to prove that the teaching of the Bible formed the basis of the whole structure. In a case of dispensation, therefore, the Pope could not speak out as freely as he would have liked; he could not, by admitting that one part of the canon law differed from the Bible, endanger every other part of it, and thereby furnish new weapons to the heretics. He was a Roman priest, the chief of the Roman clergy, and as such he could not make any concession that might imperil the supremacy of Rome.

Embarrassed by these difficulties, Clement lied and shuffled a good deal; he did not stand up boldly for that which he thought to be right. But he was influenced much more by regard for the welfare of the Church of which he was the head than by fear for his personal safety or by apprehension of another sack of Rome. And in one respect he was successful. Though the north of Germany was lost to Rome, though England was alienated, Clement contrived to retain the allegiance both of the emperor and of the King of France. By sacrificing a part of the dominion of the Church he saved the rest and consolidated its power.

3

THE DEATH OF WOLSEY

When Cardinal Campeggio took leave of the Pope at Orvieto, Henry seemed to have a fairly good prospect of success. Charles V had not yet been reconciled to the Holy See, the Pope was still excluded from his capital, and three of the cardinals remained as hostages at Naples. Nevertheless, true to his purpose, Clement instructed Campeggio to act with the greatest caution. Henry and Charles being at enmity, it was now the principal object of the Pope to avoid being drawn into the strife. Campeggio, therefore, was first to try to reason Henry out of his purpose, and if this failed he was to ask the queen to give up her rights by entering a convent, in which case the Pope was prepared to dispense for bigamy. If the queen would not give way, he was to delay as much as possible the opening of the court.[1]

While Campeggio was on his way, a great change passed over the political situation in Italy. An army raised by authority of the empire had entered Lombardy for the purpose of defending it against the inroads of the French. Though the commander, the Duke of Brunswick, did not act in concert with Antonio de Leyva, Charles's general, the latter was enabled by the presence of the German force to prevent the Count of Saint Pol from marching to Naples. The army which under Lautrec had invaded Naples and laid siege to the capital was thus placed in a bad position, which was rendered still worse when Andrea Doria, angered by some slight put upon him by the French, went over with his galleys to the emperor. The French army suffered greatly from heat and privations; large numbers, among them Lautrec himself, died of disease; the remnant, cut off from their line of retreat, were made prisoners by the very men whom they had just besieged.

Although success once more attended Charles's armies, his behaviour towards the Holy See remained as conciliatory as it had been during the time when his prospects seemed darkest. He continued to carry on negotiations with the Pope, the imperial agents being instructed to make moderate demands. Moreover, the emperor and his brother Ferdinand began to support the Holy See more energetically in Germany; they opposed the clamour for a national council, which might have led to the overthrow of the papal power in the whole kingdom. Charles's policy presented a striking contrast to that of Francis and Henry. The French during their short period of success had never done anything in favour of the Pope. They had attempted to conquer Naples for their king, but they had not thought fit either to drive the Imperialists out of the papal fortresses or to restore those papal towns their allies had occupied. Henry's agents had threatened the Pope with open rebellion, and both French and English were constantly pressing him to accept a guard of soldiers, which, as Clement knew, would be a band of disguised gaolers. The Pope therefore wished more than ever to secure the friendship of the emperor, and sent message after message to warn Campeggio not to take any definite step.[2]

The legate on his arrival – acting according to his instructions – tried first of all to dissuade Henry from his purpose. His representations, however, were met with long theological arguments; Henry was proud to show his learning, and would not listen to the counsels of Campeggio. An attempt to shake the queen's fortitude having equally failed, the cardinal had to follow the third course – to procrastinate and to hold back as much as possible.[3]

This was taken very ill by the king. Campeggio showed the decretal to Henry and Wolsey, as he had been directed to do, but he refused to part with it or even to communicate its contents to the royal council. A document which was to remain secret was of little use; the Pope might not, after all, consider himself bound by it. To obtain possession of the decretal became, therefore, one of the chief aims of the royal policy. A messenger was sent in hot haste to Sir Gregorio da Casale, Henry's agent with the Pope, with orders that he should insist on the decretal being handed to Wolsey, that it might be shown to a few members of the council.[4] If this had been done, of course the decretal would not have been returned to Campeggio as Henry promised; it would have been carefully kept as a weapon against the vacillations of Clement.

Sir Gregorio received Henry's orders at Bologna. Being ill, he sent his brother, John Casale, to the Pope to present the royal request. Clement at once detected the trap laid for him, and was greatly angered by the demand. He refused, saying he would give one of his fingers not to have signed the decretal: Campeggio ought to have burnt it as soon as it had been shown to Henry and Wolsey.[5] A few days later Sir Gregorio himself, having recovered, went to Rome, but he also was unable to shake the Pope's resolution. Sir Gregorio thereupon sent his brother Vincent to England to give an account of the whole case to the king, while the Pope despatched his most confidential secretary, Francesco Campana, nominally to explain to Henry why his request could not be complied with, in reality to tell Campeggio to destroy the dangerous document without delay.[6]

Before Campana reached London a new incident occurred. A brief had been found in Spain, addressed by Julius II to Henry and Catherine, different from the bull of dispensation for their marriage and remedying in a way its pretended defect. A certified copy was now produced in England before the two legates.[7] Henry at once asserted that the brief must be a forgery, but Campeggio was not so easily persuaded. That Henry did not believe the document to be a forgery is amply shown by the attempts he made to obtain possession of it. Charles refused to give it up, Clement declined to declare it a forgery without seeing it, and the brief had to be considered genuine.[8]

The cause was retarded by another circumstance. After the complete overthrow of the French army in Naples, the Pope had returned to Rome. Here he had several attacks of rheumatic fever, one of which was so severe that he was reported to be dead, and the rumour reached London. By Clement's death the powers conferred on Wolsey and Campeggio would have terminated; no progress was made with the cause, therefore, until it was known that the Pope had recovered. All the ingenuity of Campeggio could then serve no longer, he was at last obliged to open the legatine court. But another disagreeable incident happened which Henry and Wolsey had not foreseen. The draft of the papal commission kept at the British Museum is addressed to Wolsey and Campeggio;[9] and as the English cardinal was of older creation than his Italian colleague it was natural that it should be so addressed. It appears, however, from the minute of the proceedings that the address was changed. Campeggio and Wolsey being commissioned, the former insisted on presiding,[10] and he was thereby enabled to procrastinate even more until he should hear from the Pope.

The proceedings of the court are well known. The first sitting was held on 18 June at Blackfriars. At the second sitting, on the 21st, Catherine objected to Wolsey as a judge and to England as the place of trial, and declared that she had appealed to the Pope. Campeggio, hard pressed by Henry and Wolsey, dared not accept Catherine's protest, and the proceedings went on; but before judgement could be given, on 23 July, he prorogued the court under the pretext that this was the time of vacation at Rome.[11]

Anne watched closely the course of events during these eventful days. It is clear from one of Henry's letters to her that, better informed than the king, she distrusted Campeggio even before he reached the English shore.[12] When the legate, shortly after his arrival, showed that he was no obedient tool of the king, her suspicions increased. By and by, especially after she received reports of the Pope's change of attitude, she became convinced that there was but little probability of a favourable verdict being given by Campeggio. This she ascribed in part to secret machinations of Wolsey – who was supposed to disapprove of the claim for divorce – in part to the influence of the imperial party at Rome. She felt that if her cause was to triumph she would henceforward have to rely on her own efforts, as the means Wolsey had proposed and to which he still tenaciously clung were inadequate. But since the autumn of 1527 she had gained considerable experience, and had been able to attach a good many men to her fortunes, foremost of all the energetic and able secretary of Wolsey, Dr Stephen Gardiner. The cardinal was left with scarcely a friend, exposed to the malice of his enemies, who were made bolder every day by the prospect of his disgrace.[13]

Gardiner, who in January had been sent a second time to Rome to assist the English ministers there, returned to England on 22 June.[14] He had now a chief share of Henry's favour. A week after the prorogation of the legatine court, when the news was received that on 13 July the Pope, contrary to a secret promise made in July 1528, had revoked the commission to the legates and decided that the cause should be tried at Rome, Gardiner was made chief secretary to the king.[15] Both Henry and Anne thought they had found in him a man who might be advantageously substituted for Wolsey; and from this moment the king no longer cared for his former favourite and prime minister. Anne, Gardiner, her adherents and those peers who were not personally favourable to Catherine, formed an alliance to bring down the cardinal. Articles were framed against him, and everybody expected to see his early ruin.

Contrary to the general anticipation, a short respite was granted to the unhappy victim. His enemies, indeed, prevented him from regaining his influence by the exercise of the power he knew so well how to use in personal dealings with the king. Henry, attended by Anne and Gardiner, went hunting about the country, and Wolsey's requests to be allowed to repair to the royal presence were evaded or refused. But outwardly his position was unchanged, and no open attack upon it was allowed.

Wolsey's doom was postponed because it was still hoped that by his means the divorce might be secured. Cardinal Campeggio, after having received due notice that his powers had been revoked, prepared to return to Rome. On 19 September he presented himself at Grafton to take leave of the king. With some difficulty Wolsey had obtained permission to accompany his colleague, and to the astonishment of the courtiers Henry received both in the most gracious manner. He had a long conversation with Wolsey, treating him with the greatest kindness. On the following morning, however, the king went out early to hunt, and Wolsey saw him no more, but had to return with Campeggio to London.[16] On 5 October the Italian cardinal left and proceeded by slow journeys to Dover, which he reached on the 8th.[17] Here the royal officers of the custom house seized his luggage, and, notwithstanding his passport and his quality of legate, broke open the chests and subjected everything to a minute search.[18]

This was not an act of mere stupid insolence, nor did the king intend simply to punish Campeggio for his disinclination to proceed with the case. The incident was a part of a well-pondered plan. Henry and Anne thought that the famous decretal might still be in Campeggio's possession, and that on strict search it might be discovered among his luggage. Had this been the case, Campeggio would have been allowed – if necessary, even obliged – to depart; Wolsey would have received orders to reopen the legatine court; and as the commission gave power to the legates together, or to either of them separately, the cardinal would not have dared to disobey. Any protests of Catherine would have been met by producing the decretal and the Pope's written promise not to revoke the powers of the legates. Wolsey would have proceeded to give judgement in favour of Henry, and the trick would have been successfully played. Such, from all the circumstances, seems to have been the plan of Henry and his advisers; but it was frustrated, for the decretal had been destroyed after the arrival of Campana in January. York herald, who had accompanied Campeggio, rode post-haste to London with the woeful tidings that the document could not be found.[19] This sealed Wolsey's doom; there was no longer any reason for sparing him. The same day on which the news was received Christopher Hales, the king's attorney, preferred a bill against him for præmunire; shortly afterwards, on 17 October, he was deprived of the seals and his committal to the Tower was daily expected.[20]

For a moment Wolsey lost courage, and sat weeping and lamenting his misfortunes. He probably overrated the danger to which he was exposed; for Henry, who had not yet made up his mind to come to an open rupture with Rome, and who hoped still to induce Charles V and Clement to accede to his requests, would scarcely have dared to lay hands on a cardinal. Nor would he have embittered the strife by pushing on a prosecution for præmunire for the exercise of legatine powers in England. But Wolsey dreaded the worst, and tried to save himself by complete submission. He acknowledged that he had been guilty of an offence which he had never committed, and sought to conciliate his most powerful enemies by heavy bribes; granting pensions on the bishopric of Winchester to Norfolk, George Boleyn, and the friends of Anne,[21] and giving up to the king all his movable property, all pensions or money due to him, and the palace of York Place at Westminster belonging to the archbishopric.[22] Thoroughly humbled and stripped of his wealth, he was allowed to retire to Esher to spend the winter without further molestation.[23]

Immediately after the disgrace of the cardinal, his enemies set themselves to form a new government. There was some rivalry about the first place. The Duke of Suffolk had been foremost in the attack and claimed his reward, but the Duke of Norfolk was the abler statesman and was the uncle of Anne. This latter consideration seems to have been decisive. Norfolk was made president and Suffolk vice-president of the council. The chancellorship was thus stripped of much of its importance and splendour, and if Anne had had her way, it would have been granted to Gardiner. But Gardiner himself was not overanxious to be appointed to so difficult and dangerous an office. A bishopric seeming much more convenient, he preferred a promise of promotion to the see of Winchester, which was about to become vacant by the renunciation of Wolsey. The seals were given to a man less thoroughgoing and able in politics, but whose literary fame, high character for probity, and great breadth of view promised to shed a lustre on the cabinet – to Sir Thomas More. Sir William Fitzwilliam, the treasurer of the household, received in addition to his office that of chancellor of the duchy of Lancaster. Cuthbert Tunstall was allowed to hold for a few months more the post of keeper of the privy seal. After this he accepted the see of Durham, giving up the bishopric of London to Dr John Stokesley, an ardent advocate of the divorce, and making over the privy seal to Anne's father.

The new government was eminently aristocratic, with a strong leaning towards France. Norfolk, Suffolk, Boleyn, Fitzwilliam and More were all in receipt of pensions from Francis.[24] But as yet they were not quite agreed as to the policy to be adopted; they had arrived at power without a clear programme, the chief bond of union between them being their common hatred of the cardinal.

The first thing to be done was to provide for the meeting of parliament. Shortly after the prorogation of the legatine court, writs had been issued for the election of members to serve in a new parliament to assemble on 3 November. But the control of the elections was taken from Wolsey and confided to the Duke of Norfolk and his allies, who of course were most careful to nominate only such members as were likely to favour the intended change of policy.[25]

In the time of Henry VIII the House of Commons was not really an elective body. The sheriff generally received with the writ a letter mentioning the names of the persons whom the king wished to be elected as knights and burgesses. In a few boroughs the responsibility of making arrangements for the elections was nominally entrusted to the bishop or to some of the lords, but this was a mere matter of form, for in each case the patron was informed of the royal wish and had to see that it was fulfilled.

When the sheriff received the writ, he communicated the contents of the accompanying letter to the gentry or citizens, and called together as many electors as he thought fit. Either there were no electoral lists, or they were little regarded. Electors living at a distance often did not know when the nomination was to take place, and those who appeared were generally men who could be trusted to vote as they were directed. If anybody was bold enough to oppose the royal candidates, his opposition was rarely if ever of any avail. A show of hands decided against him. And it was not quite safe to contest a seat against the king's nominee or to vote for any one who ventured to do so. This was considered a clear proof of wilfulness, a most heinous offence under the Tudors, and a man guilty of so grave an indiscretion was soon denounced at headquarters, and generally received a letter of appearance, that is to say, an order to present himself before the royal council. By the council he was soundly rated for his presumption, and if he did not at once make humble submission, he had to appear again. If after several such appearances he remained stubborn, he might find himself as a seditious and lewd person committed to Newgate or the Marshalsea, there to meditate on the duties of a good subject. Thus the members of the House of Commons were about as freely elected as the bishops; the writ and the letter setting forth the king's wish formed together a *congé d'élire*.

And even if, by some mischance, independent candidates were returned, this did not mean that they were allowed to take their seats. In the spring of 1536, the sheriff of Canterbury received the royal writ, but inadvertently the letter of Secretary Cromwell was not handed to him. He immediately called together about seventy substantial men, who elected two representatives. Scarcely had the new members been declared duly elected, when Cromwell's letter arrived. The sheriff wrote to the secretary exculpating himself and regretting that the king's wish could not be fulfilled;[26] but he was soon undeceived. The reply of Cromwell we do not possess, but the result of it was that a week later the mayor and sheriff summoned eighty or more good and substantial men, and that they elected the two royal candidates without a single dissentient voice.[27]

A parliament thus chosen met on 3 November. The interval between the dismissal of Wolsey and the opening of the session had been employed by Henry and Anne in viewing the rich spoil they had obtained. They went down to Greenwich and then secretly to York Place, where the magnificent furniture and the plate were exhibited to them.[28] Anne was highly pleased with all she saw, and decided that this should be the future town residence of the king, one great advantage of it being that there was no apartment for Catherine. Necessary changes in the building were to be begun at once, neighbouring houses were to be pulled down to provide space for a garden, York Place was to become Whitehall.[29]

Shortly afterwards the king returned to his new dwelling to be present at the opening of parliament. Sir Thomas More read to the two houses a long speech in which the cardinal was not spared and in which a new and better policy was promised.[30] One of the first proofs of this better policy was the passing of a bill by which the king was released from all debts he had contracted towards his subjects, on the whole a sum of nearly £150,000, of which his creditors were thus cheated.[31] After this, little was done during the session, except that a great many complaints were made against the rapacity and insolence of the clergy.[32] As these complaints could scarcely have been made without the consent of ministers, they showed the real inclinations and tendencies of the cabinet.

If little was done as far as politics were concerned, a good deal was done to promote the interest of Anne and her family. First her brother, George Boleyn, a very young and totally untried man, was placed at the head of an embassy to France;[33] and Lord Rochford, while his son was employed on this honourable and lucrative errand, was raised in dignity. On 8 December he was created Earl of Wiltshire and Ormond, and daughter became Lady Anne[34] – strange to say, Lady Anne Rochford, not Lady Anne Boleyn: for what reason I do not know, except, perhaps, that Bullen, the mercer, was still too well remembered.

To mark the favour shown to Anne, a great banquet was given by the king on the day after the ceremony, Anne occupying Catherine's place, above the Duchesses of Suffolk and Norfolk and other ladies of high rank. The banquet was followed by a ball, and by such feasts and rejoicings that nothing, says Chapuis, seemed wanting but the priest to make the lovers exchange their rings. There was no longer the slightest restraint: everybody understood that Anne was to be the queen.[35]

As to the means by which her exaltation was to be brought about there was some difference of opinion. Suffolk was by no means ardent in Anne's cause, for he considered himself ill-treated, the arrogance of the Boleyns annoyed him, and he could not gain anything by the divorce. The peers generally took the same view: the cardinal having been ousted from office, and the officials thoroughly humbled, they wanted no more. Nor were the officials much more eager, for the game was a hazardous one. Of those who sat in the royal council More and Tunstall were secretly hostile, Gardiner was beginning to cool down; even Anne's uncle, the Duke of Norfolk, occasionally showed himself lukewarm, while the duchess, with whom he was still on tolerable terms, supported Catherine. Only Anne's father could be thoroughly trusted, and he was about to leave England for a considerable time.

During the spring of 1529 the reconciliation between Charles V and the Holy See had been made complete, a treaty having been concluded at Barcelona on 29 June. Charles had thereupon decided to visit the Pope in Italy. The meeting took place at Bologna; and on 29 February 1530, Charles was crowned emperor. Afterwards the two chiefs of Christendom remained together for some time in order to discuss the many grave matters by which the western world was troubled; and Henry seized the occasion to send an embassy to Charles and Clement to reason them out of their opposition to the divorce.

At first it had been intended to entrust the Duke of Norfolk with this mission, but as he had no wish to be blamed for a failure he knew to be inevitable, he prayed to be excused. He did not speak French well enough, he said, the Earl of Wiltshire would be a better ambassador.[36] The earl may also have felt reluctance to go on a useless errand, and to travel among robbers and soldiers; but, if so, his objections were overcome by the prayers of his daughter and by the prospect of an extraordinarily high salary.[37] He was to be accompanied by Dr Edward Lee, by Dr Stokesley, who was already in France collecting opinions in favour of the divorce, by Dr Thomas Cranmer, who had been his chaplain, and by Dr Edward Karne. He left on 21 January 1530, with a large retinue, was joined by Stokesley, and proceeded by slow stages towards Italy.[38] At Roanne, learning that the emperor was going to leave Bologna, he took post horses, and, abandoning his retinue, rode forward in hot haste. But he was not equal to the exertion: at Lyons he was so tired that he had to stop; his train rejoined him, and the whole company proceeded to Bologna together.[39]

The earl arrived at Bologna on 14 March. The following day he had an audience of the emperor, but it was merely formal, and he had to wait a few days before finding an opportunity of explaining his errand. He began by asking whether the emperor would permit him and his colleagues to argue the matter of the divorce before the cardinals, and whether, if the English could convince the consistory, Charles would cease to resist the king's wishes. The emperor at once interrupted him by a very pertinent question: 'Will your king, on his part, bind himself to desist from the divorce if the cardinals are not convinced by you?' The earl could but reply that he had no power to give this pledge. 'Then,' said Charles, 'I shall not promise anything either; the matter must take its regular course before the proper tribunal.' The earl now began to recite his commission, a long theological treatise, and Charles leant back in his chair while the tedious lecture proceeded. When it was ended, he calmly repeated that the matter was to take its regular course at Rome, and that he would not hear any further argument.[40] All attempts to shake his resolution proved fruitless; the most tempting bribes were rejected with scorn.

A few days later the emperor left, but before his departure the imperial ministers played a most annoying trick on the earl. Simonetta, auditor of the tribunal of the Rota, had issued a citation calling on Henry to appear in person or by proxy before him at the tribunal in Rome. Copies of this act had been sent to England, but no usher had been bold enough to serve it on the king; and the cause had been thereby delayed, much to the annoyance of the Imperialists. Wiltshire, as duly accredited ambassador, represented the person of the king, and to serve the writ on him would be sufficient for the proceedings; accordingly an usher presented himself at his lodgings and exhibited the citation. Wiltshire protested, and his colleagues and his servants would fain have knocked down the usher, but behind him stood the threatening forms of Charles's Spanish soldiers and bravi. The writ was served. As long as Charles and his guards remained at Bologna, Wiltshire dared not even remonstrate; but on the day after the emperor's departure he went to the Pope and bitterly complained of the indignity offered to him. He entreated the Holy Father, if not to recall the citation, at least to grant a delay, promising, on the part of the king, that in the interval no further steps should be taken in England. Clement, having sent a message to Charles, granted a delay of six weeks, and this was all the earl could obtain.[41] Shortly afterwards the Pope left Bologna, and Wiltshire took his way by Milan and Turin to France.

When Henry heard of the failure of Wiltshire's mission he was extremely angry, and laid the whole blame on the ambassador's incapacity and want of energy. In those with whom he had hitherto had to deal, Henry had generally observed only abject cringing or coarse egotism; either people had bowed to his caprice, or they had resisted him because it was their interest to do so. Himself destitute of generous sentiments, and having scarcely ever seen any evidence of them in others, he was unable to understand them or even to believe seriously in their existence. Here he met with an opposition which was wholly disinterested; the offers of friendship, of money and military help, which the earl had been commissioned to make to Charles V, had been treated with the same contempt as the hints thrown out that Henry might be driven by the emperor's obstinacy to enter into closer alliance with the French. This, Henry thought, could have been due only to the manner in which his wishes had been represented to Charles. He was angry and annoyed, and regretted that the ability of which Wolsey had given him so many proofs was no longer at his command.[42]

The cardinal, having thrown himself on the king's mercy, had received royal letters of protection, by which all proceedings against him had been stayed; and his friends had begun once more to rally round him. Soon after Christmas an attempt was made to obtain for him an interview with the king.[43] He fell ill, and his physician asked for a consultation with Dr Butt, the king's physician.[44] This request was complied with; and Butt, a secret friend, reported to Henry that the cardinal's life was in danger, that the chief cause of his malady was anxiety and grief for the royal displeasure, and that if he continued in the same state of mind he would shortly be dead. Henry, so Cavendish relates, exclaimed that he would not lose the cardinal for £20,000. He sent Wolsey a token of his favour, asking Anne to do the same, and she willingly assented, since, by showing herself more relenting towards the fallen minister, she hoped to be all the better able to counteract his schemes.[45] Doctor Butt returned to Esher to deliver the messages with which he had been charged, and to convey a promise that Wolsey's pardon should be made out.[46] Though the main object of the intrigue had not been attained, something, at least, had been secured; the pardon was sealed on 12 February, and, on the 14th, the temporalities of York were returned to the cardinal, as well as £6,374 in money, plate and other movables.[47] He was, moreover, allowed to leave Esher, the air of which did not agree with him, and to retire to Richmond Lodge.

If Henry really exclaimed that he would not lose the cardinal for £20,000, he spoke in a very matter-of-fact way of an intrigue he was carrying on. Like all spendthrifts, he was always in want of money, and his greed overruled nearly every other consideration. Wolsey had in his first fright ceded to the king not only all his movable property, but all sums due to him as debts and as pensions, and had offered to aid Henry in realising these assets. The pensions from Spain, and the arrears thereof, there was little hope of obtaining, for even when the cardinal was in power they had been most irregularly paid. But it was possible that the French debt and pensions might be realised, and they were so considerable as to tempt the cupidity of the king.

When in 1525 Wolsey had negotiated the peace with France which was signed at the More, he had not forgotten his personal interests. He had asked that 100,000 crowns should be given to him, and that the arrears of pension, which had been stopped during the war, should be paid with the coming instalments. These requests had been granted, and an obligation for the whole sum of 123,885 crowns, equal to about £27,000, had been made out. He was to receive from that time half-yearly 12,500 crowns, of which 4,000 crowns were to be his regular pension, and 8,500 crowns an instalment of the arrears. Had all the eight payments from November 1525 to May 1529 been made, the debt would have been reduced to 55,885 crowns. But since 1527 no payments had been made, and Wolsey, already insecure in his position, had not dared to press for them, but had tried to conciliate Francis by allowing him to employ the money in the prosecution of the war and for the ransoming of his children. It was uncertain whether the claim to the 37,500 crowns thus expended by Francis had been entirely abandoned, as the French pretended, or only postponed, as the English maintained. If the latter view was correct, the sum still due to Wolsey was about 93,000 crowns, that is to say, a little more than the £20,000 at which

Henry had rated his life. Besides, the November instalment of the pension was already due, and another would be due in May.[48]

All these sums Wolsey had made over to the king, but it was doubtful whether under the altered circumstances they could be realised. The French would certainly raise difficulties, and the help of the cardinal seemed absolutely necessary to obtain payment. This gave him a considerable advantage, as he was pretty sure to be allowed to remain in the vicinity of the court where he would be able to press Jean Joaquin, the French ambassador, for payment of the arrears and of the amount becoming due. He was made to ask urgently for these sums under the pretence that he was now very poor and in debt. The Duke of Norfolk earnestly backed his request, and gave the French to understand that Henry would be glad if the money were paid, that Wolsey might live at ease at his bishopric. But Jean Joaquin was not the dupe of Henry; he cleverly evaded all demands for payment, and asked the cardinal to give him a receipt for the amounts which Francis had been permitted to use in 1528 and in May 1529.[49]

As time went on, the resentment of Henry against his former prime minister abated. Already the friends of the cardinal dared to speak of him to the king, and made no secret of their sympathy.[50] It was their wish to procure for Wolsey an interview with Henry, that he might once more use his powers of flattery and persuasion. As the fine season, during which Henry went roaming about the country, was fast approaching, there was every chance that a meeting might take place; for, if the king came near Richmond Lodge, the cardinal might, as if by accident, find himself in his way. This was a danger which Anne and her associates viewed with considerable alarm.[51] They all agreed that the cardinal must leave, and the recovery of the French pensions became a matter of secondary importance, which was not to prevent Wolsey's departure. Even if he remained, it seemed doubtful whether it would be possible to overcome the stubbornness of Jean Joaquin.

Anne openly resented the conduct of those friends of Wolsey who dared to speak in his favour, while her uncle pressed him to leave for York.[52] It was in vain that Wolsey pleaded poverty, the bad state of the roads, and the worse state of his houses in Yorkshire; his excuses were not accepted. Norfolk was now prime minister in his turn, and spoke in the name of the king, so that the cardinal was obliged to obey. But before starting for York, a few days before Easter, he had an interview with Jean Joaquin, and, having no further interest in continuing the intrigue about his arrears, he tried to gain the goodwill of Francis by signing the three receipts for 37,500 crowns. His life thus lost £9,000 of its value to Henry.[53]

Wolsey's hope of obtaining some assistance from France was wholly illusory. Had he known what negotiations were going on between France and England, he would not have expected any advantage for himself by pleasing the French. For the new cabinet were even more eager than he to conciliate Francis; they professed the utmost anxiety to meet all his demands. The influence of Francis at the English court had increased to such an extent that he could scarcely have wished for more.[54]

Henry's chief object was now to obtain opinions from learned men and learned bodies in favour of the divorce. His pedantic folly led him to believe that the world at large and the Roman court would regard such opinions – however dishonestly come by – with a certain reverence. Fair and foul means, more foul than fair, were not spared to secure signatures for the king. In England intimidation was freely used, and nearly every divine or lawyer, fearing the royal anger, bullied and insulted by the royal commissioners, subscribed. A few resisted, but they were so small a minority that Henry could boast that in England almost everybody was on his side.

On the Continent his agents found it much more difficult to obtain favourable opinions. Though they offered bribes to any theologian who would subscribe, they met with such a reception in Germany that all hope of success in that country had to be abandoned. Roman Catholics and Lutherans concurred in holding the marriage to be perfectly lawful.[55] Spain and the Low Countries were out of the question, for not only were most of their theologians hostile to Henry, but even if it had been possible to induce any one by bribes to support him, Charles would never have allowed the English agents to make the attempt. There remained but France and Upper Italy, and here the English agents were hard at work trying to obtain subscriptions. The task was by no means easy. Frenchmen were certainly rather unfavourable to Charles and to his family; nevertheless, they would not decide against Catherine. The Faculty of Theology of the University of Paris, the famous Sorbonne, obstinately refused to give an opinion. The Faculties of Theology of Angers and Poitiers went further, and declared the marriage with Catherine to have been perfectly lawful.[56] Henry saw that if the other French universities followed the example of the Faculties of Angers and Poitiers, his cause would be entirely discredited; and as this could not be prevented by his own efforts, he urged Francis to use his influence with the doctors of Paris.[57] Francis could scarcely be expected to render such a service for nothing, and in order to obtain it the English court was obliged to make concessions of every kind, and to offer very real advantages.

But it was not only in France that the assistance of Francis seemed indispensable; in Italy too the English agents would have failed, had they not been backed by the French party. At that time the whole peninsula was divided into two hostile camps: the French and the Spanish or Imperial. In every town of Upper Italy Charles and Francis had numerous adherents or pensioners, ready to obey their behests. Henry had no such organised party at his command, and without French aid the English agents would never have been allowed to bribe as they did. The Imperialists would have asked for their expulsion, and the request would have been granted. But when the English were backed by France, they were able to disregard the Imperialists and to bribe as much as they pleased.

For the same reasons French assistance was necessary at home, where the College of Cardinals was divided into an Imperial and into a French faction. A few cardinals might be neutral, but there was no English faction, and not even a single Englishman occupied any important position in Rome. It was only through the influence of the French party that the English agents could hope to obtain an opportunity of gaining over some of those opposed to the divorce.

Under these circumstances, the English government, if bent on pursuing the course which had been adopted by Wolsey, could have no policy of its own; it could not risk defeat by alienating the goodwill of the French king. Never therefore had there been such demonstrations of affection for France. When a quarrel as to some disputed territory near Calais arose, Henry, otherwise so punctilious, exclaimed that he would permit the French to take a rod of his ground rather than allow his servants to take a foot of what belonged to France, and the matter was settled to the satisfaction of the French ambassador.[58] And so in all other matters; it was no longer necessary to buy the friendship of English ministers by such bribes and services as Wolsey had claimed; the most powerful influence, that of Anne, was bound to Francis.[59] The Earl of Wiltshire had, by command of Henry, stayed all the summer in France, partly to give an account of his mission to Francis, partly to negotiate a closer alliance.[60] George Boleyn, who was totally unfit for his new post and who longed to be back in England, had been recalled, and John Wellesbourne had taken his place.[61] But the principal negotiation remained in the hands of Wiltshire.

The earl not only acted as Henry's minister, he worked in favour of his daughter. He begged that, as soon as the French princes should be liberated by Charles, Jean du Bellay, who was now a staunch friend of the Boleyns, should go to England and promote Anne's cause; and he promised that if she were made queen she would for ever be the most devoted adherent of Francis. Du Bellay disliked the mission, but Francis was not wholly deaf to such overtures,[62] for it seemed worthwhile to make an effort to bring about a lasting enmity between Henry and Charles. Wiltshire was treated with the greatest courtesy; and the king flattered his vanity, which seems to have been great, by lodging him at the palace and by giving splendid entertainments in his honour. Moreover, his request regarding du Bellay was granted.[63]

With the help of Francis, whose ministers bullied and browbeat the Parisian doctors, an irregular opinion was obtained at one of the sessions of the faculty of theology declaring the marriage between Henry and Catherine to have been void and illegal.[64] Forty-three doctors protested against the vote as surreptitiously obtained, but the registers were taken away, so that the opinion could not be cancelled.[65] Other French universities followed the example of Paris, and with these favourable results the Earl of Wiltshire returned in the beginning of August to England. He was closely followed by du Bellay, who arrived in London on the seventeenth of the same month.[66]

The bishop, when received by the royal council, advocated a bold course. He urged that Henry should marry the Lady Anne, and expressed his belief that with the help of the French king Clement would be brought to ratify the marriage. This seemed plausible enough, for Clement himself had in former times spoken in a sense very nearly the same, but the English council were as averse from the plan as ever, for they feared that by such precipitancy England might be made even more dependent on French help. With the exception of Anne's uncle and father all the councillors voted against the scheme, the Duke of Suffolk being loudest in opposition.[67] The bishop spoke rather sharply about their action, and it seemed to him that a sudden change had come over the English court, for in other matters also he met with a cold response. The treaty which he had been commissioned to sign was not concluded, and for a moment it appeared as if the mission, instead of confirming, would shake the friendship with France.

Du Bellay failed chiefly because the members of the council were once more quarrelling. Wolsey being far off at York, they thought themselves secure, and those who found their share of the spoil insufficient now meditated the overthrow of Anne and her uncle. The Duke of Suffolk had been so enraged by the slight put upon his wife at the banquet, and by subsequent acts of insolence of Anne and her brother, that he dared to tell the king that the woman he destined for the throne had been the mistress of one of his gentlemen. Sir Thomas Wyatt seems to have been meant, but in any case Suffolk offered to prove the accusation by the evidence of unimpeachable witnesses. Henry either disbelieved or feigned to disbelieve what his brother-in-law told him, and the duke retired half in disgrace from the court. But the opposition was not thereby allayed; the divorce became every day more unpopular at the council, at court, and throughout the country.[68]

Meanwhile, Wolsey was watching his opportunity. He had by no means resigned himself to finish his life in obscurity; he continued to maintain a numerous train, he made himself popular in the north, and he never gave up the hope of returning to power. He was of course greatly pleased by

Wiltshire's failure at Bologna, and was delighted when he heard of the dissensions in the council.[69] By means of a former physician of Campeggio who had gone over to his service, he kept up an active correspondence with Jean Joaquin and with Eustache Chapuis.[70] But in these intrigues he showed little ability and little acquaintance with the character of the men whom he tried to gain over. When it was rumoured that the French ambassador had advised Henry to marry Anne Boleyn without further delay, Wolsey sent a message to Chapuis to say that he would be content to lose his archbishopric if the marriage had been concluded two years ago, for in that case the ruin brought upon him by the infamous woman would already have been avenged.[71] Wolsey, who understood Henry's character, knew that if Anne became his wife he would soon get tired of her; but in his rage he overlooked the fact that his vindictive feelings were not shared by Chapuis. To the imperial ambassador the ruin of Anne was desirable chiefly as a means of preventing the divorce; if it was to be secured by the repudiation of Catherine, he would have no hand in it. Though the court at Brussels was rather friendly to Wolsey, the ambassador gave no encouragement to the cardinal's agents and did not in any way act in his favour.[72]

Nor was the cardinal more happy in his attempt to obtain the assistance of Jean Joaquin de Vaulx. He reminded de Vaulx of his manifold services to France and of the promises made to him, but Jean Joaquin had by this time discovered that his best friends in the English council were the very men against whom his aid was wanted.[73] He would not listen to Wolsey's messages. An appeal which Wolsey is said to have made to the Pope, asking him to excommunicate Henry if he did not at once submit and send Anne away, remained equally without response.[74]

Another attempt which the cardinal made to regain his power proved even more disastrous to him. While, to make the king more pliable, he was intriguing with Chapuis, Jean Joaquin and the Pope, he tried to intrigue with Henry himself against the royal ministers. He sent off several secret agents, who were instructed to offer his services, in the hope that Henry, disgusted with the incapacity of his present advisers, frightened by the difficulties threatening him, would recall the cardinal to his presence.[75] But the men whom Wolsey had chosen for this errand were the first to betray him. It was very dangerous to negotiate such matters with so untrustworthy and dishonest a man as Henry VIII was known to be, for he might at any moment denounce the messengers to the council and hand them over to the tender mercies of Norfolk and his adherents. Wolsey's agents preferred, therefore, to play false themselves, and informed the duke of the mission entrusted to them.[76] The news created considerable alarm among the members of the cabinet. They had discovered one of Wolsey's intrigues, but it was probable that he was carrying on many more of the same kind. He might succeed and be recalled to court, in which case their influence would soon be gone; and as Wolsey was not of a forgiving temper, this was not an agreeable prospect for those who had displaced him.[77]

The common danger drew the ministers together. It was impossible to watch the cardinal's movements so closely as to prevent any secret communication with the king: the only way to counteract his intrigues was to strike at him fast and hard. The whole party set to work to bring their adversary to complete ruin, and before long they found a way of doing it. Agostino was arrested, and by threats or promises he was induced to make a full confession of all that had been transacted with Jean Joaquin and Chapuis.[78] This done, it was not difficult to raise Henry's anger against the fallen minister, and orders were sent to the Earl of Northumberland – Anne's former admirer and fast friend – to arrest the cardinal. On 4 November Wolsey found himself a prisoner at Cawood, and he was shortly afterwards sent to take his trial in London.

Norfolk was still ill at ease, for the evidence obtained would scarcely justify a sentence of death, and it could not in any case be divulged without danger. The cardinal would at the utmost be kept a prisoner at the Tower, where he would cause as much anxiety as at York since, in a moment of anger with the duke, Henry might recall Wolsey to the council board. No hurry was, therefore, made to bring him to London.

But Norfolk and Anne were spared all further trouble in this matter. Frightened by his arrest, travelling in the very worst season, already worn out by work and indulgence, Wolsey fell ill on the road. He was obliged to stop at Leicester, his illness having been increased by the journey; and a few days later, on 27 November 1530, he breathed his last.

4

THOMAS CROMWELL

The news of Wolsey's death was received by Anne and her friends with an exultation they did not care to conceal. Their great rival was gone, all danger threatening them from his vengeance seemed over; and with characteristic coarseness they expressed their hatred by violent lampoons on his character. Lord Wiltshire gave an entertainment at which a farce was performed representing the late cardinal going down to hell, and Norfolk was so pleased with the play that he had it printed. Wolsey was spoken of in such opprobrious terms that even the French ambassadors were shocked and loudly expressed their disapproval.[1]

Anne became daily more overbearing. The latest exploit in her honour had been the fabrication of the wonderful pedigree, in which good Sir William Bullen the mercer was represented as the descendant of a Norman knight. Though these pretensions were laughed at, and though Anne's aunt the duchess freely told her what they were worth, she was in no way embarrassed.[2] To show her contempt for those who opposed her, she chose a device which she had heard in France, but which she only partially remembered. '*Ainsi sera, groigne qui groigne*!' was embroidered on the liveries of her servants.[3] Anne had no luck in such matters; to her mortification she learned that she had adopted the motto of her bitter enemies, the princes of the house of Burgundy. '*Groigne qui groigne*,' she heard it repeated, '*et vive Bourgoigne*!' The liveries had to be laid aside, and Anne's servants on Christmas Day appeared in their old doublets.[4] She vented her anger by abusing the Spaniards, and wishing them all at the bottom of the sea; and when one of Catherine's ladies, bolder than the rest, bid her remember that the queen was born in Spain, she swore that she would not acknowledge Catherine to be either her queen or the wife of the king.[5]

Anne would have borne these little annoyances with greater equanimity had not more serious troubles come at the same time. The death of Wolsey, as she soon found, was not, after all, of much benefit to her. The coalition which had ruined the cardinal having been dissolved, nearly all her allies began to forsake her. The nobles, Suffolk at their head, seeing that she was more arrogant than Wolsey had ever been, were the first to go over to the opposition. Gardiner, who had obtained a promise of the bishopric of Winchester, showed himself less eager to please, and was no longer implicitly trusted.[6] More, Fitzwilliam, the comptroller Guildford and other influential officials were decidedly hostile; and even the Duke of Norfolk was said to have spoken in terms not at all favourable to Anne.[7] Her party had for the moment dwindled down to a few of her nearest kinsfolk and personal friends. Catherine took advantage of this state of things to have a serious talk with her husband. On Christmas Eve she saw him in private, and upbraided him with the wrong he was doing her, and with the scandalous example he was setting by keeping Anne Boleyn in his company. When they quarrelled, Catherine generally got the better of the king; he was cowed by her firmness, and could not prevail against her simple and straightforward arguments. But in this case the queen had courted defeat by making an insinuation which was unfounded. Henry triumphantly replied that Catherine was altogether mistaken, that there was nothing wrong in his relations with Anne, and that he kept her in his company only to learn her character, as he had made up his mind to marry her. Having grown bold by this first success, he declared that marry her he would, whatever the Pope might say.[8] Wherewith this matrimonial dispute came to an end.

Notwithstanding his valorous talk, Henry found himself not a little embarrassed. It had now become pretty clear that the Roman court would not grant the divorce; and his agents at Rome had been occupied in staving off the inevitable result of Catherine's appeal. They had already hinted that the cause could not be judged out of England, and that it ought to be settled by the authority of the English bishops. The Boleyns strongly advocated this course, the French would have approved of it, and Henry's conscience would have been satisfied by a show of a verdict in his favour. But the difficulty was, that the bishops were not at all inclined to do what he desired, and that they were daily becoming less submissive. The attacks made upon them in parliament had alarmed their cupidity; the insolence of the royal ministers angered them; a few had a remnant of conscience, and were disinclined to take part in an iniquitous judgement. Several of those who had formerly gone with the king now held back or resisted his policy.

During the first month of 1531, Henry seems nearly to have lost heart.[9] The news from Rome was so bad that he knew not what to do. The imperial agents were pressing the Pope to order Henry under pain of excommunication to send Anne from court; and now that Wolsey was dead, and the former existence of the famous decretal could neither be proved by his testimony nor made use of with his help, Clement was less unwilling to act upon the emperor's advice. If he did so, and if he followed up his threat by fulminating the censures of the Church, Henry was not yet in a position to resist, the public mind in England being unprepared for a schism. The only hope was that Francis might prevent Clement from issuing the brief; but the French king just now was out of humour with Henry, who had not complied with the most exorbitant of his demands.[10] Things looked so gloomy that, if Chapuis may be trusted, Henry thought of sending Anne from court, before he should be called upon to do so. He cannot have intended to make her remain away a long time; but, with Henry, 'out of sight' was easily 'out of mind', the opposite party was strong and numerous, and her absence might have proved the beginning of a total separation.[11]

Anne knew well that her game was not yet won. During the preceding summer, when it had appeared that Campeggio would not give sentence in favour of Henry, she had urged the king to marry her at once, without waiting for a formal dissolution of his marriage with Catherine. Henry was afraid to take so bold a course, and told her that for her sake he was making many enemies. Anne received the reproach badly, and vehemently exclaimed that his sacrifices were nothing compared with what she was ready to endure. She was well aware, she said, that there was an old prophecy that in this time a queen of England was to be burned, and she loved him so much that she did not fear even death if she could marry him.[12] But Henry was not to be moved, and Anne had to wait.

This she did not do very patiently. We hear of another quarrel between the lovers in November 1530. Anne once more upbraided him with his slackness and want of energy, and cried out that she regretted the loss of her youth and her reputation in striving after that which she could not obtain.[13] Henry tried to soothe her; and to show how much he was in earnest he allowed her to hide behind a screen while he gave audience to Chapuis, and to overhear all he said to the ambassador.[14]

But even this could not satisfy Anne. In the spring of 1531 her marriage seemed as distant as ever, and the delay did not improve her temper. She appears to have had violent quarrels with Henry, in the course of which she used such strong language that he complained about her to the Duke of Norfolk, saying she did not behave like the queen, who had never in her life used ill words towards him.[15]

It was at this most critical juncture that Anne found an able and faithful ally in a man who had just entered political life, but who had risen in it with the utmost rapidity. Thomas Cromwell was the son of a wealthy citizen, and received in youth a tolerable education. After his father's death he found himself in bad circumstances, and tried to mend his fortunes by going abroad, but he does not appear to have succeeded. On the Continent, however, he gained a fair knowledge of French, Italian and Dutch, and of the state and resources of foreign countries. Having returned to London he became a small attorney, and, as it seems, a money lender. He was brought under the notice of Cardinal Wolsey, who took him into his service and employed him in most questionable transactions, by which convents were despoiled to enrich the foundations at Oxford and Ipswich. When shortly afterwards Wolsey fell, Cromwell gave signal proof of his ability, managing to serve men of all parties. For Wolsey's enemies he secured pensions on Winchester and St Alban's, for Wolsey himself he obtained royal letters of protection and ultimately his pardon. At the same time he was not forgetful of his own interests. He solicited and obtained from the Duke of Norfolk the privilege of being nominated as one of the burgesses of the borough of Taunton; he received from the duke himself instructions how to act in parliament; and he was soon preferred to the royal service.[16] As he had made many friends at court by giving away the wealth of Wolsey, and as his talents and energy attracted attention, he quickly advanced in favour and in rank. In 1530, he was made secretary to the king, and at the time of his former patron's death he was already taking a leading part in politics, especially in all matters relating to the clergy. When the coalition broke asunder, he stood by Anne and the Boleyns, and was soon rewarded by being sworn of the king's council.

Cromwell advocated a bold and energetic policy, and wished to use for the benefit of Lady Anne his experience in dealing with clergymen. The first indication of a plan to frighten the English clergy into submission to the king's will is to be found in a letter of Cromwell to Wolsey, and it seems most probable that the idea originated with Cromwell.[17] The proposal was that all those who had ever received powers, investiture or dispensations from Wolsey as legate, should be threatened with prosecution for præmunire, if they did not entirely submit to the king. Nearly all the higher clergy belonged to this category, and with the fear of so great a penalty before them they would, it was hoped, grant everything the king wished. Such a plan could not of course fail to please Anne, to whom it held out a sure way of obtaining what she desired. The king was equally satisfied with it, as its success would make the clergy entirely dependent on him. And the party in the council which now generally opposed the measures brought forward by Anne's friends, willingly assented to a scheme which would weaken the influence of the bishops.

At that time the English clergy consisted of two very different classes having little sympathy with one another. The lower parochial clergy, who were usually neither learned nor ambitious and seldom rose to higher rank, lived with the people, and were considered the equals of small farmers and yeomen, decidedly the inferiors of well-to-do gentlemen. They tried to eke out their salaries ranging from £10 to £20 a year with the small fees they got for their services, and with presents from the wealthier parishioners. Beyond the limits of their parishes they found little to interest them; they contented themselves with performing the ceremonies of the Church and administering the sacraments, and rarely meddled with politics.

The regular clergy, who were rather numerous, were of greater importance. Many of them, like the parochial clergy, sprang from the lowest classes of society, and individually did not rise much above their kinsfolk. But even a monastery wholly peopled by such rude and lowly friars had as a collective entity considerable influence. The monks were mostly landed proprietors employing a number of servants and labourers. They often had some skill in medicine; they kept in safe custody documents and articles of value; they were in frequent communication with other monasteries of the same order, and were thus able to inform their neighbours of the news of the day. They had hundreds of little ways of making themselves useful. Besides, several of the monastic orders consisted of preachers who went from place to place to supplement the failings of the secular priests, who were generally too ignorant to deliver a sermon. In the whole archdiocese of York there were in 1534 but twelve parochial priests able to preach.[18] Some monks possessed the gift of real eloquence, and their sermons were listened to eagerly by congregations who had few opportunities of hearing anything so impressive. The regular clergy were therefore more powerful than the parochial priests, and they used their influence for the attainment of all kinds of ends, political ends not excepted.

Bishops, deans and archdeacons did not often care to manifest clerical qualities. The most correct definition of a bishop under Henry VIII would, perhaps, be: a royal official pensioned on Church funds. The way in which bishops, deans and archdeacons arrived at their dignities was generally this. A young man of humble origin and small means, who was unable or unwilling to be a soldier, had, if he was ambitious, but two careers open to him: the Church and the law. The former offered by far the most brilliant prospects, for it provided scope for a variety of talents, and the one drawback, the condition of celibacy, was often not greatly considered by a man who had not the means of maintaining a family. A man who could read, write, reckon fluently and keep accounts, and who knew enough of Latin to make out the sense of legal documents, very easily found employment with some wealthy and influential patron. Under the name of chaplain he was engaged during the week in keeping accounts, in writing letters, in acting as steward or agent, and on Sunday he said mass. If he was admitted into the household of some great nobleman or some high official, he made a good start towards arriving at a bishopric. Gaining the confidence of his new master, and being entrusted with important business, he came into contact with a great many persons of influence, and might finally arrive at that road to fortune, the royal chapel, or the chapel of the prime minister. Here he was pretty sure to obtain before long a deanery or a good parsonage, which he never visited, but left to the care of a vicar at £10 a year. By and by he might be sent on foreign missions, or be made a royal secretary, master of the rolls, or something of the kind; so that between his ecclesiastical income and the emoluments and profits of his office he could live well enough. After many years of intelligent and unscrupulous service he became ripe for a bishopric; and at the next vacancy of a fitting see, the king, making use of his quasi-right to grant *congé d'élire,* nominated him, the Pope confirmed the nomination as a matter of course, and the worthy official was consecrated a bishop. In obtaining a decided rank and a better income, he did not cease to render purely political service. Many a bishop remained to the end of his life a mere royal official, never caring for the diocese over which he was set. And for this course he had very good reasons. First, there were poor bishoprics and opulent bishoprics. A bishop of St Asaph, St David's, or Llandaff, with scarce £300 a year, very naturally desired to be translated to Ely, Winchester or Durham, the revenues of which were about £3,000 a year. Moreover, the king on granting a bishopric generally reserved a part of its revenues to be employed as pensions at his pleasure. When the recipients of such pensions died or were otherwise provided for, the prelate tried to secure the money for himself; but this was allowed only if the king was well pleased with him. It was therefore the interest of the bishop to retain the royal favour, and to serve the king who could bestow such benefits, rather than the Church which had nothing to give him. Even cardinals' hats were bestowed only on royal recommendation.

It was only when the better part of his life was spent, when his health was impaired and his energy broken, when he was no longer good enough for the royal service, that a bishop retired to his diocese and spent there at least a part of the year. But he was of course a stranger to his clergy, and his life had been so different from theirs that he rarely understood their character or won their confidence. Even if after a time he began to take some interest in his spiritual work, he was not well fitted to reform abuses; and any reforms he introduced came to a speedy end when at his death a new non-resident bishop was appointed, the diocese being then again left for many years to take care of itself.

In 1530 three English sees, those of Salisbury, Worcester and Llandaff, were held by foreigners who simply enjoyed the revenues of them. All the other bishops, with three exceptions, either were or had been royal officials. Officials also held more than half of the deaneries and archdeaconries. The episcopal bench was detested by the barons, for the bishops were not only, as a rule, more arrogant than lay officials, but they generally voted in the upper house of parliament with the government. A bishop residing in his diocese was scarcely more agreeable than a bishop who lived in London; he was a dangerous competitor for local popularity, his influence becoming often even greater than that of the smaller barons. For, once in the country, the bishop courted popularity. He entertained his neighbours, spoke kindly to the farmers and yeomen, and aided his clergy, rendering a great many little services for which his career had fitted him. He advised people who had suits at court, gave them letters of introduction, or obtained information for them. In every respect he was thus a rival to the lay peers, all the more formidable as he wielded the powers of the Church, and as an open quarrel with him was perilous for high and low.

The peers, therefore, offered no opposition to the plan of Cromwell, not being aware that the end he had in view was very different from what they desired. Shortly after the new year, in 1531, convocation met, and the clergy were informed of the danger in which they stood. At first they thought that the scheme was simply a device to obtain a larger grant of money than they otherwise would have made; and after some discussion they offered the sum of £100,000, to be paid in five years for the king's use. But to their dismay the grant was refused in the form in which they had agreed to it, and Cromwell sent them the draft of a declaration requiring them to acknowledge their offences, to crave for mercy, and to recognise the king as the supreme head of the Church of England.[19]

But the new minister had miscalculated the power which he could bring to bear on the clergy. As soon as it became apparent to what end his proceedings tended, they met with general opposition. The peers had been ready enough to assent to the humiliation and the spoliation of the hated bishops, but they did not at all wish them to be made more dependent on the king's will. The clergy also made a stand, the demand urged by Cromwell being so unheard of that even the most timid would not concede it. Every day the opposition grew, disunion crept into the royal council, and Cromwell found that he would not triumph so easily as he had anticipated. A compromise was effected, convocation agreeing to make the proposed declaration with the saving clause 'as far as God's laws allow,' a clause by which all practical value was taken out of the act.[20]

This compromise was in reality a serious defeat for Anne's party. The bills hostile to the authority of the Pope, which it had been intended to submit to parliament, were abandoned; and a strong reaction became manifest throughout the country. The bishops were rather ashamed of having made even nominal concessions; and a protest was signed by numerous priests of both provinces against any encroachments on the liberty of the Church or any act derogatory to the authority of the Holy See.[21] The Bishops of Rochester, Exeter, Chichester, Bath, Norwich, St Asaph and Llandaff were now decidedly in favour of Catherine. The Archbishop of Canterbury himself began to lean to their side. Nearly all the lower secular and regular clergy were against the divorce.

At Rome Cromwell's attempt produced even more striking consequences. It was regarded as a revolt against the Holy See; and many of those who had hitherto rather favoured the king were alienated by his proceedings. The tribunal of the Rota, and a consistory of cardinals called in on the question, had both decided that Henry was bound to plead at Rome, and that even if he did not appear in person or by proxy the cause must go on. On 5 January 1531 Paul Capisuccio, one of the auditors of the Rota, had been appointed by the Pope to hear the cause, and a mandate had been issued calling upon Henry to appear;[22] but the English agents had declined to admit the jurisdiction of the Roman tribunal, contending that it was a privilege of kings to have such causes tried in their own country. The Pope had granted delay after delay, and there had been endless discussions about the question whether Henry was bound to plead or not. But after receipt of the news of Henry's proceedings in the spring of 1531, the temper of the Roman court was roused, and the Pope by his nuncio in England, Baron de Burgo, sent warning to the king that the cause must now begin.

The message was not an agreeable one for De Burgo, and he took some days to make up his mind to deliver it. At last, on 31 May, he had audience of Henry, and explained the matter as mildly as he could. As he had expected, the king railed against the Pope, swearing that he would not submit, and threatening with the help of France to march on Rome at the head of an army. De Burgo could but shrug his shoulders at such childish bragging, but the result of the audience was that the king was more enraged than ever.

When the nuncio left, Henry, on the same evening, called a council. It was decided that another attempt should be made to induce Catherine to forego her rights, and that a deputation should be sent to her next day. Catherine was warned at once by some secret friend, perhaps by one of the commissioners. On the following morning she heard several masses to gain strength for the impending struggle. It was nine o'clock at night when she received the deputation, consisting of the Duke of Norfolk, the Duke of Suffolk, the Marquis of Exeter, the Earls of Shrewsbury, Northumberland, and Wiltshire, several other peers, the bishops of Lincoln and London, and Drs Lee, Sampson and Gardiner. Norfolk, taking advantage of the act passed in convocation, told the queen that Henry was highly displeased at having been cited to appear at Rome, that he would not submit to such an indignity, and that he was absolutely sovereign in his realms both in temporal and spiritual matters, parliament and convocation having admitted him to be so. Catherine stoutly defended her right, and with perfect good temper battled with the duke and the other counsellors. Many of them were not displeased when she made a happy retort and silenced an adversary, and some one of the party exclaimed that though they laboured a good deal a woman got the better of them. After a time the conference was broken up, the comptroller Guildford declaring that all those doctors who had first mooted the question of the divorce should be sent to Rome to defend their opinion, or to be treated according to their merits.[23]

Neither Anne nor Cromwell seem to have expected any other result. The former, who, about the new year, had thought that her purpose might shortly be accomplished, had after the indecisive action of convocation and parliament lost confidence in most of the leaders of her party. Cromwell appears to have been unwilling to argue the matter with Catherine, and he is afterwards mentioned by Chapuis as the only councillor who did not take part in the long discussions about the validity of her marriage.

But, although neither Anne nor her ally were astonished at the result of the interview, Anne wished to profit by Henry's resentment. The first whom she attacked was the outspoken comptroller. She had high words with him, threatening that he should be dismissed when she became queen. Guildford, disgusted by her insolence, went at once to Henry, and resigned his appointment. He perhaps expected that the king would make Lady Anne retract, but he was mistaken; Henry only asked him to remain in office. As, under the circumstances, Guildford could scarcely do this, he insisted on having his leave,[24] and it was granted; Sir William Paulet, a more obedient courtier, being appointed in his place. Of the other friends of Catherine, the Duchess of Norfolk, who had not been civil enough to the favourite,[25] had been sent away from court some weeks before; and the Marquis of Exeter was now also ordered to leave.[26] By these means Anne hoped effectually to silence all who spoke against the divorce and in favour of the queen.

Anne made even better use than this of Henry's annoyance at what he considered the obstinacy of Catherine. Whenever the king and the queen met, neither of them being very refined, they freely quarrelled about the question whether they were married or not, and the result generally was that Henry left the field entirely cowed. Anne might upbraid him for his want of courage, but on the next occasion the same thing would happen,[27] for the firmness, courage, and perfect good temper of Catherine had not yet lost their power over Henry's weak and vacillating mind. Besides, Catherine had a great advantage over Anne in the force of habit. Kings and queens at that time, with all their show and state, were much more of goodman and goodwife than is commonly imagined. A queen had a good deal to do with housekeeping, and rendered the king many little services which nowadays any fine lady would think beneath her dignity. Catherine took care of her husband's wardrobe, looked after the laundry, and superintended the making of his linen. Henry, accustomed to apply to her when he wanted anything in daily use, continued to do so, and she did her best to provide for his needs.[28] There were sharp quarrels about this between Henry and Anne, but it was certain that there would be no change as long as Catherine resided with the king. Anne had tried as much as possible to separate them by leading Henry away on hunting excursions, but these could not last for ever; he had to rejoin his court, and at court he found the queen. One of the principal reasons why Anne was so pleased with York Place was, as we have seen, that there would be no apartment in it for Catherine;[29] and, indeed, when Henry went there, the queen was left behind at Greenwich.[30] But the court was seldom in London; and at Greenwich, Hampton Court and Windsor, there was plenty of room for Catherine. Anne therefore wished to have her sent away from court, and by stimulating the anger of Henry she managed to obtain her object.

On Whitsunday the king and the queen dined together, and Henry, being in an unusually amiable mood, spoke in terms of affection of his daughter the princess. Next day, made bold by his seeming good temper, Catherine expressed a wish that Mary might be allowed to come to court. He received the request very badly, and answered that if Catherine wished to see her daughter she might go to the place where Mary was, and remain there as long as she liked. This would have been the beginning of a separation, for although Henry lacked the courage to send his wife away, he would have found means to prevent her return if she had once left. Catherine saw the snare, and meekly replied that for nobody in the world would she leave his company; and with this the incident came to an end.[31]

In June the court went to Hampton Court; and Henry, as was his custom at this season of the year, spent some time in hunting in his parks. The queen was not allowed to accompany him, as she had always done hitherto; he was attended only by Lady Anne and a few favourite servants.[32] About the middle of July, while Catherine remained at Windsor,[33] Henry and Anne started on a longer excursion than any they had yet undertaken together. A month after they had gone, the queen received a message to the effect that Henry wished to return to Windsor and objected to see her, and that she was to retire with her servants to the More, a house the Abbot of St Alban's had been made to cede to the king.[34] Catherine had no alternative but to obey; and a few days later Anne Boleyn made her entry as the future queen.

This was certainly a great triumph, for not only was a dangerous influence removed, but Henry's vanity and obstinacy were now engaged, and it had been made more difficult for him to draw back. Anne tried also to strengthen her cause by securing for her adherents nearly every vacancy which occurred at court, in the administration, and in diplomacy. Stokesley, a prominent advocate of the divorce, had been duly installed Bishop of London, Gardiner had become Bishop of Winchester, and the archbishopric of York, which Reginald Pole had just refused, was given to Dr Edward Lee, one of Anne's most zealous supporters. Dr Foxe, formerly Gardiner's colleague at Rome, was made almoner instead of Lee. Sir Francis Bryan, Anne's cousin and friend, was ambassador in Paris; and Sir Nicholas Carew, who had married Bryan's sister, was sent on special missions first to the emperor and then to France. Sir Nicholas Harvey, whose wife, the widow of Sir Richard Wingfield, was much liked by Anne, had been appointed ambassador at the court of the emperor;[35] and when he was considered unfit for the post, Sir Thomas Elyot, who, after the downfall of Wolsey, had attached himself to Anne, was nominated in his stead.[36]

But there was one annoying circumstance: the new bishops, as soon as they were installed, became much less ardent in their zeal for the divorce. The lay officials also cooled down. When Sir Nicholas Carew was at the imperial court, both he and his colleague, Doctor Richard Sampson, dean of the chapel, had secret audiences with the emperor, and assured Charles that they greatly regretted the demand for a divorce, and that they would do all they could to resist it, and to serve the queen.[37] Sir Thomas Elyot, too, soon became a strong opponent of the divorce, and even wrote a treatise against it which he showed to the king, and a copy of which he sent to Spain.[38] Dr William Bennet, one of the principal agents at the papal court, secretly assured the emperor that, if no weakness were shown, Henry would give way and plead his cause at Rome.[39] When on leave in England, Bennet wrote to Catherine to express his devotion to her. Whatever he had done against her, he said, he had been forced to do; and he predicted that if she remained firm she would ultimately succeed.[40] There is good reason to believe that Bennet acted as he spoke, and that at Rome, while officially and publicly pressing for a divorce, he privately let the Pope know that in his opinion it ought not to be granted, that the cause ought to be tried at Rome, and that the decision should be in favour of Catherine.[41]

This secret or open hostility of most of the courtiers and officials made it hard for Anne to obtain any decided advantage over her enemies. Her fight was a weary one, something like the work of the Danaïdes, and in the autumn of 1531, scarcely any progress had been made.

Henry would have liked to disregard papal inhibitions, to obtain some pretence of divorce in England, and to marry Anne immediately afterwards. But there were several difficulties in the way. First of all, Charles V had so warmly taken up the cause of his aunt that if such a course were adopted he might proceed to acts of open hostility. And Henry, however much he might boast of his power, knew very well that single-handed he could not withstand the emperor. If war broke out, a Dutch fleet would land a body of Spanish and German veterans on the eastern coast, and Henry would have no troops capable of opposing them. His raw, probably disaffected levies, would be scattered like chaff before the wind, and the crown would be torn from his brow. If he wished to pursue a bold policy, it was indispensable that he should conclude an alliance with France; and the tone of the French ministers had not of late been such as to reassure him. Jean Joaquin had shown no favour to religious innovations, and had occasionally behaved with something like contempt towards the king; while in France Sir Francis Bryan, and Foxe, who had been sent to assist Bryan, thought they had some reason to complain of the French.

Henry, therefore, before proceeding further, wished to make sure that King Francis would not fail him at the proper time. The new Bishop of Winchester was sent to France to take the place of Bryan and to negotiate a treaty of closer alliance.[42] He was well received, and de la Pommeraye, who had succeeded Jean Joaquin as ambassador in England, was instructed to discuss the conditions. After some haggling as to the terms, a treaty was signed at Greenwich in April 1532, by de la Pommeraye on the part of France, and by the Earl of Wiltshire and Dr Foxe on the part of England.[43]

In the new treaty it was stipulated that if the emperor attacked England Francis should assist Henry with 500 lances and a fleet mounted by 1,500 men, and that if France was attacked Henry should send 5,000 archers and a similar fleet to the assistance of the French king. The stipulation in favour of England was wholly illusory; for if Charles had invaded England, he would have done so with such rapidity that the French fleet would not have had time to arrive. The 500 lances might have served to defend Calais, but the war would have been decided before they could have reached England. On the other hand, the English fleet and the 5,000 archers might have been of some use to France in a regular campaign of four or five months. There was, moreover, this point, which had been overlooked by those who in England wished for the treaty, that it bound Francis to do less than it would have been his interest to do in any case. If Charles had overthrown the government of Henry, Catherine would have governed for Mary, and England would have sided with the emperor against France. Francis could not have allowed this, so that, treaty or no treaty, in case of attack, he would have done his best to assist Henry against Charles. In the end England would not have profited by the intervention of France, for on account of Calais the French were at heart hostile to the English, and had Francis overthrown the emperor he would soon have turned against Henry.

But the French influence was now paramount at court. The sympathies of Anne were all in favour of the land in which she had been brought up. The Duke of Norfolk was a strong partisan of France, and Cromwell had not yet sufficient authority to control foreign policy. Henry, himself but a poor politician, ascribed undue importance to the treaty, and on 30 April he ratified the act of his commissioners.[44]

While the treaty was being negotiated, attempts were made by ministers to organise their forces. Parliament had met on 15 January. It had been carefully convoked, most of the queen's partisans having either been excused from attending or having received no writ at all. Tunstall and Fisher were among the latter. Tunstall stayed away; but Fisher, more courageous, and nearer to London, attended as usual.[45] The bishops who appeared in their places were sounded as to the assistance which might be expected from them; and the great majority were found to be hostile to any measure which might smack of revolt against the authority of Rome. No hope could be entertained of a joint action of the English episcopate in favour of Henry. Another way had to be tried.

If the bishops as a body could not be made to further the king's designs, it seemed possible that their chief and representative, the primate, might be bullied or coaxed into complying with Henry's wishes. It was thought he might be induced to call in a few bishops who could be relied upon, to open a court as primate of all England, to accept in its widest sense the doctrine that the king was the supreme head of the Church of England, to disregard entirely the papal authority and all inhibitory briefs, and to proceed to try the case. Archbishop Warham had acted with Wolsey in the infamous attempt at a collusive suit in 1527; he had continued for several years afterwards most docile to the king; and when he abandoned Henry's side his timidity was in striking contrast with the energy of Fisher. *Ira principis mors est*, he had piteously replied when Catherine had asked his advice. Not unnaturally, therefore, it was supposed that the king's anger might frighten him once more into obedience.[46]

Norfolk and Wiltshire submitted the matter to him and tried to gain him over.[47] But the utmost limit of Warham's servility had been reached. He was seriously ill, dying in fact, and the inevitable having lost something of its terrors, he dared affront the royal anger although it might be death. He thought of the anger of a greater King before whom he would soon have to appear, and steadfastly declined to associate himself with a dishonourable scheme.

All spiritual authorities having refused their help, it remained to be seen whether a general consent of the laity might not be obtained. About the middle of February the Duke of Norfolk assembled a number of the leading peers and members of the Lower House, and told them he had been informed that matrimonial causes ought not to be judged by ecclesiastical but by lay tribunals. He wished to know what was their opinion on this subject, and what they would do to preserve the rights of the Crown. Lord Darcy, formerly an ally of Norfolk and a bitter enemy of Wolsey, was the first to speak. He flatly contradicted the duke, maintaining that the cognisance of matrimonial causes belonged to the spiritual courts, and that laymen had nothing to do with them. The other lords sided with Darcy, and the duke's attempt utterly failed.[48]

Henry was greatly vexed by Norfolk's failure, and for a moment he thought of marrying Anne at once. She seems to have been willing, and the French ambassador approved of the plan, which, from Henry's point of view, might, after all, have been the wisest.[49] But the council was strongly opposed to it. Anne's father, who was never in favour of a hazardous course, knew that if Henry married his daughter before Catherine was divorced, there would be a general outcry; he feared that the government would be overthrown, and that he would lose everything he had gained by a most laborious and servile life. He spoke, therefore, against an immediate marriage, and Henry, seeing his council unanimous, reluctantly gave way.[50]

From this time there was a growing enmity between Anne and her uncle, the Duke of Norfolk, which drove him at last into the camp of her enemies. She was offended with her father, too; and sharp taunts which passed between them led to a complete estrangement.[51]

Although an immediate marriage was impossible, there was nothing to prevent Anne and Cromwell from preparing the ground for further action. They wished to deprive the church of the last remnants of independence, and the end of the session was marked by an energetic attack on its privileges. Convocation was pressed by the royal ministers to declare that the clergy had no right to make ordinances in provincial councils without the royal assent. Gardiner, now installed Bishop of Winchester, argued strongly against the declaration, but all to no avail; convocation had to give way, and to admit that provincial ordinances and canons should be revised by a royal commission.[52] Warham was indignant at the injury done to his order, and from his bed he dictated a formal protest against all encroachments on the ecclesiastical power, asserting that he would not allow himself to be bound by any statute or agreement, and claiming the whole of his episcopal authority.[53] This made it very difficult for Henry to bring his case before a tribunal appointed by himself, for although he might refuse to appear at Rome, he could not with any show of reason deny that the archbishops had hitherto exercised the functions for which Warham contended. Henry himself had so often asserted that the matter of the divorce ought to be tried by the primate that it was impossible for him now to take up a different position.

Warham might have been put on his trial for some imaginary offence; but this would have created an immense scandal, and the difficulties of the divorce would only have been increased. Besides, fear of worldly consequences had no influence over a dying man. Nothing, therefore, could be done, and matters remained in suspense.

This was most annoying to Anne, for every delay became the occasion of fresh complications. During the summer an intrigue was spun against her, which, if it had succeeded, would have stopped her further career. Her former admirer, Sir Henry Percy, who had now become Earl of Northumberland, had married Lady Mary Talbot, daughter of the Earl of Shrewsbury. The marriage had not been happy, the wayward and violent young earl having soon quarrelled with his wife; and for the last two years he had abstained from her company. Being questioned by her as to the cause of his behaviour, he replied that he was not her husband, that he had long ago been betrothed to Anne Boleyn, and that in consequence of this pre-contract any subsequent marriage was illegal. The countess fancied that this statement afforded her a chance of obtaining release from one with whom she had led an unhappy life, and that it would be an obstacle to the marriage of the king and Anne. She wrote to her father giving her account of what the earl had said, and asking that the matter should be laid before the king. But Lord Shrewsbury, though an enemy of Anne, was a cautious man. Had he done as his daughter desired, he would not have gained much; the letter would have been at once communicated to Anne, who would have found means to defend herself. It was accordingly taken to the Duke of Norfolk, by whom it was handed to his niece.

Anne at once chose the boldest course. She showed the letter to the king, and insisted that the affair should be investigated. At her request Northumberland was sent for and strictly examined. Whatever the young earl might have said in a fit of passion to his wife, he was not the man to abide by it in cold blood. He knew that for having concealed a fact so closely affecting the king's honour he might almost be charged with treason, and that if, by revealing it now, he rendered the marriage of Anne and Henry nearly impossible, he would draw on himself the hatred both of the king and of the lady. Before the council he denied that any pre-contract existed between him and Anne, and this statement he solemnly repeated before the Archbishop of Canterbury.[54] Anne had once more defeated the plots of her enemies.

The hearing of the earl's deposition was the last important act of Warham's life. He was far advanced in age, and his strength had for some time been failing. The difficulties of his position, the profound alarm and displeasure he felt at the turn things were taking, preyed heavily on his mind. His body was not able to bear the strain any longer, and on 23 August he died.

5

THE MARRIAGE

The death of Warham removed the chief obstacle in the way of Anne. The stubborn resistance of the primate during the last year had hampered her efforts, and had made it impossible to obtain a divorce in England. Now this difficulty was at an end. It was Henry's duty to choose Warham's successor, and he would of course appoint a man certain to do his bidding. The new primate, when installed, would be ordered to open a court and to hear the cause, and immediately after the decision Henry would publicly marry Anne.

On 1 September, eight days after Warham's death, the courtiers were treated to a ceremony of a rather extraordinary kind. Lady Anne Rochford was on that day created Marchioness of Pembroke with remainder to the heirs male of her body. The words 'lawfully begotten,' which were generally inserted in patents of creation, were significantly left out; any illegitimate son whom Anne might have, would be entitled to the dignity.[1] A thousand pounds in lands were at the same time settled on the new marchioness, and a few days later she received a present of jewels taken by royal command from the queen.[2]

What was the reason for this extraordinary step? There seems to be but one explanation. Hitherto Anne, uncertain how long it would take to obtain a divorce, had feared that if she yielded to the king, his passion might cool before she could become his wife. After the death of Warham there was less reason to dread this result, and it is highly probable that having obtained a promise that the new archbishop would forthwith pronounce a divorce, she became the king's mistress. But even now she was cautious, and to provide against the worst, against any unforeseen event that might prevent her marriage, she asked for a title for herself and any illegitimate son she might bear, and for a grant of lands and jewels. No other theory will account for all the circumstances – the curious wording of the patent, the promotion of Anne immediately after Warham's death, the nomination of Cranmer, and the premature birth of Elizabeth.

The lovers were not to spend their honeymoon in perfect quiet. Henry, who always attached too much importance to mere professions of friendship, had expressed a wish to confirm the alliance between England and France by an interview with Francis.[3] Remembering the costliness of the famous meeting of 1520, and the bad results which had sprung from it, Francis was not very eager to grant the request; but Henry was pressing, and in the summer of 1532 de la Pommeraye, at his solicitation, went to France to arrange the conditions of an interview.[4] On de la Pommeraye's return in June the King of England surrendered one after another certain ridiculous pretensions on which he had at first insisted; and the Duke of Norfolk assured de la Pommeraye that Francis should be treated throughout as the superior.[5] It was agreed that in October the two kings should meet at Boulogne and Calais, that no exorbitant display should be made, and that the number of their attendants should be limited.[6] Francis, having no longer any pretext for declining the proposal, ratified what his ambassador had done, but asked that the agreement should be kept secret until the very eve of the meeting, so that it might appear to happen by mere chance. This, however, would not have served the King of England, and scarcely had the convention been concluded when the secret was allowed to leak out. During August it became generally known in London.[7]

Henry wished to take Anne with him to meet his royal brother of France, first, because he now found it very hard to be deprived of her company even for a few days, secondly, because he hoped that Francis might be brought to treat her as a person who was shortly to be the Queen of England, whereby a certain sanction would be given to the divorce. De la Pommeraye was asked to obtain an invitation for her from France, and wrote to Montmorency explaining the king's wishes.[8] Guillaume du Bellay, brother to Jean, Bishop of Bayonne, was now sent to England to arrange the details of the meeting; and, in reply to de la Pommeraye's suggestion, he brought a message for Henry which was capable of being interpreted as an invitation for Anne.[9]

Thereupon, early in September, privy seals were sent out to a number of Lords to hold their wives in readiness to accompany the king's cousin, the Marchioness of Pembroke, whom King Francis had invited to be present at the meeting.[10] These messages were received with much indignation; nevertheless, as disobedience might have proved dangerous, Anne would certainly not have lacked attendance had not a new difficulty arisen.

Francis had been quite willing that Anne should be brought to Calais or even to Boulogne. But when Henry had desired that the new marchioness should be met by some French lady of high rank, Francis had not shown the same readiness. The Queen of France was out of the question, for in outward things her husband retained some of the manners of a gentleman, and he would not ask her to meet the mistress of Henry – he would not oblige Leonor to greet the woman who was conspiring against the happiness of her aunt. But, Henry had suggested, might not Marguerite, the king's sister and titular Queen of Navarre, be induced to attend? She was known to be hostile to the emperor, who kept her husband out of the kingdom to which he pretended, and she belonged to that party in France which showed most enmity to the pretensions of Rome.

But Marguerite – although an enemy to emperor and to pope – objected to the divorce. She had some generous feelings, and had spoken strongly of the shameful way in which votes had been obtained for Henry.[11] She refused to go, and Francis does not seem to have been very anxious to overcome her reluctance. When de la Pommeraye brought this unwelcome message, he added that the Duchess of Vendôme might receive Lady Pembroke; but Anne was too well informed as to French court scandal not to know that the good duchess, the worthy mother of Antoine de Bourbon and grandmother of the king 'vertgalant,' had led the merriest and not the most irreproachable of lives. Her court was still anything but strict in morals, and had it been decided that she, of all the princesses of France, should accompany Francis, Anne, instead of being honoured, would have been made ridiculous. So Henry in his turn objected to Madame de Vendôme, and Anne preferred not to be met by anybody.[12] The ladies by whom she was to have been accompanied were released from the obligation to attend her.

As the time for the proposed meeting approached, the temper of the English nobles did not improve. A French alliance was very unpopular, and it was feared that if the conference took place the country might be dragged into unprofitable wars. The nobles knew also that attendance on the king would involve considerable expenditure, for, notwithstanding the sensible message of Francis as to simplicity and economy, Henry wanted his followers to make a fine display. And for all this they expected to get nothing but French sneers.[13] All the courtiers with the exception of the Boleyn faction were, therefore, violently hostile to the meeting; and the Duke of Suffolk, although he was a pensioner and partisan of France, dared even now to remonstrate with the king. Being rewarded for his pains by a volley of abuse,[14] he went to his country seat, determined, if possible, to be late in his preparations and to miss the time for the interview.[15] Lord Oxford, the high chamberlain, more prudently expressed his ill humour in conversation with his friends, asserting that the whole matter had been brewed between the king, Anne and de la Pommeraye, to the total exclusion of the council.[16] Sir Nicholas Carew, who was sent over to

France to hasten the arrival of Francis, was heard swearing that if it lay with him he would rather do his best to prevent the accomplishment of the scheme.[17] But all was of no avail; Henry had gone too far to draw back, and Anne had set her heart on the meeting.

In the beginning of October the royal party set out, going by river to Gravesend and then proceeding to a house of Sir Thomas Cheyne, the king's favourite and a great friend of Anne.[18] After a few days they went by land to Dover, and on the 11th they arrived at Calais.[19] Here they heard of the arrival of Francis at Boulogne on the 19th, and on Monday the 21st Henry rode out from Calais to meet his royal brother of France.[20]

Notwithstanding the reluctance of the English courtiers, Henry's train presented a brave show as it wound its way towards the French frontier, and at any other time the king might have felt elated by it. But at this moment the person he would have liked most to have at his side was wanting. The French had proved firm; no princess had come to Boulogne to greet the Marchioness of Pembroke, and under these circumstances Anne herself had not wished to accompany the king. Riding out to meet Francis, therefore, Henry smarted under a double injury; the honour he had wished to be shown to Anne had been refused to her, and he himself was about to be deprived of her company for three days. He had become so accustomed to her presence that he could scarcely bear to be away from her even for one day.

Francis, though firm on this point, was most obliging in every other respect. At the limit of his territory he stood ready to receive his guest, and when Henry arrived, they embraced tenderly, and after prolonged demonstrations of mutual affection rode together towards Boulogne. According to the promise made by Norfolk to de la Pommeraye, Henry was going to ride at the left of the French king; but Francis, having obtained this acknowledgment of his superior rank, desired to show all courtesy to his guest and insisted on giving him the place of honour.[21] At Boulogne the King of England was splendidly entertained for three days; and he tried to gain Francis and the French courtiers over to his views by studied amiability and liberality. With the greatest of the French noblemen he played at cards or dice, and he was careful to lose considerable sums.[22] To Montmorency, Chabot Brion, Cardinal du Prat, Jean du Bellay and Jean Joaquin de Vaulx, he offered pensions, the full value of which Francis allowed them to accept, although he would not permit them to receive regular annual payments.[23] On others Henry bestowed costly jewels or chains of gold, and when the sons of Francis came to visit him at his house he made them a present of the bonds their father had signed to obtain money for their release from Spain.[24]

On Friday 25 October, the two kings went together to Calais, where Francis was to return the visit paid to him. On his arrival he sent the provost of Paris to Anne with a valuable jewel, which he begged her to accept.[25] On Sunday, when Francis had supped with Henry, some masked ladies came in and began to dance with the French king and his courtiers. After a short space the ladies took off their visors, when it appeared that Anne was among them.[26] Whatever mortification she may have felt, she was too clever to show it; and Francis did his best to make her forget that she had been slighted. Anne's natural sympathies being in favour of France, they were soon on very good terms, and they had a long political conversation in which the French king made all kinds of vague promises.[27] 'Good reasons,' Chapuis remarks, 'the King of France had for it, for the lady serves him better than Wolsey ever did, without asking for 25,000 ducats a year.'[28] So the three days at Calais passed pleasantly enough, and when, on Tuesday the 29th, Francis took his leave, Henry upon the whole felt satisfied with the result of the meeting. The French king rode that day to Boulogne, and after a short stay went to Amiens to fulfil some of the obligations he had undertaken at Calais. Henry and Anne were detained by contrary winds, and could not cross until 13 November.[29] They spent a few days at Dover, and proceeding by slow stages arrived on the 24th at Eltham.[30]

During the interview, a treaty of alliance had been concluded against the Turks, so worded that in case of any real danger from Soliman it would have been of no effect whatever.[31] But, besides this, Francis had assented to some measures for the special benefit of Henry. The two French Cardinals of Tournon and of Gramont were to be sent to Bologna, where Clement was once more to meet the emperor. They were, if possible, to prevent the Pope from going too far in favour of Charles, and to propose a meeting between Clement and Francis. They were also to dissuade the Pope from taking vigorous measures against Henry, and to represent to him that if he procrastinated, he might arrange everything to his satisfaction at the interview with Francis, to which the King of England would send an ambassador with full power.[32] To make the Pope more pliant, a proposal of marriage between his niece, Catherine dei Medici, and a son of Francis, was again to be put forward.

Henry saw in all this a proof of the friendship and regard Francis felt for him; and the words of the French king had strengthened his confidence. Francis had been most courteous, and had professed unalterable love for his good brother of England, by whom he had promised to stand in every emergency.[33] He had repeated the advice given long ago through du Bellay, that Henry should marry Anne without further ado, and afterwards defend his cause at Rome or elsewhere.[34] The Pope, he had said, pressed as he was by the emperor, could not authorise beforehand the measures on which Henry was bent; but if the step were taken, he might accede to it as a thing past remedy. Charles himself would perhaps become less hostile, and if not, Francis would throw all his influence into the scale and neutralise the action of the emperor.

The fair speeches of Francis made a great impression on Henry's mind. Whatever distrust may have been excited by the French was now overcome; he took courage to proceed more vigorously, and without regard for the emperor. He was carried so far by his belief in the fine phrases of Francis that from being indecisive and timid he became over-eager and too self-reliant.

Anne profited by this change in Henry's temper, and she was ably helped by Cromwell and by his agents. She had already gained a most important point, the nomination of a primate on whose absolute servility she might rely. Thomas Cranmer, who was chosen to succeed Warham in the see of Canterbury, had studied divinity at Cambridge, but had married and had been obliged to leave his college. His wife having died, he had taken holy orders, had returned to his college, and had been made lecturer on divinity. When the question of the divorce was raised he sided with the king and Anne, and was rewarded by being made chaplain to Lord Rochford, Anne Boleyn's father.[35] He soon exchanged the service of the Boleyns for that of the king, and in January 1530, being then one of the royal chaplains, he was chosen to accompany his former patron, now Earl of Wiltshire, to Bologna.[36] On the return of the earl, Cranmer remained in Italy to collect opinions in favour of the divorce and to assist the English ambassadors at Rome.[37] Towards the end of the year he went back to England, where shortly afterwards he received, as a reward for his services, the archdeaconry of Taunton. When Henry and Anne became dissatisfied with Sir Thomas Elyot, then ambassador to the emperor, Cranmer was chosen to take his place;[38] and he started in the beginning of 1532 to rejoin the imperial court, which was then residing in Germany. Besides his official mission he is said to have had a secret one, namely, to try to win over to the king's cause as many German divines and doctors as possible.[39] This he did with considerable zeal but with little success, and he had soon to leave those places where at least a few doctors would have given him a favourable hearing, to attend the court of the emperor, who was preparing to repel the invasion of the Turks.[40] He followed Charles V first to Vienna and then to Italy, giving piteous descriptions of the ravages committed by the soldiers of both parties and of the dangers he himself had to encounter.[41] At Mantua he met Dr Nicholas Hawkins, from whom he received the news of his recall.[42]

The letter addressed to him to that effect in the beginning of October had not reached him on account of his travels, and he had to be content with taking cognisance of the credentials of his successor Hawkins.[43] On 18 November he took leave of Charles, and on the following day left Mantua and hastened back to England.[44]

Both by his character and by his ability Cranmer was eminently fitted to become a useful tool in the hands of Henry and Cromwell. He was now a man of forty-three, rather learned, of ready wit, a good controversialist, and withal elegant, graceful, and insinuating. An admirable deceiver, he possessed the talent of representing the most infamous deeds in the finest words. In England he had spoken so strongly in favour of the divorce and against the papal authority that he could scarcely venture to alter his tone; and in the event of his feeling any inclination to do so, it was believed – for his timidity was well known – that he would be easily frightened into any course Henry and Cromwell might prescribe.

His intellectual ability and the weakness of his moral character were not Cranmer's only titles to preferment. By accepting the archbishopric he would place himself entirely at the mercy of Henry. In Germany, at the house of Osiander, he had made the acquaintance of a young woman by whose charms he had been captivated. His opinions about the celibacy of priests were as vague and shifting as about most other subjects, and as the woman did not object to have a priest for her husband, they went through a ceremony of marriage. Cranmer had not the hardihood to acknowledge publicly what he had done, but it was not so well hidden but that some inkling of it reached Cromwell's spies. No action was taken against the archdeacon; although his marriage was clearly illegal, the matter seems not even to have been mentioned. But it was kept in good remembrance, to be made use of at the proper moment. If Cranmer, after being installed as primate, should feel tempted to follow the example of Lee and Gardiner, should stand up for the rights and independence of the Church and refuse to do the king's bidding, a slight hint might be given to him that bishops could be deprived and punished for incontinence. This would, no doubt, suffice to ensure his immediate submission; but if he held out, Henry might pretend to have just discovered the marriage; and Cranmer, accused of incontinence, sentenced and deprived, would be sent to the Tower to make way for an archbishop even more pliant, and to serve as a warning to persons disposed to betray the king's confidence.

When a bishopric became vacant, Henry generally waited a year or more before appointing a new bishop, enjoying in the meantime the revenues of the see. But in this case unusual haste was made. A week after Cranmer arrived at the English court in the middle of December, the see of Canterbury was offered to him and was gladly accepted.[45] After the customary forms had been gone through in England, the English ambassadors with Clement VII were instructed to apply for the bulls confirming his nomination, and that no delay might arise the money necessary for them was lent to Cranmer by the king himself.[46]

Had either the emperor or the Pope been fully aware of the character, opinions and position of Cranmer, the former would have vigorously opposed the confirmation of his appointment, and Clement might for once have laid aside his complaisance and refused to issue the bulls. But Cranmer at the court of Charles had given ample proof of his talent for deceit. While encouraging Henry to persist in his course, while intriguing with the Protestant doctors to obtain their votes in favour of the divorce, he had with the emperor and the imperial ministers played the part of a man who was at heart wholly opposed to the king's policy. He had spoken with so great a show of sincerity that even Granvelle had been misled.[47] Carew and Sampson, Harvey and Eliot – some of them, like Cranmer, former servants of Anne – had, when at the imperial court, been converted into stout opponents of the divorce, and were now rendering valuable service to the cause of Catherine. Why should not the archdeacon of Taunton have been converted too? Why should not his assurances be taken for truth?

It was in vain that Eustache Chapuis warned the emperor how dangerous a person Cranmer was.[48] His words had no effect: the imperial agents offered no opposition to the issuing of the bulls.

The Pope might have been informed by his nuncio as to the intentions of Henry and as to the character of Cranmer, and might of his own authority have raised some objection. But the same clever hypocrisy by which Cranmer had succeeded at the imperial court was practised in England towards de Burgo. One of Henry's ministers, his name is not found in the despatches of Chapuis, suggested to de Burgo a way in which the matter of the divorce might be brought to an end. If the Pope would depute two cardinals to hear the evidence and the pleadings at some neutral place near England, Cambray for instance, Henry would consent to send an ambassador to plead his cause before them.[49]

The nuncio swallowed the bait. Notwithstanding the warnings and protests of Chapuis, he reported the proposal to the Pope in a way most favourable to Henry;[50] and his judgement was confirmed by the two French cardinals who had arrived from Amiens. They represented to Clement all the dangers of a schism, and spoke of the strong friendship between Francis and Henry. They promised, too, that everything should be arranged to the Pope's satisfaction if he would consent to meet the French king.[51]

Clement was not indifferent to the warning conveyed by the two cardinals. He had, besides, some reason to believe what de Burgo had written. It had been generally expected that at Boulogne or Calais Henry would protest to the French cardinals and other prelates against the injustice done to him, and that he would marry Anne Boleyn either at Calais or immediately after his return to England.[52] Nothing of the kind had happened; Henry had shown no extraordinary eagerness to discuss his grievances, nor had the new Marchioness of Pembroke received anything like royal or even princely honours. People began, therefore, once more to say that the marquisate had been conferred on Anne instead of, and not as a step towards, the crown, that Henry was getting tired of his mistress, and that he was almost ready to desist from his purpose of marrying her.[53] Clement believed these reports, so that it naturally seemed to him of no great importance who was to be Archbishop of Canterbury, while he thought it desirable to avoid any conflict which might anger Henry and put English public opinion on his side. Charles V, who was at that time staying with the Pope at Bologna, was forced to admit that Clement might be right, and offered no opposition.[54] The warnings of Chapuis were dismissed as the outcome of party spirit, and on 21 February Cranmer was proposed in consistory.[55] There was some talk about the fees for the bulls by which the nomination was to be confirmed; but the documents were soon made out, and in the beginning of March they were handed to the English agents.[56]

Delay would have been extremely inconvenient for Anne, because the marquisate of Pembroke had begun to have its natural consequences. In January 1533 she had announced to Henry that she was with child. The news filled the king with joy; the child of course would be a boy, the Prince of Wales for whom he had longed so many years. But alas, no Prince of Wales, if Henry and Anne were not married betimes. If the child were not at least born in lawful wedlock, it would scarcely be rendered legitimate by a subsequent marriage. But a public marriage would overthrow the whole edifice that had been so carefully reared. The bulls for Cranmer would be refused, the divorce would not be pronounced, and the legitimacy of the child would still be doubtful. There was no way out of the difficulty but by a clandestine marriage, and on or about 25 January, in presence of a few of the most confidential attendants, the ceremony was performed.[57]

It is not quite certain who was the priest so servile and so perjured as to officiate on this occasion. Dr Rowland Lee, the king's chaplain, soon afterwards appointed to the see of Coventry and Lichfield, is generally said to have been the man; but there is no evidence for this, and the evidence which still exists tends the other way. Eustache

Chapuis asserts that the priest by whom the ceremony was performed was an Augustinian friar, whom the king rewarded by making him general of the mendicant friars.[58] This description fits perfectly with George Brown, who in the spring of 1533 was prior of Austin Friars in London. In 1534 he became provincial prior of all eremitical bodies in England, and, together with John Hilsey, was commissioned as visitor general of communities of friars of every order.[59] George Brown was certainly in favour of the divorce, and it was he who, on Easter day first prayed for Anne as queen from the pulpit.[60] He subsequently became Archbishop of Dublin, where he showed himself a strong reformer.

For a few weeks the secret of Henry and Anne was kept well enough. The nuncio, ignorant of what had taken place, and anxious to bring about a reconciliation, humoured Henry's caprices and allowed himself to be made use of by the king's ministers. Parliament had been called together for 4 February; and de Burgo was invited to accompany the king to Westminster on the 8th, and to be present at the opening of the session. Although this was rather contrary to custom, the nuncio dared not refuse. Henry sat on his throne, having on his right the representative of the Holy See, while on his left was the French ambassador.[61] Two days later de Burgo was once more pressed to accompany the king to parliament, and after having done so, he and Dinteville, the new French ambassador, were ostentatiously taken by the Duke of Norfolk and other nobles to the house of Sir William Fitzwilliam, where a banquet had been prepared for them.[62]

These demonstrations were not intended only or even chiefly to please de Burgo and the Pope, they were rather made for the purpose of misleading the English public as to the policy of the Holy See. The action of the nuncio was pointed to as unmistakable evidence that Clement approved of Henry's course; and this perplexed the king's opponents and took from them their best argument, the fear that the divorce might lead to a schism.[63]

The short time during which this game could still be played was employed, in preparing for the coming battle. The chief management of affairs had now passed into the hands of Cromwell. By his ability and energy, and by his zeal in the service of the king and Anne, he had gained the favour of both and had rapidly increased his influence. Sir Thomas More, the chancellor, had vainly tried to oppose him. In the spring of 1531 Sir Thomas with his conservative friends was still strong enough to ward off the blow aimed at the independence of the clergy. But he was already so suspected by the king, and his movements were so closely watched, that he had to ask Chapuis not to come to see him, and not to send him a letter Charles V had written to him.[64] When in the spring of 1532 further proceedings were taken to limit the power of the bishops and the authority of the Holy See, More stoutly resisted the innovations. Henry, extremely angry, insisted that the bills should pass;[65] and Sir Thomas More, seeing that it was impossible to stem the torrent, handed in his resignation.[66] It was accepted, and on 16 May he returned the seals of his office. Thomas Audeley, speaker to the House of Commons, a friend and strong adherent of Cromwell, was chosen to succeed More, but for the moment he was made only keeper of the great seal.[67]

Cromwell, no longer hampered by the opposition of More, filled every vacancy in the royal service with determined adherents of his party. William Paget, a very able young man, was made secretary to the king and employed on important foreign missions.[68] Richard Riche, a clever lawyer and absolutely unscrupulous, became attorney-general for Wales, and was afterwards preferred to the post of the king's solicitor in England.[69] Other friends and clients of Cromwell received minor appointments, and the whole administration was reorganised under his vigorous direction.

In the beginning of 1533 the party of Cromwell and Anne was still further strengthened. Sir Thomas Audeley, having shown himself an obedient and thoroughgoing servant of the king, was rewarded by being raised on 26 January to the rank of lord chancellor.[70] Those who showed themselves lax or hostile to the divorce were so constantly watched by Cromwell's agents that they dared not stir. It was about this time that the secretary began to organise that formidable system of espionage by which he afterwards made himself so terrible.

The Boleyns felt sure of success and were more overbearing than ever. Anne herself, although she did not tell people that the marriage had already been performed, talked of it as a thing quite certain to happen within a few weeks; and she already bespoke her future household servants.[71] Lord Wiltshire had hitherto never shown himself very ardent for the divorce, and had for some time been even reckoned among the opponents of it, but now he laid aside his wonted caution. On 13 February he said to the Earl of Rutland, whom he happened to meet, that the king would no longer be so timid and patient as he had been, that the marriage with Anne would soon be celebrated, and that it would be easy by the authority of parliament to silence any one who might disapprove of it. 'If this matter is brought forward in the house of peers,' he added, 'will you, who as a personal relative of the king should adhere to him, think of resisting him?' Rutland tried to escape by giving the answer that had been hit upon by Darcy the year before; but a twelvemonth had changed the state of affairs, and his objection was not allowed to pass. Wiltshire grew very violent, and Rutland, fearing the royal anger, promised to do all that was wanted.

But being at heart as opposed to the measure as ever, he sent a message to Chapuis, giving an account of what had happened. The other peers, Rutland said, would probably be treated in the same way, and it could scarcely be hoped that parliament would withstand the royal will.[72]

The spiritual peers, like their lay brethren, were pressed to support the king. Two propositions had been drawn up, setting forth that the marriage between Henry and Catherine had always been illegal and void.[73] These propositions the king urged the prelates and doctors to subscribe. Cranmer was quite willing to do so, and asked the other bishops to grant the king's request. But the Archbishop of York and Stephen Gardiner, Bishop of Winchester, refused to set their hand to the instruments, and their resistance was not for the moment to be overcome.[74]

Though officially the marriage was still a secret, some rumour of it soon began to be circulated. Anne had been unable to hide her exultation at her pregnancy. In the middle of February, in open court, she told the Duke of Norfolk that if she did not find herself with child she would go on a pilgrimage immediately after Easter.[75] A few days later, on 22 February, she came out of her apartment into the hall where a large company was assembled. Seeing one of her favourite courtiers, Thomas Wyatt, probably, she abruptly told him that three days ago she had felt such a violent desire to eat apples as she had never felt before, that when she had spoken of it to the king he had said it was a sign that she was with child, but that she had replied it was not. Thereupon she broke into a violent fit of laughter. She may have repented of her indiscretion, for she quickly retired, leaving the courtiers not a little astonished at her speech.[76] The conclusion to which they came was that Anne was either married already or quite sure of being so within a short time.

Towards the end of February, de Burgo could scarcely be ignorant that he had been duped by Henry, and that the king did not really intend to submit to the authority of the Pope. But the nuncio being a weak man, and apparently rather vain, was slow to admit that he had been wrong and Chapuis right, and slower still to act in accordance with the new state of things. Meanwhile, everything had gone smoothly at the papal court. The Pope had agreed to meet Francis, Charles offering no great opposition to the proposal; and the French cardinals had reported their success to Francis. The latter now sent Guillaume du Bellay, Seigneur de Langey, to London to settle with Henry all necessary details in connection with the approaching meeting. On 26 February, de Langey, Jean de Dinteville, Bailly de Troyes, the new French ambassador, and de Beauvais, who had just arrived from Scotland, had a long audience with the king. Henry spoke eagerly of the conference, and promised to send to it either the Duke of Norfolk or the Earl of Wiltshire with full powers to arrange everything. To the demands made by Francis in favour of Scotland he yielded, conceding several small matters which had been in dispute; and all he asked in return was that the French cardinals should be instructed to obtain a promise that the Pope would not 'innovate' anything until the interview had taken place.[77] This request was granted by Francis on condition that Henry would in the meantime abstain from further proceedings in the matter – a condition which Henry accepted. In consequence of this arrangement the Pope gladly consented to remain passive;[78] and during the latter part of March and the whole of April, notwithstanding rumours which were brought to Rome, he kept his word. Henry, on the contrary, almost as soon as Francis granted his request, broke his promise, several bills contrary to the papal authority being introduced into parliament on 14 and 15 March.[79]

Langey and Beauvais, who left London on 1 March, must already have heard something about the marriage, for their letter of 26 February to Francis contains a hint about a secret matter which had been disclosed to Dinteville. In these circumstances Henry did not think it prudent to leave Francis any longer in the dark; so George Boleyn, Anne's brother, now Viscount Rochford, was sent to France to tell the whole truth to the king. He was instructed to ask that the matter should be kept secret for a while, that no steps should be taken at Rome to defend the marriage without Henry's consent, and that Francis should order his ambassadors at the papal court to do everything the English agents required of them, placing them at the command of Bennet, Bonner, and Carne.[80]

Lord Rochford left on 13 March, and travelled post-haste to the French court.[81] He was coldly received. Francis was probably not very sorry that the marriage had taken place; but he resented the way in which he had been duped. He had been made to ask the Pope not to do anything against Henry, although Henry had already set the Holy See at defiance. Francis had been used as an instrument for deceiving the Pope, and however ready he might be to cheat on his own account he did not like to be made to cheat for other people. Besides, Henry's demands were preposterous; Francis could not degrade his ambassadors by transforming them into mere tools of English agents of inferior rank; he could not abdicate his right to have in this matter a policy of his own. The whole message – amplified by the foolish bragging of young Rochford – foreshadowed a course of action which was most distasteful to Francis. He earnestly wished to prevent an open rupture between Henry and the Holy See, and was alarmed and annoyed when he heard that in England everything tended towards this disaster. Rochford seems to have made matters even worse than they would otherwise have been by his arrogance and by his ignorance of diplomatic forms. The consequence was that all his requests, with the exception of that for secrecy, were refused, and that the French court became much less favourably disposed towards Henry than it had been before his coming.[82] Jean du Bellay now for the first time seriously blamed the conduct of his English friends; and his disapproval was the beginning of a growing coldness.[83]

But Henry went on in his course, and Anne assumed almost royal state. On 24 February she gave a great dinner at which, besides the king, the Dowager Duchess of Norfolk, the Lord Chancellor, the Duke of Suffolk and others were present. Henry was chiefly occupied in dallying with Anne; but, tearing himself away for a moment from his beloved, he called out to the old duchess to say whether the gold and plate on the sideboard were not a goodly show. It all belonged to the marchioness, and had she not a great portion, and was she not a good match? This witticism was duly acknowledged by the obedient courtiers, and quickly reported to Chapuis.[84]

A fortnight later the king and Anne went to church to hear a sermon, the burden of which was that Henry, as long as he had lived with Catherine, had remained in abominable sin, and that he was bound now to marry a good and virtuous woman, even if she were of lower degree than his own.[85] By such speeches the public mind was prepared for the final act which was drawing near.

When it was announced that the Pope had preconised Cranmer, and that the bulls for the new primate would shortly arrive, Henry plainly revealed the objects of his policy. About the middle of March a bill was submitted to parliament forbidding appeals to Rome, and settling the supreme authority in matrimonial cases on the primate and, in certain cases, on the convocation of the clergy. So open an attack on the authority of the Holy See could not but meet with considerable opposition. The House of Lords had been carefully packed, many of the members having received no writs, others having been excused from attending, while the rest had been treated as Rutland had been. But the House of Commons, elected three years before under the influence of Norfolk and Suffolk, had no desire to rebel against the papacy. Those members who belonged to the aristocratic party – and they formed the large majority of the House – did not wish to augment the power of the primate or of convocation, while the burgesses of the greater towns feared the international complications which might result from a schism and the harm it would do to their trade. Ministers had therefore to employ every artifice to ensure the passing of the bill, which was not carried for nearly three weeks.[86]

Similar artifices were employed to obtain an obedient majority in convocation, which had been summoned for 17 March.[87] Many of the clergy were excused from attending personally, and requested to give their proxy to some of their brethren, whose devotion to the king could be relied upon; and this was done to such an extent that 119 clergymen who appeared represented 200 more whose proxy they held. The first sitting took place on 26 March, and the Bishop of London, who presided, proposed the question as to the validity of the king's marriage. The opposition, knowing that direct resistance to the royal will was hopeless, raised a previous question. The matter, they said, was *sub judice* at Rome; was it permissible to discuss it here? But Stokesley was equal to the occasion; he produced a brief of Clement of the year 1530, authorising many classes of persons to state their opinion and to offer advice in the matter of the divorce. The bishop boldly asserted: '*summus pontifex voluit unumquemque declarare mentem suam et opiniones suas in dicta causa libere et impune*'. But with that dishonesty which was so characteristic of Henry's chosen agents, he omitted to say that since 1530 Clement had recalled the permission he had given, and had solemnly forbidden all clergymen and doctors to meddle with the dispute.

The opposition was in a very difficult position. They had no authentic copies of the subsequent briefs of Clement, and even if they had had them they would not have been allowed to appeal to them. Stokesley might refer to a papal brief in favour of Henry, but if his opponents had dared to produce one against the king, that would probably have been considered praemunire, and heavy punishment might have followed. Besides, the agent of the Holy See was afraid of Henry, and he had not the courage to act firmly and decisively. The English Catholics thought themselves betrayed by the Pope himself, and after a short but angry struggle most of them gave way. The two propositions drawn up by Cranmer were carried with some slight modification by nominal majorities of 253 to 19 and 41 to 6. But among the majority appear the names of Cardinal Campeggio, of Richard Nix, Bishop of Norwich, and of the Bishop of Chichester, all known to be ardent opponents of the divorce.[88]

A copy of the Acts of Convocation recording the votes was applied for by the royal agent, Dr Tregonwell; and the request was granted on behalf of the assembly by Cranmer, who had been consecrated on 30 March, and now presided in the Upper House. John Fisher, Bishop of Rochester, being so bold as to protest even at the last moment, was arrested on the following day, and kept a prisoner at Winchester House.[89] Two days later, having done all that was wanted for the present, convocation was by royal decree prorogued.[90]

Chapuis still manfully fought a losing game. When he heard of the discussions in convocation and of the passing of the Act of Appeals, he asked for an audience; and on 10 April, Maundy Thursday, he was admitted to the royal presence. He had a long discussion with Henry, to whom he represented the injustice done to the queen. The king replied that he wanted to have a son, and when Chapuis bluntly answered that he was not sure to have one by Anne, Henry smiled complacently and hinted that Chapuis did not know all his secrets. After an hour of wrangling the ambassador left, and on his return home found a message which showed that his interview could not have had any important result.[91]

The day before, a royal commission, headed by the Duke of Norfolk, had waited on Catherine, and had most earnestly entreated her to relinquish her title and to submit to the king. They had recourse to every kind of lie and artifice to shake the resolution of Catherine; representing the separate opinions of the members of Convocation as a judgement passed by a tribunal, threatening her with the king's utmost anger if she persisted, and offering her all favour if she would give way. Seeing that she intended to remain firm, Norfolk exclaimed that it mattered not, for more than two months before the king had married the other in presence of several witnesses. With that the commissioners retired, and soon afterwards Lord Mountjoy, Catherine's chamberlain, came to tell her that it was the king's pleasure she should neither call herself nor be addressed as queen, and that henceforward she was to live upon her dowry as Princess of Wales. She refused, declaring that if the king would not provide for her she would go and beg her bread from door to door.[92] Poor woman! she imagined that she was free, that she would be allowed to leave her house as she liked. A few months dispelled that illusion.

Notwithstanding Catherine's resolute maintenance of her rights, the secret was now allowed to transpire. On Thursday and Friday, 10 and 11 April, the courtiers were talking freely of the fact that on the day of the Conversion of St Paul, 25 January, the king had married Anne Boleyn. On Saturday 12 April, she appeared for the first time in royal state. Trumpeters preceded her as she went to mass, she was followed by many ladies, and her train was borne by the Duchess of Richmond, daughter of Norfolk. After the service Henry passed from courtier to courtier, telling them to pay their respects to the new queen. They felt rather awkward, for although something of the kind had been expected, they could not all at once consider 'Nan Bullen' a real queen. But Henry stood watching them, and, having no choice, one after another went and bowed to 'her grace'.[93] Anne had at last arrived at the desired goal.

6

THE CORONATION

Anne having publicly appeared as Henry's wife, it was desirable that her position should be generally acknowledged. Preachers were accordingly directed to substitute her name for that of Catherine in the prayer for the king and queen. The very first experiment made in this direction showed how strong a feeling there was against the divorce even among the most advanced class of Henry's subjects. On Easter Sunday, the day after Anne's first appearance as queen, the prior of Austin friars, preaching at St Paul's Cross, prayed loudly for her. His congregation, hearing the change in the long-accustomed formula, tumultuously rose, and nearly all left, although the service was not half over. A sharp and threatening message from the king to the lord mayor, transmitted by the latter to the guilds and freemen of the city, prevented people on the following Sunday from talking too loudly against the new marriage; but it could not hinder private criticism of the king's choice and the growth of sullen irritation.[1]

Orders were sent to the country that the prayers for the queen should henceforward be offered for Queen Anne. In most parishes compliance with these orders led to scenes similar to that at Cheapside, and in some the royal command was for a time disobeyed. Hitherto the nation at large had taken but a languid interest in the question of the divorce. After the legatine court had been closed, little had been heard about it in the country. Since the universities had been coerced into giving an opinion, no public action relating to it had been taken in England; and what was done in Rome was nearly unknown out of London. People were therefore taken by surprise when they heard the new name, and understood that the divorce and the second marriage were accomplished facts. For the next few months the matter was discussed everywhere, notwithstanding royal proclamations and commands. It had become a national question in which all Englishmen were interested.

As it was now impossible for the king to draw back, he felt that his somewhat informal proceedings ought to be ratified by a semblance at least of a judgement in his favour. This the new primate was to give, and accordingly, on 11 April, he wrote a letter to Henry asking permission to open a court and to adjudicate on the matter.[2] The letter, as Cranmer penned it was subservient enough; it was the letter of a servant to his master, not that of a judge to one of the parties. But, cringing as it was, it was not considered sufficiently submissive. Cranmer was to be taught once for all that he was entirely dependent on the royal favour, that even in his clerical capacity he must regard himself as a humble agent of the king. He had to write a second letter, even more abject than the first, in which, prostrate at the feet of his majesty, Henry's most devoted bedesman prayed for authority to proceed to the examination and final determination of the matrimonial cause.[3] Henry, while protesting that he recognised no superior on earth, graciously permitted the primate to hear and judge the case.[4] If any sense of dignity had survived in the archbishop, he would have felt degraded by the position into which he had brought himself. But Cranmer felt no degradation.

The primate wished to follow the example of Wolsey and Warham, and to work as far as possible in the dark. He feared that, if his action became generally known, the adherents of Catherine might give some trouble, and that Catherine herself might interject an appeal, or otherwise disturb his proceedings – a possibility to which he looked forward with considerable alarm.[5] But Thomas Cromwell, who chiefly directed the preparations, relied on the statute of appeal just passed, and the cause was carried on in the usual way. A citation was served on Catherine in the middle of April to appear on 9 May at Dunstable before the archbishop. Being at first rather frightened, and not knowing what to do, she asked the advice of Chapuis, who very sensibly replied that Cranmer could not prejudice her rights, and that the best course for her would be to take no heed of his proceedings, and not to admit in any way that he could have jurisdiction in her case.[6] Catherine, following the ambassador's advice, simply signed two protestations by which she declared that she would not acknowledge Cranmer, a former servant of Anne's father, as her judge.[7] In no other way did she take the slightest notice of anything done by the archbishop, so that he was able to go on with his work without let or hindrance on her part.[8]

Chapuis went to the nuncio, to whom he had brought a letter from Charles; and explaining the state of the case, he requested de Burgo to interfere by serving on Cranmer the papal brief which forbade any one to meddle with or give judgement in the matter of the divorce. But it was impossible to prevail on the nuncio to do his duty; he was personally afraid, and he still hoped to prevent the worst. The brief remained in his chest, and this obstacle was removed from the way of Cranmer.[9]

The archbishop, having opened his court on 10 May, pronounced Catherine contumacious; and when the formalities prescribed by canon jurisprudence had been fulfilled, he gave on 23 May a judgement by which the marriage between Henry and Catherine was declared to have been null and void from the beginning.[10] A few days later he held another court, and decided that the marriage between Henry and Anne was good and valid.[11] This having been done, there was no longer any reason for delaying the coronation, which in hope of this favourable issue had been arranged to take place on 1 June.

On the day after Cranmer's sentence in her favour Anne left Greenwich, where she had been staying with Henry, to come up by the river to the Tower. With the indelicacy and want of feeling so characteristic of Henry, he had thought fit to give Catherine's barge to Anne; and the arms of Catherine had been cut down from it to make way for the apocryphal emblems of the Boleyn family. In this barge, attended by a numerous retinue, and followed by nearly 200 boats, Anne went up the river. At the Tower she was received with the customary ceremonies – trumpets sounded, and cannon roared – but the people remained silent. There was none of the enthusiasm with which in all ages Englishmen have greeted a popular queen.[12]

The following day Anne spent at the Tower, and on the afternoon of Saturday 31 May, she went in great state and pomp through the city to Westminster. By order of the king becoming preparations had been made for the occasion: flags were unfurled, carpets hung from the windows, barriers kept off the crowd; and the guilds were drawn up in their best array on both sides of the road. To meet the expenses a tax had been laid on all householders, whether Englishmen or foreigners; but an exception had been made by the lord mayor and his brethren in favour of the Spanish merchants, as countrymen of Catherine.[13] This piece of delicacy shows that the Spaniards were very popular at that moment, for otherwise the court of aldermen would scarcely have paid much attention to their feelings.

The procession was headed by about a dozen French merchants residing in London, dressed all alike in violet velvet, wearing on the sleeve the colours of Anne.[14] An attempt to bring over a throng of French gentlemen to take part in the festivities had failed, so, *faute de mieux*, merchants rode in their stead.[15] After them rode English gentlemen and noblemen according to their degree. Then came the lord chancellor with Carlo Capello, the Venetian ambassador, and the primate with the Bailly de Troves. They were followed by Anne's litter, all covered with white satin, carried by two mules. A canopy was borne over her head, and at her side rode the Duke of Suffolk as earl marshal, and Lord William Howard, representing his absent brother the Duke of Norfolk, as high steward. Next came numbers of ladies in cloth of gold and velvet, riding on hackneys, and the old Duchess of Norfolk and Anne's mother riding in a chariot. Lacqueys and archers closed the procession, which from the Tower took its way by Fenchurch and Gracechurch to Leadenhall, and thence by Cheapside, Ludgate, Fleet Street, and the Strand, to York Place or Whitehall.[16]

Anne's triumphal progress was not without its little annoyances. The merchants of the Steelyard had not been able to obtain the same favours as the Spaniards, and had been obliged by the lord mayor to erect a pageant at Gracechurch near their house. They chose to represent Mount Parnassus, on which sat Apollo with the muses. The fountain of Helicon ran with Rhenish wine, to the great delight of those who were permitted to drink of it. When Anne arrived before this pageant and halted in front, the muses addressed her, singing verses in her praise.[17] But just opposite to her was that part of the pageant by which the German traders avenged themselves for having been forced to raise the structure. Parnassus was appropriately adorned with coats of arms, and above all others, in the most honourable place, was a great imperial eagle, bearing on its breast the emblems of Castille and Arragon, the arms of Anne's hated rival. Lower down came those of Henry, and, lowest of all, the coat which the heralds had made out for the Boleyns. Anne was well versed in heraldry, and detected at once the insult offered to her. For the moment she had to submit, for there was no doubt that the emperor was of higher rank than the great-granddaughter of good Alderman Bullen. But we learn from Chapuis that she deeply resented the slight, and that on the following day she tried to induce the king to punish the obnoxious merchants.[18]

The English, less secure in their position than the mighty traders of the Steelyard, were more cautious in their marks of disloyalty. Still, they too contrived to do some unpleasant things. The merchants of the staple had erected a pageant at Leadenhall; and on it sat St Anne and Mary Cleophas with four children, of whom one stepped forward to compliment Anne. The child delivered a long oration, saying that from St Anne had sprung a fruitful tree, and expressing a hope that the like would be true of this Anne also.[19] As the mother of the virgin never had any children but that one daughter, and as Anne desired above all things to have a son, this was not a very kind thing to say, and it can scarcely have helped to smooth her ruffled temper.

It was late when the procession reached Westminster, where Anne publicly accepted some wine, and then retired to her apartment. Early the next morning, attended by the same splendid throng, she went on foot to Westminster Abbey. There the coronation took place with all the accustomed ceremonies, Cranmer officiating, assisted by Stokesley and Gardiner. After the ceremony in the church there was the usual banquet in Westminster Hall, which Henry, with Dinteville and Capello, witnessed from a latticed window. The next morning there was a tournament, in which, as no French knights had come, Lord William Howard and Sir Nicholas Carew led the opposing parties. After this the king and Anne returned to Greenwich, where balls and banquets continued for a few days more.[20]

In the meantime the new form of prayer had been slowly bearing its fruit. The question of the divorce had been brought before the nation, and now the nation gave its verdict. At no time was Catherine received by the people with such demonstrations of love and loyalty. In July, by order of the king, she was removed from Ampthill to Bugden; and on the way great numbers of people flocked together to see her pass. Notwithstanding her escort, they loudly cheered her, calling out that she was still their queen, and that they would always hold her to be so.[21] And her popularity was shared by her daughter Mary, who – according to Anne – was treated in the villages through which she passed 'as if she were God Himself, who had descended from heaven'.[22] Anne had been crowned, but the nation would not acknowledge her.

Anne's old enemies, the Hanseatic merchants, continued to annoy her. A numerous fleet of German hulks came up the Thames and anchored opposite Greenwich, where she was staying; and to show their animosity the Hanseatic captains invited Chapuis to dine on board their ships. When he arrived they hoisted the hateful eagles, and in honour of the ambassador made a loud noise with shouting, drumming and firing of cannon. Anne was intensely irritated by the demonstration, and Chapuis was of course delighted at her rage. She complained to Henry, and wanted him to punish the insolence of the Easterlings and the disloyalty of the country people.[23] But the king, under the influence of Cromwell, wisely abstained from taking any notice of the offences of either. The punishment of the English peasants would have made matters even worse, and a quarrel with the Easterlings would have been most dangerous. Their fleet was strongly manned, the Steelyard was still fortified and armed, and they might have proved stronger than the king. All that Anne could do was to leave Greenwich and to retire to Windsor out of reach of Hanseatic bacchanals.[24]

However disagreeable this opposition might be, Anne had probably expected it, and would not have been made anxious by it, for she was aware that popular excitement does not last long. As for Catherine, she might be brought either to bend or to break, and then the course would be clear and easy. But that which filled Anne with serious misgivings was that her allies began to fail her.

Francis I, up to April 1533, had upon the whole been well satisfied with the way in which Henry had proceeded, and the conclusion of the marriage had pleased him rather than otherwise. But he wished Henry to continue to defend his cause at Rome as before. This would have led to an interminable suit, for neither the Pope nor the cardinals were willing to go to extremities; and during the whole time Henry would have needed the assistance of the French, and would have sunk more and more to the level of a client of Francis. When, therefore, Dinteville heard that Cranmer was to hold an archiepiscopal court and to pronounce a divorce, he strongly protested. He went to Henry and asked that Cranmer's sentence should either be postponed until after the intended interview between Francis and the Pope, or be kept strictly secret. But Henry would make no concessions: it was necessary, he said, to place the legitimacy of Anne's child beyond doubt. The bailly went away rather angrily and spoke to Norfolk, who said that he regretted what was being done as much as Dinteville, but that he could not help it.[25]

It was true that it could not be helped, for Anne was bent on it. Her interests absolutely required that Cranmer should publicly pronounce sentence in her favour; she could not possibly sanction the course proposed by Dinteville. If the question of the validity of her marriage remained in suspense, if negotiations went on with Rome, Henry might, the very moment he got tired of her, accept some compromise with the Holy See, such as the proposal for the settlement of the dispute by a court at Cambray. The award – with his secret consent – would go against him, he would virtuously submit, and Anne would be ignominiously discarded. If she miscarried, this would almost inevitably be the result; it would probably be the result if her child proved to be a girl. To such a danger she could not expose herself, and as her anti-clerical inclinations accorded with her interest, she exercised all her energy to commit Henry to an irrevocable step which would prevent him from hereafter submitting once more to the Pope.

Cromwell energetically seconded her. He seems to have had no sympathy with the ultra reformers, but he was heartily sick of the vacillations which had marked the policy of the last six years. He wished England to be independent of France, to be on good terms, if possible, with Charles V, but in any case to pursue a definite course of her own. So he helped Anne, and both together overcame any resistance which the Duke of Norfolk and his adherents dared to offer.

By this policy Anne, of course, offended the French; and it increased the hostility of those Englishmen whose animosity had hitherto been kept within bounds by the influence of Francis. The French party in England, as well as the imperial, was now decidedly hostile to Anne.

But even this was not the worst. Henry himself began to grow lukewarm. He had accomplished his purpose; he had shown the world that, pope and emperor notwithstanding, he had been able to have his own way. Anne, therefore, could no longer play upon his vanity, one of the principal motives by which she had hitherto ruled him. Moreover, he had already become rather tired of her; and thinking that in Anne's condition he was entitled to look out elsewhere for amusement, he began to flirt with the young ladies of her court. She was alarmed by this incipient infidelity, and angrily upbraided him for it; but Henry, who would have been cowed by her indignation a year ago, now brutally replied that she ought to shut her eyes to his pleasures, as others – he significantly added – her betters had done before her. Anne flew into a violent passion, and Henry threateningly bid her remember that it was still in his power to lower her as quickly as he had raised her. This made her more furious than ever, and for several days they did not speak to one another.[26]

Anne's chief hope lay in the fact that Henry firmly expected she would give birth to a boy, whom he might proclaim Prince of Wales and appoint his successor. As she was already far advanced in pregnancy, it became necessary to take care of her health; and Henry, for the sake of the child, notwithstanding occasional fits of ill-temper, showed some attention and kindness to the mother. The Easterlings having sailed away, the court returned to Greenwich, and here Anne's apartment was fitted up in splendid style. A magnificent bed which had been lying in the treasury, part of the ransom of a French prince, was given to her, that the king's child might be born in it.[27] Everything which might frighten or annoy Anne was kept from her; and when matters of state looked rather grave, Henry rode out as if to hunt, and met his council at some distance.[28] The life and health of the future Prince of Wales were not to be endangered.

There were certainly good reasons why Anne should be prevented from hearing the news which came from France and Italy. When it was known in Rome that the Statute of Appeals had passed into law, the Pope was extremely angry. He complained of having been deceived not only by Henry but by Francis, since he had refrained from proceeding against Henry in deference to the French king, who had undertaken that his authority should be respected in England.[29] The French cardinals, being anxious that the meeting should take place, tried to exculpate Francis, and were lavish of promises of all kinds. They even went so far as to declare that Francis would help to put down the German Lutherans by force of arms. The German princes were not greatly alarmed by this news; for as long as Francis paid them their subsidies, they cared little what his cardinals said. But when Henry heard of it, he was very differently impressed.[30] Francis did not in the least intend to coerce the German Lutherans, but it was not improbable that he would attempt to reconcile them to Rome, and if he succeeded in doing so, Henry would stand nearly alone in his rebellion against the Holy See. Seeing in how difficult a position he would thus be placed, Henry strongly expostulated with Dinteville, insisting that such promises would alienate the Germans and make the Pope more overbearing than ever. Dinteville tried to calm him, but in vain; Henry remained angry and suspicious.[31]

Henry's anger was intensified when, a fortnight later, he heard that Clement, although he had not refused to meet Francis, had allowed the matrimonial cause to go on. Henry's excusator having been rejected, Capisucchi, the auditor, proceeded with the matter, and letters citatorial were served on Ghinucci, as ambassador of the King of England, to appear at the Rota.[32] This was reported in England towards the end of June, and seriously alarmed the king;[33] for the nation was in so irritable a mood that it might rise against him if he were excommunicated and deprived by the Pope. As it was impossible to draw back, Henry resolved to act boldly; and on 29 June, before the Archbishop of York, he solemnly appealed from the Pope to the next general free council.[34] This was an act strictly forbidden by the rules of the Church. It would, indeed, have been impossible to maintain ecclesiastical unity and discipline, if it had been lawful for any individual, at any moment, to set the power of the Pope at defiance by appealing to a council which might never be held in the lifetime of the parties. Such an appeal was rightly considered the first open advance towards a schism; and Henry was not quite prepared to let it be publicly known at once that he had taken so momentous a step. The appeal, therefore, was not sent to Rome immediately, but kept as secret as possible, although Henry's precautions did not prevent Chapuis from hearing of it a few days later.[35]

The unwonted vigour displayed by Henry against Rome was rendered possible by the absence of the Duke of Norfolk, the chief of the conservative aristocratic party. The duke had been chosen to represent Henry at the meeting between Clement and Francis, and had left London on the day on which his niece had gone from Greenwich to the Tower. His colleagues in the embassy, Lord Rochford, Sir Francis Bryan, Sir William Paulet and a good many other gentlemen and doctors, had left on 27 May. Norfolk had remained behind to make a last attempt to win Chapuis over to the cause of the divorce, but his efforts had failed.[36] On the 30th he reached Calais, and immediately started for Amiens, where he was received by François de Montmorency, the grand master's brother, by de Humières, and by other men of high standing.[37] At Amiens he stopped, and wrote to England for fresh instructions, for he had heard that the meeting had been postponed. In reply, he was directed to proceed to Paris and to the French court, and to dissuade Francis from meeting the Pope at all. If Francis persisted, Norfolk was to accompany him, and to ask him not to conclude anything with Clement before the affairs of Henry should be satisfactorily arranged. Should the duke find that the Pope had adopted any decisive measure against the king, he was to abstain from direct negotiation with his holiness and to leave the matter to Francis, who was to be reminded of his alliance with Henry. Norfolk was also to urge Francis to make some strong demonstration against Henry's enemies.[38]

This was certainly an ungrateful task. It was most unlikely that Norfolk would succeed, and the negotiation would keep him out of England during the whole summer. The scheme had clearly been devised by Cromwell, who was already trying to oust the duke from his position as prime minister, and who wished for the next few months to rule in the royal council. But however repugnant the mission might be to Norfolk, he was obliged to proceed. At Paris, where he went first, he saw the Queen of Navarre, who, so far as opposition to Rome was concerned, was in favour of an English alliance. She received the duke very graciously, and warned him of the secret hostility of Anne de Montmorency, who at heart was an imperialist and had lately drawn the dauphin over to his party. She spoke much and well, and sent a friendly message to Anne; but she cleverly evaded all reference to the special object of Norfolk's mission.[39]

Norfolk left Paris with the intention of joining the French court. But Francis, who had been apprised of his instructions, had no great wish to see him, and the duke was not able to reach the court, which was continually moving, till 10 July. The court was then at Riom, in Auvergne.[40] He was splendidly entertained by the Duke of Albany, and was graciously received by Francis; but he was entirely unsuccessful in his mission. The meeting, Francis said, must take place, and Norfolk ought to assist at it. As, however, the French court was to proceed through parts of Auvergne, Languedoc and Provence, which were rather out of the way, Norfolk was requested to take the more commodious road by Lyons and down the Rhone. Jean du Bellay – who had lately been advanced to the more opulent see of Paris – Morette, Jean Joaquin, de la Hargerie, and others well acquainted with England were appointed to accompany him.[41] He took leave of Francis at Albany's castle of Vic le Comte, and on 21 July reached the suburbs of Lyons.[42]

At Lyons the authorities received him with great honour, the governor going out to meet him. But the ceremony was suddenly interrupted by a courier, who arrived from Rome on his way to England.[43] Thinking that Norfolk was at the French court, the English ambassadors with the Pope had sent their letters to him under cover to Anne de Montmorency;[44] but they had also given the courier a short note, which he handed to the duke. Norfolk is said by Jean du Bellay to have nearly fainted when he read it. It contained but a few lines, to the effect that sentence had been given against the king. The duke hurriedly retired to the apartment prepared for him, to take council with the bishop and with his colleagues.[45]

The news of Cranmer's proceedings at Dunstable and of the sentence he had dared to deliver, had reached Rome on the last day of May.[46] During the preceding days, Gramont being very ill, Cardinal de Tournon had in consistory proposed a plan which he had wisely concealed from Bennet. The plan was that when Francis and Clement met, the former should ask the latter not to press the matter against Henry, to which the Pope was to reply that in so abominable a case he could not but proceed, and that if the King of England remained stubborn he must be condemned and deprived. When this had been done, Francis was to send a message to Henry that if he were excommunicated it would be necessary, notwithstanding all treaties, to abandon him, since by standing by him Francis himself would incur the censures of the Church. Tournon made no doubt that Henry, so pressed, would cry for mercy, that through the influence of Francis the cause would then be heard at Cambray, and that Anne in the meantime would be sent away and Catherine allowed her rank, title and place at court.[47] This strange proposal Clement communicated to Count Cyfuentes, the Spanish ambassador. It was received by Cyfuentes with great suspicion; but Clement was once more so hopeful that he permitted the cause against Henry to lag, and Bennet was able to write most favourably of the goodwill of the Pope.[48]

The news of Cranmer's sentence changed the whole aspect of affairs. The Pope, when he heard of this usurpation of his authority, was terribly angry; and even those cardinals who had hitherto been most friendly to Henry, owned that concession and forbearance made him only more insolent. For a time the partisans of Catherine had it all their own way. Tournon abandoned his former position, [49] and the Italian cardinals were indignant at the rebellion of Henry and Cranmer. But by far the most dangerous enemy of the King of England was the Pope himself, who had been deeply hurt at the manner in which he had been duped and insulted. On 14 June, when the Cardinal of Jaen saw the Pope, Clement declared that Henry merited every pain and penalty, and that the proceedings against him were to be carried on without delay.[50] During the following days, while the congregation sat to consult about new briefs against Henry, Clement tried to stir up as many enemies as possible against the king and felt his ground with the French and the imperial agents.

About a fortnight later, Clement proposed to Cyfuentes that Francis should be incited to take part against Henry by a promise of the town of Calais, and that the emperor and the King of France should jointly make war to execute the papal censures. The count, rather startled, merely replied that it was a very grave matter. Clement, discouraged by this answer, then asked whether Mary might not marry the Duke of Norfolk's son, and thus gain many adherents and overthrow her father. True, the Earl of Surrey had a wife living, but, said Clement, that did not matter much, as he had been forced to marry her, and it had been done only *per verba de futuro*. Cyfuentes did not like this plan any better than the other, and urged the Pope to have the cause decided as soon as possible.[51]

There was no necessity to press Clement to proceed, for he was now as eager as could be desired. Several congregations and consistories were held; and on 11 July, having taken the advice of the cardinals, the Pope delivered publicly, in open consistory, a sentence annulling the proceedings of Cranmer, declaring that Henry, Anne, and the archbishop had incurred the penalties threatened in the former inhibitory briefs, and requiring them, on pain of excommunication, to undo within six weeks all that had been done.[52]

But even more had been accomplished for Catherine, although as yet it remained a secret. In one of the consistories the question had been raised whether the Pope had power to dispense for a marriage with a deceased brother's widow, and the cardinals had decided in the affirmative.[53] As all Henry's arguments rested on the denial of this position, his agents could hereafter obtain only delay; judgement could not go in his favour.

Norfolk knew that when Henry heard of these proceedings, so far as they had been made public, his vanity would once more be brought into play, and that, under the influence of those who wished for a separation from Rome, he would attack the papal authority still more bitterly and render every compromise impossible. This the duke wished to prevent, so that his first idea was to return straightway to England, where he hoped by his presence to counteract the measures of the radical party. But Jean du Bellay assured the duke and his colleagues that the sentence just given was not definitive, and that at the coming interview everything might still be settled to the satisfaction of their master. He therefore urged them to remain, and to proceed to the place of meeting. Norfolk answered that after the Pope had given sentence against his king it would not be proper for him to assist at the conference, and that if he committed so great a mistake he might lose his head for it. After an animated discussion they arrived at a compromise. The bishop, in the name of Francis, entered a formal protest against the departure of Norfolk from France contrary to the agreement between the two kings; and Norfolk, being thus provided with an excuse for remaining,[54] consented to abide for the present at Lyons. He sent Lord Rochford, Anne's brother, to England to ask for further instructions, while he despatched Sir Francis Bryan, Anne's cousin, to Francis to complain of the injury done to his master.[55]

Lord Rochford made good speed. He rode post-haste to Calais, crossed at once, and on the 28th was already at court.[56] The news he brought filled Henry with indignation and dismay, all the more because Francis seemed determined not to resent what the Pope had done. Henry – guided, no doubt, by Cromwell – decided to strike out an independent line of policy. Norfolk was to go to Francis to try once more to dissuade him from meeting the Pope, and if his representations proved unavailing he was to return to England.[57] And that the loss of the firm and close friendship of the French king might be balanced by other alliances, Stephen Vaughan, a client and friend of Thomas Cromwell, was despatched, on the day of Rochford's arrival, to Germany to negotiate an alliance with the Elector of Saxony, the Landgrave of Hesse, the Duke of Brunswick Lueneburg, and the other princes of the Schmalkaldic league.[58] Another agent, Cristopher Mundt, a German, was sent to the dukes of Bavaria who, although Catholics, were intensely hostile to the Austrian power.[59]

The intelligence brought by Rochford was kept strictly secret. The council at which it was discussed was held at some distance from court, that Anne might not hear of it, and it is probable that she was not even apprised of her brother's arrival. He remained two days in England, and on the 30th left again for France, travelling at a less furious pace.[60] He found his uncle still at Lyons, whence Norfolk, having read his new instructions, set out for Montpellier to meet Francis. Here he had a long interview with the king, who continued to preach moderation, and protested that if Norfolk could have remained, a good result might still have been hoped for at the meeting. He asked that at least another ambassador with full powers should be sent in the duke's place. Norfolk, convinced by the arguments of Francis, promised to do his best to calm his master and to obtain what the French king desired;[61] and that he might be the better able to do so, he took post horses and rode from Montpellier to Calais.[62] On the 30th he was in England.[63]

In consequence of Norfolk's representations, the Bishop of Winchester was appointed to take his place at the French court, and left on 3 September. As Gardiner, next to Norfolk, was the chief rival of Cromwell, the latter was not sorry to get rid of him for a time. With Cranmer, Audeley and Wiltshire at his back, Cromwell expected to be more than a match for the duke alone. He knew that nothing could be effected by Gardiner, who did not receive those full powers Francis had asked for, but only vague and general instructions.[64] Moreover, after Rochford had left on 30 July, the radical party had not been idle, and although Henry had already recalled his ambassadors at Rome, he sent to one of them, Dr Bonner, a copy of his appeal to the council, with orders, if Bonner should think fit, to intimate the same to Clement.[65] Bonner was an essentially coarse and violent man, who delighted in showing rudeness to the Pope; and Cromwell was pretty sure that if he found an opportunity he would not refrain from thinking fit to intimate the appeal. This, as Cromwell knew, would put an end to all hopes of a compromise.

7

MARCUS MEYER

During this time Anne's confinement had drawn near, and the king was in the very best of humours. He had consulted numerous physicians, astrologers, wizards and witches, and, as everybody knew what he wanted, they had, as right loyal sorcerers, unanimously replied that the child would be a boy – the Prince of Wales whom Henry craved for with such eagerness.[1]

The Duke of Suffolk had been a widower for full ten weeks; his wife, the king's sister, having died on 24 June. He could bear his bereaved state no longer, and on the morning of Sunday 7 September, he married Catherine Willoughby, only daughter and heiress of the late Lord Willoughby. On the death of her father, Catherine had become a royal ward, and Suffolk had paid his brother-in-law £2,600 for permission to marry her to his son, young Henry Brandon, Earl of Lincoln.[2] Henry Brandon and Catherine had been formally betrothed, but when Suffolk became a widower he caused the betrothal to be annulled, and took his son's place.[3]

This Sunday was to be a busy day at court, for a few hours after Suffolk's marriage, between three and four in the afternoon, Anne's child was born. Doctors and midwives made haste to receive the young Prince of Wales; but their faces grew long, and they slunk away crestfallen. The child was a girl.[4]

Henry was exceedingly vexed by what he considered a mischance and a humiliation. All the hopes he had so foolishly paraded before the world had come to nought; the wish of the children at Gracechurch had been too literally fulfilled. And what made the king's mortification all the greater was that he perfectly understood the exultation of his enemies. He could neither forbid nor resent the demonstrations of joy which were made all around him; but he knew that the bonfires which blazed in the streets, and the shouts with which the city rang, were intended to celebrate, not the fact that Anne had borne him a child, but the fact that the child was but a girl.

And the fact was not only vexatious and wounding to Henry's vanity, it had a real political significance. Englishmen were not accustomed to be ruled by women, and had Anne's child been a boy, some part of the opposition against the king's marriage might have been overcome. Many an Englishman might have abandoned the cause of Mary for that of a Prince of Wales, but between two girls the choice was not difficult: the nation stood by Mary.

Chapuis, of course, was delighted at the disappointment of Henry, and plotted all the more eagerly against Anne. There had been some differences between Cromwell and her; the former having wished that in Cranmer's sentence of divorce Mary should be admitted to be legitimate, as born *in bonâ fide parentum*.[5] This would have allayed much of the secret resistance offered by Mary's friends, and would have facilitated a good understanding with the emperor. For very obvious reasons Anne had opposed the idea, and she had carried the day. Something of this seems to have transpired, and Chapuis tried to make out how matters stood, and, if possible, to gain the secretary over. In July he had a long conversation with Cromwell, exhorting him to be a friend of Charles. As long as the late cardinal had associated himself with the emperor, all had gone well with him; as soon as he abandoned the imperial party, he was ruined. Let Cromwell take warning from Wolsey's fate. No friendship, Chapuis significantly concluded, could be more advantageous to England generally, and to Cromwell especially, than that of Charles. To all this the secretary listened most attentively, thanking Chapuis for the interest he took in him. 'He is a man of sense,' the ambassador wrote, 'who knows business and understands reason.'[6]

Six weeks later, it was Cromwell who tried to speak in private with Chapuis. A few days after Elizabeth's birth the secretary was flying his hawks in the fields, and Chapuis rode out by appointment to meet him. This time the ambassador thought that he might express himself more openly. He said that now the king had married Anne it might be easier to redress matters than it had been before, for Henry, having shown that he was able to do as he liked, might take Catherine back without losing any of his reputation for independence; and Cromwell ought to support so good an arrangement. The secretary listened very patiently, but replied that the time had not yet come, as the king's love for Anne was still strong and ardent. The friendship of Charles was certainly all important to England, for it would be easy for him to ruin the kingdom; but Cromwell hoped Charles would not try – the emperor would certainly not benefit by such an enterprise. As to himself, Cromwell said, he was quite ready to abandon Anne and to act for Catherine, but things of this kind could not be done in a hurry. Chapuis left him with the conviction that he was only waiting for an opportunity to change his whole policy.[7]

It seemed probable that the opportunity would soon present itself. Shortly after his last conference with Cromwell, Chapuis received strong hints that the ill will against Anne was having serious consequences. Among the ladies of her household there was a fair damsel called Elizabeth Holland, for whom the Duke of Norfolk had shown his preference in rather too public a way. The duchess, a very haughty and violent woman, had taken this very ill, and on Norfolk's return from France had absolutely refused to see him. The quarrel, which reflected some discredit on Anne, was very disagreeable to the court; and it was decided that Lord Abergavenny, the duchess's brother-in-law, should be sent to her to effect a reconciliation. He was accordingly invited to Greenwich to receive instructions.[8] Here he met Chapuis at mass, and they returned arm in arm from the chapel to the hall, the king walking immediately behind them, and Cromwell in front. Abergavenny seized the opportunity to tell the ambassador hurriedly that he should have liked to confer with him, but dared not do so. He could only say that he was a warm friend of the emperor; and to intimate the strength of his feelings, he pressed the ambassador's arm.[9] This was the first hint Chapuis received of a vast conspiracy which was being formed.

A few days later, a more precise message was sent to Chapuis by the Bishop of Rochester, who had been released after a confinement of two months, and had returned to his diocese more incensed than ever against Henry and Anne. The Pope's censures, he now told Chapuis, were against the obstinate like a leaden sword; they produced no effect. Charles ought, therefore, to take matters into his own hands, whereby he would do God as great a pleasure as in fighting the Turks.[10] Another malcontent suggested to Chapuis that Reginald Pole, who resided at Padua, and whose family were powerful, rich and discontented, might marry the princess and claim the crown, to which he had some pretensions by right of birth. In any case the emperor would do well to make sure of him.[11]

All this seemed very threatening for Anne; and it was the more dangerous, as she had some reason to complain of the conduct of the French. Francis was in a singular position. For his designs on the Low Countries he wanted Henry to be on bad terms with Charles, and to be the ally of France; and to secure this end he had favoured the divorce and the marriage with Anne. But for his designs on Italy, which he had much more at heart, he needed the friendship of the Pope; and in order to please the Pope he urged Henry to go no further, and disapproved of all steps tending towards schism. This was neither the real interest of Anne, nor did it suit her character and inclinations. During the prolonged strife she had contracted a strong feeling of hatred against the Holy See and the Roman priesthood. She desired a complete rupture, and supported every scheme likely to bring it about. 'The cause and the principal wet-nurse of heresy,' Chapuis in his quaint language styled her, and he was not much mistaken.[12]

Although Anne had not an important ally whom she could trust, she had still something in her favour. If her child was but a girl, it had a wonderful quality for a child of Henry VIII: it lived and throve, and gave rise to a hope that it might have brothers who would do the same. On 10 September it was christened.[13] Dinteville, who, notwithstanding Norfolk's request, had received no orders to be proxy for Francis, was spared the trouble by the sex of the child.[14] The dowager Duchess of Norfolk and the Dowager Marchioness of Dorset were ordered to stand godmothers, while Cranmer was godfather. After this the child remained for nearly three months at court until a separate establishment was provided for it, and it was taken to Hatfield.[15]

With this little in her favour, Anne had to allay the king's annoyance, to raise his courage, and to revive his hopes. Once more she succeeded, once more the hopes of Chapuis came to nought. Cromwell was right: the time had not yet come. She was still able to profit by all the little incidents of the summer and the autumn, and to reconstruct her power. And it happened that her task was lightened by two events which had not been foreseen.

One of these events cannot be properly understood without reference to the circumstances of the time in the north-west of Europe. The city of Luebeck, chief among the Hanseatic towns, chief too of the group of them called the Wendic towns, had obtained during the fourteenth century an almost undisputed supremacy on the Baltic. The Scandinavian kingdoms had been so thoroughly humbled by its fleets and armies that they had submitted to the terms the mighty burghers had chosen to dictate; and the Danes, by the treaty of Nystadt, had even conceded to Luebeck the right of vetoing the election of their kings. But Danes, Norwegians and Swedes cannot easily bear a foreign yoke, and at the end of the fourteenth century the three northern nations united and called Eric of Pomerania, himself a German, but no friend of Luebeck, to the throne. A long series of struggles then began between the town and the union-kings, and Luebeck slowly lost ground. When, in the middle of the fifteenth century, Christian, of the house of Oldenburg, ascended the Scandinavian throne, the position of the town was such that it could not exercise its old privileges. Luebeck was deserted by its allies, and the lesser towns began to look after their own interests, and to oppose the wishes and plans of the chief city. It had been a rule that certain classes of goods should not be imported directly to the Scandinavian ports, but should first be brought to the staple of Luebeck; but this rule was now disregarded. The Dutch towns, which had formerly been among the chief friends of Luebeck, became its most formidable opponents and rivals. They declined to submit to restrictions on their trade, and sent their ships to any port in the Baltic they chose; and when the Luebeckers tried to prevent them, they allied themselves with the union-king, who in return granted them extensive privileges in direct violation of Luebeck's treaty rights.

When Christian succeeded to the throne of the duchies of Sleswick and Holstein, and became the close neighbour of Luebeck, its difficulties were very much increased. After Christian's death, however, his territories were again divided, his elder son John inheriting the three kingdoms, Frederic, the younger son, the two duchies. John took no decisive steps against Luebeck, and there was a period of calm until his son Christian II succeeded him. Christian, who had married a sister of Charles V, followed a more active policy; but, while he energetically withstood foreign oppression, he was himself a tyrant at home, and alienated the goodwill of his subjects. A rebellion broke out in Sweden, and Gustavus Vasa, with the assistance of the Luebeckers, drove Christian out of the country. The two other kingdoms of Christian also rebelled, and Frederic of Hoistein became their king. Christian had to fly from court to court, asking everywhere to be assisted against his rebellious subjects and his treacherous kinsman.

During the early years of their reign, both Gustavus Vasa and Frederic of Denmark were friendly to Luebeck, whose help they needed. For Christian had still a party in the country, and was always trying to regain his throne. In 1531, with the aid of the Dutch cities, he fitted out a fleet; and taking some landsknechts on board, he sailed from Holland to Norway. At first he met with success, but a Luebeck fleet which suddenly appeared on the coast cut off all further reinforcements, victualled Frederic's strongholds, and transported his troops. Christian was then forced to capitulate, and Frederic treacherously seized him, and threw him into a dungeon at Gottorp.

Having obtained so decisive a victory, and having no longer anything to fear from his foe, Frederic grew cold towards those who had aided him in the hour of his need. He did, indeed, threaten the Dutch, and demand an indemnity for the assistance they had given to his rival; but he soon granted them terms which were most disagreeable to the Luebeckers. The latter were left to fight their quarrel out as best they could, Frederic putting himself to little trouble on their behalf.

Had the old constitution still been in force at Luebeck, the city might have kept quiet. But the narrow oligarchy of conservative patricians had lately been overthrown. A violently reforming democracy had taken its place, and Juergen Wullenwever, its chief spokesman, had been elected burgomaster. As a true demagogue, Wullenwever was bent on a spirited foreign policy, and under his rule a fleet was fitted out to compel the Dutch to admit the privileges of Luebeck and to pay a fine for having aided Christian. In 1533 this fleet cruised along the coast of Holland, and spread terror among the seafaring people. In August a detachment of it, consisting of five line-of-battle ships, mounted by 2,200 men, sailed towards the English Channel,[16] and at the Nore captured three vessels, one Flemish and two Spanish. Thence they proceeded to Dover, where they were allowed to victual, and finally they went to the Rye to lie in wait for fourteen Dutch hulks which were expected from Spain.[17]

Chapuis, hearing of their depredations, strongly protested against the favour shown to them; and as the Hanseatic traders had offended the court, the council were quite ready to promise that no further help should be given to the strangers. Orders to that effect were sent down to the coast, and when on 18 August the Luebeck captain, Marcus Meyer, landed to confer with the mayor of Rye, he was arrested on a charge of piracy.[18] The Luebeck ships, deprived of their leader, exposed to the cannon of the town and of the Dutch hulks, which had gained the harbour, dared not use force. They stood out to sea, and left the Channel.[19]

Marcus Meyer was brought to London, and Henry, remembering the insults offered by the Easterlings to Anne Boleyn, wanted to punish him and to make the Hanseatic merchants responsible for the damage done by his ships.[20] But the aldermen of the Steelyard protested that they had no connection with Meyer, and this they were quite able to prove. By and by, when the captain was closely examined by the royal council, he brought out certain facts which altogether changed Henry's intentions regarding him.

Marcus Meyer was one of a class of men who abounded in Germany in the sixteenth century – adventurers of talent and ambition, who delighted in daring enterprises and hairbreadth escapes. They were not without generous aims, but, leading a hard and chequered life, they could not afford to be very scrupulous, and were generally ready to enter into partnership with any one, however dishonest, who could help them to attain their ends. Meyer had originally been a blacksmith in Hamburg, but had enlisted as a soldier; and after having been tossed about a good deal, he had entered the service of Frederic of Denmark. In 1531 he passed with the rank of ensign to the Luebeckers, in whose service he rose to be a captain; and being an adherent of Wullenwever, he was appointed to the command of the soldiers on the squadron which ultimately made for the English Channel.

Meyer was not only a stout soldier, but a clever intriguer; and when examined, he expressed astonishment that he had been arrested for despoiling some of the king's bitterest enemies. He had thought Henry would be rather pleased by what he had done, but as it was otherwise, he promised that if he were set free the ships and merchandise should be restored.[21] At the same time he proclaimed the good intentions of the Luebeckers – enemies of the Pope and of the pretensions of Rome. He explained how matters stood in the north, and how advantageous it would be for Henry to conclude an alliance with Luebeck. Frederic of Denmark had just died, and a successor was about to be chosen. If a friend of Henry were elected, a confederacy might be formed between England, Denmark and Luebeck strong enough to withstand any enemy. Meyer declared that the king ought not to miss so good an opportunity, and he offered to do his best to promote Henry's interests in the matter. Perhaps he even hinted at the possibility of Henry himself being elected, and thus uniting the whole north-west under his sceptre.[22]

There was much that was absurd in this plan, but wild and fantastic combinations had an irresistible attraction for Henry, and he listened with pleasure to Meyer's glowing speeches. The captain was set free and received permission to go back to Luebeck, giving security for his return to England in November. He may not have taken advantage of this permission, as the way to Luebeck was rather dangerous for him; but an English secretary was sent thither, nominally to urge the restitution of the two Spanish ships, in reality to inform himself about the true state of the case.[23]

The hopes of an important alliance against Charles and the Holy See restored some firmness to Henry's mind. He was no longer so afraid of losing the friendship of France; he dared once more to pursue a vigorous and decided policy. In this course he was encouraged by the activity of Anne and her nearest friends, who were able to frighten the king with tales about a clerical conspiracy, and to rouse his anger by the account they gave of what the malcontents said.

Early in July a lay friar of Greenwich, Brother Laurence, who had acted for some time as a spy, went to talk to Cromwell about two friars observant whom he had been watching. They professed to have come to England for the purpose of collecting books for Friar Peto, who had fled to Flanders and had been writing against the divorce; but Laurence was able to state that they had visited Catherine at Bugden. This was immediately reported to the king, and Cromwell asked to be allowed to take any steps that might appear to him to be necessary.[24] The friars, notwithstanding their caution, were then arrested, having been dogged from Ware to London. No papers were found on them, but as they seemed unfavourable to the new state of things, and probably knew many of the secrets of their order, Cromwell applied for leave to have them racked.[25]

In his interview with Cromwell, Laurence had expressed a wish to make some revelations to the king regarding the holy maid of Kent, a nun named Elizabeth Barton, who was at this time much talked about. She had been for years subject to fits and hallucinations, and had spoken of her visions to a great many people who had been deeply impressed by them. She was very hostile to the divorce, and her prophecies were by no means favourable to Henry and Anne. The king decided that the matter should be investigated by Cranmer, who was staying at Canterbury;[26] and Cromwell sent the archbishop a list of questions he was to put to her, relating especially to predictions she was said to have uttered as to the death of the king and the queen. Cranmer had been in communication with her before he received these orders, and with his consummate talent for dissembling he had had no difficulty in making her suppose that he believed in her. He was very unwilling to act as Cromwell directed, because the questions, he thought, might put her on her guard; but being obliged to obey, he proceeded, with Dr Gwent, the new dean of arches, to execute his commission. The maid asked permission to speak privately with the archbishop, and when this was granted, she said she had been told in her trance that the next time she would know how Henry and Anne would end. Gwent wrote:

> And therefore, she desired to go to Curtopstrete, and there this week she shall have another trance, and then she shall know perfectly. And my lord has given her leave to go thither and to repair to him again, trusting that then he shall plainly perceive her foolish dissimulation. And if your interrogatory had not been, she would have confessed more things, for my lord does yet but dally with her as [if] he did believe her every word, and as soon as he has all he can get out of her she shall be sent to you.[27]

It seems that Cranmer was successful in his endeavour to lead the unsuspecting nun into a trap. She was arrested and sent to London, and shortly afterwards several monks, parsons and gentlemen shared her fate. Their papers were seized, they were submitted to a strict examination by Cromwell and his agents; and every device was employed to obtain from them a full confession of all the nun had said and a list of the persons who had seemed to attribute importance to her statements.[28] When the list was made out, it proved to be a very formidable one. It contained the names of Sir Thomas More, the Bishop of Rochester, the Marchioness of Exeter, the Countesses of Salisbury and Derby, Lord and Lady Hussey, and many others of less note.[29] It was pretended that the princess dowager and her daughter had communicated with Barton;[30] but this was contradicted by Catherine herself, and Cromwell subsequently owned that nothing had been found to compromise either her or Mary.[31] An attempt to implicate the Bishop of Winchester also failed.[32]

It does not seem to have been Cromwell's intention to proceed with any great severity against the nun and her accomplices or dupes, for the examination had shown that no real danger was to be apprehended from them. She was made to stand at St Paul's Cross, to read out a confession, and to listen to a sermon about her folly,[33] after which she was sent back to prison. Several of her adherents, however, were released on bail to the disgust of Cranmer, who advocated the adoption of stern measures.[34] As for those whose names appeared on the list of compromised persons, Cromwell's aim was to terrify them by giving them the impression that they might at any moment be sent to the Tower. A few of them were informed of the danger in which they stood, and hastened to make their most humble submission;[35] but the great majority were left in suspense whether they were to be punished or not. All this was very agreeable to Cromwell, with whose plans it perfectly accorded. Marcus Meyer had inspired Henry with fresh courage, and now the nun had provided the secretary with the means of overawing the opposition, while the king had been more than ever irritated against the conservative party. Everything appeared favourable to a revival of the energetic policy which had been followed during the spring.

Meanwhile, the Bishop of Winchester had proceeded to the French court, which he reached some time before the arrival of the Pope. On 11 October, Clement landed near Marseilles, and on the following day he made his solemn entry into the town.[36] Two or three days being spent in ceremonious visits and public consistories, negotiations did not begin until the 16th, but they were carried on very quickly, for the ground had been prepared.[37] Henry's ridiculous demand that the Pope should forthwith revoke the sentence of 11 July, and decide the whole question in his favour, was politely refused by Clement, who said that the acts of the cause were at Rome, and that without them he could do nothing. Francis, who had not seriously pressed the demand, informed the English ambassadors of Clement's answer, but declared that other means would be found to satisfy their king.[38] Gardiner seems to have taken this very ill, for he immediately sent a courier to England to apprise Henry of the disappointment of his hopes.[39]

Three days later, on the 20th, a kind of disputation was held at the lodging of Cardinal Duprat, the Chancellor of France, in which the auditor Simonetta, the nuncio, and Dr Burla, a canonist of some repute, took part. The cardinal complained of the brief of 11 July. Clement, he said, had annulled the marriage of Anne, and had declared her children illegitimate. But Anne had never been cited to answer the charge against her; and whatever might be the faults of Henry she ought not to be punished for them, nor for her own, without having an opportunity of defending herself. To this, Simonetta replied that, as Anne had known, the Pope had threatened to excommunicate any woman who should contract marriage *lite pendente* with Henry. Her marriage had been annulled because it was contrary to the papal inhibition, and she had no cause of complaint.

But Simonetta did not make a very decided stand, for there was some force in the argument of Duprat. The imperial agents had, indeed, long discussed the question whether Anne should be cited or not.[40] Chapuis had been of opinion that the Pope ought to order her under pain of excommunication to leave the court of Henry; but it seems that this was *ultra vires*. When the news of the marriage arrived, the question was once more thoroughly argued, and the imperial lawyers considered that the citation of Anne would greatly complicate the proceedings. She might send an excusator to plead that the statutes of praemunire prevented her from appearing at Rome, and by legal artifices delay the cause for years. So she was not summoned, but the imperial agents were aware that this might not be quite regular.[41]

It was on this ground that Clement intended to base the concessions he was ready to make. A deed had been drawn up by which, at Henry's request, he assented to the cause being reheard at Avignon before special legates, on condition that the king should acknowledge the authority of the Pope, and promise to submit to his final judgement. Nothing remained but to execute the deed, and Gardiner was called upon to produce the full powers he had said he held. He coolly declared that he had not spoken the truth, that he had no full powers, and that he could not bind his master to such conditions.[42] The French king, perceiving that he had again been duped by the English, became very angry, and said to Gardiner that he would no longer exert himself for a man who behaved like the King of England. Gardiner replied rather haughtily, and Francis went to the Pope and indignantly reported what had happened. Shortly afterwards, on 27 October, the marriage of the Duke of Orleans and Catherine del Medici was concluded without any previous decision regarding Henry's affairs.[43]

After some reflection Francis resolved to make another effort to settle the English difficulty. He sent Guillaume du Bellay to Gardiner, and on the 24th, at du Bellay's request, Gardiner despatched a courier to London to ask for the necessary powers to sign the agreement

Francis had proposed. It was hoped that Clement would remain until the messenger returned, and that all might still be peacefully settled.[44]

But on 25 October Henry had received Gardiner's letter of the 17th, in which the bishop reported that Clement had refused to dispose of the matrimonial cause in the offhand manner that had been suggested. Henry became pale with anger and crushed Gardiner's letter in his hand, exclaiming that he was betrayed, and that the King of France was not the true friend he had thought. He continued for some time to swear at the Pope, and could not regain his equanimity.[45]

His wrath was carefully nursed by all who wished for a final rupture with Rome. Cromwell opposed an arrangement which would increase the influence of France abroad and of the French party at the English court, while Anne was alarmed at the prospect of the question of the divorce being re-opened, and the validity of her own marriage being thereby disputed. They combined, therefore, to prevent Henry from considering the matter calmly, and they were successful. When, on 1 November, the courier who brought Gardiner's letter of the 24th arrived, the king was in a most defiant mood. He at once decided to refuse the request, and instructions to that effect were sent to the ambassadors at Marseilles.

The draft of these instructions, which is still preserved at the Record Office, seems to be in the handwriting of Cromwell, but the style resembles that of the king rather than that of the secretary:

> Upon the saying of Monsieur de Langeay, of the appointment of two legates, the one a Frenchman the other of the Pope's chosing, to determine the matter in Avignon, the same has been offered heretofore if the king's highness would condescend to make a proxy and grant the Pope's jurisdiction, that the Pope would then have made a commission to two cardinals whereof the one should be Cardinal de Monte to determine the cause at Cambray, which place is much more propice and tute and sure for the king than Avignon... Item as touching the sending of the proxy it is to be answered what needs the proxy to be sent when the French king at sundry times promised at this enterview to be proctor himself.

The writer goes on to argue against the course pursued by Francis, and directs the ambassadors to bribe, if possible, Queen Catherine's proctor. He concludes with the words: 'Item to provoke as may be the general council, which will more fear the Pope than all other things.[46]

With these instructions a courier left England on 1 November, and made such haste that on the 6th he was at Marseilles. Here he found Doctor Bonner, who had received at Lyons a copy of the king's appeal to a council, and had been ordered to join the Bishop of Winchester at Marseilles and to concert further measures with him.[47] The despatch was handed to Gardiner, who acquainted Bonner with its contents; and both were of opinion that the appeal should be intimated without further delay. But such an intimation would of course put an end to the negotiations, and it would prove that Henry had all along been trying to deceive Francis. It would, moreover, be a gross insult to the French king's guest. Francis was already in a sufficiently bad temper; and he might, perhaps, show Bonner and his colleagues that diplomatic privileges were accorded only in return for diplomatic behaviour, and that France still had dungeons and gallows for those who roused the king's anger.

On the whole, it seemed best to the English ministers to begin by feeling their ground with Francis. They accordingly told him in general terms what Bonner had been ordered to do. The king immediately tried to dissuade them from their purpose. 'Your King', he exclaimed:

thinks himself a wise man, but he is simply a fool. He is working in the interest of the queen, for by this appeal he admits that he knows of the sentence of 11 July and nevertheless disregards it. Let him know that if, in consequence of his behaviour, he is excommunicated, I have declared and declare that I shall not assist him against the Pope.[48]

But although Francis was greatly displeased, he spoke neither of hanging nor of prisons, and the English ministers came to the conclusion that the message of Bonner might be delivered without risk to their necks. So the doctor, taking Girolamo Penizzoni with him as a witness, went on the 7th to the Pope, and after some preliminary talk intimated Henry's appeal. When Clement perceived what was meant, he interrupted for a moment the reading of the different papers, and spoke bitterly of Henry's disrespect and ingratitude.[49]

While the papers were being read, Francis was announced, and the Pope hastened to complain to him of the insult he was receiving. 'Being your guest', Clement said in effect:

I allow people to enter without insisting on all the formalities which are used at Rome. These men, relying on this, have come in without asking the permission of anybody and have just done that which at Rome would entail capital punishment. I have shown myself ready to do all that I can, but the King of England has acted in a totally different manner. You ought, therefore, to forsake his alliance and to unite with the Holy See against him.[50]

Francis was not a little annoyed by Bonner's insolence; and afterwards he promised that he would no longer support Henry's cause, protesting that he was as displeased with the King of England as his holiness could be.[51] But as to an open rupture with England, that might lead to results which would be injurious to the interests even of the Holy See. If the King of England became desperate, he might throw himself into the arms of people whose alliance would be hurtful not only to the Pope and Francis, but to the whole of Christendom. Henry had asserted, Francis said, that, after all, if things came to the worst, he might take back his wife and keep the other as his mistress, and that then he and the emperor might jointly make war upon the French. In fact, the King of England had discussed this scheme with some of his most confidential ministers.[52] If it were not for this, so Francis assured the Pope, he would play Henry a trick the latter should long remember.[53]

But Clement was really angry, and urged so persistently that the insult which had been offered to him should be avenged, that Francis began to speak of Calais as the price for which he was ready to turn against Henry. The Pope readily assented, and the proposal was submitted to the two chief ministers of Francis, the grand master and the admiral. They both commended it, for they had lost patience with Henry, and were anxious that he should be abandoned.[54]

With the English ambassadors Francis had a violent quarrel. 'You will have me do for you', he said:

and when I and my council devise after what we may do, you regard us not therein, but of yourself do things clearly contrary; and as fast as I study to win the Pope, you study to lose him You see the effect of all your desires: they refuse that should receive.

Gardiner said that whatever had been done had been done with the knowledge and consent of Francis; but the king answered that he had never supposed they would go so far as they had gone. 'I desired,' he exclaimed, 'to have a proxy sent, and that was not only left behind, but also, in lieu of that, an intimation sent.'[55] Francis declared that he would have no more to do with the matter, and for the moment it seemed as if he intended to keep his word.

The Pope, after the insult he had received, was loath to stay; and Francis, who could not now expect a favourable reply from Henry, did not try to detain him. On 11 November, Clement gave his formal answer to Bonner, rejecting the appeal of Henry as utterly illegal, and on the 12th November he mounted his galley and departed.[56] Negotiations might be resumed, but instead of being conducted between the Pope and the King of France in person, they would henceforth have to be carried on by subordinate ministers.

Before leaving Marseilles, the Pope had once more tried his luck with Cyfuentes, and had spoken about the cession of Calais to the French. But in the preceding summer the reserve of the Spanish ambassador had been approved of by Charles V, who thought that Calais was much less dangerous in English hands than it would be in the hands of the French.[57] The count, therefore, would make no answer to Clement's proposals, and Francis, seeing that there was nothing to be gained by abandoning Henry, again attempted to reconcile him to the Holy See.[58]

Jean de Dinteville, the French ambassador in London, had done his best to moderate the English policy. He had had several sharp encounters with the king, and his temper had been sorely tried by Henry's insincerity and unfairness. The Duke of Norfolk, with whom Dinteville remonstrated, said that he could do nothing, as the king would not listen to any argument, and that he had already lost credit on account of the opposition he had dared to offer to extreme measures.[59] Dinteville felt relieved when, in the middle of November, de Castillon, who was to succeed him, arrived in England. He decided that, before going away, he would speak plainly to Henry; but at the farewell audience the king hardly gave him an opportunity of uttering a word, but himself broke out into vehement recriminations. He accused Francis of double-dealing, and lied with such impudence that the ambassador stood amazed. Even Norfolk was shocked by Henry's behaviour, and subsequently admitted to Dinteville that in what the king had said he had not always adhered to the truth.[60]

Dinteville was so angry that the English ministers of the French party tried to calm him. Suffolk spoke of Cromwell's influence, and Norfolk and Sir William Fitzwilliam made other excuses for the king. Anne, true to her French sympathies, and glad at heart that no compromise had been effected, was most gracious to the departing ambassador, and loud in her praise of the French;[61] and her cousin, Sir Francis Bryan, who, at the request of the French king, had hastened back to London, spoke in the same sense, and did his best to soothe the mutual irritation.[62]

But Dinteville was not to be regained so easily. On his return to France he wrote a long record of what had been said, and sent it to the court, where it was received with much displeasure. It was not made less disagreeable to Francis by the fact that Henry's accusations seemed to be something more than the passing talk of an angry man. For several weeks he remained in the same temper, abusing Francis and complaining of his want of faith.[63]

At Marseilles, Jean du Bellay had offered to go once more to England to try to bring Henry to reason. He now received long and elaborate instructions as to the past, containing a defence of the proceedings of Francis and a severe criticism on those of Henry. In carrying on negotiations du Bellay was to have great latitude, because, being more intimately acquainted with England, Henry, and the Boleyns, than anybody else in France, he would know best what could be done.[64] With this mission the bishop left, saw Dinteville on the road, and arrived at London on 17 December.[65] He found, as Francis had been warned, that Henry had decided to reject openly the papal supremacy, and that all the necessary preparations for the schism had been made.[66] But du Bellay was not disheartened. He was much liked by Anne, who trusted his friendship for her, and from her he feared no very stubborn resistance. In dealing with Henry, the bishop adopted a bold but judicious course. When the king again broke out into complaints and recriminations, accusing Francis of having violated his word, du Bellay interrupted him with a threat of instant war.[67] The decided tone of the bishop made some impression on Henry, and he went so far as to promise that he would not separate from Rome if, within nine weeks, he heard from du Bellay that the Pope, without further proceedings, would issue before Easter-day a brief annulling the sentence of 11 July, declaring the marriage with Catherine to be null and void, and confirming the marriage with Anne Boleyn.[68] If, at the end of the term of nine weeks, Henry was not informed that the Pope would do before Easter-day what was required of him, the schism would be proceeded with.[69] Du Bellay knew that the proposal presented a very slender foundation for a compromise; but he had at least prevented an immediate rupture, and he hoped that in the course of the negotiation Henry would become more tractable. With this result he left the English court on 29 December, and went in all haste to confer with Francis and Montmorency.[70]

8

THE PAPAL SENTENCE

Henry did not consider that his concessions to du Bellay bound him to remain idle until the Pope should arrive at a final decision. The policy advocated by Anne, Cranmer, and the other reformers, was indeed pursued with new vigour. If the Pope chose to submit, to annul all that had been decided at Rome, and to ratify all that had been done in England, so much the better. If not, Henry wished to be ready for definite action.

What he wanted was that his spiritual supremacy should be fully admitted, that his marriage with Anne should be acknowledged to be valid, and that Elizabeth should be recognised as heir apparent. During the session opened on 15 January parliament was to be engaged in passing the necessary measures.

But there was still so strong a feeling in England against the marriage of Henry with Anne, that the government considered it prudent to take some preliminary steps before submitting the matter to parliament. It drew up a declaration to the effect that convocation had declared the marriage of Henry and Catherine to have been null and void from the beginning, and had pronounced the marriage of Henry and Anne to be good and lawful. This declaration the higher secular clergy and the heads of houses were called upon to sign, and every artifice was employed to obtain signatures. The recusants were threatened with the king's anger, they were reviled and insulted by the royal commissioners, and all kinds of accusations were invented against them to put them in fear of their lives.[1] A great many signatures were thus secured; but the document was opposed by no less a man than John Stokesley, the Bishop of London. That convocation had condemned the marriage of Henry and Catherine was, if not strictly true, near the truth; but Stokesley remarked that it had been prorogued before the marriage with Anne had been officially acknowledged, and that it had never even been asked to give an opinion on the subject. So he begged to be excused from signing the paper. He proposed that the text of the declaration should be altered, so as to be more in accordance with the well known facts.[2] But as this would have created fresh difficulties, the suggestion did not recommend itself to Cromwell, and after some angry discussion the paper was finally suppressed.

The attempt to obtain signatures to this declaration was not the only step taken to facilitate the proceedings in parliament. An effort was also made to overcome the difficulty arising from the pretensions of Mary. The importance of this difficulty was not underrated, for Henry was well aware that most of his subjects were secretly loyal to the princess, and would do their best to defend her rights. If she herself could be made to renounce her claims as heir apparent, his way would be comparatively clear.

Soon after the birth of Elizabeth, Mary had received orders to lay aside the title of princess, but she had stoutly refused to do so.[3] When Elizabeth was taken to Hatfield, Mary's household at Beaulieu was broken up, and she was told that she would henceforward have to reside with the princess. This message was taken to her by the Duke of Norfolk, who, when she objected, answered that he had come not to argue with her but to fulfil the orders of the king. Mary thereupon asked for half an hour to prepare for the journey, and this being granted to her she retired to her chamber, where she signed a formal protest against the compulsion to which she was subjected.[4] She then allowed herself to be placed in a litter, and to be taken to Hatfield, her new place of abode. If this harsh treatment somewhat lowered her spirit, she received a little consolation from a quarter whence it was least expected. During the journey it happened that Doctor Fox, the king's almoner, and one of the royal commissioners, rode alone at the side of her litter. He seized the opportunity to say to her secretly that she had done well not to submit. For the love of God and the welfare of the realm he pleaded with her to remain firm. The other commissioners coming up, Fox once more became the harsh agent of Henry, but Mary was encouraged by perceiving that even the most trusted ministers of her father were at heart in her favour.[5]

At Hatfield Mary was entrusted to the care of Lady Shelton, a sister of Anne's father. This lady, of course, did all she could to subdue what she considered the obstinacy of her ward, but she made no impression whatever; Mary held out.

Henry, surrounded by a crowd of subservient courtiers who missed no chance of humouring his vanity, had come to believe in his own powers of persuasion. He fancied that although others might fail to influence Mary, he would have no difficulty in bringing her to his way of thinking. Accordingly, on 10 January he set out for Hatfield.[6] Knowing his fickleness and the pride he took in Mary's accomplishments, Anne feared that, instead of converting his daughter, he might himself be converted; so she sent Cromwell and some others of her friends after the king with instructions to prevent any meeting between him and Mary.[7] They were successful. Henry communicated with the princess by messengers, who were unable to shake her fortitude; but he had no direct interview with her. When he was about to leave Hatfield, having mounted his horse, he saw her standing at a balcony, and, forgetting his resentment for a moment, he lifted his cap to her. The courtiers eagerly followed the example of their master, and bowed low to Mary, after which the whole cavalcade went away towards London.[8] A few days later, conversing with Castillon, Henry could not refrain from speaking of Mary, and when the ambassador praised her virtues he sighed deeply, and tears came to his eyes. It is gratifying to know that even he retained some feeling of compassion for the daughter whom he was so deeply injuring.[9]

However praiseworthy such a feeling might be, Anne could not afford to let Henry indulge even momentary impulses of kindness for one whom she had such good reason to fear. She remembered Cromwell's attempt to have Mary legitimated, and rightly suspected him of being still favourable to her;[10] and it seemed not impossible that the king himself would by and by share the sympathies of the secretary. On 15 January Anne spoke to the king, reproaching him for allowing Mary too much liberty, and for permitting her to receive advice and encouragement. To Anne it was incredible that the answers framed by Mary could be prepared by so young a girl without help.[11]

With this opinion Henry was disposed to agree. During the summer of 1532 Mary's movements had been watched, and Lord and Lady Exeter, who were known to be her great friends, had been forbidden to visit her.[12] Now the king's suspicions had again fastened upon Lord Exeter, and about Christmas 1533, he used very threatening language to the marquis. It was Mary's confidence in the emperor, said Henry, that made her so wilful and obstinate. But she would soon have to submit, for he feared neither the emperor nor anybody else. It would be the duty of his subjects to stand by him if a conflict arose, and he did not doubt that they would do so. Persons who played him false would pay for it with the loss of their heads. He would cause such good watch to be kept that no one would be able either to send letters to, or to receive letters from, the continent without his knowing it.[13] These warnings did not frighten Lord Exeter, who continued by means of his wife to correspond with Chapuis.

To the complaints of Anne, Henry replied that henceforward Mary should be more closely guarded; and we find that shortly afterwards the Duke of Norfolk and Lord Rochford upbraided Lady Shelton for her leniency and weakness, and ordered her to treat Mary more severely, as the bastard she was. Lady Shelton, who seems to have been a good woman, and to have pitied her unhappy ward, answered with much spirit that Mary was kind and gentle and did not merit harsh treatment. Anne was enraged at this insubordination of her aunt, and became even more indignant when she heard that some Essex peasants had assembled under Mary's balcony and cheered her, calling out that she was the rightful princess.[14] It is said that Anne, after this display of loyal feeling, sent an order to Lady Shelton, directing that Mary should be beaten if she persisted in calling herself princess, and that if she would not dine at the common table she was to have nothing to eat at all.[15] But Mary was not beaten, and the king was charged the extravagant sum of ten shillings a week for the breakfast and supper which were supplied to her in her room.[16]

Anxious to use every weapon with which it was possible to strike at the opponents of the divorce, the government tried at this time to profit by the accusations against the holy maid of Kent and those who had been associated with her. After she had stood at St Paul's Cross, Cranmer had written a book railing against her vain prophecies; and he was irritated by hearing of a reply by a certain friar Dering, whom Cromwell had just saved from his clutches. Dering, when examined, declared that he had burned his book; but Cranmer declined to believe him, kept him in prison, and vehemently demanded that he should be visited with all the rigour of the law. The archbishop also asked Cromwell to have the other adherents of the nun re-examined, and urged that 'good and politic mean' should be taken at once for their trial.[17]

Cromwell had no theological hatred, but as it suited his purpose to adopt Cranmer's advice, the friar was kept in confinement, and new arrests were made. The nun could not very well be tried again, but the government framed a bill of attainder against her, and against her aiders and abettors, for high treason and misprision of treason. The general tenor of the bill was not concealed, but the names included in it were kept secret. The consequence was that everybody who had ever encouraged the nun was in no little anxiety, and, fearing that his name might be on the terrible list, was anxious to please the king. In this way the government bridled the opposition, and, as nearly as they could, ensured the passing of the bills of succession.

But during the first days of the session no measures of any moment were proposed. Henry evidently wished to hear what du Bellay might be able to do at Rome. On leaving England the bishop had repaired to the French court, which he had found at Pied de Pappe, near Avignon.[18] Here he gave an account of what he had obtained from Henry VIII;

and the French king, the constable, and the bishop concerted a plan for carrying on the negotiation. They felt confident that, if the Pope gave way in the matter of the divorce, Henry might be brought by flattery and gentle pressure to make larger concessions than he had yet offered. Their idea was that the Pope should first be thoroughly frightened, and afterwards bribed. It was agreed that he should be lured by the proposal of a marriage between his nephew Alexander dei Medici and Mary Tudor – the latter relinquishing her pretensions to the English throne, but receiving a good dowry – and that the old plan of a tribunal at Cambray should be revived in a modified form. Two cardinals were to go there by stealth, an agent of Henry was to meet them, and the cause was to be heard and judgement given in favour of the king before Catherine and her friends could become aware of the opening of the court.[19]

The advantages of this scheme, if it could have been accomplished, would have been great indeed for Francis and for du Bellay. The French king would have embroiled the Pope and Henry in everlasting enmity with Charles, and he would have secured the alliance of both. Duke Alexander would have been made dependent on France, and a firm footing would thereby have been gained in upper Italy. As for du Bellay, a cardinal's hat would have been his reward from the Pope, while Henry would have conferred on him large gifts or preferments.

All these high hopes of the French triumvirate were nearly blighted at the beginning. Du Bellay fell seriously ill on the road, suffering from such violent rheumatism that he could not bear even to be carried in a litter. But the ardent desire to try his abilities at the papal court overcame all obstacles. As soon as he recovered a little he had himself carried in a chair, and although he suffered the severest pains, he was able to reach Rome on 2 February.[20]

According to the plan laid down at Pied de Pappe, the bishop spoke at first only of the dangers which would befall Christendom if Henry were definitely alienated from Rome. When, on the 6th, he was admitted before the consistory, he explained the proposed confederation of protestant states, carefully refraining from all reference to the fact that Henry's plan would be resolutely opposed by Francis, and that it had but little chance of success. Du Bellay even magnified the danger. Heresy, he said, would spread everywhere; not only England but many other realms might be lost; even Rome, he hinted, might no longer be safe. He wished to terrify the cardinals into conceding all he asked for.[21]

In private conversation he was as violent as possible. By order of Cyfuentes, Dr Ortiz went to see him at the house of the resident French ambassador, the Bishop of Mâcon. Ortiz made inquiries as to the health of the Queen of England. 'Which queen?' said the bishop.

'The true and rightful queen,' the Spaniard replied, rather annoyed by the question. 'Queen Anne is well and triumphant,' was du Bellay's answer; to which Ortiz responded somewhat hotly that the bishop well knew that he was speaking not of Anne, but of Queen Catherine. 'Four days before I left she was very ill,' du Bellay then said, but Ortiz would not believe it, for Chapuis had said nothing about Catherine being ill, and indeed it was perfectly untrue. The doctor now began to blame Cranmer for his contempt of the Holy See. 'Cranmer,' du Bellay sharply replied, 'is held by the English to be a very saint. The English care nothing for papal censures and briefs; they have taken a lesson from the Flemish, who have torn down the papal briefs from the church doors.' The conversation continued in this strain, du Bellay evidently trying to bully the Spaniard and to frighten the advocates of Catherine.[22]

But du Bellay was not acquainted either with the character of the papal court or with that of the Pope himself. He thought Clement a weak coward of no great talent, whom he, du Bellay, might easily overreach. 'Le bonhomme', he called him at this time. A year later he spoke of Clement as the old fox, and mentioned his cleverness with a certain awe. The experience of two months had taught him that Clement VII was more than a match for him.

With the papal court du Bellay was not on good terms. When he drew a fearful picture of the expected schism, the cardinals were unanimous in deploring it deeply, but equally unanimous in considering the matter past remedy.[23] The other courtiers were either openly hostile or coldly distant; and the few pensioners of Henry spoke in a desponding tone.[24] But du Bellay did not lose heart; relying on his influence with the Pope, and on the brilliant advantages he was charged to offer, he believed failure to be impossible. It seemed to him, indeed, that matters had already taken a favourable turn, and that the Pope was becoming more and more inclined to grant all that was wanted.[25] Concession after concession was made by Clement VII.

But the Pope was quietly outwitting the overbearing Frenchman. He had not forgotten the insult offered to him at Marseilles; and, although he had no wish to displease Francis, he was determined not to interfere any longer between Henry and the due course of law. Immediately after Bonner had read the appeal to him, he had tried to bring about an alliance between the emperor and the King of France for the destruction of Henry. He had not been able to overcome the mutual distrust of the rival monarchs, but he had not given up his purpose. Two days after his return from Marseilles, he had been waited upon by Count Cyfuentes; and Clement, who had always seemed to shun a conversation about the divorce, at once eagerly asked the ambassador what was to be done in the matrimonial cause of England. Cyfuentes was rather taken aback; he said Capisucchi, the auditor who had charge of the matter, had not yet arrived, so that no steps had been taken. 'Never mind,' the Pope exclaimed, 'Simonetta may report on the matter: I want the case to be concluded.' Cyfuentes was so astonished by this eagerness of the Pope that he suspected some trick was being played upon him, and resolved to proceed with the greatest caution.[26]

But the Spaniard had soon to change his mind. The Pope was in earnest, and pressed the matter on with all his might. In consistory some of the cardinals asked who would execute the sentence if it were against Henry? The emperor, Clement declared, had bound himself to do so in person.[27] In reality the Pope had found it impossible to induce Charles V to make any promise of the kind; but the statement had its effect, and, the Pope being so zealous, every effort was made to satisfy him. Simonetta worked with a will, and when du Bellay arrived the report was ready to be submitted to the cardinals. That the sacred college might be in a position to judge of the facts of the case, an abstract of the depositions was embodied in the report, together with a number of queries and doubts respecting the legal questions involved, on which the consistory was to decide.[28]

A few days after his arrival and his reception by the cardinals, du Bellay had a private audience of the Pope, and spoke to him about remitting the cause to delegates. Clement did not absolutely refuse; he showed himself well inclined but he could not decide at once. He must have time to consider; for what would the emperor say? Du Bellay watched him with intense delight. If the Pope was already so favourable, it seemed pretty certain that he would give up everything after hearing of the great match for his nephew. On 8 February du Bellay wrote to Francis, Montmorency and Castillon, giving an account of what he had done. The two former he asked to make preparations for the mock trial at Cambray. Cardinal du Prat and Cardinal Gaddi had been proposed to the Pope as judges, and they ought, the bishop wrote, to hold themselves in readiness to leave at a moment's notice for Cambray, for quickness and secrecy were all important.[29] To Castillon, du Bellay presented everything in the most favourable light, hoping that Henry might be persuaded to grant a prolongation of the term which had been accorded. Castillon was directed to advise that an excusator should be ready to leave for Rome, there to remain hidden at the English hospital until du Bellay should want him.[30]

As these letters were despatched by a commercial courier, and as the passage of the mountains was still very difficult, they took more than a fortnight to reach Chantilly, where Francis had by this time arrived. Du Bellay's letter, and instructions to follow the bishop's advice, were immediately sent to Castillon, who received them at London on 2 March.[31]

Although the term granted by Henry was long past, the moment was not unfavourable for the requests Castillon had to make. Notwithstanding Cromwell's attempt to terrify the opposition, the bills of the government had not been so well received as had been expected. Great caution had been employed. On 31 January the lords had been called to the Star Chamber, and the treaty of alliance concluded in 1532 with France had been laid before them. They were made to believe that, whatever they might assent to, England would not be attacked by the emperor. Their fears in this respect being removed, a bill was brought in on 11 February, settling a dowry on Catherine as Princess Dowager of Wales. This of course implied that her marriage with Henry was void, and the lords, by accepting it, would admit the fact. There was some opposition, and although most of the friends of Catherine and Mary had been excused from appearing, and the bishops, as usual, had to vote for the court, the bill did not pass for ten days. When it was disposed of, the government at once introduced the bill of attainder against Elizabeth Barton, John Fisher, Bishop of Rochester, Sir Thomas More, and others her aiders and abettors. But here the lords proved more difficult to manage. The bill was read a second time on 26 February, but the opposition proved so strong that it had to be abandoned for a while.[32] In the Lower House, too, there had been a struggle. The bill about Catherine's dowry had been obstinately resisted; and one argument urged against it the government could not disregard. Henry VII had pledged the whole of the goods of his subjects for the fulfilment of the treaty of 23 June 1503, and for the payment of her revenues to Catherine; and the members for London now pointed out that if the bill passed Charles would have a perfect right to seize their property in Spain and Flanders. The danger, they said, was great, for if they could not trade in safety with Spain and Flanders English commerce would be ruined. Sharp debates took place and the bill did not pass.[33]

Nor had the king better reason to be pleased with the temper of the people than with that of parliament. With the exception of a very few fanatics and some of Anne's creatures and dependants, everybody in England looked forward to a separation from Rome with grave alarm. Henry was well aware of this, and had he had any doubts they would have been dispelled on Ash Wednesday. On that day the clergyman appointed to preach before the king maintained in his sermon that the authority of the Pope was the highest on earth. If he abused his power he was to be judged by a general council, but not otherwise. Moreover, saints ought to be honoured, and pilgrimage was acceptable to God and profitable to man's soul. Henry was of course displeased, and the courtiers cried out that the preacher had turned papist. But the king knew that what Hugh Latimer had the courage to tell him to his face the immense majority of his subjects secretly believed.[34]

The king was also vexed by Mary's steadfast assertion of her rights. Threats having failed to make any impression on her, Anne determined that she herself would try what could be done by soft and gentle means. At the end of February, she started for Hatfield; and when she arrived, she sent a message to the princess to come and salute her as the queen she was. If Mary would do so she would not only be well received, but would regain the goodwill of her father. Anne would intercede with the king on her behalf, and secure for her kinder treatment and a more brilliant position than she had enjoyed at any time of her life. But Mary was obdurate. She knew no queen in England, she said, except her mother; but she would be much obliged if the Lady Anne Boleyn would intercede with the king in her favour. Anne sent a fresh message with more tempting offers, but was again repulsed; whereupon she threatened to take vengeance on the obstinate girl who dared to withstand her will, swearing that she would break the haughtiness of this horrid Spanish blood.[35]

But all this only made the situation more complicated. Henry began to feel perplexed, and to throw on Anne the responsibility for his troubles. A possession of eighteen months had cooled his ardour; her great fault in having given birth to a daughter had not been forgiven; and her violent temper and the contemptuous manner in which she often treated the king wounded his vanity.[36] If his difficulties became too great, he might have to consider the expediency of sacrificing her. In the meantime, however, he had to think of his foreign policy; and what with the resistance to his schemes in parliament, the discontent throughout the country, and the enmity of the emperor, he felt very strongly that he could not risk a rupture with Francis.

Such was the state of mind in which Castillon found the king, when, after deciphering du Bellay's letter, he was received in private audience. He had no difficulty in obtaining from Henry the fairest assurances of goodwill. Henry spoke as if he were quite ready to do all that could be desired. But he gave no conclusive answer; he wanted first to consult his council.

The man who had most influence over Henry was certainly Cromwell. In the preceding autumn, as we have seen, he was not very unwilling to abandon Anne; but since that time he had gone too far in the other direction to be able to veer round with safety. He had of course excited the hostility of all those whom he had terrified into submission. The clergy were against him, the nobles hated him; and if his policy were changed, he would probably lose his place, and perhaps his life. For the present, therefore, he remained faithful to Anne, and so did Cranmer, Audeley, and the rest of the reformers. They represented to Henry the danger of departing from the principles he had professed; they assured him that they would ultimately carry all his measures; and they warned him of the duplicity of the Pope. Henry listened to them, and became once more firm in his purpose. The following day he sent for Castillon, whom he asked to repeat his message before the council. They heard it with frowning countenances, and most of them declared that the king could not again put himself in subjection.[37]

The ambassador tried to convince them that the course he proposed was the best for the king, for Anne, and for Elizabeth. The king ought to do all in his power to obtain a papal declaration that his marriage with Catherine was of no force, and that his marriage with Anne was good and lawful. The position of Anne and the succession to the crown would thus be assured, for all the arguments of Henry's adversaries were based on the power of the Pope to dispense and on the sentence of 11 July. Besides, the friendship of the Pope would enable Henry to defeat the intrigues of the emperor. The king ought to prefer this way, which was quite safe, to that which he was now pursuing and which was full of peril.[38]

But Castillon's eloquence was thrown away; the councillors remained decidedly hostile to his proposals. When the council broke up, the ambassador had begun to grow angry and to speak of ingratitude towards the king his master.[39]

Henry's confidence seems to have been somewhat shaken by Castillon's arguments. He took the ambassador into a garden, and, having made him promise secrecy, undertook to extend still further the term that had been granted to du Bellay. He would make no haste to have anything published against the authority of the Holy See; only the money which had formerly gone to Rome should go no longer. Du Bellay had written of a certain memorial; and when it arrived, the excusator, as had been suggested, should be despatched to Rome.[40] Castillon was delighted to hear all this. He did not see that Henry bound himself to nothing, but only provided a way of escape in the event of his circumstances becoming desperate. To Castillon, Henry's offers seemed to show real goodwill, and on the 6th he wrote, full of joy, to Montmorency, describing all that had happened. He enclosed in cipher a letter which he asked to be forwarded to du Bellay.

Without waiting for any reply, du Bellay had continued his labours at Rome. On 22 February he sent off the memorial alluded to in former despatches, containing the concessions he had been able to obtain from the Pope, and indicating the points about which there was no difference of opinion. I have not been able to find either this memorial or the letter to Francis I which accompanied it. But a letter of the same date to Castillon, a postscript of 24 February to Francis, and Castillon's reply to the whole, are extant. From these papers may be gathered how far Clement had allowed himself to be drawn.

Du Bellay's letter to Castillon is hastily written, and its style does little honour to a man who made some pretensions to literary skill. It shows that he was eager and violent, wholly unjust to his opponents, careless of the rights of Catherine, taken up with but one thing – the negotiation he had in hand. He began by saying that he had to contend with great difficulties. The Pope was terribly afraid of the emperor, and most of the cardinals were crying out, *crucifige*, 'like little devils'. If Henry separated from Rome, Francis could not remain the friend both of king and pope, and the friendship of the latter it would be impossible to jeopardise, because of the affairs of Italy. The memorial was a little hard, and ought not be shown to Henry; he should merely be told that the Pope was ready to send a cardinal and two assessors to hear the case at Cambray. They would not, however, according to present arrangements, receive powers to give sentence. To Cambray Henry might, at the request of Francis, send an excusator. At Rome, meanwhile, all the proceedings against Henry would remain in suspense, and the emperor would be very angry. Du Bellay would continue his exertions, and hoped to obtain security that sentence should be given in favour of Henry, in which case the delegates at Cambray might receive powers to pronounce it. If the Pope were no longer in fear of the emperor, and, above all, if the marriage of Duke Alexander with Mary were assented to by Henry, everything would be sure to go smoothly.[41]

Du Bellay once more assured Castillon of the goodwill Clement bore to Henry, but the poor man was daily threatened by the imperialists for what he had already done in favour of the king. If Henry would send the excusator du Bellay was willing to pledge his head that he would succeed. Castillon was to put the king on his guard against false friends, and to use every means to convince him that the course proposed by du Bellay was the safest and best for him. 'Use all the herbs of sorcery,' the bishop wrote; 'until I have your reply the devils may rage, but they will obtain nothing against us here at Rome.'[42]

Such were the principal contents of this strange letter. At first sight one naturally suspects that it was composed in order to be shown to Henry, and that the bishop gave a more favourable account of things than he himself believed to be warranted. But it is quite clear that the letter was meant to be read by Castillon alone. The bishop several times asserts that he speaks nothing but the truth, and other letters show that he wrote to Francis very much in the same strain. The letter must, therefore, be taken as representing the real opinions and hopes of du Bellay.

The letter arrived at Brie Comte Robert, near Paris, early in March, and on the 5th it was sent to Castillon with further instructions to do all he could to assist du Bellay and to bring Henry to accept an arrangement.[43] On its way to London it was crossed by the courier who carried Castillon's letter of the 6th. This letter reached Paris on the 12th, at the very moment when Montmorency was writing a reply to du Bellay's letter of 24 February, which he had just received. As the bishop's letter confirmed the good news he had already sent, and stated that he had obtained still further concessions about details, Montmorency was highly pleased and wrote to him in most eulogistic terms. Francis, Montmorency said, was very much gratified by all that had been achieved at Rome. There seemed to be every probability of success, which would be a great boon to Christendom. Du Bellay ought not to trouble himself about the opposition of the imperialists, but should go on exactly as he had hitherto done.[44] Montmorency had written so far when Castillon's letter of 6 March arrived. His satisfaction was increased by what the ambassador had to tell him, and he added a few lines to his letter to du Bellay to compliment him on the success he had had with Henry, and to express a hope that, contrary to the general expectation, a good result would be obtained.[45]

But Montmorency was mistaken. Castillon had already begun to feel that Henry was not sincere. About 10 March the ambassador had received du Bellay's letter of 22 February, and that of Montmorency of 5 March.[46] Instead of showing du Bellay's letter to Henry, he cleverly concocted another, in which all that was to remain secret or that might wound the king's vanity was carefully left out. This forged copy he took to the king and palmed it off as the genuine letter that du Bellay had written.[47] But hopeful as the tone of this paper was, Henry showed no great joy at it; his manner was not the same as it had been a week before. The concessions he had already made he did not withdraw, but he modified them in a way which made them of little consequence. He said he was ready to send an excusator, but without power to appear in his name. Moreover, out of regard to Francis, he promised that he would continue the session of parliament until after Easter, which fell on 5 April, and would delay publishing his separation from Rome. But he peremptorily refused to send a proctor to Cambray to represent him before the delegates. If the Pope was as friendly as du Bellay and Castillon said, he ought, without any further proceedings, to give the desired sentence. If he did this, Henry would be prepared to acknowledge the papal jurisdiction.[48]

That is to say, Henry refused to plead, but asked that sentence should be given in his favour. This he considered just and reasonable, and he supposed that he was making a concession by waiting somewhat longer for the fulfilment of his preposterous demand. Castillon was unable to shake his resolution.

A few days later, on 16 March, the French ambassador again asked for an audience, and was admitted into the royal presence. On the preceding day he had received letters from Francis, in which he was instructed to suggest to Henry the proposed marriage of Duke Alexander with Mary. At the same time he had received a copy of the ciphered passage of a letter of du Bellay and the Bishop of Mâcon of 24 February. This passage contained a promise that, if the proposal to hear the case at Cambray were agreed to, the Pope would remove in the meantime the censures and excommunication under which Henry had fallen on account of the sentence of 11 July 1533.[49]

Henry did not take at all well the proposal that Mary should marry Duke Alexander. It at once aroused his suspicions and wounded his vanity, for although he did everything he could to deprive Mary of her rank, he did not like to see her despised. A daughter of his, to his mind, was always a lady the greatest kings ought to honour; and to let her become the wife of a Duke of Florence seemed to him beneath his dignity. But when Castillon argued that the scheme would make the Pope his staunchest friend, and that the emperor would be entirely checkmated, Henry appeared to become less hostile and said he would think about the matter. At Henry's request, Castillon stayed for dinner; and after dinner he was called once more to the king, who had meanwhile conferred with some of his councillors, and perhaps with Anne. The match was then positively refused; but Castillon was told that if Duke Alexander wished to marry in England he might have one of the king's nieces, Lady Margaret Douglas, or Lady Mary Brandon.[50]

Henry plainly expressed his suspicion that all these overtures were meant only to delay business, according to the Pope's habit. If he did not soon perceive that the Pope intended to act honestly, he would go on with the anti-papal measures on which he had determined. As to Cambray – delegates, proxy and pleading – he remained as obstinate as ever. 'Let the Pope pronounce sentence in my favour, and I will admit his authority,' he said; 'else, it shall not be admitted.'[51]

This stubbornness was due mainly to a change which had passed over the temper of parliament. Two days after Henry's conversation with Castillon in the garden, the bill against Elizabeth Barton had been submitted to the House of Lords. Dissatisfied with the evidence against Sir Thomas More, the peers asked that he should be brought before them in the Star Chamber. The king was so enraged by what he considered an arrogant demand that he spoke of going down to the House himself, and the request was refused. Nevertheless, the name of Sir Thomas was struck out of the bill. With this victory the lords remained content, and on 12 March the measure was definitively adopted by the Upper House.[52]

The concession made by Henry sufficed to break up the compact force of the opposition, many of the lords thinking that they had done enough in saving More. On the same day that Barton was condemned, a bill forbidding the payment of 'Peter's pence' to Rome came up from the Commons; and it passed without the slightest difficulty. It was read a third time without alteration almost at the very hour when Castillon was proposing Duke Alexander's marriage.[53] This success gave Henry courage; and as his spirits rose, he became less willing to yield either to Francis or to the Holy See.

As in England, so at Rome, the prospect seemed very dark for du Bellay. The bishop had begun to doubt whether, after all, 'le bonhomme' was a perfectly appropriate name for Clement. To his dismay he found out that the Pope was better informed than himself as to all that went on in England.[54] Through Cyfuentes and Ortiz, Clement heard everything that was reported by Chapuis; and Sir John Wallop, Henry's ambassador in France, kept up a secret correspondence with the Baron de Burgo, late nuncio in England, and thus sent much intelligence to the Pope.[55] Du Bellay became somewhat alarmed, and wrote to Montmorency and to Castillon, complaining of Henry's proceedings. Henry, he said, was acting foolishly in irritating the Pope; that was not the way to obtain concessions.[56]

During this time the legal proceedings at Rome had made little progress; and Clement, when speaking to du Bellay, took the credit to himself. But the true reason was that the papers connected with the suit had got into disorder; legal forms had not been observed; and many little irregularities had to be redressed. On 27 February the matter was brought for the first time before the consistory.[57] Early in March another consistory was held, and the questions respecting the points of law were communicated to every cardinal to enable him to study them for final judgement.[58] The 23 March was fixed by the Pope as the day on which the cardinals were to reassemble to deliberate on the final sentence. Cyfuentes could not believe that the Pope really meant to have the controversy settled at so early a date; he feared some new trick, and was more alarmed than pleased.[59] Du Bellay was more easily satisfied. To him the Pope represented the delay of a fortnight as a mark of goodwill to Henry; and the bishop took it to be so; he was still full of hope and ardour. He had his laugh at the cardinals, especially at

Enkevoert and the Archbishop of Bari, who, he said, were busy with their books and fully determined to show the vastness of their learning. But they would find these questions a hard nut to crack.[60]

The 23 March was Monday of Passion Week, and the last day before Easter on which a consistory could conveniently be called. As du Bellay felt confident that the matter could not be finished at a single sitting, he was triumphant. It would stand over till after Sunday *quasimodo*, 12 April; and by that time he hoped to have such a reply from Henry as would induce the Pope to stop the proceedings.[61]

Both du Bellay and the Bishop of Mâcon asserted that they were unable to conceive how, in dealing with the questions prepared, any cardinal could declare the dispensation of Julius II to have ever been valid. If judgement was to be given, the imperialists would find themselves in great straits; for, were all the world hostile to Henry, it would be impossible for him to lose his case.[62]

The two bishops were not, of course, aware of the vote taken in July 1533 on the question of the validity of the dispensation. Cardinal de Tournon had been in Rome at that time, and had acceded to the decision, which had been carried by an overwhelming majority. But, as in duty bound, he had kept the matter secret, and the only two sovereigns who had heard of the vote were Charles V and Henry VIII. It was because Henry knew what had happened that he declined to allow judgement to be given at Rome, and distrusted du Bellay's fine promises.[63]

Clement, never forgetting for a moment that the question had been irrevocably decided, humoured du Bellay by allowing him to raise all kinds of objections against the validity of the dispensation. The Frenchman was soon to find that in this matter he had been duped, and even he might have forgiven himself for being taken in by so clever a dissembler as Clement VII. But when he wrote that Henry's case was progressing favourably, that the suit could not be lost, common sense ought to have taught him better. Had nothing else put him on his guard, his attention ought to have been arrested by the fact that of the eight Frenchmen who then wore the red hat not one had appeared. Bourbon, Lorraine, Castelnau, du Prat, Tournon, Coligny, Le Veneur and Givry were absent when a question of the greatest importance to their king was about to be settled. To Cyfuentes and Ortiz their reasons were well known. Had the French cardinals voted for Henry, they would have acted against their conscience; had they voted in opposition to him, they would have done violence to their political allegiance.[64] Cardinal de Tournon had openly declared that such was the true state of the case.[65] Du Bellay overlooked this grave symptom, and hoped where hope was folly.

On 23 March, at ten o'clock in the morning, the cardinals met, the doors were shut, and the consistory began. Like du Bellay, most people thought that the matter could not be decided at one sitting, and few expected to hear that day of anything of great importance.[66] It was remarked, however, that the cardinals allowed their dinner hour to pass without rising; and they were generally so punctual in this respect that curiosity began to be manifested. As hour after hour went by, the excitement increased; imperialists and anti-imperialists impatiently waited for news. The cardinals had sat for nearly seven hours when, at five in the afternoon, the doors opened and the reverend fathers appeared. The next moment it was known that sentence had been given.

At the beginning of the consistory, the cardinal-protector of France, Trivultio, backed by Cardinal Ridolfi, a personal enemy of Charles, and by Cardinal Pisani, proposed that final judgement should not be given at this sitting; but after a sharp and lengthy debate he was out-voted by a majority of nineteen votes to three. The discussion of the main question was now opened, and it quickly became clear that Henry had not a chance of success. Trivultio still did his best to prevent a final decision, but he had to give way. The question was put, and judgement was unanimously given in favour of the validity of Catherine's marriage. Trivultio himself and his two followers voted with the rest.[67]

Du Bellay was astounded by this result, and, when his anger had subsided, tried in vain to account for it. By whom had he been betrayed? Such had been the cleverness of Clement that he was the only person whom the indignant bishop did not suspect. On the whole, du Bellay was disposed to think that the sentence had been given with the consent of Francis, that Cardinal Trivultio had had secret instructions. He knew no longer what to do, and decided to leave at once.[68]

While he was preparing for his homeward journey, a courier arrived on 28 March from Paris, with Montmorency's and Castillon's letters.[69] From the former du Bellay learned that his conduct had been approved of, from the latter that Henry had granted a prolongation of the term first accorded, and that he was ready to send the excusator. Small as these concessions were, the bishop hoped that if they were judiciously used it might still be possible to induce the cardinals to revoke or modify the sentence, or, at least, to postpone its publication.[70]

That same day, while making his farewell visits, du Bellay chanced to meet Count Cyfuentes at the house of one of the cardinals. As the bishop's behaviour had thrown some doubts on his orthodoxy, he was anxious to justify himself. He assured the Spaniard that he had not come to Rome to contradict the good right of Catherine or to act in favour of Henry. He had neither a personal wish nor a commission from Francis to do so. He had simply wanted to point out that the

Pope would run the risk of losing the obedience of England by giving sentence against the king. Cyfuentes, seeing du Bellay so humble, answered politely; whereupon the latter went on to deplore the sentence that had been given. Only four hours ago, he had received a letter from Henry VIII telling him to believe all that Castillon would write; and the substance of Castillon's letter was that Henry would acknowledge the jurisdiction of the Pope if the question of the divorce were dealt with at Cambray. Cyfuentes coldly answered that these were but tricks to delay the publication of the sentence. If du Bellay, even when in England, had been unable to obtain any concessions whatever, how had it come to pass that by a simple letter he had made Henry accept a proposal that had always been obstinately rejected? Du Bellay knew not what to answer; he feebly said the Holy Spirit had enlightened Henry. 'Well,' Cyfuentes replied, 'in that case the Holy Spirit will move him still further to submit to the sentence.' Cyfuentes added a little anecdote about the Spanish cardinal of Santa Croce, who, when leaving the consistory, had remarked to his brethren that, now sentence had been given, the French agents would be sure to say they had received power from Henry to effect a compromise. This feeling being pretty general, du Bellay's account was everywhere received with suspicion.[71]

The statement made by the Bishop of Paris to Cyfuentes was certainly untrue. Castillon wrote on 6 and 16 March to Francis, Montmorency and du Bellay. Of these letters two only have been found, the one of the 6th to Montmorency, and the one of the 16th to Francis. From the latter it appears that between the two dates Castillon did not write either to Paris or to Rome. As in the two letters preserved, he gives a very full account of the concessions Henry showed himself willing to offer, we may safely assert that his letters to du Bellay cannot have contained any other matter of importance. The letter which the bishop received on the 28th was probably that of the 6th, which, as we know from Montmorency, arrived at Paris on the 12th. The letter of the 16th could scarcely have reached Rome on the 28th, for the roads were very bad and the mountains covered with melting snow.

Now, in the letter of the 6th to Montmorency there is not the faintest indication that Henry was as compliant as du Bellay pretended. He is represented as simply saying that he will wait before publishing the acts against the Pope, and that he will send the excusator when required, although without giving him any power whatever. From Castillon's letter of the 16th to Francis himself it is clear that Henry never went further, and that he would not hear of having the cause tried at Cambray. Du Bellay's statement had not a shadow of foundation.

But even if it had been true, it would have mattered little. Long before the letter of Castillon reached Rome, Henry had decided on the course he would adopt. On 20 March the government submitted to the House of Lords a bill ratifying the marriage of Henry with Anne Boleyn and settling the succession to the crown on Elizabeth. On Saturday the 21st, it was read a second, on Monday the 23rd, a third time.[72] As the whole question pending at Rome was settled by this bill, it would have been foolish to pretend that Henry was still ready to admit the jurisdiction of the Pope.

It was from courtesy to Francis that Drs Carne and Revett were sent about this time as excusators to Rome. They had no proxy from Henry, and their mission was a mere farce.[73]

That Henry was not sincere even in the few concessions he had made appears both from his deeds and from his words. He had told Castillon that parliament would sit until after Easter. Six days before Easter it was prorogued, and the royal assent was given to all the bills that had been passed, with the exception of that relating to 'Peter's pence'. The schism was accomplished.[74]

Henry's double dealing is frankly disclosed in the draft of a letter addressed to Wallop in April 1534. After directing the ambassador to invite Francis to revolt against the Pope, the king continues:

> And ye shall declare to our said good brother that we send not these messages and requests unto him only for displeasure that the said bishop has lately pronounced a sentence against us, contrary to the law and will of God, but ye shall assure our said good brother upon our honour that in case he had given sentence with us we would have laboured as diligently and as studiously for his reformation as we will now.[75]

Whether or not we believe what Henry here says, the conclusion forced upon us by the letter is that he had been cheating Francis all the time, and that he had never had any intention of admitting the jurisdiction of Clement.

Part 2:

FROM QUEEN & WIFE TO ADULTERESS,

APRIL 1534–MAY 1536

9

THE NORTHERN CONFEDERACY

On 31 March, in deference to the wish of du Bellay, a consistory was held, and the cardinals were asked, with a copy of Castillon's letter of the 6th before them, to reconsider their verdict, and in any case to postpone the publication of the sentence. To the first of these requests the cardinals answered that the letter was so vague, and Henry was so untrustworthy, that there was no reason why the sentence should be recalled.[1] As to the second request, neither the Pope nor the cardinals were very eager that the sentence should be immediately published; they wished to know first whether Charles V would give effect to it, and what Francis meant ultimately to do in the matter. The cardinals would not, however, bind themselves by any formal promise.

Du Bellay, finding that all his efforts were in vain, took his leave and set out for France. Happening to meet Carne and Revett at Bologna, he told them of the sentence and of what the cardinals had said, and held out hopes that even yet the sentence might be revoked; but the English agents were not very sanguine that his anticipations would be realised.[2] They stopped where they were, and shortly afterwards started for England. Du Bellay himself travelled rather quickly, and in the middle of April he was back at the French court.

The courier whom du Bellay had despatched with tidings of the sentence had travelled with extraordinary speed, and had arrived at the French court on the 1st, or on the morning of 2 April. Francis, fearing that Henry would proceed to dangerous measures if the unwelcome intelligence were not communicated to him in as gentle a way as possible, sent de la Pommeraye post-haste to the English court, which he was able to reach on 4 April.[3]

Henry received the news exactly as Francis had foreseen; but he did not allow himself to be carried away by his rage. For the more he heard of the consistory of 23 March the more he perceived the need of caution. The fact that all the French cardinals had stayed away, and that all the Italians of the French faction had voted against him, suggested to him the same doubts as those which du Bellay had for a moment entertained. He suspected that Francis, while giving him fair words, had for some reason secretly betrayed him. That cardinals could vote according to their conscience seemed incredible to Henry.

In this state of perplexity Henry was afraid to commit himself further. The league with Luebeck had not been concluded, the German Protestant princes stood aloof, Scotland was hostile and Ireland in open rebellion, while in England itself discontent had by no means been allayed by Cromwell's energetic measures. The loss of the protection of Francis in these circumstances might mean total ruin: it was a danger even Henry did not underrate. So he resolved, first of all, to make sure of the French alliance.

A few days after de la Pommeraye's arrival, Lord Rochford and Sir William Fitzwilliam were sent on a special embassy to France. They met the French king at Coussy on 21 April, and were splendidly entertained by him and by his sister the Queen of Navarre.[4] In the intervals between the feasts and the ceremonies they delivered their message. Henry requested, first, that Francis should abandon his alliance with the Pope; next, that he should invade Milan, but without taking subsidies from Clement; third, that he should adopt in France measures similar to the new English laws, which the ambassadors explained; fourth, that a meeting of the two kings should be arranged; fifth, that Francis should refuse to give the hand of his daughter Madeleine to James V of Scotland. While making these requests, Henry offered to contribute further towards the subsidies paid to the German princes.[5]

On the 24th the ambassadors received a detailed answer to their offers and demands. To the first point Francis replied that he had no alliance with the Pope. On Henry's account he had steadily refused at Marseilles to conclude any such alliance; and had the King of England been less obstinate, and sent a proxy, all would have gone in his favour.[6] As to the invasion of Milan, this was not a propitious time, but if ever Francis attempted to conquer Milan he would not, for the sake of trifling subsidies, put himself under obligations to Clement.[7] With regard to the new statutes made in England, Francis did not blame Henry for them, but he saw no reason why he should follow a similar course.[8] To the proposed meeting he had no objection; and the marriage of the princess Madeleine he was ready to forego. The contribution towards the subsidies in Germany would be gladly accepted.

But Francis in his turn put a question. Charles V, having urged the Pope to give sentence against Henry, could not honourably stand still now that his advice had been taken; he would be obliged to execute the papal mandate. Censures would be issued at Rome against the King of England and against his aiders and abettors; and Francis, if he continued to support Henry, would also be excommunicated, and would be attacked by those who were to carry out the sentence. His territory was much more exposed than England, and the war would begin on his frontiers. If he were assailed, what would his good brother of England do for him? On how large a sum of money might Francis reckon?[9]

Two days after having received this reply, the English ambassadors left Coussy to return to England. Henry was in no way offended by the venality of the French king. On the contrary, he regained the confidence he had nearly lost, and instructed Sir John Wallop, his resident ambassador in France, to thank Francis for his goodwill, and to exhort the friends of the English alliance to persevere in their efforts to establish it.[10] A few days later a second despatch was addressed to Wallop, the draft of which was largely corrected by the king himself. It treats of the proposed interview, and shows what undue importance Henry attached to this display of friendship. It also affords fresh proof of his insincerity. All his corrections are couched in ambiguous terms, and neither in the reply to Rochford and Fitzwilliam, nor in the other papers referring to the negotiation, is there any trace whatever of promises which he repeatedly speaks of as having been made by Francis. Henry would only undertake 'not vehemently to press' the French king immediately to make laws like those which had just been passed in England against the authority of the Pope. He asserted, however, that Francis had pledged himself, 'if the bishop of Rome gave him some reasonable occasion,' to 'do as much or more' than Henry had done.[11] Francis now sent de la Guiche to the English court, and to him Henry expressed a wish that the meeting should take place in August. At the same time he asked that a French fleet should be equipped to watch over his safety while he was crossing the Channel, and to protect the English coasts while he was away; and that a strong French force should be assembled at Ardres, lest Charles V – of whom he was mortally afraid – should make a bold dash at the walls of Calais and capture him in his strongest fortress.[12] In the beginning of June, de la Guiche returned with this message to Francis.

In the meantime the government were taking strong measures against all those who seemed inclined to side with the Pope. In the statute settling the succession to the crown on the children of Anne, there was a clause by which it was enacted that all adult subjects should be sworn to observe the Act. Immediately after the close of the session the oath was tendered to those whose sentiments it seemed desirable to test, and nearly every one outwardly submitted. But two men of equal fame and eminence, Sir Thomas More and Fisher, Bishop of Rochester, refused. More expressed his willingness to recognise the order of succession established by parliament; but he declined to accept the whole contents of the statute – in other words, to acknowledge the legality of the divorce and of Henry's marriage with Anne. Persisting in his refusal, he was committed for a short time to the custody of the Abbot of Westminster, and on 16 April was sent to the Tower.[13] To the same place, for the same offence, Fisher was also sent, having previously been attainted and imprisoned on a charge of misprision of treason in connection with the pretensions of Elizabeth Barton, the nun of Kent. In order to intimidate those who might be tempted to follow the example of Fisher and More, Elizabeth Barton and her associates were executed on the 20th.[14]

A few days later a royal commission waited on Catherine, and required her to take the oath. This was a gratuitous piece of insolence, for nobody could expect Catherine to comply; but it was made an excuse for depriving her of all those servants who would not swear to the statute. When Catherine refused, she was threatened with death and shut up in her chamber, and her Spanish servants were placed under arrest.[15] Chapuis strongly remonstrated, and the king, feeling that he had gone too far, gave way. Catherine was again allowed the use of her rooms, and her Spanish servants were set free.[16]

The government had now done all it could, and still but little had been achieved. Neither Catherine nor Mary had yielded, and although most of Henry's subjects had taken the oath it was pretty certain that they would willingly break it if they found an opportunity. Anne, who hated Catherine and her daughter, was enraged by what she considered a feeble and vacillating policy. She cordially despised Henry's weakness, as she called it; she wanted him to carry out his threats, and to rid her of her rival.

There was a chance that Anne herself might be able to do that from which Henry shrank; for she hoped that if he went to France she would be entrusted with the direction of the government during his absence. She had been overheard to say to her brother that, when the king was away and she was regent, she would have Mary executed for her disobedience. Rochford warned her of the king's anger if she took so bold a step without his command, but Anne vehemently answered that she did not care and that she would do it even if she was burned or skinned alive for it.[17] Chapuis, who tells the story, may have exaggerated a little, but there can be no doubt that his account is substantially true.

In April Anne had told Henry that she was once more with child.[18] Perhaps she herself believed what she so greatly wished; perhaps the announcement was only a feint to revive her waning influence, or to provide her with an excuse for remaining at home. In any case it had a very different result from that which she expected.

The violence of Anne's temper had begun to alarm Henry, and as the time for the interview approached he became very unwilling to allow her to act as regent. Rather than this, he was ready to give up the meeting he so eagerly coveted. Her supposed pregnancy was a sufficient pretext for breaking off the engagement; and in the beginning of July he sent Lord Rochford to France to obtain, through the influence of Marguerite of Navarre, the postponement of the visit till April 1535. Rochford was to say that Anne in her present state would be loath to see her husband leave her. Besides, she wished very much to meet the Queen of Navarre, and as she could not travel at this time she would be exceedingly disappointed if the interview were not put off. This reason Francis gladly accepted, for he was no longer desirous of conferring with Henry, whose proceedings annoyed him more and more. So the question of the meeting was allowed to drop, and Anne's hopes of a regency were nipped in the bud.

In the course of this summer Henry and Anne were mortified by an incident which attracted general attention. Lord Dacres of Greystock, warden of the western marches towards Scotland, had been one of the foremost opponents of the divorce. He had had frequent quarrels with Anne's friend, the Earl of Northumberland, who was warden of the eastern and middle marches; and he may have had some hand in the trick which the Countess of Northumberland, his sister-in-law, had tried to play in 1532. Northumberland had brought a long list of complaints against Dacres, and had at last been allowed to accuse him of treason. Early in May, Dacres and his cousin Sir Christopher were arrested, and the former was brought to London to be tried by his peers, while the goods of both were seized for the king's use.[19]

An acquittal in cases in which the Crown prosecuted for high treason was a thing scarcely heard of in the annals of Tudor justice. Almost everybody, therefore, expected a conviction; and the northern gentlemen and the courtiers disputed about the lands of the men about to be attainted.[20] The wife and the father-in-law of Dacres were forbidden to make suit for his life.[21] The Duke of Norfolk summoned twenty-one peers who were believed to be strong adherents of the court, and on 9 July they sat. The depositions and indictments having been read, the king's attorney asked for judgement of high treason. Dacres pleaded not guilty, offered a brief defence, and left himself in the hands of his peers. The lords then retired, and when after a short consultation they returned, Norfolk as high steward put to them the usual question. Lord Mordaunt, being lowest in rank, was asked first, and to the astonishment of the court he replied, 'Not guilty'. Peer after peer following his example, the prisoner was acquitted.[22]

Henry keenly felt this blow at his absolute authority. That the lords should dare to acquit a man whom he accused of high treason was a dangerous precedent; and in ordinary circumstances he would have turned angrily against the woman for whose sake he had aroused their opposition. Happily for Anne, he still believed her to be with child, and the hope of being father to a Prince of Wales overcame every other feeling in Henry's breast.

The rest of the summer Henry and Anne employed in a progress through the midland counties; and both did their utmost to win the hearts of those whom they met. In some instances they may have succeeded, but in general, under the surface, there remained the same discontent as before. Anne was no longer equal to the exertion of keeping her temper in difficult circumstances; and by a single moment of insolence she sometimes undid what she seemed to have accomplished by days of condescension and flattery. She began to feel tired and disheartened.

As time went on she became aware that she had been mistaken about her condition; and, as if to add to her annoyance, her sister, who had now been a widow for seven years, could not hide that she had those hopes which Anne lacked. Fair widow Carey had fallen in love with William Stafford, a soldier of the retinue of Calais, and it was afterwards pretended that she had married him. However this may have been, she was now about to bear him a son. The affair being rather scandalous, poor Mary was sent from court, and had to ask Cromwell to obtain at least a small pittance for herself and her new lord.[23]

At last Anne was obliged to tell Henry that she was not pregnant. It was no agreeable duty, for she felt sure that he would resent the failure of his hopes. And she was right. He immediately ceased to show her the attention and courtesy he had paid her during the last few months; and the court soon understood that her influence had declined.[24]

While Anne was thus beset with difficulties, she was losing the assistance of her best and most powerful ally, Francis I. The reasons for his change of policy were of a mixed kind. Personally, Francis was pretty indifferent to religion and to the papacy; but the great majority of his people still adhered to the old forms. The imprisonment of two men so far-famed as Fisher and More had excited strong indignation, and the execution of the observant friars had been resented by their whole order. The members of this order were among the principal preachers in France, and they made the French pulpits ring with denunciations of Henry's cruelty. If Francis continued to show favour to the King of England, and especially to the faction now in power, he was in danger of losing the support of his own subjects.

But this was not all. The policy of Henry might not only cost Francis the goodwill of his subjects and the friendship of the Pope, it might deprive him of the position he had gained in Germany.

At the time of Luther's revolt there was a twofold agitation in the German lands, the one for religious reform, the other for political change in a democratic sense. Luther put himself at the head of the former movement; the latter he decidedly opposed. Most of the princes, nobles, and patricians of the towns in central Germany associated themselves with him; and when the peasants rose under Muenzer to overthrow the aristocratic government, they were defeated with the help of Luther's most enthusiastic friends.

In Switzerland the reformation initiated by Zwingli was less conservative in politics. Still, it kept within bounds; it was politically respectable. Zwinglians and Lutherans had lately grown to be on friendly terms, the small differences of dogma having been nearly explained away, so that Francis was able to favour the one without offending the other.

Northern Germany was in a very different position. In that part of the country there had been no democratic rising, but the democratic idea steadily gained ground. In the towns the old oligarchies, one after another, were displaced, and a more popular form of government was introduced. The cities so constituted were generally on bad terms with the neighbouring princes and nobles, although there was no open war of any importance until 1533. Nominally, most of the northern towns had adopted Lutheranism, but their Lutheranism was not always orthodox; their divines did not absolutely submit to Wittenberg.

Francis had formed an alliance with the Zwinglians, who furnished him with strong contingents of Swiss troops, and with the Lutherans, who opposed his enemy, Charles V. With the ever-shifting factions of the northern towns he had nothing to do. He would not trust such fickle communities; nor did he believe that Charles would ever find in them real enemies. Far from Austria, the northern towns had little to fear from the emperor; and they hailed with pleasure those measures by which he diminished the power of their neighbours the princes. Their pleasure was in no way diminished by the fact that many of the princes agreed with them about religion.

It was of course the French king's chief wish to widen the breach between the Protestant princes and Charles; and a good opportunity seemed to offer itself when, on 5 January 1531, Charles's brother Ferdinand was somewhat irregularly elected King of the Romans. Duke John, elector of Saxony, who had not been properly summoned, protested against the election, and all the Lutheran princes refused to recognise Ferdinand as their superior. They were joined by Duke William of Bavaria, who had formerly been a vigorous opponent of the Lutherans. Although, next to the electors, he was the most eminent Catholic prince, he had long been jealous of the growing power of Austria; and, at the diet of Augsburg in 1530, he had been exasperated by the action of Charles in granting to Ferdinand the vacant dukedom of Wuertemberg. By this arrangement Bavaria had been nearly enclosed by Austrian territory, and had been cut off from her allies. Political reasons thus drove the Catholic duke to seek the alliance of the Protestants.

Francis had been closely watching these events; his agents, Guillaume du Bellay of Langey, Gervase Wein and others, keeping him well informed of all that went on. In May 1532, he promised to pay 100,000 crowns to the discontented princes if they would resist by force Ferdinand's claims to royal power;[25] and when the offer was accepted, he deposited the sum at Ingolstadt in Bavaria. The war, however, was postponed on account of a new inroad of the Turks. All Germany united to repel the common foe, who, baffled at Guenz by the stout defence of Jurischitz, and opposed by an excellent army under Charles V himself, had to retreat with heavy loss. The danger from the Turks having come to an end, and the emperor having gone to Italy, the moment for beginning the war seemed to have arrived; but the confederates hung back, and perhaps no battle would have been fought but for an event which disturbed all Ferdinand's calculations.

Christopher, the son of the banished Duke Ulrich of Wuertemberg, was kept in a kind of confinement at the imperial court. In the winter of 1532 he managed to escape, reached Bavaria, and threw himself on the duke's protection. He was well received, and his cause was taken up by the duke as well as by the Schmalkaldic and other princes. Francis I was friendly to him, and Guillaume du Bellay delivered a long and pathetic speech in his favour. Ferdinand, alarmed by the popularity of the young duke, offered him compensation; but Christopher insisted that Wuertemberg must be given up. Negotiations were now begun between Francis and Philip, Landgrave of Hesse, who, as an old friend of Christopher's father, was most eager to serve him. After the conference at Marseilles the French king proceeded to Lorraine, where, in January 1534, he met the Landgrave at Bar le Duc, and arrived at an understanding with him. Francis deposited an additional sum of 200,000 crowns with the Duke of Bavaria, and bought from Ulrich the county of Moempelgard, with its dependencies in the free county of Burgundy, for 184,000 ducats. With this money the Landgrave raised an army, and advanced rapidly by an unexpected route towards

Wuertemberg. Ferdinand was abandoned by all his friends. His own troops tried to make a stand, but on 13 May, at Laufen, they were utterly routed; and about the end of the month Wuertemberg was in the hands of its native duke, and Philip of Hesse was fast advancing towards Bohemia. In this emergency, without consulting the emperor, who might have been less compliant, Ferdinand accepted a treaty of peace, which was signed a few days later at Cadan in Bohemia. Ulrich retained Wuertemberg, the Protestant princes and towns were not to be molested, and in return Ferdinand was acknowledged as King of the Romans.

Francis, who did not at all wish for so speedy a settlement, protested against what he considered a breach of faith on the part of the Protestants. They answered with recriminations, asserting that the behaviour of the friends of Francis had forced them to act as they had done. And there was a good deal of truth in what they said. Philip of Hesse had concluded the treaty of Cadan, in order to be free to withstand a grave danger with which he and all German princes were threatened from the north.

Early in the spring of 1534 the Anabaptists had obtained possession of the town of Muenster in Westphalia; and as Muenster was but 50 miles from the dominions of Philip, he and his people were exposed to no small peril. The surrounding lords and princes had raised some troops, and were trying to shut the Anabaptists up in the town they held; but in these endeavours they were hampered by the action of Luebeck and its allies.

The mission of Stephen Vaughan to Germany had failed. Ignorant alike of the German language, of German customs, and of German policy, he had acted in the most clumsy way, addressing himself, of all men, to the one who was most sure to reject Henry's advances. John Frederic, elector of Saxony, to whom Henry's political methods were repugnant, was little disposed to enter into a league with him, and declined to run any risk on his behalf. Vaughan, being dismissed from the Saxon court with a very decided refusal, lost heart, and did not proceed to Cassel, where the Landgrave might have given him a better reception. He returned to Flanders without having succeeded in any of his objects.[26]

But if the German princes, the friends of Francis I, disliked Henry's proposals, the German burghers were not of the same mind. The negotiations between Luebeck and Henry had been going on without interruption. The messengers from Luebeck, who at the end of October had arrived in England to ask for the release of Marcus Meyer, had in general confirmed the account he had given of the state of affairs in North Germany and Denmark.[27] They had even added further information. Frederic I of Denmark having died on 10 April 1533, at Gottorp, his eldest son Christian was the principal candidate for the Danish throne; but Christian had refused either to form an alliance with Wullenwever and the town, or to bind himself faithfully to respect their privileges. The Luebeckers, therefore, opposed his election, while the nobles and prelates supported him, and the Danish estates were as hostile to the pretensions of Luebeck as the young duke himself.[28]

In the beginning of December the English secretary who had been sent to Luebeck returned. It was remarked that after his arrival the king was in good humour, and was particularly careful to treat Marcus Meyer with distinction.[29] The secretary had found Wullenwever quite ready for the alliance Meyer had proposed, and the city had appeared not only eager to assert its privileges, but well able with its confederates to execute its designs.

The proposed alliance seemed likely to be attended by very great advantages. If Denmark were gained, landsknechts and horsemen might be collected there and maintained at a small cost; and from Jutland a force might easily be brought over to Hull or Newcastle, especially if Hanseatic hulks assisted in transporting them. Norway and Skonen might be taken soon after Denmark, and then a great northern Protestant democratic league might be formed under the presidency of Henry. The king could not withstand the fascination of so vast a scheme. He did not, indeed, immediately grant all the demands of the Luebeckers, but he agreed to send an ambassador to the town, and asked that in return Luebeck plenipotentiaries should come to England.[30] About the same time it was decided to send agents to the other maritime towns, to the King of Poland, to the Woywode, and to the German princes, to win their favour for the league.[31] As to Marcus Meyer himself, on Sunday 7 December, he was made a Knight of the Rose, and received a chain worth £100, with the promise of a yearly pension of 250 crowns. After this he left for Luebeck to work in Henry's interest.[32]

On 15 January 1534, Meyer arrived at Luebeck.[33] He communicated to Wullenwever Henry's message, and induced the burgomaster to send a secretary to England to make a formal request for help in the projected war against Denmark. The secretary reached London in February, and promised that if Henry granted the Luebeckers money for the undertaking, they would not only repay the sum, but pay him twice as much from the revenues of Denmark. If he did not choose to appear as one of Duke Christian's enemies, a German prince – Count Christopher of Oldenburg was meant – would carry on the war; and this prince would become tributary to England for any amount he might receive. To these proposals they wished to have a speedy reply.[34]

Henry gave the secretary a very cautious answer. He encouraged Wullenwever to persevere in his bold and warlike policy, and to refuse to negotiate with the Dutch. He said he could not lightly embark on so weighty an enterprise; but he wished an embassy to be sent to him, that he might treat with duly accredited ministers; and he ended by offering Wullenwever a pension.[35] Early in March the secretary left with this reply.[36]

He had been preceded by Dr Thomas Lee, or Leigh, whom Henry had sent in January to negotiate on the spot an alliance with the Hanseatic towns.[37] At Luebeck, Lee seems to have done his best to persuade the town to adopt an active policy; and he was so far successful that the authorities made serious preparations for an attack upon Duke Christian. Wullenwever had long been in negotiation with Count Christopher of Oldenburg, formerly a clergyman and canon of the chapter of Cologne, but now a soldier of some repute. Count Christopher had levied about 3,000 landsknechts, with whom, on 12 May, he appeared before Luebeck. He sent a message to the town asking for ships to carry his troops to Denmark, where he intended to restore King Christian II; and on the following day he went himself to confer with the town council, which decided by a majority, in consequence of fiery speeches of Wullenwever and his adherents, to help the count in his undertaking.

Marcus Meyer, afraid perhaps that the council might draw back, resolved to adopt a course by which it would be absolutely committed. At the head of a small band of chosen followers he secretly left the town, and on the 14th surprised the castle of Trittau, a stronghold of the Duke of Holstein, which was of great importance to the Luebeckers. Being thus compromised, they had no alternative but to declare war against the duke; and Count Christopher's troops, together with a few Luebeckers, invaded the duchy.[38]

The war having once began, it was much easier to induce the town council to send an embassy to England to negotiate an alliance with the king. On 30 May the ambassadors left, and were joined on their way by others from Hamburg, which had also listened to the eloquence of Paget and Lee. Shortly afterwards, on 16 June, two ships flying the colours of Luebeck and of Hamburg sailed up the Thames; and when they had anchored, the ambassadors from the two towns were landed by the barges and taken in great state to their lodgings. The servants of the Luebeckers were all dressed in red, and, as if to characterise the spirit of their town, wore as motto, *Si deus pro nobis, quis contra nos*? Those of Hamburg, clad in plain black, had a more sedate inscription: *Da pacem, Domine, in diebus nostris*.[39]

On the 24th the Hanseatic ambassadors were received in state at Hampton Court. The chief of the Luebeckers, Dr Otto Adam von Pack

– a man famous for his intrigues in central Germany – addressed a long laudatory speech to the king, who gave a gracious reply, and referred the ambassadors for further negotiations to his ministers.[40] Soon afterwards, at several meetings, the conditions of the proposed league were discussed.[41]

While negotiations were proceeding at the English court, the war was being carried on in the north. Duke Christian had soon collected a force sufficient to repel the invaders, and on the mainland the Luebeckers made no further progress; but Count Christopher had taken ship at Travemuende with most of his own troops. On 19 June he set sail, and a few days later he landed on Seeland. He met with but little resistance, the whole country was overrun, and Copenhagen itself surrendered to the victor.[42]

So brilliant a beginning seemed likely to facilitate the conclusion of the Anglo-Luebeck alliance; but Henry made exorbitant demands without offering any real assistance in return. The Hamburgers, who had no pressing need of a close league, soon became very cool. The superintendent of their church, Aëpinus, had come over to join them, and, after having heard the case, had declared for the validity of the marriage between Henry and Catherine; so that his lay colleagues dared not subscribe to the articles impugning it.[43] Thus Luebeck alone remained to be treated with, for the Senate of Bremen had refused to send representatives to join those of the two towns. Pack went on with the negotiations, but could obtain no more than a loan of £3,333 to the town of Luebeck for the continuance of the war.[44] His colleagues thereupon returned home, while he remained for some time longer, plotting and scheming, and ingratiating himself with Henry.[45]

Philip of Hesse was greatly annoyed by the proceedings of the Luebeckers. The capture of Trittau, without any previous declaration of war, was contrary to his ideas of right and honour; and he was made uneasy by the state of ferment into which most of the north German towns had been thrown. He was also alarmed by the threatening movements of the free peasants of Ditmarschen, who seemed disposed to begin a new peasants' war. If Duke Christian were left to fight his way alone, the princes of northern Germany might have to face a huge and threatening democratic confederacy.

The negotiations of Henry with Luebeck were well known, and it was equally notorious that he had shown special favour to Marcus Meyer, the first aggressor in this war. Moreover, it was suspected that he secretly encouraged the Anabaptists. The German princes, therefore, were very angry with him, and their anger was in some measure extended to Francis, his ally and friend. Thus Philip of Hesse considered himself fully justified in signing the treaty of Cadan, against which Francis protested. When the treaty had been signed, some of Philip's troops were sent to Muenster, while others went to reinforce the Duke of Holstein. Ferdinand was no longer the chief enemy; the men who had to be fought were John of Leyden and Juergen Wullenwever, who was backed by King Henry of England.

Francis, dreading the loss of all his influence in Germany, and wishing to retain the friendship of the Pope and the loyal attachment of his people, had made no secret of his disapproval of Henry's policy. He and his ministers had spoken in very strong terms about Anne, and had more than once hinted that they were quite ready to abandon the English alliance. These utterances had been carefully reported to the emperor; and Clement VII, shortly before his death, had again tried to negotiate an alliance between Charles and Francis.

Charles had good reasons for wishing to be on friendly terms with Francis. The Turks had again assembled in some force on the frontier, and had made frequent inroads on Austrian territory; and the famous Admiral Khairredin Barbarossa had left Constantinople and seized Tunis, where he had secured an excellent harbour at the Goletta from which he threatened the shores of Italy and Spain. As Barbarossa and Soliman were in constant communication with Francis, Charles apprehended an alliance between the French and the Turks. This he wished to prevent by conciliating the French king, hoping meanwhile to strike a crushing blow at Khairredin. Henry, Count of Nassau, was sent from Palencia to the French court to negotiate an alliance with Francis.

By paragraphs 24–30 of his instructions Nassau was directed to speak privately about a marriage between the Duke of Angoulême, the youngest son of Francis, and the Princess Mary of England. He was to point out that in all probability Angoulême would thereby succeed to the crown of England, so that a better match could not be found for him.[46] In making this proposal Charles wished not only to benefit Mary, but to bribe Francis to forsake the alliance of Henry. For if the French king accepted his offer, the match could be concluded only by joint pressure on the King of England; and if such pressure were exercised, the alliance between Francis and Henry would, of course, be dissolved, and there would be less danger of a great coalition against the emperor.

Some time after the arrival of Henry of Nassau at the French court, finding Francis rather stubborn about Italian affairs, he suggested the idea of Mary's marriage. The French ministers eagerly listened to the proposal; but they were not ready to accept it. Francis said he was bound by ties of honour to Henry, and added the more sensible remark that Charles V was offering what he had not got. Mary was still in the power of her father, who, on hearing of the proposed marriage, might do away with her; and then the only result for Francis would be the lasting enmity of Henry and Anne. In a letter of 20 October from Blois, Charles was apprised of the objections of Francis and of the failure of Nassau's negotiation.[47]

10

THE CONSPIRACY

In 1533, after the coronation of Anne, the discontented elements of the nation had been scattered and unorganised; and before they had had time to coalesce, Cromwell's quick hand had carried the principal measures of the government. But at the trial of Lord Dacres the peers had become aware of their own strength; they had learned that they were nearly all secretly disaffected, and that the Crown would not easily obtain from them a verdict against any member of their order. Knowing this, they grew bolder; they opened their minds to one another, and looked about for remedies for the maladies of the time.

The lords having numerous adherents among the gentry, they very easily formed a strong party of resistance. As early as 17 September 1534, Eustache Chapuis received a message from two rich and influential gentlemen, who, afraid of exciting suspicion, would not come to his house, but asked him to meet them as if by chance at an appointed place in the fields. The ambassador went, and they openly told him that they wanted the emperor's help against the tyranny of the king.[1] Several ladies, thinking that their movements were less watched, dared to go to the ambassador's house, and brought Chapuis the same request in their own and in their husbands' names. So strong were the feelings of these fair plotters that one of them, a lady of high rank, forgot all prudence. She threw herself on her knees before Chapuis, and implored him to obtain the emperor's aid. Happily for her, her gentlewomen and the servants of Chapuis stood far off, and although they saw her kneel they could not hear what she said.[2]

A week later a person of very considerable importance appeared on the scene, and communicated with Chapuis. This was Lord Hussey, who until 1533 had been lord chamberlain to the Princess Mary. He owned very large estates in the midland counties, and had considerable influence at court. He now sent word that before leaving town he wished privately to speak with the ambassador. To prevent suspicion they had only a short conference, Hussey briefly stating that most of the nobility were extremely dissatisfied with the government, that they had consulted together, and that they wished to be assisted by imperial troops in forcing Henry to dismiss Anne, and to give up the course he was pursuing. For further particulars he referred Chapuis to Lord Darcy, another member of the conspiracy.

The ambassador, eager to know the whole business, sent on the following day a confidential agent to Darcy, who immediately disclosed their designs at greater length. In the northern counties alone, he said, there were already sixteen earls and barons, who in this matter were all of the same opinion.[3] If the emperor sent men of war and a few troops to the mouth of the Thames, and if a band of good hackbutters, some experienced officers and a supply of arms and ammunition were landed in the north, the lords would rise against the king. They would unfurl the imperial standard, adding a crucifix to it.[4] Their forces were already considerable – Darcy himself undertook to raise 8,000 men – and many others would certainly join them. Of his associates Darcy named but two, the Earl of Derby and Lord Dacres of Greystock, the peer who had just been acquitted of a charge of high treason. Of possible opponents in the north, Darcy knew of none except the Earl of Northumberland; and he might be easily arrested, as he had no following, and his own servants would not support him. Charles was advised to befriend James V of Scotland, who secretly aspired to the hand of his cousin, Princess Mary; and the intention of the conspirators seems to have been to proclaim James and Mary under the auspices of the emperor as feudal overlord. According to Darcy, they had no doubt of success.

The communication was so important, the details given by Darcy seemed so likely to be accurate, that Chapuis wrote at once to the emperor to ask for instructions. He did not venture to offer an opinion directly, but he clearly showed that he thought the plan feasible; and he was persuaded that if it could be carried out it would be of the greatest advantage.[5]

Charles received the ambassador's letter just after the Count of Nassau had been despatched to the French court. From a simply political point of view, the offer was tempting enough, since it might enable the emperor to obtain a firm footing in England, and secure for him a strong alliance against France. It had also a most seductive aspect for Charles's fancy. He was the last emperor who seriously thought of regaining the power that had been wielded by Charles the Great. He dreamt of being recognised as the supreme lord of the western world, of establishing that monarchy which Dante had praised, which was to heal all wounds and strife, and to extend the rule of Christendom over the whole earth. Two kingdoms had been foremost among those which had refused to submit to the authority of the Kaiser – France and England. Long ago an English king had been obliged to take an oath of fealty to the emperor, but Richard I had forgotten his promises as soon as he had recovered his liberty, and they had been wholly disregarded by his successors. For more than three centuries no emperor had pretended to exercise power in England, and only a few forms remained to remind the curious and the learned of the ancient tie.

But now the English nobles, writhing under the tyranny of Henry, appealed to the emperor. Admitting their dependence upon him, they wished to legalise their rising by fealty to the higher lord, and offered to unfurl his standard. The English leopards were to be superseded by the Roman eagle, the imperial power in England was to become a reality. It was a splendid prospect, and the resolution to turn from it must have cost Charles V a bitter pang. But dreamer as the emperor was, he was also a keen and farsighted politician. For the present, with Soliman, Barbarossa and Francis I threatening him, he could not wish for a rising which might prove the signal for general war. He wanted to fight Barbarossa separately, and for that purpose it was necessary to have peace with France, which rebellion in England would render impossible. So the English were to wait until Tunis was taken.

Chapuis was ordered to give general assurances of goodwill, and to remain in communication with Hussey, Darcy, and their confederates, but not to go any further. He was directed, too, to obtain information about Reginald Pole, regarding whom the emperor had lately received a report from Venice, describing him as a person of some importance.[6] With this part of his instructions Chapuis easily complied. Reginald was closely related to Lord Abergavenny, the ambassador's old friend, to the Earl of Westmoreland, and to Lord Latimer; and his mother, Countess of Salisbury in her own right, had been the governess of the princess and was universally respected and admired. Lord Montague, the elder brother of Reginald, and Sir Geoffrey Pole, his younger brother, had already communicated with Chapuis, and were ready to fight for Mary; and Chapuis thought that if a rising took place, and if imperial troops were sent to support it, his presence would add considerably to the popularity of the insurrection.[7]

Chapuis received his instructions at a moment when it seemed as if no rising would be necessary to drive Anne from power; for during the few weeks which had elapsed between the despatch of his letter and the arrival of Charles's reply, the conservative party had gained an important ally. In the spring of 1534 Henry had already shown signs of being weary of the woman he now called his wife. Eighteen months of possession were a long time for so fickle a lover, and he had begun to pay marked attention to a young and very handsome lady at court.

Who she was I have not been able to discover; neither Chapuis nor the French ambassador mention her name in the despatches which have been preserved. The only thing certain is, that she was not Anne's later rival, Jane Seymour.

Henry's affection for Anne had seemed to revive when she had led him to believe that there was again a chance of his having a male heir; but when she was obliged to confess that she had been mistaken he returned to the young lady, and paid court to her in a more public manner than ever. Anne became very angry, and in her bold and overbearing way tried to send her rival away from court. But she presumed too much on Henry's weakness, overlooking the fact that she had no authority except what she derived from the influence she exerted over him. As soon as he heard of her attempt to interfere with his amours, he sent her a most insulting message, informing her that she had good reason to be content with what he had done for her, because if it were still to be done he would not do it. Let her, he said, remember where she had come from, and not be overbearing.[8]

The new favourite proved to be a strong adherent of Catherine;[9] and she went so far as to send a message to Mary to be of good cheer, for things might change very soon. Whenever she could, she would do her best to serve the princess.[10]

In proportion as the power of the lady increased, that of Anne decreased; and the courtiers, ever ready to abandon a falling favourite, were eager to desert Anne, whom most of them hated. They soon had an opportunity of showing how little they really cared for her. In October Mary and little Elizabeth were taken to Richmond from the More, where they had been spending the autumn, and where Mary had been visited by the gentry of the neighbourhood. When they were at Richmond, Anne, attended by many ladies and gentlemen, went to see her daughter. No sooner had she gone in to Elizabeth than the whole throng of courtiers, the Dukes of Norfolk and Suffolk at their head, went to pay their respects to Mary. It was impossible for Anne to console herself even by an outburst of anger at the honour shown to her enemy; she had meekly to submit to what she could not but consider a deliberate affront.[11]

Of course the Boleyn faction tried every means to avert the dangers by which they were confronted. Lady Rochford, Anne's sister-in-law, began to intrigue against the favourite, hoping indirectly to shake her credit and to oblige her to leave court. But the plot was detected, and the king in his rage inflicted on her the fate she had tried to prepare for Anne's rival; so that Anne was now deprived of the company both of her sister and of her sister-in-law.[12] Occasionally she attempted to hold her ground, and once she complained of the insolence with which the favourite treated her, but Henry turned his back on her and went away. Her family shared her disgrace. Sir Francis Brian having brought an action against Lord Rochford, the influence of Henry was exerted in favour of Brian.[13]

The moment seemed favourable for an attempt to re-establish good relations between Henry and the Holy See. In September Clement VII had fallen dangerously ill, and the king had ordered Gregorio da Casale to repair at once to Rome to watch events, and, if possible, to induce the Pope on his deathbed to recall his sentence.[14] The French ambassador, who had been asked to use his influence for the same purpose, had hesitated to do so, but Casale had nevertheless remained at Rome working for his patron. Shortly afterwards Clement died, and Cardinal Farnese, formerly accounted a staunch friend of King Henry, was chosen in his place. Paul III – so the new pope decided to call himself – adopted a moderate tone, and showed himself anxious for a reconciliation. He spoke with the Cardinal of Lorraine, the most important of the French members of the sacred college, and the cardinal promised to go himself to England to bring the king back to his allegiance to Rome.[15] Casale wrote in a very hopeful manner, and the conservative party in England strained every nerve to profit by the opportunity.

All this was well known at the French court, and Francis and his ministers resolved to take advantage of it. Although they had refused the overtures made by Charles V for a marriage between Mary and the Duke of Angoulême, they had not broken off the negotiation. What they really desired was a marriage between Mary and the dauphin. If this could be brought about, Anne would be easily disposed of, for Henry would either fall with her, or he would have to give her up. In the latter case he would have to take back Catherine, from whom no further issue was to be expected. England would then, after the death of Francis, be united to France; and the new kingdom, commanding both sides of the Channel, would be the foremost power in Europe. Such were the hopes entertained by the French government; but it was not to be supposed that Charles would readily assent to a scheme that might be so perilous for the empire. The French saw that only by clever intrigue could they hope to persuade him to sanction the substitution of the dauphin for Angoulême.

The first thing they had to do was to keep up the distrust between Henry and Charles, and to obtain as much as possible from Henry's fears. About the end of October Philippe de Chabot, admiral of France, was sent on a special mission to England, and although his instructions do not seem to have survived, sufficient evidence remains as to his charge. He was to tell Henry that Charles had proposed through the Count of Nassau two marriages, one between his son Philip and the youngest daughter of Francis – which was true – the other between the dauphin and Mary – which was not true. Moreover, he was to say that Charles had offered Francis the duchy of Milan after the death of the reigning duke, and in the meantime a pension of 100,000 crowns. This also was untrue, for the offer was to hold good only if the duke should die childless, and the sum was much smaller. After this Chabot was to assure Henry that Francis intended to remain faithful to him, and to reject Charles's proposals. But Henry was to be asked to forego the title of King of France, and to accept in exchange a very chimerical title to certain estates in the Low Countries which were to be taken by Henry himself from Charles. Francis desired to be relieved of the obligation to pay the pensions due on account of the treaty of Amiens, and Chabot was to beg Henry to reconsider his policy towards Rome, and either to submit to the Pope at once or to reopen the negotiations so suddenly broken off in the spring.[16]

These instructions were very cleverly drawn, for, by a treaty signed in 1518, Mary and the dauphin had actually been betrothed, and Chabot was to base his negotiations on this treaty. If Henry repudiated it, he would set the dauphin free to marry the Infanta Doña Juana, a match which of course would strengthen the Spanish influence in France and draw Francis away from England. If, on the contrary, to prevent the match with the infanta, Henry admitted that the betrothal was still valid, the game of Francis would be half won. It was a disagreeable dilemma for the King of England, and still more disagreeable for the Boleyns.

Chabot left the French court on 20 October,[17] and having a very numerous train, he travelled slowly. On 8 November he arrived at Calais, and on the 11th he crossed to Dover.[18] Here he waited for his servants and horses, so that his entry into London was delayed until the 20th.[19] The admiral found a state of things very different from that which he had expected. The conservative party seemed to have no influence whatever; and the English government, instead of showing any desire for a reconciliation with Rome, was quietly pursuing the opposite course.

Henry and his advisers were certainly not ignorant of the state of public feeling and of the conspiracy which was being formed, for Cromwell's spies must have warned him of what was going on. But the government was not in a position to take proceedings against the conspirators. It might have secured from a packed jury the conviction of some of the lesser malcontents; but it could not venture to attack the leaders of the movement. An attempt to bring any of the lords to trial would almost certainly have failed, and failure in a matter of so much importance would have seriously damaged the authority of the Crown. Fortunately for ministers, they knew that the conspirators now hoped to gain their object by some less dangerous method than open rebellion. Moreover, the winter was setting in, a most unpropitious time for an insurrection. English peasants could not lie out in cold and damp, and if a force were raised against Henry, however powerful it might seem to be, it would dwindle away before the inclemency of the season.

The government made use of the respite to strengthen itself for the coming struggle. Henry had indeed, no choice but to go forward with the task he had begun. If he retreated now, he would encourage the opposition, and lose, perhaps, not only all that accession to the prerogative which he had gained during the last few years, but a great part of the authority which had long been obnoxious to peers and commoners alike. He would have to sacrifice his trustiest and ablest ministers, and to substitute for them at the council board the very men who resisted his pretensions. He would become so weak a king, while the peers would become so elated and so popular, that the olden times of York and Lancaster might be revived, and in the midst of the turmoil the Tudor king might disappear. It was, therefore, absolutely necessary to complete the measures which had been taken for the assertion of the royal supremacy.

Parliament met on 4 November, and ministers introduced a number of bills which clearly showed that neither the growing dislike of Henry for Anne, nor his fancy for her rival, had altered his policy. First of all came the famous Act of Supremacy, by which the king was to be declared the only supreme head on earth of the Church of England. This bill was easily carried: a fortnight after the opening of the session, two days before Chabot arrived in London, it had already passed.[20]

The admiral, being convinced that the Act of Supremacy was due to Anne's influence, took pains to indicate that the feelings of his master towards her had greatly changed. For two days after he had been received by Henry he did not even mention her name, so that at last the king asked whether he would not go and see the queen. 'As it pleases your highness,' was the cold answer. He had no message for her; and he showed that he would wait upon her only out of courtesy to the king.[21] While Chabot strongly marked his indifference to Anne, he begged for permission to see the Princess Mary. His application was refused, but he found means to let it be generally known that the request had been made. And when his gentlemen and servants were asked whether a marriage had been arranged between the dauphin and the infanta, they asserted that no such plan was thought of. How could it be? Was not the dauphin betrothed to the princess?[22]

At the same time both Chabot and the resident French ambassador, Morette, were ostentatiously polite to Chapuis; and in the same spirit Chapuis responded to their advances. There was a show of cordiality between the two embassies which boded no good to Henry and Anne.

On hearing from Chabot what his instructions were, Henry tried a counter move. He could not see why the dauphin should marry Mary, who was illegitimate; but might not Angoulême marry Elizabeth? Chabot did not absolutely reject the proposal, as it would not necessarily prevent the other match, and Henry might be persuaded to give a considerable dowry. But the French representative was careful to leave the impression that he was not satisfied.[23]

An incident which occurred on the evening before Chabot's departure from England well depicts Anne's position. On 1 December there was a ball at court, and the admiral sat with Henry and Anne on a raised platform looking at the dances. Palamede Gontier, treasurer of Brittany and chief secretary to the embassy, being in the hall, Henry wished to present him to Anne, and went to fetch him. Anne kept her eyes on the king as he made his way through the crowd, and saw that he stopped before reaching Gontier, and forgot everything in the conversation of a young lady – her rival. By constant tension of mind, Anne's health had been very much impaired; and she burst into a fit of hysterical laughter which lasted for several minutes. The admiral, indignant at her behaviour, angrily asked whether she laughed at him; and although Anne, on regaining her composure, tried to explain, she could not allay his resentment. Chabot reported the incident with remarks by no means flattering to Anne.[24]

Next day, while Chabot was standing in the hall of his house, Sir William Fitzwilliam, Sir Nicholas Carew, Cromwell and other ministers of Henry came to pay their respects to him. He received them with marked coldness, but when Chapuis was announced Chabot went to meet him, greeted him most amiably, and, leaving the Englishmen to themselves, drew the imperial ambassador aside to assure him of his goodwill and to complain of Henry. These demonstrations were intended as much for the English as for Chapuis, the admiral wishing it to be clearly understood that he was decidedly displeased with the king and with Anne.[25]

Chabot had really some reason to complain of Henry's behaviour. Even while he was in England a bill was brought in by the government to enforce obedience to the Act of Supremacy. By this bill it was to be made high treason to deny to the king and queen or their heirs the dignity, style and name of their royal estate, or to call them heretic, schismatic, or infidel.[26] The measure met with considerable opposition; and after long and animated debates in both houses it was passed only when the government accepted two amendments intended to mitigate its severity. The first of these was that the Act should not take effect until 1 February following, when it would be generally known, and nobody would be likely to incur its penalties unawares. The second amendment seemed even more important, for it decreed that only malicious denial of the king's title should be considered high treason. This clause was introduced for the purpose of shielding persons who, like Fisher and More, would offer no opinion on the question.

Fisher and More had now been prisoners for many months. The severity with which they had at first been treated had soon been relaxed; they had been allowed to obtain books and writing materials, to see their friends, and to enjoy the liberties of the Tower – that is, to take a walk either in the inner garden or on the leads behind the battlements. But after the passing of the Act of Supremacy they were asked by the council, which went to the Tower for the purpose, to accept the new law. Both desired to be excused; whereupon, to punish them for their obstinacy, the privileges they had enjoyed were withdrawn. Their books and writing materials were taken from them, and they could correspond only by stealth.[27]

Had the bill creating new kinds of treason passed in its original form, the two prisoners might have suffered immediately. As it was, the rigour of their confinement was not to last very long, and for a moment they were to have a chance of regaining their freedom. The last month of 1534 was particularly disagreeable to Henry. Chabot, as already said, had plainly shown that he was no longer the friend he had been; and, as he had hitherto been very favourable to Henry and Anne, this was an ominous sign. Nor was it much more encouraging that although couriers came from France none of them brought an answer to the proposals made to the French admiral. Chabot had, indeed, travelled home rather slowly, but even this could not account for the delay. Henry was also troubled by tidings which reached him from Spain. A considerable body of troops was being raised in that country, ships were being got ready, and an important expedition was clearly about to be undertaken. As the King of England was not aware of the real object of these preparations, he became somewhat suspicious. There were ships enough in the Biscayan harbour to bring over the whole force to the English shores, and he had no fleet to intercept them, nor an army to withstand the troops if they landed.[28]

In these circumstances Henry thought it expedient to conciliate his enemies both abroad and at home. Although most rigorous measures had been passed, the government began to act warily, and the first to feel the good effect of the change were the prisoners in the Tower. Their confinement was once more made less strict; they were allowed to write and receive letters, and to see their friends.[29] If a letter of Palamede Gontier, printed by Lelaboureur, may be considered good evidence, Fisher was even permitted to leave the Tower on bail, and to repair to the court at Westminster.[30] In any case, from the end of December to the middle of February, they were treated with comparative favour. And so were Catherine and Mary, who during this period were not molested by messages from the council.

At the same time it was thought that some arrangement might be come to with Charles V; and in Paris, towards the end of December, Sir John Wallop tried to open negotiations with Viscount Hanart, the imperial ambassador at the French court. Hanart did not pay much attention to these overtures, but neither did he refuse to listen to them. A few weeks later, on 20 January, Wallop returned to the subject. He called on Hanart, and stated that he had consulted some of his friends in England, and that in their opinion a compromise might be arrived at on the following basis. Let the emperor promise not to proceed in the matter of the divorce by violence as long as Henry lived; and in the meantime the queen would be treated well, and otherwise matters would remain in suspense. Hanart was very reserved, but he wrote an account of the conversation to Granvelle and asked for instructions.[31]

The time seemed in every way propitious for a reconciliation. The credit of the Boleyns was daily decreasing, their enemies were becoming more aggressive, and persons belonging to the class who like to be on the winning side were forsaking Anne and her relatives. She knew this, and was in great anguish of mind. She could not conceal from herself that the ally on whom she had most firmly reckoned, Francis I, was disposed to desert her cause; and she clearly understood that without his help the emperor could not be resisted. If Francis formed an alliance with Charles against England, Henry might save himself by speedy submission, but Anne would have to be sacrificed.

Happily for her, the antagonism between Charles and Francis was so deep-rooted that a real alliance was impossible. After Chabot's return Francis had hesitated, for the offers made by the emperor seemed very tempting. But the French king was well aware that the expedition which was to be undertaken against Khairredin was meant to deprive him of an ally; and he suspected that Charles's proposals were intended to amuse him and to keep him quiet while Tunis was being conquered. While he was balancing between two courses open to him, he received news which filled him with indignation against the emperor. A rumour had gone abroad in Germany that Francis had agreed to abandon the German Lutheran princes; and the French, rightly or wrongly, traced the report to an imperial source. If it were not contradicted he would lose the friendship of his German allies, and would not be able, as heretofore, to levy landsknechts to fight his battles. On 18 January Francis saw Viscount Hanart, to whom he violently complained of what he had heard. The viscount tried in vain to explain the thing away: he could not appease the king's anger or lull his suspicions.[32] Incensed against the emperor, Francis bethought himself once more of the English alliance. An answer to Henry's proposals was made out, and three days after Hanart's audience Palamede Gontier took it to the English court.

But even now the long expected message was by no means what Anne would have liked. The conditions of Francis were rather hard. No wonder, then, that she looked haggard and worn, and that when, two days after his arrival, Gontier saw her at a ball at court and gave her a letter from Chabot, she betrayed her anxiety. She complained that by coming so late he had made the king very suspicious. It was necessary, she said, that Chabot should put matters right, for she found herself in even greater difficulties than before her marriage. She entreated Gontier to pray the admiral in her name to look after her affairs, of which she could not, unhappily, inform him at such length as she wished, because of the prying eyes of the king and the courtiers. She added that she would not be able to write, nor would she have an opportunity of seeing him again, and even now she dared not remain with him any longer. And so she left him, and the treasurer followed Henry into the ball-room wondering what all this meant. 'I assure you, my lord,' he wrote to Chabot, 'by what I can make out she is not at her ease.'[33]

Immediately after his arrival, Gontier had been called to court, and had had a long audience of the king. First of all the marriage of Elizabeth with the Duke of Angoulême, which Henry had proposed, was spoken of. It would be necessary, Palamede Gontier said, that Elizabeth should be made perfectly sure of her rank, as the Duke of Angoulême could not marry a woman whose social and political status was a matter of doubt. Henry angrily protested that Elizabeth was the undoubted heir to the crown, and generally recognised as such; but if any doubt remained in the mind of Francis, he might easily set it at rest by obliging the Pope to recall the sentence given by Clement, and to declare the marriage with Catherine to have been null and void from the beginning. Henry was most anxious that this should be done, for reasons which Gontier perhaps guessed, and which ought to have made the French reluctant to commit themselves any further in the matter.

Gontier went on to state what portion Francis would expect the little girl to bring to him and to his son. It was nothing less than the renunciation by Henry of the title of King of France, and the extinction of all pensions, arrears, or payments which the French were by treaties bound to make to him – a sum of about 120,000 crowns a year. At this exorbitant claim Henry's anger broke forth, and he could not for some time regain his equanimity. In the end he said that 50,000 crowns of perpetual pension he was ready to give up, but the 60,000 which were to be paid to him personally during life he would not relinquish. No decision was arrived at, and as it had grown late the conference was postponed to the following day.

Early next morning Palamede Gontier went to Cromwell's house at Austin friars. The French had hitherto shown little attention to the secretary, having failed to realise the full extent of his power. They now tried to make up for past neglect. Gontier brought complimentary messages from the king and from the admiral, and threw out broad hints that Cromwell would profit by supporting the demands of France. The secretary listened politely, and professed goodwill towards Francis; but he made no positive promise or answer. Although Gontier flattered himself that he had made some impression on him, Cromwell remained at heart as anti-French as he had ever been.

From Austin friars the treasurer took his way to Westminster, where he met the Dukes of Norfolk and Suffolk, both of whom showed themselves most friendly. Gontier remained at court until after dinner, when he was called into the royal presence. Henry was still angry at the extravagant claims of Francis, and complained of the negotiations which had been kept up with the emperor. The following day was Candlemas, and Gontier went to the royal chapel. After the service Henry invited him into his closet, and in a more pacified tone began to talk about the proposed meeting between himself and the French king. He was much gratified to hear that the Queen of Navarre and the daughters of Francis were to come to the interview. This flattered his vanity, and put him in better humour. The audience ended with a significant request from the French king. Lord Rochford and Sir Nicholas Carew were rival candidates for the next vacant garter, and Francis asked that it might be bestowed on Carew. Henry promised to remember his good brother's wishes.[34]

That same evening – the evening of the ball at which Gontier met poor Anne – the royal council drew up the official answer to the French proposals. It was even less favourable than the reply given by the king. The perpetual pension he had declared himself willing to resign, the council would not part with. As to the marriage, they proposed that commissioners should be sent at Whitsuntide to Calais, there to debate the conditions. Should the admiral be one of them, the Duke of Norfolk, Sir William Fitzwilliam and Cromwell would go to meet him. Neither the father nor the brother of Anne were to take part in the negotiations which would settle the future fate of her daughter – another certain sign of their disgrace. The time of the conference was intentionally fixed at a distant date, that Francis might try to obtain from Paul III a reversal of the sentence given by Pope Clement.[35]

The English opponents of Henry's policy were now in high spirits. On the day after the ball at court, Morette gave a great dinner party, at which the Dukes of Norfolk and Suffolk, Sir William Weston, prior of St John, Lord Abergavenny, and other influential adherents of the papacy were present. Palamede Gontier told them of the *auto da fé* at Paris lately, when Francis himself with his sons had marched in the procession and had watched the torturing and burning of a good number of Protestants. The English lords were delighted to hear of this, and praised Francis for what he had done. There could be no doubt, Gontier wrote to Chabot, as to what they themselves would like to do in England.[36]

Henry was at this time in a state of great perplexity. Annoyed by Anne's jealousy, and angry with her for not having borne him the son and heir he had expected, he was anxious to be rid of her; and the most natural way of accomplishing his purpose seemed to be a second divorce. Cranmer, he felt sure, would make no difficulties, but would declare the second marriage, like the first, to be null and void. Having thought the matter over, he opened his mind to some of his most trusted counsellors. Who they were does not appear; but their answer averted the blow which he thought of striking at Anne. If the king, they replied, wished to repudiate Anne, he must restore the rights of Catherine, and acknowledge Mary as his heir and successor.[37] Henry had hoped that the marriage with Catherine might still be dissolved by the Pope, and that he would then be delivered from all difficulty. He had overlooked the fact that even if Paul III revoked his predecessor's sentence it would be extremely dangerous to discard Anne after all that had been done in her favour. The Catholics would be as hostile as before, and he would excite the enmity of the Protestants, who would decline to believe in new scruples of conscience. As his advisers urged, therefore, it was necessary for him to make up his mind whether he would have Catherine or Anne for wife; the choice lay with him, but was limited to these two. This was at last made apparent to Henry, and on his decision the fate of Anne depended.

11

FISHER & MORE

Anne and her friends were in serious peril, and she might have succumbed at once had she not regained the help of Cromwell. The secretary had not been much impressed by Gontier's fair words; he was still hostile to France, and saw with apprehension the growing power of the aristocratic party and of his bitter enemy the Duke of Norfolk. Having identified himself so closely with the measures against the Roman Church, he could not but fear that, if its authority were re-established, he would fare very badly at its hands. In order to prevent the possibility of a reaction, he resolved to support Anne; and perhaps it was he who explained to Henry the danger of a second divorce.

The troubles of the Boleyns had been due in a great measure to the influence of the new favourite, whose reign had now lasted nearly six months – for Henry, rather a long time. It occurred to them that their prospects might be improved if the king were under the dominion of a more friendly beauty; and in the hope that he might be fascinated they brought to court Anne's pretty cousin, Margaret Shelton, daughter of the governess of Mary. The scheme may not have been very dignified, but it was eminently successful. On 25 February, little more than three weeks after the ball at which Gontier had seen Anne in despair, Eustache Chapuis wrote: 'The lady who formerly enjoyed the favour of this king does so no longer; she has been succeeded in her office by a first cousin of the concubine, daughter of the new governess of the princess.[1]

The defeat of the imperialist favourite led to renewed agitation among the malcontents, for with the advent of Margaret Shelton disappeared the last hope that by means of female influence a reversal of policy might be obtained. Even during the preceding winter, when it had been found that the fair partisan of Catherine and Mary was not able to make Henry altogether obedient to her will, the members of the opposition had drawn together again, and numerous recruits had swollen their ranks. In the end of December 1534, the only peer north of the Trent who had been favourable to Anne, the Earl of

Northumberland, professed to be deeply offended by the insolence of the Boleyns, and to be ready to join the confederacy against his former love. This was reported to Chapuis by the earl's physician.[2] The conspirators were rather suspicious of Northumberland, whom they knew to be wayward and fickle, and they warned Chapuis to be very careful in dealing with him;[3] but if Anne's enemies were unable to consider him a trustworthy ally, it was at least certain that she could not regard even him as a faithful friend.

More important men now began to communicate with Chapuis. Lord Sandys, the chamberlain of the household, who had retired from court on the plea of sickness, sent a message to the ambassador by his physician to the effect that it would be easy for Charles V to conquer England, and that he himself would willingly rise if the emperor would undertake to support an insurrection.[4] A few weeks later, the Marquis of Exeter protested that he was prepared to shed his heart's blood in the cause of Catherine;[5] and Lord Bray, a wealthy peer who was highly esteemed for his learning and energy, applied to Chapuis for the text of a prophecy that there would be a revolt against the government, and begged for a cipher by means of which some malcontent lords might safely correspond with one another. He also wished to be permitted to speak with Chapuis about these matters. The latter request the ambassador did not think fit to comply with, as it might awaken suspicion, but otherwise he returned a friendly and encouraging answer, asking only that his correspondent would wait for a more convenient season.[6]

In February Mary had fallen seriously ill.[7] After some time the king allowed the queen's physician to attend her, and sent his own physician, Dr Butts, to consult with him.[8] The two doctors did not limit their conversation to medical matters, but very soon began to talk of politics. Dr Butts made no mystery of his opinions. He said that the life of the queen and the princess might be spared if the king fell ill, since he would then listen to reason and understand his errors, but that otherwise they could be saved only by the employment of force. It was well for the king, he added, that the emperor did not know with how little trouble he might make himself master of England.[9]

The aim of the conspirators being to proclaim Mary, Chapuis feared that if the signal for revolt were given she would be put to death; and he had sounded her whether she would be ready to save herself by flight. Finding that she was willing to do whatever might seem to him to be expedient, he decided that if he received the emperor's permission, and if Mary remained at Greenwich, she should be carried off and put on board a light rowing vessel which would carry her to Flanders; but in consequence of her illness this plan had to be abandoned.[10] It happened about this time that several of Anne's adversaries, among them her uncle, Sir Edward Boleyn, were dining with Chapuis; and with them he made an appointment to go on the Saturday following to Lord Darcy, with whom he was anxious to confer about measures for the princess's safety. Much to the disappointment of Chapuis, this engagement could not be fulfilled; and, knowing the watchfulness of Cromwell's spies, he did not venture to go alone. He despatched a confidential agent, however, and to this messenger Darcy said that if civil war were proclaimed he believed Henry would send Catherine and Mary to the Tower, and keep them there as hostages for his own security.[11] Now, Sir William Kingston, captain of the king's guard and constable of the Tower, had entered into correspondence with the conspirators, and had declared himself a devoted adherent of the two ladies. If they were entrusted to him, they would be in no danger whatever.[12] This intelligence, which was confirmed from other quarters, somewhat reassured the ambassador; but as a thoroughgoing adherent of the king might be put in Sir William Kingston's place, Chapuis was still of opinion that Mary ought to be removed from England. In April she was taken to Eltham, and he hoped that it might be possible to have her conveyed from that place to the river below Gravesend. If men were sent in pursuit, they would probably wish her good speed and take care not to overtake her.[13] The chief difficulty would be to get her out of the house, which was strongly guarded by a body of royal servants under the command of Sir John Shelton.[14]

The government, knowing much of what was going on, caused the chief conspirators to be closely watched, and when some of them applied for permission to leave the court it was not granted. Cromwell wished to keep them near, so that they might always be surrounded by spies.[15]

While Anne and her party – thanks to Margaret Shelton – seemed to be recovering their power, they were threatened by a new danger. Early in March, Cromwell caught a severe cold, and was obliged to keep his room for a few days.[16] Impatient at the confinement and wishing to speak with Chapuis, he went out too soon,[17] had a relapse to which he did not pay sufficient attention, and on Monday the 22nd, broke down altogether. He seems to have suffered from inflammation of the lungs. For a fortnight his life was in danger, and for nearly three weeks he could not transact any business.[18] During this time his enemies, the friends of Catherine and Mary, tried to exercise some influence on Henry, and he seemed not unwilling to hear them; but Cromwell recovered, and at once destroyed their hopes. Whoever had dared to speak in favour of the queen and the princess was soundly rated and threatened by the secretary.[19]

Before Cromwell's illness, it had been determined that the form of oath which had been prepared towards the close of the session, and to which the clergy attending convocation had been compelled to subscribe, should be imposed upon all who were suspected of hostility to the new measures.[20] Now another step in the same direction was taken; a proclamation was issued against those who still adhered to the Pope, or who used his name or style in the service of the Church.[21] Strict inquiry was to be made, and offenders were to be severely punished. The secular clergy in general offered little opposition, but there were monks who showed themselves less yielding. The priors of the Carthusian monasteries, men renowned for their ascetic virtue and piety, assembled at the Charterhouse, near London, and protested against the new edict. Cromwell summoned them before him, and as they boldly proclaimed their intention to disobey what they considered an unjust command they were committed to the Tower to await judgement.[22] They were not kept long in suspense. On 29 April they were arraigned at the Guildhall, found guilty, and condemned to the usual punishment of traitors.[23] No mercy was shown to them; on 4 May the three priors and a Brigitin monk from Syon were hanged, cut down alive, disembowelled, beheaded and quartered.[24] The Duke of Richmond, Henry's bastard son, the Duke of Norfolk, Wiltshire, Rochford, Norris, and other courtiers went to Tyburn to witness their death.[25]

By this time the negotiations about the proposed meeting at Calais had been nearly brought to an end. On 5 March, after a stay of five weeks, Gontier had left England to give Francis an account of his mission.[26] On the 25th he came over once more, remaining about a week in England.[27] He took back flattering and promising messages from Henry, to which the admiral of France answered in the same strain. The 23 May was fixed as the day on which the commissioners were to assemble, and Henry looked forward with confidence to the result.[28]

Cromwell was less sanguine, for he knew from the beginning what would be the effect of the execution of men so highly respected as the Carthusian monks. The English Observants, Carthusians and Brigitins were not simply English subjects, they were members of international religious societies which everywhere commanded respect and sympathy. Henry had persecuted those monastic orders which were esteemed by Catholic and Protestant alike, while he favoured the members of confraternities notorious for their sloth, their ignorance, and their immorality. Preachers on the Continent vehemently denounced the cruelty of a king who had caused men like Haughton to be executed, and men like Peyto to be banished. In France the feeling against Henry seems to have become intensely bitter, and the English alliance was most unpopular.[29]

Being certain that in these circumstances the commissioners at Calais would be unable to agree, Cromwell resolved to have nothing to do with their proceedings. He pretended that he was not yet well enough to go, and, as the Boleyns had been restored to favour, Lord Rochford was named in his stead.[30] On 19 and 20 May the English commissioners arrived at Calais, and on the 22nd they were joined by Chabot, with whom were Genoulhiac, master of the horse; Poyet, president of the parliament of Paris; and Bochetel, secretary for finance.[31] What Cromwell had foreseen came to pass. The French would not depart from the conditions proposed through Palamede Gontier, and they are said to have added a clause to the effect that if for any reason, after the conclusion of the treaty, Henry broke off the match, he would forfeit all pensions and arrears due to him by the King of France.[32] On all the points in dispute the admiral was immovable, so that after two sittings Norfolk perceived that no understanding such as Henry desired could be arrived at.

Lord Rochford crossed to Dover, and galloped straight to the court to give an account of the French demands. On his arrival he went at once to his sister, who could scarcely bring herself to believe the news he reported. On the following days she relieved her feelings by saying all the ill she could of Francis and of the French people;[33] and it was observed that whereas Morette had hitherto been invited to all her parties, he was henceforth conspicuously absent.[34]

When he had seen the king, Rochford left for Calais with the same haste with which he had come, taking with him supplementary instructions to Norfolk.[35] They were to prove fruitless. Francis, in consenting to treat with Henry regarding the marriage of Angoulême and Elizabeth, wanted to obtain such a dowry, in ready money, subsidies, or renunciation of pensions, as would make it worth his while to sanction the match without taking into account any hopes the little girl might have of succeeding to the English throne. He wished, too, to refrain from doing anything that would imperil the treaty by which a marriage between the dauphin and the Princess Mary had been arranged. And he not only objected to join Henry in his revolt against the Holy See, but strongly advised that by some kind of submission the English schism should be brought to an end. Henry, on the other hand, desired by the proposed marriage to make sure of the French alliance, and he would not accept any conditions which would render it equally advantageous to Francis to side with Mary and her adherents. He was not inclined to give a large dowry, for his vanity revolted against the idea that his, the great King Henry's, daughter was not by herself a brilliant match for a younger son of the French king.[36] He insisted that Angoulême should be sent over to him, with some idea perhaps that he would then have a hostage for the good behaviour of Francis.[37] And he advanced preposterous claims as to the position the young duke was to occupy in France, should he by right of his wife succeed to the English crown.[38]

The English commissioners in vain strove to overcome the resistance of Chabot and his colleagues. The French no longer stood in urgent need of the English alliance, since it was open to them, if they pleased, by accepting the overtures of Nassau, to come to terms with the emperor. It was Henry who was now in danger of finding himself confronted by a hostile coalition; it was he, the French thought, who ought to be ready to make sacrifices. But this he declined to do, and his commissioners succeeded only in irritating Chabot, who had not forgotten the abuse showered upon him by Henry and Cromwell early in the spring, and who had been further angered by the execution of the Carthusian priors just before the conference at Calais began.[39] The conference having been broken up, Chabot left Calais in a very bad temper on 14 June.[40]

The failure of Norfolk and his colleagues had an unhappy effect on the fate of the prisoners in the Tower. After the victory of Anne in February, they had been kept in somewhat closer confinement, but at first they had not been otherwise molested. When Cromwell recovered from his illness, and active measures were taken against the adherents of the Pope, they suffered from the change. On 30 April, the day after the Charterhouse monks were condemned to die, More was called before some of the royal councillors and warned that if he did not give way he might incur the same penalties as the Carthusians. But his fortitude was not to be shaken; he refused to yield.[41] On 4 May he was again examined, and admonished not to expose himself to the fate of those who had just been led to execution.[42] Subsequently, More, Bishop Fisher, Dr Abel, the former chaplain of Catherine, and Featherstone, Mary's former schoolmaster, were formally called upon to submit within six weeks; otherwise, they would be put upon their trial.[43]

They might still have escaped had not the suspicions of the king been aroused by the resolute tone of the French and by the rashness of the Pope. The French admiral at Calais had persisted in speaking of Princess Mary; Morette assiduously cultivated the goodwill of Chapuis; and Morette's servants talked very freely about the marriage of Mary and the dauphin. Henry began to fear that the proposals made by Count Henry of Nassau, of which Chabot had given him warning, had been secretly accepted by France, and that Francis would try to get possession of Mary in order to make her the dauphin's wife.[44]

The news from Rome was still more disquieting. The papal court had, of course, been informed of the disfavour into which Anne had fallen at the end of 1534, and of the extreme insecurity of her position during the first two months of 1535.[45] Paul III then hoped that Henry, cured of his passion for Anne, would retrace his steps; and the Cardinal of Lorraine, the most influential of all the cardinals of the French faction, promised, as we have seen, to go to England to bring about a reconciliation.[46] There seemed to be little doubt that if the cardinal fulfilled his promise, Henry would submit, as it was inconceivable that he would insult Francis by refusing the mediation of so great a man. The cardinal, however, did not go; his place was taken by Chabot; and when the Pope complained, it was replied that equally good results might be obtained at the meeting at Calais.[47] Paul III greatly doubted this, but he did not doubt that the French and Gregorio da Casale were right in the accounts they gave him of a change in Henry's temper and convictions. The Pope was not aware that there had been a reaction, that Anne was once more triumphant, and that the favourable opportunity had been lost. Believing that Fisher, who had been so leniently treated at the beginning of the year, continued to enjoy the favour of the king, he allowed himself to be persuaded to make the good bishop a cardinal.[48] This was done on 21 May; and Jean du Bellay, Henry's stout friend and advocate, and Girolamo Ghinucci, his former ambassador, were also – at the same consistory – promoted to the dignity of the purple.

As soon as Gregorio da Casale heard of the creation, he strongly protested against it. The Pope began to think that he had made a mistake, but as it was now past remedy, he tried to excuse what he had done, saying he had hoped to please rather than to offend the King of England. Casale, fearing that Henry would suspect him of having advised the nomination of Fisher, and that he might lose his pension,[49] asked that at least the red hat should not be sent to Fisher; but this request seems to have been disregarded.[50] Shortly afterwards the French ambassador, Charles de Denonville, Bishop of Mâcon, received letters about the execution of the Carthusian monks; and when they were read in consistory, they dispelled any illusion which the Pope or the cardinals may still have retained as to Henry's intentions.[51]

Paul III, now seriously alarmed, sent for Denonville, and asked him to beg Francis to intercede for the new cardinal. The ambassador, while promising to write to the king, gave little hope. The imperialists, he said, in order to make Henry suspicious of the good faith of Francis, were pretending that the honour had been granted on the recommendation of the French. If Francis pleaded for Fisher, Henry would probably believe what the imperial agents asserted, and resent his intervention.[52] Paul III was greatly distressed, and once more protested that he had not intended to displease King Henry. He was ready, he declared, to give a written attestation that he had never been asked by any prince to confer the cardinal's hat on the Bishop of Rochester.[53]

The Bishop of Mâcon wrote to his master and to Cardinal du Bellay; and Nicolas Raince, the French permanent secretary, also wrote at the urgent request of the Pope.[54] Moreover, in two letters addressed to du Bellay, Gregorio da Casale proposed that Fisher should promise, if his life were spared, to swear to the statutes in order to be allowed to go to Rome to receive the red hat. This would be very advantageous to Henry, who would be glad to get rid of his opponent.[55] Casale did not say that the scheme had been approved of by the Pope, but he had no doubt that Paul III would absolve Fisher from any sin he might commit in taking the oath.

It is most unlikely that Fisher would ever have condescended to save his life by a subterfuge such as Casale suggested; he was not the man to forswear himself, even if he had the secret permission of the Pope to do so. But he does not appear to have been put to the test. On receiving the letters of Denonville, Francis asked Henry to spare Fisher's life, and, if Cardinal du Bellay is to be trusted, Henry answered that the request should be granted;[56] but, whatever promise the king may have made, he had no mind to fulfil it. He was in an angry and suspicious mood. Not only had the Pope dared to confer a high dignity on a rebellious subject of his, but Jean du Bellay, who had seemed to be almost a Protestant, and whom he had always expected to help him in inciting Francis to open rebellion against the papacy, had accepted the red hat. Henry regarded such conduct as little short of treason.[57]

Besides, Gregorio da Casale had written to Cromwell that it was the French who, after the execution of the Carthusians, had spoken most passionately of Henry's cruelty. This confirmed Henry in his belief that he was betrayed by Francis, and that a great league had been formed against him. He felt like an animal at bay, and as he could not touch the Pope, or the King of France, or the Bishop of Paris, he resolved to wreak his vengeance on the prisoners in the Tower.

Henry felt convinced that Fisher had corresponded with the Pope, and that his promotion was a part of some vast scheme of the opposition. He considered the bishop his greatest enemy, and believed him to be far more dangerous than in any circumstances he could have been.[58] When the news of Fisher's elevation had arrived, Henry had broken out into violent threats, and had immediately sent a commission to the Tower to find whether the honour had been asked for. The cardinal asserted that the Pope had acted of his own free will, but this did not satisfy the king. Several of the jailers and some friends and kinsmen of Fisher were arrested on a charge of having served as his messengers, and were closely examined. Of course, nothing to their disadvantage was proved, but still the king was not mollified.[59]

On the 14th a royal commission again examined Fisher and More, and demanded that they should accept the Acts of Succession and of Supremacy.[60] Both refused to make any statement. Thereupon an indictment was prepared against the cardinal, and on 17 June he was brought to trial at Westminster.[61] His rights as a peer were disregarded, the government holding that by the Act of Attainder passed in the autumn of 1534, he had been deprived of his see and of the honour attached to it. A common jury it was easy to pack and easy to frighten, so a sentence for the Crown was obtained, and five days later Fisher was led to execution on Tower Hill.[62] The extreme penalty of treason had been commuted into simple decapitation, and even on the scaffold a pardon was offered to him if he would submit.[63] He remained firm, spoke a few words to the assembled crowd, laid his head on the block, and received the stroke of the axe. The king had ordered one of the preachers of the modern school to be his confessor, and even this man, prejudiced as he must have been against Fisher, was loud in praise of his goodness and sanctity.[64]

Meanwhile, Anne did her best to divert Henry's attention from his embarrassments. She organised splendid balls and mummeries, and by cleverly playing, now on his obstinacy, now on his vanity and love of show, she established her old empire over his vacillating mind.[65] It was not, therefore, difficult for the Boleyn party to persuade him that Sir Thomas More should also be brought to trial. On 26 June a true bill was found against Sir Thomas by the grand jury for Middlesex, and on 1 July he was led to Westminster Hall to be tried before a special commission.[66] He offered an eloquent defence, but it could not have any influence on the jury; he was found guilty, and sentenced to receive the punishment of a traitor. A few days later he was executed, maintaining to the last the quaint humour, the delicate tenderness, the stainless honour, which, with his fine intellectual genius, make him one of the noblest and most attractive figures in English history.

With this last and most illustrious victim Henry's cruelties, for the moment, came to an end. It soon became apparent that the executions would not have the effect which he had desired and expected. More and Fisher enjoyed so high a fame for piety, virtue and learning that their death roused a storm of indignation. In England, indeed, most people were afraid to say what they thought, but abroad Henry was loudly and universally condemned. Francis I spoke very strongly to Sir John Wallop, the English ambassador, and he might have spoken more strongly still had he not known that Wallop was at heart deeply displeased.[67] The French ministers expressed themselves with even greater freedom than their master.[68]

At Rome the French cardinals no longer opposed the publication of the sentence against Henry. Even Cardinal du Bellay ceased to defend him, and sought only to exonerate Francis from blame for the relations that had hitherto been maintained between France and England.[69] Consistories and congregations met, therefore, to prepare a bull of deprivation and excommunication; and decisive measures would have been taken had not the imperial agents at the papal court suddenly realised that there were formidable obstacles in the way. They sent a long memoir to the emperor setting forth their difficulties, and asking what they were to do.

The Pope and the cardinals, they said, shocked by the execution of the Cardinal of Rochester, wished to deprive Henry of his throne for the crimes of heresy and *lesæ majestatis*, England being still reputed at Rome to be held in fief of the Holy See. But if this were done, the kingdom would revert to the Pope as feudal overlord, and Princess Mary would lose her rights. The deprivation might, indeed, be made in favour of Mary, but such an arrangement could not be kept secret; the new cardinals would divulge it; and Henry might treat the princess as he had treated Cardinal Fisher. Upon the whole, it seemed best that the Pope should deprive Henry without saying in whose favour he acted; and then the imperial agents might appear for Catherine and Mary, and claim the vacant throne for the latter. But as every conceivable plan would be attended with danger, they did not dare to come to a final resolution without further instructions.[70]

The result of all this was that the bull of deprivation was not issued. But the indignation against the King of England remained as strong as ever, and the only question now was whether the Pope was likely to find a secular prince able and willing to carry out his sentence.

Henry was regarded with hardly less hostility by the majority of foreign Protestants than by Roman Catholics. There had always been a radical distinction between the English and the Continental reformation. The German theologians who broke away from Rome, admitting no authority but that of the Scripture, could not favour a theory of royal supremacy, which if generally acknowledged would have set up, instead of one pope, hundreds of popes.[71] They disliked Henry's proceedings, and feared that he would permanently discredit their cause. For political reasons he had favoured Wullenwever, who was strongly suspected of Protestant heterodoxy; and there is reason to think that he was at least very near entering into negotiations with the Anabaptists at Muenster, who pleased him by giving constant trouble to Mary of Hungary, the regent of the Low Countries.[72] Henry knew how much he was distrusted by moderate Protestants; and, to vindicate his character, he had caused a number of Anabaptists, who had fled from Holland to England, to be arrested in May, and to be brought before a commission. Fourteen of them had refused to retract, and had been burned as heretics.[73] This did not conciliate the German reformers, who continued to suspect Henry of being friendly to John of Leyden.

The execution of Fisher and More widened the breach between Henry and the Lutherans. Both men had been firm opponents of English Protestantism, but they had also been personal friends of the foremost Humanists; and they themselves had been among the principal representatives in England of the new learning, on which the German reformation was chiefly based. Like Luther, Fisher maintained the validity of Catherine's marriage, not because he believed in the power of the Pope to dispense from a prescription in the Bible, but because he held that there was no prescription of the kind to be found in the Bible;[74] and in matters about which public opinion was divided this was by no means the only important point on which they agreed. Fisher, therefore, was respected by Luther's followers, while for Sir Thomas More they had the strongest admiration; and the tidings that two such men had been beheaded filled them with astonishment and horror.[75]

Seeing how violent a commotion he had produced, Henry became anxious to justify himself for what he had done. Several memorials were drawn up in defence of his conduct, and in one of them, which was evidently intended for the Roman Catholics, especially for the French, the following passage occurs:

First, to assaye the mind of the most Christian majesty (oh, subtle craft!) concerning the deliverance of the late bishop of Rochester being in the ende for his unfeigned deserving condemned of treason, whom they after his death (and God's will), to excite the hatred of all cardinals, name a cardinal, he [the Pope] does say that the labour of the most Christian majesty interposed with his brother the most noble king of England, was contemned, set at nought, and mocked; where indeed no such labour was made. And yet that holy see not content with that lie makes another open lie and most falsely brings in that the intercession of the most Christian majesty has caused the said Rochester to die the rather. In this matter I call to record the conscience of the most Christian majesty, which, forsomuch as he never inter... with his friend in this cause (of whom he knows he may obtain anything that he desires) not only does see most manifestly now their lies, but also (such is his prudence) he has plainly declared that he hates all treason and inobedience, in so much that he thought that there should be given no place to... neither prayer in such case for the maintenance of the commonwealth in his estate.

Especial credit is taken for the manner in which Fisher was put to death:

> He was not killed with poison, which thing some men do use, he was not sodden in lead as the solemn use is in certain places, he was not hanged in a halter, what best agrees for a traitor, he was not burnt, he was not put to death with lingering torments, but lost his life with a sudden stroke of a sworde the which sort of death in such bitterness is most easy.[76]

This memorial was conceived with much skill, for Francis could not afford to say that he had in vain interfered for Fisher. That would detract from his reputation by showing that he had little influence in England. On the other hand, by remaining silent, he would seem to admit that he had approved of Fisher's execution, since it would be said that if he had not approved of it, he – Henry's greatest friend – would surely have tried to prevent it. The dilemma was a most unpleasant one, and Francis was indignant with Henry for forcing it upon him.

Another memorial, which seems to have been drawn up somewhat later, was intended to allay the indignation of the German Protestants; and in this production, which is in Latin, a virulent attack is made on the character of the dead men. 'As you write', the paper begins:

> that everywhere in Germany the king is believed to have punished More and Rochester for no other cause than that they sincerely adhered to evangelical doctrine and persistently opposed the king's marriage, we wonder who can be the author of this idle tale.[77]

The king's beneficence, equity, piety and mildness were so well known to the world that his reputation for these qualities could not be easily undermined by calumny.[78] With what exquisite kindness he had treated King James of Scotland, not holding him responsible for the atrocious misdeeds of his father! What generosity he had shown to Francis I, to whom, out of pure goodness, he had lent 800,000 crowns towards his ransom! The king never prevented the gospel from being preached if it were preached truly and honestly. Why, then, this impudent calumny that More and Rochester were punished because they sincerely adhered to evangelical doctrine and opposed the king's marriage? No one had been more willing than they to swear to the Acts by which the crown was settled on the offspring of Henry and Anne; and More, in his dialogues against Luther, had contended that marriages prohibited in Leviticus are not permitted to Christians. As for what was said about their defence of the gospel, the writer wondered whether any German believed that the gospel had ever had enemies more mischievous than these two.[79] Rochester and More had both written books in which they had bitterly assailed the best leaders of the sect; and in a letter to Erasmus, More had openly stated that he would be a constant enemy of heretics, for so he called those who wanted a purer doctrine. And so he had shown himself.[80] 'It makes one ashamed,' says this virtuous scribe, 'to recall what tortures he invented and inflicted upon those whom he perceived to be inclined to evangelical truth.' He caused search to be made in all quarters for heretics, offering great rewards for evidence against them; and when they were brought before him, he never committed them to prison 'until he had seen them tortured in a pitiable manner before his eyes'. That More was 'of a cruel and fierce temper' might be judged from this fact, that those whom he caught 'he was in the habit of torturing by a new method invented by himself'. He immediately caused new shoes to be put upon persons brought before him; then the victims were tied to stakes, and the soles of their feet were brought close to a blazing fire, that, to those who would not confess, the pain – .[81] Here, unhappily, a sheet of the manuscript has been lost. The document closes with a prayer that all princes may be able to imitate Henry's immense goodness of heart.[82] These accusations against More have been repeated by some later writers; but there is not a tittle of evidence that he was guilty of the cruelties imputed to him. Such charges conflict with all that we know of his character and his modes of thought; and to his contemporaries they were absolutely incredible. Henry gained nothing by the attempt to tarnish the fame of one whose virtues were so widely known and so cordially appreciated.

12

THE COLLAPSE OF THE
NORTHERN ALLIANCE

Scarcely had the blood of More dried on Tower Hill when bad news arrived from every quarter. Besides the ill feeling which the execution of two such men as Fisher and More had produced, political events were everywhere unfavourable to Henry. He was especially disappointed by the course of the war in the north, from which he had expected such great results. Duke Christian, reinforced by troops of the Landgrave, had taken the bold course of attacking Luebeck on its own ground; and Marcus Meyer had been thoroughly beaten. Cut off from the sea, the town had been forced, on 18 November 1534, to sign a treaty by which the war was to be confined to Denmark. This was of considerable advantage to the duke, who had no longer to fear for his patrimonial estates, and could employ the whole of his forces in reconquering Jutland and in opposing Count Christopher. In his difficulties Wullenwever had written to Cromwell, offering a league on better conditions, and Henry had despatched Christopher Mores to reside as ambassador in Denmark and Luebeck.[1] Mores, soon after his arrival at Hamburg, heard of the treaty with Christian, but if he came too late to be of use, his journey did not the less exasperate the German princes.

Two parties were now striving for supremacy in Denmark. Duke Christian was backed by his brothers-in-law, Gustavus Vasa, King of Sweden, and Albert, lately Master, now first Duke of Prussia. The Landgrave, the Duke of Lueneburg, and many other German Protestant princes were favourable to him, and the majority of the Danish nobility and clergy were on his side. Luebeck had as allies Count Christopher of Oldenburg, Count John of Hoya, a brother-in-law of the King of Sweden, whom the latter had deeply offended, Hoya's brother Count Eric, a certain Bernhardt von Melen, who had married a cousin of Gustavus Vasa and had also become a mortal enemy of the king, a Count of Tecklenburg, and a few of the Holstein nobles. The towns of Rostock, Wismar and Stralsund were as eager in the fray as Luebeck itself. Duke Albert of Mecklenburg, who had married a niece of King

Christian II, and the Master of Livonia were decidedly favourable to the town, while the Elector of Saxony maintained a benevolent neutrality. The peasants of Ditmarschen assisted the Luebeckers with money, and took up a threatening position on the frontiers of Holstein. In Denmark itself Luebeck could reckon on the assistance of the democratic elements, not in the towns only, but even among the peasants. In Jutland the peasantry rose at the call of a partisan of Christian II, and in a bloody battle at Svendstrup overthrew the levies of the duke and the nobility.

The two parties would have been pretty equally matched had it not been for the fact that the adherents of Duke Christian were all of one mind, desiring simply to place the duke on the Danish throne, while the adherents of Luebeck were pulling in different directions. Count Christopher had already begun to pursue an independent course, having obliged the estates of Seeland and Skonen to take an oath of fealty to him as governor of the kingdom; and this had created considerable jealousy. The intrigues of Wullenwever increased the mutual distrust. He was negotiating with three different pretenders, and the fear of offending any of the three, and of giving too much power to Count Christopher, paralysed the action of the town.

While the two parties were confronting each other in this way, Duke Christian obtained a copy of the treaty of alliance which had been proposed between Luebeck and the King of England. To find out whether the treaty had been actually signed, and, if possible, to detach Henry from the alliance with Wullenwever, he sent Peter Schwaben or Suavenius, one of his most trusty counsellors, as ambassador to England and Scotland. The instructions to Schwaben, written in Latin, and dated from Gottorp, 20 January 1535,[2] contain only a lengthy account of the facts of Christian's case and a request that Henry will not favour the Luebeckers. But it is clear from Schwaben's negotiations that he had secret instructions to offer considerable advantages to Henry for the English alliance. He seems to have been authorised to promise nearly as much help as the Luebeckers were to bind themselves by treaty to give.[3] There was this difference between Duke Christian and the Luebeckers, that the former was perfectly able to perform his promise and was a man whose word could be trusted, while the latter found it extremely difficult to levy troops, and each faction in the town was ever ready to repudiate the engagements entered into by its adversaries. Besides, by aiding the duke, Henry would have gained the friendship of his allies, especially of the Hanseatic towns on the German Ocean. Luebeck would have been forsaken by most of its confederates, and would not have been able to do the English king any great harm.

Had Henry been the wise and well-informed king he pretended to be, he would have welcomed Christian's ambassador cordially; for here was an opportunity of forming that great northern Protestant confederacy of which he had so often dreamt. In close alliance with Gustavus Vasa of Sweden and Christian of Sleswick-Holstein, Denmark, Skonen and Norway, enjoying the friendship of the Landgrave, the dukes of Lueneburg, of Pomerania, and of Prussia, he would have been a really powerful king, and might have made himself independent of Francis and well able to hold his own against the emperor. But he was neither wise nor well informed. He listened eagerly to the coloured reports and interested advice of men like Marcus Meyer, Dr Pack, and Count Eric of Hoya, who had come over to treat with him.[4] It did not occur to him that if the Luebeckers were as powerful as they said they were, they would not for the loan of 20,000 florins become his dependants. Everything they told him he believed; and he promised and acted accordingly.

When Schwaben arrived at Hampton Court on 28 February, Cromwell received him civilly, listened to his representations, denied that any treaty had been actually signed with the Luebeckers, and promised a speedy reply.[5] But when on the following day Schwaben was ushered into Henry's presence, he was treated less politely. The king would not hear him, but began a long discourse, speaking of the Luebeckers as 'our very dear and honoured friends'. He said Christian had no right whatever to rule Denmark, the throne of which was elective. The election rested with the people, not with the council; and even of the council Christian had but a small part with him. 'Why,' asked Henry, 'should not I accept the kingdom of Denmark, which has been offered to me?' As to the King of Sweden and Count Christopher, they would soon rue the day they had taken part against Luebeck. The people of that town were very powerful, they had placed Frederic I on his throne, and they would be victorious again. 'You see.' he triumphantly exclaimed, 'I too know something of these matters.' He continued for some time in this strain, and the ambassador was not even permitted to explain his mission. Schwaben handed in, in writing, the substance of what he had to say; merely informing the king that the Luebeckers had been routed in Skonen and that Marcus Meyer had been killed. Henry laughed at this, and Cromwell also showed himself less friendly than he had been the day before. Schwaben was referred for an answer to the council, and so dismissed.[6]

After this he was kept waiting for many weeks. It seems that Cromwell, who did not quite share his master's confidence in the ultimate success of Luebeck, wished to keep the negotiation open to see what course events would take. But at last Schwaben was sent away with scant courtesy and with an indecisive reply.[7]

Schwaben had been correctly informed as to the overthrow of the Luebeckers in Skonen; but Marcus Meyer, who had commanded the troops of the town, had only been made prisoner. He was taken to the strong castle of Warberg on the western coast of Skonen, where he was treated with due honour; and, as might have been anticipated, he took advantage of the comparative liberty accorded to him to conspire with the town people who were in favour of Luebeck. The result was that on the night of 11 March his friends surprised the castle, and made him its commander. But instead of handing it over to the Luebeckers, Meyer behaved at Warberg like an independent prince.[8] A message was sent to Christopher Mores, who was at Copenhagen; and when Mores went to Warberg on 26 May, Meyer asked whether Henry would not help him to hold out and to retrieve all he had lost.[9]

Henry was not at first very much inclined to assist Meyer. He had seen that Peter Schwaben, whom he had received so badly, had, in the main, given him accurate intelligence. Duke Christian had regained the whole of Jutland; and in the middle of February his captain-general, John von Rantzau, was able to elude the vigilance of the Luebeck fleet, which cruised in the Belt, and to land a strong force in the island of Funen. They seized the coast opposite Jutland, where the Belt is so narrow that the German ships could not prevent communication between the two shores. More troops followed, and shortly afterwards the greater part of the island was in the hands of Rantzau. Nor did matters look more hopeful in Skonen. Marcus Meyer, unable to follow up his success, was soon besieged at Warberg, and the entire kingdom, with the exception of a few fortified towns, was occupied by the joint forces of Duke Christian and the King of Sweden.[10]

Besides, Henry had now recognised that Christian was backed by the great majority of the German Protestants, whose goodwill he was anxious, if possible, to retain. He became, therefore, somewhat cooler in his zeal for Luebeck, Wullenwever, and Meyer, and began to think that he might act as mediator between the contending parties, who were endangering the cause of Protestantism by their political strife. By this means he hoped to earn their gratitude, and to obtain an opportunity of forming a powerful league of which he would be the natural chief. Two embassies were to set out – the one to be composed of Dr Edward Fox, bishop elect of Hereford, Dr Nicolas Heath, and Robert Barnes, a personal friend of the Wittenberg divines; the other of Dr Edmund Bonner, Richard Cavendish, and Dr Adam Pack. The former embassy was to treat with the Elector of Saxony and other German princes;[11]

the latter was to go to Luebeck, Denmark, and Holstein to mediate between the belligerents.[12]

But while the ambassadors designate were waiting for their instructions, events on the continent proceeded at a very rapid pace. On 11 June, Count John von Hoya marched out at the head of a considerable force to surprise John von Rantzau in his positions near Assens, in the island of Funen. Rantzau, hearing of the movements of Hoya, advanced against him, and gained a great victory at Oxnebjerg; Hoya himself, with Count Tecklenburg and many officers of note, being killed, while most of his troops either shared his fate or were made prisoners.

On the same day on which Hoya was routed there was a naval battle near Bornholm. The Hanseatic fleet had been divided; one part of it, near the island of Funen, hampering the progress of Rantzau, another part, near Bornholm, watching the movements of the Swedish admiral Peter Skram. Skram was in command of a numerous fleet of Swedish and Prussian ships, to which a few Dutch and Danish vessels had been added. He kept his forces well together, and on 11 June attacked the Hanseatic squadron off Bornholm. The issue of the battle was doubtful; but the Hanseatic admiral, knowing that Skram would soon be reinforced, retreated towards Copenhagen, where he expected to find the rest of his fleet. Skram, being better informed, did not pursue his adversary, but sailed towards Funen. There, near Svendborg, on the 16th, he attacked the other German squadron, took nine of its best ships, and sunk one vessel. Only a few of the German vessels made their escape.

By these battles, fought within a few days of one another, Luebeck lost its preponderance both on land and on sea, and the campaign was virtually decided. Shortly afterwards Duke Christian crossed the Great Belt, and landed in Seeland. Copenhagen was too strong to be stormed, but Duke Albert of Mecklenburg and Count Christopher were shut up in it, and the open country remained in Christian's hands.[13]

Henry must have heard at the end of June or in the beginning of July of the misfortunes of his friends. Doctor Pack tried to represent matters in as favourable a light as possible; and as the king received messages from Meyer, from Duke Albert, from Count Christopher, who now offered very favourable conditions, and from Wullenwever, he did not attach great importance to the lost battles.[14]

But there was another matter which caused him much anxiety. Hitherto Francis had rather favoured the religious dissensions in Germany; up to the summer of 1534 he had certainly not made any serious attempt to heal the schism. The league of Schmalkalden he had encouraged, and he had paid large subsidies to Philip of Hesse and to the dukes of Bavaria. He hoped that in return for this aid they would stand by him in time of need, furnish him with landsknechts, prevent Ferdinand from giving help to his brother, the emperor, and threaten the Low Countries from the south and east. By the treaty of Cadan, and by the events which followed it, Francis was taught that he could not rely on his German allies. After the conclusion of that treaty Ferdinand adopted a friendly tone towards the princes of the Schmalkaldic league, and showed that he intended to work for Rome in a temperate and conciliatory spirit.[15] The Protestants, being anxious not to endanger the concessions they had already obtained, responded with pleasure to his advances. The new Elector of Saxony proposed to visit Ferdinand at Vienna, and there was even some talk of a marriage between the eldest son of the landgrave and a daughter of the emperor.

To Francis all this was most distasteful; for if Ferdinand succeeded, he would earn the thanks of Rome, and make for himself a great reputation; and even if he failed, he would for a time possess considerable influence at Schmalkalden, at Zuerich, and at Rome, while Francis would lose his best allies. There remained but one way out of the difficulty: to beat Ferdinand on the ground he had chosen, to outdo him in his efforts to conquer heresy by kindness. For the first time since the outbreak of Luther's rebellion Francis really bestirred himself to bring the schism to an end. In the autumn of 1534 Guillaume du Bellay and Gervasius Wein were in constant communication with the Protestant theologians; and Philip Melanchthon drew up a list of articles in which he went so far as to acknowledge the primacy of the Pope. These articles were declared by the Bishop of Paris, at whose request they were prepared, to be quite acceptable.[16] The Pope himself manifested a desire to meet the German reformers half way, and at the time of Clement's death there seemed to be a fair chance of an agreement.[17]

As soon as the new pope was installed, the matter was taken up again. Paul III was as anxious to arrive at an understanding as his predecessor had been, and in the summer of 1535 the prospect appeared so bright that Francis wrote to Melanchthon, inviting him to visit France to discuss further the basis for a settlement.[18] Cardinal du Bellay and his brother strongly urged Melanchthon to accept the invitation, and the reformer was eager to undertake the journey.[19] The only thing wanted was the permission of the Elector of Saxony, the prince whom Melanchthon served; and Francis wrote to John Frederic, asking him to give the necessary leave.[20]

Henry became very uneasy when he heard of these negotiations. If the German Protestants were reconciled to the Pope, the other northern states would follow their example. England would then remain alone in its schism, and with a disaffected people and hostile neighbours,

Henry would be unable to hold out. It was, therefore, of the highest importance to him that both Francis and Ferdinand should fail; only by the maintenance of religious dissension could he hope to find allies against Charles and Paul III.

In the beginning of July, Henry decided to send Robert Barnes to Saxony, to counteract the efforts of Francis.[21] Shortly afterwards a letter was received from Sir John Wallop, announcing that Melanchthon was expected at the French court. Thereupon Barnes was ordered to depart with all speed to dissuade the great theologian from visiting a country where Protestants had just been cruelly martyred, and to invite him rather to go to England, where he would be sure of a good reception. At the same time Christopher Mundt, a German in the pay of Henry, and Simon Heynes, an English clergyman, were sent to the French court to watch the proceedings of Francis, and – in case Melanchthon went to France – to prevent him from effecting a reconciliation with the Holy See.[22]

The French were so provoked by Henry's opposition that he ought to have acted with the greatest caution; but this he was incapable of doing. Christopher Mores had returned from Denmark, and with him had come Gerhard Meyer, the brother of Henry's favourite, Sir Marcus. Gerhard Meyer had asked Henry to assist his brother with men and money, and Mores had reported on what he had seen at Warberg. For the moment the king did not grant Gerhard's request, but while Bonner and Cavendish were waiting for a fair wind to start, Dietrich Hagenow, a captain, arrived with important despatches from Meyer. Meyer offered not only to hand over to officers of King Henry the castle and town of Warberg, but to obtain for him the towns and castles of Malmoe, Landskron, Copenhagen, and Elsinore.[23]

This offer appeared so brilliant that Henry could not resist the temptation to accept it. He thought that with Warberg and the four towns in his possession he might indeed become the absolute umpire in the quarrels between the northern powers, and establish the much-talked-of confederacy. Gerhard Meyer was sent back to his brother with a most favourable message, and shortly afterwards two royal ships were fitted out to sail to Warberg. Between them they were to carry only 100 English soldiers under Mores and Hagenow, but they were to convey to Meyer a large supply of cannon, powder and shot, hackbuts, pikes, and other munitions of war. Best of all, a considerable sum of money was to be taken over to Warberg, where Bonner and Cavendish were to go to confer with Meyer.[24]

But before the ships could start, the government received from the captains of some English vessels a message which entirely altered the case. Of the English merchantmen which, in the spring of 1535, had

sailed for the Baltic, a few had already, on their outward voyage, been
seized by the Duke of Mecklenburg in the Sound and at Copenhagen.[25]
Twelve others, which had gone to Dantzig, fell in with a part of Admiral
Skram's fleet on their way home. They were stopped and boarded by
the Swedes, who treated them as enemies, and took them to Swedish
harbours.[26]

The expedition to Warberg now seemed rather hazardous
Peter Skram might waylay the royal ships, as he had waylaid the
merchantmen in the Baltic, and not only would ships, stores, and
money be lost, but clear proof would be obtained of Henry's duplicity.
Being thus deprived of an agreeable illusion, Henry violently abused
Hagenow, and ordered the soldiers to be dismissed and the ships to
be taken back to the Thames.[27] Poor Marcus Meyer was left vainly
to hope for succour. All he received was a visit from Bonner and
Cavendish, who apparently gave him some money, and exhorted his
men to remain true to him, and to reckon on the help of King Henry.[28]

About the same time that Peter Skram's inconvenient proceedings
were reported at the English court, other intelligence of even worse
import came from Hamburg. Robert Barnes had arrived there in the
beginning of August, and had intended to hold a disputation with the
divines of the place, who, headed by the famous Aëpinus, condemned
the divorce.[29] While he was preparing to defend his master's cause,
he received new and pressing orders to proceed to Wittenberg to
confer with Melanchthon; and although he was very unwilling to go
– for Wittenberg was said to be ravaged by the plague[30] – he was, of
course, obliged to obey. Before starting, he heard that on 21 August
a sitting of the council at Luebeck had led to the total overthrow of
the party of Wullenwever. Wullenwever, indeed, had been allowed to
retain the post of first burgomaster of the town, but his friends had
been compelled to leave the council. Five days later, his position having
become entirely untenable, he resigned his office, and accepted in its
stead the administration of a small outlying part of Luebeck territory.
The mighty tribune of the north, the great ally of King Henry, had
fallen from his high estate, and had been forced to make way for his
rival and enemy, his predecessor Broemse.[31]

But even now Henry did not come to the end of the troubles in which
he had involved himself by association with Meyer and Wullenwever.
Wullenwever was too ambitious not to regret the loss of his power, and
the presence of Bonner and Cavendish at Hamburg with a considerable
sum of money inspired him with a hope that he might mend his
broken fortunes. He secretly left his new home, and presenting himself
before the English ambassadors suggested the following plan. During
the last few months some 4,000–5,000 landsknechts, commanded by

This page and next page top: 1, 3 & 4. At court, Anne captured everyone's imagination. Although not beautiful by Tudor standards, her sexiness, intellect, deportment and French manners were irresistible. Possessing 'the graces of nature graced by gracious education' and 'well dressed, and every day made some changes in the fashion of her garments', she was described as 'rather tall of stature', or 'of middling stature'; 'very beautiful', or 'beautiful and with an elegant figure', she was 'eloquent and graceful … really handsome'. But, she had a 'projecting tooth under the upper lip', and 'there was found indeed, upon the side of her nail upon one of her fingers, some show of a nail', yet her defects were probably just 'certain small moles incident to the clearest of complexions'.

Below: 5. Thomas Boleyn was a favourite courtier, capable and respected diplomatist and excellent sportsman. He was highly intelligent, proficient in many languages, and keen to offer his son and daughters the best education available. Anne Boleyn resembled her father in many ways, including a sharp wit and a natural affinity for court life., as well as in looks: the two shared a slim face and pointed chin.

Bottom: 6. Blickling Hall, Norfolk: Little remains of the original building in which Anne Boleyn was born. Fragments of the house she would have known are contained within the renovations carried out during the seventeenth century.

Above left: 7. The Howard coat of arms, Framlington Castle, Suffolk: During the fifteenth century the Boleyn family rose from the merchant classes through diligent hard work and prestigious marriages. Anne's father, Thomas Boleyn, continued this trend, marrying the daughter of Thomas Howard, 2nd Duke of Norfolk.

Above right: 8. Thomas Howard, 3rd Duke of Norfolk: The Howard family, under a cloud due to their support of Richard III, gradually returned to favour under the new Tudor régime. Norfolk helped advance the interests of his brother-in-law, Thomas Boleyn, but his selfish ambition would prove fatal to two of his nieces, Anne Boleyn and Catherine Howard.

Right and next page centre and bottom: 9, 11 & 12. Hever Castle, Kent: Anne was very young when her father inherited Hever Castle, which became the family home; it is the residence most associated with Anne Boleyn.

Below: 10. Great Tournament Roll of Westminster: Henry jousts in celebration of the birth of his son, Henry, by Catherine of Aragon. Within a month the child would be dead. This was to be one of several disappointments the king and queen faced in their desire to produce an heir. Despite the love they once shared, Henry's need for a son would tear the royal couple apart.

Right: 13. Henry VIII at the height of his physical power and beauty. He had an affair with Anne's sister, who bore two children at this time, almost certainly Henry's. Her childbearing success was perhaps a factor in Henry's choice of Anne, as one of Mary's children was a boy.
Below left: 14. Mary Boleyn's relationship with Henry placed him and Anne within a forbidden degree of affinity. He used this against Anne during the divorce, to bastardise her daughter, smoothing the path of succession for his children with Jane Seymour.
Below right: 15. Thomas Wyatt fell under Anne's spell; her spirit lives on in some of his poems. Some spoke of a torrid affair but, whatever the truth, Wyatt had to step aside when Anne attracted Henry's attention.

This page: 16, 17 & 18. Henry's courtship of Anne took place against the beautiful backdrop of Hever Castle in Kent. Henry showered Anne with letters and gifts as he tried to woo her and asked her to become his mistress. Anne refused to give in to Henry unless he promised her marriage and the crown.

Opposite top: 19. Catherine of Aragon was the daughter of Ferdinand of Aragon and Isabella of Castile. She was an intelligent woman, groomed for queenship from a very early age. Despite the love they once shared, Henry's desperate need for a son would tear the royal couple apart. After being married for some twenty years, Catherine was sent away from court to make way for Anne Boleyn.

KATHERINA VXOR HENRICI . . VIII.

Below: 20. A romantic representation of the trial, before the legatine court at Blackfriars, of the validity of the marriage of Henry VIII and Catherine of Aragon; here, the queen offers a passionate defence.

Bottom: 21. A wood carving depicting Cardinal Lorenzo Campeggio (left) and Cardinal Thomas Wolsey (right) urging Catherine of Aragon to comply with the demands that she recognise the invalidity of her marriage, and free Henry to take another wife.

Above: 22. Windsor Castle provided the setting for a tragic scene: Catherine of Aragon looked upon her beloved Henry for the last time before being sent away from court for ever.

Left: 23. Charles V, the Holy Roman Emperor, was the nephew of Catherine of Aragon. He championed her cause throughout Henry's attempts to divorce her, even threatening to invade England to bring Henry to heel.

Right: 24. As this letter from Anne Boleyn to Thomas Wolsey shows, Anne took an active interest in the process of Henry's divorce from Catherine of Aragon. At this point, Anne still believes Wolsey can assist her and Henry as he seeks to resolve the great matter. *Below left*: 25. When it became clear that Cardinal Thomas Wolsey would not secure the divorce between Henry and Catherine, Anne sought to engineer his downfall. *Below right*: 26. Thomas Cranmer was a former chaplain to the Boleyn family, and he shared their reformist views. He was appointed Archbishop of Canterbury following the death of William Warham.

Above left: 27. Archbishop William Warham was a staunch opponent of the divorce. Old and frail, his efforts to thwart his king proved too much. When he died, his office was given to the reformer, Thomas Cranmer.

Above right: 28. Archbishop Thomas Cranmer assures Henry that his 'grete matter' will be successfully resolved.

Opposite bottom: 29. Calais had long been English territory. In a summit here between the two kings, Henry was anxious to secure Francis's support in divorcing Catherine.

Above: 30. Whitehall Palace, originally known as York Place, was the official seat of the Archbishops of York. It came to Henry following the downfall of Cardinal Wolsey. Henry gave it to Anne, who liked the palace because it had no rooms for Queen Catherine.

Below left: 31. Francis I of France was not always the most reliable of allies, but with meetings between the two kings at Boulogne and Calais having been crowned by professions of friendship and the confirmation of an alliance between England and France, Henry and Anne felt, at last, that it was safe to consummate their relationship.

Below right: 32. Design for a pageant tableau by Holbein: featuring Apollo and the Muses, the tableau was designed for the merchants of the Hanseatic League, who displayed it on the route of Anne's coronation procession.

33. The coronation procession of Anne Boleyn, who was crowned queen on 1 June 1533. Anne was already pregnant by this time and would give birth to a daughter, Elizabeth, three months later.

34. Greenwich Palace: Henry VIII was born in the palace, which had been extensively renovated by his father, Henry VII. It became a favourite residence of Anne Boleyn, who gave birth to her daughter, Elizabeth, here.

35. Hampton Court Palace, once the country home of the fallen Cardinal Wolsey, was one of Anne's residences as queen.

Right: 36. The Papal judgement against Henry VIII: Clement VII found the marriage between Henry VIII and Catherine of Aragon valid. Henry, although ordered to put away Anne and take back Catherine, ignored the pope; he and Anne were married, Anne was his crowned and anointed queen, and their marriage had been blessed by the birth of a daughter, Elizabeth.

Below left: 37. Sir Thomas More was unable to accept Henry as supreme head of the church in England. He was imprisoned in the Tower and, ultimately, executed.

Below right: 38. Margaret Shelton was Anne Boleyn's cousin. When Henry's eye began to wander, it was deemed prudent to offer him a mistress who would, nevertheless, protect the cause of Anne Boleyn, and Margaret was chosen. Margaret Shelton was betrothed to one of Henry's favourite courtiers, Henry Noreys, and also seems to have attracted the attentions of Francis Weston. These two men would be among those charged with adultery with Anne Boleyn and executed.

39. In 1535 Henry and Anne went on summer progress, hunting in the countryside surrounding Wolfhall in Wiltshire. Wolfhall was the seat of the Seymour family, whose daughter, Jane, would become Henry's third wife.

40. Richmond Palace was one of Henry VIII's favourite residences. Anne knew Richmond as a member of the court before marrying him, and it became one of her residences as queen.

41. A romantic representation of Catherine of Aragon's death. She clung to her status as Henry's wife and her title of queen, but to no avail. Within five months, Anne Boleyn, her replacement as Henry's wife and queen, would follow her to the grave.

Right: 42. Jane Seymour: The ambassador Eustache Chapuis, writing to his master, Charles V, made this less than complimentary assessment of Henry's new fancy: 'she is middle height, and nobody thinks that she has much beauty. Her complexion is so whitish that she may be called rather pale. She is a little over twenty-five. You may imagine whether, being an Englishwoman, and having been so long at court, she would not hold it a sin to be still a maid. At which this king will perhaps be rather pleased… for he may marry her on condition that she is a virgin, and when he wants a divorce he will find plenty of witnesses to the contrary.'

Above: 43. The king and his courtiers loved to joust, and it was here, at Greenwich Palace, during the May Day celebrations of 1536, that he and Anne watched one of their favourites, Henry Noreys, show his skill at the sport. That evening, Noreys was arrested on charges of adultery with Anne, and the queen would follow him to the Tower the next day.
Right: 44. Thomas Cromwell, threatened by Anne's influence, engineered her downfall. It was a duel to the death, which Anne had little chance of winning.

45. The tomb of Henry Howard, Earl of Surrey, and his wife: Henry Howard, a gifted poet, was Anne Boleyn's cousin and a great friend of Thomas Wyatt. Howard was one of the judges at the trial of Anne Boleyn and her brother, George, both of whom he would condemn to death.

46. In this romantic representation Anne Boleyn is condemned to death at the end of her trial at the Tower of London.

47. Queen Anne Boleyn was executed on 19 May 1536.

Uevelacker, formerly a captain under Count Christopher, had been living idly in the country between the Weser and the Elbe. Wullenwever proposed to engage these men, and undertook, after re-establishing his authority in Luebeck, to send the greater number of them to assist Duke Albert and to raise the siege of Copenhagen. Bonner and Cavendish were attracted by the scheme, and promised Wullenwever 10,000 florins, about £1,600, of the money they had in their keeping. They seem even to have advanced a part of the sum.[32]

So Juergen Wullenwever, with four of his servants, rode off to meet Uevelacker; and at night he put up at a little inn near Rotenburg. The weather having been raw, he ordered wine, and, continuing to drink, took more than was good either for him or for Henry VIII. He got drunk, and began to brag about his past greatness and his plans for the future. The innkeeper, thinking that all was not right, went out and reported what was going on to Claus Hermelink, a captain of the Archbishop of Bremen. Hermelink was an enemy of Wullenwever, and may have been allured by the money the ex-burgomaster was said to carry; at any rate, he hurried with some of his soldiers to the inn, and seized the drunken man. Next morning Wullenwever found himself a prisoner of Archbishop Christopher of Bremen.[33]

The only piece of good news sent home by the English ambassadors was that Melanchthon was not to go to France. But this was not due to their influence. A letter which Robert Barnes had written to Melanchthon from Hamburg had produced no effect; after receiving it, the German theologian was as eager to go as he had been before.[34] The journey was put off because the elector, John Frederic, refused to sanction it, pretending that he could not spare the services of so great a professor.[35] But it was whispered about that his real reason was that he was afraid of displeasing the emperor and the King of the Romans;[36] and, as this became known in England, the announcement that Melanchthon would not leave home lost a good deal of its value.

On his arrival at Jena on 18 September, Barnes found that the elector was just going to start for Vienna on a friendly visit to the King of the Romans.[37] Barnes received no immediate reply to the message he had brought to John Frederic; all that he could obtain was permission to hold a colloquy with the Wittenberg divines, and a promise that on the return of the elector the proposals of Henry should be carefully considered.[38] As to Henry's offer to join the league of Schmalkalden, John Frederic cautiously replied that, in so grave a matter, the other members of the league must be consulted.[39] They would meet in December, and then Barnes and the English ambassadors who were to follow him might make their proposals.

After the elector's departure Barnes conferred with the Protestant theologians, but their mood seemed to him by no means satisfactory.

Most of the Wittenberg divines were distinctly hostile to Henry. They did not soon recover from the shock caused by the execution of More, and Melanchthon had to defend himself for having dedicated his *Loci Communes* to a sovereign capable of such an outrage.[40] Barnes failed to convince them of the soundness of Henry's opinions about the divorce, and, half in despair, he left Jena for Leipzig, where he proposed to dispute with Cochlæus, a divine of the old school who had fiercely attacked the king.[41]

It had now become evident that no northern league of any kind could be formed, and that the idea of providing an equivalent for the French alliance would have to be given up. For the moment Henry stood quite alone. His isolation, however, was not necessarily dangerous; it would become so only if Charles V were persuaded to help the English malcontents with men and munitions of war. The lords who had entered into correspondence with Chapuis knew this quite as well as the king, and they urged the ambassador to advise Charles to send them help. After the execution of the Carthusians they became even more pressing, and Lord Bray wrote to Chapuis, entreating him not to let the opportunity pass.[42]

But Charles V was fully occupied with his expedition against Tunis, and it would be impossible for him to exercise proper control over an important undertaking in a distant country. He decided, therefore, to leave the matter in the hands of Mary, Queen of Hungary, who governed the Low Countries. Queen Mary was a very energetic and courageous woman, but she shrank from the responsibility of supporting a rebellion in England. The Low Countries were by no means quiet. Muenster, which was but a few miles from the frontier, still held out; the Anabaptists in Holland, encouraged by the successful resistance of their brethren in Germany, gave considerable trouble; and risings might occur at any moment. Besides, an expedition to England might provoke a war with France, and, in the absence of her brother, Mary could not venture to run the risk of exciting so dangerous a conflict.

It was on the absence of Charles V that Cromwell had reckoned when he began his crusade against the adherents of the papacy. The expedition to Tunis was hazardous, and it was generally predicted that the emperor would be obliged to abandon his purpose.[43] If he came back without having succeeded, he would probably be attacked by Francis, and negotiations in which this was assumed were carried on between the French and English courts.[44] The English malcontents, despairing of help from Charles, might then, by flattery, gifts, and promises, be won over to Henry's cause; and at the head of a united nation he would find little difficulty in withstanding his foes.

Cherishing such anticipations as these, Henry, Anne, and Cromwell, although aware of the extent of the conspiracy and of the insecurity of the French alliance, did not for some time feel greatly alarmed. But a few weeks after the death of Fisher and More, circumstances forced them to acknowledge that they had vastly underrated the perils to which they might be exposed through the emperor's ill will.

On 24 June the troops besieging Muenster surprised one of the towers, and, after a bloody fight, obtained possession of the town.[45] Holland, therefore, had no longer anything to fear from the Anabaptists; and Queen Mary of Hungary would be more able, and might be more willing, to assist the English malcontents.

But more alarming intelligence was soon to follow. On 23 June the emperor began the siege of the Goletta, the principal harbour of Tunis. The works were very strong, the garrison fought bravely, and Khairredin annoyed the besiegers by frequent attacks, so that the enemies of Charles became more and more confident that the expedition would be a total failure. He was resolved, however, to succeed. Never having commanded in person before, he was bent on showing that the blood of Maximilian had not degenerated in him. On 14 July a general assault was delivered, and after desperate fighting the place was taken. The whole arsenal of Khairredin, a great many galleys, hundreds of cannon, and large stores of ammunition and victuals fell into the hands of the victors.

A decided success having been obtained, Charles's generals advised him simply to fortify the Goletta, and to be satisfied with what he had achieved; but he thought otherwise. Khairredin was still hovering in the neighbourhood, and, had the imperial army left, he would have reappeared and laid siege to the harbour which had been taken from him. Besides, at Tunis there were from 18,000 to 20,000 Christian slaves, whom Charles wished to liberate. So he decided upon an advance, and early on 20 July he marched out towards Tunis. Slowly his men toiled through the burning desert which separated the Goletta from the capital. Towards noon, tired and thirsty, they came in view of some olive groves, where they expected to find water to quench their thirst; but between them and the object of their desire lay the enemy. They formed in order of battle, and advanced against Khairredin's army. A furious charge of the Moorish horse broke on the pikes of the landsknechts. After the Mohammedan horse had been driven back, the whole Christian army rushed at the Turkish and Moorish infantry, and, carrying everything before it, secured a complete victory. A great many Turks were slain, all their cannon were taken, and the imperial army could encamp around the wells it had so valiantly conquered. That same night the Christian captives in the citadel of Tunis, fearing that Khairredin, in case of a siege, would kill them all, broke their chains, rose against their warders, overpowered them, and closed the gates of the fortress. Khairredin, unable to obtain admittance, had to fly with a few thousand Turks to Algiers, while Charles entered the town of Tunis, reinstated the former Moorish king, Muley Hassan, and decided to keep the Goletta for himself.[46] The object of the expedition had been attained, and the emperor would go back to Europe with a high reputation for military ability and luck, and with more power than ever.

About the middle of August Henry heard of the taking of the Goletta, and he could console himself only by hoping that Charles would not be able to follow up his advantage.[47] But a fortnight later a courier from France brought the news of Charles's complete success. Henry, at first, could not believe it; but Cromwell, having read the despatches, had to confirm the disagreeable tidings.[48] The letters were received in the presence of a servant whom Chapuis had sent to ask some favour for the princess; and the imperial ambassador wrote to Granvelle that both the king and his minister had looked 'like dogs that had tumbled out of a window'. Cromwell, who had at a glance seen the terrible import of the news, was most crestfallen; he could scarcely find breath to mutter a few hypocritical congratulations on the event. On the following days neither Henry nor Anne could hide their vexation and apprehension.[49]

In France the peace party was greatly strengthened by the taking of Tunis. Francis had looked forward with so much confidence to the failure of the expedition that he had intended, after the emperor's return, to fall upon him, and to obtain by force of arms Milan, Asti, and the other coveted possessions in Italy. Henry had been asked to contribute towards the expenses of the war, and to close his harbours to the fleets of Charles coming and going between Spain and the Low Countries. At Calais negotiations had been carried on about the aid Henry was to give, and his ministers had been instructed to make fair promises in a general way.[50]

Now all was changed. Charles had become the hero of Christendom; and to quarrel with him, when his adherents and his army were flushed with victory, might prove disastrous. In a war declared just after the emperor had rendered so signal a service, Francis might have to encounter the united strength of Germany. For the moment, an attack upon Charles V was not to be thought of.

Forced to resign his purpose of entering upon a new struggle with the emperor, Francis felt inclined to change his policy towards England. Hitherto his object in dealing with Henry had been to obtain promises of help in the event of war. Now it occurred to him that he would have more to gain by bringing about a marriage between the dauphin and Mary. If this match could be arranged, Francis did not doubt that the emperor, out of regard for his cousin, would accede to it; and he hoped that Henry might be induced to make his peace with Rome. Mary would then be the acknowledged heir to the English throne, and after the death of Henry and Francis, their children would reign over both France and England. The accession of power obtained in this way would be far greater than any advantage that could be secured by the most successful war.

An opportunity of acting upon this policy soon presented itself. After the execution of Fisher and More, Paul III issued several briefs, setting forth the enormities committed by Henry, and requiring Christian princes to have no further dealings with him and his realms.[51] One of these briefs was addressed to Francis. As a rule, such documents were coolly received at the French court; but this time it was decided that a special ambassador should be sent to England to let Henry know of the brief, and to explain the position of Francis with regard to it.[52] The person chosen for the errand was the former ambassador-resident, Dinteville, the bailly of Troyes. He left the French court at the end of August, and arrived in England in the beginning of September.

13

THE RESULTS OF HENRY'S POLICY

The original instructions given by Francis to the bailly of Troyes seem to have been lost, but we still possess a few letters about his mission, a supplementary instruction sent to him after he had left court, and a long memorandum drawn up by Morette, Antoine de Castelnau, and Dinteville himself, which he took home and sent to court. From these papers it appears that Dinteville was first of all to communicate to Henry the contents of the brief addressed to Francis on 26 July.[1] Having done this, he was to represent that Francis, if he stood by Henry, would be attacked by the emperor and his allies, that he would have to prepare for this emergency, and that he would expect subsidies from his good brother of England. Requests for pecuniary aid had hitherto been preferred in a tentative way: no specified sum had been demanded; Henry had only been asked what he might be inclined to grant. But times had changed, and the tone of Francis had changed with them. Dinteville was instructed to insist that if Francis, for any reason whatever, chose to make war upon the emperor and to attempt the conquest of Milan, Asti, and Genoa, Henry must consider himself bound to bear one third of the expenses incurred for the French army.[2]

Dinteville was directed not only to press these demands on Henry and his ministers, but to ascertain as far as possible what were the feelings of the English people and to report in general on the state of the country. On his arrival in England, therefore, about the beginning of September, he tried to gather all the information he could; and the report he took home a month later gives a gloomy picture indeed of the misery and discontent of the nation.

Henry's policy had exerted a disastrous influence on the foreign trade of England. When the king publicly acknowledged Anne as his wife, an immediate rupture with the emperor was apprehended. The London merchants went to Chapuis, and anxiously inquired whether he was going to leave; they naturally feared that in case of war the goods which they had in the Low Countries and in Spain would be seized, and that any ship they might send out would be captured.[3] Chapuis remained at his post and war was not proclaimed, but traders in the city hesitated to undertake any large commercial enterprise. And they were right; for, although there were no open hostilities, the authorities in Flanders and in Spain were in a very unfriendly mood. In 1534 and 1535 the situation became even more complicated. Adherents of the Pope were irritated by the schism between England and the Holy See; and an angry feeling spread from Flanders and Spain to France and Italy. At the very time when Francis was professing the greatest friendship for Henry, English merchants in France were being daily insulted and robbed, and they could obtain no redress.[4] Lawyers on the continent began even to ask whether Englishmen, in consequence of the rebellion of their king and the papal censures, had not ceased to belong to the Christian republic, and had not forfeited all rights conferred by the *jus gentium* and the imperial laws.[5] Many English merchants in Flanders, Spain, and France, alarmed by the temper which had been evoked among the people around them, sold their wares and returned to England. In the summer of 1535 very few of them remained in France, and ship owners at home were afraid to send their vessels to French ports. Special safe conducts had to be taken out for those who wished to cross the Channel, and this, of course, hampered all transactions and made them less profitable.[6] Merchants got no interest on their money, and mariners were thrown out of employment.

Had Henry acted prudently, it might have been possible for his subjects to find new outlets for their energy in those countries in which papal censures were not respected; but by persisting in his alliance with Wullenwever he had irritated the opposite party, which on the Baltic and on the German Ocean was now triumphing over the friends of England. Gustavus Vasa is said to have openly boasted that he was only beginning the game against Henry;[7] and when, in retaliation for the capture of the English ships, Henry caused the goods of the Dantzig merchants to be seized, these merchants assured Chapuis that they did not care, for they meant to take out letters of reprisal by which they would get from English merchants and vessels more than their property in London had been worth.[8] Even the fishing fleet which went to Iceland and Newfoundland could not be despatched without risk. Iceland was a Danish colony, and if Christian III was not conciliated, English fishermen would meet with scant courtesy from his officials.

The circumstances which compelled English merchants on the continent to return to their own country and to abandon a profitable trade, had a corresponding influence on foreign traders in England. They feared that they might be made to pay for the injury done to

Englishmen abroad, and the latest proceedings of Henry confirmed them in this opinion. Accordingly they no longer imported foreign wares, but were rather occupied in withdrawing the capital they had invested in English commerce. A good many of them, having sold all they had, left the country altogether, while those who remained reduced their transactions as much as possible. The Venetian secretary was already inquiring whether his countrymen would be allowed to export wool from Spain, that Venice might be independent of England;[9] and the fleet which had hitherto come regularly to Southampton to import wine from Candia, and to export wool and tin, stayed away. The English government was rather alarmed by this demonstration, and tried to allay the distrust of the Venetian merchants. A fine they had incurred was partly remitted, and they were assured that they might freely export wool and kerseys.[10] But they remained suspicious, and made no use of the permission granted.

During the summer of 1535 the weather had been so bad that the harvest was very small, the yield of corn being less than half of that of average years.[11] The people had observed, Chapuis says, that it had rained ever since the execution of the Carthusians; and the bad weather was ascribed to divine vengeance for the misdeeds of the king.[12] It was in vain that the royal preachers were commissioned to say that God chastises those he loves; the people remained obdurate and angry.[13]

In former times, whenever the harvest in England had failed, the Hanseatic merchants had been large importers of grain; but after the ill-treatment they had suffered in London they sought for other markets, and thus one of the easiest sources of supply was closed.[14] England became dependent for its food on France and on the Low Countries; and both Chapuis and the French ambassadors advised their masters to forbid the export of corn, hoping in this way to be able to bring pressure to bear on Henry and to wring concessions from him.[15]

Such was the condition of England when Dinteville, in the beginning of September, arrived at the court of Henry near Winchester. Seeing how matters stood he adopted a rather high tone, and insisted on all the demands Francis had ordered him to make. But even if Henry had been disposed to grant every request of the French, he would not have been able to pay such subsidies as Dinteville had been instructed to ask for. If the French really attacked the emperor, their expenses would not be less than £100,000 a month, so that the King of England, had he yielded to Francis, might have had to find £33,333 a month. This would have been far beyond his resources, for the whole ordinary royal income even in fairly prosperous times was not more than £140,000 per annum. Henry was obliged, therefore, to refuse the demands of

Francis, and all he would promise was that he would not claim the instalment of the French pensions which had become due.[16] Angry words passed between the king and his ministers on the one hand, and the French ambassadors on the other; and after a short stay at court the bailly asked leave to return to France.

Before leaving England, Dinteville begged that he and his colleagues might be allowed to visit the king's daughters, his real object being to learn, if possible, from the Princess Mary herself how she felt inclined towards a marriage with the dauphin. Permission could not well be refused, and the three Frenchmen with their train proceeded towards Eltham, where Mary and Elizabeth were staying. One of the gentlemen of the king's chamber had been ordered to accompany the ambassadors, and to see to their comfort and honourable treatment. This person was no sooner alone with them than he informed them that he had received secret instructions from Anne to watch their movements; and they afterwards reported to their government that, so far as the queen and the princess were concerned, Henry could not trust even his personal servants, nearly all of whom were favourable to Catherine and Mary.[17]

On arriving at Eltham the ambassadors were shown into the presence of Elizabeth, but they were not allowed to see Mary. They were of course greatly annoyed at this, but they were somewhat consoled by all they heard at Eltham, and after their return to London. They were told that Mary had greatly wished to see them, but that Lady Shelton had shut her up in her room, and had caused all the windows of it to be nailed down.[18] Mary, it was said, had raged and stormed until the gentleman who had accompanied Dinteville had gone in and told her that it was the king's pleasure she should remain secluded.[19]

About this matter the French ambassadors were not well-informed. The truth was that as soon as they had manifested an intention to go to Eltham, instructions had been sent to Lady Shelton to prevent Mary from seeing or conversing with any of them; and Lady Shelton had immediately told the princess that she would have to keep her room while the ambassadors were there. Mary was rather indignant, and sent a message to Chapuis to ask whether she was to obey or not. Chapuis counselled submission, and she acted on his advice, amusing herself while the Frenchmen were in the house by playing on the virginals.[20]

The French ambassadors, however, were convinced not only that Mary had desired to see them, but that she would not dislike a marriage with the dauphin. According to an Englishman with whom they conversed, and who referred to one of Mary's servants as his authority, the princess had said many a time that the dauphin was her husband;[21]

and when Lady Shelton and other servants of Anne had told her that he had married the daughter of the emperor, she had replied that it was not true, and that they only said so to deprive her of all hope, and to make her forego her rights.[22] Another Englishman had suggested that Mary would be prepared to express her wishes in writing.[23]

The English nation seemed to the ambassadors to approve of the proposed marriage. When Dinteville and his colleagues arrived, and it was supposed that they had come to denounce to Henry the censures of the Church and to ask that the marriage of the dauphin and the Princess Mary should be concluded, they were heartily received by the common people, by the gentlemen at court, and even by the king's servants. As soon as it was known that this was not the object of their mission, they excited less enthusiasm.[24] When they returned from Eltham to spend a few days in London, they were again warmly greeted: the people, thinking they had seen the princess, cheered them as they passed, and wished them good speed.[25] The desperation of the country had become so great, the ambassadors wrote, that those who would formerly have been most opposed to the marriage of Mary with a foreign prince unwilling to reside permanently in England, now ardently desired the union. For if Mary were to marry a prince of lower degree than the dauphin, she might lose her right to the crown or obtain it only after a violent struggle, whereas, if she married the son of Francis, resistance would be impossible, and her claim would be universally admitted.[26]

Dinteville and his colleagues were not altogether wrong. The English people had almost abandoned the hope of receiving help from the emperor, and in their perplexity were ready to turn to France for assistance against the tyranny of the king. The warnings of Chapuis had come true.

The extreme unpopularity of Anne and of her kinsfolk and friends did not escape the notice of the ambassadors. The common people, they reported, were extremely angry against Anne, abusing her in no measured terms for the danger and distress into which she had brought the country.[27] The upper classes were nearly all equally bitter, some on account of the changes in religion, others for fear of war and of ruin to trade, others, and by far the greater number, from loyalty to Catherine and Mary.[28] Englishmen had no wish to see Elizabeth on the throne, with Anne Boleyn and Lord Rochford as her guardians and as regents during a long minority.

Anne herself was fully conscious of the difficulties of her position. To one of the gentlemen who accompanied Dinteville she granted a private audience, and he reported to Marguerite of Navarre the substance of their conversation. Anne said that the two things she most desired on earth were to have a son and to meet Queen Marguerite once more. She seemed ill at ease and harassed, and the eagerness with which she wished to be recommended to Marguerite showed how much she wanted sympathy and help.[29]

In proof of the great popularity of Mary the ambassador mentioned the following curious fact. When Mary had left Greenwich to go to Eltham, a great many women, in spite of their husbands, had flocked to see her pass, and had cheered her, calling out that, notwithstanding all laws to the contrary, she was still their princess. Several of them, being of higher rank than the rest, had been arrested, and, as they had proved obstinate, had been sent to the Tower.[30] On the margin of that part of the report in which this circumstance is recorded we find the words, written by Dinteville himself: 'Note, my Lord Rochford and my Lord William.'[31] The ambassador clearly meant that Lady Rochford, Anne's sister-in-law, and Lady William Howard were among those who had cheered Mary. We know from Chapuis that Lady Rochford had in the preceding autumn been sent from court, but the imperial ambassador ascribed her disgrace to intrigues on behalf of, not in opposition to, Anne. Had Lady Rochford's absence from court produced a change? That may have been so, for it is said that towards the end of the year she was on bad terms with her husband. Lady William Howard was certainly hostile to Anne, and she and Lady Rochford were great friends. Dinteville may therefore have been right.

Considering the difficulties of the government, the temper of the nation, and the supposed inclination of Mary, the French ambassadors came to the conclusion that a marriage between the dauphin and the princess might be brought about more easily than had been expected. They proposed that Paul III should be told of the offers which had been made to Francis by Henry on condition that Francis would throw off his allegiance to the Holy See, and make war on the emperor. The Pope should be warned, they suggested, that if war broke out it might be necessary to accept these offers, and that then he would lose his revenues from France as he had lost his revenues from England. The ambassadors believed that to prevent so unholy an alliance Paul III would ask the emperor himself to propose the marriage, and that Charles, for the sake of his aunt and his cousin, might be persuaded to do so.[32] If he consented, Henry would of course be immediately informed of the fact, and the French king might tell Henry that war would be unavoidable unless the proposal were accepted. Anne would oppose the marriage, but Henry would be afraid to offend both the king and the emperor. Besides, Anne's influence was on the wane; the king had again changed his mistress.[33]

Feeling sure that Henry would have to give way, the French ambassadors were not at all careful to hide their opinions and their wishes. They permitted their servants to talk openly of the advantages which would arise from the marriage of the dauphin and the princess,[34] and some indignation was caused by this freedom of discourse, for Henry was certain that if he consented to the marriage he would soon have a very precarious hold on the loyalty of his subjects. Perceiving the danger, he was angry with his former friends for trying to increase it and to profit by his difficulties.

Cromwell also was extremely angry with the French. At heart he was rather favourable to Mary, and of late his relations with Anne had not always been very good; but as he had no wish to see England become a dependency of France, he resisted the proposed match and stood loyally by Henry and Anne against the peril which was threatening them. With the French ambassadors he had been for some time on bad terms. On 29 June the Bishop of Tarbes and Morette had invited him to dinner, but he had rudely refused, saying that he knew what they wanted to tell him, and that he did not wish to hear it.[35] Shortly afterwards he had an angry discussion with the ambassadors, whom he treated with considerable insolence; and when they resented his arrogance, he used his influence to prevent the bishop from being lodged, as most of his predecessors had been, at the king's cost at Bridewell.[36]

The English ministers, being in ill humour with the French, tried to convey the impression that their relations with the emperor were improving. A new ambassador, Richard Pate, had been appointed to reside with Charles V; and Cromwell and his colleagues went about talking of the honour with which he had been received at the imperial court.[37] Henry himself considerably altered his tone, no longer speaking of the ingratitude of Charles, but, on the contrary, praising him.[38] Towards Chapuis the English ministers made a great show of cordiality. They offered him all kinds of little favours, and frequently sent for him to discuss the most unimportant matters, hoping to make the English public and the French ambassadors believe that important negotiations were going on.

Chapuis was not to be duped so easily. He would not have been unwilling to make the French feel uneasy, and to sow distrust between them and the English; but he did not wish the public to suppose that he or his master in the slightest degree approved of Henry's proceedings. When he received from the king the honour of being allowed to hunt in the royal parks – and this was considered a great favour – he quietly declared that he would make use of the privilege only if the Princess Mary were treated less harshly.[39] And so in other cases; it was always necessary to bribe him to accept any small courtesy from the king or from Cromwell, and the price he asked was often so high that it could not be granted.

The proposals made by the English ministers for the purpose of regaining the friendship of the emperor were considered by Chapuis quite unacceptable. The negotiation which Sir John Wallop had begun with Viscount Hanart in Paris had led to no result, for Henry would not consent to treat Catherine and Mary with royal honours, as the emperor desired;[40] and by the execution of the Carthusians, of Fisher, and of More, he had shown how he intended to behave towards the friends of the queen and the princess. Cromwell had suggested that a marriage might be concluded between Philip, the son of the emperor, and the little Lady Elizabeth; but, brazen-faced as he was, even Cromwell dared not press this scheme, and Chapuis contemptuously ignored all references to it.[41] He remained coldly distant, waiting for an occasion when he might advise his master to act for Catherine and Mary with vigour.

The French were not less anxious than Cromwell to please Chapuis. Morette, during the last few weeks of his embassy, affected the greatest cordiality towards him; Morette's successor, the Bishop of Tarbes, did the same; and Dinteville, during his short stay in London, conferred with the imperial ambassador, and spoke to him in a most friendly manner.[42]

On the continent, as well as in England, efforts were made to influence imperial policy in favour of France. In the month of August Queen Leonor of France had gone to the northern frontier to meet her sister Mary, Queen of Hungary. Chabot accompanied the French queen, and during the few days the two sisters spent together he had a private conversation with the Queen of Hungary, and spoke to her about the marriage of the Princess Mary of England with one of the sons of Francis. These overtures were duly reported to the emperor, and the negotiation, which had come to a standstill, was resumed.[43]

At Rome there were many symptoms of approaching trouble for Henry. The Pope was deeply irritated against him, and was preparing a bull of excommunication and deprivation. The French cardinals and ambassadors had ceased to oppose this extreme measure; they only insisted that the bull should contain no reflections on the conduct of their king, and that it should in no way tend to put him in a disadvantageous position with respect to the emperor.[44]

Paul III was not only preparing spiritual censures, he was trying to provide means for the execution of his sentence. In response to a secret appeal, Francis had agreed to help in carrying out the sentence of deprivation, if Charles would also send a contingent; and Paul III had despatched his son, Pier Luigi Farnese, to Sicily, where the emperor had arrived, to bring about an understanding. Charles V, having a deep-rooted distrust of any offer proceeding from Francis, had replied that the French king only meant to inveigle him into some false step, and that the Pope ought to obtain an authentic written promise from which it would be impossible for Francis to draw back. If such a promise were given, Charles would be ready to do his part.[45] The Pope was not disheartened; and it seemed highly probable that his secret negotiations would have results very disagreeable for the King of England.

The French party at the English court was so discredited that Anne had bitter quarrels with her uncle, the Duke of Norfolk, and, about Christmas 1534, abused him in unmeasured terms. The Duke left her presence in anger, and in the hall spoke against her with indecent violence.[46] Shortly afterwards he retired from the court, thus relieving Cromwell of all fear of serious opposition in the royal council.[47] But Anne was not yet satisfied, and seized every opportunity to bring her uncle into disgrace.[48]

In October 1535 the Bishop of Tarbes openly complained of Cromwell's insolence, and declined to call upon him. The bishop told Chapuis that he had sent a message to this effect to the secretary himself.[49] So serious a quarrel rendered diplomatic communication difficult, and the chances of an open rupture with France began to be generally discussed. The Duke of Norfolk, who intended to send his second son to France, asked Cromwell whether the friendship with Francis had come to an end; and the reply seems to have induced him to keep the young man at home.[50]

International relations being so unsatisfactory, the country became more and more discontented, and Cromwell could not venture to act with his wonted energy and fearlessness. The taxes which had been granted by parliament he was unable to levy, for fear of exasperating the people;[51] yet the royal coffers were empty, not only because the French pensions were withheld, but because, owing to the bad harvest, the farmers on the royal domains could not pay their rents. The result was that the salaries of officials were not paid, and that the whole machinery of administration began to go out of gear. The government was already despoiling small convents, the heads of houses being brought by bribes, threats, and insults to acquiesce in the dissolution of their communities. But the lands and other possessions obtained in this way brought in only a small immediate return in ready money or in things that could be at once exchanged for ready money; and the advantages of confiscation, such as they were, were dearly purchased at the cost of much popular irritation.

Altogether, Henry's position was not at this time an enviable one. When he looked around him, he saw his people thoroughly disaffected, the Pope exasperated and striving to raise against him as many enemies as possible, the King of France negotiating with the emperor for the purpose of dethroning him, the Protestant princes of Germany offended and deeply suspicious, and the fleets of Sweden, Denmark, and Prussia capturing and pillaging his ships.

Henry did not underrate his difficulties, nor did he hide from himself that most of them had sprung from the policy necessitated by his union with Anne. He fondly believed that the hatred of his subjects was mainly directed against her, and that if she were not in his way he might still triumph over his enemies. As he thought of this, the idea of discarding Anne rose before his mind even more vividly than it had done at the beginning of the year; and the idea was certainly not rendered less attractive by the fact that Anne, worn out by constant exertion and anxiety, had lost her good looks.[52] Even to Margaret Shelton, who had so recently touched his fancy, he was already becoming indifferent. During the summer he had gone on progress through the south-western counties; and on 10 September the court had been at Wolfhall, in Wiltshire, the seat of Sir John Seamer or Seymour, father of Mistress Jane Seymour, a former attendant of Queen Catherine. Whether it was on this occasion that Henry began to pay attention to his future queen is not certain, but a few weeks later the French ambassadors reported that the king had a new love.

Although Henry might be heartily tired of Anne, he remembered the advice given him in February when he had first spoken of discarding her. He must either keep her or take Catherine back. Was this the only conceivable alternative? No; Catherine might die; and if she were dead, Henry would not only be rid of his most energetic opponent, the woman to whose influence the resistance of Mary seemed chiefly due, he would be free to separate his fortunes from those of Anne.

For the last two years Henry and his ministers had spoken of the death of Catherine as an event that would soon happen. One day Gregorio da Casale told Chapuis that Henry had said she had the dropsy and in a short time would die of it. Chapuis remarked that the queen had never suffered from anything like dropsy; and he vehemently suspected that the prediction of her approaching death meant that she was to be poisoned.[53] The friends of Catherine and Mary had been warned that Anne wished to poison her rivals. Dr Ortiz had been told in Rome by the auditor Simonetta that this was her purpose.[54] The Earl of Northumberland, who at the time was still on friendly terms with Anne, made a similar communication to a gentleman at court, who reported it to Chapuis.[55] Pope Clement VII, after he had delivered sentence in March 1534, had expressed a fear that the result might be the death of the queen.[56] Anne herself spoke in a violent strain. In the summer of 1534 she plainly said that she intended to kill Mary during

Henry's absence from England; and in March 1535, when she regained her ascendancy, she was reported to have suborned a man to pretend that God had revealed to him that while the princess dowager and the Lady Mary lived Queen Anne would bear no children to the king. About the same time she denounced the two ladies as rebels and traitors who merited death;[57] and after the execution of Fisher and More she directly urged Henry to inflict the same penalty on Catherine and Mary, saying that they deserved death even more than those who had just been beheaded.[58] The hatred she had conceived for them blinded her to her own real interests.

Cromwell did not hate the queen and the princess; but he thought that if they were out of the way he would be able to compose the differences between Henry and Charles, and to avert the danger of a foreign invasion. And he made no secret of his feelings. In August 1534, he said to one of the lords that the Low Countries were too much afraid of losing their commerce to allow the emperor to make war upon England. 'But even if this were not the case,' he added, 'the death of Catherine and Mary would prevent any rupture, for then there would be no occasion for a quarrel.'[59] In March 1535, he asked Chapuis what evil or danger would arise from the death of the princess, even if it excited the indignation of the people, and what cause the emperor would have to be offended by it.[60] The ambassador gave an angry reply, having no wish to hear dark speeches which might lead to even darker deeds. But a few weeks afterwards Cromwell spoke again in the same sense, declaring that Mary was at the root of all the king's perplexities. 'And,' he added, 'I pray God... ' Here he stopped, but, as Chapuis remarked, it was not necessary to finish the sentence; his meaning was clear enough.[61]

Henry had also begun to talk in a rather ominous way. Mary having fallen ill, he went to Greenwich, where she was then staying; and in the presence of all the servants he loudly ordered Lady Shelton to tell her ward that she was his worst enemy, and that on her account he was on bad terms with most of the princes of Christendom. Chapuis interpreted this message as an encouragement to those who might feel inclined to poison the princess.[62]

During the latter half of 1533 and during the whole of 1534, Chapuis credited Anne and her friends with the most infamous designs. For the protection of Mary against certain dangers at which he occasionally hinted in his letters to the emperor, and to Granvelle and his son, he could trust only to the virtue and firmness of Mary herself.[63] But for her protection against attempts to poison her he took active measures. For some time he wished that she should reside with her mother, but this was refused, and in the end it seemed to him best that they should not live together; for if Mary stayed with her mother her enemies might poison her without exciting suspicion, whereas if she was with Lady Shelton they could not harm her without immediately causing a popular outcry.[64] Having arrived at this conviction, Chapuis tried to help the princess by influencing her guardian. He sent Lady Shelton little presents with complimentary messages, but at the same time gave her to understand that she herself would be in the greatest danger if the princess died while entrusted to her charge. In the spring of 1535 Doctor William Butt, the royal physician, was ordered to attend the princess; and he assisted the ambassador by telling Lady Shelton that it was commonly reported in London that she had poisoned Mary. The poor lady was not a little frightened, and whenever Mary was ill cried bitterly and was in the utmost anxiety.[65]

Catherine did not seem to be in the same imminent danger as her daughter. With a few of her own servants and a large staff of royal officials, she had remained at Bugden until the spring of 1534, when she had been conveyed to Kimbolton, near Huntingdon. She had been several times annoyed by commissioners calling upon her to swear to the new Acts and threatening her with the penalties for high treason; but in the autumn of 1534 she had enjoyed a short time of quiet. When, however, the young lady who had worked in her favour lost the good graces of the king, she was again treated as harshly as before, and in the summer and the autumn of 1535 she bitterly complained of the cruelty of her oppressors.[66]

The only servants of Catherine at Kimbolton, besides her female attendants, were George de Atequa, Bishop of Llandaff, her confessor; Miguel de Lasco, her physician; Juan de Soto, her apothecary; Philip Grenacre, de Soto's assistant; and Francisco Phelipe, her groom of the chamber. The royal servants, under the command of Sir Edward Chamberlain and Sir Edmund Bedingfield were far more numerous. They acted as the garrison of the castle, as the queen's gaolers, and as spies upon her conduct and upon that of her attendants. She could not leave the house without permission; and when permission was granted, she had to accept the company of royal officers, who prevented her from communicating with the people. Visitors were not admitted except by special order from the king or from Cromwell, and her letters had to be smuggled in and out by her Spanish servants.

In the summer of 1534 Chapuis had asked Cromwell for a warrant to see the queen;[67] and having waited for some time without obtaining a reply, he had set out with a large train for Kimbolton. While he was on the road, a royal messenger passed him, riding post-haste; and shortly afterwards he received a message from Chamberlain and Bedingfield that by the king's orders he would neither be admitted to the castle nor allowed to speak with the queen. After some discussion the ambassador returned to London, but not before a part of his retinue had gone close to Kimbolton, where they spoke with Catherine's attendants, some of whom were standing on the battlements, while others looked out of the windows.[68]

By such protests and demonstrations Chapuis hoped to counteract the sinister advice given to the king, and as time went on and the two ladies were neither poisoned nor brought to trial, he became less anxious. He was told that the king had no wish to hurt either of them, but intended to keep them as hostages for his own safety; and Chapuis believed what he was told, and ceased to pay much attention to floating rumours on the subject. Early in November 1535, his confidence was rudely disturbed.

14

THE DEATH OF CATHERINE

On 6 November the imperial ambassador received a message from the Marchioness of Exeter, the devoted adherent of Catherine, to the effect that 'the king had lately told his most trusted counsellors that he would no longer remain in the trouble, fear, and suspicion in which he had so long remained on account of the queen and princess, and that at the next parliament they must rid him of them; swearing great oaths that he would not wait any longer to provide for this.'[1] Some of the royal counsellors – perhaps secretly favourable to Mary – were alarmed by his violence, and could not suppress their tears. Henry brutally exclaimed that 'this was not a matter about which to cry or make wry faces, for were he to lose his crown for it he would persevere in his purpose'.[2] A fortnight later, always according to the same authority, Henry declared that:

> he would contrive that Mary should soon want neither new year's gifts nor society, and that she should be an example to show the whole world that nobody was to disobey the law. He would prove the truth of the prophecy about himself, that at the beginning of his reign he would be as gentle as a lamb, but at the end more fierce than a lion.[3]

The marchioness added that all this was as true as the Gospel.[4] And Chapuis, knowing her character and the means she had for obtaining trustworthy information, placed entire faith in what she said. He wrote that the concubine would never rest until she got quit of 'these poor good ladies'. and that for this end she was making use of every device she could imagine.[5]

> The concubine, who has for some time conspired and wished for the death of the said ladies, and who thinks of nothing so much as of how she may have them despatched, is the person who manages, orders, and governs everything, and whom the king does not dare to oppose.[6]

At the urgent request of the marchioness, Chapuis wrote to ask the emperor to save his aunt and cousin by immediate action.[7]

Although seriously alarmed, Chapuis did not at this time suspect any attempt to poison either Catherine or Mary. His idea was that the king would try to force a bill of attainder through parliament, and thus, by making the members of both houses accomplices in his offence, deprive them of all hope of the emperor's forgiveness and compel them to support subsequent proceedings.[8] As parliament was not to meet until after the new year, the ambassador thought there would be time to provide against this danger.

But when, on 3 December 1535, Chapuis called on Cromwell to ask that some money due to Catherine might be paid, he was told that a messenger had just been sent to the king to announce the dangerous illness of Catherine. The ambassador, greatly distressed, at once begged that he might be permitted to see the queen, and in the meantime to despatch one of his servants to Kimbolton. The latter request was granted by Cromwell, who signed the necessary passport, but as to the proposed visit of Chapuis, he said that it would be necessary to consult the king.[9]

When the ambassador was leaving Cromwell's house a letter from de Lasco, Catherine's physician, was handed to him, and by this he was somewhat reassured. De Lasco said that with God's help Catherine would recover, and he advised Chapuis not to insist on receiving permission to visit her. The news from Kimbolton continuing to be favourable, Chapuis acted on the doctor's advice: and he was the less inclined to press his request because Cromwell, who had promised to let him know the king's will, did not again allude to the matter.[10]

The queen had suffered from violent pains in the stomach, flatulence, vomiting, and general weakness; but the symptoms had soon passed away, and in a week she had seemed to be perfectly well again.[11] She herself did not apprehend immediate death from natural causes: she only feared that she might be the victim of some open act such as the king's violent speech had foreshadowed. On 13 December she wrote to Chapuis and Charles. To Chapuis she said that she wished to be taken to some healthier place than Kimbolton, and she asked him to obtain for her the payment of the money due to her, as she wanted to make some presents to her attendants at Christmas.[12] Charles V she entreated to interfere in her favour and in that of her daughter, now in their hour of need. In this letter her handwriting is as firm as it ever was, and her tone is that of a person who expects to live many a year.[13]

In accordance with Catherine's wishes, Chapuis saw Cromwell on the 17th, and spoke of the matters about which she had written to him; but the secretary evaded his requests. Nor was reference made to the decision of the king with regard to the desire of Chapuis to visit Kimbolton. Cromwell was evidently reluctant to introduce the subject; and as Catherine's health was restored, and there were political questions which seemed to be of more urgent importance, the ambassador still thought it might be inexpedient to press his application.[14]

Christmas passed without any disquieting tidings. On the 27th Chapuis received a message that the king, who was at Eltham, wished to speak to him; and on the following day it was arranged that he was to have audience on 2 January. But on the 29th a messenger arrived from Kimbolton at Baynard's Castle, where Chapuis resided, bringing two letters, one from Catherine's physician to the ambassador, another from the apothecary, Philip Grenacre, to Montesa, the ambassador's steward. Grenacre wrote that the queen was ill again and worse than ever. For the last two days she had been tormented by violent pains in the stomach, and by constant hic-cupping, and she had been unable to retain any nourishment whatever, either solid or liquid. She had scarcely slept an hour and a half during the whole time, and had lost all strength.[15] The doctor thought Catherine would not be able to keep up, and asked Chapuis to come as quickly as possible.[16] The ambassador, very much alarmed, immediately sent a messenger to court to renew his request for permission to visit the queen. Cromwell replied that permission would be granted, but that in the meantime the king desired to confer with Chapuis about some most important matters. The ambassador was therefore requested to be at Greenwich next day at one o'clock in the afternoon. The king would come from Eltham to meet him.

Although annoyed at the delay, Chapuis was obliged to do as the king proposed; so on the morning of 30 December he took his boat and went down the river to Greenwich Stairs. He was received with more than usual courtesy and attention. Sir Thomas Cheyne stood at the stairs to welcome him, and led him to the royal presence. They found the king in the tiltyard, surrounded by a host of courtiers. Henry greeted Chapuis with great affability, and after a little while, throwing his arm round the ambassador's neck, walked up and down with him for some time. By and by they went to the king's chamber, and Henry, ordering everybody away, began to talk politics. As Chapuis had expected, there was no very pressing business to be discussed. The French, Henry said, offered him their alliance, and if the emperor remained hostile he would be driven to accept it. He began to speak of Cromwell's suggestion that Elizabeth should become the wife of Philip of Spain, and Chapuis, wishing to keep him in good humour, did not positively reject the proposal.[17] Henry went on complaining of the emperor's ingratitude, as he called it, and told the wildest tales about all he had done for Charles, who had requited his kindness by using force at Rome to obtain the papal sentence against him. He wound up by saying that Madame – so he called Catherine – would not live long, and that after her death the emperor would have no pretext for interference in the affairs of England, and would be an entire loser by all he had done in this business. Chapuis immediately replied that the queen's death would not profit Henry, and that the papal sentence had been unavoidable.[18]

After this Chapuis took his leave of the king, who granted him permission to go to Kimbolton, and ordered Stephen Vaughan to lead him thither.[19] But before he had reached his boat, he was recalled by the Duke of Suffolk; and Henry asserted that he had just received a message that the queen was in extremis, so that Chapuis would scarcely find her still alive. He showed no sorrow, but rather satisfaction, saying that it would put an end to the difficulties which existed between Charles and him.[20]

Mary had asked that if the queen became very ill, Chapuis should obtain leave for her to go and see her mother. On hearing the bad news, the ambassador complied with Mary's request, but the king flatly refused. Chapuis insisted, and Henry, in order to get rid of him, said he would think about it and take the advice of his counsellors. More than this the ambassador could not persuade him to concede.[21]

Chapuis returned to town as quickly as possible, wrote a short letter to the emperor, and mounted horse to proceed to Kimbolton. But it was already late, and that day he could not proceed very far. Next day – St Sylvester's day – he spent on the road, and it was only on the morning of the first of January that he arrived at the gates of the castle.[22] No difficulties were made; Chapuis and his retinue were allowed to enter, and he conferred at once with the principal attendants of Catherine as to seeing her. It was arranged that the first audience should be in presence of the royal officers, whom the queen had not seen for more than a year, and of Stephen Vaughan. Immediately after dinner they were all ushered into the queen's room, where Chapuis, paying her royal honours, kissed her hand. In answer to the ambassador's compliments, Catherine thanked him for all the trouble he had taken on her behalf, and for having come to see her. His visit, she thought, would do her much good, and even if it did not do so it would be a consolation to her to die in his arms, and not to leave life like a brute.[23] Chapuis tried to cheer her, telling her that the king had agreed to let her choose hereafter the house she should live in, and to pay her the money due to her. Thinking that in the circumstances it might be permissible to use a pious fraud, he added that the king was very sorry for her illness.[24] After this he made a set speech which had been previously concerted between him and the queen through her officers. He asked her to make an effort to recover, if for no other reason, because on her life depended the union and quiet of Christendom. This he explained to her at some length, in the hope that Vaughan, who understood Spanish, might report the conversation in the proper quarters, and that it might suggest to Henry the necessity of taking more care for the preservation of her life.[25]

The whole audience lasted but a quarter of an hour, Catherine being too weak for much talk.[26] She told Chapuis to go and rest after his journey, and she herself would try to sleep a little, which for the last six days she had not been able to do for more than two hours in all. At five in the afternoon Chapuis was called by Doctor de Lasco, who, with Montesa, accompanied him to the queen's room.[27] They stayed nearly two hours, and Catherine, notwithstanding her pains and her weakness, took the greatest pleasure in the ambassador's company. She had so long been shut off from all communication, except with her servants, that to talk with a man of the intelligence, knowledge, and standing of Chapuis was a real treat for her. She complained of her own and her daughter's misfortune, and of the delay in providing a remedy – a delay whereby many had suffered in their persons and goods, and many souls had been lost; and she said that she had herself some scruples of conscience, since she had been the first cause of all this by resisting Henry's will.[28] Chapuis comforted her with the assurance that although the emperor had hitherto not been able to assist her more than he had done, things would now go better. There was a hope that the French would turn against Henry; and the Pope, on account of the death of the Cardinal of Rochester, was going to proceed *pro attentatis*. This would be very advantageous for her, because, whatever course the Pope might take, the king could not hold her responsible for it. With such talk the visit passed, and Chapuis retired.[29]

While he had been sitting by the queen's bedside another visitor had arrived. Lady Willoughby, the mother-in-law of the Duke of Suffolk, by birth a Spaniard, had formerly been an attendant of Catherine and had remained her devoted friend. Having heard of the queen's illness, she had straightway repaired to Kimbolton without asking for a passport, which would perhaps have been refused. She arrived at night at the gates, and being asked for her letters of admission, said they would come soon. She pretended that she had met with an accident on the road, and begged for God's sake to be taken in and to have a place near the fire. The royal officers dared not in so small a matter disoblige the mother of a duchess; they allowed her to enter the hall, and, in the confusion caused by the numerous retinue of Chapuis, she contrived to escape their vigilance and entered the queen's rooms, where she remained.[30]

During the next four days Chapuis had daily a long audience of Catherine. His presence really seemed to benefit her. She was encouraged by his arguments, and when he declared that all would ultimately be set right, she believed him and began to hope for a speedy settlement of her difficulties. Her health, too, appeared to improve. She was able to take a little nourishment, and slept better than during the past week. So on Tuesday, the 4th, Catherine, Chapuis, and Doctor de Lasco consulted together, and decided that the ambassador should leave Kimbolton next morning. De Lasco thought that she was out of immediate danger, and Chapuis was anxious not to abuse the privilege which had been accorded to him, but rather to act in such a way that he might be allowed to come again. He wanted, too, to obtain a more suitable residence for Catherine. On 30 December Henry had really promised that she should have a good house, and the ambassador desired to strike the iron while it was hot. On Tuesday night he took leave, and remarked with pleasure that Catherine was in better spirits; she laughed two or three times at what he said. After the ambassador left her, she sent for one of his servants, who filled the office of a jester, and listened for a while to his fancies.[31]

Next morning Chapuis rose early, and sent one of his valets to inquire how the queen had passed the night. The reply was, that she had slept better than before. The horses, therefore, were saddled and the mules loaded, but before mounting horse Chapuis had some serious talk with de Lasco. He asked the doctor whether he had any suspicion of poison. De Lasco shook his head, and said he feared something of the kind, for after the queen had drunk of a certain Welsh beer she had never been well. 'It must be,' he added, 'some slow and cleverly-composed drug, for I do not perceive the symptoms of ordinary poison.'[32] He thought that she might get over it this time. If he saw any immediate danger, he promised that he would at once send a message to Chapuis.

After this consultation Chapuis had a request to make. Being a practical man, he thought of the great lawsuit at Rome, and expressed a wish that if the queen suddenly became worse she should, shortly before her death, solemnly declare that her marriage with Prince Arthur had never been consummated. De Lasco promised that this should be done.[33]

Having thus provided for everything, Chapuis departed, and proceeded slowly towards London. At every stage he feared that a messenger would overtake him and call him back, but on the evening of the 8th he reached London without having been disturbed. Early next day he sent one of his servants to ask Cromwell when he might have audience of the king to thank him for the hospitality he had received at Kimbolton, and to speak about a change of residence for the queen. The servant came back with a short message from the secretary, announcing that Catherine had died on the 7th at two o'clock in the afternoon.[34]

After Chapuis had left Kimbolton, Catherine had passed the 5th and the 6th of January well enough. Her pains had not returned, and she had been able to sleep, and to eat a little. During the afternoon of the 6th she sat up in her bed, combed her hair, and plaited it round her head. At the customary time she went to sleep, but an hour after midnight she called for her attendants and inquired what o'clock it was. A short time afterwards she repeated the question, and being asked why she did so, she said that she wished to hear mass and to receive the Sacrament. The Bishop of Llandaff was called, and he, startled by her anxiety, offered to say mass at once before the canonical hour. But the queen refused, citing the decrees which forbade it. When four o'clock had struck, the office began, and the queen communicated with the greatest fervour, remaining afterwards in prayer. Turning to her servants, she asked them to pray for her soul, and that God might forgive the king her husband all the wrong he had done her, and inspire him to return to the right path and give him good counsel.[35]

After a while she called de Lasco and dictated two letters, one to the ambassador of her nephew the emperor, another to the king her husband, asking him to give certain sums and trinkets to persons she named. The letter to Henry she signed, 'Katherine, Queene of England'; and she gave orders that it should be forwarded to Chapuis.[36] At ten o'clock she desired to receive extreme unction. But she considered that she ought not to die in private 'like a brute', as she had said; so, for want of better men, Bedingfield and Chamberlain were called in to see her die.[37] Atequa said the office and administered the Sacrament, she herself saying the responses.[38] After this she remained in prayer until two o'clock, when she expired. Her courage never forsook her; she died, as she had lived, without fear.

However callous his office might have made him, Chapuis had a strong affection for the woman whose cause he had defended so long, and in his letters he gave free expression to the grief with which he had received the tidings of her death. The English people seem also to have heard of the event with regret. Catherine, as I have already said, had always been popular; and as the rival of Anne Boleyn, who was generally hated, she was the hope of those who wished the schism to be healed. But at court, in the small circle which surrounded the king and Anne Boleyn, the feeling was different. The news was reported to Henry on Saturday, and he took little care to hide his pleasure. He praised God who had delivered them from all fear of war; adding that the time had come when he would be able to lead the French better than he had done hitherto, because, fearing that he might form an alliance with the emperor now that the cause of dissension had been removed, they would do all he wanted.[39] The Earl of Wiltshire and Lord Rochford were equally loud and coarse in the display of their joy. The only pity was, they exclaimed, that the Lady Mary was not keeping her mother company.[40]

Next day the king appeared in the most flamboyant of dresses, all in yellow, with a white feather in his cap. Little Elizabeth, who was at court, was on that day taken to mass with extraordinary pomp, trumpets blowing before her and numerous servants following. In the afternoon a ball was given at court, at which the king was present. He was in the highest of spirits, and by and by sent for Elizabeth, whom he carried round the room in his arms, showing her to the courtiers. Balls and jousts succeeded one another, and the court rang with gaiety.[41] On 24 January, however, the king happened to fall from his horse; and although he was not hurt, he was somewhat sobered by the accident, and the following days were spent more quietly.

These strange rejoicings could not but shock every one who had any sense of decency; and one consequence of them was that all kinds of rumours began to spread. Some declared that the queen had died of a broken heart, caused by the ill treatment to which she had been subjected. According to others, she had been poisoned.[42] The poison, it was said, had been sent from Italy by Gregorio da Casale, and brought to England by his cousin Gurone, and Casale had received a pension of eight ducats a day for it. To these and other details Chapuis attached little importance;[43] but as to the main fact, he firmly believed that Catherine had been poisoned at the instigation of the king and of Anne.[44]

Was Catherine poisoned, or did she die from natural causes? That is the question we have to answer. Chapuis expected the truth to be established by the examination of the body. 'Should they open her,' he wrote on the 9th to Charles, 'the traces will be seen.'[45] But the ambassador was to be disappointed. The body of Catherine was of course opened in order to be embalmed, but it was done in such a way as to prevent any clue to the cause of her death being found. Catherine died at two o'clock in the afternoon. Chamberlain and Bedingfield at once decided that the body should be embalmed by the chandler of the house, and that it should be immediately afterwards enclosed in lead. 'The which,' they wrote to Cromwell, 'must needs shortly be done, for that may not tarry.[46] At ten o'clock in the evening, the royal officers drove everybody out of the room in which the corpse was lying, and the chandler and two assistants were called in and left alone to do their work. Doctor de Lasco wished to be present, but his request was not granted. Permission was also withheld from the Bishop of Llandaff, who was required by the customs of the Church to remain with the body.[47]

Next morning, the work being done, the chandler told the bishop that he had found all the internal organs as healthy and normal as possible, with the exception of the heart, which was quite black and hideous to look at. He washed it, but it did not change colour; then he cut it open, and the inside was the same. Moreover, a black, round body stuck to the outside of the heart. All this the chandler asked the bishop to keep strictly secret, for his life would be in danger if it became known that he had spoken.[48] But the good bishop told the doctor; and when, a few days later, a servant whom Chapuis had sent to Kimbolton inquired whether there was any suspicion of poison, the doctor answered that there could be no doubt of it after what the chandler had said, and that even without his evidence the fact had been rendered clear enough by the course and symptoms of the illness.[49]

Doctor de Lasco was somewhat biased, and his opinion must be received with considerable caution. The chandler also seems to have had a suspicion before he opened the body, otherwise he would scarcely have paid so much attention to its condition. Besides, he was not a surgeon, nor even a barber, although he had opened several bodies before.[50] The symptoms of the illness as they are described are not incompatible with the theory of death by poison; but they do not necessarily lead to this conclusion. We must, therefore, take other circumstances into account before the case can be decided.

We have seen that in the beginning of November the king manifested an intention to have an act of attainder brought in at the next session of parliament. He spoke very violently about it, and those who knew his obstinacy seem to have been of opinion that he would carry out his purpose. Now, it is quite certain that the introduction of a bill of attainder would have been the signal for instant revolt. In such circumstances even Chapuis would have favoured an insurrection, and the conspirators, driven to extremity, would have acted unanimously and enthusiastically. If Catherine had been left at Kimbolton and Mary at Hatfield or Hunsdon, an attempt would have been made to carry these two places, and it would most probably have been successful, for the royal garrisons were by no means trustworthy. Had Henry, wishing to have the ladies in his power before submitting the bill of attainder to parliament, brought them to the Tower, the rebellion would have broken out all the sooner, for his aim would then have been manifest; and, Kingston being secretly in favour of the queen and the princess, the Tower would almost certainly have been thrown open to their supporters. As the king had hardly any real adherents, and as he could not rely on the few troops he possessed, the conspirators could scarcely have failed to triumph even without assistance from the Low Countries.

It was impossible for the trusty and well-beloved councillors of Henry to approve of a proposal which was likely to lead to such a result as this. They could not but suspect that if there was to be civil war the more obnoxious of them would fall as victims to the popular fury, and that the rest, besides losing all power, might have to disgorge their ill-acquired wealth. For their own sakes Henry's threats must have filled them with alarm; and, as it happened, their personal interests coincided with the public weal. A successful insurrection would have been most disastrous to the commonwealth.

Three courses would have been open to the victorious insurgents. The first and mildest course would have been to drive away or kill Anne Boleyn and her adherents, to oblige the king to recognise Catherine as his wife and Mary as heir to the crown, to force him to give up the royal supremacy and to submit to the Pope, and to take security for the fulfilment of all these conditions by requiring the appointment of a council entirely composed of the leaders of the insurrection. But this would have been extremely dangerous for the peers. Henry was so vain that he would never have forgotten his humiliation, so vindictive that he would never have forgiven those who had brought it upon him, so false that he would not have allowed himself to be bound by any promises or oaths which might have interfered with his vengeance. Sooner or later he would have tried to recover absolute power, and if he had succeeded, not one of those who had opposed him would have been safe. This course, therefore, would not have suited the insurgents at all.

The second course would have been to dethrone Henry, either by the authority of parliament, or in fulfilment of the papal sentence, or in obedience to the imperial over-lord, and to set up Mary in his place. But it was doubtful whether Mary would give her consent to so perilous an undertaking; and even if she did so, it was not less doubtful whether she would always be willing and able to withstand her father's intrigues. If she were made queen, Henry would never cease to resist her authority, and by conspiracy and civil war he might in the end regain his throne.

The third course would necessarily have been taken. During the conflict Henry would somehow have died, and Mary would have succeeded him as his lawful heir. It would not have been the first time that an English king had been murdered to make place for his child. Edward II had been dethroned and murdered by the adherents of his son, and the reign of Edward III had been one of splendour and of at least outward success. There would have been great differences, however, in the two cases. First of all, morals had changed, and what had been possible in the fourteenth might have proved impossible in the sixteenth century. Moreover, when the bloody deed was done in favour of Prince Edward, he was a mere boy and far away; he could scarcely be held responsible. But Mary was nearly twenty; and it would be impossible for her to escape censure if a crime were committed for her benefit. Edward III was a man of considerable ability and with an undisputed title to the crown. Mary was a woman of very small ability, full of prejudices and scruples, slow of resolve, unused to action, and with a title to the crown which was by no means very clear. I have no doubt that if Mary had succeeded under conditions similar to those under which Edward III ascended the throne, she would in a few years have been as unpopular as Henry had ever been, and as she actually became at a later period. There would have been fresh rebellions with their train of misery and bloodshed, and the condition of the English people would have been even more wretched than it had been before her accession.

Salus populi suprema lex esto. In King Henry's time this famous saying had not been uttered, but the rule it sets forth had long been the standard of public morals for practical English statesmen. In a case in which the welfare of the nation coincided for once with the welfare of ministers, the rule obtained a force which must have been quite irresistible. When the royal councillors heard Henry's angry vow, when they became aware that he really meant it, when they rapidly weighed the consequences, they must have come to the conclusion that it would be necessary to use every means in their power to avert the catastrophe they foresaw. And there was but one way in which Henry could be prevented from doing what he proposed. Catherine at least must be dead before the assembling of parliament. A single death of an old and unhappy woman might save many thousands of lives, those of the trusty and well-beloved included. Cromwell and Audeley, Wiltshire and Rochford, and many others undoubtedly viewed the matter in this light. Cromwell, we know, had already spoken like Caiaphas, and there is every reason to believe that he felt as he spoke.

Early in November Henry uttered the ominous words reported by Lady Exeter. Four weeks later Catherine fell ill under circumstances which were at least suspicious. She recovered, fell ill again, and died. The danger was past, the king was free, the councillors were safe. Was there no connection between the words of the king and the death of his wife? The world thought there was, and Chapuis directly accused the king and Anne Boleyn of having murdered the queen.[51]

The events which followed Catherine's death seem to be inexplicable if she died in the ordinary course of nature. The government acted again and again as if it knew that a murder had been committed. The indecent haste made at Kimbolton to have Catherine's body embalmed as quickly and as secretly as possible, certainly looks very suspicious. Why was the body to be immediately enclosed in lead? It was winter, and Catherine had not died of any disease by which the decomposition of the body was hastened. And why was Doctor de Lasco prevented from being present at the opening?

After much solicitation Chapuis obtained permission for Doctor de Lasco and Juan de Soto to see Lady Mary for the purpose of giving her an account of her mother's death. It is significant that when they arrived at the house where Mary was kept a prisoner they were refused admittance and peremptorily ordered back.[52]

Doctor de Lasco, who was still a Spanish subject, considering himself of no farther use in England, wished to return to his native country. He applied for leave to go, but it was refused. He once more pressed his request, and was met by an offer of employment in the royal service. This the doctor declined, but he could not obtain the necessary passport.[53] The Bishop of Llandaff, also by birth a Spaniard, seeing this reluctance to let the late servants of Catherine depart, began to fear that he might have to live in a country where the papal supremacy was denied, and tried to leave in disguise. But Cromwell's spies watched him; and he was caught and sent to the Tower.[54] What reason could there be for retaining these men except the dread that once out of England they might tell an ugly tale?

On the second of May following, Anne Boleyn was arrested. That same evening, when the Duke of Richmond, Henry's bastard son, was saying good night to his father, the king burst into tears. 'The duke and his sister, the Lady Mary,' exclaimed Henry, 'might thank God for having escaped the hands of that damned poisonous wretch who had conspired their death.'[55] And shortly afterwards, at the trial of Anne, the royal officers laid it to the charge of the prisoner that she was strongly suspected of having caused the late princess dowager to be poisoned, and of having intended to do the same by the Lady Mary.[56] A scapegoat having been found, Henry's ministers did not deny that Catherine had been murdered.

With so formidable a mass of evidence it cannot but seem likely that Catherine met with foul play. If such was the case, the poison was probably administered twice in small doses, at the end of November and shortly after Christmas. Poisoning by repeated low doses was thought by the great toxicologists of the sixteenth century to be preferable to every other method. Usually the victim did not die of the direct effect of the poison, but of exhaustion caused by frequent illnesses; so that, as a rule, no traces of the drug were found in the body, and the course of the disorder did not present those strong and characteristic symptoms which might otherwise have appeared. Thus poisoners were able to baffle the efforts of the most skilful physicians, and in most cases to prevent the detection of their crime.

If a murder was committed, it is for the present impossible to say who was the actual murderer, or whose immediate orders he obeyed. The accusation brought by the royal officers in May against Anne Boleyn may have been well founded. Chapuis thought her guilty, and so did others; but Chapuis equally accused the king, and from what we know he had good reason to do so. The behaviour of Henry II towards Thomas a Becket was not worse than that of Henry VIII towards Catherine, and historians are generally agreed in saying that Henry II prompted a murder.

On the king, who made the death of Catherine a political necessity, rests the responsibility for what may have been done, not on those who in their own way fulfilled his command. Anne Boleyn may have contributed to the result, her advice may have strengthened the king in his opinion, and may have encouraged those by whom the crime was directly ordered. But the attempt to throw the whole blame on her shoulders was an attempt to exonerate the principal culprit. Her guilt, whatever it may have been, was less than that of Henry, for she was bound by no tie to the queen, and she did to Catherine what would have been done to her had Catherine possessed the power.

15

JANE SEYMOUR

On receiving the letter of Chamberlain and Bedingfield which announced Catherine's death, Cromwell immediately wrote to the Bishop of Winchester and Sir John Wallop, the English ambassadors at the French court. He instructed them to communicate the good news to Francis, and in their negotiations to modify their action in accordance with the new order of things. But before he had time to send off the letter, he received a message from Henry directing him to point out to the ambassadors that, Catherine being dead, there was no longer any reason to apprehend the hostility of the emperor. This they were to explain to the French, and Francis was to be warned that he might be forestalled by Charles V if he did not at once accept Henry's proposals. If, notwithstanding this warning, Francis still required the ambassadors to abate their claims, they were to show themselves unwilling to do so.[1] It is quite clear that Henry fully understood how much his position had been bettered by the death of his wife, and how much less he depended on the goodwill of France.

A few days after Dinteville had left England the Bishop of Winchester had been sent to assist and perhaps to watch Sir John Wallop at the French court.[2] The choice was not a happy one, for Gardiner had made himself unpopular with the French by his overbearing temper, and by the part he had taken in the intrigues at Marseilles. Probably he was chosen as much because at home they wished to be rid of him as because he was considered a very fit instrument. At the French court he met with little success. The demands of France were as exorbitant as ever, and Gardiner quickly perceived that there was scarcely any chance of an agreement. But a few days after his arrival news came from Italy which raised a hope that the French would attribute more importance to the friendship of Henry, and that they might be brought to make considerable concessions.

Maximilian Sforza, the Duke of Milan, had died without issue; and Francis, who had always pretended a title to the duchy, now claimed the succession. He at once asked the emperor to give investiture of the duchy to Henry, Duke of Orleans, his second son. To this Charles demurred, for Henry of Orleans, next to the dauphin, who was of feeble health and unmarried, was at this time heir to the French crown; and if he were made Duke of Milan, and if his elder brother died childless, the duchy would belong to the King of France, who would thus obtain a strong hold over upper and central Italy. Moreover, Henry of Orleans, in virtue of his wife, Catherine dei Medici, thought he had some claim to the Duchy of Urbino, Camerino, and other places in the Romagna. If he obtained possession of Milan, he would try to enforce his pretensions; so that the emperor, instead of securing peace by the concession demanded of him by Francis, would be involved in new quarrels and new wars.

But while Charles would not grant Milan to Henry of Orleans, he was ready to make sacrifices in order to avoid a war with France. The Tunisian expedition had been rather expensive; and Khairredin, although beaten and driven from one of his strongholds, had been able to retain Algiers, and had reconstituted a fleet with which he was once more threatening the shores and islands of Spain and Italy. The emperor was, therefore, really anxious to maintain peace with France, and in the hope that a compromise might be accepted he offered to give the investiture of Milan to the third son of Francis, the Duke of Angoulême. Negotiations were begun for the fulfilment of this plan, the Pope did his best to mediate, and the moderate party in France were favourable to an understanding.[3]

The English ambassadors watched these negotiations with keen interest, and strove to counteract them, making common cause with the admiral of France, who was at the head of the war party, and with the Italian refugees, who wished to return to their country and estates by the force of French arms. Gardiner and Wallop promised Francis some subsidies if he would invade Italy, and with the help of Chabot they prevailed over the moderate party. As a preliminary for further operations, Francis sent the Count de Saint Pol with a strong force to invade Bresse and Savoy up to the Alps. He assisted the malcontents at Geneva, who had driven out their bishop and the officials of the duke, and he urged the Swiss to overrun the Pays de Vaud. Thus, before the new year, Charles of Savoy was deprived of nearly all his lands on the western side of the Alps.

The emperor, who fully understood that this was but the beginning of a far more serious war, set himself to prepare for the worst. He tried to gain the Pope over by making great offers to his son, Pier Luigi Farnese, and endeavoured to unite the smaller Italian states in a general confederacy for the protection of the Duke of Savoy and the defence of Italy. Best of all, new troops were raised in Germany and Italy to reinforce the army the emperor had brought back from Tunis. In Spain, the Low Countries, and Italy, everything was made ready to repel an attack by the French in the coming spring.

These signs of an approaching storm were observed by Henry with unfeigned delight. He thought that if war broke out Francis would be less overbearing, and thankful for any assistance England might give him, while the emperor would no longer dare to favour the English malcontents. Even if the latter anticipation proved to be mistaken, Henry was persuaded that Charles would be unable to do him any harm. He was confident that the struggle between his lukewarm friend and his staunch opponent would be an excellent safeguard for his own tranquillity.

Henry altogether misapprehended the influences which were likely to determine Charles's course. Hitherto the emperor had been held back from active interference in favour of Catherine and Mary chiefly by the fear that any attempt of the kind would occasion a rupture with France. If for other reasons he were compelled once more to fight Francis, the principal cause of his hesitation would be removed. No sooner, therefore, did war seem to be unavoidable than he began to think rather seriously about giving the English malcontents the aid they asked for. In December, after the invasion of the territory of the Duke of Savoy by St Pol, he all but decided to assist the English lords; and an important preliminary step was taken.

Charles did not rely on the assurances of the malcontents that in case of insurrection Mary would be in no danger. He could not feel quite sure as to Kingston's loyalty to her and to the queen; and he feared a sudden outbreak of rage on the part of the king. Besides, he wished to be able to set up Mary as a pretender against Henry; and it appeared to him necessary that she should be in some place where he could constantly communicate with her. After the death of Fisher and More, Mary had repeatedly urged Chapuis to procure for her the means of flight, but the ambassador, bound by his instructions, did not dare to proceed any further in the matter. Now Charles V himself took the initiative. The Count de Roeulx, his captain-general in the Low Countries, was commissioned to send a special agent to England to prepare for Mary's flight. If all went well, the princess was to be carried off in February, and in March or April the insurrection was to follow.[4] Shortly after the new year, Roeulx's agent arrived in England, and he and Chapuis carefully considered how Mary could be safely carried away.[5]

This was only one of many difficulties in which Henry was now entangled. In November Sir Francis Bryan had been sent to help

Gardiner and Wallop in their negotiations with the French; and in the beginning of December he had met the court near Pargaix, the country seat of Chabot de Brion. Here, immediately after Bryan's arrival, the three ambassadors were told by the ministers of Francis of some despatches which had just been received from Rome.[6] They contained a copy of the sentence of excommunication and deprivation against Henry VIII which had been drawn up by order of the Pope. It had been read in the middle of November in consistory, and Cardinal du Bellay, who was at Rome, had forwarded a copy of it to Francis I. The cardinal expressed his belief that there would never be another sentence like it. 'We are well aware', he continued:

> that it is necessary for you that the sentence should be in any case a very severe one, but there are some articles so expressly designed for you that a blind man would see that they have been inserted for no other purpose than to compel you to lose either the Pope or the King of England.[7]

Du Bellay added that he and the Bishop of Mâcon would do their best to gain time until they should hear from Francis, but that they had little hope of succeeding.

Francis now found himself in a very perplexing position. If he chose to stand by Henry, he would drive the Pope into the arms of Charles; and he knew, of course, that nothing could be more detrimental to his interests in Italy, which were at this moment engrossing his attention. On the other hand, if Francis wished to obtain the goodwill of the Pope, he would have to give up his alliance with Henry. The difficulty was in part explained to the English ambassadors, who knew not what to do. Bryan decided that he would not declare his charge to Francis until he and Gardiner received fresh instructions.[8]

Henry received the news with astonishment and anger. He had never doubted that the death of Sforza would make the French more desirous of securing his friendship, and to his dismay he found that this was not the case. Some contemptuous expressions used by the admiral of France about his power greatly enraged him, and he instructed Gardiner and Wallop strongly to protest against them.[9] He appears to have been really convinced that he possessed formidable power, and that he ought to have been taken more seriously into account.

According to his wont, Henry exaggerated his own importance. He was held in very small esteem, and every prince who had anything to lose shrank from an alliance with a king who might be deposed the day after the treaty was signed. His duplicity had been so great that nobody would rely on his assurances or accept his offers without good guarantees.

Even now he was doing what he could to destroy the last remnant of goodwill which the members of the Schmalkaldic League might feel for him. In the beginning of November, after having been arrested, Juergen Wullenwever had been closely questioned by the officials of the Archbishop of Bremen as to his former doings and as to his intentions in leaving Luebeck and coming to Rotenburg. Of his negotiations with Henry VIII something was known, and a great deal more was suspected;[10] but no hint of his last negotiations with Bonner and Cavendish had been conveyed to the archbishop, to King Christian, or to any of the princes and towns by whose delegates he was about to be examined.

Hoping, probably, that Henry would intercede for him and obtain his release, Wullenwever did not wish to compromise the King of England. He remained silent as to his proceedings at Hamburg, and even on the rack he did not speak of Bonner and Cavendish, but asserted that he had acted on behalf of the Count Palatine Frederic, who pretended a right to the Danish throne.[11]

Henry was less prudent. On hearing of the arrest of Wullenwever, he wrote to the senate and to the Archbishop of Bremen in such violent terms that the latter could not but suspect that there must be very special reasons for his interference. Henry called Wullenwever his beloved friend, declared that he had been arrested against all law and equity, complained that he himself had been badly treated by the archbishop, demanded the release of the prisoner, and threatened reprisals on the persons of all Bremen citizens in England if his request were refused.[12]

This threat could have no great effect on the mind of the archbishop, who was on very bad terms with the burghers over whom he was nominally set. Wullenwever remained a prisoner, and was repeatedly examined by the officials of the archbishop, and by delegates sent by Christian III, by Duke Henry of Brunswick, and by the senate of Luebeck.

But Henry was not disheartened even by so decided a rebuff. Bonner and Cavendish wrote once more to the senate of Bremen, asking them to obtain the release of the prisoner and, like the king, threatening them with reprisals.[13] Henry himself penned a second letter to the archbishop, in which he said again that Wullenwever had not been guilty of any crime, and pretended that his friend, being in prison, was unable to defend himself or to prove his innocence. Christopher had committed a sacrilege, Henry went on, in behaving as he had done; and he was asked to believe that if Wullenwever had really offended against the emperor, Henry, as the great friend of Charles, would punish him most severely. To Henry the prisoner was to be delivered, and, if Christopher declined, signal vengeance was to be taken on his subjects.[14]

The archbishop, exasperated by this arrogant letter, replied that although it professed to be only a friendly representation on behalf of an innocent man, it read rather like a declaration of war. In this matter nothing had been done that was contrary to law or justice, for, as a prince of the empire, the archbishop had full jurisdiction over all persons in his territory. He was ready to justify his acts before the emperor and the electors, to whom Henry might complain if he chose. Should the King of England proceed against citizens of Bremen, Christopher would appeal to the princes of the empire, and sharp retaliatory measures might follow.[15]

Henry and his ministers seem to have understood at last that the archbishop was not to be frightened. The correspondence ceased, and the Bremen citizens were not molested. Bonner and Cavendish, however, tried another way. They addressed a long letter to the King of Denmark, lecturing him about his duties as a Christian, and exhorting him to forgive past offences and not to persecute Wullenwever any longer.[16] This production had no more effect than the preceding letters. The prisoner was kept in close confinement at Rotenburg.

Henry did far more harm than good to the ex-burgomaster. His violence increased the suspicions of Wullenwever's enemies, and the prisoner was more closely questioned as to his dealings with the English ambassadors. At last, on 27 January, having been racked several times, and seeing that no help was likely to come, he confessed all that had passed at Hamburg between him and Bonner and Cavendish.[17] After this he declared in his dungeon that even two kings of England would not be able to save his life.[18]

If the course taken in this matter did no good to Wullenwever, it did much harm to Henry. It had been arranged that after the arrival of Fox and Heath in Saxony, and after the return of the elector from Vienna, the proposals of Henry should be considered by the members of the league of Schmalkalden. While the princes and delegates were sitting, they heard of Wullenwever's arrest and of Henry's outrageous talk. Peter Schwaben, who was present as the ambassador of Christian III, bitterly complained of Henry's dealings with the Luebeck demagogues; and the assembly, impressed by his appeal, decided to let the King of England know that he must no longer oppose the new King of Denmark or assist those who withstood his lawful authority.[19] A few days later, in reply to Henry's proposals for a league, the princes made counter-proposals, which clearly showed how thoroughly they distrusted him. They asked that Henry should accept the Augsburg confession, and that he should give them 100,000 crowns to aid them in defending themselves against the opponents of their faith. In return they offered him a barren title of protector of the league and a promise not to assist his enemies.[20]

Henry was not told the whole truth, for he was allowed to believe that the Wittenberg theologians approved of the divorce and of his marriage with Anne. Even with the facts which were reported to him, however, he was displeased, and in his reply to his ambassadors he refused to be ordered by others as to the faith of his realm, although he declared himself ready to hear what the German theologians might have to say about further reformation. The title of protector of the league he did not immediately accept, but the 100,000 crowns he was willing to deposit for the defence of the Protestant princes and towns.[21]

Shortly afterwards a second set of instructions were forwarded to the ambassadors. In these instructions it is said that Henry 'knoweth not that the Bishop of Rome, the emperor, or any other prince picketh any quarrel with him, and much less war; and although his grace feared some hostility of them, nevertheless, by the death of a woman, all calumnies be extincted.' He asks that, in case any prince shall invade his dominions, the members of the Schmalkaldic League shall furnish him with 500 horse or with ten ships of war at their own cost for four months, and that they shall find him at his expense 2,000 horse and 5,000 foot. Finally, he requires 'that the said confederates will take upon them in all councils hereafter, and everywhere else, to promote and defend the opinion of the reverend fathers, Dr Martyn, Justus Jonas, Cruciger, Pomeran, and Melanchthon, in the cause of his grace's marriage'.[22]

Meanwhile, apart from Henry's foreign policy, the prospects of Anne had not been improving. On the day on which Catherine's death had been reported at court, she had shown the greatest exultation.[23] She had come to hate Catherine most cordially, and rejoiced at the tidings that her detested rival was no more. For, up to this time, every success Anne had gained, every distinction she had obtained, had remained incomplete. She had been proclaimed queen, and heavy penalties had been threatened against those who refused her that title. But Catherine had remained firm, and Henry had not dared to proceed against her to the full extent of his laws. And Anne knew full well that by ninety-nine out of every hundred Englishmen, by nine out of every ten even of her own servants, she herself was secretly regarded as a concubine and usurper, while the prisoner at Kimbolton was considered the lawful wife and queen. Now and then this feeling displayed itself. If wise men were afraid to speak, fools were bolder. We find it related that in July the king's jester in open court called Anne and little Elizabeth opprobrious names. Henry was so angry that Sir Nicholas Carew hid the culprit away; but after a short time the king's wrath subsided, and the jester reappeared.[24]

Fallen as Catherine was from her former greatness, she could not be wholly deprived of the honour due to the daughter of the great Catholic kings, the aunt of the Kaiser, the kinswoman of nearly every royal family in Europe. She was still spoken of with respect; and Christian princes, even when they were politically opposed to her, protested against the manner in which she was treated. Anne, on the contrary, was reminded every day of the lowness of her origin, and Henry himself often taunted her with it. No foreign prince unequivocally recognised her as the lawful Queen of England. The German Protestants, following the advice of their theologians, held that Catherine was Henry's wife. Francis I, the only king who ever expressed a kind of friendship for Anne, acknowledged the Pope's authority in the matter of the divorce, and could never be brought absolutely to admit the validity of her marriage. As to his ministers, we have seen how little respect they now showed her.

In these circumstances the death of Catherine seemed at first sight a great gain for the cause of Anne. Now that she was without a rival, it was possible to hope that all the opposition offered to her would die out, and that, having no other queen to revere, people would generally acknowledge her claims. But a very little reflection brought her to a better appreciation of her position. On the day after Catherine's death she held a small council with her brother Rochford and a few of her most tried friends.[25] The precise result of the conference does not appear, but it was remarked that Anne's joy quickly subsided. For the first time, perhaps, she understood why Henry had so ardently desired the death of his wife.[26]

But Anne Boleyn was not a woman to succumb without a struggle. She still had a considerable hold over Henry, who stood in some awe of her intelligence, her energy, and her courage. If she could contrive to help him over the worst of his difficulties, she might regain much of her power, and at least postpone her fall. Now, one of Henry's chief difficulties arose from the persistency with which Mary asserted her rights. By her stubborn resistance to his demands she encouraged her adherents to oppose him, and in case of an insurrection her friends might prove very formidable. Could Mary be brought to yield, the king would be delivered from a serious danger; the one person capable of being put forward as a pretender against him would thereby lose most of her influence.

A few days after Catherine's death Cromwell said to a servant of Chapuis that Charles had no reason to regret an event which would have a good effect on the relations of the empire and England, and that henceforward he would communicate more frequently and more fully with the ambassador. All that was wanted was, that Mary should be persuaded to submit to the king, and in this respect Chapuis would be able to do more than anybody else. Chapuis certainly ought to try to influence her, for by doing so he would not only greatly please the king, but benefit Mary who, if she gave way, would be treated better than she had ever been. These suggestions were, of course, disregarded by the ambassador, and for the moment he rather avoided Cromwell.[27]

This effort having failed, Anne determined to try whether she could not accomplish a task which was beyond the powers of others; believing that if she succeeded Henry would be less eager to abandon her, and might even reward her with as much gratitude as his nature permitted. First of all, she endeavoured to attain her object by means of what seemed to her to be very generous offers. Mary was told through Lady Shelton that if she would act as a dutiful daughter towards the king, Anne would be to her a second mother and strive to obtain for her everything she could desire. And if Mary should afterwards wish to come to court, she would be held excused from bearing Anne's train and would always walk by her side. That is to say, Mary was to take rank before every other lady at court, Anne herself excepted; she was to have all honour shown to her as at the height of her former fortune.[28] Even ladies of the blood royal were obliged occasionally to bear the queen's train, and the princesses were not always entitled to walk at the queen's side. The greatness of the offer shows how much Anne desired to see Mary at her court.

But Anne had misunderstood Mary's character. Her opposition to the divorce and to the subsequent Acts was not due only to her regard for her mother, nor was her resistance after Catherine's death influenced by worldly considerations. So when Lady Shelton implored her with tears to submit to the will of the king, Mary would give no other answer but that she wished to obey her father in everything that was not opposed to her honour and conscience.[29] The acceptance of the new statutes she considered contrary to both. She stood up not only for her mother's fair fame, but for the authority of the Pope and the tenets of the Church of Rome.

Instead of promises, threats were now tried. Anne wrote to Lady Shelton that she was not to take any further trouble with that obstinate and undutiful girl. All that Anne had hitherto done had been out of charity and pity, and she was indifferent whether Mary submitted or not. She merely wanted to save Mary before she herself should give birth to a son, as she shortly expected to do. For after the birth of a prince – she well knew – the king would not hesitate to punish Mary, and no mercy would be shown to her. This letter Lady Shelton, as if by chance, dropped in Mary's oratory; and the princess, finding it there, read it and took a copy of it, which she sent to Chapuis.[30] Mary was frightened for a moment, but she did not yield, and a message from Chapuis sustained her courage.

Anne was bitterly disappointed to find that the will she had attempted to bend was as inflexible as her own. She was seen to cry, and was extremely harassed and agitated. Almost her only hope now lay in the pregnancy to which she had alluded in her letter to Lady Shelton. The statement was true; and if she was lucky enough to bear Henry a son, he might in his joy forget everything else and once more return under her sway. But the excitement of the last few days had told upon her health, which constant anxiety had been steadily undermining; and on 29 January – the very day on which her rival and victim was buried – she miscarried in the fourth month of her pregnancy.[31]

Henry had no compassion for Anne in her trouble. He went to her bedside, and gruffly told her that he now saw that God would not give him a son; then, rising to leave, he said harshly that when she recovered he would speak to her. The unhappy woman passionately exclaimed that her miscarriage was not her fault. She had been frightened by the way in which the Duke of Norfolk had told her of the king's fall from his horse. Besides, as her love for the king was far greater than Catherine's had ever been, she could not bear to see him making love to others. This imprudent explanation enraged the king, who did not admit her right to reprove him for his unfaithfulness.[32]

Anne had alluded to a fact of which the whole court had lately become aware. The king was making love to Mistress Jane Seymour, or Seamer, the daughter of Sir John Seamer of Wolfhall in Wiltshire. In a letter to Antoine Perrenot, the son of the lord keeper Granvelle, she was described by her ally and friend Eustache Chapuis. Writing on 18 May 1536, Chapuis says that the emperor, or my lord the chancellor, may wish to hear something of the new friend of the king. He continues:

> She is the sister of a certain Edward Semel, who has been in the service of his majesty [the emperor]; she is of middle height, and nobody thinks that she has much beauty. Her complexion is so whitish that she may be called rather pale. She is a little over twenty-five. You may imagine whether, being an Englishwoman, and having been so long at court, she would not hold it a sin to be still a maid. At which this king will perhaps be rather pleased... for he may marry her on condition that she is a virgin, and when he wants a divorce he will find plenty of witnesses to the contrary. The said Semel is not very intelligent, and is said to be rather haughty.

She was formerly in the service of the good queen [Catherine], and seems to bear great goodwill and respect to the princess. I am not sure whether later on the honours heaped on her will not make her change her mind.[33]

Chapuis added a few remarks which cannot be decently translated, and Perrenot, while deciphering the letter, interspersed it with glosses of his own, which, while they do not speak in favour of the propriety of the future cardinal, show that he had no very exalted opinion of Jane's virtue.

The account given by Chapuis to the secretary seems upon the whole to have been correct. If we may judge by her portraits, Jane was indeed very pale, and by no means remarkably handsome. There is nothing in her career which indicates superior intelligence; and although Henry necessarily affected to believe in her virtue, she was no better than the other young women of a coarse and dissolute court.

But she had a very great advantage. Nearly the whole court favoured her, and the most intimate servants of the king instructed her how to humour him. The consequence was that she played her game more skilfully than any of her predecessors, with the exception of Anne, had done. While trying to fascinate Henry, and to be as much as possible in his company, she resisted his wishes, and made a great profession of high principles.[34] That he believed in her sincerity is improbable, his opinion of others being always extremely low. But he was as well pleased with a decent appearance of virtue as with virtue itself, which he had been taught by Catherine to associate with many disagreeable characteristics. Jane's influence, therefore, increased, and the whole party of Anne became seriously alarmed.[35]

The malcontents were highly pleased; but their councils were divided. Those who were nearest the court hoped that, by the aid of Mistress Seymour, they might effect their purpose without having recourse to open rebellion. The other party, on the contrary, thought that their hopes had been too often deceived, and that the safest plan would be to rise in the spring. Chapuis, who had not yet received new instructions, did not wish to commit himself: he favoured neither the one opinion nor the other, but prepared quietly for the flight of Mary and for his own safety in case of a rupture.[36]

Before Anne's miscarriage, a few days after Catherine's death, the king said in strict confidence to one of his most trusted servants, so Chapuis was informed by Lord and Lady Exeter, that he had been driven by sorcery to marry Anne, and that he thought such a marriage could not be valid. God himself clearly showed its invalidity by not granting him male offspring.[37] When Anne recovered from her confinement, Henry continued to treat her with marked coldness. She had been accustomed to follow him wherever he went; now she had to remain at Greenwich while he spent with his courtiers a merry shrovetide in London.[38] The altered demeanour of the king towards Anne was generally remarked, and held to bode no good to her.

Anne's former allies, the French, were now among her most active enemies. As soon as Francis I had received du Bellay's letters, containing a copy of the proposed sentence, he had sent off a courier to Rome with instructions to his ambassadors. They were ordered not to interfere in favour of Henry: whether the sentence against him was issued or not, whether it was severe or mild, whether it deprived him of his kingdom or only laid him under spiritual censures, was all the same to the King of France. The letter reached Rome on the evening of 9 December, and was read by du Bellay with mingled wonder and dismay. The tone of his reply shows how sorry he was that he could not use the influence of Francis on behalf of Henry and Anne.[39]

On the day after the courier arrived at Rome a consistory was held about the English business, and the Pope caused an altered draft of the sentence to be read to the cardinals. In sending a copy of this draft to their king du Bellay and Denonville wrote:

> We have followed your orders point by point. The thing appears to everybody to be badly drawn up and full of danger for the future, but it is according to your wishes. We presume you are content that the sentence should be on the one hand so severe and on the other so unjust, that you may be able to make such use of it as your affairs require. If this be so, your intention has been very well fulfilled.[40]

To the Cardinal of Lorraine and the Cardinal of Tournon, du Bellay wrote at greater length, giving them an account of what had passed in the consistory. The Pope was extremely irritated on finding that in the opinion of nearly all the cardinals the sentence was too severe, and that they thought he ought not to issue it without first citing Henry to appear and show cause why he should not be excommunicated for having killed Cardinal Fisher.[41] Cardinal Schomberg was in favour of proceeding at once, but he thought the terms of the bull too severe.[42] Schomberg, Contarini, and Gonzaga represented to the Pope that times were changed, that the papal power was somewhat less than it had been, and that regard ought to be had to the irritation which such a sentence might produce among foreign nations.[43] This roused the anger of the Pope. God, he declared, had placed him above emperor, kings, and princes, and he fully intended to make use of his power.[44] As to the sentence, it was a perfectly proper one; it had been drawn up by men whose fitness for the task was above suspicion.[45] Some cardinal – probably du Bellay – said the emperor and the King of France ought first to be consulted, but the Pope answered that he had consulted them long ago. The emperor had replied that, if the Pope did his duty, he would show by executing the sentence to the utmost of his ability that he was the true friend and protector of the Holy See. And the king, to give him his due, after having greatly blamed the abominable misdeeds of the King of England, had promised as much if the emperor kept his word.[46]

Du Bellay was taken aback by this statement, having never heard that any such promise had been made by Francis. But of late he had not been very well informed as to the policy of the king, and, mindful of his instructions, he remained silent.[47]

Schomberg, aided by Campeggio, tried to induce du Bellay to explain the position of the King of France in this matter. Campeggio urged that in issuing the sentence the Pope ought not to offend those princes who had some understanding with Henry, especially the most Christian king. It was said that the King of France was a great friend of the King of England, and that they had concluded a treaty of alliance which both kept secret.[48] Schomberg made a more direct effort to compel du Bellay to reveal what he knew. He reminded the consistory of the promptness with which Pope Clement had acted in a moment of difficulty. Some persons had made a show of promoting a reconciliation of Henry with the Church, and had pretended that he was sending a mandate, when in reality astute men were being despatched to enter a protest. Clement, perceiving this, without waiting for the customary forms, had pronounced sentence, deceiving thereby those who had hoped to take him in.[49]

At this very direct attack du Bellay fired up. He first ironically thanked Campeggio for the care with which he watched over the interests of Francis. Then he launched into a long discourse, defending his own action and that of his king. He had begun to speak of the meeting of Marseilles, and was saying that all would have been satisfactorily arranged but for the Bishop of Winchester, when the Pope broke in: 'And nevertheless,' he exclaimed, 'that very scoundrel, that accursed man, is even now ambassador with the most Christian king.'[50] Du Bellay went on to say that at Calais Francis had withdrawn from the negotiations about the marriage of Angoulême and Elizabeth, which would have made the young duke the future King of England, because Henry insisted on certain articles in the treaty that might ultimately have brought about some danger of discord between the Holy See and France.[51] 'No,' interrupted the Pope, 'your king broke off because the King of England wanted to have the Duke of Angoulême as a hostage.

That I know perfectly well.' The cardinal, according to his own account, replied with no more moderation than was necessary, and he and the Pope seem to have had a violent quarrel.[52] At last Cardinal de Cupis, who on that day acted as dean of the college, managed to quiet the Pope.[53] Du Bellay, on his part, gave up further opposition, and agreed that the Pope might issue the bull without submitting it once more to the college of cardinals.[54]

The matter remained in suspense for a few weeks, for Paul III himself, however incensed against Henry, could not but feel some misgivings as to the effect the bull might produce. No public step, therefore, had been taken when the news of Catherine's death arrived. This suggested to the Pope a possibility of new combinations; and as he thoroughly mistrusted du Bellay and du Bellay's friend, Denonville, he sent for the French secretary, Nicolas Raince, and opened his mind to him. He simply wished Francis to offer the hand of his daughter Madeleine to Henry. For the sake of so great a match, Henry might be prepared to discard Anne and to return to communion with Rome.[55] Raince seems to have reported the matter to his friends at the French court, and in subsequent letters we find hints that Francis really took up the matter and felt his ground in England, or at least gave out that he was doing so.[56]

The fact was, Francis now thoroughly understood that it was necessary to make a choice; that if he continued to stand by Henry and Anne he would entirely lose the goodwill of the Pope. And as Henry did not offer him any great advantages, the choice was soon made. The death of Catherine only confirmed Francis in his purpose, for Henry, feeling more secure, became much less tractable. The object of the new policy of the French king was to bring about an understanding with the emperor; and he formally undertook to forsake the King of England if Charles would satisfy his demands with regard to Italy. Du Bellay, who was considered too violent and too friendly to Henry and Anne, was recalled from Rome;[57] and after his departure the French agents with the Pope, so far from opposing the issuing of the sentence, seem, about the end of March, to have urged the Pope publicly to excommunicate the former ally of their master. Francis, having ceased to look for any considerable assistance from Henry, wished to have the sentence published, that Charles might be prevented from concluding an alliance with England.[58]

After the failure of Anne's attempt to subdue Mary, the princess had not been further molested, and in some minor points Cromwell had granted the requests made in her name by Chapuis. Nevertheless, feeling uneasy about her safety, the ambassador went on with his preparations for her flight. But towards the end of February he received a message to the effect that Cromwell desired to have a secret interview with him at St Austin's church. On the 24th Chapuis complied with this request, and the secretary, after complaining of some news he had received from France, began to speak of a closer alliance between Charles and Henry, and urged Chapuis to propose conditions.[59] At first the ambassador was somewhat reticent, but after some time he hinted at four conditions which might form a basis for negotiation. What answer would be given, he inquired, if Charles asked, first, that Henry should submit to the Pope and acknowledge the power of the Holy See? secondly, that the Princess Mary should be declared legitimate and reinstated in her former rank? thirdly, that the King of England should furnish help against the Turks? and fourthly, that an offensive and defensive alliance should be concluded between Charles and Henry against everybody who might wrong or attack either.[60] Cromwell quickly replied that as to the two latter points there would be no difficulty whatever; the king wished for such an alliance, and was ready to help to fight the Turk. As to the Lady Mary, this certainly was the proper time to arrange her affairs; and he felt sure it would be done to Charles's satisfaction.[61] The first demand presented the only real difficulty. 'Might not the question,' he suggested, 'be referred to commissioners?' Chapuis met this proposal with an absolute refusal; he would not hear of the matter being referred even to a council called by the emperor. Henry must admit the Pope's authority. Afterwards the points in dispute, with the consent of both parties, might be submitted to a council to be called by the Pope. Cromwell did not entirely reject these conditions; he only remarked that it would be best to begin the negotiations about some minor matter that would lead in the end to the principal question. He thought the emperor might send Chapuis full powers to treat of a reconciliation and alliance.

The French he continued to condemn in strong terms; and in doing so he used an expression which could not but arrest the attention of the ambassador. He said that the conduct of Francis was resented not only by him and his friends but by the chief of those who were in receipt of French pensions – Norfolk, Suffolk, and Fitzwilliam – even, he added, by the other party and faction. The reference was to Lord Wiltshire; and the obvious intention of Cromwell was to show that he no longer desired to be associated with the adherents of Anne.[62] He ended by asking Chapuis to be of good cheer with regard both to the rights of the Lady Mary and to all other matters still undecided. Let him remember the wonders that had been accomplished since Cromwell had had the direction of the royal affairs.[63]

Chapuis immediately wrote a detailed account of the conversation to his master, and, pointing out the advantages that might be derived from a reconciliation with England, he asked for further instructions and, if a reconciliation was to be effected, for the necessary powers. The direct route to Italy being unsafe, the courier to whom this despatch was entrusted was obliged to take a roundabout way, and, as the roads at that time of the year were bad, his journey lasted no less than five weeks. At last, on 29 March, he overtook the emperor at Gaeta on his way to Rome.[64]

16

CHARLES V & ANNE

On 28 February 1536, Charles V received a packet containing three letters from Chapuis, dated 18 December, 30 December and 9 January. He immediately sent the ambassador new instructions. Chapuis was to take up the proposals for a reconciliation and for a closer alliance which had been made by Henry on 30 December; the pretext being that since the queen was dead it might be unnecessary to adopt further measures with regard to the sentence, or to remit the matter to a council, if only Mary were fairly treated. Henry was to be advised that the best way of dealing with the princess would be to arrange for her some honourable marriage. These instructions were not seriously meant, for the emperor, seeing Henry so obstinate about Anne, thought that a good understanding was in the meantime impossible. But he considered it expedient to seem to be carrying on negotiations. King Francis would hear of them, his insolence would be somewhat checked, and he might even be brought, if he were made sufficiently angry with Henry, to treat with Charles to the advantage of Mary. In any case time would be gained, and when Charles had beaten the French he would be better able to dictate his conditions as to the princess and as to English affairs in general.[1]

The letter written by Chapuis on 24 February changed the emperor's opinion; and on the day on which he received it new and more detailed instructions were sent to the ambassador. They were highly characteristic of the emperor and of his advisers. Charles had been a staunch friend of Catherine, and even after her death he never admitted that the divorce was legal. In this respect he acted in a perfectly honourable manner, postponing his interest to what he considered right and due to his aunt. But, on the other hand, although he believed that Catherine had been poisoned, although he knew that she had been persecuted at Anne's request, he either thought of her wrongs with perfect composure, or concealed his indignation to suit the exigencies of his policy. He himself, as he had already proved, and as he proved still more decisively at a later period, was so ready to plan and order murders, that he may have felt it would be slightly absurd to resent a murder committed by an adversary. His new instructions to Chapuis were, therefore, a model of cool and able statecraft, as statecraft was understood in the sixteenth century.

As to the four points raised by the ambassador, the difficulties of the first did not seem to the emperor to be very great. It related to the sentence of divorce and to the refusal of the annates. If the claims of the princess were respected, the complications connected with the sentence might be avoided; and regarding the annates Charles would do his utmost at the court of Rome to settle the dispute to Henry's satisfaction. Chapuis was to urge that the princess should be expressly declared legitimate, and to point out that this might be done in virtue of the *bona fides parentum*. If Henry would not concede so much, he ought at least to let the matter remain in suspense, and to make no declaration to the contrary. On the other hand, Mary ought to abandon the hostile tone she had adopted, and should not ask the emperor to support her claims by force or to do more than he had done already. The emperor wrote:

> As long as the king lives, the said princess cannot pretend to anything more, nor can we or any other of her relatives proceed much further by asking for other things in her favour. It matters not what the wrong done to her late mother may have been. For she cannot in good conscience insist upon avenging this wrong on her father or consent to its being done by others, even if the life of her mother has been, as is suspected, shortened by foul means. If the sentence about the divorce be executed in order that the king may forsake his concubine, he may marry somebody else, while it is quite clear that from the said concubine he can have no progeny that can hereafter dispute the right of the princess to the succession.[2]

As clear and logical as possible. If at Henry's death the choice of the nation lay between Mary and Elizabeth, the former would be pretty sure to succeed. And as Anne's marriage was invalid, any son she might have would be illegitimate, and Mary would still have a right to the crown. It was, therefore, to the advantage of Mary and indirectly of Charles that her father should retain his mistress, and in the opinion of the emperor this consideration was more important than any other. So we find the son of Juana la Loca preaching filial respect, the murderer of Vogelsberger and so many others inculcating the duty of forgiving all offences.

But Charles thought that Mary might not be able to control her feelings; perhaps, too, he feared that Henry and Anne, to make quite sure, would prefer to poison her. He added, therefore, that if possible a husband should be found for her out of England. The Infante Dom Luis of Portugal – brother of the empress – would be a very suitable match. The concubine and her adherents, said Charles, would be unreasonable if they objected to such a marriage, for the Portuguese were peaceful neighbours. He continued:

> But should the concubine not be satisfied with the proposal either that Mary should be legitimated, or that the matter should be left in suspense – a proposal which, after all, she and all her adherents ought to welcome as a means of escape from the fear and danger in which they now continually are – and should she claim more for her daughter, or for the children she may still have, the negotiation must not for that be broken off. Her ultimate object must be found out. And after you have made to her such observations as you think may serve, you shall say that you will write to us about it, unless indeed the thing be too exorbitant. [3]

Granvelle here added a few words on the draft of the letter to the effect that Chapuis was in this matter to ask for Cromwell's help. He was to communicate the above. If there was anything the concubine or her adherents were not to know, a certain sign would be made. And the sign appears before a paragraph setting forth that if Henry had already decided to discard Anne and to take somebody else, Chapuis was not to offer too much opposition, unless the king wanted to marry a Frenchwoman. [4]

This despatch shows how far Charles was ready to go. For years he had been the bitterest enemy of Anne. Now his ambassador was ordered to treat with her, to negotiate with her a kind of truce, almost an alliance. So strong were the terms of the first draft of the letter that Granvelle, fearing Chapuis might defend Anne even against Henry himself, warned him that this was to be done only under certain conditions.

The explanation of all these concessions was indicated in the last two points noted in the instructions. Charles wanted aid against the Turk, and he wanted an alliance against Francis; at least, Henry was to defend the Low Countries or to give a good sum of money for the war. The emperor would have found it quite compatible with his religion to pocket the proceeds of the sale of the abbey lands; and had Anne been able to obtain for him so great a favour, he would have thanked her for it by smoothing over her difficulties.

The courier who carried this reply did not travel more rapidly than the one who had brought the letter of Chapuis. The consequence was that the ambassador did not receive his new instructions before 15 April.[5] In the meantime a good deal had happened to change the situation.

The influence of Jane Seymour had greatly increased. By the end of February her brother Edward Seymour had been made a gentleman of the king's privy chamber.[6] In the middle of March, when Jane was with the court at Greenwich, Henry sent her from London a letter and a purse full of sovereigns. This gave her an opportunity of making a fine show of virtue. She took the king's letter, kissed it in token of respect and devotion, but returned it unopened; then, falling on her knees, she charged the gentleman who had brought it to do the same to the king, and to beseech him in her name to remember that she was a gentlewoman sprung from a good and honourable stock, free from any taint whatever. She had no greater treasure in this world than her honour; not even fear of death would make her forget it. She would not take the purse, but said that if the king wanted to make her a present, let it be when God should send her some good and honest husband.[7] The gentleman, who seems to have been a friend of Jane, returned to Henry with the purse and the letter, and delivered the lady's message. The king was by no means displeased; the next time he saw her he greatly praised the modest and prudent answer she had sent him. She had acted most virtuously, he said; and to give her full proof that the love he bore her was honest, henceforward he would not speak to her except in the presence of some of her relatives. That the good king might suffer no loss by his scrupulous delicacy, Cromwell had to give up a room he occupied in the palace. In this room, which had the advantage of being accessible by a secret passage, Sir Edward Seymour and his wife were lodged, and there Jane received her lover.[8]

Henry was probably not aware that the highly moral speeches of Jane were not even of her own invention, but that she was taught by his attendants how to behave. Sir Nicholas Carew, Sir Thomas Eliot and other intimate servants of the king warned her not to yield to Henry unless he married her, and Jane was wise enough to follow their advice. At a given moment, they further urged, she was to tell the king that the whole nation held his marriage with Anne in abomination, and that nobody considered it valid. All around there were to be people who would confirm what she said, if the king ordered them on their allegiance to tell him the truth. For this purpose the help of Chapuis was desired; and the Marchioness of Exeter, who kept the ambassador well informed of all that went on at court, sent him a message on 1 April imploring him to lend his aid.[9]

Chapuis, who had not yet received his new instructions, felt rather inclined to grant the request of Lady Exeter. Since the meeting at

Austin friars Cromwell had shown himself more and more friendly to the imperial ambassador and to the imperial party. In the beginning of March he happened to speak to Doctor de Lasco, whom Henry wanted to place with Mary; and the doctor observed that when Cromwell pronounced the princess's name he raised his cap – a mark of respect with which he had never before honoured her.[10] A little cross of gold which Catherine from her deathbed had sent to Mary, had been taken away by the royal officials. A few days after speaking to de Lasco, Cromwell had it sent back to the princess.[11]

But Cromwell did more than all this. In the reply which the English ambassadors at the Saxon court were to make to the Schmalkaldic princes, there was, as we have seen, a paragraph requiring the league to defend the opinion of Luther, Melanchthon and Pomeranus in the matter of the divorce. This paragraph the ambassadors were obliged to suppress, for they knew that the Lutheran theologians had maintained, and continued to maintain, that the marriage with Catherine was valid.[12] At first the royal ministers tried to keep the matter secret; but as it soon began to be talked about, the opinion of the Lutheran divines was laid before a number of bishops and doctors that they might draw up a fitting answer.[13] This was an excellent opportunity for those among them who were adverse to further innovation; and the opportunity was not lost. Members of the reforming party found themselves in a very unpleasant position, and the result of the conference was decidedly unfavourable to Protestantism. Cranmer was unable to restore the credit of his adherents, for he himself was in disgrace with the king. At the very time when Henry wished to be reconciled to Charles, the archbishop had chosen to preach most violently against what he called the usurpations of the imperial power, the supremacy of which he angrily denied.[14]

Seeing the tendency of events, Cromwell apparently began to think in earnest of the possibility of a reconciliation with Rome. The *malleus monachorum*, as he has been called, was heard to protest against the way in which the abbeys were despoiled. He took the side of the conservative churchmen against those who had been hitherto considered Anne's principal supporters; and he did so with a boldness and energy which offended both the vacillating king and Anne.[15] About the end of March the court was full of rumours regarding a serious quarrel between Anne and the secretary.

At a dinner given by Chapuis to the Marquis of Exeter, Lady Kildare, and Lord Montague, the latter told the ambassador of the ill feeling between Cromwell and Anne, and mentioned a report that Henry was bent on a new marriage.[16] Shortly afterwards Chapuis had an interview with Cromwell, to whom he bluntly spoke of what he had heard. If it were true, he said, the secretary ought to prepare for the coming struggle better than Wolsey had done. Did the king really wish to make another marriage, it would be a very good thing, as all his difficulties might then be overcome. Cromwell demurely replied that if the fate of Wolsey overtook him, he would try to bear it patiently. He had been no promoter of the marriage with Anne; he had only found the means by which it could be accomplished when the king vehemently desired it. As to a new marriage, the king in former days had certainly rather loved the fair sex, but Cromwell thought that henceforward he would live more chastely and not change again. But he said this in a way which convinced Chapuis that he meant the contrary; as he spoke, he put his hand before his face to conceal a smile. One thing he assured Chapuis of; if the king re-married, he would not choose his bride in France. During the whole interview Cromwell was most friendly; and when they were about to part, he begged Chapuis to accept a very fine horse as a gift from him.[17]

After this conversation Chapuis felt pretty sure that Cromwell would no longer maintain the cause of Anne. The intrigue which had been proposed by Lady Exeter seemed, therefore, to have every chance of success; and the ambassador considered whether he ought not to become the chief mover in the attempt to drive 'the concubine' from the throne. He saw, however, that the interests of Mary might be imperilled if Henry were free to marry again. Accordingly, before deciding finally, he wrote once more to Mary, and, placing the two sides of the question before her, asked to be informed what her wishes were.[18] As he had expected, she immediately replied that she did not care how her own interests might be affected, if her father could be saved from the sinful life he was leading. She wished Chapuis to do as Lady Exeter had desired, and hoped he would succeed. This decided the ambassador's course. During the following days he had several interviews with Cromwell and with the leading conspirators, and some arrangements had been made when the despatches from Charles arrived.[19]

On receipt of the emperor's letters Chapuis sat down to decipher them at once. As they were rather long he had to work until late at night, but he made a short abstract of such points as he was to communicate, and early next morning he went to Cromwell to request that he might have an audience of the king. The secretary, on hearing what Chapuis had to say, was so pleased that he would have liked to open negotiations without delay. But it was Easter Sunday, and Henry, who always shrank from forming a definite judgement, was glad to have a pretext for putting off the audience. Cromwell had to reply that the ambassador would be received on Tuesday the 18th.

The news that Charles was disposed to be on good terms again with Henry was not kept a strict secret. A good many of the courtiers heard of it, while Anne and her nearest kinsfolk and friends seem to have been more particularly informed as to the proposed articles. Consequently, when Chapuis arrived on Tuesday morning at Greenwich Palace, he was welcomed by a throng of joyous courtiers, Lord Rochford, Anne's brother, being foremost among them. With Rochford the ambassador had a most friendly conversation, the young lord making loud protestations of his desire for an alliance between England and the emperor. Even then, however, as Chapuis remarked, he spoke as a strong Lutheran which, of course, was not to the taste of the imperial minister.

After a short while Cromwell went to greet Chapuis, and to ask him in Henry's name whether he would not see the queen and kiss hands. The king would be pleased if he did so, but left him entirely free. Chapuis cleverly answered that it might be better to wait until he had conferred with the king about the new proposals; and with this opinion Cromwell agreed. Henry also, when the secretary reported to him what Chapuis had said, declared himself satisfied.[20]

The truth is, if Chapuis had thought that he would have gratified the king and advanced the interests of his master by allowing himself to be presented to Anne as queen, he would gladly have gone. As he wrote to Granvelle, he would have been ready, had Henry been tractable, to offer, not a pair of candles, but a hundred, on the altar either of the devil or of the she-devil. But he had been warned that she was in disgrace, and that it would be of no use to pay his court to her.[21]

Coming out of his apartment to go to mass, Henry plainly showed that the refusal of Chapuis had not displeased him. He was most gracious to the ambassador. After this the king went on, and Rochford again placed himself by the side of Chapuis to accompany him to the chapel. There was a great rush after them, for as Anne was also going to mass she and Chapuis would be brought face to face; and the host of idle courtiers were curious to see how they would behave to each other. Chapuis was placed close to the door by which Anne was to enter, probably in order that he might be quite near her. It had not been observed that after the opening of the door he would be concealed behind it. Anne, however, knowing that he was there, turned round as she passed. He made her a deep bow, and she responded with as deep and gracious a salute. Then she swept on to her place at the king's side.[22] A good many people who had hoped that Chapuis would be rude to his former enemy were grievously vexed, and Mary herself was astonished when she heard that the ambassador of the emperor had bowed to 'that woman'.[23]

After mass Henry went to Anne's rooms, where he was accustomed to dine. The foreign ambassadors and most of the courtiers followed him, but Chapuis – with Rochford always at his side – dined with the principal noblemen in the chamber of presence. Anne seems to have been disappointed that Chapuis did not attend her to her apartments, for she asked the king why he had not come with the other ambassadors. Henry, annoyed by the question, answered that Chapuis had good reasons for staying away.[24] Nevertheless, Anne was resolved to throw in her lot with the imperial faction; and after dinner she spoke strongly against Francis. 'It was a great shame,' she said, 'that the King of France treated his uncle the Duke of Savoy so badly, and intended to invade Milan in order to prevent further action against the Turks. It seems,' she exclaimed, alluding to the infamous disease of Francis, 'that the King of France, tired of life on account of his illness, wants to shorten his days by going to war.'[25] These remarks were of course repeated, and they were meant to show that there was an open rupture between her and her former friends.

In the afternoon Henry left Anne's rooms, and taking the ambassador into the recess of a window, prepared to hear his communication. When Chapuis had submitted his proposals, Henry broke out into the most extravagant talk, declaring that he would make no concessions, and boasting in a preposterous way about his greatness and power, and about the benefits he had heaped upon Charles. Chapuis, although irritated by this bragging, allowed the king to go on, that he might have his fill of vainglory and slowly quiet down.[26] But Henry would not quiet down; he refused to listen to reason, and insisted, among other things, that Charles should acknowledge himself to have been altogether in the wrong, and should either have the papal sentence quashed or declare that it had been obtained against justice by threats.[27]

By and by, the king called Cromwell and the Lord Chancellor Audeley into the recess, and asked Chapuis to repeat his message to them. When they had heard it, the ambassador retired and began to speak with Sir Edward Seymour, keeping, however, a watchful eye on the little group at the window. He could soon perceive that there was an acrimonious dispute between the king and Cromwell. After a protracted discussion the secretary called out that he was so thirsty he could not bear it any longer, and, snorting and puffing with anger, he left the king and Audeley, and went to sit on a chest where Henry could not see him.[28]

After a while Henry left the chancellor; and Chapuis, perceiving that for the moment nothing more could be done, made ready to depart. Henry was a little more gracious when the ambassador came to take his leave, but he made no concessions. Chapuis was accompanied by many of the courtiers to the gates, where he mounted his horse. They were rather crestfallen, and some of the councillors said plainly that they were very sorry for what had happened. On the road Chapuis was overtaken by Cromwell, who was also riding back to London; and the secretary did not hide his vexation at the obstinacy and folly of the king. He was in a state of such excitement that when he arrived at his lodgings at Roll's house he had to take to his bed, where he remained for several days.[29]

Antoine de Castelnau, Bishop of Tarbes, the resident French ambassador, soon heard of the negotiations opened by Chapuis; so, curious to know what had been the result, he went on the following day to Greenwich. He saw the Duke of Norfolk, who assured him that, whatever the emperor might offer or propose, the king would not withdraw from the alliance with Francis.[30] Afterwards Castelnau was received by the king, who complained that Francis did not show him sufficient respect, and that a special envoy who should have been sent to him long ago had not yet arrived. The bishop tried to soothe his anger, and at last the king told him about the mission of Chapuis. The four propositions of the imperial ambassador had now swollen into five, besides curiously altering their nature. The first referred to the day when Charles V would enter Rome. Secondly, Charles asked Henry to intercede with the French king in favour of the Duke of Savoy. Thirdly, fearing that Francis might invade Milan, Charles begged Henry to help him if he were so attacked. Fourthly, Henry was entreated to forget all that had passed between him and the emperor on account of Catherine, and to renew the old treaties of friendship and confederation. The fifth proposition set forth a demand for aid against the Turk.[31] Henry pretended that as to Savoy he had replied in a manner quite favourable to Francis. He warned the bishop that Charles was raising a large army with which to repel the French, and advised the king not to advance any further, but to fortify the conquests he had made, and to await the emperor's attack. Castelnau thanked Henry for the friendly feeling he had exhibited, and immediately after his return to London wrote an account of the audience to his master. He added that at this moment Henry seemed most favourably inclined.[32]

Anne's position was now a very strange one. After years of unrelenting hostility the emperor had proposed the terms of a truce which appeared likely, as the death of Catherine had appeared likely, to be of great advantage to her. If she could have had her way, the offers of Charles would have been accepted; and had she been willing to give up Protestantism, she might then have persuaded Henry to submit to the Pope, who would have given absolution to both of them and recognised the validity of their marriage from the time of Catherine's death. But it was too late to hope for these great results. New influences were at work – some of them of Anne's own creation – over which she had no control, and which brought her to the scaffold.

When Henry obstinately refused to submit to the Pope, it was not only his vanity which was at play; he was impelled also by greed and by fear of rebellion. By an act of parliament passed in March a good many abbeys had been dissolved, and their lands vested in the king.[33] His coffers had thus been filled, and he had been enabled to meet the expenses of government and of an extravagant court without exasperating his people by odious taxes. Submission to Rome meant for him the loss of this agreeable and plentiful source of income; it meant retrenchment and economy – a prospect which had no attractions for him. But it meant even more. A good part of the abbey lands seized by the king's officers had been granted away to his servants and courtiers, or to the lords and gentry in the neighbourhood of the confiscated estates. These favoured persons, and others who expected similar bounties, had a direct interest in opposing a reconciliation with the Holy See, which might have endangered the peaceful possession of what they held and cut off all hope of new spoliation. As long as Henry was firmly resolved not to return to communion with Rome, it may have been excellent policy to give away abbey lands, but his generosity at the expense of the church made it very difficult for him to alter his course.

Among those to whom large grants had been made were the Duke of Norfolk, the Duke of Suffolk, and several other recipients of French pensions. They became the leaders of the party opposed to submission to the Pope; and as Cromwell had begun to speak against the destruction of the abbeys, and had resisted further grants, they looked upon him as their great enemy.[34] During the illness which kept Cromwell at Roll's house, Norfolk ruled supreme at the council board, and he employed his time very well. The official party without their chief presented but a poor front; they could not thwart so powerful a peer. The object of Norfolk now was to throw Henry into the arms of Francis, to make reconciliation with Charles and with the Holy See impossible, and to displace the imperialist first secretary. He succeeded so far that on the 22nd Henry summoned Castelnau to his presence, and asked him to go to France and explain the whole position to Francis, and to obtain the speedy conclusion of a treaty of alliance. As Henry seemed ready to grant terms most advantageous to Francis, the bishop consented, and returned to London to prepare for his journey.[35]

Henry was not, however, without misgivings. Had he, by rejecting the proposals transmitted by Chapuis, definitively closed the door to a reconciliation with the emperor? That would be extremely awkward, for if it were made known the French would become as arrogant as ever. He was already half sorry for what he had done. Sending for de Lasco, about whose future service with Mary he pretended that he wanted to speak, he closely questioned the doctor as to the way in which Chapuis had talked since his audience at Greenwich. He was evidently afraid of the anger of the ambassador.[36]

It was in this state of mind that Cromwell found his royal master when after his brief illness he returned to court. The secretary had had time to review quietly the whole situation, and he had arrived at the conclusion that vigorous action on his part had become inevitable. By opposing the further destruction of abbeys, by stoutly advocating the imperial alliance and the concessions necessary to obtain it, he had kindled the anger of Henry, of the greedy courtiers, and of the French faction. His position was threatened, Norfolk was gaining on him, and by some means or other he must strengthen his hold over the king. It would be necessary to teach Henry that he could not afford to dispense with his secretary's services. He would have to be confronted by some difficulty which he could hope to dispose of only with the aid of the powerful and complicated organisation over which Cromwell presided.

At this moment there was a difficulty which, if brought to a crisis, might be made to serve. Henry had been so well worked upon by Jane Seymour and her friends that he ardently wished to be rid of a woman with whom he was no longer in love, and who could not bear him the son he desired. He had already on several occasions spoken of his marriage with Anne as invalid, and of his intention to proceed with another divorce. He had assured Jane Seymour that his love for her was honourable, and had clearly shown that he intended to marry her. But, as usual, he had not courage to strike the blow with his own hand; he was waiting for some one to take the responsibility of the deed.

Of course Cromwell might have helped to obtain a divorce; but he saw that it would be neither in his own nor in the king's interest to proceed in this manner. To have applied for a divorce would have been to proclaim to the world that Henry, on entering the holy bonds of matrimony, was careless whether there were impediments or not; it would have been to raise a very strong suspicion that the scruples of conscience he had pleaded the first time, were courtly enough to reappear whenever he wanted to be rid of a wife. Henry's reputation would have greatly suffered, and as he knew this himself, although he chafed at his fetters, he dared not cast them off. A second reason – which more especially affected Cromwell – was that Anne, if she were simply divorced, would still remain Marchioness of Pembroke, with a very considerable fortune, and with some devoted friends. Rochford had gained experience, and showed no little ability, and he, acting with his sister, might form a party which would be most hostile to the secretary.

Besides, a divorce could have been secured by Norfolk as easily as by Cromwell. There would really have been no difficulty at all. Cranmer would not have dreamt of disobeying the royal commands; he did in fact pronounce the marriage to be void. Of the other bishops one half were bitterly opposed to Anne, while most of those whose promotion she had aided were supple courtiers who would do the king's bidding. Indeed, we hear of some zealous servant, who, perceiving what was wanted, went on 27 April to consult Stokesley, the Bishop of London, as to whether the marriage between the king and Anne was valid or not. Stokesley, although he hated Anne and the Boleyns, was too cautious to offer an opinion. He said that he would reply to such a question only if it were put by the king himself; and he added that, should the king intend to ask him, he would like to know beforehand the kind of answer that was desired.[37]

For all these reasons it was necessary that Anne should be got rid of in a quicker and more violent way. Difficulties and dangers were to be invented, that Cromwell might save the king from them. Anne was to be found guilty of such heinous offences that she would have no opportunity of avenging her wrongs. Her friends were to be involved in her fall, and the event was to be associated with horrors that would strike the imagination of the king and withdraw the attention of the public from the intrigue at the bottom of the scheme. Calamity was to be brought upon her, too, in a way that would satisfy the hatred with which she was regarded by the nation, and take the ground away under the feet of the conspirators. Thus Cromwell, as he afterwards told Chapuis, resolved to plot for the ruin of Anne.[38]

17

THE ARREST

Whether Henry was at once informed that Anne was to be killed is not certain. Probably he was only told by Cromwell that he was menaced by grave dangers, and that it would be necessary to appoint commissioners to hold special sessions at which offenders against him might be tried. On 24 April, in accordance with these representations, the king signed a commission by which the Lord Chancellor Audeley, the Dukes of Norfolk and Suffolk, the Earl of Oxford, lord high chamberlain, the Earl of Westmoreland, the Earl of Wiltshire, lord privy seal, the Earl of Sussex, Lord Sandys, chamberlain of the household, Sir Thomas Cromwell, chief secretary, Sir William Fitzwilliam, treasurer, Sir William Paulet, comptroller of the household, and the nine judges or any four or more of them were empowered to make inquiry as to every kind of treason, by whomsoever committed, and to hold a special session to try the offenders.[1] That this was virtually a death-warrant for Anne, Henry must have known, or at least suspected; but his conscience remained quiet: the deed would be done by others.

The commission was not made public; nor was it communicated to the persons to whom it was addressed. That would have been contrary to all the traditions of the Tudor service. It was kept strictly secret; and only a few chosen instruments were to be employed until the case should be sufficiently prepared. To make out a case against Anne was now the great object of Cromwell, and he began his task with characteristic energy.

The tacit understanding between Henry and Cromwell which led to the signing of the commission restored the secretary to his former influence. When, therefore, the Bishop of Tarbes, ready to leave for France, repaired to court on 25 April, and asked for the articles he was to submit to his master, he found that they had not been drawn up; and he was kept the whole day at Greenwich, the council sitting and debating until late at night.[2] Although Henry, acting on Cromwell's advice, treated the French coldly, he was not prepared to conciliate the emperor, as he showed clearly enough in a despatch sent at this time to Richard Pate, the English ambassador at the court of Charles V. In giving directions for the composition of this despatch – for it was evidently in substance the work of the king – Henry seems to have resolved to have once more what Chapuis had called, a week before, 'his fill of glory'. He asserted that through his influence Charles had been made King of Spain and Emperor; he rejected and complained of all the conditions Charles had proposed for a reconciliation; he protested that he would not be dictated to; and finally, in a ciphered paragraph at the end, he instructed Pate to ascertain the most favourable terms the emperor might be brought to offer.[3] It was an extremely foolish letter, but Cromwell allowed it to pass, well knowing that a complete change in the state of affairs would shortly render it inoperative. In return for this concession to the king's vanity, he was allowed to add to the articles agreed upon with Castelnau certain demands which, as he knew, Francis would never grant. The consequence was that when the bishop, already somewhat angry at the delay, returned to court on the 27th and heard what was proposed, he indignantly refused to go to France on such an errand. For the moment there was no further danger of a closer alliance with Francis.[4]

Cromwell was thus in a position to devote himself to the work of collecting evidence against Anne. The old stories about her ante nuptial misconduct would not of course suffice. Even with regard to irregularities of which she had been accused after marriage there was a difficulty; for by the statute passed in the autumn of 1534 any statement capable of being interpreted as a slander upon the king's issue might be accounted treason, so that people were rather loath to repeat what they might have heard to Anne's discredit. Cromwell decided, therefore, to have her movements watched closely, in the hope that she might be caught in some imprudence. As most of her servants were secretly her enemies, he did not doubt that some of them would gladly give information against her, if they could do so without risking their own lives.

On the 23rd there had been an election to a place in the Order of the Garter, rendered vacant by the death of Lord Abergavenny. Sir Nicholas Carew and Lord Rochford had been candidates for it, and in ordinary circumstances the brother-in-law of the king would certainly have carried the day. But it was Sir Nicholas, Anne's open enemy, who had been elected. This incident, although insignificant in itself, was of great service to Cromwell, for those who disliked Anne began to think that it could not be very dangerous to speak against her, when she had not influence enough even to obtain a favour for her brother. On the day after the election her opponents sent a triumphant and cheering message to Mary.[5]

It seems to have been Anne's own imprudence which gave Cromwell his first clue. She was exceedingly vain; and, like her daughter Elizabeth, who inherited many of the qualities of her strange character, she delighted in the admiration of men, and fancied that every man who saw her was fascinated by her charms. Her courtiers soon found out that the surest road to her favour was either to tell her that other men were in love with her, or to pretend that they were in love with her themselves. She was extremely coarse, and lived at a most dissolute court; so that the flattery she asked for was offered in no very modest terms. Lately, her health had been giving way, and her mirror had been reminding her that she was getting rather old and losing her good looks. This caused her to crave more than ever for adulation; and her increased coquetry gave rise to scandalous stories, and provided Cromwell with the kind of charges he wanted. On 29 April, at Greenwich, Anne found a certain Mark Smeton, a groom of the chamber to Henry, and a player on the lute, standing in the bow of the window of her chamber of presence. She went up to him, and, according to her own statement, asked him why he was so sad. Smeton replied it was no matter; and she then said, 'You may not look to have me speak to you as I should to a nobleman, because you be an inferior person.' 'No, no,' Smeton replied, 'a look sufficeth me, and so fare-you-well.'[6]

The conversation seems to have been overheard, and to have been reported by Cromwell's spies. Smeton's manner, or that of Anne, had excited suspicion; and when, on the following day, the unhappy musician took his way to London, he was arrested at Stepney and rigorously examined.[7] It is not known how much Smeton confessed at this first examination. He may not have admitted that he had committed adultery with Anne; but he was no hero, and fear of the rack or the hope of pardon probably led him to make statements by which she was seriously compromised and by which other persons were implicated. He was kept in close confinement at a house in Stepney, but his arrest and examination were not immediately made known, for Cromwell wanted further evidence before striking the blow.

Among the friends of Anne there was a young courtier named Sir Francis Weston, the son of Sir Richard Weston, under-treasurer of the exchequer. He had first been a royal page, but had risen to the rank of groom of the privy chamber, and was now one of the gentlemen of it. For the last eight years, by reason of his office, he had resided constantly at court, and he had obtained a good many grants and pensions. In May 1530, he had married Anne, the daughter and heiress of Sir Christopher Pykering; and having thus become a man of considerable property, he was created, at the coronation of Anne, a knight of the Bath.

Another of Anne's friends was Henry Noreys, also a gentleman of the king's chamber, and the keeper of his privy purse. Noreys had been for many years a favourite attendant of Henry. He had at once sided with Anne when she had begun her struggle; and he had been among the foremost of those who had worked the ruin of Wolsey. Ever since the death of the cardinal he had belonged to the little group of personal adherents of the Boleyns. He had married a daughter of Lord Dacres of the South; but having been for some time a widower it had occurred to him that he would please both Henry and Anne if he took as his second wife pretty Margaret Shelton, who, although she had lost her hold on Henry's caprice, had remained at court. So a marriage had been arranged between him and Mistress Margaret. But of late he had become somewhat cold, and Anne attributed his estrangement to jealousy, for she had observed that Sir Francis Weston had been paying rather marked attentions to her cousin. Accordingly, on 23 April she had some private talk with Sir Francis, and upbraided him for making love to Margaret and for not loving his wife. The young man, knowing how great was her appetite for flattery, answered that he loved some one in her house more than either his wife or Margaret Shelton. Anne eagerly asked who it was, and he replied, 'It is yourself.' She affected to be angry, and rebuked him for his boldness; but the reprimand cannot have been very terrible, for Weston continued his talk, and told her that Noreys also came to her chamber more for her sake than for that of Madge, as Margaret Shelton was called.[8]

Finding all this very interesting, Anne took occasion to speak to Noreys, hoping perhaps that he would gratify her with the same kind of compliments as those which had been paid to her by Weston. She asked him why he did not marry her cousin, to which he replied evasively that he would wait for some time. Displeased by this cautious answer, Anne said he was waiting for dead men's shoes, for if aught came to the king but good, he would look to have her. Noreys, being older and more experienced than Weston, understood how dangerous a game he was being made to play. He strongly protested that he dared not lift his eyes so high; if he had any such thoughts, he would his head were cut off. Anne then taunted him with what Weston had told her. She could undo him if she would, she said. About this they seem to have had some words, Noreys being evidently afraid that he might be drawn into a perilous position. Perhaps Anne herself began to feel uneasy, for she ended the conversation by asking Noreys to contradict any rumours against her honour. This he consented to do, and on Sunday, the last day of April, he told Anne's almoner that he would swear for the queen that she was a good woman.[9] Cromwell apparently heard of this conversation, and concluded that the time had almost come for making the case public. Henry was informed of what was about to be done, that he might be ready to play his part.

The following day being May Day, a tournament was held at Greenwich, Henry Noreys and Lord Rochford being among the challengers. The king and Anne were present, and seemed to be still on tolerable terms. When the tilting was over, Henry bade Anne farewell, and, as had lately become his custom, rode off towards London. On the way he called Noreys to his side, and telling him he was suspected of having committed adultery with the queen, urged him to make full confession. Although the king held out hopes of pardon, Noreys refused to say anything against Anne, and protested that his relations with her had been perfectly innocent. Henry then rode away, and Noreys was immediately arrested, and kept, like Smeton, a close prisoner.[10] He was taken to the Tower by Sir William Fitzwilliam, who, it was afterwards asserted, tried hard to persuade him to confess that he was guilty. Whether, as was further stated, Noreys said anything that compromised Anne is not known, but he certainly did not confess that he had committed adultery with her.[11] Having left him at the Tower – to which Smeton had been brought about the same time – Sir William Fitzwilliam went to Greenwich, where the commissioners were to examine Anne herself.

That evening nothing further was done. Anne was still treated with the outward respect due to a queen, but she knew that her enemies were working against her, and that she was threatened by the greatest dangers. At ten o'clock at night she heard that Smeton was confined in the Tower, and shortly afterwards it was reported to her that Noreys had been sent there too. Combining these facts with Henry's growing coldness to herself, and his increasing affection for Jane Seymour, Anne began to fear that she would have to take the same way.[12] She was absolutely without means of defence. Henry had gone to Westminster to be out of the way, and she could not bring her personal influence to bear on him. The few friends she had were equally out of reach, most of them having gone with the king to London; so she could do nothing but await her doom. Even flight was impossible, for had she been able to leave the palace and to go on board a ship to elude the vigilance of the searchers and to cross the sea she would not have been safe. Neither Charles nor Francis would have afforded her an asylum; her flight would have been taken as a clear proof of guilt, and she would have been given up in accordance with the treaties which forbade the various sovereigns to shelter one another's traitors.

So passed the night. On the following morning Anne received a message requesting her to appear before the council. She obeyed, and was then told of the powers given to the royal commissioners. She was also informed that she was suspected of having committed adultery with three different persons – Smeton, Noreys, and a third whose name does not appear – and that the two former had already confessed the crime. Her remonstrances and protestations had no effect.[13] She subsequently described the behaviour of the commissioners as generally rude. The Duke of Norfolk, who presided, would not listen to her defence; Sir William Fitzwilliam seemed the whole time to be absent in mind; Sir William Paulet alone treated her with courtesy.[14]

At the end of the interrogation, the royal commissioners ordered Anne to be arrested, and she was kept in her apartment until the tide would serve to take her to the Tower. At two o'clock her barge was in readiness, and in broad daylight, exposed to the gaze of the populace who had assembled on the banks or in boats and barges, she was carried along the river to the traitors' gate.[15] She was accompanied by the Duke of Norfolk, Lord Oxford, and Lord Sandys, with a detachment of the guard.

Lord Rochford had already been caught in the toils which had been woven for Anne's destruction. He was an able and energetic man, strongly attached to his sister; and it was foreseen that in so dreadful an emergency he would, if left at large, do everything in his power to save her. So he was arrested towards noon at Westminster, and taken to the Tower.[16] Anne's friends were closely watched, but it was not thought necessary to interfere with the liberty of Lord Wiltshire. He was a mean egotist and coward, and from motives of prudence had always disapproved of his daughter's bold and violent courses. There was, therefore, no reason to fear that he would try to defend her.

At the Tower Anne was received by Sir William Kingston, the constable, of whom Chapuis had reported that he was wholly devoted to Catherine and Mary. To his keeping she was handed over by the commissioners. Up to this moment she seems to have maintained an appearance of firmness; but when the gates had shut behind the departing councillors, when she found herself surrounded by the gloomy walls of the Tower, in the custody of the constable, her courage gave way. She realised the full horror of her situation, and as Kingston beckoned to her to proceed, fearful visions of loathsome prison cells rose before her mind. She tremblingly asked Kingston whether he was leading her to a dungeon. He reassured her, saying that she was to go to the lodging she had occupied before her coronation. This somewhat relieved her distress. 'It is too good for me,' she exclaimed. But, the tension of the last hour having been too much for her shattered nerves, she fell on her knees and burst into hysterical fits of laughter and weeping. When she calmed down she was taken to her apartment, where four gentlewomen under the superintendence of Lady Kingston had been deputed to wait on her. Suspecting what had happened to her brother, she made a few anxious inquiries about him, and Kingston, who seems to have felt some pity for her, merely answered that he had left Lord Rochford that morning at Whitehall. She asked that the eucharist might be exposed in a closet near her room, that she might pray for mercy; and then she began to assert her innocence of the crimes with which she was charged. But these were matters to which Kingston would not listen, and he went away, leaving her to the care of her female gaolers.[17]

The news of Anne's arrest and imprisonment ran like wildfire through the city. It was known that she was accused of having committed adultery with Noreys, or with Noreys and Smeton, and that Lord Rochford and others were somehow involved in the case, but as yet nothing was heard of the charge of incest. Rochford was said to have been arrested for having connived at his sister's evil deeds.[18]

The fate which had overtaken Anne excited little sympathy. Even among the Protestants, who formed at this time in England but a small class, there were some who disliked her. The great majority of the people, detesting the changes of recent years, accused her and her family of having plunged England into danger, strife, and misery in order to satisfy their own ambition and greed. The difficulties abroad and the consequent slackness of trade, the severity of the new laws and the rigour with which they were enforced, were held to be due altogether to Anne's ascendancy; and it was expected that with her downfall there would be a total change of policy, which would place England once more in a secure and prosperous condition.

But there was a man whom the tidings filled with dismay. For some months Cranmer had been ill at ease. The ultra reformers, Anne's friends, had not been favoured since her influence had begun to decay; and the archbishop, who relied chiefly on them, had found himself under a cloud.[19] In the country he received a letter from Cromwell, informing him of the arrest of Anne and of the reasons for it, and ordering him to proceed to Lambeth, there to await the king's pleasure, but not to present himself at court. He obeyed with a heavy heart, for such an order from the secretary boded no good, and Cranmer was not the man to face danger calmly. Next morning, at Lambeth, he wrote a letter to the king, beseeching him not to visit the faults which might be found in the queen on the Church she had helped to build up.

The archbishop had just finished writing when he received a message to appear before the council at Westminster. Such a message at such a time seemed even more ominous than Cromwell's letter, but it was peremptory, and had to be obeyed. Cranmer took his barge, crossed the river, and went to the Star Chamber, where he found the Lord Chancellor Audley, the Earls of Oxford and Sussex, and Lord Sandys. By the terms of the commission of 24 April they formed a quorum; and it is probable that they subjected Cranmer to an examination. But he seems to have been either unable or unwilling to furnish fresh evidence against Anne. The commissioners acquainted him with the proof which they had, or pretended to have, of her guilt; and the primate, cowed by the manner in which he was treated, declared himself satisfied with it. He returned to Lambeth, and there added a postscript to his letter, saying he was exceedingly sorry such things could be proved against the queen.[20]

After this, of course, Cranmer made no attempt to help his former patron. Nor do we hear that her friends at court dared in any way to interfere. The only person who tried to be of service to her was a poor lawyer of Gray's Inn, one Roland Buckley, the brother of a friend of Noreys, Sir Richard Buckley, knight chamberlain of North Wales. As soon as Roland heard of the arrest of Anne and Noreys, he wrote to Sir Richard, who was in favour with the king, beseeching him to come to court and to intercede on their behalf.[21] The letter was entrusted to one of Sir Richard's servants, who rode in haste towards Wales. But in Shropshire the messenger was stopped and examined, and the letter was taken from him. It was sent to the Bishop of Lichfield, the President of Wales, while Griffith – that was the messenger's name – was retained in gaol at Shrewsbury. The bishop forwarded the letter to Cromwell, and inquired what was to be done, so that Sir Richard never knew of his brother's message until it was too late.[22]

While Anne's friends were prevented from acting in her favour, her enemies laboured to complete her ruin. They searched eagerly for evidence against her, and examined every one who seemed likely to know anything to her disadvantage. Sir William Fitzwilliam and Sir William Paulet, aided by Sir Edward Baynton, seem to have distinguished themselves in this way at Greenwich, where Anne's personal servants had remained.[23] Cromwell went frequently to the Tower, and appears to have principally conducted such little examination of the prisoners as took place.[24]

Anne herself was not examined any further. At first, orders had been issued that, except in the presence of Lady Kingston, she was to hold no communication with the four women deputed to serve her; but it was soon decided that this would neither be practicable nor expedient. So her attendants were allowed to talk with her, on condition that everything of any importance which she might say to them should be reported to the constable. In a state of hysterical excitement Anne was unable to weigh her words and to control her tongue. On the morning after her arrest she spoke of Noreys, and told Mrs Cosyns, one of her attendants, of the conversation she had had with him. She then talked of Weston, whose indiscretion she seemed greatly to fear. The whole conversation was immediately reported to Kingston, who in his turn sent an account of it to Cromwell.[25] The consequence was that Sir Francis Weston went to swell the number of the prisoners at the Tower.[26]

About the same time, on the afternoon of Thursday, 4 May, William Bryerton, one of the gentlemen of the king's chamber, was also arrested.[27] Like Weston, Bryerton had grown up at court, where, before receiving the office he held at the time of his arrest, he had been a page and a groom of the privy chamber. He was of a good family; and his uncle, Sir William Bryerton, or Brereton, one of Henry's ablest captains, had done excellent service in Ireland. As young Bryerton had married a lady of small fortune – the widow of Sir John Savage – his position was not equal to that of Weston; but he was able to make a very good figure at court, and, like other light-hearted courtiers, he was much in the society of Anne and her friends. The immediate occasion of his arrest does not appear; it may have been some further indiscretion on the part of Anne, or some statement wrung from her former servants or others about court.

On the following day the list of prisoners was completed by the arrest of Thomas Wyatt, Anne's cousin, and Sir Richard Page.[28] Wyatt, it will be remembered, had been suspected – if not more – of being Anne's lover before she yielded to the king. Sir Richard Page, a gentleman of the privy chamber, had been, like the other prisoners, on very friendly terms with Anne, to whom he had rendered sundry little services, which she had requited with gifts and otherwise.[29] Besides the persons who were actually sent to prison, a good many others were bound under heavy fines to present themselves before Cromwell or before the royal council. They were thus kept in suspense and fear, and could not exert themselves in favour of the accused.

It now remained to prepare the indictments against such of the prisoners as were to be brought to trial. Besides Anne, five of them were singled out. Mark Smeton, who had already confessed that he had committed adultery with the queen, was one of them. It was necessary to bring him publicly to trial, for his confession was the only direct evidence against Anne which Cromwell was able to produce. By promises of pardon he might be induced both to plead guilty and to tell more than he had yet told, but condemned he must be. The other four were Lord Rochford, Noreys, Weston, and Bryerton. Cromwell fully understood that it would be most dangerous to allow these men to escape. Had it been Henry's intention, after the death of Anne, to effect a reconciliation with Rome, the three last named might have been allowed to escape; but if he wished to keep a middle course it was his interest to eliminate from the party of the reformation as many as possible of those who might drive it to extremes, and thereby force the government to lean to the other side. Besides, Rochford and Noreys, if released, would certainly try to avenge their own wrongs and the fate of Anne; and they would probably be aided by Weston and Bryerton. It was deemed advisable, therefore, that they should all die.

As to Wyatt, he does not seem to have been on very intimate terms with Anne for some years. He was arrested rather that he might give evidence than that he might be brought to trial; and a few days after his imprisonment Cromwell wrote to his father, Sir Henry Wyatt, that the young man would be spared.[30] It was decided, too, that Sir Richard Page, who was connected with the Fitzwilliams and the Russells, should be allowed to escape.

The examination of the prisoners producing no further evidence, the bills of indictment were drawn up. The original documents are still preserved. There are two findings of the grand juries of Middlesex and Kent; and when read together they tell a very strange tale. Anne was accused of having repeatedly committed adultery with Henry Noreys, William Bryerton, Sir Francis Weston, and Smeton, and of having been repeatedly guilty of incest with her brother Lord Rochford. She was also accused of having conspired with these five men to bring about the death of the king, and of having said that she did not love him, and that after his death she would marry one of her lovers. It was set forth, moreover, that Anne and her confederates had by their misdeeds brought Henry into contempt and had slandered his issue, and that the sorrow caused by their treasonable behaviour had so injured his health as to put his life in danger.[31]

If we consider this long and heavy charge, its improbability at once becomes apparent. It is unnecessary to dwell on the extreme corruption and coarseness which it presupposes in Anne and her lovers; for of the corruption and coarseness of Henry's court we have ample proof. But even if it be admitted that Anne was one of the most depraved women of an extremely base court, it is most unlikely that she behaved in the manner described in the two indictments. According to her accusers, she never acted on impulse, but invariably made cool arrangements with her lovers as to the place and time when and where she was to meet them, although, according to the very detailed accounts presented in the indictments, she ought to have thought herself unobserved and in no danger of surprise. She is charged, not with giving way to temptation gradually, but with plunging at once into a vicious life; and it is assumed that she was guilty of adultery within a month after the birth of Elizabeth, and of incest a month before she was delivered of her stillborn babe. There was no evidence whatever to support such accusations as these.

The second part of the indictment, that which relates to conspiring the king's death, is open to even greater doubt than the first. Towards the end of 1535, and in January 1536, Anne would have been inconceivably foolish had she wished Henry to die. In November Catherine was still in good health, and if Henry had suddenly died there would have been an immediate rising in favour of her and of her daughter. Anne would not have been able to offer even a semblance of resistance, Cromwell himself would have turned against her, Kingston would have shut the gates of the Tower in her face, and the gaolers at Kimbolton and Hatfield would have been the first to try to obtain forgiveness by raising the banner of Catherine and Mary.

At first sight it may seem that Anne was in less danger after Catherine's death. But Anne's enemies were exasperated by that event, and they drew together even more closely than they had done at any previous period. Besides, Anne had at that time the very best reasons for not risking anything. She was with child, and she knew that if she bore the king a son she would be safe. The pretended conspiracy to murder the king, and the alleged promise to marry one of her lovers, seem to have been nothing more than an amplification of Anne's conversation with Noreys at the end of April – the conversation of which she spoke the day after her committal to the Tower. Such amplifications were too common in the time of the Tudors.

But while I am strongly of opinion that the indictments were drawn up at random, and that there was no trustworthy evidence to sustain the specific charges, I am by no means convinced that Anne did not commit offences quite as grave as most of those of which she was accused. She may have been guilty of crimes which it did not suit the convenience of the government to divulge. At the subsequent trial some hints to this effect were thrown out, and although proof was not adduced they were likely enough to have been true.[32]

18

ANNE'S LAST DAYS

After leaving Greenwich on May Day, Henry went to York Place, his new palace at Westminster. Here he spent the night, and here on the following day Lord Rochford was arrested. It was at York Place, too, that Henry had the touching scene with the Duke of Richmond described in a former chapter.

The tears shed by the king over the danger which the Duke of Richmond had escaped did not flow long. They seem to have been the only tears the whole affair drew from his eyes, for on the following day he was in excellent spirits. Although accustomed to dissemble, he could not hide his joy that means had been found to rid him of Anne and to enable him to take a new wife. As he had allowed his exultation to appear at the death of Catherine, so he showed his delight at the coming fate of Anne. Never had the court been so lively as now, when the titular queen and some of the foremost courtiers lay in the Tower awaiting sentence of death. Feasts and banquets followed one another, and the inhabitants of the river-banks were often roused from their sleep by the music which enlivened Henry as he went home in his barge from some prolonged festivity.[1]

Notwithstanding the coarseness of the age, notwithstanding the indifference of most people of the time to bloodshed, notwithstanding the hatred with which the Boleyns were regarded, Henry's raptures provoked general disgust. Even his courtiers disapproved of his behaviour, and although they vied with each other in providing amusement for him they spoke contemptuously of his merriment. Among others, the Bishop of Carlisle gave a supper to Henry and to some of the ladies at court. Here the king showed exuberant mirth. He spoke with the bishop of the arrest of Anne, and said he had long foreseen that such would be her end. He had even written a tragedy on the subject; and drawing a book out of his doublet he showed it to the bishop. The latter went next day to see Chapuis and told him of Henry's conduct, using expressions, it seems, not very flattering to the king.[2]

But Henry not only pretended that he had foreseen all that was happening; it is evident that he took an active part in shaping the course of future events. He was regularly informed of every step taken against Anne and her associates, and he interfered a good deal with the proceedings.[3] Although, as on most other occasions, it was chiefly about matters of detail he was asked to decide, his wishes probably influenced the form in which the indictments were drawn up.

The indictments were to be laid before the two grand juries of Middlesex and Kent, where the crimes were said to have been committed. On 9 May precepts to this effect were addressed to the sheriffs, Humphrey Monmouth and John Cotes for Middlesex, and Sir Edward Wotton for Kent.[4] They immediately returned a list of jurors, of whom those for Middlesex were to attend at Westminster, and those for Kent at Deptford.[5] That these juries were packed there is no reason to believe. It would have been quite superfluous to take so much trouble, the proceedings before the grand jury being in such cases considered a mere formality. Never had a bill presented by the royal officials of the Tudors been ignored, and the confidence of the government was so complete that the principal commissioners did not even attend at the sitting. Only some of the judges presided; and before them, on the 10th at Westminster, and on the 11th at Deptford, true bills were found.[6]

Even before the indictments had been found, the day for the trial of the four commoners had been fixed. They were to be tried on the morning of Friday the 12th, at Westminster Hall.[7] On the 11th Cromwell went to Hampton Court, to which Henry had retired, and settled with the king the details of the coming trial, returning to town in the evening. No one but the king and the secretary had anything to do with the final arrangements. The Duke of Norfolk even, who remained at court on the 11th, knew nothing of what was to happen on the following day. Afraid to commit himself, he asked Sir William Paulet how matters stood, but found him equally ignorant. The duke declared he would not act without special orders from the king, and sent a message to that effect to Cromwell.[8] Shortly afterwards he received the news that he was expected to sit the next morning.

On Friday morning, then, the court over which Audley presided opened at Westminster Hall. With the exception of one of the judges, Sir Thomas Englefield, all the commissioners sat, Lord Wiltshire among them.[9] The four prisoners were brought up by Sir William Kingston; and when the indictments had been read, they were asked whether they would plead guilty or not. Smeton, having already confessed the adultery, pleaded guilty as to this part of the charge, throwing himself on the mercy of the king. As to the rest of the charge he declared himself innocent. Noreys, Weston, and Bryerton pleaded not guilty to all the charges. A jury was immediately sworn to try the case. Here, I must say, the list looks rather suspicious.[10] Of the twelve knights who composed the jury most were royal officials. Sir Thomas Wharton was comptroller in the north. Sir Richard Tempest, a near kinsman of Anne's aunt and enemy, Lady Boleyn, was steward of Wakefield and constable of Sandale. Sir William Musgrave was constable of Bewcastle and keeper of the park of Plumpton, and had a yearly pension of £20 out of the revenues of Sorby. Moreover, he had signed a bond for 2,000 marks to Cromwell and others the king's officers, payment of which might be demanded. Sir Thomas Palmer was one of the ushers of receipts of the exchequer. Sir Edward Willoughby was keeper of Hendley park. Sir William Sidney had been keeper of the great scales of London. Sir Walter Hungerford was the son-in-law of Lord Hussey, Anne's bitter enemy, and had just obtained from royal favour a writ of summons to the House of Lords. Sir Giles Alington was the son-in-law of Lady More, Sir Thomas More's widow. As to the four others, Sir William Askew, Robert Dormer, William Drewry, and John Hampden, I have found no proof of their holding any office or pension under the Crown; but they had all been justices of the peace in their counties, some even sheriffs. They were, therefore, men trusted by the government.

Before such a jury the accused had but small chance. Even had the jurors felt no prejudice against Anne and her friends, they could not have approached the consideration of the case with perfect impartiality; for they knew that if they acquitted the three gentlemen they would draw on themselves the anger of the king and his ministers, and that in the event of Henry trying to take vengeance for their verdict they would not find any allies upon whom they could rely. Besides, in the time of the Tudors it was the accused person who had to prove his innocence rather than the king's officers who had to prove his guilt; and in this instance the prisoners were more than usually hampered in their defence. Until the indictments were read in court, they probably did not know the specific acts with which they were charged: and it was impossible for them, without preparation, to recall what had happened on the days when their offences were said to have been committed. Their condemnation was inevitable, and a verdict of guilty was returned on all counts. Sir Christopher Hales, the attorney-general, asked for judgement against Smeton on his own confession, against the other three on the verdict; and the court condemned them to suffer the usual torture and death as traitors.[11]

It was now the turn of Anne and Rochford. But as it had become too late to call together a sufficient number of peers for the following day, their trial had to be postponed to Monday the 15th.[12]

By this time Anne had somewhat recovered from the shock she had received on the day of her arrest. She was quieter, and we hear less of such hysterical attacks as were reported on the 3rd and 4th of May. It seems that she did not quite realise her position. She fancied that she was liked by the greater part of the English people, and hoped that the bishops preferred by her influence would interfere in her favour.[13] She had not even heard of Cranmer's cowardice. As to the past she appears to have been undisturbed by scruples of conscience. She felt no remorse for the part she had taken against Catherine, Fisher, More, and the other martyrs; and at that time, and among persons of her class, any crimes of a different kind which she may have committed were scarcely considered to be morally wrong. What she remembered was her steady kindness to her friends and adherents; and she expressed a firm hope that if she died she would go straight to heaven.[14]

It was only after she had been several days in the Tower that she heard that her brother lay a prisoner in a cell not far from her. She had probably expected as much, for when Kingston confirmed the news she showed no extraordinary emotion. At the same time she was told of the arrest of Weston, Bryerton, Wyatt, and Page. She manifested no fear of them, but chatted about them very freely with her gaolers. Of the two prisoners who escaped, Wyatt and Page, she seems to have said nothing that could expose them to danger.[15]

Even in this time of dire distress Anne abated nothing of her overbearing temper. She had complained of the rudeness of the councillors at Greenwich; she now expressed her astonishment that they did not wait on her to hear her further defence. She complained, too, of the ladies whom the king had deputed to wait on her, and did not hide her dislike for them.[16] Chapuis she greatly abused, ascribing chiefly to his influence the action that had been taken against her. Ever since he had been at court, on 18 April, she said, the king's manner towards her had altered.[17]

In this way Anne spent her days in the Tower until the moment arrived for her trial. On 13 May the Duke of Norfolk, who had been named Lord High Steward of England for the occasion,[18] issued a precept to summon twenty-six peers in or near London to appear on the 15th at the Tower, there to decide as a jury between Anne and Lord Rochford on the one hand and the king on the other.[19] The peers thus summoned were the Duke of Suffolk, the Marquis of Exeter, the Earls of Arundel, Oxford, Northumberland, Westmoreland, Derby, Worcester, Rutland, Sussex, and Huntingdon, and the Lords Audeley, Lawarr, Mountague, Morley, Thomas Dacres of the South, Cobham, Maltravers, Powes, Mounteagle, Clinton, Sandys, Wyndsor, Wentworth, Burgh, and Mordaunt.[20]

That this panel was quite fairly chosen I have no doubt. The whole lay peerage at that time consisted of sixty-two persons. Of these, four were women, and two under age. Four of the peers – the Earl of Kent, and Lords Dudley, Say, and Talboys – never sat, being too poor. The Earl of Cumberland and Lord Dacres of the North were employed on the marches towards Scotland, while Lord Lisle was deputy of Calais. The Duke of Norfolk acted as high steward. Of the remaining forty-six, excluding Lord Rochford and Lord Wiltshire, several had at their urgent request been excused from attending the parliament which was going to open, while twenty-six had been summoned and had appeared.

Among those who sat, there were, indeed, many enemies of Anne: the Duke of Suffolk, who had opposed her from the beginning, the Marquis of Exeter, Catherine's and Mary's staunch friend, the Earl of Northumberland, whose former passion for Anne had been changed into hatred, the Earl of Derby and the Lords Mountague and Sandys, who had joined the conspiracy against her. But, on the other hand, such bitter enemies of Anne as Lord Dacres of the North, Lord Hussey, Lord Bray, and Lord Darcy had not been summoned, as they would certainly have been if it had been thought necessary to have a packed jury. Probably the Duke of Norfolk omitted no peer whom he knew to be in or near London.

It was not thought fit that a woman who, according to the statutes, was still Queen of England, should be led as a prisoner through the city to Westminster. Anne and Rochford were, therefore, to be tried in the Tower, and the great hall was prepared for the court. A platform was erected, benches were made for the peers, a dais on which was a raised chair was spread for the high steward, and barriers were placed to keep off the crowd.[21]

On Monday morning, 15 May, Norfolk and the peers took their seats.[22] The Lord Chancellor Audley sat next to the duke, for although, as a commoner, he could not officially interfere, he might privately advise the high steward. Sir John Allen, the Lord Mayor, with a deputation of aldermen, wardens, and members of the principal crafts of London, attended by order of the king. The part of the hall not occupied by the court was crowded with people who wanted to see a queen of England tried for adultery and treason.[23]

As soon as the members of the court had taken their places Anne, attended by Lady Kingston and Lady Boleyn, was brought in by Sir William Kingston and Sir Edmund Walsingham, the Lieutenant of the Tower.[24] A chair had been provided for her, and she sat down to hear the indictments read.[25] When the reading was over, and the usual question had been put to her, she pleaded not guilty. On behalf of the Crown Sir

Christopher Hales argued in favour of the indictments,[26] and he was
assisted by Cromwell, who, having formerly been a lawyer, appeared as
counsel for the king. They did not keep strictly to the indictments, but
heaped accusation upon accusation. Anne's conversation with Noreys,
reported by Kingston, was adduced as evidence that she had agreed to
marry Noreys after the king's death. From this it appeared that they
desired his death; and this, again, was held to prove that they had
conspired to bring it to pass. Besides arguing in this tortuous fashion,
Hales and Cromwell brought forward new charges. They accused Anne
of having given certain lockets to Noreys, from which they concluded
that she had contrived to have Catherine poisoned, and had conspired
to bring Mary to the same end. They furthermore asserted that she
and her brother had spoken contemptuously of the king, of his literary
productions, and of the way in which he dressed, and that she had
shown that she was tired of him.

In the presence of immediate danger Anne regained her composure,
and defended herself temperately and ably. She denied absolutely the
crimes laid to her charge. That she had given money to Weston she
admitted; but she had done the same to several other young courtiers
– in their case, as in his, without any criminal intent. Although she was,
of course, unable to produce rebutting evidence, she spoke so well, and
so thoroughly upset the whole structure of the prosecution, that before
an impartial tribunal she would scarcely have been convicted.[27] But
her efforts were of no avail. The question which presented itself to
the minds of the lords was, not whether she was guilty of the charges
contained in the indictments, but whether she was to die or not. This
question they answered in the affirmative. After the pleadings they
retired, and soon came back with a verdict of guilty.

The Duke of Norfolk thereupon gave sentence that Anne, Queen of
England, was to be burnt or beheaded at the king's pleasure. She heard
the sentence without shrinking, and having obtained leave to say a few
words she declared that she did not fear to die. The thing which grieved
her most, she asserted, was that the gentlemen included in the indictments,
who were absolutely innocent, should suffer on her account, and all she
asked was to be allowed a short time to prepare for death.[28] Kingston and
Walsingham then led their prisoner back to her apartment, and her place
at the bar was taken by her brother. Before his trial began, however, the
Earl of Northumberland was obliged, by illness, to leave the Tower. He
was dying of a nervous disorder, and it may be that although he had hated
Anne of late most cordially, he felt some compunction for condemning
her to death. The court went on with its work without him.

Rochford was accused of having on one occasion remained a
long time in Anne's room; and against charges of this kind, which

were neither authenticated nor proof of guilt, he defended himself energetically. To the charge that he had used expressions showing that he doubted whether Elizabeth was Henry's child, he made no reply. Rash, overbearing, and mocking as he and Anne were, he may have uttered some such jest; and he was now to pay for it with his life.[29] In the course of his trial it was asserted that Anne had told Lady Rochford that Henry was no longer able to beget children. This statement, which Cromwell did not wish to be made public, was written on a piece of paper, and handed to the accused, who was forbidden to read it aloud. But Rochford, having become fully aware that there was no hope of pardon, disregarded the prohibition, and loudly proclaimed the contents of the sheet.[30]

After the matter had been argued at great length, Rochford defending himself cleverly and stoutly, the peers were once more called upon to pronounce their verdict, and in answer to Norfolk they found the accused guilty on all counts. Judgement was given,[31] and then Lord Rochford was allowed to speak a few words. He said in general terms that he was worthy to die, but he craved from the king's mercy that his debts might be paid out of his fortune, which was by the judgement forfeited to the Crown. After this he was taken back to his cell, and the court rose.[32]

The condemnation of Anne had been generally expected, but it had been believed that her brother would be acquitted. At the trial he defended himself so vigorously and so eloquently, that among the common people who were present wagers were laid at ten to one that he would get off.[33] The fact was that during the last few days there had been a strong revulsion of popular feeling. At first the downfall of the chiefs of the Boleyn faction had been hailed with joy by all whom their pride and insolence had galled, by every one who expected some share in the plunder that was likely to be divided after such a catastrophe, and by those who hoped that there would now be a complete political and religious reaction. It had been assumed that there was some real foundation for the charges brought against the prisoners; beyond a very limited circle no one knew the exact nature of the crimes of which they were accused, or the kind of evidence that was to be adduced in proof.

The trial of the commoners at Westminster disclosed the true state of affairs. For the first time the English people heard of the charge of incest, which, even in so corrupt a society as that of Henry's court, was considered almost incredible. The public, too, were gravely informed that Henry had taken the infidelity of the queen so much to heart, had felt such overwhelming sorrow, that his health had been injured.[34] This they were told at the very time when they heard the sounds of rejoicing coming from the royal barge, when Henry was known to be in unusually high spirits. Moreover, the king's dallying with Jane Seymour, which now began to be talked about, raised a suspicion that Anne was to die in order to make way for an equally depraved rival. When all these considerations were added to that feeling of good nature which impels Englishmen to spare a vanquished foe and to favour the weaker party, the unpopularity of Anne soon decreased. Many of those who had been most furious against her became anxious that no harm should be done either to her or to Rochford.[35]

But there was no hope for any of the prisoners. An attempt was made to save Sir Francis Weston, whose family was powerful and rich, and had generally sided against the Boleyns. The French ambassadors are said to have interfered in his favour, but their request – if made – was not granted.[36] On the day after the trial of Anne and Rochford, the five men condemned to suffer death were told to prepare for execution on the following morning.[37] This they did as well as they could. They confessed, made out lists of their debts, and wrote farewell letters to their families, whom, it appears, they were not permitted to see. One of these farewell letters, that of Sir Francis Weston, has been preserved at the Record Office. It is written at the end of the list of his debts, amounting in all to about £900. It runs:

Father and mother and wife, I shall humbly desire you for the salvation of my soul to discharge me of this bill, and for to forgive me of all my offences that I have done to you, and in especial my wife, which I desire for the love of God to forgive me and to pray for me, for I believe prayer will do me good. God's blessing have my children and mine. By me a great offender to God.[38]

By royal order the scaffold was prepared, not at Tyburn, but on Tower Hill; and instead of being hanged, disembowelled, and quartered, the prisoners were simply to be beheaded.[39] They were allowed to address the people, who had come in great numbers to witness their execution. Except in the case of Lord Rochford, of whose words conflicting versions remain, their speeches have not been preserved.[40] So much, however, seems certain, that the prisoners did not assert their innocence, but that on the other hand not one of them confessed that he had been guilty of those offences for which he had been condemned.[41] The former fact has been held to prove that they virtually admitted their guilt; but this is not a legitimate inference. On such occasions condemned persons were permitted to speak only if they promised not to say anything against the king or in opposition to the sentence they had received; and up to the last moment the government had very effectual means of enforcing the covenant. For it might interrupt the execution, and order an offender to be hanged, drawn and quartered; or his family might be made to smart for the violation of his pledge. Hence scarcely any of Henry's victims dared to maintain their innocence. When Lady Salisbury did so in 1541 she was considered by the government to have been guilty of an extraordinary piece of impertinence; and her family might have fared ill had any of them remained in the king's power.

So Lord Rochford, Weston, Noreys, Bryerton, and Smeton were executed on Wednesday 17 May. Their bodies were exposed to no further ignomy, but thrown into simple shells and buried in the Tower.

Meanwhile, attempts had been made to secure the aid of Anne for the accomplishment of a scheme in which the king was profoundly interested. Having no legitimate heir male, and being in doubt whether Jane Seymour would ever contrive to bear him a son, Henry had begun to think of his bastard son, Henry Fitzroy, Duke of Richmond. It occurred to him that if he had no legitimate male offspring it might be possible to obtain the sanction of parliament for the recognition of the duke as heir to the crown. But as yet little Elizabeth stood in the way; she had been solemnly proclaimed heir presumptive, and her title could not be easily disregarded. It was desirable, therefore, that Anne's daughter should be declared illegitimate.

This object might have been attained if Henry had been willing to adduce proof that Elizabeth was not his child. The words attributed to Rochford, whether really spoken or not, and the general rumour that Elizabeth was the daughter of Noreys, would have been held sufficient evidence by a subservient primate and a willing parliament. But Henry would not hear of this; he insisted that Elizabeth should be recognised as his daughter, yet be proclaimed a bastard. This was, of course, impossible, unless it were decreed that his marriage with Anne Boleyn had been invalid from the beginning. In support of such a decree Henry might have used the argument which in the opinion of nearly every foreigner and of most Englishmen was the best, namely, that he was legally and validly married to Catherine when he took Anne for his wife. But had this reason been advanced, he would have acknowledged that he had been guilty of adultery or bigamy, and that he had been in the wrong, and had shown bad faith throughout the whole of the proceedings connected with the divorce case. Moreover, by a divorce from Anne based on this ground Mary would have been declared legitimate.

This argument being considered inadmissible, the statements of the Countess of Northumberland with regard to a previous marriage, or a binding precontract, on the part of Anne, were remembered, and Cromwell was directed to follow up the matter. On Saturday 13 May, the day after the condemnation of the commoners, Sir Raynold Carnaby, a friend of Northumberland, was sent to him to obtain if possible a retractation of what he had formerly said, and an admission that there had been a precontract between him and Anne. But the earl either had spoken the truth and honestly adhered to it, or he was aware that he would put himself in serious danger by making such a confession as was desired. If a precontract existed, his denial of it before the king's marriage with Anne might well have been construed as an act of treason. So he stoutly upheld his former deposition before Warham, Lee, and the council, that there was no precontract between him and the queen.[42]

There remained but one other conceivable reason for a divorce – a forbidden degree of affinity. Now Mary Boleyn, Anne's sister, had been Henry's mistress; and as illegitimate relations, according to the canon law, formed as strong an obstacle as legitimate relations, there was a forbidden degree. Scandalous as the proceeding might be, the marriage was to be annulled on this ground.

The person who was required by the new rules to pronounce sentence was Anne's friend, Thomas Cranmer. However loth he might be to take an active part against his former patron, however annoyed at having to declare invalid that which he had solemnly declared to be valid, he had no choice. He knew that the king might undo him at any moment; he had been sufficiently frightened by Cromwell's peremptory messages; he was ready for anything that might be asked of him. On the morning of the day following the trial of Anne he went to the Tower, and was admitted to her presence. What he told her and what she said to him is not known; but when he left her, she was convinced that she would be pardoned and allowed to leave the country. She told the ladies who were guarding her, that she would be sent to Antwerp.[43] It is, therefore, probable that the primate gave her hopes that her life might be spared if she would consent to a divorce.

On the 17th, at nine o'clock in the morning, the primate opened his court at Lambeth. The Lord Chancellor, the Duke of Suffolk, the Earls of Oxford and of Sussex, Sir Thomas Cromwell, and others of the king's council were present. Doctor Richard Sampson appeared for the king, Doctors Nicholas Wotton and John Barbour for Anne. Whether the two latter had really received any powers from her does not appear. They may have been named by Henry in accordance with the precedent set in 1527 on the occasion of the collusive suit against Catherine; but, on the other hand, it is not improbable that one of Cranmer's objects in going to see Anne at the Tower was to induce her to appoint Wotton and Barbour as her proctors.

In any case the two men who appeared for Anne did nothing to defend her cause. Had they had the interest of their client at heart, they might have raised such difficulties that, if Henry had obstinately insisted on securing a divorce, he would have been compelled to come to terms with Anne in order to obtain her consent, and thus her life might have been spared. But Wotton and Barbour were royal officials, anxious to please the king; so Cranmer was allowed to give sentence. He solemnly declared the marriage between Henry and Anne to have been null and invalid from the beginning.[44]

Anne might now be allowed to die. Her hopes of life had not lasted long, for Kingston had soon undeceived her. After the sitting at Lambeth her execution was fixed for the morning of the 18th, and she was told of it. She slept little that night; her almoner was in attendance, and from two o'clock onwards she remained in prayer with him. In the morning she sent for Kingston, and asked him to be present when she was to receive the sacrament and to assert her innocence of the crimes laid to her charge.[45] Shortly afterwards the communion was celebrated, and both before and after receiving the host she declared on the salvation of her soul that she had never been unfaithful to the king.[46] After this she patiently waited; but as time passed on she became restless, and asked her attendants when she was to die. They answered that she would not be executed before noon.[47] In reality, the execution was not to take place until the following day.

The explanation of this change of plan is not perfectly clear. It seems that Anne, faithful to her French education, considered it more honourable to die by the stroke of a sword than to have her head hacked off with an axe. The hangman of Calais, the only subject of Henry who knew how to behead with a sword, had, therefore, been sent for;[48] and he may not have arrived at the expected time. It is more probable, however, that the delay was due to a different cause.

The government now regretted that so many people had been allowed to hear the incredible accusations against Anne and her brother, and their able and eloquent defence. Many strangers had been present at the trials; and it was feared that after their return to their homes they would give a very unfavourable account of the king's proceedings. On Thursday morning, therefore, Cromwell wrote to Kingston that all foreigners were to be expelled from the Tower. In reporting that this order had been obeyed, Kingston expressed the opinion that if the exact time was not made public there would probably be few spectators;[49] and it is not unlikely that the government decided to postpone the execution in the hope that this suggestion would prove to be right.

When Anne's attendants told her that she would not die before noon, she sent for Kingston and complained to him of the delay.[50] She had hoped, she said, to be past her pain. The constable tried to console her; it was no pain, he said, it was so quickly done. Anne spoke of the executioner's skill and of the smallness of her neck; and then, the long waiting having unstrung her nerves, she had another attack of hysterical laughter, by which the constable was sorely puzzled. 'I have seen many men and also women executed,' he wrote, 'and that they have been in great sorrow; and to my knowledge this lady has much joy and pleasure in death.'[51] The rest of the day Anne spent partly in praying, partly in chatting with her attendants on her past life and on her future fame. Those ingenious persons, she said, who had forged so infamous a name for the late queen would have no trouble in finding one for her. They would call her Queen Lackhead. And therewith came another burst of hysterical laughter.[52] There was but one thing which preyed on her mind, her behaviour to the Princess Mary. She repeatedly spoke of it, saying that she had been brought to this end by divine judgement for being the cause of Mary's ill-treatment and for having tried to bring about her death.[53] Of the common story that Anne, kneeling, asked Lady Kingston to beg Mary to pardon her, I have found no trace; and it may be dismissed as an embellishment of later writers.

In this way the time went on. During the night Anne seems to have taken scarcely any rest, her nerves being too excited for sleep. She continued to talk to her ladies, and conversed and prayed with her almoner. As the morning of Friday 19 May approached, Kingston informed her that she would shortly be executed, and he handed her a purse with £20 which she was to distribute, according to custom, as alms before her death. A little before nine he returned, and announced that the moment had come.[54]

During the night a platform had been erected in the courtyard of the Tower. It rose but a few feet above the ground, for it had been deemed inexpedient to raise a high scaffold which might be seen from afar.[55] In the courtyard the Lord Chancellor, the Dukes of Suffolk and of Richmond, Sir Thomas Cromwell, and others of the council were assembled to witness Anne's death. The Lord Mayor, with some aldermen and representatives of the crafts of the city, attended by order; and as their coming had attracted attention, they had been followed by a considerable number of people. But strict watch had been kept at the gates, and although Englishmen had been freely admitted, all foreigners had been excluded.[56]

Anne now appeared, led by Kingston and followed by the four ladies. She wore a dressing-gown of grey damask, which she had chosen because it was low round the neck and would not interfere with the executioner's work.[57] For the same reason she had tied up her hair in a net, over which she wore the customary head-dress. In this guise she was handed over by Kingston to the sheriffs, who led her up to the platform.

Permission was granted to her to address the crowd, and she did so in few words and very simply. She had not come to preach, she said, but to die. She asked those who were present to pray for the king, who was a right gentle prince and had treated her as well as possible. She said that she accused nobody on account of her death, for she had been sentenced according to the law of the country. So she was ready to die, and asked the forgiveness of all whom she might have wronged.[58] Having said these words, she herself took off her head-dress, which she handed to one of the ladies. Then she once more asked the bystanders to pray to God for her.[59]

During the whole time that she had been on the scaffold, she had been nervously looking round[60] towards the place where the executioner stood leaning on his heavy sword, Now she knelt down, and one of her attendants bound a handkerchief round her eyes. After this the ladies also knelt down, silently praying, while she repeated the words: 'Oh God, have pity on my soul.' The executioner stepped quickly forward and took his aim; the heavy two handled blade flew hissing through the air, and Anne's head rolled in the dust.

Head and trunk were taken up by the ladies, wrapped in a sheet, laid in a plain coffin, and carried to the Tower chapel.[61] Here they were buried with little ceremony. No inscription, except a few letters, was put upon Anne's grave, and the exact spot was soon forgotten. It was discovered only a few years ago.

Such was the end of a strange and eventful career. For a moment it seemed as if Anne would leave no trace in history; but the schism of which she had been the first cause, and to which in one form or another the ruling powers were already deeply committed, could not be undone. Her influence survived, too, in the little girl at Hunsdon, who grew up to be very like her, although Elizabeth never showed a spark of tenderness for the memory of her mother and would have been ashamed to own that she resembled her. From Anne the English people received one of the greatest of their rulers, and for this gift they may well forgive such misdeeds as were not atoned for by long and cruel anxiety and a terrible death. Anne was not good; she was incredibly vain, ambitious, unscrupulous, coarse, fierce, and relentless. But much of this was due to the degrading influences by which she was surrounded in youth and after her return to England from France. Her virtues, such as they were, were her own. So we may pass no harsher judgement on her than was passed by Cromwell when, speaking confidentially to Chapuis of the woman whose destruction he had wrought, he could not refrain from extolling her courage and intelligence.[62] Among her good qualities he might also have included her warm and constant attachment to her friends.

Conclusion

For more than a week after Anne's arrest, the English government remained silent as to the causes which had led to it and to the imprisonment of so many other persons of note. This reticence gave rise to such very extraordinary rumours both at home and abroad,[1] that Cromwell at last thought it wiser to inform the English agents at foreign courts how the matter was to be spoken of. On 14 May he wrote to Gardiner and Wallop:

The queen's abomination, both in inconvenient living and other offences towards the king's highness was so rank and common that her ladies of her privy chamber and her chamberers could not contain it within their breasts, but, detesting the same, had so often consultations and conferences of it, that at last it came so plainly to the ears of some of his grace's council that with their duty to his majesty they could not conceal it from him, but with great fear, as the case enforced, declared what they heard unto his highness. Whereupon in most secret sort certain persons of the privy chamber and others of her side were examined, in which examination the matter appeared so evident, that besides that crime with the accidents, there broke out a certain conspiracy of the king's death, which extended so far that all we, that had the examination of it, quaked at the danger his grace was in, and on our knees gave Him laud and praise that he had preserved him so long from it and now manifested the most wretched and detested determination of the same. Then were certain men committed to the Tower for this cause: that is Marke and Norres, and her brother; then was she apprehended and conveyed to the same place; after her was sent thither, for the crimes specified, Sir Francis Weston and William Brereton. And Norres, Weston, Brereton and Mark be already condemned to death upon arraignment in Westminster Hall on Friday last. She and her brother shall be arraigned tomorrow and will undoubtedly go the same way. I write no particularities, the things be so abominable, and therefore I doubt not but this shall be sufficient instruction to declare the truth if you have occasion so to do.[2]

Similar accounts were published in England, but the people declined to believe the official version, and continued secretly to blame the government for the way in which the trials had been conducted. After a time their interest in Anne's fate died out, but a few of her adherents always held her memory dear, and we find among the records of the following years a note or two of proceedings against persons who maintained that Henry had put her to death unjustly.[3] In France poems were written in her honour,[4] and in Germany the Protestants expressed strong disapproval of the king's act.[5] About 1544, Jean de Luxembourg, Abbot of Ivry, wrote an *Oraison de Madame Marie de Cleves*, in which it is said that Henry was suspected of having already ill-treated, that is to say murdered, three wives.[6] And Constantine, in his memorial, reports a saying of the councillors of the Duchess of Milan to the effect that 'her great aunte was poisoned, that the second was innocently put to death, and the third lost for lack of keeping in her childbed'.[7] By and by, however, those who had known Anne passed away, the real person was forgotten, and fantastic portraits of her were drawn both by admirers and by enemies. And so her history was distorted by party spirit until it became a mere myth.

The fortnight before Anne's execution Henry had spent in the most pleasant manner. After a short stay at York Place he went to Hampton Court, and Jane Seymour was sent to a house of Sir Nicholas Carew, about 7 miles from London.[8] Here the king frequently visited her, but he soon found that the distance was too great. On 14 May she removed to a house on the Thames, only a mile from the court; and in this residence she was served with quasi-regal pomp, having numerous servants and living in splendid style.[9] On the 15th she received a message from the king that at three in the afternoon she would hear of Anne's condemnation; and shortly after dinner, Sir Francis Bryan, Anne's cousin, arrived with the welcome intelligence.[10] When, on the Friday following, the death of Anne was announced to Henry, he immediately took his barge and went to spend the day with Jane Seymour at the place where she lived.[11] Next morning, at six o'clock, she secretly joined him at Hampton Court, and there, in the presence of a few courtiers, they were married.[12] A few days later the marriage was acknowledged, and Jane appeared as queen.

The hopes entertained by the conservative and papal party after the arrest of Anne were doomed to disappointment. The first news of her imprisonment reached Rome by way of Flanders,[13] about the middle of May. Paul III at once sent for Gregorio da Casale, and told him what had happened, saying that God had enlightened the conscience of Henry. The Pope showed himself most anxious for a reconciliation, and eagerly pointed out to Casale that by forming an alliance with the Holy See, Henry would gain so much authority that he might lay down the law both to Charles V and to Francis. He, the Pope, had always been at heart Henry's friend, and whatever he had done against him he had been forced to do. The slightest advance Henry might make would be gladly responded to.[14]

Casale asked the Pope whether he might write all this to the King of England; but Paul III replied that if after the insults and injuries he had received he took the first step in the matter, people would cry shame on him. Casale was to keep everything that had been said strictly secret; he was only to assure his employers of the Pope's goodwill, and to urge them not to miss so fortunate an opportunity of making peace with the papacy. If Paul III saw any favourable sign, he would send Messer Latino Juvenale, Casale's uncle, or some other agent, to England, who would go nominally for the purpose of transacting some private business of his own.

Notwithstanding the Pope's request that the conversation should be kept secret, Casale gave Henry a full account of it; and he expressed a hope that the intended mission of Latino Juvenale would not be prevented, as it could do no harm and might do good.[15] Casale seems to have encouraged the friendly disposition of the Pope; for little more than a week after the date of his letter an agent was despatched to England.

The person chosen for this errand was Marco Antonio Campeggio. He received his instructions from his brother, Cardinal Campeggio, who had acted as papal legate in the time of Wolsey. He was to ask that the cardinal should be reinstated in the revenues of his former see of Salisbury; but this was to be only the ostensible occasion of his visit. If a favourable chance offered itself, he was to urge on the royal ministers that for the honour of God and the quiet of the realm the king ought to seek for a reconciliation with the Holy See, which would deal with him graciously.[16] Henry was to be advised to give proof of a friendly temper by repressing the preaching of new heresies, and to obtain peace of conscience by begging for absolution for his offences, as his predecessors had often done, earning thereby praise and glory.[17] Those whom Marco Antonio would find favourable were the Dukes of Norfolk and Suffolk, the Bishops of Durham and Winchester, and Campeggio's agent.[18]

As these instructions are now in the British Museum among the Cotton Manuscripts, they must have been formerly at the State-paper Office; and from this I conclude that Marco Antonio really came to England and negotiated with the English ministers. This opinion is confirmed by the fact that at the Record Office there is a letter from Cardinal Campeggio to the Duke of Suffolk, accrediting Marco Antonio.[19]

The Pope not only tried direct offers, he had recourse to indirect means. He spoke with Denonville and with Nicolas Raince, strongly advocating the marriage of Henry and the Princess Madeleine of France. Raince wrote to Cardinal du Bellay that the Pope had referred to this proposal again and again, and that his holiness could think of no more effectual way of obtaining a hold over the King of England.[20]

But on the day after the departure of Marco Antonio Campeggio, Denonville received letters from England in which it was said that Henry again intended to marry one of his own subjects. Nicolas Raince mentioned this to the Pope, who was greatly disappointed. Paul III continued, however, to believe that the French match might be brought about.[21] A few days later he spoke of a marriage between the dauphin and the Princess Mary; and Denonville and Raince wrote about it to the French court.[22]

It was only in July, presumably after he had heard from Marco Antonio, that the Pope understood that Henry was not inclined to give up the spiritual supremacy he had arrogated to himself, and that he did not propose either to ask for absolution or to submit in any way to Rome. Paul III then spoke angrily of Henry and even more angrily of Cromwell, and abandoned all hope of regaining the allegiance of England by peaceful means.[23]

Francis I also heard with annoyance of Henry's marriage with Jane, for – apart from his apparent desire to have the King of England for his son-in-law – he probably foresaw that Henry would soon be perfectly reconciled with the emperor, and that he himself would thereby lose a valuable ally and client. This anticipation was realised. After some time Charles was on very good terms with Henry, although he never gave up his defence of the memory of his aunt. For many years he and Queen Mary of Hungary irritated Henry by addressing him as 'wellbeloved uncle', and it was with great difficulty that Chapuis at last persuaded them to give up the use of the obnoxious name.

Mary gained little by the death of Anne. Contrary to the general expectation, Henry refused to admit her legitimacy or to restore her to her former rank. The Duke of Richmond soon died, but as long as he lived Henry appears to have wished to make him his successor, and Mary could escape the danger of imprisonment and death only by laying aside her pretensions to be the Princess of England. During the whole of Henry's reign she continued to play with the idea of flight and of rebellion, but even when the means were at her disposal she shrank from carrying out her purpose.[24]

To Henry's courtiers the death of Rochford and his friends brought a golden harvest. Rochford and Noreys, being royal favourites, had enjoyed numerous pensions and a good many lucrative sinecures. As soon, therefore, as it was known that they had been arrested, an active correspondence took place regarding the sharing of the spoil.

To Gardiner and Wallop Cromwell wrote: 'Your lordship shall get in CC £ of the III that were out among these men... the 3rd C is bestowed of the vicar of hell.' At the end of the letter he added: 'And you master Wallop shall not at this time be forgotten, but the certainty of that ye shall have I cannot tell.'[25] Gardiner was by no means satisfied with this arrangement. In 1529, Wolsey had been forced to grant to Rochford and Noreys pensions for life of £200 and £100, out of the revenues of Winchester. These pensions Gardiner had been obliged to pay, but now that the pensioners were to die the bishop thought that all the payments should cease. He protested in vain, however; he was even sharply reprimanded for complaining, and the 'vicar of hell', as Sir Francis Bryan was called, got his pension. What was the share of Sir John Wallop, I have not been able to make out.

The Duke of Richmond was not quick enough. He wrote on the 8th to the Bishop of Lincoln to secure the office of Steward of Banbury held by Noreys.[26] But, three days before, the bishop had already offered it, with the stewardship of the university of Cambridge, to Cromwell.[27] Robert Barnes applied for the mastership of Bedlam, worth, as he said, but £40.[28] The other offices of the five men executed on 17 May were distributed in a similar manner.

In the summer of 1536, seeing that the change of queens had made no great change in politics, the conspirators rose against the king. But they had waited too long. The emperor gave them no help, for he was fully occupied in Provence, and at that very time he was treating with Henry about an alliance against France. Besides, many of the great lords had become reconciled to the new order of things, which, after all, they found rather profitable. Most of them had received considerable grants out of the lands of the dissolved abbeys; and they hoped that their chances of sharing in the spoil were not even yet exhausted. Moreover, the insurgents were embarrassed by the indecision and stupidity of Mary. She had scruples about encouraging open rebellion against her father; and the majority of her personal friends, knowing her mind, held back from the insurrection. The pilgrimage of grace, therefore, was suppressed with comparative ease, and Lord Darcy, Lord Hussey, and many other adherents of Mary were brought to the block.

Chapuis remained for several years as ambassador at the English court, on excellent terms with Henry and with his principal advisers. In the beginning of 1539, the relations between Charles and Henry having become less friendly, he was recalled,[29] and the Dean of Cambray took his place.[30] When the coldness passed away, and the emperor desired once more to be on good terms with Henry, Chapuis returned to England;[31] and he remained there until the king crossed to Calais to take the command of his army before Boulogne. Chapuis was present at the siege, and after the campaign he went back with Francis van der Dilft, who had been chosen to succeed him as ambassador.[32] Having spent more than four months in schooling van der Dilft for his new post, he had a farewell audience of the king, on 4 May 1545; and Henry did not conceal his regret, for he had come to like the man by whom he had been so ably and so stoutly resisted.[33] At this time Chapuis was ill and crippled by gout; but he was still vigorous enough to be employed in treating with the English commissioners in the Low Countries. The last mention of him I have found is in 1546; the date of his death I do not know.

All of Henry's German favourites, Juergen Wullenwever, Dr Adam von Pack, and Marcus and Gerhard Meyer came to a violent end. Having been kept for many months a close prisoner, first at Rotenburg and afterwards at Steinbrueck, Wullenwever was brought to Wolfenbuettel, where, on 24 September 1537, he was sentenced to death and immediately executed. Doctor Pack left Hamburg in March 1536, to return to England; but while passing through the Low Countries he was detained and thrown into prison. At first Cromwell protested so strongly against his arrest that Chapuis wrote to Flanders; and on 16 April he wished to explain why the doctor had been seized. But having by this time heard of the proposals of Charles V, Cromwell did not want to quarrel about minor points; so he interrupted the ambassador with the remark that these were small matters of no importance. The authorities of the Low Countries, finding that Pack was to be left to his fate, tried to extort information from him by putting him to the rack, and soon afterwards he died in prison.

Marcus Meyer held out at Warberg for some time after Henry abandoned him; but in May he was obliged to surrender. In direct violation of the terms on which he capitulated, he was tried by a tribunal of his worst enemies, condemned, and executed. A few weeks later his brother Gerhard shared his fate.

And now I close these pages. My object has been to show that very little is known of the events of those times, and that the history of Henry's first divorce and of the rise and fall of Anne Boleyn has still to be written. If I have contributed to dispel a few errors, or have in any way helped towards the desired end, I shall be satisfied. The task I set myself will have been fulfilled.

Appendix Note A:

THE BIRTH & EARLY LIFE
OF ANNE BOLEYN

It has been generally held that Anne Boleyn was born in 1507, the authority for this date being a passage and a marginal note in Camden's *History of Elizabeth*. Dr Lingard, Mr Froude, and Dr Brewer accept the statement of Camden as good evidence; but in this opinion I am unable to agree with them. Camden wrote more than fifty years after Anne's death, and in many instances his account of her early life can be proved to be quite incorrect. In this case also he is, I think, mistaken. Happily some evidence has been preserved as to Anne's age. At Basel there is a picture of her, painted by Holbein, which bears the inscription: HR 1530 – *ætatis* 27. It bears also the words, added later: Anna Regina. From this portrait, the authenticity of which is above suspicion, it would appear that in 1530 Anne Boleyn was in her twenty-seventh year, which would place her birth in 1503 or 1504. She may have been rather older, for women so vain as Anne generally give themselves out for somewhat younger than they are.

Most historians have been of opinion that Anne Boleyn was sent to France with Mary Tudor when Mary went to marry King Louis XII. Mr Brewer strongly opposes this view. In the first volume of his *Calendar* he says: 'I take this opportunity of correcting a common error. It was not Anne, but Mary Boleyn, her elder sister, who attended the princess into France… '[1] and in the third volume he says:

My own opinion is, that she went into France with her father, Sir Thomas, when the latter was sent ambassador to that kingdom in 1519, and that she remained there until 1522. Those who adopt the popular statement will have to account for the improbability that a child not more than seven years of age should have been sent in the train of Queen Mary in preference to her elder sister – that she should have been called Miss Boleyn when, not only in the document referred to, but in others, younger sisters are distinguished by their Christian names… [2]

In the preface to the fourth volume he returns to the subject, and expresses his opinion as confidently as in the passages just quoted.[3]

But the charge which Mr Brewer brings against his opponents, that they have followed, 'with little examination, and some additions,' the account which Cavendish gives in his *Life of Wolsey*, is not justified.[4] Cavendish's book does not contain, as Mr Brewer pretends, 'the earliest notices we have of her career'.[5] Long before Cavendish wrote his *Life of Wolsey*, notices about Anne's life had appeared in France, and a long account in verse of her rise and fall had been published. A Spanish manuscript chronicle, written before the year 1552 by some officer in the service of Henry VIII or Edward VI,[6] contains a great many curious passages about her, and there are references to her in many letters and other papers of the same period. English historians have made little use of these sources, but abroad some of them have been known and referred to by a good many writers.

From the account of Anne Boleyn in verse I have already quoted,[7] a passage which distinctly says that she accompanied Mary Tudor when the latter was married to Louis XII. Of this account there are two manuscript copies, both apparently of the first half of the sixteenth century, preserved in the French Bibliotheque Nationale.[8] In each of them it is stated that the account was composed on 2 June 1536 – that is to say, a fortnight after Anne's death. The printed version published at Lyons in 1545, though differing slightly from both manuscripts, contains the same statement as to the date of the composition of the poem.[9]

Charles de Bourgueville, who lived in the beginning and in the middle of the sixteenth century, wrote a book called *Les Recherches et Antiquites de la Province de Neustrie*, which is a kind of diary mixed with antiquarian, historical, and political discussions. In this book, among the events of the year 1533, the writer notes the marriage of the King of England with 'a young lady called Anne Boullenc, who was brought up in France.' 'She came there,' he adds, 'when King Louis XII married Queen Mary, sister of the King of England.'[10]

So we have two independent witnesses to a fact which at the time when they wrote must have been known to a great many persons. Between 1520 and 1550 there must have been in France many hundreds of men and women who had known Anne Boleyn while she was at the court of Francis, and the date when she came over could not have been so soon forgotten.

In the *Cronica del Rey Enrico Otavo de Ingalaterra* it is said that Anne was most courteous towards Francis I, 'because this Anne Boleyn was brought up in France at the court of the king'.[11] This could not have been said had she gone to the French court when she was past fifteen, and remained there less than three years.

After the death of Anne a courtier told Chapuis – so Chapuis reports – that Henry had refused the hand of the daughter of Francis I because she was too young, and because in the said concubine he had had too much experience of what the corruption of France was.[12] If Anne had lived less than three years in France it would have been absurd to speak of her as a sample of French morals.

That Anne remained a Frenchwoman in many of her habits and modes of thought is indicated by little idioms and expressions which she is reported to have used. For instance, she said of Sir William Fitzwilliam that during her examination at Greenwich he was in the forest of Windsor. This phrase puzzled Sir William Kingston, and even Dr Lingard could not explain it. It is simply an adaptation of a Parisian idiom: 'être dans la forêt de Fontainebleau,' for being absent in mind.

After what I have said the reader will probably agree with me in thinking that if all this evidence had been known to Mr Brewer he would have admitted that it was Anne who went to France in 1514. Had he done so, he would have found it difficult to maintain that Anne Boleyn was the younger and Mary Boleyn the elder sister. For, on his own showing, the younger sister remained at home and would not have been called Miss Boleyn.

It is true that Mr Brewer adduces what he considers good direct evidence for the opinion that Mary was the elder sister:

> Any doubt on that head, is entirely dispelled by the petition presented to Lord Burghley, in 1597, by Mary's grandson, the second Lord Hunsdon, claiming the Earldom of Ormond in virtue of Mary's right as the elder daughter. It is inconceivable that Lord Hunsdon could have been mistaken in so familiar a fact; still less that he should have ventured to prefer a petition to the queen, in which her mother was described as the younger sister, if she had in truth been the elder.[13]

I do not know whether Mr Brewer had ever read the letter of Lord Hunsdon to which he refers. It certainly cannot have been present to his mind when he wrote this passage. The letter is not, as Mr Brewer says, a petition; it is a letter asking for the advice and the favour of the Lord Treasurer, as Lord Hunsdon intends to prefer a petition to the queen. That he ever presented such a petition to Elizabeth there is no evidence to show.

In the letter to Lord Burghley, Lord Hunsdon says:

> My late Lord father, as resolved by the opinion of Heralds and Lawyers, ever assured me that a right and title was to descend on me to the Earledom of Ormond... the brief of whose title was, I well

remember, in that Sir Thomas Bullen was created Viscount Rochford
and Earle of Ormond to him and his heirs general… the Earledom of
Ormond, he surviving his other children before that time attainted,
he in right left to his eldest daughter Mary, who had issue, Henry,
and Henry myself.

Subsequently Lord Hunsdon says that Mary Boleyn was 'the eldest
daughter and sole heir' of Sir Thomas Bullen, whose manors, lands, and
tenements descended to her.[14]

From the fact that Mary Boleyn inherited her father's estates Lord
Hunsdon seems to have inferred that she was the eldest daughter; but
she was her father's 'sole heir', not as his eldest daughter, but as his only
surviving descendant; Elizabeth being at that time considered a bastard,
and legally non-existent. The argument based on Lord Hunsdon's letter,
therefore, falls to the ground; and the fact that he was not recognised
as Viscount Rochford and Earl of Ormond, but that his nephew, after
the death of Elizabeth, was created Viscount Rochford, goes some way to
prove that Anne was older than Mary.

There is nothing to break the force of Mr Brewer's argument that it
must have been the elder sister who was spoken of as Miss Boleyn, and
who was sent to France with Mary Tudor. And as it was Anne who went
with Mary Tudor, and who was called Miss Boleyn, she must have been
the elder sister.

As to Anne's life in France, Sanders says that she was brought up at first
near Briere,[15] and J. Brodeau, in his life of Charles Dumoulin, improving
on this statement, asserts that she was brought up in Brie by a relative of
Dumoulin.[16] But 'near Briere' certainly does not mean 'in Brie,' but near
the little town of Briare, which Englishmen at that time generally spelled
Briere. Both the Duke of Norfolk and Peter Vannes spell it so.[17]

It is probable, however, that Anne was brought up neither 'near Briere'
nor 'in Brie.' Claude of France, the wife of Francis I, was a very good
woman who took pleasure in superintending the education of young
girls. She is said to have had large numbers of them at court, as many as
300 at a time, who were taught by the best masters. 'When Mary returned
to this country,' says the writer of the history in verse, 'she [Anne] was
retained by Claude, the new queen, at whose court she became so graceful
that you would never have taken her for an Englishwoman, but for a
Frenchwoman born'.[18] There can be little doubt, therefore, that Anne
spent most of the time she was in France at the court of Queen Claude.

That she returned to England in 1522, about the new year, is proved
by the papers cited by Mr Brewer. These papers also settle the date of the
negotiations for her marriage with one of her Irish cousins. Mr Brewer at
first thought that the negotiations referred to Mary Boleyn, but this error

he corrected. He continued, however, to be mistaken about the person whom Anne was to marry. The husband proposed for her was not, as Mr Brewer thought, Sir Piers Butler,[19] but the son of Sir Piers, Sir James.

In speaking of her life between 1522 and 1526, Mr Froude quotes a letter addressed to a Mr Melton and speaking of a Mistress Anne, as if there could be no doubt that it referred to Anne Boleyn.[20] A French writer, M. Albert du Boys, translating the letter, fancied that he might safely add to 'Anne' the little word 'Boleyn.' And so he did.[21] But there is not the slightest reason to think that the letter to Mr Melton belongs to a time when the writer could possibly have alluded to Anne Boleyn as 'Mistress Anne'. The writer says: 'I must go to my master, wheresoever he be, for the Lord Privy Seal desireth much to speak with me, whom if I should speak with in my master's absence, it would cause me to lose my head.' Who was this Lord Privy Seal, whom to speak with might have cost the writer his head? It is most improbable that the reference was either to Thomas Rowthall or to his successor Cuthbert Tunstall, for the one was commonly called my Lord of Durham, and the other my Lord of London, the episcopal dignity being considered the higher of the two. I cannot remember any letter in which either of these two bishops is spoken of as 'the Lord Privy Seal'. The letter, therefore, appears to have been written after Tunstall had relinquished his office to Lord Wiltshire, who was sometimes called Lord Privy Seal. But it was only in 1530 that Anne Boleyn's father obtained the office, and as at that time she was called Lady Anne, the allusion in the letter must be to another of the numerous ladies called Anne, and not to her.

Cavendish's account of the flirtation between Anne Boleyn and Sir Henry Percy is rejected by Mr Brewer, because in his opinion it cannot have taken place after Sir Henry was betrothed to Lady Mary Talbot.[22] I cannot understand the argument, for Cavendish distinctly tells us that it did take place after the betrothal, and that Sir Henry asked Cardinal Wolsey to have the betrothal annulled. There is nothing impossible or very improbable in this account, and, as Cavendish was certainly with Wolsey at the time, I see no reason to disbelieve his statement. It is confirmed by the fact that Chapuis and other contemporary writers repeatedly assert or imply that Anne was on very intimate terms with young Percy about the beginning of 1527 or about the end of 1526.[23]

Appendix Note B:

WAS MARY BOLEYN HENRY'S MISTRESS?

The question whether Mary Boleyn was the mistress of Henry VIII is now generally answered in the affirmative. Notwithstanding all the evidence which has come to light, however, Mr Froude still maintains the opposite view. He says:

> The argument from the Pope's silence, and from the absence of all mention of the Mary Boleyn connection in every authoritative document where it would most have been expected, has always appeared to me so weighty as to overbalance floating scandal, rhetorical invective, and conclusions drawn by inference from ambiguous legal documents. The story may have been true, and if it was true it was peculiarly disgraceful, but it is not proved. In my own opinion the balance of probability is the other way, but those who believe it will find their case strengthened by the deliberate words of the Imperial ambassador. [1]

As Mr Froude thus states the case for Henry and Mary Boleyn, I will now state the case against them; after which the reader may form his own opinion on the subject. I agree with Mr Froude that if the story was true 'it was peculiarly disgraceful'; but it is fair to add that as morals at the English court were at that time extremely low, Henry's conduct ought not to be judged by a very elevated standard.

Mary Boleyn was married in February 1521, not, as Mr Brewer says, in 1520, to Mr William Carey, not, as Mr Froude says, to Sir Henry Carey. Mr Froude asserts that:

> the liaison, if real, must have taken place previous to 1521. In the January of that year Mary Boleyn married Sir Henry Carey, and no one pretends that it occurred after she became Carey's wife. Nothing was known about it at the time, nor was it ever heard of till many years after, during the agitation of the first divorce. [2]

This is not the fact. It has been 'pretended' that Mary Boleyn was Henry's mistress after she became Carey's wife. There is still at the Record Office a paper containing the confession of a monk of Syon, in which the following passage occurs: 'Moreover, Mr Skydmore did show me young master Care, saying that he was our sovereign lord the king's son, by our sovereign lady the queen's sister, whom the queen's grace might not suffer to be in the court.'[3]

Not only, then, was it said that Anne's sister was Henry's mistress after her marriage, but it was stated that Henry Carey was the king's son. I hasten to say that I know of no other evidence in support of the latter assertion.

In 1527, Henry VIII, wishing to divorce Catherine and to marry Anne Boleyn, applied for a dispensation to marry any woman, even if she stood in the first degree of affinity to him, *ex quocunque licito seu illicito coitu conjuncta*, provided she were not the widow of his late brother. Why should this extraordinary and superfluous clause have been inserted, if Mary Boleyn had not been the king's mistress? Mr Froude, indeed, contends that the clause proves nothing against his hero. 'The dispensations,' he suggests, 'granted to Emmanuel of Portugal, who married two sisters and afterwards his niece, may have nearly resembled this. Legal documents of the kind were made as broad as possible to cover all questions which might afterwards be raised.'[4] Had Mr Froude taken the trouble to make inquiry as to the dispensations he speaks of, he would have found that they contain no such clause. I have examined many briefs and bulls of dispensation, and I have discovered no clause of the kind in any of them.

Dr Ortiz, the Spanish theologian sent to Rome to defend Catherine's interest, was informed by the courtiers of Clement, that Dr Knight, who had been deputed to ask for the dispensation, had made no secret of the reasons for which it was wanted. 'It is certain truth,' Dr Ortiz wrote to the empress, 'that some time ago he [Henry] sent to ask his holiness for a dispensation to marry her, notwithstanding the affinity between them on account of his having committed adultery with her sister'.[5]

In 1529 Charles V had already heard of the matter. On 5 January 1530, he gave audience to Dr Richard Sampson, one of the English ambassadors who had been sent to convince the emperor of the necessity of the divorce. Charles declared that Henry's conscientious scruples did not seem to be justified, especially 'if it were true, as his said Majesty had heard (although he himself would not positively affirm it), that the said king had kept company with the sister of her whom he now, it was stated, wanted to marry'. To the other observations of the emperor, Sampson replied; to this he made no answer.[6] Was not that a tacit admission of the truth of what the emperor had heard?

In 1532, Eustache Chapuis speaks of the former adultery of Henry with Mary Boleyn as a well-known fact of which there can be no doubt. 'Even if,' he writes, 'he could separate from the queen, he could not have her [Anne], for he has had to do with her sister,'[7] In the following year several persons were arrested in England because they had blamed the king for marrying the sister of his former mistress.

Before Henry's marriage with Anne, Sir George Throgmorton spoke to him of a rumour that he, Henry, had had improper relations both with her mother and with her sister. The king replied, 'Never with the mother;' and Cromwell, who was present, added, 'Nor with the sister either.'[8] All this was set forth by Sir George Throgmorton in a letter addressed to Henry himself, after the death of Anne Boleyn. 'The sting of the imputation,' as Mr Brewer justly remarks, 'consists not in the character of the writer, but in the tacit admission made by the king.'

In 1533, parliament passed an Act promulgating a table of degrees of consanguinity and affinity, within which marriage was forbidden; and it is remarkable that while this table covered the case of Henry and Catherine, it was so framed as to permit marriage with a sister of a discarded mistress. Up to this time the canon law had been in force; and, in that law, so far as forbidden degrees were concerned, no difference was made between legitimate and illegitimate intercourse. As soon as the marriage between Henry and Anne was to be null and void, the provisions of the canon law began again to command respect; and in 1536 parliament passed a new Act ordering every man who had married the sister of a former mistress to separate from her, and forbidding such marriages in the future.

Before this Act was passed, Chapuis had again stated as an indubitable fact that Mary Boleyn had been the mistress of Henry, and he had added that it was on this ground that Cranmer had pronounced a divorce between Henry and Anne.

Such, in the main, are the arguments for the opinion that Mary Carey had been the mistress of Henry. The case for the defence, as stated by Mr Froude in the passage I have quoted, is, that the Pope did not take official cognisance of the connection, and that no mention of it is made in any 'authoritative document where it would most have been expected'.

The answer to the first of these two arguments is very simple. The Pope did not take official cognisance of a fact which had never been brought officially before him. For reasons which I have explained in the text, the imperial agents opposed the marriage with Anne, on no other ground than that it was a contempt of court. They asserted that

Catherine was Henry's wife; and beyond this they did not need to go. The two sentences of Clement, therefore, simply pronounced the marriage with Catherine to be valid. The bull of Paul III excommunicated and deprived Henry for a great many acts which were perfectly public and undeniable, such as the casting off of Catherine, the concubinage with Anne, the rebellion against the spiritual authority of the Holy See, and the execution of Cardinal Fisher. It would have been mere folly in the Pope to have weakened his case by making any assertion which could have been disputed; for if he had done so, Henry would have complained to all the world that the Pope was slandering him. So Paul III wisely abstained from speaking about Mary Boleyn.

As to the second argument, I know not where Mr Froude supposes that mention of 'the Mary Boleyn connection' ought to be expected. I have shown that it is mentioned in a good many documents which are still preserved. That it is not acknowledged in any document issued with Henry's authority is true, but that proves nothing except that he was, perhaps, just a little ashamed of 'peculiarly disgraceful' immorality.

THE AUTHENTICITY OF THE BRIEF OF DISPENSATION

The brief dated 26 December 1503 by which Julius II granted a dispensation to Henry and Catherine to contract marriage, although the former marriage of Catherine with Prince Arthur had been consummated, has been frequently spoken of as a forgery. Its authenticity was denied by Henry VIII and his ministers; and this view, which was adopted by Bishop Burnet, has been supported by Mr Froude. As the genuineness of the brief has been considered probable by Dr Lingard, Dr Brewer, and Mr Pocock, it might have been unnecessary to argue the question afresh, had not the opinion of Bishop Burnet and Mr Froude been defended in the *Quarterly Review*, January 1877, in an article attributed to a writer who enjoys a deservedly high reputation for fairness, ability, and learning.

'The brief was unheard of,' says the Reviewer, 'until the need for it became apparent.'[1] This, however, is not proved. In documents belonging to the years 1504 and 1505 there are several allusions to a brief which seems to have been this very parchment. From a letter written on 17 March 1505 by the Bishop of Worcester to Henry VII,[2] we know that a duplicate of the dispensation was sent in the autumn of 1504 to Queen Isabella of Spain, and this duplicate is nowhere said to have been an exact copy of the intended bull. It is highly probable, therefore, that it was the brief dated 26 December 1503.

'It was unknown to Charles V,' the Reviewer continues, 'when, on 31 July 1527, he suggested that the Pope should supply the defects of the bull. It was uncertain whether Clement would consent, when, towards the end of the year, the brief made his consent unnecessary. Its existence was unexplained.' Unexplained at the time it was, but this is not of much importance if, as I have suggested, the brief was sent to Queen Isabella in the autumn of 1504.

'It was said to have been obtained,' adds the Reviewer, 'about the time of the marriage, in 1509; but it was dated 1503.' In proof of the former statement the Reviewer cites a few lines from a very rare and curious book, *Philalethæ Hyperborei... Parasceve*, ascribed by some to Cochlæus, by others to Ludovicus Vives. But he mistakes, I think, the true bearing of this evidence. Philalethes does not say that Catherine, or the emperor, or their agents, pretended that the brief had been obtained about the time of the marriage, in 1509. Nor does he himself give this date. He merely repeats what is said by Catherine's adversaries. They, he declares, point out that the words *forsan cognita* occur in the bull, but that in the brief which Ferdinand obtained about the time of the marriage *forsan* does not occur. This they make use of, 'as an invincible ram,' to prove that Catherine's marriage was consummated. In opposition to them, Philalethes adduces a letter written on 23 August 1503 by Ferdinand to Don Francisco de Rojas, his ambassador at Rome, in which the king states that the marriage was not consummated. On the question of the date of the brief Philalethes offers no opinion; and he does not think it worthwhile to inform his readers whether Catherine's enemies had any good reason for asserting that the document was issued *circiter tempus nuptiarum*.[3] This argument of the Reviewer must also, then, be dismissed as proving nothing at all against the brief.

'It was obtained by Ferdinand, yet Ferdinand did not possess a copy.' How is this known? There is not a tittle of evidence to show that Ferdinand had not, besides the original, even several copies of the brief. 'It was sent to England, but it was admitted that it had left England before the marriage for which it was required.' I know of no evidence for this assertion, and none is adduced by the writer. The brief seems to have been found among the papers left by Dr de Puebla to his sons, for one of them, Ruiz de Puebla, declared that he had placed it in the hands of the emperor in the beginning of 1528.[4] How it came to be among the papers of the doctor there is nothing to show, and I have nowhere found anything which may be called an admission that it was in England, or that it left that country, at any specified date.

But even admitting that the writer correctly describes the facts, they would not prove his case. The brief sent to Queen Isabella when on her deathbed may have been despatched to England to facilitate the marriage which Ferdinand desired, and when at a later period the bull of dispensation was brought from Rome by the Bishop of Worcester, the brief, being considered superfluous, may have been kept by de Puebla. This is a perfectly natural account of the circumstances, and offers an easy explanation of the difficulty raised by the writer in the *Quarterly Review*.

'Ferdinand did not want it, for, on his theory, it was quite unnecessary.' The writer must have forgotten that he himself had just cited a letter from Ferdinand of Aragon to Don Francisco de Rojas, his ambassador at Rome, which points to the opposite conclusion. In this letter the Catholic king states, indeed, that such a brief is not rendered necessary by the real state of the case, but he adds that as the English are very suspicious and fond of raising difficulties, the ambassador is to obtain a dispensation; and his directions as to the contents of the proposed dispensation exactly correspond to the form in which the brief is made out.[5]

'If he [Ferdinand] had asked for it the brief would have been addressed to him, and a copy would have been treasured up in Spain.' This is not a necessary inference. The bull of dispensation was asked for by Henry VII and by Ferdinand, and it was addressed to neither of them.[6]

The Reviewer asserts that the brief 'was addressed to Henry VII'; but in reality, like the bull, it was addressed to Henry, the son of Henry VII, and to Catherine, the daughter of Ferdinand and Isabella.[7]

'But Henry did not want it; for he was more than content with the original bull, which he never intended to use, and could never wish to amplify.' True; but this tells rather against than for the writer's argument, for it explains very well why the brief, if it really was sent to de Puebla, did not remain in England, but was taken back to Spain.

'The brief was discovered among the papers of the Ambassador de Puebla, who had left England before the marriage, and who was now dead. A list of all his papers relating to the marriage is still extant, and the brief is not among them.' We have no list of *all* de Puebla's papers relating to the marriage. What is known about the matter is that in the beginning of 1528 Ruiz de Puebla handed over the brief to the emperor, that afterwards, about 1529, he was requested to bring up all papers relating to the marriage, that he then made search for them and found those enumerated in the list which the Reviewer asserts to be complete, that several years later he made another search and found more papers relating to the marriage, and that he declared all this in 1545 before a notary in Spain.[8]

'Two men,' the Reviewer continues, 'were living who could have given valuable testimony. De Puebla's heir, Fernandez, had possession of his papers.' From the deposition of Ruiz de Puebla above referred to, it clearly appears that this was not so. It was the brother of Fernandez who had possession of the papers of Dr Ruy Gonzalez de Puebla.

'He [Fernandez] was reputed an honest man, and it was desirable to have him examined. It appeared, however, that he had just been sent to one of the few places in Europe which were beyond the reach of Henry and the jurisdiction of Charles – to the dominion of the Earl of Desmond.' Gonçalo Fernandez was despatched from Toledo in February 1529.[9] On 28 April following, the Earl of Desmond signed a petition to Charles V which Fernandez was to take back with him; and towards the end of May the English ambassador at the Spanish Court reported that he had returned to Spain from Ireland.[10] The absence of Fernandez, on which the Reviewer lays so much stress, lasted therefore not more than about three months, and on his return the English ambassadors might have questioned him if they had chosen to do so.

'Accolti,' the Reviewer proceeds, 'the cardinal who in the name of Julius had drawn up the dispensation a quarter of a century earlier, was now the most zealous opponent of the divorce in the Court of Rome. He could have settled the doubt whether a second dispensation had, in fact, been given. Accolti remained impenetrably silent.'

The bull and the brief are countersigned by the papal secretary Sigismundus; and from this it would appear that both were drawn up by him. The bull is also countersigned by D. de Comitibus, by whom it was written out. There is no evidence that Accolti, who was not a cardinal when the dispensations were granted, had anything to do with the drawing up of the writings; and the Reviewer's assertion that Accolti 'could have settled the doubt whether a second dispensation had, in fact, been given,' seems to me to be wholly unwarranted.

As to Accolti being the most zealous opponent of the divorce, so far from this being the case, he was for a time considered decidedly favourable to Henry. Under the name of 'the old man' he is frequently mentioned by the English agents at Rome, who took his advice as to the way in which they were to proceed. The English agents and he were constantly haggling about the terms on which he would sell his support, and great promises were made to him. His nephew, Benedict de Accoltis, was nominated by Henry to the See of Coventry and Lichfield with a promise of promotion to the more opulent Bishopric of Ely. Under these circumstances it would have been strange indeed if Cardinal Peter de Accoltis had volunteered any statement which might have damaged the cause of Henry. If he knew anything about the issuing of a brief of dispensation, it was certainly not his interest to make a public statement to that effect.

'Though addressed to Henry VII, the brief was unknown in England.' I have already stated that the brief was not addressed to Henry VII, and it is impossible to prove that it was unknown in England. It was of the utmost importance to the king that the brief should be held to be spurious, and had any royal official known of a copy of it in England he would have been careful to keep the secret. An Englishman might have lost his head for asserting that there was proof that such a brief had been made out.

'It formed the strongest security for the honour and the legal position of a Spanish princess: yet it did not exist in the archives of Spain.' The

Reviewer had, no doubt, read the preface to the first volume of Mr Bergenroth's *Calendar*; but the contents of it seem to have escaped his memory. In that preface Mr Bergenroth distinctly states that during the reign of Ferdinand and Isabella there were no archives of Spain. The papers were scattered about in strong boxes in different palaces and convents, and in one instance Mr Bergenroth shows that they were actually deposited abroad.[11] The institution of the royal archives of Spain dates from 1543, when Charles V decided that state papers were to be preserved in the castle of Simancas.

The circumstance noted by the Reviewer as an argument against the authenticity of the brief, speaks rather in favour of it. If the brief had been forged, the secret would have been confided to as few persons as possible; for the more accomplices there are in such transactions the greater are the chances of detection. Besides Charles himself, no one ought to have known of it but Gattinara, whose aid would probably have been indispensable, and the actual forger. Why should Ruiz de Puebla have been let into the secret? Why was it not simply pretended that the brief had been found by Gattinara in some of the royal areas? That this was not done is almost sufficient proof, in the absence of contradictory evidence, that the brief was not a forgery.

'It constituted the most extreme exertion of the Pope's prerogative known till then: yet Rome preserved no record of its existence.' The statement that the dispensation to marry a late brother's wife was the most extreme exertion of the Pope's prerogative known till 1503 is open to question. The dispensation given to King Henry IV of Castille to commit bigamy seems to me to go somewhat further.

'In April 1529, Charles was in doubt as to the value of the brief. He was willing to submit it to the Pope. His mind would not, he said, be at rest until he knew whether it had been found in the Roman registers. His doubts were soon satisfied. The registers were subjected to the scrutiny of Spanish and English agents. They found no trace of the brief.' This objection would have had some force, had it not been lately shown that the real date both of the bull and of the brief was later than the professed date. According to a letter of the Bishop of Worcester, the brief was made out in the autumn of 1504, the bull perhaps even later.[12] If the English and Spanish agents looked for the dispensation under the date of December 1503 – as they probably did – it was, of course, impossible that they should find it. The Reviewer's argument would have been of some importance if he could have shown that the bull of dispensation had been properly entered in the registers, but that the brief had not been so entered. This, however, nobody has yet shown.

'Errors were detected in the text. A vital flaw was detected in the date.' There are a good many errors in the text, and there is a flaw in the date. But it is a mistake to say that the flaw in the date is a vital flaw. An error in the date of a dispensation did not then, and would not now, make the dispensation invalid. If it had done so, a great many people would have had to suffer.

There is no doubt that in the end of the fifteenth century it became the custom of the Roman court, in dating briefs, to regard the year as beginning on 25 December. A few years after the issue of the bull and the brief of dispensation, the same Sigismundus who had drawn them up dated a brief directed to the Archbishop of Rouen: 'Datum Romæ, apud Sanctum Petrum, sub annulo piscatoris die XXVIII[a] decembris M[o] D[o] VIIII[o], pontificatus nostri anno sexto.'[13] The brief of Clement VII announcing his escape from the castle of St Angelo is dated: 'Die ultima decembris MDXXVIII pont. nostri anno quinto.'[14] But although at the time of the divorce it was laid down at Rome that the year was to be reckoned in bulls from 1 January, and in briefs from 25 December, this rule was not strictly adhered to; the greatest diversity continued to exist in the computation. There is, therefore, nothing very extraordinary in the fact that the new papal secretary, having in 1504 to make out a brief which was to go forth as one that had been written in the preceding year, dated it either intentionally or by mistake in an unusual manner. The flaw is certainly not, as the Reviewer says, 'a vital flaw'.

'Charles never sent it to Rome for judgment.' This may be admitted; but the emperor strongly objected to part with the brief, and declared his intention of submitting it himself to the inspection of the Pope. He did not go to Rome until the spring of 1536 on his return from Tunis, when the divorce suit had long been decided; but in 1529 he met the Pope at Bologna, and there, as I believe, he laid the brief before Clement and his cardinals and auditors. That the brief was never sent to Rome, therefore, proves nothing against its authenticity.

The Reviewer adds: 'It was no longer necessary. The brief had served to delay action in the legates' court until the Pope was reconciled with Spain.' From this it might be concluded that after the Pope was reconciled with Spain the brief was no more heard of; but the truth is that its authenticity was assumed in all the discussions which preceded the sentences of July and August 1533 and of 23 March 1534. In July 1533, it was decided by the college of cardinals that Julius II was entitled to grant such a dispensation as that which is contained in the brief; and in March 1534, it was considered that for the sentence in favour of the queen such a dispensation was necessary. Soon after leaving the consistory, Cardinal Campeggio told the Spanish agents that if the queen's case had depended on the proof of her virginity he would have had grave doubts about the justice of it. But he had regarded it as settled that the marriage was forbidden only by the human law, and so he had never doubted of the result. It is scarcely correct, therefore, to say that after the reconciliation of the Pope with Spain the brief was no longer necessary.

The brief is in the Vienna Archives among the papers which came from Brussels; and we may safely say that it would not have been preserved had Charles V known that it was a forgery. And it is incredible that if it was a forgery he was ignorant of the fact. I may add that I have carefully examined the brief, and that I found in it nothing which seemed to indicate that it had been forged. It has been inspected by several other persons well versed in palaeography, and from none of them have I heard any expression of doubt as to its authenticity. Unless, therefore, the Reviewer can bring forward more important evidence, or show that impartial and capable judges who have seen the brief agree with him, the document about which there has been so much discussion must be accepted as genuine. It will give me much pleasure if the arguments I have advanced induce him to reconsider his judgement in the matter.

THE DATE OF ANNE'S MARRIAGE

According to some historians, Henry and Anne were married on 14 November 1532; according to others, on 25 January 1533. The former date has been adopted by all who have wished to make it appear that there was no stain on the birth of Elizabeth. I do not know of any documentary evidence for it, and so far as I am aware none has ever been brought forward by the numerous panegyrists of Henry.

For the later date there is evidence which to my mind seems perfectly conclusive, unless, indeed – as is possible – Henry and Anne were never formally married at all. Cranmer, writing on 17 June to Dr Hawkyns, his successor at the Imperial Court, says that Anne Boleyn's marriage took place about St Paul's day last; that is to say, about 25 January.[1] It has been objected to this that Cranmer was a most inexact man, and wrote nearly five months after the date he mentions. I fully admit that Cranmer was inexact; but it appears impossible that he should have said the ceremony took place in the end of January if it really took place in the middle of November, especially when it was not the interest of the archbishop or his friends to adopt the later date.

Cranmer's statement is corroborated by several passages in the despatches of Chapuis. On 15 April 1533, Chapuis reports that on the 9th the Duke of Norfolk and other commissioners had waited on Queen Catherine, asking her to relinquish her pretensions, and that, when she had refused, Norfolk had declared it did not matter, for, more than two months before, the king had married Anne Boleyn, though none of them had been called to be present at the ceremony.[2] This agrees very well with the later date. If the true date had been 14 November, Norfolk would certainly have said that the king had married Anne Boleyn more than four months before.

Shortly afterwards Chapuis wrote that it was generally said the ceremony had been performed on the day of the Conversion of St. Paul.[3]

The statement of Cranmer is, therefore, fully borne out by the Imperial ambassador, and it cannot be fairly denied that the king and his adherents spoke of 25 January as the date of the marriage. As they had no reason whatever to adopt a later date than the true one, but, on the contrary, for the sake of the expected prince, had every reason to adopt the earliest date possible, the official account must be accepted as altogether beyond dispute.

Appendix Note E:

BISHOP FISHER IN THE
SPRING OF 1535

In November 1534, Fisher and More were treated with greater rigour than at any previous period of their imprisonment; and shortly before Christmas Cromwell advised the bishop to write to the king. Fisher hesitated, as he said, for fear of offending Henry, but he addressed a letter to Cromwell himself, representing his miserable state, and asking either to be released from prison or at least to be allowed to see a priest during the holy days and to have the use of some books of devotion.[1]

Cromwell's answer to this request I have not found, but towards the new year the severity with which the prisoners had been treated was certainly very much relaxed. We hear from William Roper, Sir Thomas More's son-in-law, that about that time Sir Thomas was visited by Cromwell, who spoke in a friendly manner, and assured him that he would not again be pressed with questions, or asked to make any declaration or to take any oath. The king, Cromwell said, was well disposed towards him, and would show him all possible favour.[2]

A few days later it was reported that Fisher and More had made their submission and were restored to the good graces of the king. Of course this was not true; but we know that about the middle of January Sir Thomas More was once more allowed to correspond with his friends.[3]

On 5 February Palamede Gontier wrote that on the 1st, at the Court at Westminster, he had given the admiral's letters to the Duke of Norfolk, who had inquired about Chabot's health, 'and the same did Messieurs of Suffolk and Fischer'.[4]

When I first read this passage of Gontier's letter, I felt nearly sure that it was a mistake; but after some time I became less confident. If the name Fischer does not refer to the bishop, it can only stand for Wiltshire. But, according, to the French orthography of the time, Wiltshire was written either Wulchier, Vulchier, or Wuilchier; and if Lelaboureur read and printed 'Fischer' for any one of these forms, he was guilty of a very gross mistake indeed. That he committed so grave a blunder is highly improbable, for he was well aware that Anne's father was Earl of 'Wilt' and Ormond, and that Fisher was a prisoner in the Tower. Besides, there is ample evidence in this letter that when Lelaboureur met with the name of an unknown person he printed it correctly. He printed Ovaston and Borgonny, which are certainly the forms Gontier was likely to use in spelling the names of Sir William Weston and Lord Abergavenny.

There are but two reasons why it might seem probable that there is a mistake. First, in the very long letter no mention is made of the *'Comte de Wulchier'*. But the reader naturally expects to find some reference to Lord Rochford; and his name does not occur any more than that of his father. The truth is that at that time the Boleyns were out of favour. It is significant that when commissioners were designated to treat of the marriage of little Elizabeth with the Duke of Angoulême neither her grandfather nor her uncle were appointed, and that they are not mentioned among the guests at a great supper party which was given a few days later by the French ambassador.

The second circumstance which might suggest a doubt whether 'Fischer' means the bishop, is that in another part of the letter Gontier says that on 2 February, while he was in the ballroom, 'Messieurs of Nortfolk, Suffolk, Fischer, the Chancellor, Cromwell, and others sat in council.' This passage would present no difficulty if 'Fischer' was Lord Wiltshire; but it needs explanation if Gontier alluded to the bishop, for it is most unlikely that Fisher was called from the Tower to take part in the proceedings of the royal council. But Gontier was not present at the sitting, and, not seeing Bishop Fisher in the ballroom, he may have concluded that he was in the council chamber. And there the bishop may really have been, for he was very often before the council both at the Tower and elsewhere. Even this passage, therefore, does not prove that the reference is to Lord Wiltshire.

Nevertheless, it would be hard to accept Gontier's statement as it appears in Lelaboureur's volume, were it not that it is supported by other evidence. At the British Museum a paper is preserved setting forth the sums which Sir Edmund Walsingham, the Lieutenant of the Tower, charged the king for the maintenance of the prisoners. When the charge was only for a part of the time during which the prisoners were confined, or when they themselves had paid a portion of the amount due, a note to that effect was made. In this paper we find the following record: *The Bishop of Rochester for XIIIIth monthys after XXs. le weke summa... LVI li.*[5] That is to say, the Lieutenant of the Tower charged for the maintenance of Bishop Fisher during fourteen months of four weeks each, or during a year and twenty-seven days. But Fisher was sent to the Tower on 16 or 17 April 1534, and executed on 22 June 1535, between which dates one year and sixty-six or sixty-seven days intervened – forty days more than Sir Edmund charged for. There is no note that this is a charge only for a part of the time, or that the prisoner had paid the £6 which are not included in the account; and as it cannot be supposed that Sir Edmund demanded less than he was entitled to demand, we are driven to the conclusion that between 17 April 1534, and 22 June 1535, Bishop Fisher was forty days absent from the Tower.

Dr Hall, the author of the *Life of Fisher* published by Baily, tells a long story how the lords of the council first sent for the bishop and asked him to swear to the Act of Supremacy, pretending that Sir Thomas More had done so; how when Fisher refused they sent him to the garden; how the Lord Chancellor thereupon assured More's daughter, Margaret Roper, that the Bishop of Rochester had taken the oath and was at liberty, and restored to the royal favour; how Margaret believed him, and reported to her father what she had heard, and begged him to follow Fisher's example; and how More declined to take the oath, doubting the truth of Audley's statement. If any of these incidents really took place, they must have happened early in 1535.[6]

Hall is by no means a perfectly trustworthy historian, and his account is certainly not altogether correct. But it is clear from his book that he had seen a good many documents; so it is more probable that he inaccurately described what he had read than that he invented the whole story.

After all, there is nothing very improbable in some parts of the story of Hall or in the statement of Gontier. In the beginning of 1535 Henry wished to conciliate his enemies, and he was well aware that for this reason alone it would be good policy to show some favour to Fisher and More. Moreover, we learn from Roper that, so far as Sir Thomas More was concerned, the council 'in the beginning were resolved that with an oath not to be acknown whether he had to the supremacy been sworn or what he thought thereof he should be discharged'.[7] Now if Bishop Fisher had taken such an oath, and had promised, as he was ready to do, that he would not again declare his opinion about the king's proceedings, it would have been excellent policy to set him free. For most people, seeing him at liberty and silent about the king's new laws, would have concluded that he had yielded, which was just what the government wanted, since the supposed submission of one who was so highly respected might induce the malcontents to give way.

On the whole, therefore, I am inclined to think that shortly after Christmas 1534, Fisher was released on bail on the above stated conditions; that this was the cause of the rumour that he and More had submitted; and that Gontier really saw the bishop at Westminster. When Anne regained her ascendancy, about the middle of February 1535, this lenient treatment came to an end. She hated Fisher, and was never in favour of conciliatory measures.

Appendix Note F:

ARREST OF ANNE &
HER ACCOMPLICES

With regard to the real cause of Anne's fall, the correspondence of Chapuis has cleared up all doubt. But there still remains the question: What reasons did the government put forward to justify the arrest of the woman whom they called the queen, and of her friends?

There is an old story that Lady Wingfield, on her deathbed, revealed the crimes of Anne, and that it was upon this information that the government acted. It is not said by whom the deposition of Lady Wingfield was taken, nor how it was transmitted to the king. The story presents a good many difficulties, and it is made all the more improbable by the fact that in contemporary accounts no mention is made of any such deposition.

Chapuis gives no information on the subject, except that he expresses strong disapproval of the manner in which the trial was conducted, and censures the fact that depositions were not produced against the prisoners.[1] The writer of the French life of Anne Boleyn gives a very strange and highly-coloured account. One of the members of the privy council, he says, had to reprove his sister for being too exuberant. The lady, seeing her fault discovered, tried to palliate her guilt by saying that the queen did much worse, and that Mark Smeton might tell the whole story of her scandalous life. The privy councillor was much frightened by this speech, for, on the one hand, if he kept the facts secret he might afterwards be blamed and punished; on the other hand, if he revealed them, he might be accused of slandering the king's issue. He took the advice of two of his friends, most intimate servants of the king; and in the end all three went to Henry and told him what they had heard. The king ordered them to be silent, and caused Anne to be watched and finally arrested.[2]

According to a French manuscript printed by Mr Pocock, the gentleman in question was Anthony Brown, wrongly said to be the king's physician, and his sister had formerly been a mistress of the king.[3] The writer of this paper certainly had access to some documents or other good sources; nevertheless I am not satisfied of the truth of the French accounts. They may be merely a reproduction of one of the many stories that were current at the time both at home and abroad.

The author of the Spanish *Cronica del Rey Enrico otavo* reports the story which seems to have been accepted by the Spanish merchants who resided in London towards the close of Henry's reign. He gives a very detailed account of the proceedings. Smeton, he says, was the last of Anne's lovers, and an old woman called Marguerita, servant to Anne, acted as their *confidente*. Having before that time been rather poor, Mark received considerable gifts from Anne, which he spent on dress, horses, and other showy objects. He became very overbearing, and treated the other courtiers with insolence. Finally he had a violent quarrel with Thomas Percy, who complained of him. Anne, on hearing of this, sent for Percy and ordered him to make up his quarrel with Mark. Percy was forced to obey, but, bearing the other a grudge, he went to Cromwell, told him of what Anne had done for Mark, and pointed out that the musician could not have by perfectly fair means all the money he was in the habit of spending. Cromwell thereupon asked Percy secretly to watch his enemy, which Percy did; and the result was, that, on 29 April, early in the morning, he saw Mark coming out of Anne's apartment. This he reported to the secretary; and on May Day, in the morning, Cromwell sent for Mark, and subjected him to torture by causing a knotted cord to be violently tightened round his head. Mark, unable to bear the pain, confessed, and said that Noreys and Bryerton had been his rivals. Cromwell wrote down the confession, and sent it to Henry at Greenwich, who received it in the afternoon, and immediately took his barge and left for Westminster. Noreys and Bryerton were secretly arrested, and Wyatt was also sent to the Tower, but treated with great kindness, Cromwell being his friend. The next day Anne and the duke her brother were arrested; and Anne was examined by Cranmer, the chancellor, Norfolk, and Cromwell. By and by she and her brother were sent to the Tower. Then the old woman Marguerita was arrested and put to the rack, when she incriminated Noreys and Bryerton, but swore that Wyatt was innocent. Rochford, Noreys, Bryerton and Mark were all condemned, and executed together; the old woman was burnt at night within the Tower; and Anne after her conviction was beheaded with a sword by the executioner of Saint Omer.[4]

In many particulars this account is of course false. The writer knows nothing of Weston, he calls Rochford a duke, he makes Cranmer the president of the committee before which Anne appeared, and he falls into other and even greater mistakes. He has heard of Mistress Margaret, but he believes her to be an old woman, and evidently confounds her with the Lady Wingfield of Spelman.

The parts of the story, however, which relate to the insolence of Smeton, to his quarrel with Thomas Percy – there was a Sir Thomas Percy at court, brother of the Earl of Northumberland – and to his arrest and extorted confession, may well be true. They perfectly agree with the account of Constantine and with the official account of Cromwell.

Mr Froude, in the Appendix to the second volume of his *History of England*, gives one more version of the proximate cause of Anne's arrest. 'Lord Howard,' he says, 'wrote at the same time to Granvelle saying that he understood the "concubine" had been surprised in bed with the king's organist.'[5] In proof of this statement about Lord Howard, Mr Froude quotes the following passage: 'Le visconte Howard a escript a Sr de Granvelle que au mesme instant il avoit entendu de bon lieu que la concubine dudict Roy avoit este surprise couchée avec l'organiste dudict Roy.'[6] Unhappily Mr Froude does not say who was the writer of this extraordinary passage, to whom it was addressed, and where it may be found. Moreover, absolutely nothing is known of the existence of a 'Viscount Howard' in the time Henry VIII. There was a Lord Howard, but as he was also the Duke of Norfolk, he was always called by the latter title.

The official account of the causes of Anne's arrest does not go into details. In the letter written on 14 May to Gardiner and Wallop, Cromwell does not name the persons who first denounced Anne. He says her servants could not hide 'the queen's abomination' any longer; and this perfectly agrees with the Spanish account. Cromwell further says that her servants and others were most secretly examined. This, again, agrees with the account of the chronicler and of Constantine. The plot to murder Henry is, of course, an embellishment of Cromwell's. On the whole, the statements of Cromwell, Constantine, and the Spanish chronicler support each other so well that the balance of evidence seems to be decidedly in favour of the account I have given in the text.

The order in which the arrests were made is now pretty certain. The first arrested was certainly Mark Smeton. This appears from Constantine's account, corroborated by Cromwell's, Chapuis's and Bulkeley's letters, as well as from the *Histoire de Anne de Boullant*, from the French account printed by Mr Pocock, and from the Spanish chronicle. Noreys was certainly arrested on the evening of May Day; Rochford on 2 May about noon. Anne was called before the council in the morning, and taken to the Tower about two o'clock in the afternoon. Weston and Bryerton were both arrested on Thursday 4 May. In the account of Constantine, printed in the *Archæologia*, Bryerton is said to have been arrested on Thursday afore May Day.[7]

But from the context it is clear that Bryerton was arrested after the other men were in the Tower, so that *afore* is either a clerical error or a misprint for *after*. Any doubt on this head is dispelled by Cromwell's letter to Gardiner and Wallop. As to Page and Wyatt, they seem to have been arrested about the same time as Bryerton and Weston, or at latest on the day following; for it appears from the letter of Kingston to Cromwell that Anne was told of the arrest of the two former on the same occasion on which she was told of that of Rochford and the two latter gentlemen.[8]

According to the writer of the Spanish chronicle, Wyatt was told on the day before the execution of Rochford – that is, on the day after the conviction of Anne – that he would not be proceeded against. Thereupon, the chronicle proceeds, Wyatt wrote a letter to the king; and in this letter he took credit for having warned Henry not to marry Anne Boleyn, because she was a bad woman. For his boldness he had been banished from court for two years. Now he wished to state that his reason for speaking as he had done was that Anne Boleyn had been his mistress.[9] Whether this be true or not, it is difficult to say; but it is certain that Thomas Wyatt admitted that he had committed some kind of moral offence, for reference to it is made in the letters of his father, Sir Henry Wyatt, to Cromwell and to the king.[10] The chronicler correctly states that Wyatt was immediately restored to royal favour, and that he was shortly afterwards sent as ambassador to Spain.

GROUNDS FOR THE DIVORCE OF ANNE

Dr Lingard, in his *History of England*, expressed the opinion that the marriage between Henry and Anne was decreed by Cranmer to have been null and void from the beginning, because of the former relation of the king to Anne's sister Mary Boleyn. For this he was taken to task by an 'eminent writer'. In the Appendix to the fourth volume of his *History* he replied to his critic; and every impartial reader will, I think, be convinced by his able and temperate answer.[1] Mr Froude, however, rejects the theory, repeating some of the old arguments of Dr Lingard's opponent, and adding others which he considers very important.

It may be well, therefore, to re-state briefly the whole case. I have already given my reasons for believing that Mary Boleyn had been the mistress of Henry VIII; but I fully agree with Mr Froude that the two questions are to a certain extent independent of one another, and that, even if Mary Boleyn had been Henry's mistress, the divorce may have been granted by Cranmer on different grounds.

The first of Mr Froude's arguments is that in the statute by which Elizabeth was disinherited there occurs in the preamble the following passage:

> … certain just true and lawful impediment unknown at the making of the said Acts and since that time confessed by the said Lady Anne before the most reverend father in God, Thomas, archbishop of Canterbury, Metropolitan and Primate of all England, sitting judicially for the same by the which plainly appeareth… [2]

In answer to this it may be said, first of all, that if preambles to Acts of Parliament were to be accepted as trustworthy evidence as to the facts they recite, English history would be a very strange tale – even stranger than it appears in Mr Froude's pages. Again, the Act sets forth that Anne confessed an impediment before Cranmer 'sitting judicially for the same'. Now, when Cranmer sat at Lambeth on 17 May, Anne was represented by Dr Wotton and Dr Barbour; and, as Dr Lingard urged some forty years ago, any confession which she may be said to have made must have been made in her name by her proctors. Mr Froude evidently feels that there is some force in this argument, for to strengthen his case he says of Anne that: 'On Wednesday she was taken to Lambeth, where she made her confession in form, and the Archbishop, sitting judicially, pronounced her marriage with the king to have been null and void.'³ But Mr Froude adduces no evidence for this remarkable statement. It is most unlikely that if Anne had been taken from the Tower to Lambeth and back, no reference would have been made to the fact by chroniclers and newsletter writers, by Kingston, and by Chapuis. The official record of the court held by Cranmer expressly excludes the possibility of her having appeared before him at that time. All the persons who were present are enumerated, and her name is not in the list. It is stated that she was represented by N. Wotton and J. Barbour, and the words *personaliter comparens*, which are always found in such records when the party chiefly concerned was in court, are wanting. No weight, therefore, can be attached to Mr Froude's argument, unless he can show that Cranmer held two different courts for the same purpose, that Anne was really taken to Lambeth to appear at one of them, and that her marriage was twice annulled by the archbishop.

In *Chronicle of England under the Tudors*, written apparently by some cousin of Thomas Wriothesley, who became Lord Chancellor and Earl of Southampton, occurs the following passage:

> And the same day in the afternoon at a solemn court kept at Lambeth by the Lord Archbishop of Canterbury and the doctors of the law, the king was divorced from his wife, Queen Anne, and there at the same court was a privy contract approved that she had made to the Earl of Northumberland afore the king's time, and so she was discharged and was never lawful Queen of England, and there it was approved the same.⁴

Mr Froude accepts this as sound evidence; but he does not say that the only copy of the manuscript of the *Chronicle* known to exist is certainly later than the year 1592. Though it is pretty certain that the original *Chronicle* was written by a contemporary, all we have of it is a copy made at a much later date by a scribe who can be proved to have taken considerable liberties with the text. It is, therefore, impossible to decide how much of the manuscript is the work of the author, and how much is due to interpolations and alterations by the copyist.

This fact detracts considerably from the authority of the *Chronicle*. The phrase about the divorce stands quite apart from the statement that a pre-contract was proved, and the latter explanatory sentence may well have been an interpolation.

But even admitting for argument's sake that the passage was written by the chronicler himself, it cannot be regarded as an important contribution to the discussion of the question. The writer was certainly not a man of high station who had access to the very best information. At the time when his chronicle seems to have been written, his cousin, Thomas Wriothesley, had not risen to eminence, and Sir Thomas Audeley, who appears to have been his patron, was wise enough not to tell the secrets of the king. The chronicler, therefore, had no special knowledge as to secret events; and even about matters regarding which he might have been expected to have accurate information he falls into some very palpable mistakes. He asserts that Henry and Jane Seymour were secretly married at Chelsea, while all other evidence tends to show that the ceremony was performed at Hampton Court.[5] And in the passage quoted by Mr Froude there are also some very grave errors as to fact. For the chronicler says that the court was held on the afternoon of 17 May, while it appears from the official record that it was held between nine and eleven o'clock in the morning. He says, moreover, that Cranmer sat with the doctors of the law, while Cranmer, according to the same official account, sat alone.[6] A writer who makes two such mistakes is certainly not a very trustworthy authority, and his assertion, if it be his, is not to be taken as of equal weight with that of Chapuis.

It is true that Mr Froude tries to discredit the account of Chapuis by asserting that he had at first offered two explanations of the divorce.[7] But in the despatches of Chapuis I have not found these two explanations. The ambassador did say in a letter to Granvelle that he had heard from some people that Cranmer had declared Elizabeth to be the daughter of Noreys, and not of the king, while, according to others, Cranmer had decreed that the marriage between Henry and Anne was invalid on account of the king's former cohabitation with Mary Boleyn.[8] I think it is only Mr Froude who will call this two explanations of the divorce. Chapuis, in June, simply confirmed his first statement as to the grounds of Cranmer's sentence.[9]

A further reason for disbelieving the account of the chronicler and the theory of Mr Froude is that, if the marriage had been pronounced void on account of a pre-contract, this would have had some consequences of which we do not find any trace. First of all, it would have prevented Elizabeth from being declared a bastard, for the good faith of even one of the parents was sufficient to legitimate the issue. As Henry could not well have said that when he married Anne he knew there was a pre-contract with Northumberland, he would necessarily have been held to have acted in good faith. Secondly, the same pre-contract which would have annulled the marriage of Anne and Henry would have annulled that of Lord and Lady Northumberland. We know that the countess wished to be separated from the earl; she would certainly, therefore, have asked for a divorce if it could have been obtained. There is not the slightest evidence that she even thought of making such an application after Anne's death.

If all these arguments be added to those adduced by Dr Lingard, it cannot be seriously doubted that the cause of nullity which Henry was afraid to avow, was his former connection with Mary Boleyn.

NOTES TO PART 1

Part 1: From Courtier's Daughter to Queen of England, 1502–March 1534

Introduction

1. P. Pasqualigo to —, 3 May 1515, *Giustiniani's Despatches*, vol. i. p.90.
2. E. Chapuis to Charles V, 15 March 1533, Vienna Archives P.C. 228, i. fol. 27: 'Que depuis peu de temps en ca les francois avoient desrobe la beaulte et corpulence des anglois et que sembloit proprement quils fussent anglois non point francois.'
3. Castillon to Francis I, 12 August 1538, Paris, Bibl. Nat. MSS Français, vol. 2954, fol. 145: 'Car il noblie jamais sa grandeur et se tait de celle des aultres.'
4. *Diary of Petrus Svavenius*, edited by C.F. Wegener. *Aarsberetninger fra det kongelige Geheime Archiv*, vol. iii. p.171: 'Caesar simplex est et latine nescit, sicut et Gallus... Quod si in me et Gallum rejiceretur arbitrium nos convocaremus eruditissimos quosque... '
5. Count Cyfuentes to Charles V, November 1533, Br. Mus. Add. MSS 28,586, fol. 62: Que stava maravillado dello que el dicho Rei de Anglaterra se tenia por sabio y que en verdad era un loco... '
6. Henry VIII to R. Pate, 25 April 1536, *State Papers*, vol. vii. p.684: 'Whenne We made Him, first King of Spayne, thenne Emperour whenne the empire was at our disposition,' and Chapuis to Charles V, 30 December 1535, Vienna Archives, P.C. 229½, i. fol. 151.
7. Henry VIII to Gardiner and Wallop, 4 January 1536, British Museum Add. MSS 25,144, fol. 119: 'We be of no lesse but much greater auctoritie to direct France than We or owre progenitors have been at any time.'
8. Marilhac to Montmorency, 25 October 1539, Paris, Bibl. Nat. MSS FR. 2955, fol. 93: 'Il est de telle qualité, Monseigneur, quil ayme mieulx un bon visaige que plus grands biens quon luy pourroit faire.'
9. Jean du Bellay to Montmorency, 18 June 1528, Paris, Bibl. Nat. MSS Fr. vol. 3077, fol. 71: 'Une des filles de chambre Monsgr. de Mdlle. de boulan se trouva mardi actainte de la suee, a grand haste le Roy deslogea et alla a douze miles dicy, et ma lon dict que la demoyselle fut envoyee pour le suspect au viconte son pere qui est en caint.'
10. M. de Marilhac to Montmorency, 6 July 1540, Paris, Bibl. Nat. MSS Fr. vol. 2955, p.185: 'Comme la plus timide personne en tel cas quon sache.'
11. Chapuis to Charles V, 17 January 1534, Vienna Archives, P.C. 229, i. No. 6: 'Touttefois considerant la dame la facilite du Roy ou ligierete (qui loseroit dire)... '
12. Castillon to Francis I, 19 June 1538, Paris, Bibl. Nat. MSS Fr. vol. 2955, p.107: 'Il a je ne scais quelle folle fiance de moy et mesmerveille quil pense que je vous en celle rien. Je lui laisse touteffois et fais semblant. Sil vous plaist en faire ainsy jusques a ce que plus ouvertement je le vous face declarer jen tirerois plus en avant.'
13. E. Chapuis to Charles V, 13 December 1529, Vienna Archives, P.C. 227, i. Fol. 81: 'Et pour ce retourd yl ont quelque peu suspecte la Royne pour ce quelle monstra avoir quelque compassion et pitie de la Ruyne du dict Cardinal... '

14. G.G. de Fuensalida, knight commander of Membrilla, to Ferdinand of Aragon, 20 March 1509, G. Bergenroth, *Calendar of State Papers* (Spanish), Supplement to vols. i. and ii. p.23, and Don Luis Carroz to Almazan, 28 May 1510, ibid. p.36.

15. Catherine of Aragon to Ferdinand, 9 March 1509, G. Bergenroth, *Calendar*, Supplement to vols. i. and ii. p.16.

16. John Stile to Henry VII, 26 April 1509, J. Gairdner, *Memorials of King Henry VII*, Appendix, p.435.

17. L. Pasqualigo to his brother, 17 September 1513, R. Brown, *Calendar of State Papers*, Venetian, vol. ii. p.146.

18. Sanuto Diaries. R. Brown, *Calendar*, vol. ii. pp.139 and 140.

1. Anne & Wolsey

1. Dreux de Radier, *Mémoires Historiques*, vol. iv. p.219, and Julien Brodeau, *La Vie de Maistre Charles du Molin*, p.6: 'J'ay un tiltre du Samedi apres la St. Martin, 1344, de Baudouin de Biaunoir, Sire d'Avesnes proche de Peronne, qui nomme entre ses hommes de fief Vautier de Boulen.'

2. Chapuis to Charles V, 21 and 31 December 1530, Vienna Archives, P.C. 226, i. Nos. 51 and 52.

3. About the date of Anne Boleyn's birth and the history of her early life see Appendix, Note A.

4. *Epistre contenant le proces criminel fait a lencontre de la Royne Boullant d'Angleterre*, ascribed to Lancelot de Carles, to Marot and to Crispin de Milherve, printed first at Lyons 1545, by 'Charles ausmonier de Mr le Dauphin;' and again by Crapelet, at Paris, in his Lettres de Henry VIII a Anne Boleyn:

   Or Monseigneur je crois que bien scavez
   Et de longtemps la connaissance avez
   Que Anne Boullant premierement sortit,
   De ce pays quand Marie en partit.
   Pour s'en aller trouver le Roy en France
   Pour accomplir des deux Roys l'aliance.

5. Cambridge, Corpus Christi College MSS vol. 119, fol. 21.

6. See Appendix, Note B.

7. Crapelet, *Love Letters of Henry VIII*, Letter No. iv. p.110.

8. E. Chapuis to Charles V, 10 May 1530, Vienna Archives, P.C. 226, i. 50: 'Sire il y a longtemps que le duc de Suffocq ne sest trouve en cort et dit lon quil est banni pour quelque temps a cause quil revela au Roy que la dame avoit este trouvee au delit avec un gentilhomme de court qui desja en avoit autreffois este chasse pour suspicion.'

9. Sanuto Diary, 1 September 1514, R. Brown, *Venetian Calendar*, vol. ii. p.188.

10. Brewer, *Letters and Papers of Henry VIII*, vol. ii. p.xxxiv. note, &c.

11. British Museum, Cotton MSS Caligula, D ix. 248, and Brewer, *Letters and Papers*, vol. iv. p.1109.

12. Proceedings before Cardinal Wolsey, 17 to 31 May 1527, R.O. and Brewer, *Letters and Papers*, vol. iv. pp.1426 to 1429.

13. Proceedings before Cardinal Wolsey, 17 to 31 May 1527, R.O. and Brewer, *Letters and Papers*, vol. iv. p.1429.

14. The Bishop of Rochester to Wolsey, R.O. and Brewer, *Letters and Papers*, vol. iv. p.1434.

15. Don Iñigo de Mendoza to Charles V, 18 May 1527, Vienna Archives, P.C. 224, i. No. 18; and Gayangos, *Calendar of State Papers*, Spanish, vol. iii. part ii. p.193.

16. Don Iñigo de Mendoza to Charles V, 13 July 1527, Vienna Archives, P.C. 224, i. No. 22; and Gayangos, *Calendar*, vol. iii. part ii. p.276.

17. Wolsey to Henry VIII, 1 July 1527, *State Papers*, vol. i. p.194.

18. Don Iñigo de Mendoza to Charles V, 16 August 1527, Vienna Archives, P.C. 224, i. No. 27; and Gayangos, *Calendar*, vol. iii. part ii. p.327.
19. Wolsey to Henry VIII, 29 July 1527, *State Papers*, vol. i. fol. 230.
20. J. Gairdner, *Letters and Papers*, vol. vi. p.ix. footnote.
21. Knight to Henry VIII, 13 September 1527, R.O. and *State Papers*, vol. vii. p.3.
22. Draft of Commission to Wolsey, British Museum, Cotton MSS Vitellius, B. ix. fol. 218, printed by N. Pocock, *Records of the Reformation*, vol. i. No. XIII .
23. Knight to Henry VIII, 12 September 1527, R.O. and *State Papers*, vol. vii. p.1.
24. Wolsey to Henry VIII, 5 September 1527, R.O. and *State Papers*, vol. i. p.267.
25. Cardinal Cibo to Cardinal Salviati, 27 July 1527, *Lettere de' Principi*, vol. ii. fol. 233; Cardinal Salviati to —, 17 August 1527, *Ibid*. vol. ii. fol. 235; and Wolsey to Henry VIII, 5 September 1527, *State Papers*, vol. i. p.270.
26. Don Iñigo de Mendoza to Charles V, 26 October 1527, Vienna Archives, P.C. 224, No. 35; and *Spanish Calendar*, vol. iii. part ii. p.432.

2. The Legatine Court

1. Oxford, Corpus Christi College, MSS cccviii. fol. 3, holograph, published by E.L. Hicks in the *Academy*, 15 March 1879.
2. Knight to Henry VIII, 4 November 1527, *State Papers*, vol. vii. p.13.
3. Knight to Henry VIII, 4 December 1527, *State Papers*, vol. vii. p.16.
4. Dr Ortiz to the Empress, 7 February 1533, British Museum Add. MSS vol. 28,585, fol. 217: 'Y para poderse casar con esta Ana es cierta verdad que a tiempo que embio a demandar dispensacion a Su St para poderse casar con ella no estante la afinidad que entre ellos avie por aver mal usado de su hermana...'
5. Knight to Wolsey, 1 January 1528, Burnet, *Collectanea*, part i. book ii. No. 4.
6. Knight to Henry VIII, 9 and 10 January 1528, Pocock, *Records*, vol. i. No. xxvii. and *State Papers*, vol. vii. p.46; Knight to Wolsey, 9 and 10 January 1528, Pocock, *Records*, vol. i. No. xxviii., and Brewer, *Letters and Papers*, vol. iv. p.1687.
7. Wolsey to Gregorio da Casale, 12 February 1528, *State Papers*, vol. vii. p.50; Wolsey to Cardinal Santi Quattro, Brewer, Letters and Papers, vol. iv. p.1745.
8. Crapelet, *Lettres de Henry VIII*, Love Letter, No. xiv. p.134.
9. Cardinal Wolsey to Gardiner and Foxe, Brewer, *Letters and Papers*, vol. iv. p.1741.
10. Knight to Henry VIII, 21 April 1528, R.O. and Pocock, *Records of the Reformation*, vol. i. No. Lv.
11. Lord Rochford to Wolsey, 20 August 1528, Brewer, *Letters and Papers*, vol. iv. p.2020; Anne Boleyn to Wolsey, Brewer, *Letters and Papers*, vol. iv. p.3166.
12. Henry VIII to Cardinal Campeggio, Brewer, *Letters and Papers*, p.1740; Gardiner and Gregorio da Casale to Wolsey, 13 April 1528, Pocock, *Records of the Reformation*, vol. i. No. li.
13. T. Henneage to Wolsey, 3 and 16 March 1528, Brewer, *Letters and Papers*, vol. iv. pp.1779 and 1806.
14. Foxe to Gardiner, 11 May 1528, Pocock, *Records*, vol. i. No. liii.
15. Foxe to Gardiner, May, 1528, Pocock, *Records*, vol. i. No. liv.
16. Du Bellay to Montmorency, 18 June 1528, Paris, Bibl. Nat. MSS Français, vol. 3077, fol. 71; and *Le Grand*, vol. iii. p.129. The abstract in Mr Brewer's *Letters and Papers* is incorrect. Du Bellay wrote: 'Une des filles de chambre, Monsgr de Madlle. de Boulan se trouva mardi actainte de la suée.'
17. T. Henneage to Wolsey, 23 June 1528, Brewer, *Letters and Papers,* vol. iv. p.1931.
18. Henry VIII to Anne Boleyn, Crapelet, Love Letter No. iii. p.108, and Love Letter No. xii. p.128.
19. Brian Tuke to Wolsey, 23 June 1528, Brewer, *Letters and Papers*, vol. iv. p.1931,
20. Henry VIII to Anne, Crapelet, Love Letter No. xii. p.128.
21. Brian Tuke to Wolsey, 23 June 1528, *loc. cit.*
22. J. Russell to Wolsey, 28 June 1528, Brewer, *Letters and Papers*, vol. iv. p.1938.
23. T. Henneage to Wolsey, 23 June 1528, Brewer, *Letters and Papers*, vol. iv. p.1931.

24. Henry VIII to Anne Boleyn, Crapelet, Love Letter No. xiii. p.130.

25. T. Henneage to Wolsey, 23 June 1528, *loc. cit.*

26. Henry VIII to Anne Boleyn, Crapelet, Love Letter No. xiii. p.130; and Dr Bell to Cardinal Wolsey, 7 July 1528, *State Papers*, vol. i. p.310.

27. Dr Bell to Cardinal Wolsey, 10 July 1528, *State Papers*, vol. i. p.313.

28. Dr Bell to Wolsey, 10 July 1528, *loc. cit.*; and T. Henneage to Wolsey, 11 July 1528, *State Papers*, vol. i. p.315.

29. Henry VIII to Wolsey, Fiddes, *Life of Cardinal Wolsey*, Appendix, p.174.

30. T. Henneage to Wolsey, July 14, 1528, *State Papers*, vol. i. p.316.

31. Henry VIII to Wolsey, Fiddes, Appendix, p. 174.

32. Henry VIII to Wolsey, Lord Herbert of Cherbury, *Life of Henry VIII*, p.67; and Wolsey to Henry VIII, *State Papers*, vol. i. p.317.

33. Isabel Jordan to Wolsey, Brewer, *Letters and Papers*, vol. iv. p.1978; and Thomas Benet to Wolsey, 18 July 1528, *State Papers*, i. p.314.

34. Anne Boleyn to Wolsey, Burnet, *History of the Reformation*, vol. i. p.56; and Anne Boleyn and Henry VIII to Wolsey, *ibid.* p.55.

35. Italian News, 13 June 1528, Brewer, *Letters and Papers*, vol. iv. p.1916.

36. Instructions to Sir Francis Bryan, August 1528, Brewer, *Letters and Papers*, vol. iv. p.2024; and T. Clerk and Taylor to Wolsey, 31 August 1528, Brewer, *Letters and Papers*, vol. iv. p.2031.

37. Campeggio to Jacopo Salviati, 16 September 1528, Theiner, *Vetera Monumenta Hibernorum*, p.567; and T. Clerk and Taylor to Wolsey, Brewer, *Letters and Papers*, vol. iv. p.2053.

38. T. Clerk to Wolsey, and T. Clerk to Gardiner, 18 September 1528, Brewer, *Letters and Papers*, vol. iv. pp.2060 and 2062; and Cardinal Campeggio to Jacopo Salviati, 17 October 1528, Theiner, *Vetera Monumenta*, p.570.

39. Examination of John Fisher, Record Office, Henry VIII, Box Q, 155.

3. The Death of Wolsey

1. Cardinal Campeggio to Jacopo Salviati, 21 June 1529, Brewer, *Letters and Papers*, vol. iv. p.dclxx; and Giovanni da Casale to Wolsey, 17 December 1528, Burnet, *Collectanea*, part ii. book ii. No. xvii.

2. G.B. Sanga to Cardinal Campeggio, 2 and 16 September 1528, Porcacchi, *Lettere di XIII huomini illustri*, pp.39 and 41.

3. Cardinal Campeggio to G.B. Sanga, 17 October 1528, Laemmer, *Monumenta Vaticana*, No. xxii.

4. Wolsey to Gregorio da Casale, 1 November 1528, *State Papers*, vii. p.102.

5. Giovanni da Casale to Wolsey, 17 December 1528, Burnet, *Collectanea*, part i. book ii. No. xviii.

6. F. Bryan and P. Vanni to Wolsey, 28 December 1528, British Museum, Cotton MSS Vitellius, b. x. 186; and Cardinal Campeggio to Jacopo Salviati, 21 June 1529, Brewer, *Letters and Papers*, vol. iv. p.dclxx.

7. Julius II to 'Dilecto filio Heinrico Char^mi in Chro filii nri Henrici Anglie Regis Ill^i nato Ill° et dilecte in Chro filie Catherine Char^mi et in Chr° filii nri Ferdinandi Regis et Char^me in chr° filie nre Elizabeth Regine Hispaniarum et Sicilie Catholicorum Nate Ill^e 26 December 1503, Vienna Archives, P.C. 228, iv. No. 1; and Don Iñigo de Mendoza to Charles V, 18 November 1528, Vienna Archives, P.C. 226, i. No. 15.

8. P. Vanni to Henry VIII, 28 March 1529, *State Papers*, vol. vii. p.154; and G.B. Sanga to Cardinal Campeggio, 10 April 1529, Porcacchi, *Lettere di XIII huomini illustri*, p.63. As to the authenticity of the brief see Note C. in the Appendix.

9. Commission of 8 June 1528, Cotton MSS Vitellius, B. x. 97, and Pocock, *Records*, vol. i. p.167.

10. Procedure in Divorce Court, 21 June 1529, Pocock, *Records*, vol. i. p.223.

11. Procedure in Divorce Court, Pocock, *Records*, vol. i. pp.206–11 and 216–31.

12. Crapelet, Henry to Anne Boleyn, Love Letter No. xvii. p.140.

13. Jean du Bellay to Anne de Montmorency, 18 September 1529, Legrand, vol. iii. fol. 354, &c.
14. Cardinal Campeggio to J. Salviati, 24 June 1529, Theiner, *Vetera Monumenta*, p.584.
15. Miçer May to Charles V, 4 August 1529, British Museum, Add. MSS 28,579, fol.20; and Gardiner to Vanni, 28 July 1529, Brewer, *Letters and Papers*, vol. iv. p.2591.
16. Thomas Alward to Thomas Cromwell, 23 September 1529, British Museum, Cotton MSS Vitellius, B. xii. 173, printed by Ellis, first series, i.307.
17. Cardinal Campeggio to Jacopo Salviati, 7 October 1529, Theiner, *Vetera Monumenta*, p.587.
18. Henry VIII to Cardinal Campeggio, 22 October 1529, Brewer, *Letters and Papers*, vol. iv. p.2677; and E. Chapuis to Charles V, 25 October 1529, Vienna Archives, P.C. 226, i. No. 23, printed by Bradford, *Correspondence of Charles V*. Carlo Sigonio, in his Life of Cardinal Campeggio, gives a highly coloured account of this affair, but adduces no authority.
19. Accounts of Bryan Tuke, Gairdner, *Letters and Papers*, vol. v. p.315.
20. Bill of Indictment, Brewer, *Letters and Papers*, vol. iv. p.2686; Memorandum of the Surrender of the Great Seal, Rymer, *Fœdera*, xiv. p.349 ; and G. Cavendish, *Life of Cardinal Wolsey*, p.251.
21. Grant to G. Boleyn, R.O., Brewer, *Letters and Papers*, vol. iv.p.2730; and Wolsey to Cromwell, *State Papers*, vol. i. p.355, &c.
22. Indenture, 22 October 1529, R.O., Brewer, *Letters and Papers*, vol. iv. p.2678.
23. Letters of Protection, 18 November 1529, Rymer, *Fœdera*, xiv. p.351.
24. Pensions payées en Angleterre, Paris, Bibl. Nat. MSS Français, vol. 2997, fol. 54.
25. Gardiner to Wolsey, R.O., Brewer, *Letters and Papers*, vol. iv. p.2668.
26. John Hobbys, sheriff of Canterbury, to Cromwell, 12 May 1536, R.O., *Cromwell Correspondence*, vol. v. fol. 108.
27. The mayor and sheriff of Canterbury to Cromwell, 20 May 1536, R.O., *Cromwell Correspondence*, vol. v. fol. 102.
28. E. Chapuis to Charles V, 25 October 1529, Vienna Archives, P.C. 225, i. No. 23.
29. E. Chapuis to Charles V, 6 February 1530 and 14 May 1531, Vienna Archives, P.C. 226, i. fol. 24 and 227, i. fol. 43.
30. E. Chapuis to Charles V, 8 November 1529, Vienna Archives, P.C. 225, i. No. 24.
31. *Statutes of the Realm*, vol. iii. p.315.
32. Grievances charged by the Commons upon the Spiritualty: Hall, *Union of the Houses of York and Lancaster*, p.765.
33. Instructions to G. Boleyn and Dr Stokesley, *State Papers*, vol. vii. p.219.
34. Patent, 8 December 1529, Brewer, *Letters and Papers*, vol. iv. p.2718.
35. E. Chapuis to Charles V, 13 December 1529, Vienna Archives, P.C. 227, i. fol. 81.
36. E. Chapuis to Charles V, 13 January 1530, Vienna Archives, P.C. 226, i. fol. 4.
37. Bryan Tuke's Accounts, 20 January 1530, Gairdner, *Letters and Papers*, vol. v. p.317.
38. E. Chapuis to Charles V, 25 January 1530, Vienna Archives, P.C. 226, i. fol. 7.
39. J. du Bellay to Montmorency, 20 February 1530, Paris, Bibl. Nat. MSS Fr. 3080, fol. 90.
40. Charles V to Eustache Chapuis, 25 March 1530, Vienna Archives, P.C. 228, ii. fol. 50.
41. Charles V to Chapuis, 25 March 1530, Vienna Archives, P.C. 228, ii. fol. 55: 'Disant le comte de Wilschire que combien quil neu procuration speciale pour asseehurer que le dict Roy son maistre ne innoveroit rien de son couste cependant par voie de fait ny autrement que touteffois il avoit bien tel credit de son dict maistre quil sen vouloit bien faire fort…'
42. E. Chapuis to Charles V, 10 May and 11 July 1530, Vienna Archives, P.C. 226, i. fols. 50 and 59; J.J. de Vaulx to Francis I, 2 and 4 April 1530, Paris, Bibl. Nat. MSS Fr. vol. 3019, fol. 126.
43. E. Chapuis to Charles V, 6 February 1530, Vienna Archives, P.C. 226, i. fol. 24.
44. Dr Agostino to Cromwell, 19 January 1530, Brewer, *Letters and Papers*, vol. iv.

p.2747.

45. E. Chapuis to Charles V, 6 February 1530, Vienna Archives, P.C. 226, i. fol. 24: 'Sire un cousin du medecin du Cardinal ma dit que la dame lavoyt envoye visiter durant sa maladie et se presenter de luy estre favorable vers le Roy quest chose dure a croyre attendu ce que dessus et linimitie quelle luy a toujours porte, ce nestoit ou quelle pensast quil dehust mourir ou quelle heu voulu monstrer sa dissimulacion et affayterie de quoy au dire du commung elle est bonne ouvriere.'

46. G. Cavendish, *Life of Cardinal Wolsey*, p.287.

47. Rymer, *Fœdera*, xiv. pp.366 and 374.

48. J.J. de Vaulx to Francis I, 5 March 1530, Paris, Bibl. Nat. MSS Fr. 3014, fol. 78.

49. J.J. de Vaulx to Francis I, 15 March 1530, Paris, Bibl. Nat. MSS Fr. 3014, fols. 80, 81.

50. Eustache Chapuis to Charles V, 6 February 1530, Vienna Archives, P.C. 226, i. fol. 24: 'Jean Joaquin a charge... de rabiller les affaires du Cardinal avec le Roy que seroit sans la dame fort ayse... La pratique bien demesle ne pourroit estre plus advantageuse pour eulx mais elle nest sans grand danger de demoure imparfaytte et dirrite ceulx que ont le credit et maniement aux quieux y va la vie... Maistre Rossel ma dit que a cause quil avoit porte quelque parolle au Roy en faveur du dict Cardinal que la dame avoit bien demoure ung moys luy tenant trognie et refusant luy parler.'

51. E. Chapuis to Charles V, 6 February 1530, *loc. cit*: 'Jentends que pour remedier a cet inconvenient yl aye este ordonne quil napprocheroit de la court de cinq ou sept milles de ce pays.'

52. Chapuis to Charles V, 6 February 1530, *loc. cit.*

53. J.J. de Vaulx to Francis I, 27 March 1530, Paris, Bibl. Nat. MSS Fr. vol. 3126, fol. 106.

54. J.J. de Vaulx to Francis I, 22 March 1530, Paris, Bibl. Nat. MSS Fr. vol. 3012, fol. 79, &c.

55. Dr Martin Luther's *Saemmtliche Schriften*, vol. x. p.716, Sermon, anno 1522: 'Das' [to marry a late brother's widow] 'ist nun nicht mehr geboten doch auch nicht verboten,' and *Ibid.* vol. x. pp.744 and 745, Sermon, anno 1525?: 'Daraus folget dass ich meines Weibes oder Braut Schwester nach ihrem Tode ehelichen mag, darzu auch des Bruders Weib nach seinem Tode im Gesetz befohlen war zu nehmen.' At a later period Luther disapproved of such marriages, but he never admitted that a marriage once concluded with a deceased brother's widow was illegal and void.

56. Opinion of Angers, 7 May 1530, Legrand, vol. iii. p.507; and Opinion of Poitiers, 23 April 1530, Vienna Archives, P.C. 226, ii. fol. 25.

57. G. du Bellay and J.J. de Vaulx to Francis I, 15 February 1530, Paris, Bibl. Nat. MSS Fr. 3019, fol. 112: 'Sicome col mezo de V. M^{te} la M^{ta} sua non dubita que tutti ben sentirano altramente chin suo favor non puo venire, cossi disse ley. E perche la prestezza importa... '; and J.J. de Vaulx to Francis I, 5 March 1530, Paris, Bibl. Nat. MSS Fr. 3014, fol. 78: 'E se con tal mezo S. Sta inclinera al intento desso S^{mo} Re in buona hora se manco Sua M^{te}, parendoli haver justissima causa, per satisfatione della sua conscientia per aventura prendera degli expedienti che a lei e al suo buon consiglio pareran piu al proposito... '; and J.J. de Vaulx to Francis I, 27 March 1530, Paris, Bibl. Nat. MSS Fr. 3126, fol. 106.

58. J.J. de Vaulx to A. de Montmorency, 15 November 1530, Paris, Bibl. Nat. MSS Italiens, vol. 1131, fol. 44.

59. E. Chapuis to Charles V, 15 September 1532, Vienna Archives, P.C. 227, iii. fol. 61: 'Le dict Sr Roy de France na rien perdu a la mort du Cardinal d'Yorch recouvrant cette dame car oultre quelle est plus maligne et a plus de credit que navoit lautre il ne luy bailie vint cinq mille escus comme il faisoit au susdit Cardinal ains tant seulement flatteries et promesses de soliciter le divorce.'

60. J. Breton de Villandry to A. de Montmorency, 6 May 1530, Paris, Bibl. Nat. MSS Fr. 3018, fol. 58.

61. J.J. de Vaulx to Francis I, 27 March 1530, Paris, Bibl. Nat. MSS Fr. 3126, fol. 106; and Accounts of Sir Bryan Tuke, 20 March 1530, Gairdner, *Letters and Papers*, vol. v. p.318.

62. J. du Bellay to A. de Montmorency, 26 June 1530, Paris, Bibl. Nat. MSS Fr. 3079, fol. 35: 'Je crois Mgr. Vous souvient dun propos que je Vous tins a Bayonne qui avoit est mis en avant envers Mr de Vuilcher pour resserrer lamitie de ces deux Roys quil na oublie envers son maistre de sorte quil este arreste que incontinent messieurs delivres je cours en Angleterre pour cet effect . . . il est vray quon se fust bien passe de tant se haster... il ny a plus ordre de rompre la chose mais vostre venue la pourra beaucoup amender.'

63. J. du Bellay to A. de Montmorency, 'De Moulins ce mardi,' Paris, Bibl. Nat. MSS Fr. 3079, fol. 45; and J. Breton de Villandry to A. de Montmorency, 6 May 1530, *loc. cit.*

64. Francis I to the President of Paris, 17 June 1530, Brewer, *Letters and Papers*, vol. iv. p.2903; Guillaume du Bellay to A. de Montmorency, 12 June, 8 July and 15 and 18 August 1530, Paris, Bibl. Nat. MSS Fr. 3020, fol. 113; 3080, fol. 153; 3079, fols. 91 and 99; Jean du Bellay to A. de Montmorency, 15 August 1530, *Ibid.* vol. 3077, fol. 93; and Opinion of the Faculty of Theology of Paris, 2 July 1530, Rymer, *Fœdera*, vol. xiv. p.393.

65. Names of doctors in favour of Catherine, Vienna Archives, P.C. 226, ii. fol. 28.

66. E. Chapuis to Margaret of Savoy, 20 August 1530, Vienna Archives, P.C. 227, iv. fol. 45.

67. E. Chapuis to Charles V, 5 September 1530, Vienna Archives, P.C. 226, i. fol. 73: 'Et dient que le duc de Susphoc a este celluy qua le plus resiste.' The abstract of this letter given by Mr de Gayangos in his *Calendar*, vol. iv. part i. p.708 to 710, is very inaccurate.

68. E. Chapuis to Charles V, 10 May 1530, Vienna Archives, P.C. 226, i. fol. 50: 'Sire il y a longtemps que le duc de Suffocq ne sest trouve en cort et dit lon quil en est banni pour quelque temps a cause quil revela au Roy que la dame avoyt este trouvee au delit avec ung gentilhomme de court que desia en avoit autreffois este chasse pour suspicion et ceste derniere foys lon lavoit faict vuyder de cour a linstance de la dicte dame qui faignoit estre fort courroussee contre luy mais enfin le Roy a intercede vers elle que le dict gentilhomme retournast a la court;' and George Wyatt, *Life of Sir Thomas Wyatt*.

69. E. Chapuis to Charles V, 23 April 1530, Vienna Archives, P.C. 226, i. fol. 43.

70. E. Chapuis to Charles V, 23 April and 15 June 1530, Vienna Archives, P.C. 226, i. fols. 43 and 64.

71. E. Chapuis to Charles V, 10 May 1530, Vienna Archives, P.C. 226, i. fol. 50: 'Et vouldroit le dict Cardinal quil luy eust couste son archevesche que cella eu este attempte il y a deux ans car mieulx neust il peu estre vange de ceste garse que la deffayt.

72. Giles de la Pommeraye to A. de Montmorency, 28 December 1529, Paris, Bibl. Nat. MSS Fr. 20502, fol. 44: 'Le Cardinal de Yort ne demourera gueres longuement ... les flamands ne luy donnent le tort'; and E. Chapuis to Charles V, 27 November 1530, Vienna Archives, P.C. 226, i. fol. 96.

73. J.J. de Vaulx to Francis I, 27 March 1530, Paris, Bibl. Nat. MSS Fr. 3126, fol. 106; and E. Chapuis to Charles V, 13 November 1530, Vienna Archives, P.C. 226, i. fol. 93.

74. E. Chapuis to Charles V, 13 and 27 November 1530, Vienna Archives, P.C. 226, i. fols. 93 and 96.

75. E. Chapuis to Charles V, 27 November 1530, *loc. cit.*

76. E. Chapuis to Charles V, 11 July 1530, Vienna Archives, P.C. 226, i. fol. 59. Norfolk said of Wolsey: 'Touteffois de sa vie ne parleroit au Roy ny le verroit; ce quil avoit bien pense fayre il y a peu de jours et a cet effect avoit invente la plus caute et subtille occasion du monde, mais les moyens de lexecution avoint este bien fols car le dict Cardinal sestoit declayre a troys qui feroient faulce monnoye pour le dict duc.'

77. E. Chapuis to Charles V, 6 February 1530, Vienna Archives, P.C. 226, i. fol. 24.
78. E. Chapuis to Charles V, 27 November 1530, Vienna Archives, i. fol. 96: 'Mais depuis quilz ont eu le medecin du dict Cardinal entre les mains ils ont trouves ce quilz serchoient... il a chante comme ils demandoient.'

4. Thomas Cromwell

1. E. Chapuis to Charles V, 23 January 1531, Vienna Archives, P.C. 227, i. fol. 11: 'Sire le comte de Vulchier naguiere donna a soupper au sieur de la Guiche ou pour mieux le festoyer fust jouee une farse de lallee du Cardinal en enfert de quoy le dict de la Guiche blasme fort le dict comte et encoires plus le duc pour ce quil a commande le fayre mectre en impression. Lon a fayt et continuellement fait lon grande chiere au dict de la guiche toutteffois ilz nen scavent tant faire quil ne sen gaudisse et ne leur die de [leur die en] leurs entreprinses pouvre gouvernement et conseil.' The passage, as quoted by Mr de Gayangos in his *Calendar*, vol. iv. part ii. p.41, I have not been able to find in Chapuis' despatch.
2. E. Chapuis to Charles V, 31 December 1530, Vienna Archives, P.C. 226, i. fol. 109: 'Lon ma dict que la duchesse de Norphocq luy a naguyres derechiefz desclayre et deschiffre larbre de sa genealogie la blasonnant bien asprement. Le Roy en est bien deplaisant mays il fault quil aye pacience.'
3. E. Chapuis to Charles V, 21 December 1530, Vienna Archives, P.C. 226, i. fol. 106.
4. E. Chapuis to Charles V, 31 December 1530, Vienna Archives, P.C. 226, i. fol. 109: 'Sire la dame na permis que ces serviteurs a ces festes ayent portes leurs accoustrements faytz avec la devise grognie que grognie. Je ne scais si elle attend la determination de ce parlement ou sy quelqung luy a dit que le propre et vray refrain dicelle devise est de y ajouster vive borgougne.'
5. E. Chapuis to Charles V, 1 January 1531, Vienna Archives, P.C. 227, i. fol, 1: 'La dame sen tenant asseure est plus brave quung lion jusqua dire a une dame de la Royne quelle vouldroit que tant dispaigniolz quil y a au monde fussent en la mer et luy disant lautre que pour lhonneur de la Royne quelle ne debvroit ainsi parler elle lui replica quelle ne luy challoyt de la Royne ni des siens et quelle aymeroit mieulx que ladicte Royne fust pendue avant quelle confessa quelle fust sa maystresse ne famme du Roy.'
6. E. Chapuis to Charles V, 6 June 1531, Vienna Archives, P.C. 227, i. fol. 47.
7. E. Chapuis to Charles V, 29 April 1531, Vienna Archives, P.C. 227, i. fol. 41: 'La ducesse de Norphoc a cecy rapporte a la Royne luy disant davantaige que son mary en estoit merveilleusement marry et tribule, disant quil veoit bien quelle [Anne Boleyn] seroit cause de fayre detruire tout le parentaige.'
8. Catherine of Aragon to Clement VII, December 1530, Vienna Archives, P.C. 227, ii. fol. 1.
9. E. Chapuis to Charles V, 31 January 1531, Vienna Archives, P.C. 227, i. fol. 13: 'La duchesse de Norfock a envoye hier dire a la Royne quelle sera tousiours de son party et quelle print bon cueur car ses adversaires estoient au bout de leur sens estans plus estonnez et nouveaulx en ceste affaire que le premier jour.'
10. Instructions to the Bishop of Bayonne, Paris, Bib. Nat. MSS Fr. 3020, fol. 59; and E. Chapuis to Charles V, 31 October 1530 and 8 March 1531, Vienna Archives, P.C. 226, i. fol. 87 and 227, i. fol. 27.
11. E. Chapuis to Charles V, 31 January 1531, Vienna Archives, P.C. 227, i. fol. 13: 'Le Roy... delibereroit veu quaultrement il ny pouvoit remedier prandre lhonneur a soy et de son propre mouvement avant quil y soit aultrement force de separer la dame davec luy. Il est bien a supposer que son intent est de la rappeler tost mais je pense que sy une fois elle est en voye dieu et la Royne pourvoyeroint bien a son retour.'
12. E. Chapuis to Charles V, 11 July 1530, Vienna Archives, P.C. 226, i. fol. 59: 'Il y a desia quelque temps que le Roy luy disoit quelle luy estoit merveilleusement oblige car pour son amour il pregnoit picque a tout le monde... que cela estoit peu de faict au regart delle que scavoit bien que par les anciennes prophecies que disoint que en

ce temps yl y devoit avoir une Royne que seroit bruslee mais quant bien elle devroit mille fois morir si ne rabbatroit elle rien de son amour.'

13. E. Chapuis to Charles V, 27 November 1530, Vienna Archives, P.C. 226, i. fol. 99.

14. E. Chapuis to Charles V, 13 November 1530, Vienna Archives, P.C. 226, i. fol. 93.

15. E. Chapuis to Charles V, 29 April 1531, Vienna Archives, P.C. 227, i. fol. 41: 'Elle devient touts les jours plus fiere et plus brave usant de parolles et auctorite envers le Roy de quoy il sest plaint plusieurs foys au due de Norphoc disant quelle nestoit point de la condicion de la Royne laquelle en sa vie ne luy avoit dict mauvaise parolle. La ducesse de Norphoc a cecy rapporte a la Royne... '

16. Ralf Sadleyr to Cromwell, 1 November 1529, British Museum, Cotton MSS Cleopatra, E. IV. fol. 178; and Brewer, *Letters and Papers*, vol. iv. p.3180.

17. Cromwell to Cardinal Wolsey, 21 October 1530, Brewer, *Letters and Papers*, vol. iv. p.3019: 'The parliament ys prorogyd [until the] vi daye of January. The prelatts shall not appere [in the] premunire. Ther ys another way devysyd in [place thereof] as your Grace shall ferther know.'

18. Record Office, Report of Edward Lee, Box R, No. 60.

19. Wilkins, *Concilia*, iii. pp.725–745; and Chapuis to Charles V, 14 February 1531, Vienna Archives, P.C. 227, i. fol. 15.

20. Chapuis to Charles V, 21 February 1531, Vienna Archives, P.C. 227, i. fol. 18.

21. Chapuis to Charles V, 22 May 1531, Vienna Archives, P.C. 227, i. fol. 45: 'Sire depuis quatre jours les ecclesiastiques de larchevesche dyort et de levesche de Durem ont envoye au Roy une grande protestation et reclamation contre la souveraincte que le Roy veult pretendre et usurper sur eulx. Ceulx de larchevesche de Canturbery ont de mesme public une autre protestacion de laquelle envoye un double a Mgr de Granvelle et se trouve le Roy bien desplaisant des dictes choses.' Protestation of the clergy of Canterbury, Vienna Archives, P.C. 227, ii. fol. 26, signed by Peter Ligham in his own name and in that of the clergy of Canterbury, Robert Shorten, Adam Travis, Ric. Fetherstoune, Richard Henrisoun, Thomas Petty, John Guarr, Rowland Phelippes, Wylliam Clyffe, archdeacon of London, J. Fitzjames for the clergy of Bath and chapter of Wells, Thomas Parker for the clergy of Worcester, Rob. Ridley for the clergy of London, Nicolas Metcalfe, archdeacon of Rochester, Rob. Johanson for the clergy and chapter of Rochester, Ralph Suede for the clergy and chapter of Coventry and Lichfield, John Willo for the clergy of Rochester, and John Rayne for the clergy of Lincoln.

22. Brief of Pope Clement VII., 5 January 1531, Vienna Archives, P.C. 226, ii. fol. 3.

23. E. Chapuis to Charles V, 6 June 1531, Vienna Archives, P.C. 227, i. fol. 47.

24. E. Chapuis to Charles V, 6 June 1531, Vienna Archives, P.C. 227, i. fol. 47.

25. E. Chapuis to Charles V, 14 May 1531, Vienna Archives, P.C. 227, i. fol. 43: 'A lappetit aussi de la dicte dame la duchesse de Norphoc a este envoyee en sa maison pour ce quelle parloit trop liberallement et se declayroit plus quilz ne vouloint pour la Royne.'

26. E. Chapuis to Charles V, 17 July 1531, Vienna Archives, P.C. 227, i. fol. 55: 'Le jeune Marquis a eu deffense de non se trouver en court de quelque temps pour ce quil a ete charge de fere assemblee de gens en cornouaillies et au pays de lenviron, la Royne croit que se soit invention de la dame pour ce que le dict Marquis luy est tant serviteur.' Both M de Gayangos and Mr Gairdner think that the 'young Marquis' is the Marquis of Dorset; but it is quite clear from other letters of Chapuis that the Marquis of Exeter is meant.

27. E. Chapuis to Charles V, 8 October and 6 December 1529, Vienna Archives, P.C. 225, i. Nos. 22 and 28.

28. E. Chapuis to Charles V, 15 June 15 1530, Vienna Archives, P.C. 226, i. fol. 54.

29. E. Chapuis to Charles V, 14 May 1531, Vienna Archives, P.C. 227, i. fol. 43.

30. E. Chapuis to Charles V, 8 November 1529, Vienna Archives, P.C. 225, i. No. 24.

31. E. Chapuis to Charles V, 14 May 1531, Vienna Archives, P.C. 227, i. fol. 43: 'Sire disnant ces jours le Roy avec la Royne que il a accoutume la pluspart des festes il entra a parler des treves... et apres tombant en propos de la princesse yl accusa la

Royne de cruaute a cause quelle navoit faict continuellement resider son medecin aupres de la dicte princesse et ainsy fust icelluy disne rempli dhumanite et de bonnayrete. Le lendemain que cela fust advenu la Royne sur confiance desdictz gracieux propos requit au Roy vouloir permettre que ladicte princesse les vint veoir, laquelle requeste il rebroua assez rudement et luy dit quelle pouveoit aller veoir ladicte princesse si elle vouloit et y demourer aussy. A quoy tres prudemment et gracieusement luy repondit la Royne que ne pour fille ne pour autre personne du monde elle ne vouleoit eslougnier sa compaignie et a tant demeura icelle practique.'

32. E. Chapuis to Charles V, 24 June 1531, Vienna Archives, P.C. 227, i. fol. 53: 'N'ayant en sa compaignie que la dame, le grant escuyer et deux autres et y a pres de quinze jours quil na faict autre.'

33. E. Chapuis to Charles V, 17 July 1531, Vienna Archives, P.C. 227, i. fol. 55.

34. E. Chapuis to Charles V, 19 August 1531, Vienna Archives, P.C. 227, i. fol. 61.

35. E. Chapuis to Charles V, 10 June 1530, Vienna Archives, P.C. 226, i. fol. 52.

36. E. Chapuis to Charles V, 10 September 1531, Vienna Archives, P.C. 227, i. fol. 63.

37. Charles V to E. Chapuis, 14 March 1530, Vienna Archives, P.C. 226, ii. fol. 19: 'Le grand escuyer et doyen nous ont parle chascun deulx particulierement demonstrans avoir gros regret de la poursuite que le dict Sr Roy faict contre nostre dicte tante et quilz desireroient dy pouvoir faire service et davantaige ma dict ledict grant escuyer quil vous advertiroit de ce quil pourroit entendre concernant nostre service et celluy de nostre dicte tante...'

38. E. Chapuis to Charles V, 5 June and 11 July 1532, Vienna Archives, P.C. 227, iii. fols. 42 and 50.

39. Charles V to Chapuis, 11 May 1530, Vienna Archives, P.C. 226, ii. fol. 35: 'Que le Roy dangleterre... se condescendroit a ce que laffaire soit connue et videe a Rome.'

40. E. Chapuis to Charles V, 4 January 1532, Vienna Archives, P.C. 227, iii. fol. 1.

41. Micer Mai to Charles V, 29 February 1532, British Museum, Add. MSS, 28,584, fol. 206.

42. Francis I to Mr de la Pommeraye, 13 January 1532, Paris, Bibl. Nat. MSS Fr. vol. 4126, fol. 5.

43. Camusat, *Meslanges historiques*, ii. fols. 84–88.

44. Camusat, *Meslanges historiques*, ii. fol. 88.

45. E. Chapuis to Charles V, 22 January 1532, Vienna Archives, P.C. 227, iii. fol. 8.

46. E. Chapuis to Charles V, 6 June 1531, Vienna Archives, P.C. 227, i. fol. 47.

47. E. Chapuis to Charles V, 14 February 1532, Vienna Archives, P.C. 227, iii. fol. 15.

48. E. Chapuis to Charles V, 14 February 1532, Vienna Archives, P.C. 227, iii. fol. 15.

49. E. Chapuis to Charles V, 16 April 1532, Vienna Archives, P.C. 227, iii. fol. 26. The French ambassador said to Chapuis: 'Que si ce Roy avoit envie de soy remarier quil nestoit pas bien conseille de perdre temps et argent a faire tant de poursuites ains a lexemple du Roy Loys devrait sans autre proces exposuer celle quil veult.'

50. E. Chapuis to Charles V, 29 May 1533, Vienna Archives, P.C. 228, i. fol. 77: 'Apres ce il [the Duke of Norfolk] se commenca descharger quil navoit este ne promoteur ne fauteur de ce mariaige ains lavoit tousjours dissuade et neust este luy et le pere delle, que contrefit le malade et le frenetique pour avoir meilleur moyen de contredire, ce mariaige se fust fait il y a ung an passe, dont la dame fust fort indignee et contre lung et contre lautre.'

51. E. Chapuis to Charles V, 29 May 1533, Vienna Archives, P.C. 228, i. fol. 77: 'Puis huict jours ayant la dame print une piece comme font icy les femmes ensainctes pour supplir aux robes que se trouvent tropt estroites son dict pere luy dict quil falloyt louher et regracier dieu de la veoer en tel estat, et elle en lieu de merciement en presence des ducz de Norphoc et Sufforc et du tresorier de lhostel respondit quelle estoit en meilleur estat quil neust voulu.'

52. E. Chapuis to Charles V, 13 May 1532, Vienna Archives, P.C. 227, iii. fol. 32: 'Le chancelier et les evesques contrarient ce quilz peuvent de quoy le Roy est tres indigne especiallement contre le dict chancellier et levesque de Vuinchestre et sobstine fort le Roy de fere passer la chose;' and Strype, *Ecclesiastical Memorials*, vol. i. part i.

p.130.

53. Protestation of Archbishop Warham, 24 February 1532, Burnet, *Collectanea*, part iii. book ii. No. xxv.

54. E. Chapuis to Charles V, 22 July 1532, Vienna Archives, P.C. 227, iv. fol. 57; and Earl of Northumberland to Cromwell, 13 May 1536, Burnet, *Collectanea*, part iii. book iii. No. 49.

5. The Marriage

1. Order of the Ceremony, Gairdner, *Letters and Papers*, vol. v. p.522; and Patent of Creation, 1 September 1532, *Ibid*. p.585.

2. Grant of Annuity, Gairdner, *Letters and Papers*, vol. v. p.585; and E. Chapuis to Charles V, 5 September and 1 October 1532, Vienna Archives, P.C. 227, iii. fols. 57 and 63.

3. Francis I to Giles de la Pommeraye, 13 January and 15 September 1532 (the latter wrongly dated 1531), Paris, Bibl. Nat. MSS Fr. 4126, fols. 2 and 5.

4. Giles de la Pommeraye to the Bishop of Auxerre, 21 June 1532, Paris, Bibl. Nat. MSS Dupuis, vol. 547, fol. 93; and E. Chapuis to Charles V, 13 May 1532, Vienna Archives, P.C. 227, iii. fol. 32.

5. Giles de la Pommeraye to A. de Montmorency, Paris, Bibl. Nat. MSS Fr. vol. 3094, fol. 145.

6. G. du Bellay to A. de Montmorency, 10 September 1532; and 'Ordo observandus in conventu...' Paris, Bibl. Nat. MSS Dupuis, vol. 547, fols. 133 and 135.

7. E. Chapuis to Charles V, 29 July and 9 August 1532, Vienna Archives, P.C. 227, iii. fol. 52, and P.C. 227, iv. fol. 60.

8. G. de la Pommeraye to A. de Montmorency, 23 July 1532, Paris, Bibl. Nat. MSS Fr. vol. 3003, fol. 23. This letter has been ascribed by Legrand (vol. iii. p.553), by Mr Froude, and by Mr Gairdner to Jean du Bellay. But by a comparison with the postscript to the paper in vol. 3094, fol. 145, which is a holograph, it clearly appears that the letter must have been written by de la Pommeraye. The copy at Paris is dated 23 July while Legrand prints 21 July.

9. E. Chapuis to Charles V, 15 September 1532, Vienna Archives, P.C. 227, iii. fol. 61.

10. E. Chapuis to Charles V, 15 September 1532, Vienna Archives, P.C. 227, iii. fol. 61: 'Et davantaige a eu charge le dict Langey de prier et requerer de la mesme part ce Roy de vouloir mesner et conduire dela de la mer en sa compaignie la nouvelle marquise. Syl na eust telle charge yl souffist que le dict ambassadeur le donne ainsi dentendre et quil avoue le Roy, lequel a dernierement escript a plusieurs seigneurs quilz tinssent prestes et en ordre leur femme pour accompaigner sa tres chiere et tres aymee cousine la Marquise de Pembrot laquelle a la priere de son bon frere et perpetuel allie le Roy de France il a de mesner a cette assemblee.'

11. Dr Ortiz to the Empress, 7 February 1533, British Museum, Add. MSS vol. 28,586, fol. 217.

12. E. Chapuis to Charles V, 1 October 1533, Vienna Archives, P.C. 227, iii. 63. Carew sent word to Chapuis: 'Et davantaige que ce roy nestoit pas tropt content a cause que lon luy avoit donne quelque fumiere et espoir que le Roy de France meneroit avec luy en contrecharge de la dame sa sueur madame delanson et que maintenant ilz disoient quelle estoit malade et que en son lieu se trouveroit Madame de Vandosme de quoy ceulx cy ne se contentent disant que comme la dicte Dame de Vandosme a ete autreffois bonne compagne quelle aura quelque compagnie correspondente au temps passe et de male reputacion, que sera une honte et injure pour les dames de pardeca.'

13. G. de la Pommeraye to A. de Montmorency, 23 July 1532, Paris, Bibl. Nat. MSS Fr. vol. 3003, fol. 23.

14. E. Chapuis to Charles V, 5 September 1532, Vienna Archives, P.C. 227, iii. fol. 57.

15. E. Chapuis to Charles V, 15 September 1532, Vienna Archives, P.C., iii. fol. 61.

16. E. Chapuis to Charles V, 5 September 1532, *loc. cit.*

17. E. Chapuis to Charles V, 1 October 1532, Vienna Archives, P.C. 227, iii. fol. 63.
18. E. Chapuis to Charles V, 1 October 1532, Vienna Archives, P.C. 227, iii. fol. 63.
19. *Chronicle of Calais*, printed for the Camden Society, p.41; and Peter Ligham to Bishop Fisher, 12 October 1532, Gairdner, *Letters and Papers*, vol. v. p.600.
20. Account of the meeting at Boulogne, Camusat, *Meslanges*, ii. fol. 106.
21. Account of the meeting at Boulogne, Camusat, *Meslanges*, i. fol. 106.
22. Privy Purse Expenses of Henry VIII, British Museum, Add. MSS 20,030; and Gairdner, *Letters and Papers*, vol. v. pp.760 and 761.
23. Accounts of R. Fowler, 1 November 1532, R.O. Henry VIII Box N; and Permission granted by Francis I to Cardinal Duprat, A. de Montmorency, and Ph. de Chabot Brion, 18 March 1534, Paris, Bibliotheque de l'Arsenal, Registres Conrart, vol. xv.
24. Account of the meeting at Boulogne, Camusat, *Meslanges*, ii. fol. 108.
25. Account of the meeting at Boulogne, Camusat, *Meslanges*, ii. fol. 108.
26. Wynkin de Worde, *The Manner of the Tryumphe*. Gairdner, *Letters and Papers*, vol. v. p.624.
27. J. de Dinteville to A. de Montmorency, 7 November 1533, Bibl. Nat. MSS Dupuis, vol. 547, fol. 276.
28. E. Chapuis to Charles V, 15 September 1532, Vienna Archives, P.C. 227, iii. fol. 61.
29. *Chronicle of Calais*, p.44.
30. E. Chapuis to Charles V, 26 November 1532, Vienna Archives, P.C. 227, iii. fol. 71.
31. Treaty of 28 October, 1532, Camusat, *Meslanges*, ii. fol. 109.
32. Instructions to the Cardinals of Tournon and of Gramont, 13 November 1532, Camusat, *Meslanges Historiques*, ii. fol. 114.
33. Instructions to Lord Rochford, *State Papers*, vol. vii. p.429.
34. J. Hanart to E. Chapuis, 18 January 1533, Vienna Archives, P.C. 228, ii. fol. 17; and Instructions to Lord Rochford, *loc. cit.*
35. Catherine of Aragon's Appeal to the Pope, from Ampthill (no date), Vienna Archives, P.C. 227, ii. fol. 61.
36. E. Chapuis to Charles V, 20 January 1530, Vienna Archives, P.C. 226, i. fol. 15; and Accounts of Sir Bryan Tuke, Gairdner, *Letters and Papers*, vol. v. p.317,
37. Cranmer to R. Crocke, Pocock, *Records of the Reformation*, No. cxxx.
38. Henry VIII to Charles V, 25 January 1532, Vienna Archives, P.C. 227.
39. E. Chapuis to Charles V, 22 January 1532, Vienna Archives, P.C. 227, iii. fol. 8: 'Lambassadeur que ce roy a advise den voyer resider devers vostre Majeste aulieu de celuy qui est apresent (duquel ceulxcy ne soy contentent, ne scay pourquoy) partira dans peu de jours. Cest ung des docteurs de ceulx que furent a Boulogne avec le comte de Vulchier, duquel et de sa fille il depend entierement. Il a escript en faveur du divorce et est de ceulx qui ont translate en Anglois le livre du Roy. Je doubte quil oseroit bien avoir charge passant par les universites dallemaigne de veoir sil pourroit les tirer a son oppinion, soit lutheriens ou autres ;' and E. Chapuis to Charles V, 30 January 1532, Vienna Archives, P.C. 227, iii. fol. 10: 'Il plaira Vostre Majeste y faire tenir loeul.'
40. Cranmer to Henry VIII, 4 September 1532, Strype, *Memorials of Archbishop Cranmer*, Appendix No. ii.
41. Cranmer to Henry VIII, 20 October 1532, Pocock, *Records of the Reformation*, No. ccxciii.
42. N. Hawkins to Henry VIII, 21 November 1532, *State Papers*, vol. vii. p.386.
43. Henry VIII to Charles V, 1 October 1532, Vienna Archives, P.C. 227, iv. fol. 71.
44. Charles V to Henry VIII, 18 November 1532, Vienna Archives, P.C. 227, iv. fol. 76; and N. Hawkins to Henry VIII, 21 November 1532, *loc. cit.*
45. E. Chapuis to Charles V, 29 January 1533, Vienna Archives, P.C. 228, i. fol. 3.
46. E. Chapuis to Charles V, 29 January 1533, *loc. cit.*
47. N. de Granvelle to E. Chapuis, 26 September 1535, Vienna Archives, P.C. 229½ ii. fol. 48: 'Je mesbahys fort des termes estranges que comme lon a entendu du couste de Rome tient larchevesque de Canturbery mesmes en laffaire des Royne et Princesse, actendu que durant le temps quil estoit resident en ceste court il blasmoit

mirablement ce que le Roy dangleterre son maistre et ses autres ministres faisoient
en laffaire du divorce encontre les dictes Royne et Princesse.'

48. E. Chapuis to Charles V, 9 February 1533, Vienna Archives, P.C. 228, i. fol. 8.
49. E. Chapuis to Charles V, 29 January 1533, Vienna Archives, P.C. 228, i. fol. 3.
50. E. Chapuis to Charles V, 9 February 1533, Vienna Archives, P.C. 228, i. fol. 8; and
     Charles V to E. Chapuis, 5 January 1533, Vienna Archives, P.C. 228, ii. fol. 23: 'N^{re}
     Sainct Pere (en grant secret et confidence) nous a faict entendre comment son nonce
     extant en Angleterre avoit eu propos a quelqung des gens dudict Sr Roy, mesmes
     de ceulx dont il se fye, que luy avoient declare que si N^{re} dict Sainct Pere vouloit
     remettre la connaissance et examen de la cause hors de Rome fust a Cambray ou
     autre part ailleurs que en Angleterre que le dict Roy pourroit estre induit a soy
     soubmettre expressement dois maintenant au jugement de sa sainctete.'
51. Instructions to the Cardinals of Tournon and of Gramont, 13 November 1532,
     Camusat, *Meslanges*, ii. fol. 103; Cardinals of Tournon and of Gramont to Francis I,
     21 January 1533, Camusat, *Meslanges*, ii. fol. 23; and François de Dinteville, Bishop
     of Auxerre, to A. de Montmorency, 7 January 1533, Camusat, *Meslanges*, ii. fol.
     117.
52. E. Chapuis to Charles V, 9 August 1532, Vienna Archives, P.C. 227, iv. fol. 60: 'Bien
     que de quelque autre part lon ma averti que la dicte dame fait tout son effort pour
     recouvrer dames qui la voysent accompaigner a ceste entrevue et si cela estoit il
     seroit fort a doubter que pour mieux auctoriser le cas ce Roy la vouldroit esposer en
     lassistance de lautre;' and E. Chapuis to Charles V, 26 August 1532, Vienna Archives,
     P.C. 227, iii.fol. 55.
53. E. Chapuis to Charles V, 9 August 1532, Vienna Archives, P.C. 227, iv. fol. 60:
     'Je luy [la Pommeraye] demanday si le jeusne due de Lorraine estoit en court de
     France pour espouser laisnee fille de France que autreffois luy avoit este promise.
     Sur ce il demeura ung espace tout pensif... Lesquelz propos joinct la myne dudict
     ambassadeur me font souspeconner que ce Roy, voyant que ne pour son honneur
     ne pour la sehurete de son estat ne selon conscience, avec quil se pust separer de
     la Royne, actendu quil a eu affaire avec la sueur de cestecy, il ne la peut avoir, quil
     vouldra entendre en la fille de France. Ne scais si les autres seront tant despourveuz
     de sens quilz voulsissent hazarder une telle princesse en dangier destre desclaree un
     jour une concubine et adultere. Et maugmente ma dicte suspecon ce que quelqung
     ma faict entendre quil estoit quelque propoz de envoyer de court la dame avec
     touteffois grand honneur et reputacion;' and E. Chapuis to Charles V, 26 August
     1532, *loc. cit.*
54. Charles V to E. Chapuis, 5 January 1533, Vienna Archives, P.C. 228, ii. fol. 23.
55. N. Hawkins to Henry VIII, 22 February 1533, *State Papers*, vol. vii. p.425.
56. *Ibid*; and Bull of Clement VII, IX. Cal. Martii, anno 1532, Gairdner, *Letters and
     Papers*, vol. vi. p.190.
57. Archbishop Cranmer to N. Hawkins, 17 June 1533, *Archæologia Britannica*, vol.
     xviii. p.81; E. Chapuis to Charles V, 23 February, 15 April and 10 May 1533, Vienna
     Archives, P.C. 228, i. fols. 20, 41 and 61; and E. Chapuis to N. de Granvelle, 23
     February 1533, Vienna Archives, P.C. 228, ii. fol. 43. See Appendix, Note D.
58. E. Chapuis to Charles V, 28 January 1535, Vienna Archives P.C. 229½, i. fol. 9: 'En
     recompense de ce quil fit loffice a lepousement.'
59. Patent to G. Browne and J. Hilsey, 13 April 1534, Gairdner, *Letters and Papers*, vol.
     vii. p.223.
60. E. Chapuis to Charles V, 27 April 1533, Vienna Archives, P.C. 228, i. fol. 55.
61. E. Chapuis to Charles V, 9 February 1533, Vienna Archives, P.C. 228, i. fol. 8.
62. E. Chapuis to Charles V, 15 February 1533, Vienna Archives, P.C. 228, i. fol. 16.
63. E. Chapuis to Charles V, 10 May 1533, Vienna Archives, P.C. 228, i. fol. 61.
64. E. Chapuis to Charles V, 2 April 1531, Vienna Archives, P.C. 227; i. fol. 34.
65. E. Chapuis to Charles V, 13 May 1532, Vienna Archives, P.C. 227, iii. fol. 32: 'Le
     chancellier et les evesques contrarient ce quilz peuvent de quoy le Roy est tres indigne
     especiallement contre ledict chancellier et levesque de Vuinchestre et sobstine fort le

Roy de fere passer la chose.'

66. E. Chapuis to Charles V, 22 May 1532, Vienna Archives, P.C. 227, iii. fol. 36: 'Il a rendu les sceaulx se demectant de loffice soubs couleur que son traictement estoit trop petit aussi quil ne pouvoit la peyne. Tout le monde en est bien marry et non sans cause car il ny eu oncques ny aura plus homme de bien en loffice.'

67. Memorandum on the delivery of the great seal, Rymer, *Fœdera*, vol. xiv. p.433.

68. E. Chapuis to Charles V, 11 July 1532, Vienna Archives, P.C. 227, iii. fol. 50.

69. Patent, 13 May 1532, Gairdner, *Letters and Papers*, vol. v. p.484; and Patent, 10 October 1533, Gairdner, *Letters and Papers*, vol. vi. p.552.

70. Memorandum on the delivery of the great seal, 26 January 1533, Rymer, *Fœdera*, vol. xiv. p.446.

71. E. Chapuis to Charles V, 9 February 1533, Vienna Archives, P.C. 228, i. fol. 8.

72. E. Chapuis to Charles V, 15 February 1533, Vienna Archives, P.C. 208, i. fol. 16.

73. Propositions enclosed in the letter of Chapuis to Granville, 23 February 1533, Vienna Archives, P.C. 228, ii. fol. 44: 'I. Ex attestationibus testium nobilissimorum virorum scriptura etiam tractatus inter ill[mos] et potent[mos] principes Sere[me] Regie M[ti] et Clar[me] Dñe Catherine parentes conclusi confirmatis atque aliarum allegationum… corroboratis, videtur nobis canonica ac legitime fide constare Ill[mum] principem Arthurum clarissimam dominam Catherinam predictam carnaliter cognovisse, nec debere judicem quemcumque ex hujusmodi productis aliter pronuntiare, sed oportere eum hujusmodi exhibita considerantem motum animi sui in nostram opinionem inclinare. Ita quidem sentimus et opinamur non obstante juramento predicte dñe Catherine… III. Conclusio est uno ore omnium theologorum quod non valet matrimonium secundum si primum matrimonium erat carnali copula consumatum. Atque ad probandum… unde creditur quod clerus anglie vult fateri copulam esse plene probatam, quo admisso statim conveniunt theologi quod matrimonium secundum est invalidum.'

74. E. Chapuis to Charles V, 23 February 1533, Vienna Archives, P.C. 228, i. fol. 20; and E. Chapuis to N. de Granvelle, 23 February 1533, Vienna Archives, P.C. 228, ii. fol. 43.

75. E. Chapuis to N. de Granvelle, 23 February 1533, Vienna Archives, P.C. 228, ii. fol. 43: 'Mgr celluy que ma adverty des esposailles du Roy avec sa dame est tel que la Royne ma commande de pouvoir escripre au rapport dicelluy comme delle mesmes. Depuis escripte la lettre de Sa Ma[re] jen ay parle a ung autre que ma dit quil avoit sentu quelque vent, adjoustant que le Roy avoit este precipite de ce fere tant pour lyer lesleu de Canturbery que pour ce que la dicte dame se treuve grosse ou au moins elle le feindoit ainsi; et semble quelle veult donner entendre au monde quelle est ensaincte ou quil est ainsy, car il y a environ huict jours que parlant au Due de Norphoc en presence de plusieurs elle luy dit quelle vouloit aller incontinent apres pasques a ung pellerinage de nostre dame en cas quelle ne se trouvast ensaincte.'

76. E. Chapuis to N. de Granvelle, 23 February 1533, *loc. cit.*: 'Et hier encoires elle se desclayra ung peu plus en avant en plus grande compaignie et sans grands propoz ne raison car ainsy quelle sortoit de sa chambre elle commenca dire a ung quelle ayme bien et lequel le Roy a autreffois chasse de la court pour jalousie delle que puis trois jours en ca elle avoit heu une inextimable et tresauvaige envie de manger des pommes ce que en sa vie ne luy estoit advenu et que le Roy luy avoit dit que sestoit signe quelle devoit estre grosse et quelle luy avoit reddit quil nen estoit riens. Sur ce elle se print a rire si fort en sen retournant en sa chambre que presque toute la court luy pouvoit ouyr desquelz propoz et gestes la pluspart de ceulx questoient en la presence furent esbays et honteux.'

77. G. du Bellay, de Beauvoys, and J. de Dinteville to Francis I, 26 February 1533, Paris, Bibl. Nat. MSS Dupuis, vol. 547, fol. 291.

78. Cardinal de Tournon to Francis I, Camusat, *Meslanges*, ii. fol. 8.

79. E. Chapuis to Charles V, 15 March 1533, Vienna Archives, P.C. 228, i. fol. 27.

80. Instructions to Lord Rochford, *State Papers*, vol. vii. pp.427-37.

81. E. Chapuis to Charles V, 15 March 1533, Vienna Archives, P.C. 228, i. fol. 27.

82. Francis I to Jean de Dinteville, 20 March 1533, Paris, Bibl. Nat. MSS Dupuis, vol. 547, fol. 221.
83. J. du Bellay to J. de Dinteville, 20 March 1533, Paris, Bibl. Nat. MSS Dupuis, vol. 547, fol. 218: 'Jusqua ce jour je ne veis onc homme si desraisonnable…je crois quil mandera que je suis bien mauvais anglois pour ce que je ne luy ay voulu accorder les pires raisons et les plus jeunes que passerent onc a mer.'
84. E. Chapuis to Charles V, 8 March 1533, Vienna Archives P.C. 228, i. fol. 23.
85. E. Chapuis to Charles V, 25 March 1533, Vienna Archives P.C. 228, i. fol. 27.
86. E. Chapuis to Charles V, 31 March 1533, Vienna Archives, P.C. 228, i. fol. 33.
87. E. Chapuis to Charles V, 23 February 1533, Vienna Archives, P.C. 228, i. fol. 20.
88. Account of the Proceedings in Convocation, Pocock, *Records*, No. cccxxvi.
89. E. Chapuis to Charles V, 10 April 1533, Vienna Archives, P.C. 228, i. fol. 37.
90. Account of Proceedings, Pocock, *Records*, No. cccxxvi; and Determination of Province of Canterbury, Pocock, *Records*, No. cccxxvii.
91. E. Chapuis to Charles V, 10 April 1533, Vienna Archives, P.C. 228, i. fol. 37.
92. Eustache Chapuis to Charles V, 10 April 1533, *loc. cit,*
93. Eustache Chapuis to Charles V, 15 April 1533, Vienna Archives, P.C. 228, i. fol. 41.

6. The Coronation

1. E. Chapuis to Charles V, 27 April 1533, Vienna Archives, P.C. 227, i. fol. 55.
2. Archbishop Cranmer to Henry VIII, 11 April 1533, *State Papers*, vol. i. p.390.
3. Archbishop Cranmer to Henry VIII, 11 April 1533, *State Papers*, vol. i. p.391.
4. Henry VIII to Archbishop Cranmer, *State Papers*, vol. i. p.392.
5. Cranmer to Cromwell, 17 May 1533, British Museum, Cotton MSS Otho, C. x. fol. 166.
6. Chapuis to Charles V, 27 April 1533, Vienna Archives, P.C. 227, i. fol. 55.
7. Protestation of Catherine that she does not recognize Cranmer as her judge: notarial copy by George, Bishop of Llandaff, 30 April 1533, from Ampthill; signed by Catherine, by George, Bishop of Llandaff, and, as witnesses, by Thomas Abel, pryst, el licenciado Lassao, Francisco Phelipe, Johan Soda – Vienna Archives, P.C. 228, ii. fol. 56; and Appeal to the Pope, no date, from Ampthill, draft, Vienna Archives, P.C. 228, ii. fol. 61.
8. E. Chapuis to Charles V, 27 April 1533, *loc. cit.*
9. E. Chapuis to Charles V, May 10, 1533, Vienna Archives, P.C. 228, i. fol. 61.
10. T. Bedyll to Cromwell, 12 May 1533, *State Papers*, vol. i. p.394; Archbishop Cranmer to Henry VIII, 12May 1533, *State Papers*, vol. i. p.394; Archbishop Cranmer to Cromwell, 17 May 1533, British Museum, Cotton MSS Otho C. x. fol. 166; Archbishop Cranmer to Henry VIII, 23 May 1533, *State Papers*, vol. i. p.396; and Sentence given at Dunstable, Burnet, *Collectanea*, part i. book ii. No. 47.
11. Sentence given at Lambeth, 28 May 1533, Rymer, *Fœdera*, vol. xiv. p.467.
12. E. Chapuis to Charles V, 29 May 1533, Vienna Archives, P.C. 228, i. fol. 77.
13. E. Chapuis to Charles V, 18 May 1533, Vienna Archives, P.C. 228, i. fol. 69.
14. Narration de l'entree et couronnement, Camusat, *Meslanges*, ii. fol. 17.
15. E. Chapuis to Charles V, 15 April 1533, Vienna Archives, P.C. 228, i. fol. 41.
16. E. Hall, *Chronicle of the Union of the Houses of Lancaster and York*, fol. 215; and Narration de l'entree, *loc. cit.*
17. E. Hall, *Chronicle of the Union of the Houses of Lancaster and York*, fol. 215.
18. E. Chapuis to Charles V, 11 and 30 July 1533, Vienna Archives, P.C. 228, i. fols. 88 and 91.
19. E. Hall, *Chronicle*, fol. 215.
20. Narration de l'entree, etc., Camusat, *Meslanges*, fols. 17 and 18; and Sir E. Baynton to Lord Rochford, 9 June 1533, R.O. Henry VIII, Box I.
21. E. Chapuis to Charles V, 30 July 1533, Vienna Archives, P.C. 228, i. fol. 91.
22. E. Chapuis to Charles V, 11 July 1533, Vienna Archives, P.C. 228, i. fol. 88.
23. E. Chapuis to Charles V, 30 July 1533, Vienna Archives, P.C. 228, i. fol. 91.

24. Chapuis to Charles V, 30 July 1533, *loc. cit.*
25. J. de Dinteville to Francis I, 23 May 1533, Paris, Bibl. Nat. MSS Dupuis, vol. 547, fol. 128; and Camusat, *Meslanges*, ii. fol. 128: 'Sire larchevesque de Canterbery besongne sur le grand affaire du Roy vostre dict bon frere pour juger sy lautre Royne estoit sa femine ou non, et croy que dans trois jours la sentence en sera donnee. Je lay supplie a mon pouvoir quil luy pleust vouloir faire dilayer le jugement aumoins jusques a ce que nostre dit St Pere feust arrive a Nice ce quil ne ma voulu accorder, puis je lay suplie quil luy pleust faire tenir le jugement secret, en sorte que nostre dit St Pere nen peust estre adverty que premierement ne eussiez parle ensemble. Il ma dit estre impossible de le pouvoir tenir secret et quil faut quil soit publiquement entendu et mesmes avant le coronation… Sire mondit Sieur de Norfort ne sy trouve moins empesche que moy comme plus au long vous pourra compter jusque il vous voye.'
26. E. Chapuis to Charles V, 3 September 1533, Vienna Archives, P.C. 228, i. fol. 102: 'Remplie de jalousie et non sans juste cause usa de quelque parolle au Roy dont il ne fust content et luy dit quil falloit quelle serrat les yeulx et quelle endurast aussi bien que avoint faict les autres que valloint mieulx quelle et quelle debvoit savoir quil estoit en sa main de la rabaisser en ung moment plus quil ne lavoit exalte; a cause desquels propoz il y a eu du groing et facons de faire de sorte que le Roy a este deux ou trois jours sans parler a elle… '
27. E. Chapuis to Charles V, 3 September 1533, Vienna Archives, P.C. 228, i. fol. 102.
28. E. Chapuis to Charles V, 30 July 1533, Vienna Archives, P.C. 228, i. fol. 91.
29. Bennet to Henry VIII, 14 June 1533, *State Papers*, vol. vii. p.469.
30. Bennet to Henry VIII, 28 May 1533, *State Papers*, vol. vii, p.463.
31. J. de Dinteville to J. du Bellay, 9 June 1533, Camusat, *Meslanges*, ii. fol. 130.
32. Paul Capisucchi to Ghinucci and Bennet, 12 May 1533, R.O. Henry VIII, box i. No. 156.
33. E. Chapuis to Charles V, 11 July 1533, Vienna Archives, P.C. 228, i. fol. 88.
34. Appeal of Henry VIII, 29 June 29 1533, Rymer, *Fœdera*, vol. xiv. p.478. In presence of E. Archbishop of York, Ric. Sampson, W. Fitzwilliam, Th. Cromwell, and Th. Argall and J. Godsalve, notaries.
35. E. Chapuis to Charles V, 11 July 1533, Vienna Archives, P.C. 228, i. fol. 88.
36. E. Chapuis to Charles V, 29 May 1533, Vienna Archives, P.C. 228, i. fol. 77.
37. Norfolk to Henry VIII, 30 May 1533, R.O. Henry VIII, Box I. No. 176; and A. de Montmorency to J. de Dinteville, 31 May 1533, Camusat, *Meslanges*, ii. fol. 127.
38. Henry VIII to Norfolk, Rochford, Paulet, Browne, and Bryan, June 1533, *State Papers*, vol. vii. p.473.
39. Marguerite de Navarre to J. de Dinteville, 22 June 1533, Paris, Bibl. Nat. MSS Dupuis, vol. 726, fol. 98; and Norfolk to Henry VIII, from Paris, middle of June 1533, Gairdner, *Letters and Papers*, vol. vi. pp.308 to 311. Mr Gairdner places this letter after 23 June, which is clearly a mistake, for on 23 June Norfolk was already at Briare, fifty miles south of Paris, on his way to Auvergne.
40. Sir W. Paulet to Cromwell, 15 July 1533, *State Papers*, vol. vii. p.481.
41. Francis I to J. de Dinteville, 15 July 1533, Paris, Bibl. Nat. MSS Dupuis, vol. 547, fol. 250.
42. Sir Anthony Browne to Cromwell, 24 July 1533, R.O. Henry VIII, Box I. P. No. 70.
43. Account written by Jean du Bellay to serve for the memoirs of Martin du Bellay, Paris, Bibl. Nat. MSS Dupuis, vol. 33, fol. 53: 'Ainsi quilz entroient dedans la ville les accompagnans les gens dela dicte ville et gouverneur en grand honneur, voicy un gentilhomme qui venoit de Rome en poste et extreme diligence devers le Roy dangleterre qui vient dire a loreille du Due de Norfoc quil sen alloyt signifier au roy dangleterre comment sentence avoyt este donne contre luy par Pape Clement.'
44. A. de Montmorency to J. du Bellay, 22 July 1533, Paris, Bibl. Nat. MSS Dupuis, vol. 265, fol. 232.
45. Account of Jean du Bellay, *loc. cit.*: 'Et luy en baille une petite letre dont le pouvre duc demeure si estonne que soubdainement cuyda deffaillir et ayant dict ceste nouvelle a levesque de Paris apres estre le mieulx rasseure quil peult se retirat secretement

au logys et commencent a communiquer par ensemble quel remede se pourroyt trouver... '

46. W. Bennet to Henry VIII, 13 June 1533, *State Papers*, vol. vii. p.469.

47. Count Cyfuentes to Charles V, 29 May 1533, British Museum, Add. MSS 28,585, fol. 260.

48. Bennet to Henry VIII, 28 May 1533, *State Papers*, vol. vii. p.462.

49. Dr. Ortiz to Charles V, 9 September 1533, British Museum, Add. MSS 28,586, fol. 1.

50. Cardinal de Jaen to Charles V, 14 June 1533, British Museum, Add. MSS 28,585, fol. 270.

51. Cyfuentes to Charles V, 5 July 1533, British Museum, Add. MSS 28,585, fol. 309.

52. Sententia diffinitiva, V Idus Julii, 1533, Vienna Archives, P.C. 228, ii. fol. 102; Pocock, *Records*, Appendix, No. xxxiv; and Secretary Ferrarys – to 15 July 1533, Paris, Bibl. Nat. MSS Dupuis, vol. 462, fol. 48.

53. — to Catherine of Aragon, British Museum, Cotton MSS Vitellius, B. xiv. fol. 50; Gairdner, *Letters and Papers*, vol. vi. p.473; and Dr. Ortiz to Charles V, 4 March 1534, British Museum, Add. MSS 28,586, fol. 148.

54. Account of Jean du Bellay, Paris, Bibl. Nat. MSS Dupuis, vol. 33, fol. 52: 'Ils disoient que apres que leur maistre avoyt receu une telle honte que destre condemne par le pape et declare excommunie il ne seroyt honneste queulx se trouvassent avec le Roy comme supplyans vers le dict pape et disoient que silz avoyent faict une telle faulte leur vie seroit envers luy en tres grand dangier et de faict neust este lasseurance que leur bailloyt levesque de Paris que ceste sentence quil presupposoyt avoir este donnee par contumace se pourroyt reparer par lordre de droict a ceste entrevue et une facon de protester quil feist a lencontre deulx au nom du roy silz sen alloyent si soubdainement (desquelles protestes ilz se pouroyent couvrir envers leur maitre) ils rompoyent des l'heure toute pratique de paction et sen retournoyent soubdenement en Angleterre.'

55. Account of Jean du Bellay, *loc. cit.*: 'Levesque de Paris qui suyvant et sachant lintention de son maistre estre pour le bien de la chrestienete que la chose si bien commencee se continuast feist tant envers le dict duc et aultres deputez quapres plusieurs disputes ilz se contenterent que pour suyvre leur premiere opinion qui estoit daller en poste prendre congie du Roy pour retourner devers leur maistre le frere de la Royne seulement y iroyt en poste et extreme diligence pour scavoir ce quil luy plairoyt quilz feissent et Bryant iroyt vers le Roy pour l'advertir aussy de ce qui leur estoyt survenu et se plaindre de loutraige du pape.'

56. E. Chapuis to Charles V, 30 July 1533, Vienna Archives, P.C. 221, i. fol. 91.

57. Account of Jean du Bellay, *loc. cit.*: 'Par la fin retourna le frere de la Royne avec les plus grandes querimonies du monde voulant, sil eust peu, tirer le Roy de son coste contre le pape monstrant que luy avoyt rompu sa foy et promesse, desprise le Roy, etc.'; and Francis I to J. de Dinteville, 27 August 1533, Paris, Bibl. Nat. MSS Dupuis, vol. 33, fol. 137.

58. E. Chapuis to Charles V, 30 July 1533, Vienna Archives, P.C. 228, i. fol. 91.

59. Vaughan to Cromwell, 3 August 1533, *State Papers*, vii. p.489; and Vaughan and Mundt to Henry VIII, 27 August 1533, *State Papers*, vii. p.501.

60. Chapuis to Charles V, 30 July 1533, Vienna Archives, P.C. 228, i. fol. 91: 'Afin que la dame ne sen pust appercevoir pour non dommaiger ce quelle pourte et pour mieulx couvrir le cas sous umbre daller a la chasse le Roy est party de Windezore ou il la laissee et est alle a Guillefort ou il a appelle outre ceulx de son conseil plusieurs docteurs... '

61. Francis I to the Bailly de Troyes, 27 August 1533, Paris, Bibl. Nat. MSS Dupuis, vol. 547, fol. 137.

62. *Chronicle of Calais*, p.44; and Norfolk to Lord Lisle, 28 August 1533, Gairdner, *Letters and Papers*, vol. vi. p.442.

63. E. Chapuis to Charles V, 3 September 1533, Vienna Archives, P.C. 228, i. fol. 102.

64. Account of Jean du Bellay, Paris, Bibl. Nat. MSS Dupuis, vol. 33, fol. 54; and

Instructions to Jean du Bellay, Paris, Bibl. Nat. MSS Dupuis, vol. 121, fol. 35.
65. Henry VIII to Bonner, 18 August 1533, Pocock, *Records*, Appendix, No. xxxv.

7. Marcus Meyer

1. E. Chapuis to Charles V, 3 and 10 September 1533, Vienna Archives, P.C. 228, i. fols. 102 and 105.
2. Debts of the French Queen and the Duke of Suffolk, R.O. and Gairdner, *Letters and Papers*, vol. vii. p.613.
3. E. Chapuis to Charles V, 3 September 1533, *loc. cit.*
4. E. Chapuis to Charles V, 10 September 1533, *loc. cit.*
5. Memorandum on the back of a letter of John Mille to Cromwell, 25 April 25 1533, R.O. *Cromwell Correspondence*, vol. xxviii. fol. 74: 'Item touching in the judgment that the great personage might be brought in to be notyd *in bona fide parentum.*'
6. Chapuis to Charles V, 30 July 1533, Vienna Archives, P.C. 228, i. fol. 91.
7. E. Chapuis to Charles V, 27 September 1533, Vienna Archives, P.C. 228, i. fol. III: 'Actendu que les choses sont trop fresches et lamour du Roy tropt vehement et ardent.'
8. E. Chapuis to Charles V, 27 September 1533, *loc. cit.*: 'Je cuydois Sire quil eust este appelle en court pour quelque affaire dimportance mais ce nestoit que pour une folie a scavoir lenvoyer vers la Ducesse de Norphoc quest sueur de sa femme pour faire lappoinctement entre elle et le due son mari lequel elle ne vouloit veoer ne ouyr a cause quil est amoureux dune demoyselle de la concubine du Roy que sappelle Hollande... '
9. E. Chapuis to Charles V, 27 September 1533, *loc. cit.*: 'Il [Abergavenny] eust charge dernierement que fuz en court de me ramener de la messe et lors me dit quil eust eu bien desir de deviser avec moy mais quy ny avoit ordre et seullement me signiffioit que ny avoit gentilhomme au monde que de meilleur cueur feist service a Vostre Maieste que luy et que pourroit estre que Vostre Maieste sen appercevroit quelque jour. Et pour ce que le Roy poursuidoit tout de pres et Cremuel qui nous precedoit et nous alloit tenant les oreilles ny eust ordre de plus long practique; touteffois Sire laffection quil monstroit avoir de me declairer son intencion linduisoyt de cop sur cop me fere feste et me sarrant le braz par soubz lequel il me mesnoit.'
10. E. Chapuis to Charles V, 27 September 1533, *loc. cit.*: 'Que les armes du pape pour ceulx cy que sont obstinez sont plus fresles que de plomb et quil convient que Vostre Maieste y mecte la main et que en ce elle fera œuvre tant aggreable a dieu (que) daller centre le turcq.'
11. E. Chapuis to Charles V, 27 September 1533, *loc. cit.*: 'Le dict filz est maintenant a Padue a lestude pour la grande et singuliere vertu duquel joinct quil est du parentaige du Roy du couste du pere et de mere et pour la pretension que luy et ses freres pourroient avoir au royaulme la Royne desireroit austant colloque la princesse sa fille par mariaige qua autre quelle sache. A quoy la dicte princesse ne feroit reffuz ains sen tiendroit plus que contente.' I have quoted so largely from this letter of Chapuis because the quotations in M de Gayangos' *Calendar* are not quite correct.
12. E. Chapuis to Charles V, 1 April 1536, Vienna Archives, P.C. 230, i. fol. 50: 'Pour remedier aux heresies dyci dont la concubyne est la cause et principale nourisse.'
13. Account of the christening, Gairdner, *Letters and Papers*, vol. vi. p.464.
14. J. de Dinteville to Francis I, 5 October 1533, Paris, Bibl. Nat. MSS Dupuis, vol. 547, fol. 269.
15. Minutes for the council and acta in consilio, 2 December 1533, *State Papers*, vol. i. pp.414 and 415; and E. Chapuis to Charles V, 9 and 16 December 1533, Vienna Archives, P.C. 228, i. fols. 140 and 143.
16. E. Chapuis to Charles V, 23 August 1533, Vienna Archives, P.C. 228, i. fol. 98.
17. E. Chapuis to Charles V, 3 September 1533, Vienna Archives, P.C. 228, i. fol. 102.
18. Reimer Kock's *Chronicle of Luebeck*; and E. Chapuis to Charles V, 3 September 1533, *loc. cit.*

19. Sir Edward Guldeford to Cromwell, 21 and 22 August 1533, Gairdner, *Letters and Papers*, vol. vi. p.433; G. Waitz, *Luebeck unter Juergen Wullenwever*; and Wurm, *Die politischen Beziehungen Heinrich VIII zu Marcus Meyer.*

20. E. Chapuis to Charles V, 3 September 1533, *loc. cit.*

21. E. Chapuis to Charles V, 3 September 1533, *loc. cit.*

22. Wurm, *Die politischen Beziehungen*; Waitz, *Wullenwever*, etc.

23. E. Chapuis to Charles V, 15 September and 9 December 1533, Vienna Archives, P.C. 228, i. fols. 107 and 140.

24. Cromwell to Henry VIII (not dated), R.O. Henry VIII, Box Q, No. 147.

25. Cromwell to Henry VIII, 23 July 1533, R.O. Henry VIII, Box P, No. 361.

26. Cromwell to Henry VIII, 23 July 1533, R.O. Henry VIII, Box P, No. 361.

27. R. Gwent to Cromwell, 11 August 1533, R.O. *Cromwell Correspondence*, vol. xv. No. 70.

28. Examination of Elizabeth Barton, R.O. Henry VIII, Box Q, No.141; Examination of John Mores, R.O. Henry VIII, Box Q, No.154; Examination of — of Syon, R.O. Henry VIII, Box Q, No. 127; and Sir Christofer Hales to Cromwell, 24 and 25 September 1533, R.O. *Cromwell Correspondence*, vol. xvi. Nos. 33 and 38.

29. List of names, R.O. Henry VIII, Box Q, Nos. 148 to 150.

30. *Ibid.*; and Account of J. de Dinteville, Paris, Bibl. Nat. MSS Dupuis, vol. 547, fol. 323.

31. E. Chapuis to Charles V, 20 November 1533, Vienna Archives, P.C. 228, i. fol. 125.

32. Examination of John Mores, *loc. cit.*

33. E. Chapuis to Charles V, 24 November 1533, Vienna Archives, P.C. 228, i. fol. 130.

34. Archbishop Cranmer to Cromwell, 16 December 1533, and 5 January 1534, R.O. Cranmer's Letters, Nos. 8 and 10.

35. Lady Exeter to Cromwell, Wednesday, R.O. *Cromwell Correspondence*, vol. x. fol. 199; and Henry Gold to Cromwell, *Ibid.* vol. xiv. fol. 4, etc.

36. Secretary Berthereau to J. de Dinteville, 15 October 1533, Paris, Bibl. Nat. MSS Dupuis, vol. 547, fol. 273.

37. *Ibid.*; and Account of Jean du Bellay, Paris, Bibl. Nat. MSS Dupuis, vol. 33, fol. 52.

38. E. Chapuis to Charles V, 3 November 1533, Vienna Archives, P.C. 228, i. fol. 120; and J. de Dinteville to Francis I, 2 November 1533, Paris, Bibl. Nat. MSS Dupuis, vol. 547, fol. 276.

39. Gardiner, Bryan, and Wallop, to Lord Lisle, 17 October 1533, Gairdner, *Letters and Papers*, vol. vi. p.526; and E. Chapuis to Charles V, 3 November 1533, *loc. cit,*

40. Cyfuentes to Charles V, 24 October 1533, British Museum, Add. MSS 28,586, fol. 42.

41. Memorial sent from Rome by R. de Avalos, British Museum, Add. MSS 28,586, fol. 94.

42. Instructions to du Bellay, *Legrand*, iii. p.571; and Account of J. du Bellay, Paris, Bibl. Nat. MSS Dupuis, vol. 33, fol. 62.

43. Cyfuentes to Charles V, 6 November 1533, British Museum, Add. MSS 28,586, fol. 49.

44. Instructions to J. du Bellay, *Legrand*, vol. iii. p.571; Account of du Bellay, Paris, Bibl. Nat. MSS Dupuis, vol. 33, fol. 57; and Cyfuentes to Charles V, 6 November 1533, British Museum, Add. MSS 28,586, fol. 49.

45. E. Chapuis to Charles V, 3 November 1533, Vienna Archives, P.C. 228, i. fol. 120.

46. Instructions to the Ambassadors, R.O. Henry VIII, Box P; abstracted, Gairdner, *Letters and Papers*, vol. vi. p.333.

47. Henry VIII to Bonner, 18 August 1533, Strype, *Memorials of Cranmer*, App. No. iv.; Henry VIII to Bonner, British Museum, Cotton MSS Vit. B. xiv. fol. 52; and Bonner to Henry VIII, 16 October 1533, Gairdner, *Letters and Papers*, vol. vi. p.525.

48. Cyfuentes to Charles V, 9 November 1533, British Museum, Add. MSS 28,586, fol. 62.

49. Bonner to Henry VIII, 13 November 1533, Burnet, *Collectanea*, part iii. book ii. No. 23.

50. Account of J. du Bellay, *loc. cit.* fol. 56: 'Je presuppose que vous scavez... comment apres toutes concertations a lheure que le Roy venoyt pour sur ce point la et a linstant mesmes prendre avec le pape a ung jour une resolution de faire affaire il rencontra les ambassadeurs dangleterre qui venoyent de signiffier au pape lappellation au futur concile, comment il trouva le pape en colere, comment il etc.

 Le pape done vinct a grandement se lamenter que non seulement le Roy dangleterre les eust tous deulx desprisez en faisant ceste innovation mais eust grandement abuse de la couverture du Roy car soubs couleur que le pape estoit logie chez luy au moyen de quoy sa sainctete donnoyt entree indiferement a chacung sans user de la ceremonie que a Rome il est accoustume de user a ses audiences ces docteurs sestoyent venuz insinuer et se presenter sans demander congie a huissier chambrier ne aultre et avoyent faict chose que a Rome eust este capitale cest de luy signifier ceste appellacion (chose que veritableinent les dicts docteurs confessoient bien avoir faict pour la dicte rayson sachant quil ne leur seroyt loisible de la pavoir faire ailleurs). Concluoyt la dessus le pape sestant de son coste tout voulu mectre en son debvoir et le Roy dangleterre faict au contraire que le Roy le debvroyt reputer pour enemy et se mectre contre luy avec le sainct siege apostolique.'

51. Cyfuentes to Charles V, 9 November 1533, *loc. cit.*; and Account of J. du Bellay, *loc. cit.* fol. 60: 'Le Roy que ne povoyt nyer ne excuser lerreur quavoyent faicte ces deputez et voyant la principale occasion de son voyage estre par cest acte demeure a neant, se trouva fort ennuye car a la verite il ne povoit nyer au pape quil neust raison de dire ce quil disoyt. Et apres avoir faict parler aux ambassadeurs dangleterre (je croy que ce fust par vous) et veu le peu de fondement quil trouvoyt de leur coste ne sceust faire de moins que de consentir au pape de ne luy parler plus de ceste affaire et a venir traicter des aultres.'

52. Account of Jean du Bellay, *loc. cit.* fol. 60: 'Mais den venir jusques la que de se declarer contre le Sr Roy dangleterre il remonstra le dommaige quil feroyt aux affaires publiques et mesmement au sainct siege car telle chose pourroyt advenir que encores serviroyt bien ung mediateur et aultre ne sen povoit trouver que luy; aussy que faisant icelle declaration cestoyt le vray moyen de desesperer le dict Roy et de le contraindre de se venir jecter entre les mains de gens dont lalliance pourroyt estre dommeagable non a eulx deulx seulement mais a toute chrestiente. Joinct quil estoyt eschappe au roy dangleterre de dire a quelqung que la ou le Roy son frere luy fauldroyt au pis aller il seroyt tousjours quicte pour reprendre sa femme au contentement de lempereur, entretenant laultre pour sa mye, et quil mectoyt telz partys en avant au dict empereur contre le roy avec lequel il estoyt en... quilz le renieroyent eulx deux ensemble et de faict cestoyent propoz quil avoyt secretement concertez avec ses plus privez et familiers.'

53. Cyfuentes to Charles V, 9 November 1533, *loc. cit.*: 'Que sino tuviera necessidad de tenerlo por amigo a causa que otros no lo tomassen le haria una burla que se le acordasse.'

54. *Ibid.*

55. The English Ambassadors at Marseilles to Henry VIII, November, 1533, British Museum, Arundel MSS 151, fol. 192; and Gairdner, *Letters and Papers*, vol. vi. p.571.

56. Bonner to Henry VIII, 13 November 1533, Burnet, *Collectanea*, part iii. book ii. No. 23.

57. Relacion de Cartas de Roma, 5 July 1533, British Museum, Add. MSS 28,585, fol. 309.

58. Cyfuentes to Charles V, 9 November 1533, British Museum, Add. MSS 28,586, fol. 62.

59. J. de Dinteville to A. de Montmorency, 7 November 1533, Paris, Bibl. Nat. MSS Dupuis, vol. 547, fol. 276: 'ce dit Sieur Roy... me vouloit faire a croire que mes instructions portoient de luy dire que jamais le Roy ne feroit le mariaige de Mgr dorleans que le pape ne depeschat son affaire selon son intention, mais jamais je ne luy voulu accorder quainsi feust ...je devisay bien amplement avec Mr de Norsfort

auquel je remonstroit... que sil [Francis] entendoit que ses peines et labeurs outre la grande despence quil faict feussent si mal reconnus de la part de ce Roy, que je ne doubtays point quil sen ennuyeroit et fascheroit... et que lon peut bien tant presser et fascher son amy que lon sen faict importun... Mgr je vous puis bien asseurer quilz sont plusieurs du conseil de ce Roy qui trouvent ces raisons dessus dictes veritables et tres bonnes et principallement Mr de Norsfort, mais il ma dict quil trouve le Roy son maistre si tres embrouille en son cerveau de ceste affaire quil ne se fie a homme vivant et que... il congnoist tres bien que luy et la Royne sont en souspecon bien souvent contre luy pour lamour de ce dit affaire.'

60. Report of J. de Dinteville, November, 1533, Paris, Bibl. Nat. MSS Dupuis, vol. 547, fol. 321.: 'Il ne scait si lon veult faire a lancienne facon de France quy est de mener et entretenir les gens pendant quilz en ont affaire sans venir au poinct mays de user de dissimulation qui est chose par ou on ne le menera pas'... and 'Nota, que Mr de Norsfort dit nen avoir du tout tant dict' ... and 'Quant a lentreveue dont il a este adverty quon a parle deulx deux il ne peult penser pour quelles raisons... combien quil y a plus de deux moys que le dict sieur maye touche quelque mot de la dicte entrevue. Nota quil ne veult quil soit sceu.

61. *Ibid.* fol. 323 and 324: 'Nota que tout le conseil dangleterre est bien marry de quoy leur Roy est si aigre... Mr le Tresorier est fort marry de quoy son maistre est tant passionne... de dire a Mr le grandmaistre les propoz de Monsgr de Suffoc touchant Cramouel'; and E. Chapuis to Charles V, 16 December 1533, Vienna Archives, P.C. 228, i. fol. 145.

62. E. Chapuis to Charles V, 16 December 1533, *loc. cit.*: 'La dame disculpe fort les francois sy a faict Brian Turcq depuis son retourd de Marseilles.' *Brian Turcq*, which would mean Sir Bryan Tuke, is a clerical error for *Briant*, which means Sir Francis Bryan. Tuke was not at Marseilles, and that Sir Francis was sent in October from France to England we know from the Account of Jean du Bellay, Paris, Bibl. Nat. MSS Dupuis, 33, fol. 57: 'Prevoyant le Roy la precipitation ou ilz estoient pour se jecter avoyt prier et persuader Bryant par plusieurs bons moyens daller en diligence faire arrester toutes choses jusques a la venue du dict evesque de Paris...'

63. Mr de Castillon to J. du Bellay, 17 November 1533, Paris, Bibl. Nat. MSS Dupuis, vol. 33, fol. 19: 'Je ne vous mettre qung mot des choses de se pays cest quelles sont en telz termes que le Roy dangleterre commence fort a dimynuer de lamytie et fiance qui pencoyt avoyr a jametz avec le Roy voyant que sy froydement il a precede avec le pape veu les aliances et longtemps quil ont este ensemble. Et davantaige il se resoult de toutallement se mettre et luy et son pays hors de lobeissance du pape voulant faire prescher la sainte parolle de dieu par tout son pays ayant ferme foy que par icelle nostre seigneur laydera en son bon droit. Qui est une chose tres mauvaise pour lexemple que les aultres princes y pourront prendre, touteffois il en est tout resolu et la pluspart des seigneurs dautour de luy et de tout le pays y sont ja enclins'; and E. Chapuis to Charles V, 6 December 1533, Vienna Archives, P.C. 228, i. fol. 132.

64. Account of du Bellay, Paris, Bibl. Nat. MSS Dupuis, vol. 33, fol. 52.

65. E. Chapuis to Charles V, December 1533, Vienna Archives, P.C. 228, i. fol. 149.

66. Henry VIII to Sir John Wallop, December 1533, *State Papers*, vol. vii. p.524.

67. Account of Jean du Bellay, *loc. cit.*, fol. 61: 'Et pource que encores avoyt le dict Roy adjouste parlant a quelqung que le Roy luy avoit promis de jamais ne faire ce mariaige sans son consentement expres et quen ceste promesse luy avoyt failly, des aultres choses qui ne touchoyent son honneur il estoit pour en pardonner une bonne partie a la passion et colere de son frere. Mays quand a ce qui touchoyt son honneur il ny avoyt homme au monde a qui il en laissast passer le gros dung cheveu et pour ce le prioyt en fraternite et amitie commune que sil avoyt tenu ce propoz quil sen departit car sil y vouloyt perseverer il scavoyt bien ce quil avoyt accoustume de respondre quand on le chargeoyt de son honneur et en avoyt veu peu dannees au precedent lexperience et que luy nen povoit pas moins actendre.'

68. Castillon to Francis I, 16 March 1534, Paris, Bibl. Nat. MSS Français, vol. 5499, fol. 197: 'Quand Monsieur de Paris partit dicy la conclusion que ce Roy print avec luy

estoit que si sans forme de proces nostre Sainct Pere luy vouloit accorder sa demande et que ce fust devant pasques il ne procederoit point a la separation de lobeissance de leglise romaine. Mais si dedans ce terme it navoit la dicte sentence il en feroit la publication.'

69. J. du Bellay to Castillon, 8 February 1534, Paris, Bibl. Nat. MSS Français, vol. 5499, fol. 191: 'Que je ne soye prins de si pres que du xxvme de ce moys;' and J. du Bellay to Francis I, 8 February 1534, Paris, Bibl. Nat. MSS Français, vol. 5499, fol. 189: 'Quil vous plaise ordonner une bonne depesche en angleterre pour impetrer ung peu plus de temps que celuy quon a donne a moy de Paris.'

70. E. Chapuis to Charles V, 3 January 1534, Vienna Archives, P.C. 229, i. fol. 1.

8. The Papal Sentence

1. Friars of Greenwich to E. Chapuis, December 1533, Vienna Archives, P.C. 228, iii. fol. 14; Account of the Proceedings of the Bishop of Chester and Master Bedell at the Convent at Greenwich, Vienna Archives, P.C. 228, iii. fol. 16; and the Friars of Greenwich to Henry VIII, 11 December 1533, Vienna Archives, P.C. 228, iii. fol. 18.

2. Stokesley to Bedell, 4 January 1534, R.O. Box Q, No. 181.

3. Mary Tudor to Henry VIII, 2 October 1533, P. Heylin, Ecclesia *Restaurata*, ed. 1660, p.10.

4. Chapuis to Charles V, 16 December 1533, Vienna Archives, P.C. 228, i. fol. 143: 'II luy dit quil nestoit venu pour disputer ains pour accomplir la voulente et commandement du Roy questoit tel que dessus et voyant la dicte princesse quil ny avoit excuse ne replicque que peust servir elle demanda respit de demy heure pour entrer en sa chambre ou elle demoura environ le dict espace, pour faire et passer a ce quentendis une protestacion que luy avois envoye afin que si par force ou tromperie il la vouloient faire renuncer a ses drois ou marier a leur appetit ou la faire entrer en clostre que cela ne luy pust prejudicier et revenant de sa dicte chambre elle dit au duc que puis quil playsoit ainsy au Roy son pere quelle ny vouloit desobeyr;' and Protestation of Mary, holograph, attested by Maurice Mistralis de Aviernez as notary; Vivianus Montesa, Pern, Machet, and Gleyrod, witnesses at London. Vienna Archives, P.C. 229, ii. fol. 50.

5. E. Chapuis to Charles V, 10 January 1534, Vienna Archives, P.C. 229, i. fol. 4: 'Et ma aussy fait scavoir que le docteur foux que fust lung des commis avec le duc de Norfocq pour la mener ou elle est et linciter a la dicte renunciation luy avoit dit en passant ainsy quilz estoient en chemin quelle avoit respondu le plus vertueusement du monde et que pour lamour de dieu elle continua a tenir ferme autrement tout ce royaulme estoit en danger de ruyne et perdicion. Je crois Sire que cela aydera beaulcoup a la dite princesse pour estre constante... '

6. E. Chapuis to Charles V, 10 January 1534, *loc. cit.*: 'Voyant le Roy que ceulx quil avoyt cydevant envoye devers la princesse pour luy persuader la renuntiation de son tiltre navoyent rien peu faire, il est party aujourdhuy pour experimenter si son triacle sera plus fin que celluy des aultres; et va charge de belles parolles et promesses mais beaulcoup plus de horribles menasses... '

7. E. Chapuis to Charles V, 17 January 1534, Vienna Archives, P.C. 229, i. No. 6: 'Toutteffoys considerant la dame la facilite du Roy ou ligierete que louseroys dire et que par la grande beaulte, vertu et prudence de la dite princesse son pere pourroit abolir le courroux quil a contre elle et esmeu par les dictes vertuz et de compassion paternelle estre induict a la mieulx traicter et luy laisser son tiltre la dicte dame Anne envoya tout incontinent en diligence Cremuel apres le Roy et depuis aultres messaigiers pour empescher que le dict Roy en sorte du monde ne parlast a la princesse ny la vit.'

8. E. Chapuis to Charles V, 17 January 1534, Vienna Archives, P.C. 229, i. No. 6: 'Sire estant ce Roy vers sa nouvelle fille la princesse lenvoya pryer et supplier quelle luy peust baiser les mains. Il ny eust ordre dimpetrer la dicte requeste, quoy voyant la dicte princesse ainsi quil vouloit monte a cheval elle allast sur une terrasse au hault

de la mayson pour le veoir; de quoy adverty le dict Sgr Roy ou par adventure par fortune il se retourna ung peu devers elle et la voyant getter a genoulx et joinctes mains il luy inclina la teste mectant la main au chappeau, lors tous ceulx que la assistoient que devant ne ousoient haulser leurs testes pour la regarder resjouiz et animes de ce que le Roy avoit fait la saluerent tres reverentement avec signifficacion de bonne volonte et compassion.'

9. E. Chapuis to Charles V, 11 February 1534, Vienna Archives, P.C. 229, i. fol. 32: 'Sire lambassadeur de France ma compte que revenant ce Roy de veoyr sa nouvelle fille yl dit a icelluy ambassadeur quil navoit voulu parler a la princesse a cause quelle se rendoit tant obstinee envers luy et que cela tenoit elle du sang despagne. Et luy disant le dict ambassadeur que a ce quit entendoit elle avoyt este fort bien nourrie, les lermes luy vindrent aux yeulx et si ne se peult tenir de la louer de plusieurs choses.'

10. Cromwell's Memoranda, end of 1533, British Museum, Cotton MSS, Titus B. i. fol. 461, and Gairdner, *Letters and Papers*, vol. vi. p.251: 'Those things with my Lady Mary which are not meet for the princess to be also brought thither. To remember what danger is in war and that the commons were better to bear a contribution to find in the estate that she now is in and to avoid war than to diminish anything.' The last sentence is struck out.

11. E. Chapuis to Charles V, 17 January 1534, Vienna Archives, P.C. 229, i. fol. 8: 'Sire lon me vient de dire que avant hier la dame ayant entendu les responces si prudentes de la princesse elle avoit faict grand querymonie au Roy de ce quil ne faisoit tenir si court la princesse quelle ne feust si bien conseillee ni advisee quelle avoit este jusques yci, et que nestoit a croire que ses responces et propoz vinssent sans suggestion dautruy.'

12. E. Chapuis to Charles V, 22 July 1532, Vienna Archives, P.C. 227, iv. fol. 57: 'Le due de Norphoc a ces jours, premiererment en particulier et puis en presence du conseil du Roy, deffendu au Marquis que sur lindignacion du Roy que luy ne sa femme deussent aller en lieu que se treuve la princesse le mesme a este dit au frere du grand prieur de Saint Jehan qua sa mayson tout aupres de la dicte princesse et a este commande a celluy qua la garde delle que fasse bon guet sur ceulx que la yront veoir et de tout cecy me vint hier advertir la marquise mesmes.'

13. E. Chapuis to Charles V, 17 January 1534, Vienna Archives, P.C. 229, i. No. 6: 'Et y a environ xx jours que le dict Sr Roy dit au Marquis que la confiance que la dicte princesse avoit a Vre Ma^te la rendoit difficile et obstinee, mais que la feroit venir au point car il ne craignoit ni Vre Ma^te ni aultre, mais que le dict Marquis et aultres ses vassaulx luy feussent loyaulx quil pensoit quilz seroient et que aussy ne besoignoit que nul deulx ne chancellast ny variast le moings du monde quil ne vouldroit perdre la teste et quil feroit faire si bon guect quilz ne scaurroient escripre ny recepvoir lectres de dela la mer quil nen soit adverty.'

14. E. Chapuis to Charles V, 21 February 1534, Vienna Archives, P.C. 229, i. fol. 37: 'A laquelle gouvernante le duc de Norfoch et le frere de la dicte Anne dirent naguyeres beaulcoup de grosses parolles a cause quelle usoit trop dhonnestete et humanite a leur semblant envers la dicte princesse que comme il disoit ne debvoit estre honoree ny traictee que comme une bastarde quelle estoit. A quoy respondist laultre que oyres que ainsy fust voyre quelle fust bastarde dung pouvre gentilhomme que sa bonte doulceur et vertu meritoient tout honneur et bon traictement;' and 'Ains a cause que les paysans dautour dela la voyant pardessus une galerie la saluoient a haulte voix pour leur vraye princesse elle est maintenant tenue plus de court.'

15. E. Chapuis to Charles V, 11 February 1534, Vienna Archives, P.C. 229, i. fol. 32: 'Quelle luy dounast des buffes comme a une mauldicte bastarde quelle estoit… '

16. Privy purse expenses of the Lady Elizabeth.

17. Archbishop Cranmer to Cromwell, 5 January 1534, R.O. Cranmer letters, No. 10.

18. J. du Bellay and C. de Denonville, Bishop of Mâcon, to Francis I, 8 February 1534, Paris, Bibl. Nat. MSS Français, vol. 5499, fol. 189. Of this letter, as well as of others referring to this matter, abstracts have been published in the seventh volume of the *Letters and Papers*, edited by Mr Gairdner. Owing to the involved style of du Bellay

and Castillon, and to the errors of copyists, these abstracts differ very considerably from the true sense. I am informed that the mistakes are to be corrected in the forthcoming volume of the *Letters and Papers*, but in the meantime I feel obliged to quote more fully from the letters than I would otherwise have done.

19. J. du Bellay and C. de Denonville to Francis I, 8 February 1534, *loc. cit.*: 'Aujourdhuy nous susmes entrez sur le moyen des deleguez en quoy a este garde lordre quil vous avoit pleu recorder a moy de Paris allant a la messe a pied pappe...' and J. du Bellay to Castillon, 22 February 1534, Paris, Bibl. Nat. MSS Français, vol. 5499, fols. 191–6.

20. J. du Bellay to Castillon, 8 February 1534, Paris, Bibl. Nat. MSS Français, vol. 5499, fol. 191: 'Monsieur. J'ay tant faict avec layde de dieu que je suis icy et afin que vous ne pensiez que ce ayt este sans peyne jen ay este jusqua ne pouvoir endurer que homme me portassent en une chaire. Pour le mieux jen eschaperay pour ung peu de sciatique, ce ne sera pas grand chose au mestier que je meyne;' and Cyfuentes to Charles V, 14 February 1534 British Museum, Add. MSS 28,586, fol. 129.

21. Cyfuentes to Charles V, 14 February 1534, *loc. cit.* Dr Ortiz to Charles V, 14 February 1534, British Museum, Add. MSS vol. 28,586, fol. 125; and J. du Bellay and C. de Denonville to Francis I, 8 February 1534, *loc. cit.*: 'Il [the Pope] a este dopinion que nous trouvissions au consistoire pour y faire entendre ce que luy avions dicts touchant les inconvenients qui estoient prests de soubsvenir en la Chrestienete et mesmement au saint siege, aposant que si incontinent il ny estoit donne ordre. Ce qui a este faict...'

22. Dr Ortiz to Charles V, 13 February 1534, British Museum, Add. MSS 28,586, fol. 125.

23. J. du Bellay and C. de Denonville to Francis I, 8 February 1534, *loc. cit.*: 'Et ont este trouvees les advertissements et remonstrances faictes ladessus sy bonnes que toute la compaignye sen sent merveilleusement obligee et tenue a vous. Mais quand se vient aux remedes et expediens la plus grande partye sy trouvent si empeschez que qui ne leur tiendroit la bride bien royde ilz auroient bientost faict ung mauvais sault.'

24. G. Ghinucci to Andrea Ghinucci, 9 February 1534, British Museum, Cotton MSS Vitellius, B. xiv. fol. 116; and G. Gianetto to Sir John Wallop, 14 February 1534, *ibid.*, Vitellius, B. xiv. fol. 118.

25. J. du Bellay and C. de Denonville to Francis I, 8 February 1534, *loc. cit.*: 'Nous ne voyons que de la se puisse rien esperer de bon; et si riens sy peult faire il faudra que ce soit nostre Sainct Pere qui le face secretement et a part a quoy nous taschons par tous moyens de le persuader.' J. du Bellay to A. de Montmorency, 8 February 1534, Paris, Bibl. Nat. MSS Français, vol. 5499, fols. 189b: 'Et ma faict et faict journellement pour respect du Roy plus de recueil que je ne merite et suys bien abuze ou il a grant envye en tant que touche le dict Sieur de bien faire.'

26. Cyfuentes to Charles V, 13 December 1533, British Museum, Add. MSS, 28,586, fol. 70.

27. Cyfuentes to Charles V, 23 January 1534, British Museum, Add. MSS, vol. 28,586, fol. 117.

28. Dr Ortiz to Charles V, 25 February 1534, British Museum, Add. MSS vol. 28,586, fol. 124.

29. J. du Bellay to Francis I, 8 February 1534, *loc. cit.*: 'Aussy nous semble que actendant lautre despeche sera bon de faire tenir bien secretement prestz pour leur voyage Messieurs le legat et de Guadis qui ont estez nommez a nostre dict Sainct Pere suyvant ce quil Vous avoit pleu les me proposer, car sil se peult riens obtenir, il fauldra quilz usent de telle diligence que les choses soyent faictes devant quesventees.'

30. J. du Bellay to Castillon, 8 February 1534, *loc. cit.*: 'Aussy vour prye donner ordre que lexcusateur se tienne secretemment tout prest pour venir a lhospital de Rome quand je vous envoyeray mes memoires qui sera pour la premiere depesche.'

31. Castillon to A. de Montmorency, 6 March 1534, Paris, Bibl. Nat. MSS Dupuis, vol. 33, fol. 46.

32. *Journals of the House of Lords*, vol. i.

33. E. Chapuis to Charles V, 7 March 1534, Vienna Archives, P.C. 229, i. fol. 54.

34. — to Mr Fowler, London, 20 February, (dated 26th Henry VIII, but clearly written in spring 1534), British Museum, Cotton MSS Vitellius, B. xiv. fol. 119.

35. E. Chapuis to Charles V, 7 March 1534, Vienna Archives, P.C. 229, i. fol. 54.

36. E. Chapuis to Charles V, 10 January 1534, Vienna Archives, P.C. 229, i. fol. 4: 'Mais ou la dame veult quelque chose yl ny a personne qui ose ne puisse contredire, ny le Roy mesmes que luy est comme lon dict incrediblement subject pour ce que quand il ne veult faire ce quelle veult elle faict et fainct la forcenee ainsy que lon ma adverty.'

37. Castillon to A. de Montmorency, 6 March 1534, *loc. cit.*: 'Le lendemain que jeuz adverty ce Roy de lesperance en quoy me mectoit Monsr de Paris il menvoya querir et me prya luy reciter de nouveau devant son conseil ce que luy avoys le jour davant dict de par Monsr de Paris et aprez que leur eu compte a veoir leur contenances la pluspart deulx ny trouvoit poinct de fondement et disoient que le Roy navoit que faire de se mectre en telle subjection. Je trouvay aussi le Roy tout refroidy des propoz qui mavoit tenuz le jour de davant.'

38. Castillon to A. de Montmorency, 6 March 1534, *loc. cit.*: 'A lheure je les priay de mescouter et leur dis tout ce que je pensoys que pouvoit esmouvoir se Roy non seullement de prandre par les mains de nostre Sainct Pere la declaracion de son premier mariaige estre nulle et celuy ci bon, mais que daventaige par tous les moyens quon pourroit pencer il devoit chercher paix et amytie avec luy. Et quant au premier que me sembloit ny en avoir point de meilleur, pour mettre en seurete la Royne et apres oster toutes contradicions que pourroient cy apres survenir que les enfans de ce mariaige ne feussent vraiz heritiers, que si par lauctorite de nostre dit Saint pere les choses estoient faictes et confermees. Et que tout se que ses malveillans scavent mettre en avant nest fonde que la dessuz. Quant au second quil ne scauroit mieulx rompre le dessain de lempereur qui parle si hault et fait des menees que jentens ne sont a laventaige de se roy que avec lamytie du Roy mon maistre prandre celle de nostre Sainct pere. Car lempereur en sera dautant afoybly et luy plus fortifie qui sont toutes choses premierement pour layse et repoz du Roy secondement au temps a venir pour la seurete de la succession de se Royaume aux enfans qui viendroient de se dit mariaige.'

39. *Ibid.*: 'Oultre quon auroit bien peu de regard au Roy son bon frere, qui a tant fait et travaille pour cest affaire, que, si le peut mettre a bonne fin, toutes ses paines et employs reveinsent a rien.'

40. Castillon to A. de Montmorency, 6 March 1534, *loc. cit.*: 'Et apres Monseigneur quelques autres petits propoz le Roy me mena en ung jardin ou il macorda, me priant toutes foys que je le tinse secret car je pense quil craindroit bien quon pensast que sy soubdainement il se fut condescendu a telle requeste, qui ne se hasteroit de riens faire publier contre lobéissance du pape et quil atendroit comme se porteroient plus avant les choses du coste de Rome; bien quil reformera que si grand somme de deniers qui souloit aller au pape nyroit plus. Daventaige que me fait plus pencer que se veult remectre au bon train, cest que quand Monsr de Paris envoyra les memoires qui mescript quil doit envoyer, il pourveoira a lexcusateur pour lenvoyer a Rome ainsi que Monsieur de Paris escript. Conclusion: il me semble que combien que le feu soit partout se royaume contre nostre Saint Pere que par le moyon du Roy et linclinacion que ce Roy y a la pluspart des affaires de nostre dit sainct pere sy rabilera.'

41. J. du Bellay to Castillon, 22 February 1534, Paris, Bibl. Nat. MSS Français, vol. 5,499, fols. 191–6: 'Je laisse le pape en une perplexite si grande que ceulx qui le cognoissent disent ne lavoir jamais veu en plus grande... voyant de combien cela luy importe. Mais il est icy si captif de lempereur et si fort menasse quil nose luy desobeyr en rien et voila toute la maladie; joinct que la pluspart de ces cardinaux cryent sur luy en ceste matiere crucifige comme beaulx petits diables'... 'pour parler a vous a estomac ouvert je suis seur que quand le dict sieur aura faict ce quil veult faire il sen trouvera bien empesche'... 'et ung aultre grand inconvenient sen en suit que je ne voy point comment il sera possible que le Roy puisse demourer amy de tous deux et de cestuy cy ne peult il departir pour les practiques ditalye'... 'quant au memoire que jenvoye

de ce que le pape ma consenty on na que faire de le luy communicquer car il est ung peu dur; seulement luy fault dire que le pape est content denvoyer ung Cardinal a Cambray avec deux adjoinctz qui cognoistront de la matiere jusques a la diffinitive exclusivement. Il peult respondre sil luy plaist que pour complaire au Roy son frere il est content de veoir que ces deleguez vouldront dire'... 'et demoureront icy toutes choses au croc dont lempereur enragera tout vif. Je veux que cependant quilz yront dicy a Cambray on regarde si on se pourra asseurer quilz donnent la sentence comme nous la demandons et lors nous poursuyurons de leur faire amplier leur pouvoir jusques a la diffinitive inclusivement. Le vray moyen de sasseurer sera que le pape se treuve plus en liberte de lempereur quil nest et surtout qui pourroit asseurer entre eulx le mariage du duc Alexandre a la fille du Roy ce seroit la conclusion des escriptures ce coste icy.'

42. J. du Bellay to Castillon, 22 February 1534, Paris, Bibl. Nat. MSS Français, vol. 5,499, fols. 191-6: 'Le pape na moings denvye dapprouver le mariage du Roy que luy mesmes'... 'Je ne suys pas trop papiste mais par ma foy il me faict grand pitie de le veoir en la peyne ou il est. Seulement pour se formaliste pour le Roy dangleterre comme il faict, ouvertement et en beaulx plains consistoires il est menasse et non pas de poires cuictes'... 'sil men veult laisser faire je prens a ma charge sus mon honneur de luy rendre son cas despeche'... il naura quenvoyer lexcusateur et quil me laisse faire le demourant. Si je ne luy conduictz les choses a son appetit, ne intervenant rien de nouveau; je me veulx rendre a luy quil me fasse trencher la teste'... 'et vous soubzvienne de celluy que nous presumions vouloir sa ruyne. Je vous respondz quil est vray mais je scay a qui je parle. Considerez tout cecy et aultant que Vous aymez ce prince et que Vous scavez que je layme mettez y toutes les herbes de la Saint Jehan; actendant vostre responce les diables pourroient enrager quilz nobtiendront riens icy contre nous.'

43. Castillon to Francis I, 16 March 1534, Paris, Bibl. Nat. MSS Français, vol. 5,499, fol. 197; and A. de Montmorency to J. du Bellay, 12 March 1534, Paris, Bibl. Nat. MSS Dupuis, vol. 265, fol. 230. Cipher, undeciphered: 'Jay tousjours faict envoyer *en angleterre* tout ce que Vous y avez escript et mesmes *le chiffre quavez adresse au sieur de Castillon* duquel jay monstre au Roy le double que Vous mavez envoye que le dict seigneur a trouve tres bon et *a escript au dict Castillon* par courrier que jay depesche expres pour le pourter plus seurement *quil eust a se conduire envers le Roy dangleterre selon cela.*'

44. A. de Montmorency to J. du Bellay, 12 March 1534, *loc. cit.*: 'Monsr jay receu toutes Vos lettres et veu celles quavez escriptes au Roy qui a tousjours veu et entendu le tout par la ou il a tresbien cogneu que navez rien oublie ni obmis a faire entendre a nre St pere de ce quil Vous avoit ordonne luy dire et quavez pu penser estre pour servir *en laffaire du Roy dangleterre duquel il espere que moyennant la bonne conduicte du dict affaire* que Vous avez *si bien commancee a dresser par vostre prudence sen rapportera bonne issue* qui luy seroit tel plaisir que povez penser. Vous advisant que le dict Seigneur est merveilleusement content *de Vous et de la negociation que Vous avez faicte jusques icy par de la;* de la ou il ne veult pas *que bousgez encores,* que premierement *il ne le Vous mande.* Et quant *au doubte et souspecon de quoy ont les imperiaulx* de vostre allee et demeure vers nostre Saint pere ne vous en soulciez autrement car le dict Seigneur vouldroit *que pour ung soupecon quilz en ont de Vous quilz en eussent quatre.*'

45. *Ibid.*: 'Jay eu tout a ceste heure *responce de Castillon* qui Vous escript de la bonne volunte en laquelle Vous avez mis *le Roy dangleterre qui me faict esperer que vostre allee portera oultre loppinion de beaulcoup de gens quelque bel fruict pour la crestiente.*'

46. Castillon to Francis I, 16 March 1534, Paris, Bib. Nat. MSS Français, vol. 5499, fol. 197.

47. Forged letter, dated 21 February 1534, R.O. Box Q, No. 160; and Gairdner, *Letters and Papers*, vol. vii. p.85.

48. Castillon to Francis I, 16 March 1534, *loc. cit.*: 'Maintenant par vostre moyen ce Roy est contant denvoyer ung excusateur ne faisant pas semblant de luy envoyer

expressement pour la peur quil a destre lie de se submectre a la jurisdiction de Rome car il sembleroit par la quil voulust renoncer a celle de Monsieur de Canturbery qui est tout leur fondement car par la leur mariage a este faict. Et encores en vostre faveur veult continuer son parlement jusques apres pasques pour differer de faire publyer la dicte separation. Et pense beaucoup avoir accorde pour lamour de vous. Pourtant Sire affin que entendiez ce poinct le Roy vostre frere ma dict et declaire quil nenvoyra poinct de procuration devers les deleguez; mais bien, si sans forme de proces le pape luy veult accorder son affaire comme il dict que justement ne luy peult reffuser, et quil luy monstre ceste bonne volonte quon dict quil luy porte, il ne se separera point de son obeissance et differera comme il a accorde en faveur de Vous jusques apres Pasques.'

49. J. du Bellay and Denonville to Francis I, 24 February 1534, Paris, Bibl. Nat. MSS Français, vol. 5499, fol. 193.

50. Castillon to Francis I, 16 March 1534, *loc. cit.*: 'Il trouva de plain sault ceste ouverture fort nouvelle et estrange. Et apres quelques devises... il me prya de disner avec luy et que aprez disner nous acheverions ce propoz. Il alla en sa chambre et croys quil en parla a deux ou troys de son conseil. Conclusion Sire, apres disner il me feist responce que touchant sa fille Marie il estoit delibere den faire pour toujours comme dune chose de rien et que de celle la il nen falloit jamais parler...'

51. Castillon to Francis I, 16 March 1534, *loc.cit.*: 'Mais quon veuille ung peu dilligenter. Car il a tousjours opinion que ce sont tous delaiz pour (comme il dict que nostre Sainct pere a de coustume) de plus en plus prolonger son affaire et quil ne laissera pour toutes ces ouvertures a poursuivir les choses de par de ca comme il a ja commence si bientost il ne se apercoit que ses menees soient sans dissimulation.'

52. *Journal of the House of Lords.*

53. *Journal of the House of Lords.*

54. J. du Bellay and Denonville to Francis I, 15 March 1534, Paris, Bibl. Nat. MSS Français, vol. 5499, fols. 193–6.

55. Cyfuentes to Charles V, 23 January 1534, British Museum, Add. MSS vol. 28,586, fol. 117.

56. J. du Bellay and Denonville to Francis I, 15 March 1534, *loc. cit.*: 'Il est vray quil se trouve plus fasche de la matiere quil nestoit au commencement pour veoir que de tant plus que sa sainctete se mect en debvoir de bien faire plus ilz se mectent de la a le vituperer par yronies et choses diffamatoires... Il seroit bien raisonnable que le Roy dangleterre se moderast ung peu de son coste...'

57. Dr Ortiz to Charles V, 15 and 25 February 1534, British Museum, Add. MSS 28,586, fols. 125 and 142; Acts of the Consistory at Rome, Gairdner, *Letters and Papers*, vol. vii. p.632.

58. J. du Bellay and Denonville to Francis I, 15 March 1534, *loc. cit.*

59. Cyfuentes to Charles V, 10 February 1534, British Museum, Add. MSS 28,586, fol. 156.

60. J. du Bellay and Denonville to Francis I, 15 March 1534, *loc. cit.*: 'En tant Sire que touche la matiere du Roy dangleterre les gens de lempereur ont faict extreme instance de faire proceder au principal tellement que desja y a este besougne par deux consistoires et ont este baillez les doubtes a chascun des cardinaulx afin quilz estudiassent dessuz pour mieulx selon droict et raison en pouvoir opiner. Et de ceste heure sont tous ces clercs voire jusques aux cardinaulx de Bar et Denquefort empesche a remuer leurs livres estant chascun bien delibere de y desployer le tresor de sa science.'

61. *Ibid.*: 'Et levent les dicts ministres de lempereur fort les cornes davoir gaigne ceste partye suz le Roy dangleterre, mais ilz ont la baye car on leur a baille tel os a ronger que Vous pouvez estre asseure que de quasimodo ilz ny donneront coup qui puisse porter dommaige au dict Sieur. Il est vray quil estoit besoin de y gaigner deux consistoires a compter jour pour jour et pour ce faire nostre dict Sainct pere est alle par advis des medecins prendre lair ceste semaine a Ostie. Si durant tout ce temps il vient responce du dict Roy dangleterre et quil accepte ce qui luy a este envoye, lors

on parlera autre langaige... '

62. J. du Bellay and Denonville to Francis I, 15 March 1534, *loc. cit.*: 'Quand bien... tout seroit alle en Angleterre les piedz contre mont si ne voyons nous pas bien comment ilz peussent donner sentence contre le dict Roy dangleterre au principal. Car Sire sur les doubtes que leur a bailles nostre Sainct pere dont nous Vous envoyons le double, il ny en a gueres, tant partiaulx puissent ilz etre, qui osassent, en telle boutique quung consistoire, maintenir la dispence avoir jamais este bonne. Parquoy Vous pouvez Sire croire que quant on en viendroit jusques la il sen trouveroit de bien empeschez. Qui nous faict derechef Vous dire que ce sera ung grand malheur si le dict Roy dangleterre ne veult entendre raison, veu que quant bien sa matiere se mectroit icy suz le bureau et que tout le monde luy seroit contraire en cas quil ne la peust gaigner a tout le moings ne la pourroit il perdre.'

63. Dr Ortiz to Charles V, 4 March 1534, British Museum, Add. MSS 28,586, fol. 148.

64. Dr Ortiz to Charles V, 24 March 1534, British Museum, Add. MSS 28,586, fol. 191.

65. Dr Ortiz to Charles V, 9 September 1533, British Museum, Add. MSS 28,586, fol. 1.

66. Cyfuentes to Charles V, 10 March 1534, British Museum, Add. MSS 28,586, fol. 156.

67. J. du Bellay and C. de Denonville to Francis I, 23 and 24 March 1534, Paris, Bibl. Nat. MSS Français, vol. 5499, fols. 199b and 201; Cyfuentes to Charles V, 24 March 1534, British Museum, Ad. MSS 28,586, fol. 197; Dr Ortiz to Charles V, 24 March 1534, British Museum, Add. MSS 28,586, fol. 191; Dr Ortiz to Catherine of Aragon, 24 March 1534, British Museum, Add. MSS 28,586, fol. 195, etc.

68. J. du Bellay and C. de Denonville to Francis I, 23 March 1534, *loc. cit.*

69. Cardinal of Jaen to F. de los Covos, 30 March 1534, British Museum, Add. MSS vol. 28,586, fol. 200; Cyfuentes to Charles V, 2 April 1534, British Museum, Add. MSS 28,586, fol. 213.

70. J. du Bellay and C. de Denonville to Francis I, 1 April 1534, Paris, Bibl. Nat. MSS Français, vol. 5499, fol. 201.

71. Cyfuentes to Charles V, 2 April 1534, British Museum, Add. MSB. 28,586, fol. 213.

72. *Journal of House of Lords.*

73. E. Chapuis to Charles V, 25 March 1534, Vienna Archives, P.C. 229, i. fol. 67; and Castillon to Francis I, 16 March 1534, Paris, Bibl. Nat. MSS Français, 5499, fol. 197.

74. *Journal of House of Lords.*

75. Instructions to Sir John Wallop, April 1534, R.O. Henry VIII, Box B, No. 10a, b and c.

NOTES TO PART 2

Part 2: From Queen & Wife to Adulteress, April 1534–May 1536

9. The Northern Confederacy

1. Cardinal of Jaen to Covos, 30 March 1534, *loc. cit.*
2. Carne and Revett to Henry VIII, 7 April 1534, *State Papers*, vol. vii. p.552; and Cyfuentes to Charles V, 26 April 1534, British Museum, Add. MSS vol. 28,586, fol. 238.
3. E. Chapuis to Charles V, 5 April 1534, Vienna Archives, P.C. 229, i. fol. 74; and Francis I to Henry VIII, British Museum, Cotton MSS Cal. E. i. fol. 35.
4. Martin Valles to F. de los Covos, April 1534, British Museum, Add. MSS 28,586, fol. 244.
5. Reply given by Francis I to Rochford and Fitzwilliam, Paris, Bibl. Nat. MSS Français, vol. 3005, fol. 129. The instructions said by Mr Gairdner, *Letters and Papers*, vol. vii. p.195, to have been addressed to Rochford and Fitzwilliam, do not agree very well with this answer. I am inclined to think, therefore, that they are not those which were really given to the two ambassadors.
6. Reply to Rochford and Fitzwilliam, *loc. cit.*: 'Et premierement quant au propoz quilz luy ont tenu de vouloir habandonne le pape. Le dict Seigneur a respondu quil na nulle alliance avec luy. Par quoy nestant en nulle sorte son allie il ne peult et ne scauroit riens rompre en cest endroict. Et la cause qui la garde de sallier avec le dict pape a ete la faulte du pouvoir que navoient point les ambassadeurs de son dict bon frere luy estant a Marseille. Au moyen de quoy il ne voulut rien traicter tout seul.'
7. *Ibid.*: 'Quant a lemprinse de Milan dont iceulx ambassadeurs luy ont aussi parle. Le dict Seigneur a tres bien entendu tout ce quilz luy ont dit de la part de son dict bon frere touchant la dicte emprinse, mais quil ne se voulsist point ayder en nulle sorte dudict pape… Cognoissant tres bien le dict Seigneur quant a ce poinct la petite ayde quil pourroit avoir dudict pape qui ne scauroit estre que de cent ou deux cents mil escus, parquoy il sest tres bien garde de se vouloir obliger envers luy pour si peu de chose que cela. Mais de faire la guerre a ceste heure le dict Seigneur ny veoit pas grand propoz.'
8. Reply to Rochford and Fitzwilliam, *loc. cit.*: 'Touchant les nouvelles ordonnances faictes par le dict Seigneur Roy dangleterre en son royaume. Le dict Seigneur Roy son bon frere a tres bien entendu tout ce que les dicts ambassadeurs luy en ont dict. Et veu quil ny a rien contre le droict divin et loultrage quon a faict a icelluy son bon frere, il ne les scauroit trouver maulvaises et luy semble bien quil neust sceu faire de moins. Mais quant a luy de faire le semblable veu quil na pareille occasion et que ce seroit se perturber et travailler actendu quil est en repoz il luy semble ne le devoir faire.'
9. Reply to Rochford and Fitzwilliam, *loc. cit.*: 'Plus a prie le dict Seigneur Roy iceulx ambassadeurs de remonstrer de sa part a son dict bon frere comme estans de presens le pape et lempereur desesperez il fault que icelluy empereur face de deux choses

lune; ou quil vienne a lexecution de la sentence ou que a sa tresgrande honte, apres lavoir faict donner il laisse les choses comme elles sont; ce que le dict Seigneur Roy ne peult croyre quil face, puys que il en est si avant. Parquoy venant a lexecution sera force de user de fulminations et mectre en proye non seulement le royaume de son dict bon frere, mais pareillement touts ceulx qui luy ayderont. De quoy ne voulant le dict Seigneur sexcuser de faire laide et diffension a son dict bon frere tel quil doibt ... indubitablement luy sera le premier assailly, parquoy... desire il bien scavoir le cas advenant quel ayde es secours il auroit de luy.'

10. Henry VIII to Sir John Wallop, R.O. Box I, and Gairdner, *Letters and Papers*, vol. vii. p.252.
11. Henry VIII to Sir John Wallop, R.O. Box R, l0c.
12. Answer to de la Guiche, *State Papers*, vol. vii. p.559
13. E. Chapuis to Charles V, 16 April 1534, Vienna Archives, P.C. 229, i. fol. 83.
14. J. Husee to Lord Lisle, 20 April 1534, Gairdner, *Letters and Papers*, vol. vii. p.208.
15. E. Chapuis to Charles V, 29 May 1534, Vienna Archives, P.C. 229, i. No. 37: 'Il envoya bientôt apres devers la Royne larchevesque de Yorch, les evesques de Duren et de Chestry et aultres personnes, que oultres plusieurs estranges propos luy dirent quelle regardast a ce quelle feroit, car si elle refusoit de jurer et obeyr elle encourroit peyne de la vie, et comme elle ma envoye dire luy parlairent dun gibet; quoy ouyant la dicte Royne, elle leur demanda lequel deulx devait estre le bourreaulx et que sil estoit question la faire morir que ce fust en public non point en secret. En la fin refusant de jurer ils la confinarent en ung quartier de son logis, les demoiselles furent serrees en une chambre, ses confesseur, medecin et apothiquaires deffendus de parler a elle et de non sortir du logis, de quoy adverty... '
16. E. Chapuis to Charles V, 7 June 1534, Vienna Archives, P.C. 229, i. fol. 109.
17. E. Chapuis to Charles V, 23 June 1534, Vienna Archives, P.C. 229, i. fol. 44.
18. *State Papers*, vii. p.565.
19. Inventories of 9 and 14 May 1534, R.O. Henry VIII, Box Q.
20. E. Aglionby to Cromwell, 28 June 1534, R.O. Henry VIII, Box Q.
21. Earl of Shrewsbury to Cromwell, 29 June 1534, R.O. Henry VIII, Box Q.
22. R.O. Baga de Segretis, Bundle VI.
23. E. Chapuis to Charles V, 19 December 1534, Vienna Archives, P.C. 229, i. No. 70; and Mary Stafford to Cromwell, Gairdner, *Letters and Papers*, vol. vii. p.612.
24. E. Chapuis to Charles V, 24 September 1534, Vienna Archives, P.C. 229, i. No. 57; and Cyfuentes to Charles V, 30 September 1534, British Museum, Add. MSS vol. 28,587, fol. 31.
25. Receipt of Dukes William and Lewis of Bavaria, Paris, Bibl. Nat. MSS Fr. vol. 3016, fol. 76.
26. Stephen Vaughan to Henry VIII, 6 September 1533, *State Papers*, vol. vii. p.501; and S. Vaughan to Cromwell, 25 September and 21 October 1533, *State Papers*, vol. vii. pp.509 and 516.
27. Senate of Luebeck to Henry VIII, 1 October 1533, R.O. Henry VIII, Box I.
28. G. Waltz, *Luebeck unter J. Wullenwever*; Paludan Mueller, *Grevenfeide*, etc.
29. E. Chapuis to Charles V, 9 December 1533, Vienna Archives, P.C. 228, i. fol. 141; and E. Chapuis to Charles V, 16 December 1533, Vienna Archives, P.C. 228, i. fol. 148.
30. E. Chapuis to Charles V, 23 December 1533, Vienna Archives, P.C. 228, i. fol. 153.
31. *State Papers*, vol. i. pp.413, 414.
32. E. Chapuis to Charles V, 9 December 1533, Vienna Archives, P.C. 228, i. fol. 140; and Gairdner, *Letters and Papers* vol. vii. p.110.
33. Bartholdt, *Juergen Wullenwever von Luebeck*.
34. British Museum, Cotton MSS Nero, B. iii. fol. 105, and Wurm, p.17.
35. Henry VIII to Wullenwever, British Museum, Cotton MSS Nero, B. iii. fol. 106.
36. E. Chapuis to Charles V, 7 March 1534, Vienna Archives, P.C. 229, i.fol. 54.
37. Warrant to Cromwell, 31 January, 1534, R.O. Henry VIII Box Q.
38. Waitz, *Luebeck unter Juergen Wullenwever*; Paludan Mueller, *Grevenfeide*, etc.

39. E. Chapuis to Charles V, 23 June 1534, Vienna Archives, P.C. 229, i. fol. 115.
40. Chapuis to Charles V, 7 July 1534, Vienna Archives, P.C. 229, i. fol. 119.
41. Chapuis to Charles V, 16 July 1534, Vienna Archives, P.C. 229, i. fol. 123.
42. G. Waitz. *Luebeck unter Juergen Wullenwever.*
43. E. Chapuis to Charles V, 27 July 1534, Vienna Archives, P.C. 229, i. fol. 124; and E. Chapuis to.Charles V, 28 January 1535, Vienna Archives, P.C. 229½, i. fol. 9.
44. Paludan Mueller, *Aktstykers til de Nordens historie*, i. p.265, etc.
45. E. Chapuis to Charles V, 10 September 1534, Vienna Archives, P.C. 229, i. fol. 137.
46. *Papiers d'Etat de Granvelle*, vol ii. p.146.
47. *Papiers d'Etat de Granvelle*, vol. ii. p.221.

10. The Conspiracy

1. E. Chapuis to N. de Granvelle, 23 September 1534, Vienna Archives, P.C. 229, ii. fol. 79: 'Mgr je ne vous scaurais escripre davantaige de nouvelles de par de ca de ce que verrez aux lettres a sa Ma^te saulf que ce peuple ne me laysse vivre a force dimportunite pour me faire escripre et solliciter a sa dicte Majeste de pourvoir au remede dyci avant que les choses se gastent plus et soy offrant lopportunite des affaires dirlande. Il ny a point six jours que deux seigneurs de sorte et estat non me ousant venir trouver en la maison me requerirent saillir aux champs pour deviser avec moy que ne fut que pour me parler de ce que dessus et masseurer que a la moindre motion de Sa Majeste presque tout le royaulme se declareroit.'
2. *Ibid.*: 'Plusieurs dames de la part de leur mari et daultres men sont venus parler et me feist lune ces jours presque grant honte car en presence de ses demoiselles et serviteurs questoient beaulcop assistans aussi les miens elle se gecte devant moy a deux genoux pour moy recommander la dicte affaire dont deppendoit non seullement le salut de la Royne et princesse mais aussi de tant de povres ames. Ceulx questoient en la compaignie veirent les larmes et facon de faire mais ilz ne sceurent de quoy se traictoit.'
3. E. Chapuis to Charles V, 30 September 1534, Vienna Archives, P.C. 229, i. fol. 139: 'Et que au quartier du nort dont il estoit il scavoit bien quil y avoit seze contes et autres groz... que sont de son oppinion.' The abstract of this letter, printed in Mr Gairdner's Calendar, is not quite correct.
4. *Ibid.*: 'Et plus moyennant lassistence de Vostre Majeste vouldroit faire dresser la banniere du crucifix ensemble celle de Vostre Majeste.'
5. E. Chapuis to Charles V, 30 September 1534, *loc. cit.*
6. Mr Hardy's *Report upon Venetian Archives*, p.69; and Chapuis to Charles V, 3 November 1534, Vienna Archives, P.C. 229, i. fol. 151.
7. Chapuis to Charles V, 3 November 1534, Vienna Archives, P.C. 229, i. fol. 151.
8. E. Chapuis to Charles V, 24 September 1534, Vienna Archives, P.C. 229, i. fol. 139.
9. E. Chapuis to J. Hanart, 13 October 1534, Vienna Archives, P.C. 229, ii. No. 60: 'Monsr lambassadeur... le Roy depuis quelques jours a commence destre amoureux dune tres belle et tres adroicte demoiselle et va journellement croissant lamour et le credit et la bravete de la concubine decroissant; et y a quelque bon espoir que continuant la dicte amour les affaires de la Royne et princesse aux quelles la dicte damoyselle est tres affectionee se porteront bien.'
10. E. Chapuis to Charles V, 13 October 1534, Vienna Archives, P.C. 229, i. fol. 142.
11. E. Chapuis to Charles V, 24 October 1534, Vienna Archives, P.C. 229, i. fol. 147: 'Mercredi avant que departir de Mur elle fust visitee de presque tous les gentilshommes et gentilzfemmes de la court, quelque fascherie quen eust la dame. Avant hier jeudi estant a Richemont avec la petite garse, la vint la dame pour veoir sa fille accompagnee des deux dues de Norphocq et Suffocq et daultres que trestous la vindrent visiter et saluer et une partie des dames que fust chose nouvelle, et ne voulut sortir de sa chambre jusques la dame fust partie pour non la veoir.' Mr Gairdner's abstract of this letter is not quite correct.
12. E. Chapuis to J. Hanart, 13 October 1534, Vienna Archives, P.C. 229, ii. fol. 85: 'Ung

homme de la dicte princesse me vient de dire que le dict Roy avoit faict vuider de la court la femme du Seigneur de Rocheffort, pource quelle avoit conspire avec la dicte concubine de procurer et tenir main de par ung moyen ou aultre faire vuider de la court la dicte damoiselle;' and E. Chapuis to Charles V, 13 October 1534, *loc. cit.*

13. E. Chapuis to Charles V, 19 December 1534, Vienna Archives, P.C. 229, i. fol. 164.

14. G. da Casale to J. du Bellay, 22 September 1534, Paris, Bibl. Nat. MSS Français, vol. 19,751, fol. 113; and G. da Casale to Cromwell, 24 September 1534, *State Papers*, vol. vii. p.570.

15. G. da Casale to Norfolk, 15 October 1534, *State Papers*, vol. vii. p.574; and G. da Casale to Rochford, 15 October 1534, *State Papers*, vol. vii. p.575.

16. Reply to Chabot de Brion's proposals, *State Papers*, vol. vii. p.584; E. Chapuis to Charles V, 28 November and 19 December 1534, Vienna Archives, P.C. 229, i. fol. 157 and 164; and Palamede Gontier to Chabot, 5 February 1535, Lelaboureur, *Memoires de Mr de Castelnau*, vol. i. p.405.

17. Girolamo Penizon to Cromwell, 22 October 1534, R.O. Henry VIII, Box Q, fol. 81.

18. *Chronicle of Calais*, p.45; and Lord Rochford to Norfolk, 11 November 1534, Gairdner, *Letters and Papers*, vol. vii. p.535.

19. E. Chapuis to Charles V, 18 November 1534, Vienna Archives, P.C. 229, i. fol. 153; and J. du Mouchiau to Lady Lisle, 23 November 1534, Gairdner, *Letters and Papers*, vol. vii. p.548.

20. Chapuis to Charles V, 18 November 1534, Vienna Archives, P.C. 229, i. fol. 153.

21. Chapuis to Charles V, 28 November 1534, Vienna Archives, P.C. 229, i. fol. 157.

22. Chapuis to Charles V, 5 December 1534, Vienna Archives, P.C. 229, i. No. 68.

23. Reply to Chabot de Brion, *State Papers*, vol. vii. p.584; and E. Chapuis to Charles V, 5 December 1534, Vienna Archives, P.C. 229, i. fol. 160.

24. E. Chapuis to Charles V, 14 January 1535, Vienna Archives, P.C. 229½, i. fol. 1: 'Le soir du festin que le Roy luy feist que feut la veillie de son partement estant assiz aupres de la dame pendant que lon dansoit, sans occasion ne propoz se meit a rire le plus desmesurement du monde de quoy le dit admiral monstra estre bien marry et fronsant le nez luy dict: comment madame vous mocquez Vous de moy ou quoy? Dont apres avoir saouler son ris sexcusa vers luy disant quelle se ryoit a cause que ce Roy luy avoit dit quil alloit demander le secretaire dudict admiral pour lenvenir vers elle pour luy faire feste et que le dict Roy avoit rencontre en chemin une dame que luy avoit fait oblye le surplus…'

25. E. Chapuis to Charles V, 5 December 1534, Vienna Archives, P.C. 229, i. fol. 160.

26. Statutes of the Realm, 26 Henry VIII, cap. xiii.

27. *More's Works*, p.1446; and Interrogatory of J. Fisher, § 5, printed by J. Lewis, in *Life of J. Fisher*, vol. ii. p.410.

28. Hanart to Granvelle, 14 January 1535, British Museum, Add. MSS 28,587, fol. 207.

29. *More's Works*, p.1450.

30. Palamede Gontier to P. Chabot de Brion, 5 February 1535, Lelaboureur, *Memoires de Mr de Castelnau*, vol. i. p.405, *et seq.* See Appendix, Note E.

31. Hanart to Granvelle, 31 January 1535, British Museum, Add. MSS 28,588, fol. 70.

32. J. Hanart to Charles V, 31 January 1535, British Museum, Add. MSS 28,587, fol. 207.

33. P. Gontier to Chabot de Brion, 5 February 1535, *loc. cit.*

34. P. Gontier to Chabot de Brion, 5 February 1535, *loc. cit.*

35. Henry VIII to Chabot de Brion, *State Papers*, vol. vii. p.596; Chabot de Brion to Henry VIII, 17 April 1535, *State Papers*, vol. vii. p.592; and P. Gontier to Chabot de Brion, 5 February 1535, *loc. cit.*

36. Gontier to Chabot de Brion, 5 February 1535, *loc. cit.*

37. E. Chapuis to Charles V, 2 May 1536, Vienna Archives, P.C. 230, i. fol. 80: 'Et plustost se fust declaire ce dict Roy neust est que quelcung de son conseil luy donnoyt entendre que ne sauroyt separer de la dicte concubyne sans tacitement confirmer non seullement le premier mariaige mais aussy que plus il crainct lautorite du pape.'

11. Fisher & More

1. E. Chapuis to Charles V, 25 February 1535, Vienna Archives, P.C. 229½, i. fol. 13: 'La damoiselle questoit naguieres en faveur de ce Roy ne lest plus et a succede en son lieu une cousine germaine de la concubine quest fille de la moderne gouvernante de la princesse.'

2. E. Chapuis to Charles V, 1 January 1535, Vienna Archives, P.C. 229½, i. fol. 34.

3. E. Chapuis to Charles V, 28 January 1535, Vienna Archives, P.C. 229½, i. fol. 9.

4. E. Chapuis to Charles V, 14 January 1535, Vienna Archives, P.C. 229½, i. fol. 1.

5. E. Chapuis to Charles V, 25 February 1535, *loc. cit.*

6. E. Chapuis to Charles V, 4 March 1535, Vienna Archives, P.C. 229½, i. fol. 42: 'Sire hier vint ung docteur religieux avec lequel jay de longtemps familiarite qui me vint demander une pronosticacion que parle de la mutynacion qui doit estre contre les gouverneurs de ce royaulme de laquelle pronostication chacun estoit requis de la part de millor Brez, quest ung seigneur scavant riche et de bon cueur... il vouldroit escripre a plusieurs bons personnages pour selon que pouvoit comprendre dudict religieulx les inciter contre... gouvernemens desperant de la tardance du remede de Vostre Maieste.'

7. E. Chapuis to Charles V, 9 February 1535, Vienna Archives, P.C. 229½ i. fol. 22.

8. E. Chapuis to Charles V, 25 February 1535, *loc. cit.*

9. E. Chapuis to Charles V, 25 April 1535, Vienna Archives, P.C. 229½, i. fol. 74: 'Il a dit au dict de la Royne quil ny avoit que deux moyens pour remedier aux affaires des Royne et princesse, et a ceulx de tout le royaulme. Le premier estoit si dieu vouloit visiter ce roy de quelque petite maladie, lors oultre que de luy mesmes se recougnoistroit, il prendroit, aussy en pacience et de bonne part les remonstrances que luy en seroynt faictes; lautre moyen seroit dattempter la force...et que tardant lung ou laultre remede elles estoient en dangier de leur vie, et que bien en prenoit au dict Roy son maistre que V Mte nestoit bien informee de la facilite quil y auroit de venir a chief de lemprinse dont seroit maintenant la propre saison.'

10. E. Chapuis to Charles V, 9 and 25 February and 4 March 1535, *loc. cit.*

11. E. Chapuis to Charles V, 7 March 1535, Vienna Archives, P.C. 229½ i. fol. 46.

12. E. Chapuis to Charles V, 4 March 1535, Vienna Archives, P.C. 229½, i. fol. 42: 'Que me faict croire que survenant la dicte evocacion ce roy ne se hasteroit de faire oultraige ausdites dames actendant lissue des affaires. Il est a penser quil sen saisiroit et les feroit mectre en la tour et croys que en tel cas les dictes royne et princesse ne seroint tant a son commandement quil penseroit bien, pour estre le cappitaine a ce que il monstre serviteur de vostre maieste et des dictes dames et homme de bien ayant communique avec aucuns des susmencionez;' and E. Chapuis to Charles V, 7 March 1535, *loc. cit.*: 'Je suis seur que tumbant elles en main et garde de celluy dont rescripvis dernierement quelles seroyent hors de dangier et ne desire moings le bien que les autres comme ay sceu encoires aujourdhuy de bien bonne part et ne desire que locasion de pouvoir monstrer sa bonne volente.'

13. E. Chapuis to Charles V 5 April 1535, Vienna Archives, P.C. 229½, i. fol. 64: 'la maison ou elle gist est a douze mille de ceste riviere et quant pourroit une fois tenir la dicte princesse a cheval il seroit plus aise de la saulver quil nestoit a grinuic, car lon lembarqueroit plus avant que gravesen de la ou est tout le dangier de ceste riviere; 'and E. Chapuis to N. de Granvelle, 5 April 1535, Vienna Archives, P.C. 229½, iii. fol. 4: 'et serreroient les yeulx donnant une benediction a ceulx qui la saulveroient.'

14. E. Chapuis to Charles V, 5 April 1535, *loc. cit.*: 'et que la ou elle estoit maintenant yl ny avoit ordre de soy saulver de nuyt.'

15. E. Chapuis to Charles V, 1 January, 25 February and 23 March 1535, *loc. cit.*

16. E. Chapuis to Charles V, 4 March 1535, Vienna Archives, P.C. 229½, i. fol. 42: 'Quil sestoyt hier trouve malade dune reume que luy avoit faict enfler ung yeul et la joue.'

17. E. Chapuis to Charles V, 7 March 1535, *loc. cit.*: 'Le VIeme Cremuel me vint trouver ne layant pu faire premier a cause de son indisposicion.'

18. Diarium Petri Suavenii, edited by C. F. Wegener, *Aarsberetninger*, vol. iii. pp.234-

36: 'Sabato [6 March] renunctiatum, non dari otium ad me audiendum propter raucedinem et nescio quam valetudinem malam'... 'Die lunae post Palmarum [22 March], coepit aegrotare tertiana febri ... Dominica Quasimodo geniti [4 April] accessi ad aedeis Crumwelli propterea quod dicebatur nonnihil convaluisse. Nemo inveniebatur, qui me adesse vellet significare... Die Jovis [7 April]... jam nonnihil convaluisset et homines ad se admitteret.'

19. E. Chapuis to Charles V, 17 April 1535, Vienna Archives, P.C 229½, i. fol. 68.
20. Palame Gontier to Chabot de Brion, 5 February 1535, *loc. cit.*
21. Henry VIII to the Earl of Sussex, 17 April (1535), Strype, *Memorials*, vol. i. part ii. p.208. Mr Gairdner places this letter in the year 1534, but I think it belongs to 1535, for in the latter year Tunstall received a similar privy seal: Cuthbert Tunstall to all men, 9 June 1535, R.O. Henry VIII, anno xxviii, bundle ii.
22. Examination of Carthusian monks, 20 April 1535, R.O. Henry VIII, Box R, No. 36.
23 Records of the trial, R.O. Baga de Segretis, Pouch VII, Bundle I; and Third Report of the deputy keeper of public records, App. II. p.237.
24. E. Chapuis to N. de Granvelle, 8 May 1535, Vienna Archives, P.C. 229½ iii. fol. 7.
25. E. Chapuis to Charles V, 8 May 1535, Vienna Archives, P.C. 229½, i. fol. 76.
26. E. Chapuis to Charles V, 7 March 1535, *loc. cit.*
27. E. Chapuis to Charles V, 5 April 1535, Vienna Archives, P.C. 229½, i. fol. 64.
28. Henry VIII to Chabot de Brion, *State Papers*, vol. vii. p.596; and Chabot de Brion to Henry VIII, 17 April 1535, *State Papers*, vol. vii. p.592.
29. Advertisements from France, 24 and 25 October 1534, R.O. Henry VIII, Box Q, Nos. 84 and 85; and T. Thebalde to Lord Wiltshire, 7 June 1535, R.O. Henry VIII, Box R, No. 1.
30. E. Chapuis to Charles V, 8 May 1535, *loc. cit.*
31. *Chronicle of Calais*, p.45; and Chabot to Henry VIII, 17 April 1535, *loc. cit.*
32. J. Hanart to Mary of Hungary, 5 June 1535, Brussels, Archives du Royaume, Negotiations de France, vol. ii. fol. 18: 'Jentends que sur la matiere de leurs alliance y a de grosses difficultes sur les demandes que se font pour asseurence du mariage. Ceulx de ce couste demandent payne de comise le tribut et toutes les pensions quil payent chacun an en angleterre et que la fille soit dois maintenant juree pour princesse.'
33. E. Chapuis to Charles V, 5 June 1535, Vienna Archives, P.C. 229½, i. fol. 89: 'Sire apres les deux premieres communications entre les deputez de ces deux Roys le Sr de Rochefort partist de Calais et arriva icy le XXV du mois passe et avant que parler au Roy il sadressa a la dame sa seur et divisa bien longuement avec elle et ne luy dust rapporter dudict Calais chose que luy aggreast car et lors et mainteffois depuis ainsy que ma dict le grant escuyer elle a maulgree et dit mille maulx et opprobres du Roy de France et generallement de toutte la nation.'
34. E. Chapius to Charles V, 16 June 1535, Vienna Archives, P.C. 229½, i. fol. 97: 'la dame... fit plusieurs braves mommeries, elle y appella plusiers et na ete content lambassadeur de France dy etre oblye.'
35. Articles and Instructions for Norfolk, *State Papers*, vol. vii. p.608.
36. Henry VIII to Chabot de Brion, *State Papers*, vol. vii. p.596.
37. Articles and Instructions for Norfolk, *loc. cit.*: Secondarylie, touching the traduction hither into this Realme the saide Duke of Angolesme to be educate and brought up here, the saide Duke of Norfolk and his colleges shall eftsones in that behalf, by all meanes they can, presse the saide Admyrall... ; 'and Cyfuentes to Charles V, 16 July 1535, British Museum, Add. MSS 28,587, fol. 345.
38. Articles and Instructions, *loc. cit.*: 'Thirdely, where as the kinges Highnes by the said former instructions hathe gyven in charge to the said Duke of Norfolk and his colleges that amongst other it be specyallie provyded, in case the saide Duke of Angolesme shall succede the Kinges Highnes in the emperiall Crowne of this Realme in the right and title of the saide Lady Pryncesse, that then his saide dukedom of Angolesme, and all other his domynyons, landes, and possessions within the realme of Fraunce, or elles where in any of the Frensh kinges domynyons, shalbe clerely

exonerated and frely discharged, by the consent of their Parliamentes, from all
exactions, servytutes, homages, and fealties... the saide Duke of Norfolk and his
colleges shall in that poynt styke fyrmely to the conducing of the same to effecte... '

39. Chabot de Brion to Cardinal du Bellay, 8 June 1535, Paris, Bibl. Nat. MSS Fr. vol.
19,577: 'Vous entendrez le tout par ce qui est escript au Roy presentement, Vous
asseurant Monsieur que jen voudroys bien estre depesche pour la tricoterie de mode
estrange de marchander quon nous tient qui nest point mon naturel... '

40. *Chronicle of Calais*, p.45.

41. Account of Thomas More, *More's Works*, ed. 1557, p.1451.

42. *Ibid*. p.1452.

43. E. Chapuis to Charles V, 8 May 1535, Vienna Archives, P.C. 229½, i. fol. 76.

44. E. Chapuis to N. de Granvelle, 25 July 1535, Vienna Archives, P.C. 229½, iii. fol.
19.

45. Cyfuentes to Charles V, 7 November 1534, British Museum, Add. MSS 28,587, fol.
125; and Account from Rome, British Museum, Add. MSS 28,586, fol. 9.

46. G. da Casale to Norfolk, 15 October 1534, *State Papers*, vol. vii. p.573:
'Lotharingius... dicit se velle in Angliam ad Serenissimum Regem venire;' and G. da
Casale to Cromwell, 8 November 1534, *State Papers*, vol. vii. p.579.

47. Cyfuentes to Charles V, 3 March 1535, British Museum, Add. MSS 28,587, fol.
243.

48. G. da Casale to Cardinal du Bellay, 21 May and 2 June 1535, Paris, Bibl. Nat. MSS
Fr. vol. 19,571, fols. 117 and 118.

49. G. da Casale to Cardinal du Bellay, 21 May 1535, *loc. cit.*: 'Hora questa cosa sara
giudicata molto male in Inghilterra, maxime da quelli che sa V. S. R^{ma}, dubito che
quei tali com sospettosi dirano che questo sia stato mio motivo onde nascerebbe la
mia ruina totale... '

50. G. da Casale to Cromwell, 29 May 1535, *State Papers*, vol. vii. p.604; and Report
of Spy from Boulogne, R.O. Henry VIII, Box R.: 'Monseigneur, il passa ung homme
mardi la nuyt en engleterre que le pappe envoye au Roy avec ung chappeau rouge
pour levesque de Rocestre qui est prisonier en la tour de Londres avec une bulle
dexcommunication pour fulminer le Roy sil ne mect le dict evesque dehors et sil
luy empesche de prendre le chappeau. Ledict messaigier vint mardi quant Monsgr
ladmiral.'

51. G. da Casale to Cromwell, 1 June 1535, *State Papers*, vol. vii. p.605; and the Bishop
of Mâcon to Francis I, 29 May 1535, Paris, Bibl. Nat. MSS Dupuis, vol. 265, fol.
138.

52. The Bishop of Mâcon to Francis I, 29 May 1535, *loc. cit.*, cipher undeciphered: 'Me
priant affectueusement Vous vouloir encoires suplier davoir le Cardinal de Rocestre
pour recommande doubtant que sans voustre ayde il nen aura pas moins que les
executez. Il se dict que les ministres dudict Empereur avoient escript en flandres de
faire publier en angleterre par les marchants flamens ayant trafficque avecques les
angloys que la promotion dudict Roffence avoit este faicte a voustre poursuite et
requeste affin danimer le dict Roy a lencontre de Vous et seroit bon quil Vous pleust
y faire donner ordre pour y obvier et ouster ce scrupulle au dict Roy. Jay adverty
noustre dict Sainct Pere de tout cecy luy remonstrant que au moyen de ce bruit il sera
bien difficille que puissiez persuader ny moyenner affaire du dict Roffence vers le
dict Roy dangleterre.'

53. *Ibid.*: 'Il me dict quil feroit telle attestation que Vous adviseriez que Vous ny autre
prince chrestien ne luy feist parler dudit Roffence, que la verite estoit quil lavoit fait
cardinal pour son scavoir et vertu le cognoissant par ses œuvres estre necessaire
pour le futeur concille, et lavoit plustoust fait cardinal pour en gratiffier le dit Roy
dangleterre que en hayne de luy.'

54. The Bishop of Mâcon to Cardinal du Bellay, 2 June 1535, Paris, Bibl. Nat. MSS Fr.
vol. 19,577; and Nicolas Raince to Cardinal du Bellay, 21 May [sic.], 1535, *ibid*.

55. G. da Casale to Cardinal du Bellay, 21 May 1535, *loc. cit.*: 'Potria anchora S. M^{ta}
far intendere al Re dInghilterra che questa cosa tornera a suo commodo, perche

questo vescovo il quale non ha mai voluto giurare la osservantia de nuovi statuti fatti in Inghilterra, il che ha dato gran dispiacere al Re, al presente, si per liberarsi di prigione, si per la gran dignita, forse fara quel che vuole il Re, perche lo lasci vinire in qua, et cio seguendo, la Mᵗᵃ Chrᵐᵃ et quel principe potrano anchora far capitale di Roffense come dun gran cardinale. Questa cosa quando fosse con destrezza maneggiata col Re proprio potrebbe forse riuscire. Ma ci bisogna usare destrezza grande;' and G. da Casale to Cardinal du Bellay, 2 June 1535, *loc. cit.*: 'Sopra questo affare potria la Mᵗᵉ Chrᵐᵃ persuadere al Re dInghilterra, che poi che la cosa e fatta dovrebbe cercare al meno cavarne qualche utilita. Come saria col liberarlo e lascarlo esser cardinale farlo assentire et conjurare alla osservatione de statuti, il che egli non havendo voluto fare infra si trova in prigione. Et forse glielo fara fare per un tanto premio et honore. Et quando pur sia per stare nella sua ostinatione si puo mostrare che lascandolo venire in Francia fara doi effeti, luno che levera questo impedimento dInghilterra laltro che essendo il Chrᵐᵒ et il Re dInghilterra tanto amici venendo qualche occasione potranno valersi dun tanto huomo Cardinale.'

56. G. da Casale to Cromwell, 27 July 1535, *State Papers*, vol. vii. p.618.

57. E. Chapuis to Charles V, 16 June 1535, Vienna Archives, P.C. 229½, i. fol. 97: 'Sire ce Roy a ce que jentends nest seullement picque destre faict ledict evesque Cardinal mais a cause de celluy de Paris auquel en toutes choses avoit grande confidence mesmes pour ce que avant cette creation il se tenoit pour maulvais papiste. Il na aussi gros plaisir de lauditeur de la chambre.'

58. E. Chapuis to Charles V, 30 June 1535, Vienna Archives, P.C. 229½, i. fol. 103: 'Cremuel me dit que le pape estoit cause de sa mort et que le dict pape avoit faict tres mal et tres follement de lavoir faict Cardinal actendu que cestoit le pire enemy que le Roy son maistre eust.'

59. E. Chapuis to Charles V, 16 June 1535, *loc. cit.*: 'Sire des que ce Roy entendict levesque de Rochestre estre cree Cardinal tres despit et fasche que se trouva il dit et asseura par plusieurs foiz quil dounroit ung autre chappeau audict evesque et quil envoyeroit apres la teste a Rome pour le chappeaul Cardinal.'... 'Et cependant pour ce que il ny a legitime occasion de les faire morir le Roy va serchant sil se trouvera quelque chose contre eulx, mesme si le dict evesque a fait poursuyte du chappeaul, et pour ce entendre sont constituez plusieurs prisonniers tant de ses parents que de ceulx que le gardoient en prison;' and Examination of J. Fisher, *Archaeologia Britannica*, vol. xxv. p.99.

60. Examination of J. Fisher, 14 June 1535, *State Papers*, vol. i. p.431; and Examination of Sir Thomas More, 14 June 1535, *State Papers*, vol. i. pp.432 to 436.

61. Records of the trial, R.O. Baga de Segretis, Pouch VII Bundle II; and Third Report of the Deputy of Public Records, App. II, p.239.

62. About the date of Fisher's execution there is some uncertainty. It is differently stated as 21, 22 or even 23 June. Lord Herbert says it was 22 June, and in this he agrees with the account given by Chapuis. E. Chapuis to Charles V, 30 June 1535, Vienna Archives, P.C. 229½, i. fol. 103: 'Le xxii yl eust trenchee la teste au lieu que le duc de boquinguam et nest a penser le regret et compassion que tout le monde en avoit.'

63. *Ibid.*: 'Il fust sollicite a merveilles depuis quil fut sur lechaffaud de consentir a ce que vouloit le Roy luy offrant sa grace mais y ny eust ordre et mourust tres vertueusement.'

64. E. Chapuis to Charles V, 30 June 1535, *loc. cit.*: 'Il luy fust donne pour confesseur ung sien grand enemy quest le plus grand lutherien du monde et faulteur de toutes les diableries que sont yci, si ne cesse il de dire que lon a faict morir lung des meilleurs et plus saincts homme du monde.'

65. E. Chapuis to Charles V, 16 June 1535, *loc. cit.*: 'Et pour le desennuyer de ces fascheries la dame luy a ces jours faict ung festin en une sienne maison ou elle fit plusieurs braves mommeries... la dicte dame a si bien banquete et momme que a ce que ma aujourdhuy envoye dire la princesse le Roy est plus rasste [*sic* rassote] delle quil ne fust oncques quest chose qua augmente grandement la craincte de la princesse.'

66. Records of the trial, R.O. Baga de Segretis, Pouch VII, Bundle III; and Third Report

of the Deputy Keeper of Public Records, App. II, p.240.

67. Cromwell to Sir John Wallop, 23 August 1535, Burnet, *Collectanea*, part iii. book ii. No. xxxv.

68. A. de Montmorency to Cardinal du Bellay, 26 July 1535, Paris, Bibl. Nat. MSS Fr. 19,577: 'Apres avoir faict coupper la teste au C^al Rochestot ils ont faict le semblable a Monsieur Morus qui estoient deux tels personnaiges que scavez;' and Gregorio da Casale to — 30 July 1535, *State Papers*, vol. vii. p.621, footnote: 'Dicunt etiam quod Cardinalis Turnonensis, suis literis Romam missis, hujus hominis mortem descripsit adeo pie, ut ommes commoverit ad lachrymas.'

69. Cardinal du Bellay to Francis I, 3 September 1535, Paris, Bibl. Nat. MSS Fr. 5499, fol. 206; and *Memorial on the English Cause, ibid.* fol. 212.

70. *Memoir on the English Cause*, British Museum, Add. MSS vol. 28,587, fol. 334.

71. Anton Musa to Stephan Rothe, 16 January 1536, *Corpus Reformatorum*, vol. iii. No. 1389.

72. Memorandum by Paget, Gairdner, *Letters and Papers*, vol. vii. p.230.

73. E. Chapuis to Charles V, 5 June 1535, Vienna Archives, P.C. 229½, i. fol. 89.

74. Examination of John Fisher, R.O., Box Q, 155, and B. M. Cotton MSS Cleopatra, E. fol. 196, etc.

75. *Glaubwuerdiger Bericht, von dem Todt T. Mori*, Strassburg, 1535, and *Beschreibung des Urtheils Herrn T. Morus*, s. 1.

76. Memorial about Fisher's death, R.O. Henry VIII, Box K, No. 11. I have altered the spelling of the passages above quoted.

77. Latin Memorial about More's and Fisher's death, R.O. Henry VIII, Box S: 'Quod scribis passim per Germania idque constantissima fama vulgatum, regem haud aliam ob causam in Moro ac Roffense animadvertisse qua quod Evangelicam doctrinam syncere assererent, et regias item nuptias impugnarent miramur profecto quis ejus fabulæ author esse possit.'

78. *Ibid.*: 'Neque enim induci possumus ut credamus erudita Germanorum ingenia tam facile vanissimis vulgo rumoribus posse abduci ut quidlibet credant de quolibet et regis benignitatem, equitatem, pietatem, clementiam orbi scimus multo notoria quam ut a quovis calumnie impetu facile subruantur.'

79. Latin Memorial about More's and Fisher's death, R.O. Henry VIII, Box S: 'Iam quod de propugnato evangelio fabulantur miramur si quisquam Germanorum sit, qui credat Evangelium nocentiores unquam his duobus hostes habuisse.'

80. *Ibid.*: 'Idem in epistola ad Erasmum (quam Paulo antequam maiestatis postularetur ediderat) ingenue et palam se perpetuum hostem hereticis (sic enim purioris doctrine studiosos omnes appellat) non sine stomacho futurum denunciat. Id quod Archigrammateus adhuc regni exactissime haud dubie prestitit.'

81. Latin Memorial about More's and Fisher's death, R.O. Henry VIII, Box S: 'Pudet commemorare quos ille cruciatus excogitaret exercueratque in eos quos veritati evangelice persenserat esse addictiores, conquisitos undique et magno interim indicibus proposito praemio, unquam ante carceribus committere solebat, quam in oculis suis miserabiliter excruciatos conspixisset. Fuisse autem Moro atrox et saevum ingenio vel hoc judicat, quod novo et a se invento questionis genere deprehensos venationis torquere solitus sit, cruciatus vero erat hujusmodi, Adductos ad se, protinus novis calceis indui et cippis constringi fecerat. Deinde eorum plantas igni flagrantissimo admoveri, scilicet ut ne confitentibus quidem dolor... '

82. Latin Memorial about More's and Fisher's death, R.O. Henry VIII, Box S: 'Quem ut assequi pauci possent, ita ut omnes principes imitare possent immensam illius misericordiam precamur, qui gloriosam illam aeternitatis adoptionem, studiosis misericordie benignissime policitur, fallere non potest.'

12. The Collapse of the Northern Alliance

1. Wullenwever to Cromwell, 17 October 1534, R.O. Box Q, No. 78; and Expenses of Christofer Mores, R.O. Box Q, No. 88.

2. C.F. Wegener, *Aarsberetninger*, vol. iii. p.217.

3. Proposals of P. Schwaben, C.F. Wegener, *Aarsberetninger*, vol. iii. p.251.

4. E. Chapuis to Charles V, 3 November 1535, Vienna Archives, P.C. 229, i. No. 62.

5. Diarium Petri Suavenii, C.F. Wegener, *Aarsleretninger*, vol. iii. p.233.

6. Diarium Petri Suavenii, *loc. cit.* p.233: 'Die lunae sum auditus in horto. De foedere non negavit rex, caussam autem scire voluit, quamobrem sibi oblatum Danicum regnum acceptare non liceret... Danicum regnum electivum non haereditarium esse. Lubecenses revera amicos regis... electionem non apud consiliarios, sed apud plebem quoque haerere. Paucos ex consiliariis Christiano adhaerere; nihil hoc esse... Se quoque aliquid scire... Dixi postea de defectione Scanicorum, de caede Lubecensium, de morte Marci Meyers. Eorum nihil creditum est.'

7. Diarum Petri Suavenii, *loc. cit.* p.240; and E. Chapuis to Charles V, 18 April 1535, Vienna Archives, P.C. 229½, i. fol. 68.

8. G. Waitz, *Wullenwever*, vol. ii. pp.196, 197 and 212.

9. Accounts of Christofer Mores, R.O. Box Q, No. 88; and E. Chapuis to Charles V, 30 June 1535, Vienna Archives, P.C. 229½, i. fol. 103.

10. G. Waitz, *Luebeck unter Juergen Wullenwever*, vol. ii. pp.186, 187, 220, 221.

11. *State Papers*, vol. vii. p.636, footnote; *Corpus Reformatorum*, vol. ii. p.939, footnote.

12. G. Waitz, *Luebeck unter Juergen Wullenwever*, vol. iii. p.469.

13. G. Waitz, *Luebeck unter Jusrgen Wullenwever*.

14. Albrecht of Mecklenburg and Christof of Oldenburg to Henry VIII, 12 and 15 May 1535, *Aktstykker*, vol. ii. pp.80–2, etc.

15. L. von Ranke, *Deutsche Geschichte*, vol. iv. pp.51–5.

16. Articles by Melanchthon, 1 August 1534, *Corpus Reformatorum*, vol. ii. No. 1205, A: 'Concedunt nostri politiam ecclesiasticam rem licitam esse, quod videlicet sint aliqui episcopi qui praesint pluribus ecclesiis; item quod Romanus Pontifex praesit omnibus episcopis. Hanc canonicam politiam, ut ego existimo, nemo prudens improbat... ' 'Melanchthon to Camerarius, 13 September 1534, *Corpus Reformatorum*, vol. ii. No. 1215; and Cardinal du Bellay to Mr de Saint Caletz (November 1534), Paris, Bibl. Nat. MSS François, vol. 5499, fol. 199.

17. Cardinal du Bellay to Mr de Saint Caletz, Paris, Bibl. Nat. MSS Fr. vol. 5499, fol. 199.

18. Francis I to Melanchthon, 23 June 1535, *Corpus Reformatorum*, vol. ii. No. 1279.

19. Cardinal du Bellay to Melanchthon, 27 June 1535, *Corpus Reformatorum*, vol. ii. No. 1280; and G. du Bellay to Melanchthon, 16 July 1535, *Corpus Reformatorum*, vol. iv. *Supplementa*, No. 56.

20. J. Friedrich to Francis I, 18 August 1535, *Corpus Reformatorum*, vol. ii. No. 1303.

21. Credentials for R.Barnes, 8 July 1535, *Corpus Reformatorum*, vol. ii. p. 936, footnote.

22. Norfolk and Rochford to Cromwell, Burnet's *Collectanea*, part iii. book iii. No. xlii.

23. J. Gostwyk to Cromwell, 31 July 1535, R.O. Cromwell letters, xiv. No. 37; Bonner and Cavendish to Cromwell, 24 July 1535, British Museum, Cotton MSS Nero, B. iii. No. 51; *Wurm*, p.27; *Waitz*, vol. iii. pp.179 and 468; and *Aktstykker*, vol. i. p.430.

24. *Waitz*, iii. p.180; *Aktstykker*, i. p.459; and E. Chapuis to Charles V, 6 and 13 September 1535, Vienna Archives, P.C. 229½, i. fols. 123 and 125.

25. Albrecht of Mecklenburg to Henry VIII, 12 May 1535, *loc. cit.*

26. Robert Legge, Thomas Gyggs, and William Bolle to —, 6 September 1535; G. Schanz, *Englische Handelpolitik*, vol. ii, p.487; Christian III to Henry VIII, 16 November 1535 *ibid.* p.490; and Report of Dinteville, Paris, Bibl. Nat. MSS Dupuis, vol. 547, fol. 200.

27. E. Chapuis to Charles V, 25 September 1535, Vienna Archives, P.C. 229½, i. fol. 128.

28. G. Waitz, *Luebeck unter J. Wullenwever*, vol. iii. pp.180, 181, and Regkman's Chronicle.

29. E. Chapuis to Charles V, 28 January 1535, Vienna, P.C. 229½, i. fol. 9; and R. Barnes to Cromwell, 22 August 1535, British Museum, Cotton MSS Vitellius, B. xxi. fol. 34.

30. R. Barnes to Cromwell, 25 August 1535, R.O. *Cromwell Correspondence*, vol. iii. fol. 78.

31. G. Waitz, *Luebeck unter Juergen Wullenwever*.

32. Examination of J. Wullenwever, 27 January 1536, Waitz, *Luebeck unter Juergen Wullenwever*, vol. iii. p.494: '54, Gefragt, was er leztmals tzu Hamburck mit den Engelischen gehandelt. Daruf bekannt das die Engelischen ime angetzeigt das sie von dem konige in Engeland befelch haben, hertzog Albrechten, wo er ein fues im reich hette, mit einer summa geldes als zehen thausent gulden zu erledigung konig Christierns vorzustreckenn. Doch wollen sie erstlich sich erkundigenn ob die knechte so Ubelacker bei einander hette pfalzgraff Friederichen zustendig, das sein F.G. dieselbigen zu eroberung des reichs Dennemark gebrauchen wolten, als dan wolten sie sich der sachenn mit den knechten nit undernemen. Daruf hat er Wollenweber sich gegen inen erboten, das er selbst zu Ubelacker und den knechten reiten und eigentlich bei innen erkunden wolte, ob sie pfalzgraf Friederich zu gebrauchen in willens. So sei er uf dem wege alhier ins gefencknus gebracht.'

33. Account from Luebeck, 15 November 1535, Waitz, *Luebeck unter Juergen Wullenwever*, vol. iii. p. 469: 'Wollenweber isth hier auszgerithen selb vierde ane wyllen und wyssen des Roths, szo das er isth gekomen zcue Hamborck, von do isth er gerithen noch Buchszthehode, von do nam er zwene diener mith, und isth geritthen noch Rodenborch, das hoereth dem bischoffe von Brehmen zcu, do isth er die Nacht ueber gebliben. In summa in der Herberge isth er truncken undt voll worden...'

34. Melanchthon to Camerarius, 5 August 1535, *Corpus Reformatorum*, vol. ii. No. 1295; and Melanchthon to H. Baumgartner, 11 August 1535, *Corpus Reformatorum*, vol. ii. No. 1297.

35. The Elector of Saxony to Francis I, 18 August 1535, *Corpus Reformatorum*, vol. ii. No. 1303.

36. The Elector of Saxony to Dr Brueck, 19 August 1535, *Corpus Reformatorum*, vol. ii. No. 1304.

37. Dr Brueck to the Elector, 18 September 1535, *Corpus Reformatorum*, vol. ii. No. 1328.

38. The Elector of Saxony to Henry VIII, 28 September 1535, *Corpus Reformatorum*, vol. ii. No. 1330.

39. The Elector of Saxony's answer to Barnes, *Corpus Reformatorum*, vol. ii. No. 1329.

40. Melanchthon to Camerarius, 24 December 1535, *Corpus Reformatorum*, vol. ii. No. 1381: 'Mori casu afficior, nec me negotiis illis admiscebo. In dedicatione nondum illa audieramus, et ego amico cuidam volui consulere.'

41. Dr Brueck to the elector, 15 November 1535, *Corpus Reformatorum*, vol. ii. No. 1355.

42. E. Chapuis to Charles V, 8 May 1535, Vienna Archives, P.C. 229½, i. fol. 76.

43. G. da Casale to Cromwell, 27 July 1535, *State Papers*, vol. vii. p.618.

44. Articles and Instructions to the Duke of Norfolk, *State Papers*, vol. vii. p.608.

45. L. v. Ranke, *Deutsche Geschichte*, vol. iii. p.400.

46. *Papiers d'Etat de Granvelle*, vol. ii. pp.361–86; and Diary of Charles V, by Mr d'Herbays, MSS Biblioteca Naçional, Madrid.

47. E. Chapuis to Charles V, 25 August 1535, Vienna Archives, P.C. 229½, i. fol. 121.

48. E. Chapuis to Charles V, 6 September 1535, Vienna Archives, P.C. 229½ i. fol. 123.

49. E. Chapuis to N. de Granvelle, 13 September 1535, Vienna Archives, P.C. 229½, iii. fol. 23: 'Le dict roy... et Cremuel... ont estes estonne de la bonne nouvelle comme chiens tumbants de fenestres et mesme Cremuel lequel a male peyne pouvoir parler.'

50. Instruction to the Commissioners at Calais, *State Papers*, vol. vii. p.608.

51. Baronius, *Annales*, vol. xxxii. p.366, 26 July 1535.

52. Jean Breton to Cardinal du Bellay, 31 August 1535, Paris, Bibl. Nat. MSS Fr. vol.

19,577; and A. de Montmorency to Cardinal du Bellay, 28 September 1535, Paris, Bibl. Nat. MSS Fr. vol. 19,577.

13. The Results of Henry's Policy

1. J. Breton de Villandry to Cardinal du Bellay, 31 August 1535, Paris, Bibl. Nat. MSS Fr. vol. 19,577: 'Le Roy a depesche Monsr le bailly de Troyes pour aller en angleterre pour laffaire du brief que Nre St Pere escripvit dernierement au Roy touchant le faict dudict Roy dangleterre;' and A. de Montmorency to Cardinal du Bellay, 28 September 1535, Paris, Bibl. Nat. MSS Fr. vol. 19,577.
2. Francis I to J. de Dinteville, 29 August 1535, Paris, Bibl. Nat. MSS Dupuis, vol. 547, fol. 307.
3. E. Chapuis to Charles V, 15 April 1533, Vienna Archives, P.C. 228, i. fol. 41.
4. J. Coke to Cromwell, 12 May 1534, R.O. Henry VIII, Box Q; and Reports from France, 24 and 25 October 1534, R.O. Henry VIII, Box Q, Nos. 84 and 85.
5. Allegations of Robyn Carre, Gairdner, *Letters and Papers*, vol. vii. p.625.
6. E. Chapuis to N. de Granvelle, 3 August and 25 September 1535, Vienna Archives, P.C. 229½, iii. fols. 22 and 25.
7. E. Chapuis to Charles V, 13 October 1535, Vienna Archives, P.C. 229½, i. fol. 130.
8. E. Chapuis to Charles V, 21 November 1535, Vienna Archives, P.C. 229½, i. fol. 137: 'Les marchandisez de ceulx de Danzic sont tousiours icy en sequestre; partie de ceulx a qui sont lesdictes marchandises mont dit quilz navoient garde de sollicite la relaxation dudict sequestre soy tenant pour certains quilz trouveront assez moyens destre recompensez au double et du principal et des interetz.'
9. E. Chapuis to Charles V, 11 August 1534, Vienna Archives, P.C. 229 i. fol. 128.
10. E. Chapuis to Granvelle, 13 December 1535, Vienna Archives, P.C. 229½, ii. fol. 69.
11. Memorandum of the French ambassadors, Paris, Bibl. Nat. MSS Dupuis, vol. 547, fol. 200.
12. E. Chapuis to Charles V, 13 October 1535, *loc. cit.*
13. E. Chapuis to N. de Granvelle, 1 November 1535, Vienna Archives, P.C. 229½, iii. fol. 28.
14. E. Chapuis to Charles V, 13 October 1535, *loc. cit.*
15. Memorandum of French ambassadors, *loc. cit.*; and E. Chapuis to N. de Granvelle, 1 November 1535, *loc. cit.*
16. Duke of Suffolk to Mr de Saint Martin, 25 September 1535, R.O. Henry VIII, Box S.
17. Memorandum of the French ambassadors, *loc. cit.*
18. E. Chapuis to Charles V, 13 October 1535, *loc. cit.*: 'Sire les ambassadeurs et bailli ont este visiter la petite bastarde de ce Roy, de quoy faire les ambassadeurs avoint a ce quilz me dirent touts deux souvent este requis et instes de la concubine dudict Roy, et quilz avoint tousiours differe jusqua la venue dudict baillif, lequel avoit este doppinion dy aller, pensant que en quelque sorte ils entreverroint la princesse, questoit la chose du monde quilz desiroient austant, et sans lespoir de laquelle ils ny feussent allez. Mais que leur defortune navoit point permis quils la veissent, et ce a cause quelle avoit este non seullement, comme ils disoint, serree dans sa chambre, mais aussi furent cloues les fenestres par ou elle pouroit estre veue.'
19. Memorandum of the French ambassadors, *loc. cit.*: 'Lautre part Vous scavez le tumulte qui fut entre sa gouvernante et elle, quant nous feusmes veoir sa petite seur, et quil nous a este dict quelle fust mise comme par force dans sa chambre, pour quelle ne parlast a nous et quil ne feust possible de la rapaiser et contenir dedans sa chambre que le gentilhomme qui nous menoit ne luy eust premierement asseure, que le Roy son pere luy avoit commande de luy dire quelle ne se monstra point cependant que nous serions la.'
20. E. Chapuis to Charles V, 13 October 1535, *loc. cit.*: 'Ce que ne crois ains que suivant ce que luy avoit escript, veuillant que ce avoir mon advis, elle se tint tout vouluntierement en sa chambre, jouant de lespinette pour dissimuler lennuyt dicelle visitacion.'
21. Report of the French ambassadors, *loc. cit.*: 'Item vous scavez que ung homme nous a asseure que une des femmes de la dicte princesse, luy avoit racompte, que

plusieurs fois elle luy avoit oui dire que mon dict Sieur le Dauphin estoit son mari… '

22.   Report of the French ambassadors, *loc. cit.*: 'Quant sa gouvernante et autres dames que la Royne qui est a present a commises pour sa garde luy disoient que mon dit Sieur le Dauphin estoit marie avec la fille de lempereur, leur respondit quelle ne le croyait pas, veu quil ne peut avoir deux femmes et quil ne peut ignorer quelle ne soit sa femme, et que jamais elle nen perdra lesperance, et quelle scavoit bien quon faisoit courre ce bruict pour luy en ouster, et par ce moyen luy faire quitter son droict.'

23.   *Ibid.*: 'Semblablement Vous scavez que ung sest faict fort de luy faire mettre par escript sa volonte, affin que les choses ne soient fondees legerement.'

24.   *Ibid.*: 'Outre plus Mr vous noublierez dire sur vostre venue et que cela feust espards parmy le menu peuple on disoit que Vous veniez pour denuncer au Roy les excommuniements et pour demander madame la princesse pour Mr le Dauphin, dont le peuple estoit si trescontant quil ne cessoit de faire priere pour Vous, comme plusieurs vous ont asseure estre vray. Pareillement Vous scavez le bon receuil que les propres gentilshommes de ceux du Roy vous faisoient, qui estoient meilleur, que depuis quils ont sceu que vostre charge ne touchoit rien de cela.'

25.   Report of the French ambassadors, *loc. cit.*: 'Item que lon nous dict ainsi que nous feusmes arrivez a Londres que le peuple faisoit priere pour nous ayant entendu que nous estions alle veoir madame la princesse.'

26.   *Ibid.*: 'Item le trouble a este si grand et la desesperation dudict peuple si grande, que ou le temps passe il ne trouvoit bon quelle fust mariee audict sieur Daulphin, pour le desir quilz ont davoir un Roy en Angleterre, qui se tint au pays, a present ils ne desirent rien plus que cela, disant que si moindre que luy vient a lepouser elle demourera desheritee oubien faudra quelle aye son droict par guerre et avec grandes incommoditez de tout le peuple.'

27.   Report of the French ambassadors, *loc. cit.*: 'Item aussy que le peuple menu prevoyant toutes ces choses est fort anime contre la Royne, jusques a en dire mille maux et improperes.'

28.   *Ibid.*: 'Item que tout le peuple est merveilleusement mal contant, les uns, et quasi tous hormis les parens de la Royne qui est a present, pour raison des dictes dames, les autres pour la subversion de la religion, les autres craignans la guerre et voyans que lentrecours de marchandise cessera tant dedans le royaume que dehors.'

29.   — to Marguerite de Navarre, 15 September [1535], Paris, Bibl. Nat. MSS Fr. vol. 3,014, fol. 98. This letter has been ascribed by Mr J. Stevenson, in his *Calendar of State Papers*, to a much later period, and he asserts that the Queen of England spoken of is Mary Tudor. The whole context shows that this is not the case. The letter is certainly not addressed to Jeanne d'Albret (who succeeded Marguerite); and besides, the court of Philip and Mary never was at Winchester in September.

30.   Memorandum of the French ambassadors, *loc. cit.*: 'Item, dernierement quant elle fust remuee de Grenewich, une grande trouppe de femmes, tant bourgeoyses que autres (au desceu de leurs maris) luy furent au devant, en pleurant et criant, que nonobstant tout ce quavoit este faict, elle estoit Princesse, et en furent mises les plus grandes en la tour, tousiours persistant en leur opinion.'

31.   *Ibid.*: 'Nota. Millor de Rochefort et Millor de Guillaume.'

32.   Memorandum of the French ambassadors, *loc. cit.*: 'Si le pape estoit adverty des traictes que le Roy dangleterre pretend faire avecque le Roy, il entrera en doubte de perdre largent de France comme il a faict celluy dangleterre si guerre se meust, et il moyenneroit bien envers lempereur quil prieroit le Roy entendre au mariage que dessus et croy que le dict empereur y ayderoit pour lamour quil porte a sa niepce.'

33.   Memorandum of the French ambassadors, *loc. cit.*: 'Item si le dict Empereur vient a prier de ce que dessus, il pourra lors adviser de faire entendre au Roy dangleterre lintention de lempereur et luy persuader de le consentir pour eviter toutes guerres, veu que le dict Sieur ne denie point quelle ne soit sa fille et quil scait bien que le mariaige en est faict.

Et si le dict Sieur Roy dangleterre ne le trouvoit bon a cause de la persuasion que sa femme luy pourroit faire au contraire, si craindra il bien de mettre contre soy le Roy et lempereur pour la seule affection quil porte a sa dicte femme, qui est beaucoup moindre quelle na este, et diminue tous les jours veu quil y a nouvelles amours comme Vous scavez.'

34. E. Chapuis to Charles V, 5 June 1535, Vienna Archives, P.C. 229½, i. fol. 89.
35. E. Chapuis to Charles V, 30 June 1535, Vienna Archives, P.C. 229½, i. fol. 103.
36. E. Chapuis to Charles V, 11 July 1535, Vienna Archives, P.C. 229½, i. fol. 105.
37. E. Chapuis to N. de Granvelle, 11 July 1535, Vienna Archives, P.C. 229½, iii. fol. 17.
38. E. Chapuis to Charles V, 11 July 1535, Vienna Archives, P.C. 229½, i. fol. 105.
39. E. Chapuis to Charles V, 3 August 1535, Vienna Archives, P.C. 229½, i. fol. 119.
40. Sir John Wallop to J. Hanart, 17 May 1535, Vienna Archives, P.C. 229½, ii. fol. 39.
41. E. Chapuis to Charles V, 7 March 1535, Vienna Archives, P.C. 229½, i. fol. 46: 'Sire sur ce il [Cromwell] mentra a parler de mariage du prince despaigne avec ceste bastarde quilz appellent princesse, mays voyant la myne quen tenois il nen dit que deux parolles, et sans ce que luy disse riens il en fit la responce quil croyoit bien que Vostre Maieste ny vouldroit entendre pour respect de la princesse sa cousine;' and E. Chapuis to N. de Granvelle, 17 February 1536, Vienna Archives, P.C. 230, ii. fol. 5.
42. E. Chapuis to N. de Granvelle, 11 July 1535, *loc. cit.*; and E. Chapuis to Charles V, 13 October 1535, *loc. cit.*
43. Account of the negotiation of Pier Luigi Farnese with Charles V, November 1535, Vienna Archives, P.C. 229½, ii. fol. 60; and Charles V to J. Hanart, 23 October 1535, *Papiers d'etat de Granvelle*, vol. ii. p.387.
44. Cardinal du Bellay to — , Paris, Bibl. Nat. MSS Fr, vol.5499, fol. 212: 'Quant au faict dangleterre troys Cardinaulx ont charge de y veoir et aux premiers jours faire leur rapport en consistoire de ce quilz y auront trouve affin quil y soit oppine de ce qui se y doibt faire pour procedder a lencontre du Roy;' and Cardinal du Bellay and Denonville to Francis I, 3 September 1535, Paris, Bibl. Nat. MSS Fr. vol. 5499, fol. 2176: 'Et en tant Sire, que touche laffaire dangleterre dont il Vous plaist nous faire mention par Vos lettres la chose nest passe plus avant et ne sen est parle depuis que moi du Bellay Vous ay dernierement escript quon avoit ordonne aux deputez de se faire prests pour faire leur rapport en consistoire... et maidoit beaucoup pour mes defenses la demonstration que Vous feistes durant pappe Clement quand Vous menvoyastes icy et la faulte qui y fust faicte telle et si grande que le dicte pappe confessa que en aviez tant faict quil se contantait desormais que quoique feist le dict Roy dangleterre Vous ne Vous empeschissiez pour le Sainct Siege contre luy ne aussy pour luy contre le Sainct Siege... Aussi que icelluy Sainct Siege debvra considerer de ne Vous rechercher de chose qui Vous soit trop pernitieuse et contre la rayson.'
45. Account of the negotiation of Pier Luigi Farnese, *loc. cit.*
46. E. Chapuis to Charles V, 1 January 1535, Vienna Archives, P.C. 229½ i. fol. 34.
47. E. Chapuis to Charles V, 25 February 1535, *loc. cit.*
48. E. Chapuis to Charles V, 11 July 1535, *loc. cit.*
49. E. Chapuis to Charles V, 1 November 1535, Vienna Archives, P.C. 229½ i. fol. 115.
50. Norfolk to Cromwell, 9 September 1535, R.O. Henry VIII, Box R, No. 137.
51. E. Chapuis to Charles V, 1 November 1535, *loc. cit.*
52. Dr Ortiz to the Empress, 1 September 1535, British Museum, Add. MSS 28,588, fol. 12: 'Ayer... partio de aqui un camarero del Rey de Inglaterra llamado Tomas Petiple el qual... dice que... todos llaman a la Ana Reyna la qual dice que esta muy fea y que todo el pueblo esta como atonido y espantado que no saben de que parte a de venir el juizio de Dios sobre ellos'
53. E. Chapuis to Charles V, 17 January 1534, Vienna Archives, P.C. 229, i. fol. 8: 'Et oultre lespoir quil a sur ses subjectz il a aussi grant ... sur la mort de la Royne laquelle il dict encoires de nouveaulx a lambassadeur de France ne pouvoir vivre longuement a cause quelle est ydropique de laquelle maladie elle ne fust oncques attaincte. Dont est a doubter, comme jay cydevant escript a Vostre Maieste quilz sement telles choses pour luy faire venir une ydropisie artificielle dont dieu la veuille preserver. Et ma

faict advertir Gregoire de Cassal desdictz propos du Roy audict ambassadeur de France et ma faict dire quil pensoit avant que partir dyci de renuncer au service de ce Roy et dresse la banniere blanche.'

54. Dr Ortiz to Charles V, 9 September 1533, British Museum, Add. MSS 28,586, fol. 1.

55. E. Chapuis to Charles V, 11 February 1534, Vienna Archives, P.C. 229, i. fol. 32.

56. Dr Ortiz to Charles V, 24 March 1534, British Museum, Add. MSS 28,586, fol. 191.

57. E. Chapuis to N. de Granvelle, 23 March 1535, Vienna Archives, P.C. 229½, iii. fol. 1: 'Ces jours la concubine a suborne ung que dit avoir eu revelacion de dieu que estoit impossible quelle conceust enfans pendant que les dictes dames seroint en vie. Je doubte quelle laura faict parler au Roy et ces jours elle la envoye a Cremuel. Elle ne cesse de lautre couste de dire quelles sont rebelles et traictresses meritant la mort.'

58. E. Chapuis to Charles V, 25 July 1535, Vienna Archives, P.C. 229½, i. fol. 107: 'Elle ne cesse de cryer apres ledict Roy quil ne faict bien ny prudemment soufrir vivre lesdictes royne et princesse que meritoint beaulcop plus la mort que ceulx quavoient este executer.'

59. E. Chapuis to Charles V, 29 August 1534, Vienna Archives, P.C. 229, i. No. 53: 'Et quant cela ne seroit la mort de la Royne et de la princesse amortiroit tout car cela estant yl ne resteroit aulcune querelle.'

60. E. Chapuis to Charles V, 23 March 1535, Vienna Archives, P.C. 229½, i. fol. 59: 'Me repliquant de nouveau quel domaige ne dangier seroit que la dicte princesse feast morte oyres que le peuple en murmurast et quelle raison auroit V^{re} M^{te} en faire cas.'

61. E. Chapuis to Charles V, 17 A.pril 1535, Vienna Archives, P.C. 229½, i. fol. 68. Cromwell said: 'Que la princesse estoit celle que mettoit la difficulte et que troubloit les affaires et que pleust a Dieu – il ne ousa dire plus avant mays aussy ny estoit il besoing.'

62. E. Chapuis to Charles V, 23 March 1535, Vienna Archives, P.C. 229½, i. fol. 59: 'Ains luy feist signiffier par sa gouvernante quil navoit pire enemys au monde quelle et quelle estoit cause quil estoit mal de la pluspart des princes chrestiens, et ce declairoit le dict Roy publiquement quest bien pour donner cueur et ardiesse a ceulx que luy vouldroient machiner quelque chose.'

63. E. Chapuis to Charles V, 16 December 1533, Vienna Archives, P.C. 228, i. fol. 143: 'La princesse, laquelle, comme il est a doubter et croire, veullent faire mourrir ou de deul ou daultre sorte ou faire renoncer son droict ou marier bassement ou la fere tresbucher en lascivuite pour avoir occasion de lexereder et faire tout aultre mauvais traictenient;' and E. Chapuis to N. de Granvelle, 17 January 1534, Vienna Archives, P.C. 229, ii. fol. 6: 'Monsgr lon ma dit que ce Roy vouloit faire dyvorcer le comte de Nortambellan davec sa femme et luy donner la princesse. Je crois bien que sil estoit sans femme que le Roy luy bailleroit vollentiers ladicte princesse pour les respectz que Vous escripray une autre fois, ce sont choses estranges mais actendu les precedentes il ne sen fault esbayr.'

64. E. Chapuis to Charles V, 11 February 1534, Vienna Archives, P.C. 229, i. fol. 32: 'Javoye aussi pense pour aultre remede que la princesse (apres avoir faict solempnes et suffisantes protestacions de la force que luy est faicte et du dangier apparent ou elle estoit) quelle ouffert au Roy destre contente de non estre appelle princesse pourveu quelle feust en liberte daller resider avec la Royne sa mere. Mais se faisant il seroit paradventure dangier que la dicte Anne prit alors plus dardyment de executer sa maulvaise voulente craignant la reconciliation avec le pere et penseroit que a lheure a moindre soupcon elle pourroit ce faire soubz umbre damytie que maintenant ou la hayne et inimitie est ouverte... '

65. E. Chapuis to Charles V, 25 February 1535, Vienna Archives, P.C. 229½, i. fol. 13. Chapuis spoke to Cromwell: 'Louhant que ceste moderne gouvernante en deust avoir la charge que me semble le plus seur, car la luy ostant de la main il y auroit dangier que lon ne luy donnast quelque venin lent, ce, pendant quelle demeurra entre ses mains, je pense quelle ne vouldroit faire ne permettre telle chose pour la

suspicion quest desia contre elle. Il y a longtemps que luy ai faict dire par tierce main le mal que luy pourroit survenir mesadvenant de la dicte princesse, et ay aussy tenu main que le medecin du Roy luy a dit que ces jours le bruict estoit tout commung par Londres quelle avoit empoisonne la dicte princesse que la mise en une merveilleuse craincte de sorte quelle ne faict que plorer quant elle veoit la dicte princesse ainsy indisposee.'

66. Sir E. Chamberlain and Sir E. Bedingfield to Cromwell, 22 March 1535, R.O. Henry VIII, Treasury papers, No. 3907; and Sir William Fitzwilliam to Cromwell, Pocock, *Records*, vol. ii. No. cccliv.

67. E. Chapuis to Charles V, 16 July 1534, Vienna Archives P.C. 229, i. fol. 123.

68. E. Chapuis to Charles V, 27 July 1534, Vienna Archives, P.C. 229, fol. 124.

14. The Death of Catherine

1. E. Chapuis to Charles V, 6 November 1535, P.C. 229½, i. fol. 119: 'Sire tout a cest instant la marquise de excestre ma envoye dire que ce Roy a dernierement dict a ces plus privez conseillers quil ne vouloit plus demeurer es fascheries, crainctes et pensemens quil avoit de longtemps este a cause des Royne et princesse et quil [quilz] regardassent a ce prouchain parlement len faire quicte; jurant bien a certes et tres obstinement quil nactendroit plus longuement de y pourvoir.'

2. E. Chapuis to Charles V, 21 November 1535, Vienna Archives, P.C. 229½, i. fol. 137: 'Me fesant dire davantage icelluy personnaige que voyant ce Roy aucuns de ceulx auxquels il tenoit les susdicts propos larmoyer, il se print a dire quil ny convenoit ne larmes ne grymasses car oyres quil deust perdre sa courrone il ne layroit de mettre en effect et experience ce que dessus.'

3. E. Chapuis to N. de Granvelle, 21 November 1535, Vienna Archives, P.C. 229½, iii. fol. 30: 'Ce Roy puis quatre ou cinq jours devisant de la princesse avec quelcung deust dire que bientost il pourvoyroit quelle nauroit besoing ny de train ne de compaignie et quelle seroit dexemple pour monstrer a tout le monde que nul ne devoit desobeir aux loix et quil vouloit veriffier ce que avoit este predict de luy assavoir que a lentree de son regne il seroit doulx comme ung agneaul et a la fin il seroit pire que lyon.'

4. E. Chapuis to Charles V, 6 November 1535, *loc. cit.*: 'Et ce ma mande dire la marquise pour chose de croyre veritable comme evangile.'

5. E. Chapuis to Antoine Perrenot, 6 November 1535, Vienna Archives, P.C. 229½, iii. fol. 29: Il fault tenir pour chose plus que vraye ce que jescripz a sa maieste et croyre que ceste dyablesse de concubine ne cessera jusques elle ait une fin et soit quictes de ces pouvres bonnes dames a quoy elle travaille par tous les moyens quelle peult imaginer.'

6. E. Chapuis to Charles V, 21 November 1535, *loc. cit.*: 'Sire ce sont choses par trop estranges execrables et pource mal aisees a croyre, mais considerant ce que yci est passe et passe journellement, la continuacion est longtemps de telles menasses; et davantaige la concubine que pieca a conjure et conspire la mort des dictes dames et que ne pense a rien tant qua les faire despescher est celle que mande commande et gouverne le tout et a laquelle le dict Roy ne scauroit contredire.'

7. E. Chapuis to Charles V, 6 and 21 November 1535, *loc. cit.*

8. E. Chapuis to Charles V, 21 November 1535, *loc. cit.*: 'Le cas est fort dangereux et fort a doubter il voudra comme jay desia autrefois escript a Vostre Maieste faire participant voyre aucteurs de tel meschiefs ceulx de son parlement et estats du Royaulme afin que par ce moyen perdant lespoir de la clemence et misericorde de Vostre Maieste trestous fussent plus determines a se deffendre quant il en seroit besoing.'

9. E. Chapuis to Charles V, 13 December 1535, Vienna Archives, P.C. 229½, i. fol. 114: 'Sire estant il y a environ dix jours alle trouver Mre Crumuel tant pour le solliciter du payement de certains arreraiges de la Royne, que aussy entendre quelques nouvelles icelluy Crumuel me dit quil ne faysoit quachever de depescher ung homme pour advertyr le Roy son M^{re} de lindisposicion de la Royne qu se trouvoit tres malade; que furent les premieres nouvelles quen avoye ouyez. Je luy demandey licence pour

laller et mander visiter. Yl mottroya incontinent que y puisse envoyer des miens en depescha sur ce lettres, quant a mon aller quil en parleroit audt Sr Roy, et a son retour de la court me resouldroit de lintencion et voulente dud. Sr Roy.'

10. E. Chapuis to Charles V, 13 December 1535, Vienna Archives, P.C. 229½, i. fol. 114: 'Ainsi que je sortois dudict Crumuel jay recu une lectre du medecin de la dicte Royne disant que a layde de dieu ce ne seroit rien de sa maladie... graces a dieu elle est tousiours depuis esmendee et soy treuve bien maintenant.'

11. E. Chapuis to Charles V, 9 January 1536, Vienna Archives, P.C. 230, i. fol. 3: 'Cestoit une douleur desthomac si aspre et violente quelle ne pouvoit rien retenir dans le corps.'

12. E. Chapuis to Charles V, 18 December 1535, Vienna Archives, P.C. 229½, i. fol. 141.

13. Catherine to Charles V, 13 December 1535, Vienna Archives, P.C. 229½, ii. fol. 68.

14. E. Chapuis to Charles V, 18 December 1535, Vienna Archives, P.C. 229½, i. fol. 141: 'Sire, inste de la Royne madame Vostre tante je fuz encoires hier faire rencharge a Monsgr le Secre Cremuel sur le changement de logis de la d. Royne, et pour luy faire avancer pour ses festes ce peu de reste de ses arreraiges dont cy devant ay escript a V^{re} M^{te}.'

15. Philip Grenacre to Montesa, British Museum, Add. MSS 25,114, fol. 117: 'Et sella a cause de unne tres grande doleur de son estomak avec ung soubglon que ung dict nicquet que le tient contignualment.'

16. E. Chapuis to Charles V, 30 December 1535, Vienna Archives, P.C. 229½, i. fol. 151.

17. E. Chapuis to Charles V, 30 December 1535, Vienna Archives, P.C. 229½, i. fol. 151; and E. Chapuis to N. de Granvelle, 17 February 1536, Vienna Archives, P.C. 230, ii. fol. 5: 'Monseigneur jay cydevant oblye descripre comme ces festes de noel disant a ce Roy que mesbayssays que de tout le temps que maistre Crumuell et moy avons eu propoz sur la nouvelle intelligence na oncques ouvert nul party, il maffirma plusieurs foys que si, voyre plus que raysounable, et que en ce Cremuel sestoit advance plus que ne devoit, et luy demandant la specification dudict party, ou de honte ou je ne scay pourquoy a pene me scavoit le dict Roy achever de dire que cestoit du mariaige de sa petite fille, a quoy luy respondit quil estoit vray que le dict Cremuel men avoit parle, sed verecunde et tymide ac si porrigeret assem elephanto de sorte que ne le tenoyt pour estre dict mais puisque luy mesme lavoit declare quen rescriproye a toutes aventures avec le surplus des nouveaulx propoz quil mavoit tenu et ne me semble en rien luy rejecter le dict party pour non le desperer de navoir moyen de reconsiliacion et amytie avec Sa Maieste et quil feust contrainct traicter avec les francais.'

18. E. Chapuis to Charles V, 30 December 1535, *loc. cit.*: 'Sire a la fin le dict Sr Roy me vint a dire quil pensoit que la Royne quil ne nomma que madame ne le feroit icy lodgement et que venant a morir V. M. naura cause de se empescher des affaires de ce royaulme et se pourra tenir par le bec des poursuites faictes en ce negoce. Je luy dit que la mort de lad. Royne ne pouvoit en rien prouffiter, et que en tous advenements la sentence estoit necessaire.'

19. E. Chapuis to Charles V, 9 January 1536, *loc. cit.*: and Sir Edward Chamberlain and Sir Edmund Bedingfield to Cromwell, 5 January 1536, British Museum, Cotton MSS Otho C. x. fol. 215.

20. E. Chapuis to Charles V, 30 December 1535, *loc. cit.*: 'Sire estant party dud. Sr Roy il me feist rappeller par le due de Suffocq pour me dire que en cest instant luy estoint venues nouvelles que la Royne estoit en extreme et que a peyne la trouveraije en vie, disant davantaige que cela seroit hoster lempeschement que mestoient les scrupules dentre V. M. et luy.'

21. E. Chapuis to Charles V, 30 December 1535, *loc. cit.*: 'Je luy demanday licence que la princesse puist aller veoir la Royne sa mere ce quil refusa de prime face et luy ayant fait quelques remonstrances yl dit que bien yl y penseroit et auroit adviz. Lad. princesse avoit este dadvis que feisse telle requeste.'

22. E. Chapuis to Charles V, 9 January 1536, Vienna Archives, P.C. 230, i. fol. 3. Chapuis says that having stayed four days at Kimbolton he took leave of the queen on Tuesday. He must therefore have arrived on Saturday morning, the first of January, not on the second, as Chamberlain and Bedingfield wrote.

23. E. Chapuis to Charles V, 9 January 1536, Vienna Archives, P.C. 230, i. fol. 3. 'Et du moins quand il plairoit a dieu la prandre a sa part ce luy seroit consolacion de pouvoir mourir entre mes braz et non point la desemparer comme une beste.'

24. *Ibid.*: 'Aussy pour sa plus grande consolation que le d. Sr. Roy estoit tres desplaisant de son indisposicion.'

25. E. Chapuis to Charles V, 9 January 1536, *loc. cit.*: 'Sur ce luy suppliay vouloir prendre cueur et sefforcer pour guerir et sy elle ne le vouloit faire pour aultre quelle considerast que de sa salut et vie dependoit ung tres grand bien pour lunion et tranquillite de la chrestiennete, pour la persuasion de quoy usay plusieurs propoz, comme yl avoit este preadvise par interposite personne entre la Royne et moy; et ce affin que mon conducteur et aucuns en eussent peu faire le rapport ou estoit besoing et que par tel moyen lon eust plus de regard a la conservacion de sa vie;' and Chamberlain and Bedingfield to Cromwell, 5 January 1536, *loc. cit.*

26. Chamberlain and Bedingfield to Cromwell, 5 January 1536, *loc. cit.*

27. *Ibid.*: and E. Chapuis to Charles V, 9 January 1536, *loc. cit.*

28. E. Chapuis to Charles V, 9 January 1536, *loc. cit.*: Ses devises estoient… soy quereller de sa deffortune et de celle de la princesse sa fille et pareillement de la tardance de remede des affaires, dont tant de gens de bien avoient soufferts en la personne et biens et tant de ames sen alloient en perdicion… se tenant par avant en doubte et scrupule de conscience pour estre les dicts maulx precede a loccasion de son affaire.'

29. E. Chapuis to Charles V, 9 January 1536, *loc. cit.*

30. Chamberlain and Bedingfield to Cromwell, 5 January 1536, *loc. cit.*

31. E. Chapuis to Charles V, 9 January 1536, *loc. cit.*: 'Ainsy prins mon congie delle le mardy au soir la laissant bien allegre et le mesme soir la veiz rire deux ou troys foys, et environ demy heure que fust party delle elle voulust encoires soy recreer avec ung de mes gens que faict du plaisant.'

32. E. Chapuis to Charles V, 9 January 1536, *loc. cit.*: 'Je demanday par plusieurs fois au medecin syl y avoit quelque suspicion de venin, il me dit quil sen doubtoit car depuis quelle avoit beu dune cervoise de galles elle navoit fait bien et quil falloyt que ce fust poyson limitee et artificieuse car il ne voit les signes et apparences de simple venin…'

33. E. Chapuis to N. de Granvelle, 21 January 1536, Vienna Archives, P.C. 230, i. fol. 21: 'Javoye appointe avec le medecin de la Royne, que survenant quelque danger en elle il se souvint et tinsse main quelle affirmat in extremis quelle navoyt oncques este cogneue du prince artus.'

34. E. Chapuis to Charles V, 9 January 1536, *loc. cit.*: Crumuel… ma envoye dire les tres griefves tres douleureuses et tres lamentables nouvelles du trespaz de la feue bonne tres vertueuse et tres saincte Royne que feust vendredi lendemain des roys environ les deux heures apres midy.'

35. E. Chapuis to Charles V, 21 January 1536, Vienna Archives, P.C. 230, i. fol. 7: 'Le jour des Roys… sur le soir elle seulle sans ayde de personne se peignant lya ses cheveulx et saccoustra la teste; et le lendemain environ une heure apres minuit elle commenca a demander quelle heure sestoit et si le jour approuchoit et de ce senquist elle plusieurs foys dempuis, et non pour aultre comme a la fin elle desclayra synon pour pouvoir ouyr messe et recepvoir le sainct sacrement. Et combien que levesque de Landafs son confesseur se offrye a dire messe avants les quatres heures, elle ne le voulust permettre, allegant plusieurs raysons et auctorites en latin pourquoy il ne se debvoit faire. Venant le jour elle ouyst sa messe et receu son sainct sacrement avec une ferveur et devotion quil nest possible de plus et dempuis continua dire plusieurs belles oraysons, et prier les assistans quilz voulsissent pryer et faire pryer pour le salut de son ame et que Dieu voulsist perdonner au Roy son mary le tord et sans rayson quil luy avoit faict et que sa divine bonte le voulsist inspirer au droit chemin et luy donner bon conseil.'

36. *Ibid.*, and Account of Catherine's Burial sent by Chapuis, Vienna Archives, P.C. 230, iv. fol. 1: 'Pource quellast a ceste heure la ordonne faire une escripture a son nom adressant au Roy comme a son mary et a lambassadeur de la Maieste de lempereur son nepveux laquelle elle souscripvit et signa par telles mots: Katherine Royne dangleterre;' and Catherine to Henry VIII, British Museum, Cotton MSS, Otho C.X. fols. 216, 217.

37. Bedingfield and Chamberlain to Cromwell, 7 January 1536, *State Papers*, vol. i. p.452.

38. E. Chapuis to Charles V, 21 January 1536, *loc. cit.*: 'En apres elle receu lextreme unction respondant elle mesme a tout loffice tres bien et tres devotement.'

39. E. Chapuis to Charles V, 21 January 1536, *loc. cit.*: 'Le Roy le samedi quil eust la nouvelle il dit louhe soit Dieu quy nous a libere de toute suspicion de guerre et que le temps estoit venu quil conduyroit mieulx les francois que jusques icy car doubtant quil ne se ralye avec Vostre Maieste puisque la cause que troubloit lamytie estoit estainte ils feroint tout cequil vouldroit.'

40. *Ibid.*: 'Sire il nest a penser la joye que ce Roy et les faulteurs de ce concubinage ont monstre de la mort de la dite bonne Royne specialement le comte de Vulcher et son fils que deurent dire que estoit dommaige que la princesse ne luy tinsse compaignie.'

41. E, Chapuis to Charles V, 21 January 1536, *loc. cit.*: 'Le jour suibvant que fust le dymanche ce Roy fust tout accoustre de jaune de pied en cap ce ne fust la plume blanche quil avoit au bonnet, et fust la petite bastarde conduitte a la messe avec trumpettes et autres grans triumphes. Lapres dine le Roy se trouva en la sale ou dancoient les dames et la comme transporte de joye fist plusieurs choses a la fin il fust querre sa petite bastarde et la pourtant entre ses bras yl lalloit monstrant a lung puis a lautre. Les jours ensuyvant depuis il en a use correspondentement et si a couru quelques lances a grinuyc.'

42. *Ibid.*: 'Plusieurs deulx confessent voire sement que le regret est cause de sa mort et ce pour exclure la suspicion du surplus'... il n'est a croyre... lindignacion quilz ont contre le Roy luy donnant la coulpe de sa mort laquelle partie imagine avoir ete par venin et les autres par regret... '

43. E. Chapuis to N. de Granvelle, 29 January 1536, Vienna Archives, P.C. 230, ii. fol. 2: 'Plusieurs suspeconnent que si la Royne est morte de poyson que Gregaire de Casal layt envoye par ung sien parent modeneys nomme gorron... et que ceulx cy pour avoir poison plus lente et que ne donnoit indice de soy lavoient envoye querre la; ce que ne puis croire bonnement car la chose seroit en trop grand dangier detre divulgee.'

44. E. Chapuis to Charles V, 21 January 1536, *loc. cit.*: 'Sire ce Roy et la concubine, impacient de plus longue tardance voyant mesmement que en Rome lon procedoyt a certes et que y allant Vostre Maieste les provisions se renforceroint, ils ont voulu vuyder le proces de la bonne Royne comme yl est apparent par ce que Vostre Maieste verra cy apres.'

45. E. Chapuis to Charles V, 9 January 1536, loc. cit.: 'Sil viennent a louvrir lon en verra les indices.'

46. Chamberlain and Bedingfield to Cromwell, 7 January 1536, *State Papers*, i. p.452.

47. E. Chapuis to Charles V, 21 January 1536, *loc. cit.*: 'La bonne Royne expira deux heures apres midi et dedans huict heures apres elle feust ouverte par le commandement de ceulx quen avoient la charge de la part de ce Roy et ne fust permis que le confesseur ne medecin de la Royne y assista ne personne du monde, synon le feseur de chandelles de la mayson et ung sien serviteur et ung compaignon lesquels louvrirent.'

48. *Ibid.*: 'Lequel sortant de faire la dicte ouverture vint a declairer au dict evesque de Landaf confesseur de la dicte Royne, mais en grand secret comme chose ou yl luy alloit la vie, quil avoit trouve le corps de la dicte Royne et tous les membres interieulx tant sains et nets quil nestoit possible de plus excepte le cueur lequel estoit tout neoir et hideux a veoir, et que voyant que ores que il le avoit tres fort lave en trois eaue il ne changeoit point de couleur, il le fendit par le milieu et trouva le dedans de la

mesme couleur laquelle aussy peu se voulsist changer pour laver que feit, et dit aussy que trouva certaine chose noire toute ronde questoit tres fort attache au dehors dudict cueur.'

49. E. Chapuis to Charles V, 21 January 1536, *loc. cit.*: 'Interrogeant mon homme le medecin si la Royne estoit morte de poison il luy respondist que la chose estoit trop verifiee par ce que en avoit este dit a levesque confesseur, et quant cela neust este descouvert la chose estoit assez clair considerant le discours qualite et accidens de la maladie.'

50. *Ibid.*: 'Et oires que ce ne soint berbiers ne sirurgiens touttefois ils ont souvent faict tel office, aumoings le principal… '

51. E. Chapuis to Charles V, 21 January 1536, *loc. cit.*

52. E. Chapuis to Charles V, 29 January 1536, Vienna Archives, P.C. 230, i. fol. 22: 'Je suis esbay oyres que ce Roy meust permis y envoyer les susdicts que lon leur a permis entrer aussy peu que mes gens; lon la garde de parler au monde mais elle sen revanche bien… '

53. E. Chapuis to Charles V, 7 March 1536, Vienna Archives, P.C. 229½, i. fol. 20: 'Ce Roy doubte que le medecin de la dicte feue royne vuille desloger dicy et tache le plus quil peult pour y obvier de retirer le dict medecin a son service ou du moings lentretenir yci quelque temps; et pour traicter dudict affaire cremuel ma a ce matin envoye prier luy envoyer ledict medecin, auquel il a faict plusieurs remonstrances pour accepter ledict service du roy son maistre, et luy respondant icelluy medecin que acceptant si soubdainement ledict service ce seroit donner occasion au monde de mal penser et mal dire… ledict Cremuel replicqua… que cependant le dict Sr Roy feroit donner secretement bon traictement audict medecin lequel touteffois ne sest voulu resoldre, remectant le tout a mon advis.'

54. *Ibid.*: 'Sire levesque de Landaf confesseur de la feue Royne dangleterre… se deslibera le propre jour de la date de mes dernieres lectres que furent du XXVe du passe de vuyder secretement de ce royaulme et sen retirer pour quelque temps en flandres ou en aragon dont yl est natifs ayant premierement este devers V^re M^te et devers Sa S^re mais il porgecta et dressa si mal et si symplement son cas, quil fust descouvert et constitue prisonnier dans la tour de ceste cite et ne scait lon encoires quelle issues auront ses affaires, du moings je pense quilz ne le permectront sortir de ce Royaulme pour craincte quil ne sollicite ou dise quelque chose contre eulx.'

55. E. Chapuis to Charles V, 19 May 1536, Vienna Archives, P.C. 230, i. fol. 82: 'Sire le mesme soir que la dicte concubyne feust menee a la tour allant le due de Richemont donner le bonsoir au Roy et luy demander la benediction a la coustume dangleterre, le dict Roy se print a larmoyer, disant que luy et sa sueur, enctendant la princesse, estoient bien tenus a dieu davoir eschapper les mains dicelle mauldicte et veneficque putain quavoit delibere les faire empoisonner; dont fault il dire que le dict Roy en scavoit quelque chose.'

56. *Ibid.*: 'Ce principallement dont elle fust chargee, estoit… quelle avoit receu et donnee certaines medailles au dict Noris que se pouvoint ainsi interpreter quelle avoyt faict empoysonner la feue Royne et machine de fayre le mesme a la princesse.'

15. Jane Seymour

1. Cromwell to Gardiner and Wallop, 8 January 1536, British Museum, Add. MSS vol. 25,114, fol. 126.

2. Gardiner to Cromwell, 21 October 1535, R.O, Henry VIII, box S.

3. Memoir by N. de Granvelle, *Papiers d'etat de Granvelle*, vol. ii. p.395.

4. E. Chapuis to Charles V, 10 February 1536, Vienna Archives, P.C. 230, i. fol. 26.

5. E. Chapuis to Charles V, 17 February 1536, Vienna Archives, P.C. 230, i. fol. 30.

6. Chabot de Brion to Cardinal du Bellay, 3 and 10 December 1535, Paris, Bibl. Nat, MSS Fr. vol. 19,577.

7. Cardinal du Bellay and Denonville to Francis I, 22 November 1535, Paris, Bibl. Nat. MSS Fr. vol. 5499, fol. 2446: 'Nous vous envoyons Sire le double de la dicte

sentence conceue ainsi que dict est, qui este telle que jamais aultre nen approchera. Il nous semble bien que en quelque evenement que ce soit il faut pour vous quelle soit fort rigoureuse mais il est a notter quil y a aulcuns articles qui sont si expressement couchez pour vous, que ung aveugle verroit quilz ne sont mis a aultre effect que pour Vous faire perdre par necessite ou le pape ou le roy dangleterre.'

8. Chabot de Brion to Cardinal du Bellay, 10 December 1535, *loc. cit.*

9. Henry VIII to Gardiner and Wallop, 4 January 1536, British Museum, Add. MSS vol. 25,114, fol. 119.

10. Johann von Werden to Duke Albrecht of Prussia, 4 December 1535, G. Waitz, *Luebeck unter Juergen Wullenwever*, vol. iii. p.470: 'Genedyger furst, ich befynde bey myr awssz mennychfeltygen ursachen, dasz eynen hemlyche swynde practicke zwyschen dem konynge zu Engelandt Wollenweffer unnd Merckus Meyer musz seyn geweszen; szo werde ich berycht, wyhe meyn g. h. von Bremen inhnen geret zu peynlycher froge hot stellen lasszen;' and the Bishop of Ermeland to Duke Albrecht of Prussia, 13 December 1535, G. Waitz, *Luebeck unter Juergen Wullenwever*, vol. iii. p.471.

11. Examination of J. Wullenwever, 31 December 1535, and 1 January 1536, G. Waitz, *Luebeck unter Juergen Wullenwever*, vol. iii. pp.475–7.

12. Henry VIII to Christoph, Archbishop of Bremen, 15 December 1535, Buchholtz, *Geschichte der Regierung Ferdinand I.*; vol. ix. p.351: 'Intelleximus V. R. D... praeter fas et aequum dilectum amicum nostrum Georgium Wolweber a suo itinere interceptum... Modus hic agendi indignior est, quam suo intimi nostri amici tractare debeant iniquiorque et inhumanior quam nostra in cives vos benevolentia expectasset. Caeterum... eam impense rogamus ut velit eum e carceribus statim liberare; alioquin eandem R. D. V. neutiquam ignorare volumus, nos hac injuria... provocatos parem vicissitudinem in tot, quot hic adsunt Bremenses cives esse ostensuros... gravissime nos pati tam duras injurias in amicos nros a quocunque inferri.'

13. Translation of Bonner and Cavendish's letter to the Senate of Bremen, 7 January 1536, G. Waitz, *Luebeck unter Juergen Wullentwever*, vol. iii. p.473: 'Dieweil doch derselbige furtrefflich berumbter Mann sein lebenlang nichts dergleichenn verschuldet hat... Dann sein ko. Mᵗ hat beschlossenn solichs an allenn Bremischen kauffleuten in Enngelandt zu rechen.'

14. Henry VIII, to the Archbishop of Bremen, 10 February 1536, printed by G. Waitz, vol. iii. pp.473, 474, according to the draft in British Museum, Cotton MSS Vitellius, B. xxi. fol. 97, and extracted by Buchholtz, vol. ix. p.352, from the original: 'Nullum ideo jus in eo detinendo D.V. competit... quin potius ejus partes essent, meminisse synceram ac firmam inter Cesarem et nos amicitiam esse, eoque jure famulum hunc nrum criminis causa (quod tam atrociter illi a vobis impingitur) ad veritatem perspecta, in Cesaris manum et arbitrium multum quam vos justius nos posse consignare, vel admissi in Cesam. Mm. (quem ut fratrem amamus) facinorus si reus convincatur, nos esse de eo supplicium pro culpa exacturos... D.V. ... in admissi sacrilegii apertam labem incurrisse patebit ... nil quoque nos obstare videmus, quomimus tantam injuriam et indignitatem, quacunque ratione possimus, et in quoscunque id commodum videbitur, retaliemus.'

15. Christoph of Bremen to Henry VIII, 1 March 1536, Buch holtz, *Geschichte der Regierung Ferdinand* I, vol. ix. pp. 352–4: 'So schmeckt solch Schreiben mer nach einer betrolichen herben Absag wider uns und die Unsern... so haben wir auch... als ein Fuerst des h. R. Reichs von kays. Maj. unser hohe und nider Gericht und Regalie krafft derselben einen Uebelthetter rechtfertigen zu lassen uns wol gepuret... den wuerden wir verursacht, solche hochgedachten unsern Obrigkeiten und gemeinen Stenden des h. R. Reichs anzuzeigen und gleichmessig Anhaltung Hilff und Beswerde ueber E. k. M. Underthanen und Verwandten zu Waszer unde Lande wo die angetroffen moechten werden, Uns und den Unsern zu gestatten zu bitten... '

16. Bonner and Cavendish to Christian III of Denmark, 13 March 1536, British Museum, Cotton MSS Vitellius, B. xxi. fol. 127, printed by G. Waitz, vol. iii. p.474,

but wrongly taken by him to be a letter to Henry VIII: 'Quid vero turpius, quam sub titulo publico privatam injuriam et contumeliam ulcisci, denique que tua sunt querere, non que Jhesu Christi ?... Nunc autem oramus et obtestamur tuam Celsitudinem ut hanc effrenatorum hominum licentiam, quo in bonorum omnium perniciem grassatur et in proscriptionem evangelii sedulo laborat, tua auctoritas non compescat modo...'

17. Examination of J. Wullenwever, 27 January 1536, G. Waitz, *Luebeck unter Juergen Wullenwever*, vol. iii. pp. 490–6.

18. Juergen Wullenwever to Joachim Wullenwever, G. Waitz, vol. iii. p.483: 'Du moest dorch den marckgreven hartych Hynryck styllen, edder ick kame umme den hals, wenne ick ock twe konnynge von Engelant tho bate hadde.'

19. The Elector of Saxony and the Landgrave of Hessen to Henry VIII, 23 December 1535, *State Papers*, vol. vii. p.538.

20. Proposals of the Elector and Landgrave, 25 December 1535, *Corp. Ref.* vol. ii. No. 1383.

21. Answer to the proposals of the Elector and Landgrave, Burnet, *Collectanea*, part iii. book iii. No. 45.

22. Answer of the king's ambassadors, Burnet, *Collectanea*, part iii. book iii. No. 46. This paper is a draft of the answer which the ambassadors were to make, but which they subsequently had to alter.

23. E. Chapuis to Charles V, 29 January 1536, Vienna Archives, P.C. 230, i. fol. 22: 'La concubine de ce Roy nonobstant quelle eust monstre grande joye des nouvelles du trespas de la bonne Royne pour lesquelles elle avoit donne ung bon present au messaigier...'

24. Decipher of a note of Chapuis, Vienna Archives, P.C. 229½, iii. fol. 20: 'Le roy dangleterre a cuyde tuer son fol quest ung innocent pour ce quil disoit et parloit bien des Royne et princesse et disoit Ribalde a la concubine et bastarde a sa fille et a este banni de court et la recelle le grand escuyer.'

25. Indictment found at Deptford, 11 May 1536, R.O. Baga de Segretis, Pouch ix. Membrane 21.

26. E. Chapuis to Charles V, 29 January 1536, *loc. cit.*: 'Touteffois elle avoit souvent larmoye soy doubtant quil en oseroit faire delle comme de la bonne Royne.'

27. E. Chapuis to Charles V, 21 January 1536, *loc. cit.*

28. E. Chapuis to Charles V, 21 January 1536, *loc. cit.*: 'La concubine a ce que ma envoye dire la dicte princesse luy a fait gecter la premiere amorse et luy a fait dire par sa tante quest gouvernante de la dicte princesse que si elle vouloit se demettre de son obstinacion et obeyr comme une bonne fille a la volente du Roy son pere quelle luy seroit la meilleure amye du monde et comme une autre mere et procureroit luy faire avoir ce quelle scauroit demander, et que si elle vouloit venir en court elle seroit exemptee luy haulser la quehue de sa robe et si la mesneroit tousjours a son couste...'

29. *Ibid*.: 'Et ne cesse la dicte gouvernante et a chauldes larmes de prier la dicte princesse davoir regard aux dictes affaires a quoy na aultre respondu la dicte princesse synon quil ny avoit fille au monde que voulsust estre plus obeissante a son pere en ce quelle pourroit faire saulvant son honneur et sa conscience...'

30. Anne Boleyn to Lady Shelton, Vienna Archives, P.C. 230, i. fol. 34.

31. E. Chapuis to Charles V, 10 February 1536, Vienna Archives, P.C. 230, i. fol. 26.

32. *Ibid*. and Chapuis to Charles V, 24 February 1536, Vienna Archives, P.C. 230, i. fol. 42: 'Sire jentends de plusieurs de ceste court quil y a passe trois mois que ce Roy na parle dix fois a la concubine et quant elle abortit il ne luy tint guayres aultres propoz synon quil voyoit bien que dieu ne luy vouloit donner enfans masles, et en sen allant comme pour despit il luy dit assez de male grace que aprez quelle seroit releve quil parleroit a elle et me semble que la dicte concubyne disoit deux choses estre en cause du dict inconvenient, lune la chute du Roy, lautre pour ce que lamour quelle luy pourtoit estoit trop plus grande plus fervente que celle de la feue Royne, de sorte que le cueur luy rompoit quant elle veoit quil en aimoyt des autres. Duquel propoz le dict

Roy a este fort marry et en fait bien le semblant veu que ces jours de feste et bonne chiere yl est yci et laissa lautre a Grinuich la ou autrefois ne la pouvoit habandoner une heure.'

33. E. Chapuis to Antoine Perrenot, 18 May 1536, Vienna Archives, P.C. 230, ii. fol. 20.
34. E. Chapuis to Charles V, 1 April 1536, Vienna Archives, P.C. 230, i. fol. 50.
35. E. Chapuis to N. de Granvelle, 18 March 1536, Vienna Archives, P.C. 230, ii. fol. 10: 'Les nouvelles amours de ce roy avec la demoyselle dont ait cydevant escript vont tousiours en avant a la grosse raige de la concubyne.'
36. E. Chapuis to Charles V, 29 January 1536, *loc. cit.*; and E. Chapuis to Antoine Perrenot, 29 January 1536, Vienna Archives, P.C. 230, ii. fol. 1: 'Si le cas me preignoit bien comme ceulx cy sont barbares et diaboliques vous verriez de terribles exclandres toutesfois le mandant sa maieste lon postposera le tout, je dis de mon couste.'
37. E. Chapuis to Charles V, 29 January 1536, *loc. cit.*: 'A ce matin lon mest venu dire de la part de la dame mencionne en mes lectres du six de novembre et de son mariz quilz estoient advertiz dung des principaulx de court que ce Roy avoit deu dire a quelcung par grand secret et comme en confession quil avoit faict ce mariaige seduict et contrainct de sortileges et que a ceste cause yl tenoit ce dict mariaige nul et que bien le monstroit dieu que ne leur permectoit avoir lignee masculine et quil tenoit quil en pouvoit prendre une autre, ce quil donnoit a entendre avoyt envie de faire. La chose mest bien difficile a croyre, oyres quelle soit venue de bon lieu.
38. E. Chapuis to Charles V, 24 February 1536, *loc. cit.*
39. Cardinal du Bellay to the Cardinals of Lorraine and of Tournon, 22 December 1535, Paris. Bibl. Nat. MSS François, vol. 5499, fol. 275–6: 'Lequel Trany estoit pour faire ce que les serviteurs du Roy luy eussent dict et la pluspart des aultres avec et jen avois seurete… mais ayant la nuict precedente et a propoz receu ses lettres du troysieme je suyvy son intention car nottez que jeusse peu faire tourner le de sur ung coste ou sur lautre'… 'le jour du feu Trivoice sen sceut tres bien exempter depuis que je luy euz faict responce quil ny alloit de linterestz du Roy ne pro ne contra.'
40. Cardinal du Bellay and C. de Denonville to Francis I, 22 December 1535, Paris Bibl. Nat. MSS Français, vol. 5499, fols. 269 *b*: 'Le lendemain au matin fut mis sur le bureau laffaire dangleterre dont nous estions en grande peine. Et en icelluy y avons suivy vostre intention de poinct en poinct… La chose semble a chascun mal digeree et de mauvaise consequence, mais elle est selon vostre desseing; et presuposons bien que Vous estes content que la sentence soit si aigre dune part et si injuste de lautre que Vous puissiez Vous en ayder selon ce que Vos affaires le requerent. Si ainsi est Vous avez tres bien Vostre intendit.'
41. Cardinal du Bellay to the Cardinals of Lorraine and of Tournon, 22 December 1535, Paris, Bibl. Nat. MSS Français, vol. 5499, fol. 275–6: 'Jusques a Capua tous sont dadvis que non debere Incipi ab executione et que citatio seu monitio (?) deberet procedere sententiam maxime quum ageretur de novo et graviore delicto pro quo nondum Rex fuerat citatus.'
42. *Ibid.*: 'Capua mitiga encore plus les paines mais tolust la citation… '
43. *Ibid.*: 'Et aux aultres qui estoient Capua, Contarin, et Mantue pour ce quilz vouloient que, habenda esset Ratio temporum quum imminuta sit aliquo modo auctoritas sedis apostolice… Censuimus agendum nec provocandas omnes nationes In nos ob interdicta commertia.'
44. *Ibid.*: 'Et sur ce point fut le grand feu de la colere. Et Dieu scait sil menassa bien et reitera de nespargner empereurs, Roys et princes puisque Dieu la constitue sur eulx.'
45. Cardinal du Bellay to the Cardinals of Lorraine and of Tournon, 22 December 1535, Paris, Bibl. Nat. MSS Français, vol. 5499, fol. 275–6: 'Pour conclusion quil falloit quelle se despeschast et incontinent comme bien faicte, bien digeree et bien couchee et en bons termes quoy quon en dist et ne quon laccusast que plusieurs estoient davis de limer le style, et quil y avoit commis viros omni ecceptione majores et sic est finis.'

46. *Ibid.*: 'Pource quaulcuns vouloient quon en advertist premierement le Roy et lempereur il sen courouca et dist lavoir desia faict et que le dict empereur avoit respondu que la ou il seroit icy procedde comme il doibt il monstreroit en lexecution quil est vrai advocat et protecteur de leglise et quil se y mecteroit jusques au bout. Et le Roy, et ne et ipsum frauderet sua laude, apres avoir fort blasme et abominez les meschancetez faict par le Roy dangleterre en avoyt promis aultant que dessuz moyennant que le dict empereur ny faillist de son coste.'
47. *Ibid.*: 'Si cela est vray je ne scais, car Monsr de Mascons ne moy nen sceumes jamais rien entendre de dela quelques instances que nous ayons faictes.'
48. Cardinal du Bellay to the Cardinals of Lorraine and of Tournon, 22 December 1535, Paris, Bibl. Nat. MSS Français vol. 5499, fol. 275–6: 'Campiege disoit considerandum esse ne fœderati principes lederentur presertim Rex Christianissimus, quem audiebat magnam amicitiam habere cum Rege Anglo et inter eos aliqua fœdera esse et pacta, qua ipse nesciret qua essent, ut esse solent inter principes amicos secreta.'
49. *Ibid.*: Capua en persuadant de incontinent donner la sentence dist: ne nobis, inquit, accidat ut accidisset Clementi nisi mature providisset. Clam quum essent qui ostenderent velle Ilium Reconciliare ecclesie et fingeretur mittendum mandatum, interim huc mitebat clam viros astutos qui facerent protestationes quod previdens Clemens subitum nec expectatis terminis pronuntiavit sententiam, illis deceptis qui his artibus eum volebant fallere. Voila ses motz.'
50. Cardinal du Bellay to the Cardinals of Lorraine and of Tournon, 22 December 1535, Paris, Bibl. Nat. MSS Français, vol. 5499, fol. 275–6: 'Et tamen, dist le pape perseverant en sa collere ou furie en tous propoz et contre chascun, ille idem nebulo ille maledictus vir etiam nunc est orator apud regem christianissimum.'
51. *Ibid.*: 'Concluant que le Roy avoit laisse a saproprier pour son filz de ung tel Royaulme que celuy dangleterre pour le respect du Sainct Siege pour aultant quaux conditions proposes par le dict Roy dangleterre il y avoit ung article qui de degre en degre a la fin engendroit par indirect quelque dangier de discorde a ladvenir entre ledict Sainct Siege et la France.'
52. Cardinal du Bellay to the Cardinals of Lorraine and Tournon, 22 December 1535, Paris, Bibl. Nat. MSB. Français, vol. 5499, fol. 275–6: 'Mais la nostre Sainct pere me vint rompre la parolle disant que le Roy avoit laisse de traicter pour ce que le Roy dangleterre voulait le duc dangoulesme pour ostage me replicquant par plusieurs foys et en collere quil le scavoit bien et eust vouluntiers dict mieulx que moy. A quoy je use en mes responces dhumilite non plus grande que je debvoye.'
53. *Ibid.*: 'Trany faisant le doyen mist peine de le rappaiser de sorte que pour ce coup nous ne feusmes poinct envoyez au chasteau Sainct Ange.'
54. Cardinal du Bellay and Denonville to Francis I, 22 December 1535, *loc. cit.*: 'Jay faict soubz main que la dicte sentence afin destre moins valide ne fust plus remise au consistoire et a nostre Sainct pere arreste en soy quelle passera oultre non en la forme que je Vous disoy premierement mays en celle que je Vous envoye le double cotte.'
55. Nicolas Raince to Cardinal du Bellay, 23 May 1536, Paris, Bibl. Nat. MSS Français, vol. 19,577.
56. N. Raince to Cardinal du Bellay, 3 Apri 1536, Paris, Bibl. Nat. MSS Français, vol. 19,577; and E. Chapuis to Charles V, 1 April 1536, *loc. cit.*
57. Viscount Hanart to the Empress, 10 March 1536, British Museum, Add. MSS 28,588, fol 226: 'Anoche despues de venido de la corte questa a VI leguas de aqui en el delfinado supe *que el cardinal de paris es venido en posta de Roma* dice el vulgo en esta villa que *viene... por miedo de sue malas platicas... en perjuycio* de Vras Majestades.'
58. Charles V to E. Chapuis, 13 April 1536, Vienna Archives, P.C. 230, iii. fol. 19.
59. E. Chapuis to Charles V, 24 February 1536.
60. E. Chapuis to Charles V, 24 February 1536: 'Je luy vins a dire de moimesme que pour retourner a renovacion de intelligence et amitie dont il mavoit parle, si Vostre Maieste comme prince tres catholique et protecteur de leglise requeroit prealablement

le Roy son maistre de soy remettre en lobeissance apostolique et reconciler a lunion de leglise et pareillement si demandoit Vostre Maieste la princesse estre declaree legitime et reintegre en son estat et tiercement si Vostre Maieste requeroit le Roy dangleterre dentrer en lighe contre le turcq pour y faire entrer la Germanie qua pieca ouffert une tresgrande ayde pour icelle entreprinse pourveu que les autres princes y entrevinssent et quartement si Vostre Maieste le requerroit de lighe generale offensive et deffensive contre ceulx que pourroient tenir et avoir tort de lung ou de lautre, quest ce que le dit Roy son maistre vouldroit responde et faire sur le tout.

61. *Ibid.*: 'Au regard de la princesse que maintenant estoit la propre et opportune sayson dentendre a pourvoir de remedier aux affaires de la dicte princesse au contantement de Vostre Maieste et que la porte en estoit ouverte.'

62. E. Chapuis to Charles V, 24 February 1536: 'Et aussy ceulx questoient comme il disoit de lautre part et faction cest assavoir le comte de Vulcher.

63. *Ibid.*: 'Que au surplus eusse bon expoir et que considerasse les merveilles quil avoit yci faictes depuis quil avoit eu le gouvernement des affaires du Roy son maistre.'

64. E. Chapuis to Charles V, 24 February 1536: Indorsement: 'Receues le 29eme de Mars a Gayette.'

16. Charles V & Anne

1. Charles V to E. Chapuis, 29 February 1536, Vienna Archives, P.C. 230, iv. fol. 5; and Lanz, *Correspondenz Kaiser Karls V*, vol. ii. p.212.

2. Charles V to E. Chapuis, 28 March 1536, Vienna Archives, P.C. 230, iv. fol. 12: 'Viyant le dit Roy dangleterre la dicte princesse ne peult pretendre davantaige ni a aultre action ny nous et autres ses parents pouvons passer plus avant quant a requerir dadvantage en sa faveur quoy quil soit des injures faictes a sa feue mere dont elle ne peut persister en bonne conscience a la vendicacion contre son dict pere ne encoires consentir quil se fist quant oires la vie de sa dicte feue mere fut este advancee sinistrement comme lon sen doubte et si lon veut poursuivre lexecucion de la sentence dudict divorce affin que le dict Sr Roy delaisse sa concubyne il se pourra marier marier [sic.] a aultre ou il est tout certain et evident que de lad. concubine il ne peut avoir lignee que empesche le droit de succesion de lad. princesse.'

3. Charles V to E. Chapuis, 28 March 1536, Vienna Archives, P.C. 230, iv. fol. 12: 'Et pourtant quant oires la d^{te} concubine ne se vouldroit contenter de lung ou lautre des moyens avantdits de la declaration ou suspencion que touteffois elle et touts ses adherens devront tenir pour tres grand bien pour soy quicter de la crainte et dangier ou continuellement ils sont et oultre ce voulsist requerir et pretendre plus pour sa fille et au dicts enfans quelle pourra avoir, ne fault point tant en faire rompre la pratique, mais assentir du tout ce aussy a quoy elle sarrestera, et aprez luy avoir remonstre ce que verrez servir aux propoz Vous remectre a nous en avertir si [non] que la chose soit par troup exhorbitante... '

4. Charles V to E. Chapuis, 28 March 1536, Vienna Archives, P.C. 230, iv. fol. 12: 'En vous aydant dudict Crumuell... et sil y a chose que doige estre tenue secrete ou dissimulee a la dicte concubine ou ses adherens il sen usera selon ce+.'

5. E. Chapuis to Charles V, 21 April 1536, Vienna Archives, P.C. 230, i. fol. 58.

6. E. Chapuis to N. de Granvelle, 18 March 1536, *loc cit.*

7. E. Chapuis to Charles V, 1 April 1536, *loc. cit.*: 'Sire tout a cest instant la marquise ma envoye dire ce que desia mavoit affirme maistre heliot ascavoir que ses jours passez estant ce Roy en ceste ville, et la demoyselle maistresse semel laquelle yl sert a grynuitz yl luy envoya une bourse pleine de souverains ensemble une lectre que la dicte demoyselle ayant baise la lectre la retourna au messagier sans la vouloir ouvrir et se gectant a genoulx elle supplia au dict messagier vouloir supplier au Roy de sa part vouloir considerer par sa prudence quelle estoit gentil-feme issue de bons et hounorables parens sans nul reproche et quelle navoit plus grande richesse en ce monde que son honneur, lequel pour mille mors elle ne vouldroit blesser et que syl luy vouloit faire quelque present

dargent elle luy supplioit que ce fust quand dieu luy enverroit quelque bon party de mariaige.'

8. E. Chapuis to Charles V, 1 April 1536, *loc. cit.*: 'Sire icelle marquise ma envoye dire que par ce lamour et fantaisie dicelluy Roy sestoit augmente vers la dicte demoiselle merveilleusement et quil luy avoit dit quelle en avoit use tres vertueusement et que pour luy donner a cognoistre quil ne laymoit synon damour honneste il ne deliberoit desormais de parler avec elle synon en presence de quelqun de ses parens et a ceste cause le dict Roy a faict desloger maistre cremuel dune chambre a laquelle le dict Seigneur Roy peut aller par certaines galleries sans estre veu ne apperçu, et illec a losge laisne frere de la dicte damoyselle avec sa femme pour illec faire venir la dite demoyselle...'

9. E. Chapuis to Charles V, 1 April 1536, *loc. cit.*: 'Laquelle est bien endoctrine de la pluspart des privez du Roy qui hayent la concubyne quelle ne doije en sorte du monde complaire a la fantaisie du Roy sy nest par tiltre de mariaige de quoy elle este toute resolue. Il luy est aussy conseille quelle die hardyment au Roy quelle abhominacion a tout ce peuple de ce mariage et que nul ne le tient pour legitime et au poinct quelle proposera la dicte affaire yl ny doit avoir que gens attiltres que proposeroient le mesmes pourveu que le Roy les contraigne sur le jurement et fidelites quilz luy ont, et desireroit ladicte Marquise que moy ou quelque autre de la part de Vostre Maieste tint la main audict affaire...'

10. E. Chapuis to Charles V, 7 March 1536, Vienna Archives, P.C. 229½ i. fol. 20.

11. E. Chapuis to Charles V, 18 March 1536, *loc. cit.*

12. Melanchthon to Camerarius, 5 February and 30 March 1536, and Melanchthon to Th. Vitus, 6 February 1536, *Corpus Reformatorum*, vol. iii. Nos. 1396, 1409, and 1397; and Opinion of Lutheran divines, Seckendorf, *De Lutheranismo*, p.112, etc.

13. E. Chapuis to Charles V, 1 Apri 1536, *loc. cit.*: 'Aussi sont les dicts prelats en besogne pour respondre a certaine escripture faite par luter et ses compaignons laquelle levesque ambassadeur de ce Roy estant avec eux a envoye par laquelle le dict luter et ses adherents concluent que le premier mariage fut tolerable et que fut tel ou non sans nul doubte la princesse estoit legitime et est vray que le dict ambassadeur pour complaire a son maistre a escript que combien quil pense que les dits luter et autres saichent lopposite de ce quilz avoient escript touttefois ilz ne le ousoint dire pour crainte de Vostre Maieste.'

14. E. Chapuis to Charles V, 1 April 1536, *loc. cit.*; and Cranmer to Cromwell, 29 March and 20 April, 1536, R.O. Cranmer Correspondence, Nos. 44 and 45.

15. *Ibid.*

16. E. Chapuis to Charles V, 1 April 1536, *loc. cit.*: 'Estant venu ces jours disner avec moy le jeusne Marquis, la veufve comtesse de Childra, monsieur de Montagu et certains autres gentilzhommes ledict sieur de Montagu apres plusieurs queremonies du desordre des affaires dyci me vint a dire que la concubyne et Cremuel estoient en picque et quil se bruyoit de quelque nouvel mariaige pour ce Roy, que conformoit a ce que mestoit escript de France...'

17. E. Chapuis to Charles V, 1 April 1536, *loc. cit.*: 'Et ce me disoit sy froydement quil me donnoit suspicion du contraire, mesmes que le me disant ne saichant quelle contenance tenir yl sappoya sur la fenestre ou nous estions mectant la main devant la bouche pour se garder de soubrire ou pour le couvrir, disant en apres que dune chose se pouvoient bien assurer les francois que advenant le cas que le dict Roy son maistre voulsist autre femme quil ne la yroit sercher vers eulx...'

18. *Ibid.*

19. E. Chapuis to Charles V, 2 May 1536, Vienna Archives, P.C. 230, i. fol. 80: 'Sire je tiens Vostre Maieste assez souvenante de ce quescripvis a icelle au commencement du mois passe touchant les propoz que je tins a maistre Cremuel sur le divorce de ce Roy davec la concubyne. Surquoy, depuis ayant entendu la volunte de la princesse, selon laquelle comme deslors escripviz entendoye me gouverner laquelle volunte estoit que deusse tenir main audict affaire principalement pour lhonneur et descharge de conscience du Roy son pere, et quelle ne socioit en facon du monde que

le dict Roy son pere puist avoir hoirs legittimes que luy hostassent la sucession, ne de toutes les injures faictes ne a elle ne a la feue Royne sa mere lesquellee en lhonneur de dieu elle perdonnoit de tresbon cueur a tout le monde, jay tenu plusieurs moyens pour ayder a leffect tant envers ledict maistre Cremuel que diverses autres personnes que me sembloit convenir... '

20. E. Chapuis to Charles V, 21 April 1536, Vienna Archives, P.C. 230, i. fol. 58: 'Avant que le Roy sortit pour aller a la messe Cremuel me vint demander de la part dudict Roy sy vouloit point aller visiter et baiser la dicte concubine, et que en ce feroit plaisir a icelluy Roy, touteffois quil sen remectoit a ma voulente... '

21. E. Chapuis to N. de Granvelle, 24 April 1536, Vienna Archives, P.C. 230, ii. fol. 16: 'Je reffusay de laller visiter jusques a ce queusse parle au Roy. Si jeusse veu quelque apparence ou espoir en la responce et propoz du Roy je fusse aller ouffrir non point deux seullement mais cent chandelles au diable ou diablesse combien que aussy une autre chose men faisoit perdre lenvye, assavoir quil me fust dit quelle nestoit fort en grace du Roy... '

22. E. Chapuis to Charles V, 21 April 1536, *loc. cit.*: Je fuz conduyt a la messe par le sieur de Rocheffort frere de la concubyne et venant le Roy a loffrande yl y eust grand concours de gens, et une partie pour veoir quelle mine la concubine et moy nous tiendrons. Elle en usa assez cortoisement car comme jestoys derrier la porte par ou elle enstroit elle se retournast du tout pour me faire la reverence conforme a celle que je luy fiz.'

23. E. Chapuis to N. de Granvelle, 24 April 1536, *loc. cit.*: 'Encoires que je ne baississe ne parlasse a la concubyne touteffois et la princesse et plusieurs autres bon personnaiges ont eu quelque mal a la teste des mutuelles et par honnestete inevitables reverences que furent faictes a leglise... '

24. E. Chapuis to Charles V, 21 April 1536, *loc. cit.*: 'Apres la messe le dict Roy sen alla disner au logis et chambre de la concubine ou tout le monde laccompaigna excepte moy que fuz conduit par Rocheffort a la chambre de presence dicelluy Roy ou disna avec touts les principaulx de la court, et a ce que ma dict quelque homme de bien la dicte concubyne interrogea le Roy pourquoy nestoit la entre comme faisoyent les autres ambassadeurs et que icelluy Roy avoit respondu que ce nestoit sans bon respect.'

25. E. Chapuis to Charles V, 21 April 1536, *loc. cit.*: 'Ce neantmoings a ce que ma dict personne que affirme lavoir ouy icelle concubyne apres disne deust dire que cestoit grande honte au Roy de France de ainsy traicter son oncle le due de Savoye et de vouloir movoir guerre contre Milan pour entrerompre lemprinse contre les Turcqs, et quil sembloit proprement que le dit Roy de France ennuye de sa vye a cause de ses maladies a envye dachever par guerre plus brefvement ses jours.'

26. *Ibid.*; and E. Chapuis to N. de Granvelle, 21 April 1536, Vienna Archives, P.C. 230, ii. fol. 14: 'Pour le saouler de gloire et non lirriter... '

27. E. Chapuis to N. de Granvelle, 21 April 1536, *loc. cit.*

28. E. Chapuis to Charles V, 21 April 1536, *loc. cit.*: 'Et la y eust de la dispute et courroux assez aigre comme il sembloit entre le dict Roy et Cremuel, et apres ung grand espace de temps le dict Cremuel romphant et grondisant se part du conclave de la fenestre ou estoit le dict Roy prenant excuse que estoit tant altere quil nen pouvoit plus, comme aussy estoit, et se alla asseoir sur ung coffre hors de laspect dudict Roy.'

29. E. Chapuis to Charles V, 21 April 1536, *loc. cit.*; and E. Chapuis to N. de Granvelle, 21 April 1536, *loc. cit.*

30. Francis I to J. de Dinteville and A. de Castelnau, 29 April 1536, Paris, Bibl. Nat. MSS Dupuis, vol. 547, fol. 303: 'Le Roy a tres bien entendu... les propoz et langaige que luy tint a son arrivee a Grenuic Mr de Norfort et lasseurance quil luy donna derechef que quelque praticque ou ouverture que le dict Empereur peust faire ne mettre en avant audit Roy dangleterre les choses ne seroient jamais autres quelles ont este par cydevant et sont de present entre son maistre et le dit sieur Roy... '

31. Francis I to J. de Dinteville and A. de Castelnau, 29 April 1536, Paris, Bibl. Nat. MSS Dupuis, vol. 547, fol. 303: 'Et pource diront iceulx Evesque de Tarbe et Bailly de Troyes audit sieur Roy dangleterre comme le Roy a tres bien entendu ce que ledit

de Tarbe luy a faict scavoir touchant la lettre que luy avoit dernierement escript ledit
Empereur contenant les cinq chefs et articles contenuz et declarez es lettres dudit
Evesque. Le premier faisant mencion du jour que devoit entrer icelluy Empereur a
Romme, le second du faict de la guerre que le Roy faict au duc de Savoye et la requeste
que icelluy Empereur faict au dit sieur Roy dangleterre a ce quil veuille interceder
envers le Roy pour icelluy duc de luy rendre et restituer ce qui a este gaigne sur luy.
Le tiers quil crainct que le Roy luy veuille faire la guerre a la duche de Milan et layde
quil luy demande advenant icelluy cas. Le quart quil veuille oblier ce qui est passe
entre eux pour raison de sa feue tante, estant a present cessee loccasion, le priant au
surplus pour lever et oster tous les suspecons et racines dinimitie et dissentions de
vouloir renouveller les viels traites de leur amitie et confederation, et le dernier quil
se delibere de dresser une armee contre le turcq pour la diffension de la chrestiennete,
priant icelluy Roy dangleterre de luy vouloir estre pour cest effect contribuable… '

32. Francis I to J. de Dinteville and A. de Castelnau, 29 April 1536, Paris, Bibl. Nat. MSS
Dupuis, vol. 547, fol. 303.

33. Statutes of the Realm, 27 Henry VIII, cap. 28.

34. E. Chapuis to Charles V, 1 April 1536, *loc. cit.*

35. E. Chapuis to Charles V, 29 April 1536, Vienna Archives, P.C. 230, i. fol. 78.

36. E. Chapuis to N. de Granvelle, 24 April 1536, Vienna Archives, P.C. 230, ii fol. 16.

37. E. Chapuis to Charles V, 29 April 1536, Vienna Archives, P.C. 230, i. fol. 78: 'Le frere
de monsieur de Montaguz me dit hier en disnant que avant hier que levesque de
Londres avoit este interrogue si ce Roy pourroit habandonner la dicte concubyne et
quil nen avoit point voulu dire son adviz ne le diroit a personne du monde que au seul
Roy et que avant de ce faire yl vouldroit bien espier la fantaisie dudict Roy vuillant
innuyr que le dict Roy pourroit laisser la dicte concubyne toutteffois connaissant
linconstance et mutabilite de ce Roy il ne se vouldroit mectre en dangier de la dite
concubyne. Ledict evesque a este la principale cause et instrument du premier divorce
dont de bon cueur il sen repent et de meilleur vouldroit poursuivre cestuy mesme a
cause que la dicte concubyne et toute sa race sont si habominablement lutheriens.'

38. E. Chapuis to Charles V, 6 June 1536, Vienna Archives, P.C. 230, i. fol. 92: 'Et que sur
le deplesir et courroux quil avoit eu sur la responce que le Roy son maistre mavoit
donne le tiers jours de pasques il se meist a fantaisie et conspira le dict affaire… '

17. The Arrest

1. R.O. Baga de Segretis, Pouch VIII, Membranes 10 and 14.

2. E. Chapuis to Charles V, 29 April 1536, *loc. cit.*

3. Henry VIII to Richard Pate, 25 April 1536, British Museum, Harleian MSS vol. 282,
fol. 7; and *State Papers*, vol. vii. p.683. The editors of the *State Papers* and Mr N.
Pocock ascribe this letter to the year 1537. That it belongs to the year 1536 is clear
from the letter written by Chapuis on 21 April.

4. E. Chapuis to Charles V, 29 April 1536, *loc. cit.*

5. E. Chapuis to Charles V, 29 April 1536, *loc. cit.*: 'Le grand escuyer maistre Caro eust
le jour Sainct George lordre de la jarretiere et fust subroge au lieu vacant par la mort
de monsieur de Burgain, qua este ung grand crevecueur pour le seigneur de Rocheffort
que le poursuyvoit mais encoires plus que la concubyne que na eust le credit le faire
donner a son dict frere, et ne tiendra audict escuyer que la dicte concubyne quelque
cousine quelle luy soit ne soit desarconnee et ne cesse de conseiller maistresse Semel
avec autres conspirateurs pour luy faire une venue et ny a point quatre jours que luy
et certains de la chambre ont mande dire a la princesse quelle feit bonne chiere et que
briefvement sa contrepartie mectroit de leau au vin car ce Roy estoit desia tres tant
tanne et ennuye de la concubyne qui nestoit possible de plus.'

6. Sir William Kingston to Cromwell, Cotton MSS, Otho C. x. fols. 224–6, printed in
Singer's edition of Cavendish's *Life of Wolsey*, p.456.

7. Constantyne's Memorial to Cromwell, *Archæologia*, vol. xxiii. pp.63–5; and
Cronica del Rey Enrico otavo de Ingalaterra.

8. Sir W. Kingston to Cromwell, 3 May 1536, British Museum, Cotton MSS, Otho C. x. fol. 2253, printed by Singer, p.451.

9. Sir W. Kingston to Cromwell, 3 May 1536, *loc. cit.*

10. Constantyne to Cromwell, *Archæologia*, vol. xxiii. pp.63–5; and *Histoire de Anne de Boullant*, etc.

11. Sir E. Baynton to Sir W. Fitzwilliam, British Museum, Cotton MSS, Otho C. x. fol. 209*b*.

12. Sir W. Kingston to Cromwell, British Museum, Cotton MSS, Otho C. x. fol. 224*b*.

13. Sir William Kingston to Cromwell, 3 May 1536, *loc. cit.*

14. Sir William Kingston to Cromwell, Cotton MSS, Otho C. x. fol. 224*b*.

15. E. Chapuis to Charles V, 2 May 1536, Vienna Archives, P.C. 230, i. fol. 80: 'Laffaire… est venue beaulcop mieulx quasy que personne peust penser et a la plus grande ignominie de la dicte concubyne laquelle par jugement et pugnicion de dieu a ete amenee de plein jour dois Grynuych a la tour de ceste ville de Londres ou elle a este conduicte par le due de Norphoch, les deux chambellan du Royaulme et de la chambre et luy a lon laisse tant seullement quatre femmes.'; *Histoire de Anne de Boullant*; *Wriothesley's Chronicle of the Tudors*, etc.

16. E. Chapuis to Charles V, 2 May 1536, *loc. cit.*: 'Le frere de la dicte concubyne nomme Rocheffort a este aussy mis en la dicte tour mais plus de six heures apres les aultres et trois ou quatre heures avant sa dicte seur… '; *Wriothesley's Chronicle*; and Cromwell to Gardiner and Wallop, 14 May 1536, British Museum, Add. MSS 25,144, fol. 160.

17. Kingston to Cromwell, 3 May 1536, *loc. cit.*

18. Roland Buckley to Sir Richard Buckley, 2 May 1536, R.O., Henry VIII, 28th, Bundle II.: 'Sir ye shall untherstande that the queene is in the towere, the ierles of Wyltshyre her father my lorde Rocheforde her brother, maister norres on of the king previe chamber, on maister Markes on of the kings preyve chamber, wyth divers others soundry ladys. The causse of there committing there is of certen hie treson comytyde conscernyng there prynce, that is to saye that maister norres shuld have a doe wyth the queyne and Marke and the other acsesari to the sayme… '; and E. Chapuis to Charles V, 2 May 1536, *loc. cit.*: 'Le bruyt est que cest pour adultere auquel elle a longuement continue avec ung joueur despinette de sa chambre lequel a este dois ce matin mis en ladicte tour, et maistre Norris le plus prive et familier sommeiller de corps de ce Roy pour non avoir revele les affaires… '

19. Cranmer to Cromwell, 22 April 1536, R.O., Cranmer Letters, No. 45.

20. Cranmer to Henry VIII, 3 May 1536, British Museum, Cotton MSS, Otho C. x. fol. 225, printed by Burnet, etc.

21. Roland Buckley to Sir R. Buckley, 2 May 1536, *loc. cit.*: 'The are lyke to suffyre, all there morre is the pitte, yff it plesyde good otherwyse I praye you macke you redy in all the haste that can be and come downe to youre prynce for you your seffte may do morre than xx men in your absence, therefore mayke haste for ye may be ther or onny a worde be of theyr deth, when it is onnes knowe that the shall dede all wilbe to latte therefore mayke haste… '

22. Council of Wales to Cromwell, 7 May 1526, R.O., *Cromwell Correspondence*, xxv. No. 2.

23. Sir E. Baynton to Sir W. Fitzwilliam, British Museum, Cotton MSS, Otho C. x. 209*b*; *Wriothesleys Chronicle*, i. p.37, etc.

24. Sir W. Kingston to Cromwell, British Museum, Cotton MSS, Otho C. x. fols. 222 and 224*b*.

25. Kingston to Cromwell, 3 May 1536, Cotton MSS, Otho C. x. fol. 225.

26. Cromwell to Gardiner and Wallop, 14 May 1536, *loc. cit.*; and *Histoire de Anne de Boullant*.

27. *Ibid.*; and Constantyne to Cromwell, *Archæologia*, xxiii. pp.63–5. As to the dates of the arrests, see Appendix, Note F.

28. *Histoire de Anne de Boullant*:
    Maistre Waston et Barton le suivirent,
    Pages et Oviet ce mesme chemin feirent,

29. List of Anne's debts, R.O., Henry VIII, Box I.
30. Sir Henry Wyatt to Cromwell, 11 May 1536, R.O., Henry VIII, 28th, Bundle II.
31. Indictment found at Westminster, 10 May 1536, R.O. Baga de Segretis, Pouch VIII, Membrane 7, and Pouch IX, Membrane 18; and Indictment found at Deptford, 11 May 1536, R.O. Baga de Segretis, Pouch VIII, Membrane 11, and Pouch IX, Membrane 21, most incorrectly abstracted in the Appendix to the Third Report of the Deputy Keeper of Public Records.
32. E. Chapuis to Charles V, 19 May 1536, Vienna Archives, P.C. 230, i. fol. 82.

18. Anne's Last Days

1. E. Chapuis to Charles V, 19 May 1536, *loc. cit.*: 'Et desia sonne tres mal aux oreilles du peuple que le dict Roy ayant receu telle ignominie sest monstre beaulcop plus joyeulx depuis la prinse de la dicte putain quil ne feist oncques et est presque continuellement alle banquetter deca et dela avec les dames et quelque fois il est demoure jusques apres mynuit et sen retournant par la riviere la pluspart du temps il estoit accompagne de diverses sortes dinstrument et de lautre part les chantres de sa chambre que faysoient leur debvoir que sentoit fort a lnterpretation de plusieurs la joyssance destre quicte de maigre vieille et meschante bague avec expoir de reschargement quest chose fort peculieyre et agreable audict Roy.'
2. *Ibid.*: 'Il souppa naguaires avec plusieurs dames en la maison de levesque de Carlion, yl monstra une joye desespere comme me vint dire le lendemain icelluy evesque et me rappourta aussy que entre plusieurs propoz que le dict Roy luy avoit tenu particulierement il luy dict quil y avoit desia longtemps quil presagissoit lissue de ces affaires et que sur ce yl avoit cy devant compose une tragedie quil pourtoit avec luy et ce disant icelluy Roy tira de son seing ung petit livret escript de sa main, mais le dict evesque ne luy point dedans. Peut estre que cestoit certaines ballades que le dict Roy a compose desquelles la putain et son frere comme de chose inepte et gouffe se gaudissoient que leur feut objecte pour grand et grief cryme.'
3. Sir William Paulet to Cromwell, 11 May 1536, R.O., *Cromwell Correspondence*, vol. xxxiv; etc.
4. Precept of the justices, 9 May 1536, R.O. Baga de Segretis, Pouch VIII, Membranes 8 and 12.
5. List of grand juries, R.O. Baga de Segretis, Pouch VIII, Membranes 9 and 13.
6. Indictments, R.O. Baga de Segretis, Pouch VIII, Membranes 7 and 11.
7. Baga de Segretis, Pouch VIII, Membrane 6.
8. Sir W. Paulet to Cromwell, 11 May 1536, R.O., *Cromwell Correspondence*, vol. xxxiv.
9. Baga de Segretis, Pouch VIII, Membrane 1.
10. Baga de Segretis. Pouch VIII, Membrane 5.
11. R.O. Baga de Segretis, Pouch VIII, Membranes 2 and 3.
12. R.O. Baga de Segretis, Pouch IX, Membranes 14, 16 and 19.
13. Sir W. Kingston to Cromwell, British Museum, Cotton MSS, Otho C. x. fol. 228.
14. Sir W. Kingston to Cromwell, British Museum, Cotton MSS, Otho C. x. fol. 225.
15. *Ibid.*
16. Sir W. Kingston to Cromwell, British Museum, Cotton MSS, Otho C. x. fol. 225 and 228.
17. E. Chapuis to N. de Granvelle, 18 May 1536, Vienna Archives, P.C. 230, i. fol. 90: 'Celle que la eu en charge et garde ne men scelera chose du monde, desja des le commencement elle menvoya advertir de quelques choses et entres autres que ladicte Messaline ne pouvoit considerer ne imaginer que personne du monde leust mis en disgrace de ce Roy que moy, car oncques puis que fus en la court le dict Roy ne la regarda de bon oeyl. Bien men prent quelle nest exchappee car selon quelle estoit humaine et piteuse elle meust voulu faire menger aux chiens.'

18. Commission to the Duke of Norfolk, 12 May 1536, R.O. Baga de Segretis, Pouch IX, Membrane 17.
19. Precept to Ralph Felmingham, 13 May 1536, R.O. Baga de Segretis, Pouch IX, Membrane 16.
20. Panel of Peers, R.O. Baga de Segretis, Pouch IX, Membrane 15.
21. Wriothesley's *Chronicle of England*, edited by W. D. Hamilton.
22. Record of Session, R.O. Baga de Segretis, Pouch IX, Membranes 1–6
23. Wriothesley's *Chronicle*.
24. Record of Session, *loc. cit.*
25. Wriothesley's *Chronicle* and *Histoire de Anne de Boullant.*
26. Record of Session, *loc. cit.*
27. E. Chapuis to Charles V, 19 May 1536, *loc. cit.*: 'Ce principallement dont elle fust chargee estoit davoir cohabite avec son frere et autres complices, quil y avoit promesse entre elle et noris de se espouser aprez le trespas de ce Roy, que denotoit quilz luy desiroient la mort et quelle avoit receu et donne certaines medailles audit Noris que se pouvoynt ainsi interpreter quelle avoyt faict empoysonner la feue Royne et maschine de faire le mesme a la princesse. Lesquelles choses elle nya tottalement et a chacune donna assez coulorie responce, bien confessa elle quelle avoit donne de largent a Waiston comme aussy elle avoit faict a plusieurs autres jeunes gentilzhommes. Il luy fust aussy objecte et au frere aussy quilz sestoient mouque du Roy et de ses habillemens et quelle en plusieurs facons demonstroit ne aymer le dict Roy ains estre ennuye de lui... peut etre que cestoit certaines ballades que le dit Roy a compose desquelles la putain et son frere comme de chose inepte et gouffe se gaudissoient que leur feut objecte pour grand et grief cryme.'
28. E. Chapuis to Charles V, 19 May 1536, *loc. cit.*: 'La concubyne fust condempnee premierement et avoit ouye sa sentence que fust destre bruslee ou davoir transchee la teste au chois du Roy. Elle tint bonne mine disant quelle se tenoit toute saluee de la mort et que le plus que luy deplesoyt estoit que les susmencionnez questoient innocents et loyaulx au Roy deussent morir pour elle et ne supplia autre chose synon luy donner ung peu despace pour disposer sa conscience'; and *Histoire de Anne de Boullant:*

> Aprez quilz lont coupable publiee
> Et que luy ont peine de mort livree
> Le president millort due de Norfort
> Pour endurer de lespee leffort
> Ou bien du feu selon le bon vouloir
> Du Roy, na faict semblant de se douloir
>
> Car jay tousiours au Roy este fidelle
> Et pour ce veulx que ce dernier parler
> Ne soit que pour mon honneur consoler
> Et de mon frere et de ceulx que jugez
> Avez a mort, et dhonneur estrangez
> Tant que vouldrois que les peusse deffendre
> Et delivrer pour coupable me rendre
> De mille morts, et puis quil plaist au Roy
> Je recepvray la mort en ceste foy...

The French poet is mistaken when he says that Anne was condemned after Rochford. This certainly was not the case.
29. E. Chapuis to Charles V, 19 May 1536, *loc. cit.*: 'Le frere fust charge davoir cohabite avec elle par presumption quil sestoit une foys treuve longtemps avec elle et de certaines autres petites folies. Et au tout il respondit si bien que plusieurs des assistens voulurent gaiger dix pour ung quil seroit absoublz... il luy fust aussy

objecte quil avoit deu semer quelque parolles par lesquelles il mectoit en doubte si la fille de sa sueur estoit fille du Roy a quoy il ne respondist riens.'

30. *Ibid.*: 'Je ne veulx omectre quentre autres choses luy fust objecte pour crime que sa sueur la putain avoit dit a sa femme que le Roy nestoit habile en cas de soy copuler avec femme et quil navoit ne vertu ne puissance et ce ne luy voulut lon dire devant le monde mais luy fust monstre par escript avec protestacion quil ne le recita. Mais tout incontinent il declaira laffaire au grand despit de Crumuel et aucuns autres quilz ne vouldroient cet endroit engendrer suspicion que pourroit prejudiquer a la lignee que le dict Roy pretend avoir.'

31. R.O. Baga de Segretis. Pouch IX, Membrane 1–6.

32. R.O. Baga de Segretis, Pouch IX, Membrane 1–6: 'Le frere apres sa condampnacion dit que puis quil falloit quil morut il ne vouloit plus soubstenir son innocence ains confessay quil avoit bien desservy la mort, seullement supplioit au dict Roy vouloir permectre que de ses biens feussent payez ses debtes quil nomma'; and *Histoire de Anne de Boullant*:

Il ne sesmeut ne les juges il blasme
Mais seulement les prie de tant faire
Envers le Roy quil veuille satisfaire
A ses amis qui luy avoient preste
De leur argent a sa necessite

Et cependant en Dieu deliberoit
Que de bon cueur ceste mort souffriroit.

33. *Ibid.*; and Constantino to Cromwell, *loc. cit.*: There was said that much money would have been laid that day and that [at?] greate odds that the Lord Rochford should have been quit... '; 'I heard say he had escapyd had it not byn for a letter.' Was this an allusion to the paper shown to Rochford at the trial? I am inclined to think it was.

34. Indictments found at Westminster and at Deptford, *loc. cit.*

35. E. Chapuis to Charles V, 19 May 1536, *loc. cit.*: 'Combien que tout le monde dyci soit bien joyeulx de lexecution de la dicte putain touteffois yl y a peu de gens qui ne murmurent et treuvent bien estrange la forme qua este tenue a la procedure et condemnacion delle et des autres et se parle diversement dudict Roy et ne sera pas pour appaiser le monde quand lon sappercevera de ce quest passe et se passe entre luy et maistresse Jehanne Semel.' E. Chapuis to N. de Granvelle, 18 May 1536, *loc. cit.*: 'Vous ne veites oncque prince ne autre homme que manifesta plus ses cornes ne que les pourta plus alegrement. Je Vous laisse penser la cause.'; 'and Constantine to Cromwell, *loc. cit.*: 'Dean:... I never heard of the queens that they should be thus handled, George: In good faith neither I; neither yet I never suspected, but I promise you there was much muttering of Queen Anne's death. Dean: There was indeed.'

36. E. Chapuis to Charles V, 19 May 1536, loc. cit.: 'Quelque instance quaye faicte levesque de Tarbes ambassadeur ordinaire de France et le Seigneur de Tinteville lequel arryva yci avant hier pour en saulver ung nomme vaston.'; and *Histoire de Anne de Boullant.*

37. Sir W. Kingston to Cromwell, 16 May 1536, British Museum, Harleian MSS vol. 283, fol, 134; and Singer's *Cavendish*, p.459.

38. Record Office, Henry VIII, Anno 1536–37, Bundle I.

39. Dr Lingard and Mr Froude say that Smeton was hanged, and the former asserts that 'the Portuguese writer is certainly in error when he supposes Smeaton to have been beheaded.' I think 'the Portuguese writer' is right. First of all, there were no gallows on Tower Hill, and the erection of gallows for the occasion would have caused no little trouble and expense. Secondly, the account of 'the Portuguese writer' is confirmed by Chapuis in letters to Charles V, 17 and 19 May 1536, *loc. cit.*: 'Sire ce jourdhui a este tranchee devant la tour la teste au seigneur de Rochefort et aux

quartre autres susnommes;' by the French account, Paris, Bibl. Nat. MSS Dupuis, vol. 373, fol. 111: 'Apres le dict Rocheford furent decappittez quatre gentilzhommes nommez Messieurs Westen, Norris premier gentilhomme de la chambre du Roy, Brecter et Marc;' by the *Histoire de Anne de Boullant*:

Sinon que Marc...
...Ainsi finablement
Apres les quatre et suivant leur chemin,
Receut le coup de sa piteuse fin;

and by Hall, Grafton, Holinshed, Wriothesley, and the chronicler of the Gray Friars.

40. The account of Lord Rochford's speech given by Wriothesley in his *Chronicle of England* (edited by Mr Hamilton for the Camden Society) agrees best with: 'Ce que dict Millor de Rochefort... Paris, Bibl, Nat. MSS Dupuis, vol. 373, fol. 111, and with the account sent by Chapuis: 'Execution criminelle faicte en angleterre le xvieme [sic] de May 1536,' Vienna Archives, P.C. 230, iii. fol. 31.

41. French account, Paris, Bibl. Nat. MSS Dupuis, vol. 373, fol. 111: 'Qui ne dirent pas grant chose synon que lon priast Dieu pour eulx et quilz prenoient la mort en gre;' *Histoire de Anne de Boullant*:

Les quatre qui restent encores apres
Ne dirent riens comme si par expres
A Rochefort eussent donne creance
De parler seul selon leur conscience
Sinon que Marc qui tousiours persistoit
En son propoz et au peuple attestoit
Que telle mort recepvoit justement
Pour ses meffaictz... ;

and Constantine to Cromwell, *loc. cit.* Constantine says that he was present at the execution and 'heard them and wrote every worde they spake.' According to Constantine, Noreys was silent; Bryerton said: 'I have deserved to die if it were a thousand deaths; but the cause whereof I die judge ye not. If ye judge, judge the best'; Mark Smeton: 'Masters, I pray you all pray for me for I have deserved the death'; and Weston: 'I had thought to live in abomination yet this twenty or thirty years and then to have made amends; I thought little I would have come to this.'

42. Earl of Northumberland to Cromwell, 13 May 1536, Burnet, *Collectanea*, Part III. Book III. No. 49.

43. Sir W. Kingston to Cromwell, 16 May 1536, *loc. cit.*

44. Wilkins' *Concilia*, vol. iii. fol. 804. See Appendix, Note G.

45. Sir W. Kingston to Cromwell, 18 May 1536, British Museum, Cotton MSS Otho C. x. fol. 227.

46. E. Chapuis to Charles V, 19 May 1536, *loc. cit.*: 'La dame que la eu en garde ma envoye dire en grand secret que la dicte concubyne avant et apres la reception du sainct sacremant luy affirma sur la dampnation de son ame quelle ne sestoit meffaicte de son corps envers ce Roy.'

47. Sir W. Kingston to Cromwell, 18 May 1536, *loc. cit.*

48. *Chronicle of Calais*, p.47; and account of Mr Gostwyk, R.O. Henry VIII, 28th, Box II: 'To Sir William Kingston for a composition for such Iuells and apparail as the late queene had in the tower – 100*l*. To the same Sir William Kingston for money delyvered unto her to gyve in almes before her deathe – 20*l*. To the executioner of Calays for his rewarde and apparail, C. crownes – 231. 6*s*. 8*d*. To the said Sir William Kingston for the said late queenes diett at her being in the tower – 251. 4*s*. 6*d*.'

49. Sir W. Kingston to Cromwell, 18 May 1536, *loc. cit.*

50. E. Chapuis to Charles V, 19 May 1536, *loc. cit.*: 'Elle se confessa hier et comuniqua

pensant destre execute et ne monstra oncques personne meilleure vollonte daller a la mort quelle et en sollicitoit ceulx quen debvoient avoir charge; et estant venu commandement de differer lexecution jusque a aujourdhuy elle sen monstra fort dolante priant le cappitaine de la tour que pour lhonneur le dieu il feit supplier au Roy que puis quelle se trouvoit en bon estat et disposee a recepvoir la mort que lon la voulsist depescher incontinant.'

51. Sir W. Kingston to Cromwell, 18 May 1536, *loc. cit.*

52. E. Chapuis to N. de Granvelle, 6 June 1536, Vienna Archives, P.C. 229½ iii. fol. 12: 'La dame Anne la nuyt avant quelle fut decapitee commença a jazer le plus playsement du monde et entre aultres choses elle dit ces glorieuses et ingenieuses personnes que forgearent ung nom inaudit a la bonne Royne ne seront cy empeschez luy en trouver ung car il la pourroient appeller la Royne Anne sans teste et disant telz propoz se mit a rire si tres fort que oncques ne fust vu telle chose, bien sachant touteffoys quelle mourroit lendemain sans nul remede.'

53. Ibid.: 'Elle dit le jour devant quelle fust executez et depuys quant lon la voulust mener a lexecution quelle ne pensoit estre la conduytte par le jugement divin sinon pour avoir estee cause du male traytement de la princesse et avoir conspire a sa mort ... '

54. E. Chapuis to Charles V, 19 May 1536, *loc. cit.*: 'Lexecution et decollation de la concubyne qua este faicte maintenant a neuf heures du matin dedans la tour.'

55. French account of Anne's death, Paris. Bibl. Nat. MSS Dupuis, vol. 373, fol 112: 'Leschaffault qui nestoit pas plus hault que de quatre ou cinq marches.'

56. Wriothesley's *Chronicle*; and E. Chapuis to Charles V, 19 May 1536, *loc. cit.*: 'Ou se sont trouvez presents le chancellier et maistre Cremuel et plusieurs aultres du conseil du Roy, et autre assez grand nombre de subjectz mays lon ny a voulu souffrir estraingiers... '

57. French account of Anne's death, *loc. cit.*: 'Accoustree dune robbe de nuyt de damas gris fourre pour faire plus beau col.'

58. *Ibid.*: 'Lors elle commença a dire que elle ne estoit pas venue la pour prescher ains estoit la venue pour mourir, Disant a messieurs les assistans quilz priassent bien dieu pour le Roy, car il estoit tout bon et quil lavoit tant bien traictee quil nestoit possible de mieulx et quelle ne accusoit personne de sa mort juges ne aultres gens quelz quelz fussent, car cestoit la loy du pays qui la condempnoit, parquoy elle prenoit bien la mort en gre demandant pardon a tout le monde.' This account agrees very well with the versions preserved by Wriothesley and Constantine. The version of the *Histoire de Anne de Boullant* is a paraphrase of that just quoted, differing only in a few details. The letter of the 'Portuguese writer' is a mere translation of this account.

59. *Ibid.*: 'Lors elle print elle mesme son accoustrement de teste et le bailla a une damoyselle et ne luy demoura que une coeffe quelle avoit mise pour tenir ses cheveulx... disant aux assistants quilz priassent dieu pour elle.'

60. French account of Anne's death, *loc. cit.*: 'Regardant tousiours derriere elle... '

61. *Ibid.*: 'Et sagenoilla et lune de ses damoselles luy bandist les yeulx; sans se faire tenir aucunement elle attendit la le coup avant quon eust dit une pastenostre, disant tousjours Mon Dieu ayez pitie de mon ame. Lesdictes quatre damoyselles estant tousjours sur

leschaffault agenoilles. Et a ceste heure la pouvre dame fut expedyee lune des susdictes damoyselles print la teste et les aultres le corps et midrent tout dedant ung linceul et apres dedans une biere qui estoit toute apprestee et la feirent apporter dedans une eglise qui est devant ladicte tour ou lon dit quelle et les dessusdictz ont este enterrez. Requiescat in pace.'

62. E. Chapuis to Charles V, 6 June 1536, Vienna Archives, P.C. 230, i. fol. 92: 'Et sur ce me louha grandement le sens expert et cueur de la dicte concubyne et de son frere.'

19. Conclusion

1. Charles V to E. Chapuis, 15 May 1536, Vienna Archives, P.C. 233, iii. fol. 26: 'Le Viconte Hanart a escript au Sgr de Granvelle du ix. de ce mois que au mesme instant il avoit entendu de bon lieu que la concubyne du Roy dangleterre avoit este surprise couchee avec lorganiste dudict Roy.'

2. Cromwell to Gardiner and Wallop, 14 May 1536, *loc. cit.*

3. Depositions against John Hill and William Saunders before the justices of Oxfordshire, 26 June 1536, R.O. Henry VIII, 28th Bundle ii. John Hill was accused of having said that the king had caused Norris, Weston and the others 'to be put to death only of pleasure... ' and 'how that the king for a frawde and a gille cawsed Mr Norrys, Mr Weston and the other queen to be putt to death, bycause he was made sure unto the queens grace that nowe is half a yere before.' William Saunders spoke in a similar manner.

4. *Epigrammata*, Lib. iii. p.162, published by Etienne Dolet, Lyons, anno 1538: 'Regine Utopiae, falso adulterii crimine damnatae, et capite mulctatae Epithaphium.

Quid? quod tyrannus crimine falso damnatam
Me jussit occidi, minus me jam laudas?
Necnon velut turpe maledicta suffundis?
Nulla nota turpis sum, ob acceptum vulnus.
Nimirum honesta turpido est sine culpa
Mori, et innocentem cedere aliquando fatis.

I have been unable to find the book itself, so I quote from Crapelet.

5. Melanchthon to Camerarius, 9 June 1536, *Corp. Ref.* vol. iii. No. 1437: 'Posterior Regina magis accusata quam convicta adulterii ultimo supplicio affecta est.'

6. This book is very rare, and I have never been able to see the original. But there is in the Grenville library an Italian translation from, which I quote: 'Un re il quale era sospettato dhavere di gia mal trattate tre donne.'

7. Constantine's Memorial, *loc. cit.*

8. E. Chapuis to Charles V, 19 May 1536, *loc. cit.*: 'Et pour couvrir laffection quil a a la dicte Semel il la faict tenir a sept mille dyci en la maison du grand escuyer.'

9. *Ibid.*: 'Ce Roy... lequel le jour avant la condempnacion dicelle putain envoya querre par le grand escuyer et plusieurs aultres maistresse Semel et la feist venir a ung mille de son logis la ou elle est servye tres splendidement de cuysiniers et certains officiers dudict Roy et tres richement accoustree.'

10. E. Chapuis to Charles V, 19 May 1536, *loc. cit.*; 'Et ma dict une syenne parente que disna avec elle le jour de la dicte condempnacion que des le matin icelluy Roy avoit envoye dire a la dicte Semel que a troys heures apres mydy il luy envoyeroit nouvelles de la condampnacion de la dicte putain, ce quil feist par maistre Briant quil envoya en toute diligence.'

11. E. Chapuis to N. de Granvelle, 20 May 1536, Vienna Archives, P.C. 230, ii. fol. 22: 'Sil este vray ce que ma este dit, assavoir quicelluy Roy tout incontinent quil heust hier les nouvelles de la decapitation de la putain il monta en barque et alla trouver la dicte maistresse Semel quil a faict loger a ung mille de luy en une maison sur la riviere.'

12. *Ibid.*: 'Jay este adverty de plusieurs et divers bons lieux comme ce matin aux six heures mestresse Semel est venu par la riviere secretement au logis de ce Roy et a

neufz heures a este faict la promesse et desponsation et entend le dict Roy que le tout doit estre tenu secret jusques aux festes de penthecoste... '

13. N. Raince to Cardinal du Bellay, 23 May 1536, Paris, Bibl. Nat. MSS Français, vol. 19,577.

14. G. da Casale to Henry VIII, 27 May 1536, British Museum, Cotton MSS Vitellius, B. xiv. fol. 198: 'Primum igitur se omnipotentem deum bonorum omnium largitorem deinde M^{tem} Vram obsecrare, ut animum inducat sese ita comparare, ut tanta gloria adeunda occasionem non praetermittat. Quod si V. Regia M^{tas} huic Romana Ecclesia conjuncta fuerit, ipsam sine dubio tantum habiturum auctoritatis, ut caesari simulque Gallorum Regi jubere possit et utrunque cogere ad pacem... '

15. G. da Casale to Henry VIII, 27 May 1536, British Museum, Cotton MSS Vitellius, B. xiv. fol. 198; and G. da Casale to Cromwell, 27 May 1536, *State Papers*, vol. vii. p.656.

16. Cardinal Campeggio to Marco Antonio Campeggio, 6 June 1536, British Museum, Cotton MSS Vitellius, B. xiv. fol. 205: 'Anchorache la reintegration delle cose mie habi da esser il principal pretesto dell andata vra in anglia pur non restareti se con qualchedun de questi grandi pigliasti confidentia con bon proposito ricordar che a laude de dio quete di quel regno... sarebbe bene che soa m^{ta} pensasse e facesse ogni opera per reintegrarsi con la sede appostolica quel mi rendo certo che sempre se li renderia benigna, et che per poter conseguir questo il ver principio seria che reprimessi li predicatori di nove heresie... '

17. Cardinal Campeggio to Marco Antonio Campeggio, 6 June 1536, British Museum, Cotton MSS Vitellius, B. xiv. fol. 205: 'Anchor vi forzareti far... la conscientia soa procurasse ottener le debite absolutione... antecessori soi con molta laude et inemoria... procurorno...

18. *Ibid.*: 'Li particulari amici e fautori me... confidentia sono li Ill^{mi} duca di Norfolch, di Sopholch... Dunelmen, Wintonien ne voglio scordarmi il nro R^{do} M... homo della virtu e bonta che sapete il qual e mio procuratore... '

19. Cardinal Campeggio to the Duke of Suffolk, 5 June 1536, *State Papers*, vol. vii. p.657.

20. N. Raince to Cardinal du Bellay, 23 May 1536, *loc. cit.*: 'De belle prime face Sa S^{te} levant les mains au ciel me dict quon ne pourroit mieulx faire que de trouver moyen de faire le mariage de madame fille aisnee du Roy et du Roy dangleterre comme il mavoit autrefois dict et mesmement quand je luy dis la premiere nouvelle de la mort de la Royne Catherine... Croyez Mgr que Nostre dict St pere a une singuliere devotion au sainct [faict ?]... et men a parle depuis chacune fois que jay este a luy et encor aujourdhui et si en parla samedy quand Mgr lambassadeur y fust.'

21. N. Raince to Cardinal du Bellay, 8 June 1536, Paris, Bibl. Nat. MSS Français, vol. 19,577: 'Je fis lecture a Nostre dict S. P. de Vre chiffre a Mondict Sr de Mascon tant dangleterre que dailleurs. Sa S^{te} ne print pas bien cette nouvelle volonte de mariage en plus basse condition et en eust deplaisir pour ce quil vouldroit quon parvint a lautre party quil desire comme Vous entendez bien.'

22. N. Raince to Cardinal du Bellay, 27 July 1536, Paris, Bibl. Nat. MSS Français, vol. 19,577: 'Il [the Pope] desire fort dentendre ce que lon repondra a ce que Mgr lambassadeur et moy escripvimes par le depesche du 20eme Juin touchant le mariage de la princesse Marie pour Mgr le daulphin et ne passe pas ce propos sans que S. S^{te} parle de Vous.'

23. N. Raince to Cardinal du Bellay, 27 July 1536, Paris, Bibl. Nat. MSS Français, vol. 19,577: 'Mgr. N^{re} dict S. P. me parla du Roy dangleterre ainsi comme jescript au Roy en bien grosse colere et se attache continuellement contre Cramouel.'

24. E. Chapuis and D. de Mendoça to Charles V, 31 August 1538, Vienna Archives, P.C. 231, ii. fol. 54; etc.

25. Cromwell to Gardiner and Wallop, 14 May 1536, *loc. cit.*

26. The Duke of Richmond to the Bishop of Lincoln, 8 May 1536, R.O. 28th Henry VIII, Bundle ii.

27. The Bishop of Lincoln to Cromwell, 5 May 1536, R.O. 28th Henry VIII, Bundle ii.

28. Robert Barnes to Cromwell, R.O. *Cromwell Correspondence*, vol. iii. fol. 77.

29. Mary of Hungary to E. Chapuis, 10 March 1539, Vienna Archives, P.C. 231, iv. fol. 6.
30. The Dean of Cambray to Mary of Hungary, 19 March 1539, Vienna Archives, P.C. 231, iv. fol. 8.
31. E. Chapuis to N. de Granvelle, 3 September 1540, Vienna Archives, P.C. 232, ii. fol. 1.
32. E. Chapuis and F. van der Dilft to Charles V, 2 January 1545, Vienna Archives, P.C. 236, i. fol. 7.
33. E. Chapuis to Charles V, 9 May 1545, Vienna Archives, P.C. 236, ii. fol. 26.

Appendix Note A: The Birth & Early Life of Anne Boleyn

1. J.S. Brewer, *Letters and Papers*, vol. i. p.lxv, footnote.
2. *Letters and Papers*, vol. iii. p.ccccxxx.
3. *Letters and Papers*, vol. iv. p.cccxxxiii. and p. cccxxxiv.
4. *Letters and Papers*, vol. iii. p.ccccxxx.
5. *Ibid.*
6. *Cronica del Rey Enrico Otavo de Ingalaterra*, edited by the Marquis de Molina, Madrid, 1874.
7. Vol. i. p.41, footnote.
8. *Histoire de la Royne Anne de Boullant*. Paris, Bibl. Nat. MSS Français, vol. 1742 and vol. 2370, fol. 1.
9. *Epistre contenant le proces criminel*, etc., par Carles aulmosnier de Mr le Daulphin.
10. *Les Recherches et Antiquites de la Province de Neustrie* par Charles de Bourgueville. Caen, 1583, p.123: 'Une demoiselle nommee Anne Boullenc laquelle avoit ete nourrie en France et y estoit venue lorsque le Roy Louis douzieme epousa la Royne Marie soeur du Roy d'Angleterre.'
11. *Cronica del Rey Enrico Otavo*, p.41: 'Y la Reina Annale hizo muy gran acatamiento porque esta Anna Boloña habido sido criada in Francia in la corte del Rey... '
12. E. Chapuis to N. de Granvelle, 6 June 1538, Vienna Archives, P.C. 229½, iii. fol. 12: 'Quil avoit trop experimente en la dicte concubine que cestoit de la pourriture de France.' Both Mr Froude and my copyist read 'nourriture,' but the stronger expression seems to me to be the true reading.
13. *Letters and Papers*, vol. iv. p.ccxxvi.
14. Lord Hunsdon to Lord Burghley, 6 October 1597, R.O. Elizabeth, Domestic Series, vol. 264, fol. 283.
15. N. Sanders, *de Origine Schismati*, 1588, p.16.
16. J. Brodeau, *Vie de Maistre Charles du Moulin*, p.7.
17. Norfolk to Henry VIII and Peter Vannes to Cromwell, 23 June 1533, *Letters and Papers*, vol. vi. pp.307, 308.
18. *Histoire de la Royne Anne de Boullant, loc. cit.*:

> Apres que Marie fust revenue
> En ce pays, elle fust retenue
> Par Claude, qui Royne apres succeda
> Ou tellement ses graces amenda
> Que ne leussiez oncques jugee angloyse
> En ses facons, mais naifve francoyse;

and *Cronica del Rey Enrico Otavo de Ingalaterra*.

19. *Letters and Papers*, vol. iv. p.ccxxxviii.
20. J.A. Froude, *History of England*, vol. i. p.184: Mr Melton – 'This shall be to advertise you that Mistress Anne is changed from that she was at when we three were last together... '
21. Albert du Boys, *Catherine d'Aragon*, p.146: 'Cette lettre est pour Vous avertir du

grand changement qui sest opere dans Anne de Boleyn depuis trois ans que nous l'avons veue, pendant que nous etions ensemble.'

22. *Letters and Papers*, vol. iv. p.ccxliii. footnote.
23. E. Chapuis to Charles V, 2 May 1536, *loc. cit*: 'Yl y avoit des temoings tous conformes testiffians mariage avoir este passe neufz ans faict et charnellement consume entre elle et le conte nortanberlan.'

Appendix Note B: Was Mary Boleyn Henry's Mistress?

1. *History of England*, vol. ii. App. p.655.
2. *History of England*, vol. ii. App. p.653.
3. R.O. 26th Henry VIII Box Q, No. 127.
4. *History of England*, vol. ii. App. p.653.
5. Dr Ortiz to the empress, 7 February 1533, British Museum, Add. MSS 28,585, fol. 217.
6. Account of the conversation of the emperor with Dr Sampson, sent to E. Chapuis, 5 January 1530, Vienna Archives, P.C. 226, ii. fol. i.
7. E. Chapuis to Charles V, 9 August 1532, Vienna Archives. P.C. 227, iv. fol. 60.
8. Brewer, *Letters and Papers*, vol. iv. p.cccxxix. footnote.

Appendix Note C: The Authenticity of the Brief of Dispensation

1. *Quarterly Review*, No. 285, January 1877, p.38.
2. Gairdner, *Letters and Papers Illustrative of the Reigns of Richard III and Henry VII*, vol. i. p.243.
3. *Philalethæ Hyperborei... Parasceve*. Lueneburg, 1533: 'Primum tanquam invinicibilem arietem objiciunt, quod cum in ipso dispensationis diplomate, sive bulla habeantur haec verba forsan cognitam, in Brevi vero quod circiter tempus nuptiarum ut conficeretur ab Ferdinando Rege Catholico procuratum est, dudum ex Hispaniis allato simpliciter sit adscriptum cognitam non addito dubitandi adverbio forsan.'
4. Gayangos, *Calendar*, vol. iv. part i. p.881; and Gairdner, *Letters and Papers of Henry VIII*, vol. v. p.171.
5. G. Bergenroth, *Calendar*, vol. i. p.309; and *Philalethæ Hyperborei... Parasceve*, fol. c. iii.
6. Julius II to Henry, son of Henry King of England and Catherine, daughter of Ferdinand and Isabella, 26 December 1503, R.O.
7. Julius II to Henry, son of Henry King of England, and to Catherine, daughter of Ferdinand and Isabella, 26 December 1503, Vienna Archives, P.C. 228, iii. fol. i.
8. Deposition of Ruiz de Puebla, 14 September 1545, Gayangos, *Calendar*, vol. iv. part i. p.881; and Gairdner, *Letters and Papers*, vol. v. p.171.
9. Instructions to Gonçalo Fernandez, February 1529, Gayangos, *Calendar*, vol. iii. part ii. p.907.
10. Ghinucci and Lee to Wolsey, 31 May 1529, Brewer, *Letters and Papers*, vol. iv. p.2485.
11. G. Bergenroth, *Calendar*, vol. i. pp. iv. and v.
12. The Bishop of Worcester to Henry VII, 17 March 1505, Gairdner, *Letters and Papers of Richard III and Henry VII*, vol. i. p.243.
13. Paris, Bibl. Nat. MSS Français, vol. 2960, fol. 4.
14. Paris, Bibl. Nat. MSS Français, vol. 3010, fol. 64.

Appendix Note D: The Date of Anne's Marriage

1. T. Cranmer to Hawkyns, 17 June 1533, Gairdner, *Letters and Papers*, vol. vi. p.300.

2. E. Chapuis to Charles V, 15 April 1533, Vienna Archives, P.C. 228, i. fol. 41.
3. E. Chapuis to Charles V, 10 May 1533, Vienna Archives, P.C. 228 i. fol. 61

Appendix Note E: Bishop Fisher in the Spring of 1535

1. J. Fisher to Cromwell, 22 December 1534, *Archæologia*, vol. xxv. p.93.
2. More's works, edition of 1557, p.1452; and Roper's *Life of Sir Thomas More*.
3. More's works, p. 1450.
4. Palamede Gontier to Chabot de Brion, 5 February 1535, Lelaboureur. *Memoires de Mr de Castelnau*, vol. i. p.405.
5. British Museum, Cotton MSS Titus B.I fol. 165.
6. Baily, *Life of John Fisher*, pp.157–63.
7. W. Roper, *Life of Sir T. More*, p.89.

Appendix Note F: Arrest of Anne & Her Accomplices

1. E. Chapuis to Charles V, 19 May 1536, *loc. cit.*
2. *Histoire de Anne de Boullant.*
3. Pocock, *Records of the Reformation*, vol. ii. No. ccclix.
4. *Cronica del Rey Henrieo otavo*, pp.68–87.
5. *History of England*, vol. ii. Appendix, p.636.
6. *Ibid*, footnote.
7. Constantine's account, *Archæologia*, vol. xxiii. pp.63–5.
8. Sir W. Kingston to Cromwell, British Museum, Cotton MSS, Otlio C. x. fol. 225.
9. *Cronica del Rey Enrico otavo de Ingalaterra*, pp.88–91.
10. Sir Henry Wyatt to Cromwell, 11 May 1536, *loc. cit.*; and Sir Henry Wyatt to Henry VIII, no date, R.O. Henry VIII, 28th, Bundle I.

Appendix Note G: Grounds for the Divorce of Anne

1. Lingard, *History of England*, vol. iv. Appendix, note K.
2. *Statutes of the Realm*, 28th Henry VIII, chapter vii. paragraph i.
3. Froude, *History of England*, vol. ii. p.395.
4. C. Wriothesley, *A Chronicle of England*, edited by W. D. Hamilton, for the Camden Society, 1875–7, vol. i. p.40.
5. Wriothesley's *Chronicle*, p.43.
6. Wilkins, *Concilia*, iii. p.803.
7. Froude, *History of England*, vol. ii. App. p.651.
8. E. Chapuis to N. de Granvelle, 19 May 1536, Vienna Archives, P.C. 230, i. fol. 90.
9. E. Chapuis to N. de Granvelle, 8 July 1536, Vienna Archives, P.C. 230, i. fol. 145.

More Tudor History from Amberley Publishing

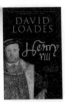

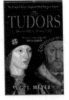

HENRY VIII
David Loades

'David Loades Tudor biographies are both highly enjoyable and
instructive, the perfect combination' *ANTONIA FRASER*

£12.99   978-1-4456-0704-7   512 pages HB   113 illus, 49 col

ANNE BOLEYN
Elizabeth Norton

'Meticulously researched and a great read'
THEANNEBOLEYNFILES.COM

£9.99   978-1-84868-514-7   264 pages PB   47 illus, 26 col

THE TUDORS VOL 1
G. J. Meyer

'His style is crisp and popular'
PROFESSOR DAVID LOADES

£12.99   978-1-4456-0143-4   384 pages PB   72 illus, 54

THE TUDORS VOL 2
G. J. Meyer

'A sweeping history of the gloriously infamous Tudor era'
KIRKUS REVIEW

£12.99   978-1-4456-0144-1   352 pages PB   53 illus, 15

ANNE BOLEYN
P. Friedmann

'A compelling and lively biography... meticulously researched and
supremely readable classic of Tudor biography' *DR RICHARD REX*
'The first scholarly biography' *THE FINANCIAL TIMES*

£20.00   978-1-84868-827-8   352 pages HB   47 illus, 20 col

CATHERINE PARR
Elizabeth Norton

'Norton cuts an admirably clear path through tangled Tudor intrigue'
JENNY UGLOW
'Wonderful... a joy to read'
HERSTORIA

£9.99   978-1-4456-0383-4   312 pages HB   49 illus, 30

MARY TUDOR
David Loades

£12.99   978-1-4456-0818-1   328 pages HB   59 illus, 10 col

MARGARET BEAUFORT
Elizabeth Norton

£9.99   978-1-4456-0578-4   256 pages HB   70 illus, 40

IN BED WITH THE TUDORS
Amy Licence

£20.00   978-1-4456-0693-4

272 pages HB   30 illus, 20 col

THE BOLEYNS
David Loades

£10.99   978-1-4456-0958-4

312 pages HB   34 illus, 33 col

BESSIE BLOUNT
Elizabeth Norton

£25.00   978-1-84868-870-4

384 pages HB   77 illus, 75 col

ANNE BOLEYN
Norah Lofts

£18.99   978-1-4456-0619-4

208 pages HB   75 illus, 46 col

Available from all good bookshops or to order direct
Please call **01453-847-800 www.amberleybooks.com**

Tudor History from Amberley Publishing

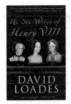

THE TUDORS
Richard Rex

'The best introduction to England's most important dynasty'
DAVID STARKEY
'Gripping and told with enviable narrative skill... a delight'
THES
'Vivid, entertaining and carrying its learning lightly'
EAMON DUFFY
'A lively overview' **THE GUARDIAN**

£9.99   978-1-4456-0700-9   256 pages PB 143 illus., 66 col

CATHERINE HOWARD
Lacey Baldwin Smith

'A brilliant, compelling account' **ALISON WEIR**
'A faultless book' **THE SPECTATOR**
'Lacey Baldwin Smith has so excellently caught the
atmosphere of the Tudor age' **THE OBSERVER**

£9.99   978-1-84868-521-5   256 pages PB 25 col illus

MARGARET OF YORK
Christine Weightman

'A pioneering biography of the Tudor dynasty's most
dangerous enemy'
PROFESSOR MICHAEL HICKS
'Christine Weightman brings Margaret alive once more'
THE YORKSHIRE POST
'A fascinating account of a remarkable woman'
THE BIRMINGHAM POST

£10.99   978-1-4456-0819-8   256 pages PB 51 illus

THE SIX WIVES OF HENRY VIII
David Loades

'Neither Starkey nor Weir has the assurance and command
of Loades' **SIMON HEFFER, LITERARY REVIEW**
'Incisive and profound. I warmly recommend this book'
ALISON WEIR

£9.99   978-1-4456-0049-9   256 pages PB 55 illus, 31 col

MARY ROSE
David Loades

£20.00 978-1-4456-0622-4
272 pages HB 17 col illus

MARY BOLEYN
Josephine Wilkinson

£9.99 978-1-84868-525-3
208 pages PB 22 illus, 10 col

JANE SEYMOUR
Elizabeth Norton

£9.99 978-1-84868-527-7
224 pages PB 53 illus, 26 col

HENRY VIII
Richard Rex

£9.99 978-1-84868-098-2
192 pages PB 81 illus, 48 col

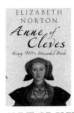

THOMAS CROMWELL
Patrick Coby

£20.00 978-1-4456-0775-7
272 pages HB 30 illus (20 col)

ANNE BOLEYN THE YOUNG QUEEN TO BE
Josephine Wilkinson
£9.99 978-1-4456-0395-7
208 pages PB 34 illus (19 col)

ELIZABETH I
Richard Rex

£9.99 978-1-84868-423-2
192 pages PB 75 illus

ANNE OF CLEVES
Elizabeth Norton

£9.99 978-1-4456-0183-0
224 pages HB 54 illus, 27 col

Available from all good bookshops or to order direct
Please call **01453-847-800 www.amberleybooks.com**

More Tudor History from Amberley Publishing

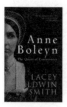